THE BLUE BOOK OF BROADWAY MUSICALS

BY

JACK BURTON

WITH ADDITIONS BY LARRY FREEMAN

Copyright 1952-1969
CENTURY HOUSE
Library of Congress Card No. #69-55070

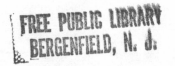
CENTURY HOUSE
WATKINS GLEN   NEW YORK

Foreword

This is the second book in a trilogy on popular music, the first of which, "The Blue Book Of Tin Pan Alley", was restricted to the biographies and song listings of approximately one hundred of the country's most prolific composers.

The present anthology, however, is far more embracing in the field of operetta, musical comedy and revue since it aims to cover all the musical productions that have had a Broadway first night since the turn of the century—and—they total in excess of fifteen hundred!

Like "The Blue Book Of Tin Pan Alley", this anthology is divided into five main decades, each of which was marked by new trends in musical productions and by the appearance of new authors, lyricists and composers on the Broadway scene. Following a general introduction to each chronological period, the shows and their songs are listed according to the composers of their scores. All songs from musical productions that have had a sheet music sale of a million or more copies are marked by an asterisk (*), and the casts listed are those that appeared in the original Broadway production and not on the road. The index of shows, lengths of runs, and albums of recordings are given at the end of the book. Of the many hundreds of shows listed only about forty have had a 500-performance run. JACK BURTON   Dec. 30, 1951

The original issue, which carried the Broadway story from its beginning through 1950, now requires extension and emendations. As a long-time student of popular music (cf. Larry Freeman, THE MELODIES LINGER ON, Century House, 15.00), it has become my responsibility to cover the last twenty years herein. Following the style set by Mr. Burton, each composer's scores first give the name of the show and the year it was originally produced on Broadway, followed by incidental information and a list, by title, of its songs. I have not, however, been interested in whether a given show caught on or flopped; nor do I give (as did Mr. Burton) a list of revivals of past shows appearing in these last twenty years. The student interested in such detail, is referred to the "Best Plays" annuals, also "Theater Arts" and "Biographical Encyclopedia & Who Who's of the American Theatre" (J. H. Heineman, 1966) which lists all Broadway and off-Broadway productions from 1959 through 1964. Larry Freeman, 1969

Yorker Yankee Village
Watkins Glen, N. Y.

Contents

It is realized that errors in Mr. Burton's original compilation still remain in this re-issue; but thanks to collector friends like Hilary Knight, an effort has been made to correct by insert. In this later compilation, Dr. Freeman has not listed original casts nor given the number of continuous performances; in an attempt to keep this new volume to usable reference size, he has lumped the work of less active composers together by show names under the title, "Miscellaneous Scores", also has only told where available recordings can be found rather than listing these. The high cost of bringing such a limited edition reference work up-to-date necessitates selling it as part of the two-volume set along with Burton's BLUE BOOK OF HOLLYWOOD MUSICALS. While we make no claim to absolute completeness, it is hoped that this up-dated version will prove as helpful to students as the original.

The Candle and Gaslit Era
(pre 1900)

It was just two hundred years ago—on the night of January 14, 1751—that the first musical production to be staged in what is now the United States was presented on the lower end of Manhattan Island, the reputed cost of this strip of land, $24, wouldn't get you two choice seats for *Guys And Dolls* at current scalper's prices.

The scene of this epochal first night, the Nassau Street Theater, located between John Street and Maiden Lane and the former residence of the Hon. Rip Van Dam, was a two-story, high-gabled structure with ten box seats priced at eight shillings each, 161 pit seats at five shillings each, and 121 gallery seats at three shillings each—grossing a total take that was peanuts compared to the weekly receipts of $50,000 that *Call Me Madam* or *South Pacific* yields.

The stage was raised five feet from the pit floor, a green curtain hung from the ceiling, two paper screens formed the wings, and the house and stage were illuminated by twelve wax candles, six of which comprised the footlights and six being stuck in a barrel hoop that served as a chandelier. The orchestra consisted of three pieces—English horn, flute and drum—and the vehicle that established New York City as the nation's fountainhead of musical comedy and revue was John Gay's *The Beggar's Opera*, which incidentally was given the full jazz treatment a hundred and ninety-five years later by Duke Ellington in his *Beggar's Holiday*.

This premiere of all American musical premieres was one of a series of benefit performances staged by a troupe of English players, headed by Thomas Kean, who being in debt for their passage money to the captain of the sailing vessel that had brought them to the New World, were held in semi-bondage until they could raise the funds to repay him, and to insure a capacity house and sufficient box office receipts to get them out of hock to the ship's owner, a comedy, *Miss In Her Teens,* and an olio, consisting of a harlequin dance, a clown dance and a drunken peasant sketch, also were presented.

Of course, Nassau Street is a 15-minute subway ride from Times Square, but since Broadway is the synonym for show business, the New World premiere of *The Beggar's Opera* in 1751 marks the opening chapter in the fabulous story of Broadway, where during the past 200 years, the American musical comedy and revue have developed and progressed from humble and unpretentious beginnings into productions unmatched in excellence and world-wide eminence.

The modern Broadway musical is no 100 proof, bottled-in-bond, American-distilled product, but a blend of several ingredients, some of native and some of foreign origin, and combines the best features of other closely allied forms of theatrical entertainment—pantomime, extravaganza, ballet, Viennese opera, English light opera, French opera-bouffe, farce comedy, vaudeville and minstrelsy.

Minstrelsy, in fact, might be termed the keystone of the Broadway musical since it pioneered pure and unadulterated American stage entertainment, performed by native-born troupers either Negro or blackface, with songs by American composers and comedy as typically American as the mint julep and the Mississippi side-wheeler.

The virgin seeds of American minstrelsy were planted in 1843 with the formation of the Original Virginia Minstrels by Billy Whitlock, who plunked the banjo, Frank Brower, who rattled the bones, Dick Pelham, who banged the tambourine, and Dan Emmett, a violinist, who seventeen years later gained immortality by writing a walk-around for Dan Bryant's Minstrels that became the battle song of the Confederacy—*Dixie*. Since the invention of grease paint and burnt cork were still twenty-five years away, this quartet colored their faces with ham fat, a makeup that made "ham" a synonym for actor in stage parlance.

The Original Virginia Minstrels set the basic pattern for other and more pretentious minstrel troupes—Christy's Minstrels, which played New York City in 1846; Dan Bryant's Minstrels, which pirated and popularized the songs of Stephen Foster; and Callendar's Original Georgia Minstrels, which gave James Bland, the first of our great Negro songwriters and author-composer of *Carry Me Back To Ol' Virginny,* an outlet for his rare talent and introduced Negro minstrelsy to the British Isles with Charles and Daniel Frohman acting as company managers.

In the closing two decades of the nineteenth century, the far-more-famous and still-remembered successors to these trail-blazers of minstrelsy—the troupes of Al G. Fields, Lew Dockstader, Hi Henry, Neil O'Brien, Haverly, McIntyre and Heath, Primrose and West, George Thatcher and George "Honey Boy" Evans—brought melody and mirth not only to Broadway but to tank towns from the Atlantic to the Pacific and schooled such eminent Broadway stars as Al Jolson and Frank Tinney in the blackface art.

Today's Broadway musical also owes a debt to Tony Pastor, who rates an accolade as the granddaddy of the Broadway revue, the offspring of the variety shows he presented at his three famous music halls, the first of which he opened in 1865 and the third and most famous, on Fourteenth Street, sixteen years later. Graduate of the circus sawdust, celebrated singer of topical songs and a knowing showman, Tony Pastor made the variety show, born in the squalor of Bowery dives, a wholesome and refined attraction for both the family and the carriage trade, and introduced on well-balanced bills many of the future greats of musical comedy—Weber and Fields, Lillian Russell, Montgomery and Stone, the Four Cohans, Pat Rooney and Harrigan and Hart.

Harrigan and Hart, with their composer, David Brahams, also had a hand in shaping the mold of the Broadway musical of today, and of this trio, Ned Harrigan made the most important contribution since he had both vision and the creative ability to translate that vision into a theatrical reality. Fascinated by the polyglot population of New York City, he created a series of musical farces based on the triumphs and tribulations of Dan Mulligan and his social-climbing wife, Cordelia, and the struggle for political power between the Mulligan Guards and their Negro rivals, the Skidmore Cadets, that were hailed by such eminent critics as William Dean Howells and Brander Mathews as "the springs of true American comedy."

Teeing off with *The Mulligan Guard Ball* in 1879, Ned Harrigan wrote and produced twenty-four Broadway productions in a 17-year span in addition to starring in all of them and writing the lyrics for such highly popular songs of a half-century and more ago as *The Babies On Our Block, The Market On Saturday Night, When Poverty's Tears Ebb And Flow, Danny By My Side* and *Maggie Murphy's Home.* In the sunset of his success, Harrigan leased the theatre bearing his name to Richard Mansfield, who in 1895 renamed it The Garrick, and here thirty years later, Richard Rodgers and Larry Hart made their initial bid for Broadway fame with their first song hit, *Manhattan,* written for the *Garrick Gaieties.*

When Father Knickerbocker finally gets around to celebrating the 200th anniversary of the Broadway musical, he will be sadly remiss if he doesn't raise his glass in a toast to Charles Hoyt, who as a creator and producer of musical farces fell heir to the mantle discarded by Ned Harrigan soon after the team of Harrigan and Hart was dissolved in 1885.

While Ned Harrigan restricted the locale of his plays to the sidewalks and the slums of New York, Hoyt chose a wider canvas on which to portray his satires on such topical, nation-wide themes as woman's suffrage, the temperance crusade and the grandiose ambitions of small-time politicians, and reached the crest of his success in 1893 when his *A Trip To Chinatown* smashed all Broadway long-run records with 656 performances—a mark that stood for twenty-six years until shattered in 1919 by Harry Tierney's *Irene.*

A Trip To Chinatown also was the first Broadway musical to produce a bonanza in sheet music sales with Percy Gaunt, the musical director of the production, writing both words and music for four smash hits: *The Bowery, Reuben, Reuben, I've Been Thinking; Love Me Little Love Me Long* and

Push Dem Clouds Away, while an interpolated number, introduced by J. Aldrich Libby, sold better than a million copies—Charles K. Harris' *After The Ball.*

Equally as prolific as Ned Harrigan, Charles Hoyt is credited with the following highly successful productions both on Broadway and the road:

A Bunch Of Keys (1883), starring Willie Edouin; *A Rag Baby* (1884), directed by Julian Mitchell, who later served George M. Cohan and Florenz Ziegfeld in a similar capacity; *A Hole In The Ground* (1888); *A Tin Soldier* (1889) in which Paul Dresser, author-composer of *On The Banks Of The Wabash* and *My Gal Sal,* played a leading role; *A Midnight Bell* (1890) in which Maude Adams made her stage debut; *A Texas Steer* (1891), starring Tim Murphy; *A Parlor Match* (1892), starring Evans and Hoey, in which Anna Held sang *Won't You Come And Play Wiz Me?; A Temperance Town* (1893); *A Dog In The Manger* (1894); *A Contented Woman* (1895), a satire on woman's suffrage; *A Runaway Colt* (1895); *A Milk White Flag* (1895); *A Black Sheep* (1896) with two hit songs: *The Clock Will Never Strike Again* and *She Is My Picnic Girl; A Stranger In New York* (1897), which had the country singing *Miss Helen Hunt* with its double entendre last line "Go to Helen Hunt for it"; and *A Brass Monkey* (1901), based on the acute sufferings induced on this legendary creature by extremely low temperatures.

When counting the Broadway milestones, there is one so highly polished it can't be overlooked. That's bald-head row, which first cast its refulgence over the Great White Way on the night of September 12, 1886 when *The Black Crook* had its American premiere at Niblo's Garden, located at the corner of Broadway and Prince Street, where feminine pulchritude was shockingly revealed sans all Victorian modesty. This extravanganza, which marked the birth of the leg show, was the mating of a French ballet troupe of a hundred girls, imported by Henry C. Jarrett, a theater manager, and his angel, Harry Palmer, a Wall Street broker, and a melodrama by Charles M. Barras.

This unusual union was a marriage of convenience since the Academy of Music where Jarrett planned to produce his French ballet burned down before the show was ready to open, while the manager of Niblo's Garden, who had agreed to stage the Barras melodrama, thought better of the idea while the thriller was in rehearsal and was open to any suggestion that would inject life into a certain flop. The nuptials also had the earmarks of a shotgun wedding since Barras at first refused to be a party to such an unholy alliance, and only gave in after going without food for several days, finally sacrificing his pride of authorship for the price of a meat ticket, a down payment of $1500 and a share in the royalties, which eventually made him a man of no little affluence.

The reception accorded *The Black Crook* and the furor it caused rocked both Broadway and the nation, for in this Mother Eve of later Minsky's shows, the plunging neckline had its genesis and six of the ballet girls appeared unskirted and in flesh-colored tights. The clergy branded the show as a menace to national morality, the *New York Tribune*, overlooked when advertising space was bought, took up the editorial cudgel in defense of virtue, and the inevitable happened: *The Black Crook* became one of the most profitable enterprises in theatrical history, playing the road to packed houses for at least thirty years after a Broadway run of 474 performances, returning to New York City for eight revivals during the nineteenth century, and challenging such hardy perennials as *Uncle Tom's Cabin* and *Rip Van Winkle* for the longevity record. In fact, there was "life in the old girl yet" as late as 1929 when a revised edition of *The Black Crook* was staged at Hoboken, N.J. with Agner de Mille as the prima ballerina.

The plaudits that bald-head row showered upon the buxom beauties of *The Black Crook* nightly from the 7:45 curtain to the 1:15 finale eventually reached London, and in 1868, the arrival of Lydia Thompson and her company of British blondes for an American engagement at Wood's Museum was greeted with cries of indignation from press and pulpit and the nightly display of the SRO sign in front of the theater. The leg show was again front page news, especially in Chicago where the voluptious Lydia, smarting from the abuse heaped upon her by *The Chicago Times*, suddenly became highly volatile and subjected Wilbur S. Story, the editor, to a public horsewhipping.

But of these pioneering Minskys, Edward E. Rice was the first to produce burlesque-extravaganzas as Henry Ford later built Lizzies—on a quantity basis. After attending a performance of *The Black Crook*, Rice, a clerk in the Boston Cunard Line office, and his companion, J. Cheever Goodwin, a Harvard graduate and reporter on *The Boston Traveler*, decided they could write a much better show than they had just witnessed and set about to do so. While racked by early birth pains, these collaborators had their pristine urge to write for the stage sharpened by the phenominal success scored by *Humpty Dumpty*, which ran for 483 performances on Broadway, repeated its Manhattan triumphs on the road, and established its star and producer, George L. Fox, as one of the all-time greats of pantomime. And shortly before his success so unbalanced Fox that he started a movement to have a monument erected in his honor in Union Square and had to be carted off to a mental hospital, Edward Rice in 1880 set up an imposing milestone on Broadway with his *Evangeline*, the first American musical with an original score, the music by the former Cunard Line clerk, a self-taught pianist, who for the next fifteen years, ranked as the leading creator and producer of extravaganzas, with *Evangeline* being a perennial favorite on the road till well into the twentieth century.

The foreign influence still reflected in the Broadway musical had its beginning as early as 1844 when William Michael Balfe's *The Bohemian Girl* had
its American premiere, but the most telling impact came thirty-five years later
when the D'Oyle Carte Opera Company opened in *Pinafore* at the Fifth
Avenue Theater, and for the next decade, the light operas of Gilbert and Sullivan not only challenged the popularity of the Mulligan musical farces in
which Harrigan and Hart co-starred but provided a pattern and an inspiration for the American composer, lyricist and librettist.

But despite the excellence of their collaboration and the acclaim their
operas received, Gilbert and Sullivan during the 1880s ran a poor second to
Edward Jacobowski, English by birth but of Polish parentage, whose *Erminie*
enjoyed a continuous run of 1256 performances in New York City, Boston
and Philadelphia after a Broadway premiere at the Casino Theater on May
10, 1886. Rudolph Aronson, the producer, could have had the American
rights to the production for $500 but turned the offer down, a rejection that
cost him $120,000 in royalties.

Another English composer for whom Broadway spread out the red carpet
of welcome during this period was Edward Solomon, the first of Lillian Russell's three husbands, who combined business with pleasure by starring his
wife, whose hour-glass figure was the envy of American womanhood, in most
of his operas that were produced in this country.

The Viennese operettas, compared to these English importations, played a
down-stage role during this period, and although Johann Strauss made a
personal American appearance in the 1890s and several of his operas were
presented in New York prior to that visit, the Blue Danube school of music
had fuller expression in the opening years of the twentieth century in the
scores written by Victor Herbert and Gustave Luders, who while being the
adopted sons of Uncle Sam, had been trained in the technique of the Waltz
King.

In passing, a nod of recognition is due the Kiralfy Brothers, three Hungarian acrobats and pantomimists, who when they turned producers in 1875,
went in for striking mechanical effects and realistic stage settings. They were
the Joseph Urbans of their day, and the first to use subdued color in their
scenic backgrounds in order that the attention of the audience would be
focused on the actors and the action. In their first production, *Around The
World in Eighty Days* (1875), they reached a new high in scenic realism
with settings that brought the Suez Canal, the Taj Mahal and Calcutta in
something approaching their natural splendor to the eyes of little-traveled New
Yorkers, and eight years later, in *Excelsior,* introduced "spectacular electric
lighting effects under the personal supervision of Thomas A. Edison".

In the early 1880s, as well, the country's leading exponents of musical comedy—singers, dancers and comedians—were provided with a de luxe show case in which to display their talents—the celebrated Casino, built in 1881 and located at the southwest corner of Broadway and Thirty-first Street. Since the theater district at that time centered around Fourteenth Street, the Casino was dubbed "Aronson's Folly" by the Broadway skeptics who held that the location was too far north to attract the city's playgoers. But Rudolph Aronson, who promoted the venture with the financial backing of such notables as Cyrus W. Field, William K. Vanderbilt, Chauncey Depew, Tom Platt, Pierre Lorillard and J. P. Morgan, proved such a pessimistic prediction unfounded by staging productions of such outstanding merit at the Casino that residents of New York and visitors to the city were willing to go out of their way to see and enjoy them.

A spacious and imposing structure of Moorish design, the Casino housed both a theater and the first open-air roof garden in the United States, the latter decorated with rich oriental tapestries and giant palms and provided with tables at which patrons might dine and drink while watching an operetta or musical extravaganza in which the top names in show business appeared.

Mecca of late nineteenth century sightseers, the Radio City of New York's yesterday, the Casino was the doorway to fame for such Broadway celebrities as David Warfield, Lois Fuller, Lillian Russell, Anna Held, Eddie Foy, DeWolf Hopper, Lulu Glaser, Adele Richie, James K. Powers and Jefferson de Angelis, and fired the American composer, struggling for recognition from producers partial to the Made-in-England musical product, with ambition, hope and dreams of success.

Some of these dreams came true during the Gay Nineties.

Reginald de Koven, American-born despite his Oxford accent and the *grand seigneur* of music as he strode down Broadway in his silk hat and sable-lined overcoat, made theatrical history with his *Robin Hood,* which presented by The Bostonians, put *Oh Promise Me* on the music racks of the nation's pianos and launched Harry B. Smith on a career in which he wrote 300 librettos.

Victor Herbert also found his place in the spotlight, and the eight comic operas he wrote during the closing decade of the dying century were the stepping stones that led to Broadway's Hall Of Fame where the former cellist at the "Met" soon was to be enshrined as the equal if not the superior of Johann Strauss and Sir Arthur Sullivan in the light opera field.

Gustave Kerker, in addition to directing the orchestra at the Casino, not only wrote the scores of ten productions that were staged at that famous playhouse, but captivated London with his *The Belle of New York,* the first made-in-America musical to play the British capital where it was the sensation for two seasons.

John Stromberg, like Kerker, discovered gold and fame in the orchestra pit, and became a leading figure in a Broadway rags-to-riches success story that made the Weber & Fields Music Hall the talk of the town, writing the songs for ten productions staged by two ambitious Dutch comedians, who doubling as producers, gave burlesque a lift that brought praise instead of censure from the press and lured the elite of Manhattan to the box office with catchy tunes, genuine talent and side-splitting travesty in addition to well-filled tights.

The bulging-bosomed, broad-beamed Amazons of *The Black Crook* already had gone the way of all flesh—into oblivion, and the toast of Broadway in the Gay Nineties were the Gaiety Girls from George Edwardes' London Gaiety Theater, who in long, billowy skirts and picture hats endowed the chorus line with charm, beauty and refinement.

There was truly American music—an unmistakable red, white and blue strain—in the martial numbers John Philip Sousa wrote for his early operas— *El Capitan* and *The Bride Elect,* and near the century's close, the Negro troupers, who had been relegated to the side streets of Manhattan despite their natural and proven ability as singers, dancers and comedians, finally made the Broadway grade when *Clorindy* or *The Origin Of The Cake Walk* with music by Will Marion Cook and book and lyrics by Paul Lawrence Dunbar, opened on the Casino Garden Roof for a summer run.

In one hundred and fifty years, the theater had moved up town from Nassau Street to Times Square, and the Broadway musical, in seven-league boots, had kept pace with it.

Highlights In Broadway Musical History Before The Century's Turn

1751. THE BEGGAR'S OPERA
By John Gay, with music by Dr. Christopher Pepusch. Principal songs: *Let Us Take To The Road, Lillibullero, Green Sleeves, Hither Dear Husband,* and *When A Wife's In A Pout.*

1844. THE BOHEMIAN GIRL
Book and lyrics by Alfred Bunn, and music by William Michael Balfe. Principal songs: *I Dreamt That I Dwelt In Marble Halls, With Heart Bowed Down* and *Then You'll Remember Me.*

1847. THE GOLDEN AX
A pantomimic fairy tale with patriotic tableaux that included "The Battle Of Bunker Hill" as a rousing finale.

1848. MARITANA
Book and lyrics by Edward Fitzball, and music by Edward Wallace. Principal songs: *Scenes That Are Brightest* and *Yes, Let Me Like A Soldier Fall.*

1855. POCAHONTAS
An extravaganza-burlesque in which the author and producer, John Brougham, played the role of John Smith.

1856. HIAWATHA
Another John Brougham production.

1857. NOVELTY
An extravaganza presented by the Ronzanni troupe of French and Italian acrobats and dancers with the laying of the Atlantic cable serving as a spectacular finale.

1862. JACK AND THE BEANSTALK
A pantomime in which George L. Fox established a Broadway record of 150 consecutive performances at the Bowery Theater.

1866. THE BALLOON WEDDING
An extravaganza starring the Six Hanlon Brothers, an acrobatic troupe, and introducing a ballet in which the girls sang as well as danced—an innovation.

1866. THE BLACK CROOK
Produced at a reputed record cost of

$25,400 at Niblo's Garden where the stage was completely rebuilt to provide trap doors and sliding floors for quick scene changes.

1868. THE WHITE FAWN
A sequel to *The Black Crook*.

1868. HUMPTY DUMPTY
Produced by George L. Fox, star of this pantomimic extravaganza, who introduced such novelties in the production as a troupe of roller skaters, a baby ballet, headed by a 5-year-old premiere danseuse; and a bicycle act by Little Venus and Young Adonis, aged 2½ and 4½ years respectively.

1868. IXION, or THE MAN AT THE WHEEL
The American debut of Lydia Thompson and her troupe of British blondes in which the star played the title role in male attire.

1869. THE FORTY THIEVES
The second of the Lydia Thompson burlesques to be staged in New York City.

1870. PIPPIN, or THE KING OF THE GOLD MINES
This ended the Broadway vogue of Lydia Thompson and her bleached blondes.

1874. EVANGELINE.
With music by Edward E. Rice, its producer, and book and lyrics by J. Cheever Goodwin. In this production, George K. Fortesque, later of the Bostonians, made his debut as a female impersonator in the role of "the ponderous Catherine", and a white heifer, played by two actors who performed an exccentric dance, was a Broadway innovation and a stage celebrity for the next twenty years.

1874. LONDON BY NIGHT
An extravaganza that featured impressive cycloramas and mechanical effects, produced at the New York Colosseum, located at Broadway and Thirty-fifth Street.

1875. AROUND THE WORLD IN EIGHTY DAYS
Produced by the Kiralfy Brothers at Niblo's Garden.

1879. THE BROOK
The first American musical with songs and story closely integrated, written and produced by Nate Salsbury, who later became the managing director of Buffalo Bill's Wild West Show.

1879. THE MULLIGAN GUARD BALL
The first of the Harrigan and Hart productions, presented by a cast that included Annie Yeamans, the comedienne, and John Wild and William Gray, the 1879 edition of Moran and Mack. Principal songs: *The Mulligan Guard Ball, The Skidmore Fancy Ball, We're All Young Fellows Bran' New, Singing In The Hallway Door* and *The Babies On Our Block*.

1879. THE MULLIGAN GUARDS' CHOWDER
Principal songs: *The Skids Are Out Today, Oh, Girly, Girly; The Little Widow Dunn, Casey's Social Club* and *Never Take The Horseshoe From The Door*.

1879. THE MULLIGAN GUARDS' CHRISTMAS
Principal songs: *The Little Green Leaf In Our Bible, The Sweet Kentucky Rose, The Pitcher Of Beer, The Mulligan Braves, The Skids Are On Review*, and *Tu-ri-ad-i-lum, or Santa Claus Has Come*.

1879. PINAFORE
The first of the Gilbert and Sullivan operas to be staged in this country.

1879. THE SORCERER
In this Gilbert-and-Sullivan opera, John Howson played the title role, a caricature of the Rev. T. DeWitt Talmadge, with Lillian Russell and Digby Bell in the supporting cast.

1879. THE TOURISTS IN A PULLMAN PALACE CAR
A farce comedy with interpolated songs from Gilbert and Sullivan's *Box and Cox, Il Trovatore* and *The Chimes of Normandy* plus several original tunes: *Nursery Rhymes, The Telegraph Boy* and *The End Of The Route*.

1879. HOBBIES
A musical farce comedy in which Nat C. Goodwin gave impersonations of such eminent tragedians as Edwin Booth, Lawrence Barrett and Joseph Jefferson.

1879. THE CHIMES OF NORMANDY
Score by Robert Jean Planquette.

1879. GIROFLE-GIROFLA
Score by Charles Lecocq. The first of the French opera-bouffes to be presented in this country by Maurice Grau.

1880. THE PIRATES OF PENZANCE
World premiere of this Gilbert-and-Sullivan opera was staged in New York City to protect the American copyright.

1880. THE MULLIGAN GUARDS' SURPRISE
Principal songs: *Full Moon Union, Dat Citron Wedding Cake, I'll Wear The*

Trousers Oh! and *Whist, The Boogie Man.*

1880. THE MULLIGANS' PICNIC
Principal songs: *Mary Kelly's Beau, Second Degree Full Moon Union, Going Home With Nelly After Five, All Aboard For The M.G.P., Roderick O'Dwyer, Hurry, Little Children, Sunday Morn; The Beauty of The Limerick* and *Locked Out After Nine.*

1880. THE MULLIGAN GUARDS' NOMINEE
Principal songs: *The Skids Are Out To-Night, Hang the Mulligan Banner Up, A Nightcap, Oh, He Promises* and *Down In Gossip Row.*

1880. MULLIGAN'S SILVER WEDDING
Principal songs: *The Castaways, Don't You Miss The Train, John Reilly's Always Dry, The Mirror's The Cause Of It All, South Fifth Avenue, Third Degree Full Moon Union* and *Wheel The Baby Out.*

1880. HIAWATHA. The second in a series of Edward E. Rice's extravaganzas with Alice Atherton in the title role.

1880. THE ROYAL MIDDY
A Viennese operetta with music by Franz Richard Genee in which the chorus girls wore sailor pants that accentuated the feminine derriere.

1881. PATIENCE
The American premiere of this Gilbert and Sullivan opera.

1881. THE MAJOR
In this production, the first at the new Theater Comique, Ned Harrigan abandoned the Dan Mulligan role and appeared as Major Gilfeather, a la-de-da Englishman. Principal songs: *That's An Old Gag With Me, The Veteran Guard Cadets, Henrietta Pye, Clara Jenkins' Tea, I Really Can't Sit Down, Miranda, When We Are One* and *Major Gilfeather.*

1881. THE SNAKE CHARMER
In this Viennese opera by Edmund Audran, Lillian Russell graduated from Tony Pastor's Music Hall into a comic opera star.

1881. BILLIE TAYLOR
The first of the Edward Solomon operas to be produced in this country, and revived in 1885 with Lillian Russell in the starring role.

1881. ZANINA
Another Viennese opera by Franz Richard Genee in which six nautch dancers had feature billing.

1882. SQUATTER SOVEREIGNTY
A Harrigan and Hart production. Principal songs: *Paddy Duffy's Cart, Widow Nolan's Goat, Miss Brady's Piano Fortay, The Maguires, The McIntyres* and *The Forlorn Old Maid.*

1882. THE BLACKBIRD
DeWolf Hopper was a member of the cast of this short-lived Harrigan and Hart production. Principal songs: *John Cope, The Mountain Dew* and *The Trouper's The Pride Of The Ladies.*

1882. MORDECAI LYONS
A Harrigan and Hart production. Principal songs: *The Old Bowery Pit, Cash, Cash, Cash!, She Lives On Murray Hill, When The Clock In The Steeple Strikes Twelve* and *Mordecai Lyons.*

1882. McSORLEY'S INFLATION, or THE McSORLEYS
A Harrigan and Hart production. Principal songs: *The Old Feather Bed, The Market On Saturday Night, McNally's Row Of Flats, The Charleston Blues, The Salvation Army, Oh!* and *I Never Drink Behind The Bar.*

1882. IOLANTHE
The American premiere of this Gilbert and Sullivan opera.

1882. THE QUEEN'S LACE HANDKERCHIEF
This Johann Strauss operetta was the opening attraction at the New York Casino.

1883. A BUNCH OF KEYS
The first of the Charles Hoyt musical farces, starring Willie Edouin and presented at the San Francisco Theater.

1883. THE MUDDY DAY
This Harrigan and Hart production took its title from the name of a mud scow that made regular trips down the bay. Principal songs: *On Board The Muddy Day, The Golden Choir, Silly Boy, The Bunch Of Cherries, The Family Overhead,* and *The Turin Verein Cadets.*

1883. CORDELIA'S ASPIRATIONS
A Harrigan and Hart production. Principal songs: *My Dad's Dinner Pail, Just Across From Jersey, Sam Johnson's Colored Cake Walk,* and *Waiters' Chorus, or Two More To Come.*

1883. THE MERRY WAR
An operetta with music by Johann Strauss.

1883. LA VIE PARISIENNE
An operetta by Jacques Offenbach.

1883. *POP*
An Edward E. Rice production, starring George K. Fortesque.

1883. *EXCELSIOR*
A Kiralfy Brothers' production with spectacular electric lighting effects supervised by Thomas A. Edison.

1883. *THE PRINCESS OF TREBIZONDE*
A Jacques Offenbach operetta in which Lillian Russell, Emma Carus and Digby Bell headed a Casino Theater cast.

1884. *DAN'S TRIBULATIONS*
A Harrigan and Hart production. Principal songs: *Cobwebs On The Wall*, *Coming Home From Meeting*, *My Little Side Door* and *The French Singing Lesson*.

1884. *ADONIS*
This Edward E. Rice extravaganza, which hung up a Broadway run of 603 performances, made a national matinee idol out of Henry E. Dixey.

1884. *PRINCESS IDA*
The American premiere of this Gilbert and Sullivan opera.

1884. *FALKA*
Francis Wilson made his comic opera debut in this production with music by Francois Chassaigne.

1885. *McALLISTER'S LEGACY*
A Harrigan and Hart production. Principal songs: *Molly, Mr. Dooley's Geese, Pat And His Little Brown Mare, Blow The Billows Blow!* and *Oh My, How We Pose!*

1885. *INVESTIGATION*
When the final curtain fell on this musical farce, the historic partnership of Ned Harrigan and Tony Hart came to an end. Hart starred later in *A Toy Pistol* and two or three other plays before his death, while his place in the Harrigan troupe was taken by Dan Collyer. Principal songs: *On Union Square, The Boodle, Hello Baby, As Long As The World Goes Round* and *The Man Who Knows It All*, or *Muldoon The Solid Man*.

1885. *OLD LAVENDER*
A Ned Harrigan production. Principal songs: *When Poverty's Tears Ebb and Flow, Extra, Extra!, Get Up, Jack! John Sit Down!; Please To Put That Down* and *Sweetest Love*.

1885. *THE GRIP*
A Ned Harrigan production. Principal songs: *The Aldermanic Board, No Wealth Without Labor, Oh, Dat Low Bridge!,*

School Days and *The Soldier Boy's Canteen*.

1885. *THE MIKADO*
In the American premiere of this Gilbert-and-Sullivan opera, which ran for 250 performances on Broadway, DeWolf Hopper played the role of Ko-Ko.

1885. *POLLY, THE PRIDE OF THE REGIMENT*
A light opera by Edward Solomon, and starring Lillian Russell.

1885. *THE BLACK HUSSAR*
In this light opera by Karl Millocker, DeWolf Hopper made his entrance wearing a coal stove for a suit of armor in the open door of which a fire blazed. Principal song: *Read The Answer In The Stars*, a topical number.

1885. *DIE FLEDERMAUS*
The American premiere of Johann Strauss' most famous operetta.

1886. *THE LEATHER PATCH*
A Ned Harrigan production. Principal songs: *Baxter Avenue, It Showered Again, Denny Grady's Hack* and *Put On Your Bridal Veil*.

1886. *THE O'REAGANS.*
A Ned Harrigan production. Principal songs: *Mulberry Springs, The Little Hedge School, Strolling On The Sands, The U. S. Black Marines* and *When The Trumpet In The Cornfield Blows*.

1886. *PEPITA*, or *THE GIRL WITH THE GLASS EYES*
This Edward Solomon opera, starring Lillian Russell, marked the transition of Chauncey Olcott from a minstrel trouper to an Irish tenor.

1886. *ERMINIE*
In this operetta with music by Edward Jacobowski, Josephine Hall played Erminie, Francis Wilson Cardeaux, Marie Jansen Javotte and William S. Daboll Ravannes. Principal songs: *At Night On My Pillow Lying, The Darkest Hour* and *Dear Mother, In Dreams I See Her*.

1886. *THE LITTLE TYCOON*
Produced by Augustin Daly, this musical springboarded Willard Spencer into the limelight as one of the first American composers to achieve signal successes in the comic opera field. It had its premiere at the Temple Theater in Philadelphia, the home of the composer, where it ran for 500 performances. Principal songs: *On The Sea, Doomed Am I To Marry A Lord, Love Comes Like A Summer Night,*

Heel And Toe We Always Go, Love Reigns, Oh, Why The Apprehension? Sad Heart Of Mine, Checkmated We, Tell Me Daisy, Speak Low Walls Have Ears, Sham The Great Tycoon, The Cats On Our Back Fence and *Yes I'll Be A Little Tycoon.*

1886. NANON
An operetta by Franz Richard Genee. Principal song: *Anna In Rapture I Come To Thee.*

1886. LITTLE JACK SHEPPARD. A burlesque produced by Nat C. Goodwin in which Lois Fuller made her American debut as a skirt dancer.

1887. McNOONEY'S VISIT
A Ned Harrigan production. Principal songs: *Ho, Molly Grogan; The Black Maria, Have One On Me* and *Toboggan Slide.*

1887. PETE
A Ned Harrigan production. Principal songs: *Where The Sweet Magnolia Grows, The Old Barn Floor, The Bridal March, The Old Black Crow, Slavery's Passed Away, Massa's Wedding Night, Haul The Woodpile Down* and *Wander Through The Orange Grove.*

1887. CONRAD, THE CORSAIR
An Edward E. Rice production with music by John J. Braham.

1887. RUDDYGORE
The New York premiere of this Gilbert and Sullivan operetta.

1887. DOROTHY
A musical from London's Gaiety Theater with music by Alfred Cellier and starring Lillian Russell.

1887. PRINCESS OF TRIBIGONDE
Music by Jacques Offenbach.

1888. WADDY GOOGAN
A Ned Harrigan production. Principal songs: *The Midnight Squad, Isabelle St. Clair, Old Boss Barry* and *Where The Sparrows And The Chippies Parade.*

1888. THE YEOMAN OF THE GUARD
The American premiere of this Gilbert and Sullivan operetta.

1888. MONTE CRISTO, JR.
An imported burlesque from London, produced under the direction of George Edwardes.

1888. THE LADY OR THE TIGER
The first Broadway musical with a book based on a best-selling novel, Frank R. Stockton's story of the same name, with

libretto by Sydney Rosenfeld and music by Julius Lyons.

1888. THE BRIGANDS
A New York Casino production of Jacques Offenbach's operetta.

1889. THE LORGAIRE
A Ned Harrigan production. Principal songs: *La Plus Belle France, I'm A Terror To All, My Molly Is Waiting For Me, Dolly My Crumped Horn Cow* and *Paddy and His Sweet Potteen.*

1889. THE SEVEN AGES
An Edward E. Rice extravaganza, based on the Shakespeare soliloquy in *As You Like It,* and starring Henry E. Dixie.

1889. THE GONDOLIERS
The American premiere of the last of the Gilbert-and-Sullivan operettas.

1889. FAUST UP-TO-DATE
A burlesque from London's famous Gaiety Theater.

1890. THE MERRY MONARCH
This was the first successful comic opera of Woolson Morse, who composed his songs on a harmonica, directed the productions and painted the scenery. Francis Wilson starred in the title role.

1890. POOR JONATHAN
This Karl Millocker operetta in which Lillian Russell and Jefferson de Angelis co-starred was distinguished by its last-act setting—West Point.

1890. REILLY AND THE FOUR HUNDRED
This was Ned Harrigan's opening production at his new Harrigan Theater in which Ada Lewis gained fame as a tough, gum-chewing Bowery girl. Principal songs: *The Jolly Commodore, I've Come Home To Stay, Taking In The Town, Uncle Reilly, The Great Four Hundred, Jim Jam Sailors Superfine* and *Maggie Murphy's Home,* introduced by Emma Pollock.

1891. WANG
Although a failure when first produced under another name, this proved to be the most successful of Woolson Morse's comic operas with DeWolf Hopper and Della Fox in the leading roles. Principal songs: *Welcome Madam Frimousse, Every Rose Must Have Its Thorn, Ask The Man In The Moon, A Pretty Girl (A Summer's Night), The Man With A Elephant On His Hands, To Be A Lone Widow, Coronation March* and *Get On Board.*

1891. THE LAST OF THE HOGANS
A Ned Harrigan production. Principal

songs: *Hats Off To Me, Old Neighborhood, Knights Of The Mystic Star, The Last Of The Hogans, On De Rainbow Road, Take A Day Off Mary Ann* and *Danny By My Side,* a song that was given a husky revival by Al Smith in 1933 at the celebration marking the fiftieth anniversary of the Brooklyn Bridge.

1891. *MISS HELLYETT*
This light opera with music by Edmund Audran had a book by David Belasco, who starred Mrs. Leslie Carter in the production.

1891. *LA CIGALE*
This light opera, starring Lillian Russell, was the first American production with music by Ivan Caryll.

1891. *THE TYROLEAN*
This light opera, starring Marie Tempest, was offered as a dual attraction with the American premiere of *Cavalleria Rusticana*—the birth of the double feature.

1891. *THE TAR AND THE TARTAR*
A light opera by Adam Itzel, Jr. in which the first barefoot dancers appeared on the Broadway stage.

1892. *THE ISLE OF CHAMPAGNE*
A comic opera with book and lyrics by Charles A. Byrne and Louis Harrison, music by William Wallace Furst, and starring Thomas Q. Seabrooke in the role of King Pommery II. Principal songs: *We're The Light Brigade, Pop! Ah!; Fly Little Bird, Old King Mumm Could Make Things Hum, There's A Land In The Silvery Shimmery Moon* and *Song Of All Nations.*

1893. *PRINCESS NICOTINE*
In this comic opera, with music by William Wallace Furst, Lillian Russell was called upon to sing eight high Cs at each performance, a feat that elicited the admiration of the Metropolitan prima donna, Nellie Melba.

1893. *A GAIETY GIRL*
This English importation, with music by Sydney Jones, introduced the demure Gaiety Girls to Broadway audiences, and put new ideas of glamour in the heads of the Stage Door Johnnies. Principal songs: *Private Tommy Atkins* and *Sunshine Above.*

1893. *PANJANDRUM*
This comic opera with music by Woolson Morse had its locale in the Philippines, which few Americans realized was on the

map until five years later when Dewey steamed triumphantly into Manila Bay.

1893. *1492*
This Edward E. Rice production, with book by R. A. Barnet and music by Carl Pfleuger, was a nightly sellout attraction in Chicago during the World's Columbian Exposition, and Richard Harlowe, the female impersonator, stopped every performance with his singing of *Isabella.*

1893. *A TRIP TO CHINATOWN*
The most successful of all the Charles Hoyt's productions with a Broadway run of 656 performances.

1893. *THE RAINMAKER OF SYRIA*
The first of the Leo Fall operettas to be produced in this country.

1893. *DON JUAN*
A comic opera with music by Sydney Jones. Principal song: *Linger Longer Lou.*

1893. *THE WOOLEN STOCKING*
A Ned Harrigan production. Principal songs: *The Sunny Side Of Thompson Street, Callahan's Gang, Sergeant Hickey Of The G.A.R., Little Daughter Nell* and *They Never Tell All They Know.*

1894. *DR. SYNTAX*
In this comic opera with music by Woolson Morse and co-starring DeWolf and Edna Wallace Hopper, a boat race between the Yale and Harvard crews rang down the last act curtain.

1894. *LITTLE CHRISTOPHER COLUMBUS*
This Edward E. Rice production had a score by Gustave Kerker and Ivan Caryll, and was staged in London before its Broadway premiere.

1894. *PRINCESS BONNIE*
A comic opera by Willard Spencer that before its Broadway opening, had a 1039 performance run in Philadelphia.

1894. *THE PASSING SHOW*
This first of the modern revues, with music by Ludwig Englander and starring Adele Richie, set the pattern for productions bearing the same title that were staged annually at the Winter Garden after the turn of the century.

1895. *EXCELSIOR, JR.*
In this Edward E. Rice production, Fay Templeton impersonated the dauntless hero of Henry W. Longfellow's poem and Arthur Dunn gave a burlesque imitation of a newly crowned piano virtuoso, Ignace Paderewski.

1895. *ALADDIN, JR.*
An extravaganza with book by A. Cheever Goodwin, music by W. F. Bachelor, W. F. Glover and Jesse Williams, and produced by David Henderson. Principal song: *Little Alabama Coon,* an interpolated number by Hattie Starr, sung by Frankie Raymond.

1895. *A DAUGHTER OF THE REVO-LUTION*
An extravaganza with book and lyrics by J. Cheever Goodwin and music by Ludwig Englander in which a series of historical tableaux were introduced, including Washington's crossing of the Delaware.

1896. *BOHEMIA*
This comic opera had a book by Clyde Fitch and lyrics and music by William Wallace Furst. Principal song: *Love Makes The World Go Round.*

1896. *THE GEISHA*
A comic opera with book and lyrics by Harry Greenbank, music by Sydney Jones, and introducing Isadora Duncan as a ballerina. Principal songs: *The Amorous Goldfish, Chin-Chin Chinaman, Chon-Kina, The Jewel Of Asia* and *The Toy Monkey.*

1896. *THE MINSTREL OF CLAIRE*
Chauncey Olcott's first starring vehicle in which he introduced *Olcott's Home Song.*

1896. *MARTY MALONE*
A Ned Harrigan production. Principal song: *The Pride Of The London Stage.*

1898. *CLORINDY, or THE ORIGIN OF THE CAKE WALK*
The first colored musical to play Broadway with music by Will Marion Cook and lyrics by Paul Lawrence Dunbar. Principal song: *Who Dat Say Chicken In Dis Crowd?*

1898. *THE RUNAWAY GIRL*
A comic opera with music by Ivan Caryll and Lionel Monckton, which repeated in America its triumph in London, where it had a 593-performance run at the Shaftesbury Theater. Principal songs: *The Sly Cigarette, The Convent Bell, I'm Not That Sort Of Girl, I'm Only A Poor Singing Girl, No One In The World, Follow The Man From Cook's, We Have Left Pursuit Behind Us, The Soldiers In The Park, Beautiful Venice, The Boy Guessed Right The Very First Time, The Pickaninnies,* and *Oh How I Love Society!*

1899. *THE ROUNDERS*
A musical comedy with book and lyrics by Harry B. Smith, music by Ludwig Englander, and produced by a cast headed by Dan Daly, Harry Davenport, Joseph Cawthorn, Thomas Q. Seabrooke, Mabelle Gilman, Irene Bentley, Harry Clifford, Phyllis Rankin and Marie George. Principal songs: *What's The Use Of Anything* and *The Same Old Story.*

1899. *IN GAY PAREE*
A revue with book and lyrics by Edgar Smith, music by Ludwig Englander, and presented by a cast that included Harry Davenport, Mabelle Gilman, Marie George, Robert F. Cotton, Edward D. Tyler, George Beane, Charles Dickson, Samuel Edwards and Perkins Fisher.

1899. *THE ROMANCE OF ATHLONE*
In this Irish comedy-drama, Chauncey Olcott sang *My Wild Irish Rose* for the first time.

1899. *THE ROGERS BROTHERS IN WALL STREET*
The was the first of the annual Rogers Brothers' musicals with book and lyrics by John J. McNally and music by Maurice Levi, and starring Max and Gus Rogers in a cast that included Louise Gunning, Maud Raymond, Ada Lewis, Lee Harrison, Georgia Caine and John G. Sparks. Principal song: *The Belle Of Murray Hill.*

Pre-1900 Scores of Composers Who Wrote Twentieth Century Musicals

Reginald De Koven Scores

1887. *THE BEGUM*
Book and lyrics by Harry B. Smith. Col. John A. McCaull, a Confederate Army veteran and prominent theatrical producer, agreed to stage this comic opera before reading the book or hearing the score after having been regally entertained at the De Koven home. "The Begum" had its premiere at the Chestnut Street Opera House in Philadelphia with a cast headed by DeWolf Hopper, Digby Bell, Jefferson de Angelis, Harry MacDonough, Mathilde Cottrelly and Hubert Wilke.

1889. *DON QUIXOTE*
Book and lyrics by Harry B. Smith. While written as a co-starring vehicle for DeWolf Hopper and Digby Bell, these comedians

were unable to play in it because of previous commitments and the Bostonians were engaged to present it.

—HEART OF MY HEART

1890. *ROBIN HOOD*

Book and lyrics by Harry B. Smith. This comic opera, which was destined to make theatrical history, was staged at a total production cost of only $109.50, the cast appearing in costumes used in "Il Trovatore," "Martha" and "The Bohemian Girl." The Chicago Opera House was the scene of the premiere June 9, 1890, with members of the famous Bostonians in the following roles: Edwin Hoff as Robin Hood, H. C. Barnabee as the Sheriff of Nottingham, W. H. MacDonald as Little John, Eugene Cowles as Will Scarlet, George B. Frothingham as Friar Tuck, Peter Lang as Guy of Gisborne, Jessie Bartlett Davis as Allan-a-Dale, Josephine Bartlett as Dame Durden, Grace Reals as Annabel and Marie Stone as Maid Marian.

—THEN HEY FOR THE MERRY GREENWOOD
—SIR CAVALIER, YOU'RE WELCOME HERE
—BROWN OCTOBER ALE
—SWEETHEART, MY OWN SWEETHEART
—ARMORER'S SONG
—TINKER'S SONG
—THE LEGEND OF THE CHIMES
—FAREWELL TO OLD SHERWOOD
—'TIS THE MORNING OF THE FAIR
—AS AN HONEST AUCTIONEER
—COME THE BOWMAN IN LINCOLN GREEN
—THOUGH IT WAS WITHIN THIS HOUR WE MET
—I AM THE SHERIFF OF NOTTINGHAM
—AN OUTLAW'S LIFE'S THE LIFE FOR ME
—CHEERILY SOUND THE HUNTER'S HORN
—THE TAILOR AND THE CROW
—OH, SEE THE LAMBKINS PLAY
—A TROUBADOR SANG TO HIS LOVE
—THERE WILL COME A TIME
—*OH, PROMISE ME
Lyrics by Clement Scott.
When the final curtain dropped on the opening performance of "Robin Hood," Jessie Bartlett Davis flew into a rage. She declared there was no song in the score that suited her contralto range, and threatened to leave the company unless De Koven supplied her with at least one solo that did justice to her voice. The composer was stumped momentarily and then recalling an unpublished melody he had written three years before, he stamped into the orchestra pit, sat down at the piano and played and sang the song from memory. Miss Davis was delighted. It was just what she wanted and "Reggie was a dear!" The next night she sang "Oh Promise Me" for the first time.

1892. *THE KNICKERBOCKERS*

Book and lyrics by Harry B. Smith. Presented as a successor to "Robin Hood."

—A PURITAN DAMSEL
—UPON OUR LITTLE FARM
—HANS RAP
—IF YOU AND I SHOULD MEET
—IF THERE IS A LAD
—SING YOUR MERRIEST LAYS
—A MAIDEN VEXED (The Spinning Song)
—I HAVE A SWAIN IN THE ARMY
—HASTEN, TIME
—AN OVERWORKED TRUMPETER
—SONG OF THE FLINT AND STEEL
—I HAVE A PIPE
—ONLY IN DREAMS
—WAR TO THE KNIFE
—DO YOU SIGH FOR LOVE OR GLORY?
—SLEEP YOU PRETTY CREATURES
—TWELVE HOURS A DAY
—HERE'S A SONG TO THE FLAG
—THE SONG OF THE CUCKOO CLOCK

1893. *THE ALGERIAN*

Book and lyrics by Harry B. Smith, and presented by a cast headed by Adele Richie, Marie Tempest, Julius Steger and Joseph Herbert.

—BRETON BOAT SONG
—ONE DAY A LITTLE MAID
—THE WEATHER VANE
—TARTARIN, THE TERRIBLE
—WHEN BAYA'S RAVEN TRESSES
—ALGERIAN SERENADE
—OH, RASH MUEZZIN!
—OLD VILLANELLE
—LIGHTLY, LIGHTLY THE SHIFTING SHADOWS
—TAMBOURINE SONG
—SITTING THE LUTE A-STRIKING
—NUBIAN DANCE
—MARCH OF THE WATCH
—REVEILLE

—CASTLES IN SPAIN
—AND NOW, THE COLONEL

1893. *THE FENCING MASTER*
Book and lyrics by Harry B. Smith, and
co-starring Laura Shirmer Mapleson and
Hubert Wilke.
—THE LIFE OF A ROVER
—I PLAY ALL GAMES OF CHANCE
—AH YES, I LOVE THEE
—WE ARE VERY POOR MUSICIANS
—WILD BIRD THAT SINGETH
—EVERY KNIGHT MUST HAVE A
   STAR
—THE NIGHTINGALE AND THE ROSE
—WILL-O'-THE-WISP

1894. *ROB ROY*
Book and lyrics by Harry B. Smith, and
presented by a cast headed by Lizzie Mac-
Nichol, Juliet Cordon, William Pruette,
Richard Carroll and Joseph Herbert.
—WHO'S FOR THE CHASE, MY BON-
   NIE HEARTS?
—THEN I SHALL LIVE LOVE FOR
   THEE
—DING, DONG
—WE COME TO THE SOUND OF THE
   DRUM
—THE WHITE AND THE RED,
   HUZZAH!
—MY HOME IS WHERE THE HEATH-
   ER BLOOMS
—MY HEART IS IN THE HIGHLANDS
—THE MERRY MILLER
—THE LAY OF THE CAVALIER
—SONG OF THE BALLADMONGERS
—COME, LADS OF THE HIGHLANDS
—MY TRUE LOVE IS A SHEPHERDESS
—DEAREST HEART OF MY HEART
—RISING WHEN THE SUN IS GRAY
—WHO CAN TELL WHERE SHE
   DWELLS?
—SONG OF THE TURNKEY
—SERENADE
—RUSTIC SONG

1896. *THE MANDARIN*
Book and lyrics by Harry B. Smith, and
first produced by the De Koven-Smith
Opera Company at the Herald Square
Theater, New York, with a cast headed by
Adele Richie, George Honey and George
C. Boniface Jr.
—TELL ME, LOVERS, I PRAY

1897. *THE HIGHWAYMAN*
Book and lyrics by Harry B. Smith. When
first produced with Jerome Sykes in the
leading comic role of Foxy Quiller, this
comic opera was a disappointment; but
when it was revived twenty years later,

Jefferson de Angelis played Quiller and
John Charles Thomas was cast as Dick,
an Irish soldier of fortune, and "The
Highwayman" was a notable success.
—BREAD, CHEESE AND KISSES
—MARCHING AWAY
—THE HIGHWAYMAN
—VIVE LA BAGATELLE
—GRETNA GREEN
—KITTY O'BRIEN
—THE FARMER AND THE SCARE-
   CROW
—MOONLIGHT SONG
—DO YOU REMEMBER, LOVE?
—GYPSY SONG
—WHILE THE FOUR WINDS BLOW
—ON THE TRACK
—FAREWELL TO THE KING'S HIGH-
   WAY

1899. *THE THREE DRAGOONS*
Book and lyrics by Harry B. Smith and
starring Jerome Sykes.
—WITH A CACHUCA, FANDANGO
   AND BOLERO
—FILL UP AGAIN, WARRIORS
—WHO WOULDN'T BE A SOLDIER'S
   BRIDE?
—OFFICERS OF THE CAVALRY
—WHEN CUPID COMES TAPPING AT
   THE DOOR
—I'M A SELF-MADE NOBLEMAN
—'TWAS OVER WINDING MOUNTAIN
   ROADS
—SAY THAT YOU CANNOT FORGET
—CARNIVAL IS KING TONIGHT
—THE NAUGHTY LITTLE CLOCK
—WE'RE A PARTY OF GAY SERENAD-
   ERS
—THE BOLD DRAGOON
—IN LISBON GAY
—HAIL, OUR KING
—THE SMART SET
—SOLDIERS OF ALL NATIONS
—HE IS A BLUFF
—ONE HEART TO THEE
—THE LEGEND OF THE DONKEY
—PHILOSOPHY
—IN BATTLE OR UPON PARADE

1899. *PAPA'S WIFE*
Book and lyrics by Harry B. Smith. This
was an early Florenz Ziegfeld production
in which he starred his future wife, Anna
Held, in a cast that included Henry Bergman, George Marion, Henry Woodruff,
Eva Davenport, Dan Collyer and Charles
A. Bigelow. In this musical comedy, Ziegfeld demonstrated for the first time that
he was a connoisseur of feminine pulchri-

tude by presenting sixteen of the most
beautiful chorus girls ever to grace a
Broadway stage.
—WEDDING ANTHEM
—IN THE CONVENT THEY DIDN'T
  TEACH ME THAT
—A PRIVATE AFFAIR
—CUT HIGH, CUT LOW
—AUTOMOBILE SONG
—I'D LIKE TO HAVE A PHOTOGRAPH
  OF THAT
—THE DISSOLUTE MOSQUITO
—THIS WINE'S ALL RIGHT
—PROFESSOR, WON'T YOU TEACH
  ME ALL YOU KNOW?
—OH, THAT'S THE WORST OF GIRLS!
—FROM LA FEMME A PAPA

Julian Edwards Scores

1892. *JUPITER*
A comic opera with book and lyrics by
Harry B. Smith, and starring Digby Bell
in a cast that included Laura Joyce Bell,
Louise Montague, Trixie Friganza and J.
Aldrich Libby.
—I'LL MAKE A LAW TO STOP IT
—THE COBBLER'S SONG
—FLY FAST, FOND DOVE
—A VERY OLD GAG
—SAILING TO THE MOON
—YOU MAY SOAR AND SEARCH
—LIFE IS SUCH A STUPID BORE
—I'LL WAIT FOR THEE
—I CALL ALOUD FOR THEE
—I PRAY THEE HEAR ME
—COME DRAW NIGH

1893. *FRIEND FRITZ*
A comic opera with book and lyrics by
Stanislaus Stange, and co-starring John
Mason and Marion Manola.
—THE HEART THAT LOVES
—I WOULD NOT IF I COULD
—SNOW KING'S DEATH
—BACHELOR'S SONG
—NOBODY KNOWS
—SONG OF THE WEDDING RING
—I'LL FOLLOW THE RULE

1895. *MADELEINE*
A comic opera with book and lyrics by
Stanislaus Stange, and starring Camille
D'Arville and Charles Dickson.
—SONG OF THE HUSBANDS
—MARY HAD A LITTLE LAMB
—THE LEGEND OF GRIMM
—'TWAS BUT A DREAM
—I LOVE YOU SO

—'TIS SAD TO LOVE IN VAIN
—DICKIE AND THE BIRDIE
—THE DOCTOR AND THE SCRIBE
—THE BRIDAL SONG
—SERENADE
—HEART, FOOLISH HEART
—I WOULD HAVE TOLD YOU LONG
  AGO

1896. *THE GODDESS OF TRUTH*
A comic opera with book and lyrics by
Stanislaus Stange, and starring Lillian
Russell in a cast that included Leo Dit-
richstein and Joseph Herbert.
—THE SWEET OLD STORY
—A PRINCESS I
—ON PROBATION
—THE LITTLE WEATHER VANE
—I AM BULGARIA'S KING
—'TIS THE SPIRIT NOT THE LETTER
—AH LOVE, SWEET FRAGRANT
  FLOWER
—HUSH! SAY NOTHING
—AUF WEIDERSEHN
—LOVE THE MAGICIAN
—I WISH YOU WOULDN'T DO THAT
—IF YOU SHOULD
—WHEN A GOOD KING REIGNS
—ONE SMILE FROM THEE

1896. *BRIAN BORU*
A comic opera with book and lyrics by
Stanislaus Stange, and starring Jefferson
de Angelis in a cast that included Max
Eugene, John C. Slavin and Amelia Sum-
merville.
—I'M A GIANT'S LITTLE BABY
—THE IRISH PATRIOT
—GUARDIANS OF BEAUTY
—THE EARTH'S RICHEST DOWER
—FARE-THEE-WELL
—THERE'S A LAD THAT I KNOW
—A PICTURE IN MY HEART
—SIMPLE IRISH COLLEENS
—MY NAME IS PAT O'HARA
—SING THE SONG OF GREAT BRIAN
—SING A MERRY ROUNDELAY
—AN ENGLISHMAN'S TOAST
—THE OPEN GATES
—NO SPY AM I
—A FOOL AM I
—PADDY AND HIS PIG
—WHEN ERE YOU LEAVE
—SHEATHE THE SWORD
—BOYS AND GIRLS
—FILL UP THE LOVING CUP
—PRIDE GOES BEFORE A FALL
—CLINK, CLANK
—WHERE IS THY HEART, OH BRIAN
  THE BRAVE?

—FOR IRELAND
—ALL HOPE HAS FLOWN
—THE IRISH CUCKOO

1898. *THE JOLLY MUSKETEER*
A comic opera with book and lyrics by
Stanislaus Stange, and starring Jefferson
de Angelis in a cast that included Van
Rensselaer Wheeler, Harry MacDonough
and Maud Hollins.
—THE WISHING WELL
—THE KING'S OWN MUSKETEERS
—LOVE FOR AN HOUR
—THE WICKED MAN
—FRIENDS
—THAT SWEET OBLIVION DRINK
—JUST TO PRATTLE AWAY
—WILFUL WOMAN

Victor Herbert Scores

1894. *PRINCE ANANIAS*
Book and lyrics by Francis Neilson. First
presented by The Bostonians at the Broad-
way Theater, New York, December 20,
1894.
—UNDER AN OAK
—WHO MIGHT YOU BE?
—IT NEEDS NO POET
—AN AUTHOR-MANAGER AM I
—THE HAMLET OF FANCY
—WHEN I WAS BORN I WEIGHED
  TEN STONE
—I AM NO QUEEN
—AMARYLLIS
—AH, CUPID, MEDDLESOME BOY
—LOVE NE'ER CAME NIGH
—TITLED WIDOWS ARE WE
—A ROYAL SADNESS SITS ON ME
—LOVE IS SPRING

1895. *THE WIZARD OF THE NILE*
Book and lyrics by Harry B. Smith. In
this comic opera, which was Victor Her-
bert's first hit, Frank Daniels played the
comedy role of "Kibosh," a Persian wiz-
ard, and repeatedly asked, "Am I a wiz?",
a phrase that soon found its way in the
American vernacular of that day.
—SONG OF THE OPTIMIST
—I AM THE RULER
—I HAVE BEEN A-MAYING
—IF I WERE KING
—STONE CUTTERS SONG
—STAR LIGHT, STAR BRIGHT
—AH, LOVE, WE KNOW
—ORIENTAL MARCH
—THERE'S ONE THING A WIZARD
  CAN DO
—ON CLEOPATRA'S WEDDING DAY

—MY ANGELINE
—THE ECHO SONG
—IN DREAMLAND

1896. *THE GOLD BUG*
Book and lyrics by Glen MacDonough.
This was not a comic opera but a farce
with music for which Victor Herbert
wrote only three numbers, and while not
a distinguished production, it served to
introduce to New York audiences for the
first time one of the greatest Negro teams
in stage history—Bert Williams, the comedian, and George Walker, his cake-walk-
ing partner.
—THE GOLD BUG MARCH

1897. *THE SERENADE*
Book and lyrics by Harry B. Smith. First
produced as a successor to "Robin Hood"
by the Bostonians in Chicago and later at
the Knickerbocker Theater, New York,
with Alice Neilsen in the starring role.
—HIST! HUSH!
—SONG OF THE CARBINE
—PEERING LEFT, PEERING RIGHT
—WITH CRACKING OF WHIP
—THE FUNNY SIDE OF THAT
—I LOVE THEE, I ADORE THEE
—THE SINGING LESSON
—GAZE ON THIS FACE SO NOBLE
—THE SERENADE
—FOR LOVE—PIFF! PAFF!
—IN OUR QUIET CLOISTER
—IN FAIR ANDALUSIA
—THE MONK AND THE MAID
—WOMAN, LOVELY WOMAN
—THE ANGELUS
—CUPID AND I
—HERE MERRILY THE BANDIT
  TRIBE
—DON JOSE OF SEVILLE
—I ENVY THE BIRD
—DREAMING, DREAMING

1897. *THE IDOL'S EYE*
Book and lyrics by Harry B. Smith, and
starring Frank Daniels.
—PRETTY ISABELLA
—CUBAN SONG
—BALLOON SONG
—I JUST DROPPED IN
—I'M CAPTAIN CHOLLY CHUMLEY
—THE LADY AND THE KICK
—THOU ART GUILTY
—WITH DANCES WILD
—HERE IN THE TEMPLE I'VE WAIT-
  ED FOR THEE
—THE TATTOOED MAN
—TALK ABOUT YO' LUCK
—FAIRY TALES

—COME, BE OFF!

1898. *THE FORTUNE TELLER*

Book and lyrics by Harry B. Smith, with a cast headed by Alice Neilsen, Marguerita Sylva, Eugene Cowles, Joseph Cawthorn and Joseph Herbert.

—ALWAYS DO AS PEOPLE SAY YOU SHOULD
—ROMANY LIFE
—GYPSY JAN
—HUNGARY HUSSARS
—HO, YE TOWNSMEN
—SERENADES OF ALL NATIONS
—THE LILY AND THE NIGHTINGALE
—GYPSY LOVE SONG (LITTLE GYPSY SWEETHEART)
—THE POWER OF THE HUMAN EYE
—SIGNOR MONSIEUR MULDONI
—SPEAK, IRMA, I IMPLORE THEE
—HERE WE ARE A GYPSY TROUPE

1899. *CYRANO DE BERGERAC*

Book by Stuart Reed and lyrics by Harry B. Smith, with Francis Wilson and Lulu Glaser.

—I AM A COURT COQUETTE
—WALTZ SONG
—CHORUS OF POETS
—SINCE I'M NOT FOR THEE
—SERENADE
—SONG OF THE NOSE
—DIPLOMACY
—THE KING'S MUSKETEERS
—CADETS OF GASCONY

1899. *THE SINGING GIRL*

Book and lyrics by Harry B. Smith, with a cast that included Alice Neilsen, Eugene Cowles, Joseph W. Herbert, Joseph Cawthorn, John C. Slavin and May Boley.

—THE WELL BELOVED
—IF YOU WERE ONLY MINE
—SONG OF THE DANUBE
—LOVE IS A TYRANT
—THE SIREN OF THE BALLET
—CHINK, CHINK
—GRETNA'S WALTZ SONG

1899. *THE AMEER*

Book and lyrics by Fred W. Ranken and Kirke LaShelle, starring Frank Daniels.

—IN OLD BEN FRANKLIN'S DAY
—THE ARMOURED KNIGHT
—WITH STEALTHY FOOTSTEPS FALLING
—SWEET CLARISSA
—CUPID WILL GUIDE THEE
—THE LITTLE POSTER MAID
—OLD MAIDS ARE WILLING TO PLEASE
—FOND LOVE, TRUE LOVE

Gustave A. Kerker Scores

1890. *CASTLES IN THE AIR*

Book and lyrics by Charles Alfred Byrne, and presented at the New York Casino by the DeWolf Hopper Opera Bouffe Company. After witnessing this production, Oscar Hammerstein, the producer and grandfather of the author of "Show Boat" and "Oklahoma," made a bet that he could write an operetta in 48 hours, and after locking himself in a room at the Gilsey House for two nights and days, came out with the book and score for "The Kohinoor."

—THE WEDDING BELL
—WE LOOK AND SMILE AND BOW JUST SO
—THE YOUNG MAN ATHLETIC
—THE CRICKET
—JUST US TWO
—CASTLES IN THE AIR
—WHAT IN THE WORLD COULD COMPARE TO THIS?
—IS IT A DREAM?
—THIS LITTLE PIG WENT TO MARKET

1895. *KISMET*

Book and lyrics by Richard Carroll, and starring Lizzie MacNichol with Harry Davenport and Aubrey Boucicault in the supporting cast.

—DO YOU LIKE TUTTI-FRUTTI?
—JUST ONE KISS
—PHYSICAL CULTURE
—TERROR, TERROR
—TUZZIE MARIE
—WHY AM I NOT LIKE THE REST OF THE GIRLS?

1896. *IN GAY NEW YORK*

Book and lyrics by Hugh Morton, and presented by a cast headed by Virginia Earle, Louise Hunter, Walter Jones, David Warfield, Lee Harrison, John Slavin, Richard Carle and Madge Lessing.

—CRIPPLE CREEK BANDITS
—GIRLIE GIRL
—IN GAY NEW YORK
—JIM JAM
—LURLINE
—MOLLIE
—TAKE ME DOWN TO CONEY ISLAND
—A TRIP AROUND THE TOWN
—IT'S FORTY MILES FROM SCHENESTADY TO TROY
—TURN YOUR GREAT EYES ON ME

1896. *THE LADY SLAVEY*
Book by George Dance, lyrics by Hugh
Morton, and presented at the New York
Casino with a cast headed by Charles
Danby, Dan Daly, Richard Carle, Vir-
ginia Earle, Marie Dressler and La Petite
Adelaide.
—BABY, BABY
—BEAUTIFUL HUMAN FLY
—CACHUCA SONG
—COME DOWN MY HONEY DO
—GOLF SONG
—NELLIE KEPT ON SMILING
—TWINKLE TWINKLE
—WHOOP DE DOODEN DO

1897. *AN AMERICAN BEAUTY*
Book and lyrics by Hugh Morton, and
starring Lillian Russell with Jerome Sykes
and Alexander Carr in the leading com-
edy roles.
—FAT BOY
—HEIGH HO FOR THE FEMININE
SEX
—INHERITED FROM MY AUNT
—LITTLE DICKEY DOUBLEDAY
—TRULY, TRULY
—WHEN I MET YOU
—LITTLE DOTTIE, LITTLE TOTTIE

1897. *THE WHIRL OF THE TOWN*
Book and lyrics by Hugh Morton.
—CABLE CAR GRIPMAN
—DARLING LITTLE YUM YUM
—FROM THE BATTERY TO HARLEM
—I'M A CAPTAIN BOLD AND
HAUGHTY
—A GIRL IS NOTHING BUT A ROSE
—ONE, TWO, THREE
—MY ESTELLE
—LITTLE YALLER BOY
—MARY ELLEN BROWN
—LITTLE BIRDS LEARNING TO FLY
—THE OLD DAYS
—NANCY HOGAN'S BALL
—TRICKY LITTLE SARAH
—LEAD ON EBENEZER
—OH, WILLIE BOY!

1898. *YANKEE DOODLE DANDY*
Book and lyrics by Hugh Morton. A mu-
sical extravaganza in which Edna Wallace
Hopper, Thomas Q. Seabrooke, Walter
Jones and Julius Steger got feature billing.
—BOYS OF YANKEE LAND
—CHERRY HILL FUSILEERS
—FAIR HONORIA
—FLORA
—FROM THE DISTANT TOWN OF
CADIZ
—THE GIRL WITH THE STRAW-

BERRY MARK
—GOLLY, CHARLIE!
—IF YOU DO IT IN THE PROPER
SORT OF WAY
—I LOVE A GIRL WHO IS MADE OF
STUCCO
—INFANT INCUBATOR
—HAVE YOU SEEN MANDY?
—HERE'S TO OUR ALMA MATER
—JUANITA
—MAY I?
—MR. JOHNSON'S CHOWDER
—OH, HOW WOULD YOU LIKE TO
PET?
—THE OLD, OLD STORY
—POOR O'HOOLAHAN
—LOUISA
—MEET ME DOWN AT HUYLER'S
—OH, WILLIE! DON'T YOU LOVE
ME?
—ROXIANA DOOLEY
—WINE,WINE, WINE
—WHEN THE CLOCK STRIKES TWO
IN THE TENDERLOIN

1898. *THE BELLE OF NEW YORK*
Book and lyrics by Hugh Morton, and
starring Edna May after the first perform-
ance.
—WHEN I WAS BORN THE STARS
STOOD STILL
—TEACH ME HOW TO KISS
—THEY ALL FOLLOW ME
—GOOD OLD GLORY
—BELLE PARISIENNE
—WE'LL DANCE IN THE MOONLIGHT
—A SIMPLE LITTLE GIRL
—I'M THE BELLE OF NEW YORK
—A NICE YOUNG MAN
—CORA ANGELIQUE
—THE PURITY BRIGADE
—ON THE BEACH AT NARRAGAN-
SETT
—THE ANTI-CIGARETTE SOCIETY
—CONUNDRUMS
—MY LITTLE BABY
—WHEN WE ARE MARRIED
—YOU AND I

1898. *THE TELEPHONE GIRL*
Book and lyrics by Hugh Morton, and
co-starring Clara Lipman and Louis
Mann.
—AND THE BELL GOES TING-A-LING-
LING
—I WOULDN'T DO ANYTHING
WRONG
—ROUGH RIDERS
—WOULD YOU IF YOU COULD
—UPTOWN DOWNTOWN

John Philip Sousa Scores

1884. *DESIREE*
Book by Edward Tabor. This was De-Wolf Hopper's first starring vehicle, and in the cast were Ida Mosher, his second wife, and Rose Leighton.

1893. *THE GLASS BLOWERS*
Book by Leonard Liebling. In his autobiography, "Marching Along," Sousa makes no mention of this comic opera, although he used most of the songs from its score in "The American Maid" twenty years later.
—IT WOULD BE VERY HARD TO GET
—CLEOPATRA'S A S T R A W B E R R Y BLONDE
—IN THE DIMNESS OF TWILIGHT
—THE MATRIMONIAL MART
—THIS IS MY BUSY DAY
—NEVERMORE   —CHEER UP
—WE CHANT A SONG OF LABOR
—MY LOVE IS A BLOWER
—THE DINNER PAIL —THE BIVOUAC
—THE CRYSTAL LUTE
—THE AMERICAN GIRL
—I CAN'T GET 'EM UP
—WHEN YOU CHANGE YOUR NAME TO MINE   MARCONIGRAMS
—RED CROSS NURSE

1898. *EL CAPITAN*
Book by Charles Klein, lyrics by Tom Frost and Sousa. This production, which starred DeWolf Hopper in the role of Don Errico Medigua, had his wife, Edna Wallace Hopper, playing the feminine lead.
—NOBLES OF CASTILIAN BIRTH
—OH BEAUTIFUL LAND OF SPAIN
—FROM PERU'S MAJESTIC MOUNTAINS
—IF YOU EXAMINE HUMANKIND
—BAH! BAH!
—DITTY OF THE DRILL
—OH, WARRIOR GRIM!
—HERE COMES EL CAPITAN
—SWEETHEART, I'M WAITING
—WHEN SOME SERIOUS AFFLICTION
—A TYPICAL TUNE OF ZANZIBAR

1897. *THE BRIDE-ELECT*
Book and lyrics by John Philip Sousa, and starring Christie MacDonald.
—IF NINETY-NINE PERCENT THE PAPERS PRINT
—COME CAVALIER
—KIND FRIENDS, THIS DEFERENCE
—SHOULD YOU MARRY ME
—OH, STARS!
—LET POETS SING
—HERE'S A PACK
—HE'S HERE
—LOVE LIGHT OF MY HEART
—WE CANNOT SEE REASON WHY
—THE ICE BABY
—UNCHAIN THE DOGS OF WAR
—THESE ARE OUR SENTIMENTS
—THE ICEMAN WORKS
—CUCKOO
—THE GOD OF LOVE PRESIDES
—TO MARRY OR NOT TO MARRY

1898. *THE CHARLATAN*
Book by Charles Klein. Co-starring De-Wolf Hopper and Nellie Bergen.
—M O N T E B A N K S, COME WAKEN FROM YOUR DREAMING
—SHE WAS A MAID OF SWEET SIMPLICIT-EE
—GOOD MORNING
—THE PHILOSOPHER'S TALE IS TOLD
—AS THE AGENT
—AMMONIA
—PLUTO'S PARTNER I
—SOCIAL LAWS
—VENUS, GODDESS OF LOVE
—WHEN THE WINTRY MORN IS BRIGHT
—LOVE'S THE PLEASURE
—I'M THE SEVENTH SON OF A SEVENTH SON
—BEFORE THE TWILIGHT SHADOWS CHANGE
—THE MATRIMONIAL GUARDS
—DAY OF JOY
—THE LILIES OF YOUR LOVE MAY DIE
—FRIENDS, DEAR FRIENDS
—IT'S A WELL ESTABLISHED FACT
—AFTER DUE CONSIDERATION
—OH, SUNLIT SEA!
—THE LEGEND OF THE FROGS
—THE COLLEGE MAN

John Stromberg Scores

1896. *THE ART OF MARYLAND*
Book and lyrics by Joseph Herbert. Following five vaudeville acts, in which Lottie Gilson, the "Little Magnet," and Weber and Fields in their pool table skit were the headliners, a burlesque on "The Heart of Maryland," Mrs. Leslie Carter's starring vehicle, was presented by the following cast: Joe Weber, Lew Fields, Sam Bernard, John T. Kelly, Charles K. Ross, M. Fenton, T. Shattuck, Beaumont Sisters.
—I LOVE YOU DEAR   —MISS LUCY
—I'M THE HEAVY-HANDED VILLIAN
—APPEARANCES AGAINST HER

1896. *THE GEEZER*

Book and lyrics by Joseph Herbert. Acted by the same cast as presented "The Art of Maryland," this travesty on "The Geisha" ran for four months and then was replaced by "Under the Red Globe," a burlesque of "Under the Red Robe."

—THE HEN AND THE DOOR KNOB
—THE PASSIONATE CODFISH
—KISSING SONG —ALOFT, BELOW!
—LI HUNG CHANG
—ULTRA PROPRIETY
—WHAT WOULD LORDSHIP SAY?

1897. *THE GLAD HAND*

Book and lyrics by Joseph Herbert. For the opening production of the 1897-'98 season, a cast composed of Weber and Fields, John T. Kelly, Charles Ross, Mabel Fenton, Sam Bernard, Peter F. Dailey, Frankie Bailey and Bessie Clayton presented "Secret Servants," a burlesque on William Gillette's "Secret Service," following vaudeville in which Cissie Loftus, McIntyre and Heath had top billing.

—HOW I LOVE MY LOU
—IF YOU LOVE ME TRULY
—THE GLAD HAND

1897. *POUSSE CAFE*

Book and lyrics by Edgar Smith. During the run of this production, the following burlesques were presented by the cast of "The Glad Hand": "The Wee Minister," a travesty on "The Little Minister"; "The Worst Born," a travesty on "The First Born"; "The Wayhighman," a travesty on "The Highwayman," and the "Con Curers," a travesty on "The Conquerors."

—IN GAY PAREE
—THE SELF-MADE MAN
—ALL THAT SORT OF ROT
—FOREIGN VAUDEVILLIANS
—HOW I LOVE MY LOU
—I AM A DOLL —SONG TOW
—I LOVE THEE, OLEANDER
—OH, WHAT A ROW AND A RUMPUS!
—HORNY-HANDED FARMERS
—SURE BLARNEY'S THE ART OF STEALING A HEART
—THE FARMER AND THE CON MAN

1898. *HURLY-BURLY*

Book and lyrics by Edgar Smith. David Warfield made his appearance as a Jewish comedian in this production, and Fay Templeton also was a newcomer in the Weber and Fields company, which presented burlesques on "Cyrano de Bergerac" ("Cyanose de Brick-a- Brac"), "The Christian ("The Heathen"), "Catherine."

—THE OPENING OF THE SEASON

—MOONLIGHT SERENADE
—THE PROGRESSIVE POKER GAME
—LITTLE OLD NEW YORK IS GOOD ENOUGH FOR ME
—WHO'LL HELP ME SPEND MY MONEY?
—A LOIDY WHAT IS STUDYING FOR THE STOIGE
—DINAH, KISS ME HONEY DO
—I THINK I SHALL LEARN, DON'T YOU? —CLINK, CLINK
—IN THE MUSIC HALL BAR WHEN THE CURTAIN IS DOWN
—GREAT CLEOPATRA COMES
—A LARGE COLD BOTTLE AND A SMALL HOT BIRD
—KEEP AWAY FROM EMMALINE

1899. *HELTER-SKELTER*

Book and lyrics by Edgar Smith. During this, the second Weber and Fields production of the 1898-'99 season, the following Broadway hits were burlesqued: "Lord and Lady Algy," "Zaza," "The Great Ruby," "The King's Musketeer."

—WHAT, MARRY DAT GIRL!
—MAUD —LOVES MY LOU

1899. *WHIRL-I-GIG*

Book by Edgar Smith, lyrics by Harry B. Smith. Lillian Russell made her first appearance as a Weber and Fields' star in this production, the other members of the cast including Peter Dailey, David Warfield, Charles J. Ross, Frankie Bailey, Bonnie Maginn, Mabel Fenton, May Robson and Weber and Fields. During the run of this production, the following burlesques were presented; "The Girl From Martin's," a travesty on "The Girl From Maxims"; "Barbara Fidgety," a travesty on "Barbara Frietchie," and "Sapolio," a travesty on "Sappho." The seats for the opening performance were sold at auction two weeks before the premiere and netted $10,500, two stage boxes bringing $1,000, and such notables as Stanford White, Louis Sherry, William Randolph Hearst, Richard Croker and James R. Keene bidding as high as $750 for choice locations.

—STRIKE, STRIKE —OLD GLORY
—MARIE ANTOINETTE —TALLY HO!
—KING GILHOOLEY —IN PARIS GAY
—QUEEN OF BOHEMIA
—SAY YOU LOVE ME, SUE
—WE'RE THE MOB ERRATIC
—COME ALONG —I'M A HUMORIST
—WHEN CHLOE SINGS A SONG
—DE SUN DO MOVE
—THE COLONEL
—THE BLUE AND THE GRAY

ome song covers of the 1910 era were
dorned with pictures of the *Ziegfeld Follies'*
velies, but George Gershwin's *Swanee* out-
ripped them in music counter sales.

Victor Herbert's songs graced the music racks of the nation's pianos in the 1900s along with the hits popularized by Blanche Ring, Nora Bayes and Marie Cahill.

The Decade of Rising Revolt
(1900-1910)

The new century not only injected new life and vitality into the Broadway musical but set up a rumble along the Great White Way other than that caused by the sandhogs blasting for the new subway.

It was a rumble of protest against the partiality shown by many American producers for comic operas and revues of foreign extraction, and the leader of the uprising was a cocky kid trouper but two years past voting age—George M. Cohan, who held that the U. S. A. had the creative talent and domestic backgrounds for homemade musicals that would better Europe's best. What's more, he set about to prove it.

Of course, the producers' preference for these foreign attractions was justified by the box office receipts. The outstanding musical of the 1900-1910 decade was *Florodora,* an English importation that ran for 505 performances at the Casino Theater, where the original "pretty maidens" in the *Florodora Sextet* parlayed stage door romances into marriages that made them ladies of wealth and title. Almost as successful was Franz Lehar's Viennese opera *The Merry Widow,* which during its 416-performance run at the New Amsterdam wore out six Sonias and one Prince Danilo and established a millinery vogue. And American producers also pocketed a handsome net from the success of such highly popular shows as *The Messenger Boy, The Toreador, The Girl From Kay's, The Earl And The Girl, The Little Cherub* and *The Orchid* after signing fat royalty checks that were deposited in the Bank of England and not with J. Pierpont Morgan.

Other Broadway entrepreneurs reaped a golden harvest from the Blue Danube school of music which produced *The Chocolate Soldier* and dominated the scores of Victor Herbert, who was about to be crowned king of light opera composers following the success of Montgomery and Stone in *The Red Mill* and the triumph of Fritzi Scheff in *Mlle. Modiste.*

In fact, George M. Cohan went to the post a long shot and was slow in getting away from the barrier, but in 1903 the Yankee Doodle Boy rode into the winner's circle with *Little Johnny Jones,* and although the critics lambasted the author-composer-star for his flag-waving, the audience loved it, for here was something refreshingly new in the American theater. His songs packed a punch, his heroes and heroines were American guys and gals you'd meet in Joe's bar and the 5-and-10, and his librettos put New Rochelle, N. Y., Richmond, Va. and Boston on the musical comedy map. This "real live nephew of my Uncle Sam" had fired the opening shot in Broadway's War of Independence, and its Yorktown came twenty years later when George Gershwin, Jerome Kern and Richard Rodgers demonstrated beyond question a talent for writing homespun American music that made them the Monte Cristos of the musical comedy world.

But George M. Cohan was not alone in his crusade. Out of the Middle West came Gustave Luders to enrich the Broadway stage with the music he wrote for *The Burgomaster, King Dodo* and *The Prince Of Pilsen*. Raymond Hubbell, another songwriter from Chicago, made *The Runaways, Fantana* and *A Knight For A Day* the opening chapter in a Broadway success story that covered a quarter-century. There was a promise of future greatness in the interpolated songs an unknown composer named Jerome Kern wrote for twenty or more productions during this decade. And the reception accorded *Three Twins* brought Karl Hoschna into the spotlight and changed Otto Harbach from a $50-a-week advertising agency copy writer into a librettist-lyricist gifted with imagination, originality and rare talent.

The patriotic germs with which George M. Cohan was infected were catching, and other creators of Broadway musicals found inspiration for their librettos and music in such American achievements as the discovery of the North Pole, the invention of the airplane and motion picture, the annexation of the Philippines, and the victory of the American Cup defender over Sir Thomas Lipton's Shamrock. The Gibson Girl came to life on the Broadway stage, where Buster Brown and Foxy Grandpa cut their comic strip capers; the finish of the Vanderbilt Cup race was framed in the proscenium of the Broadway Theater, and the entrance of the United States Marines or a detachment of blue jackets from the U. S. fleet guaranteed a rousing first act curtain.

Although there were skeptics who didn't hold with George M. Cohan that America could produce musicals to equal Old World productions, there was no question but that this country already possessed a stockpile of stage talent that rivaled in richness the gold reserve now buried at Fort Knox.

It was a decade of great comedians—Richard Carle, Joseph Cawthorn, Bickel and Watson, Otis Harlan, John Slavin, Alexander Clark, James T. Powers, Francis Wilson, Sam Bernard, Eddie Foy, Tom Lewis, Victor Moore, Raymond Hitchcock, DeWolf Hopper, Jefferson de Angelis, Harry Bulger, William Norris, Frank Moulan, Louis Harrison, Frank Lalor, Ralph Herz, Weber and Fields and Montgomery and Stone, who achieved overnight stardom in *The Wizard of Oz*.

In addition, the marquee boards carried the names of such celebrated comediennes as Marie Dressler, Marie Cahill, Stella Mayhew, Trixie Friganza, Mabel Hite and Mae Irwin. The composer was sure his high Cs would be well protected by such easy-on-the-eyes songbirds as Christie MacDonald, Grace Van Studdiford, Vera Michelena, Paula Edwards, Lulu Glaser, Louise Gunning, Fritzi Scheff, Lina Abarbanell and Ethel Jackson, and to join them in singing soulful duets, he had such leading men to choose from as Donald Brian, Jack Gardner, Eugene Cowles, Edgar Atchinson-Ely, Jack Norworth and Van Renssellaer Wheeler.

Add to this roster of stars such queens of bald-head row as Fay Templeton, Adele Richie, Anna Held, Adele Rowland, Elsie Janis, Bessie McCoy Davis, Hattie Williams, Ethel Levey, Blanche Ring, Julia Sanderson, Marguerite Clark, Emma Carus, Kitty Gordon, Nora Bayes, Bessie Wynn, Virginia Earle and Lillian Russell, and you have a round-up of box office magnets that paupers the Hollywood Who's Who of today.

It was a decade of grim tragedy, too—tragedy set to music. During a Yuletide season matinee performance of *Mr. Bluebeard* at the Iroquois Theater, Chicago, a crossed wire set fire to the filmy costumes of the girls in the Butterfly Ballet, and in a frantic rush for the exits, 602 lives were lost despite the heroic attempt made to quell the stampede by Eddie Foy,the comedian, who stepped up to the footlights and shouted to the orchestra leader: "Play, for God's sake, play!"

Three years later at the old Madison Square Garden in New York, Stanford White met death to the strains of a song—*I Could Love A Million Girls*— when Harry Kendall Thaw walked casually over to the architect's table and shot him—a sensational murder that made Evelyn Nesbitt Thaw, the *cause celebre,* a headline attraction at Oscar Hammerstein's Victoria Theater and changed a one-night flop, *Mamzelle Champagne,* into an SRO attraction for the next ten weeks.

With chains of local op'ry houses linking coast to coast and border to border, the traveling musical shows played to packed houses, and the most envied of all the one-night-stand troupers was Jess Dandy, who played the German brewer, Hans Wagner, in *The Prince Of Pilsen* for four solid years on the road with three return Broadway engagements to break the monotony of nightly sleeper jumps. The minstrels, however, sang their last lay in 1909 when the Cohan & Harris troupe turned out for the last 11:45 ever to thrill Broadway and Lew Dockstader retired to his tulip beds in Mount Vernon, N. Y., leaving his throne vacant until a new king of blackface was crowned two years later—Al Jolson.

This opening decade of the new century was marked by two first nights that made Broadway history. The first was on April 12, 1905 when the curtain at the New York Hippodrome, built at cost of $1,750,000 by Frederic Thompson and Elmer S. Dundy, owners and developers of Luna Park, lifted for the first time. Seating 5,200 persons and with a stage 100 feet deep, a 60-foot apron large enough to contain two regulation circus rings, and a huge steel-and-concrete tank fourteen feet deep, this cradle of sensational musical spectacles made London's Drury Lane Theater, the home of English extravaganzas, a peep-show by comparison.

Ring also in red the night of July 8, 1907 when Florenz Ziegfeld founded without fanfare of trumpets but with a prophetic drum roll at the conclusion of the first act, a fabulous theatrical institution on feminine pulchritude— *The Ziegfeld Follies*. And for the next quarter-century, chorus girls from the Battery to the Golden Gate had a common theme song and ambition:

> "I want to be glorified by Mr. Ziegfeld,
> As only Mr. Ziegfeld can."

After a retarded childhood and a checkered adolescence, the Broadway musical had finally come of age.

Alfred E. Aarons Scores

1900. *MAM'SELLE 'AWKINS*
With Herman Perlet. A musical comedy with book and lyrics by Richard Carle, who was a member of the cast that included Josephine Hall, Etienne Girardot, George C. Boniface Jr., Marguerite Sylva, Maude Creighton, Lawrence Wheat and Rose and Nellie Beaumont.
—OUR LAND OF DREAMS
—I'M SORRY DAT I LEFT MY HAPPY HOME
By Irving Jones.
—DRINK AND LET'S BE GAY
—DOLLY
—DON'T START NO ARGUMENT WITH HIM
—EVERYBODY WONDERED WHY HE KNEW
Music by Howard Talbot.
—DON'T BELIEVE A TALE LIKE THAT

1900. *THE KNICKERBOCKER GIRL*
A musical comedy with book and lyrics by George Totten Smith, and presented by a cast headed by Josephine Hall, Sydney Deane, Harry Kelly, Alice Clifford, Grace Belmont and Nellie Beaumont.
—BROTHER BILL
—CONTRARY MARY
By M. E. Rourke and Ellis R. Ephram.
—SHE'S MY GIRL
—PRETTY POLLY PRIMROSE
—SHE'S ALL RIGHT
—MY LINDA LOVE
—I LOVE YOU
—DEVOTION
—LALLA

—ESPANOLA VIVA
—A LITTLE BIRD IS LOOKING ALL THE TIME
—HEAR THE BAND

1900. *THE MILITARY MAID*
A musical comedy with book and lyrics by George V. Hobart, and presented by a cast headed by Josephine Hall, Henry Bergman, David Torrance, Taylor Granville and Sallie Berg.

1904. *A CHINA DOLL*
A musical comedy with book and lyrics by Harry B. and Robert B. Smith, and presented by a cast headed by W. H. MacDonald, Helen Roynton, Arthur Cunningham, Albert Hart, George C. Boniface Jr. and Corrine.
—LITTLE CHINA DOLL
—THE BUTTERFLY AND THE CLOVER
—CAFE CHANTANT
—APPLE MARY MAGUIRE
—ONE UMBRELLA WOULD BE BIG ENOUGH FOR TWO

Charles Alphin Score

1908. *SKI-HI*
A musical comedy with book and lyrics by the composer, and presented by a cast that included Lottie Kendall, Harry Short and Tom Kendall.
—THE DANCE OF SING LING FOO
—HONEY DO YOU LOVE ME DEARLY?
—MY TOKIO QUEEN
—PRETTY LITTLE JAPANESE LADY
—TAMAMURA
—THE GIRL WORTH THE WHILE

Frederick V. Bowers Score

1902. *KING HIGHBALL*
A musical comedy with book and lyrics by Charles Horwitz, and starring Marie Dressler.
—THE GIRL FROM MARS

Robin Hood Bowers Scores

1904. *THE MAID AND THE MUMMY*
A musical comedy with book and lyrics by Richard Carle, who headed a cast that included Edward Garvie, Edgar Norton, Adele Rowland, May Boley, Annie Yeamans and Janet Priest.
—OH, IT'S GREAT TO BE CRAZY
—SAD EXPERIENCES
—MY EGYPTIAN QUEEN
—I'M SO DIZZY
—PECULIAR JULIA
—I FELL IN LOVE WITH POLLY
—MY GASOLINE AUTOMOBILE
—FLO
—THE SALES LADY
—LETTERS

1906. *THE VANDERBILT CUP*
A musical comedy with book by Sydney Rosenfeld, lyrics by Raymond Peck, and based on the annual automobile road racing classic. Elsie Janis headed the cast and in the finale, defeated Barney Oldfield nightly and two matinees weekly.
—THE LITTLE CHAUFFEUR
—MY HOUSE BOAT BEAU
—VANDERBILT CUP GALLOP
—SOMEWHERE IN THE WORLD THERE'S A LITTLE GIRL FOR ME
—WINE, WOMEN AND SONG
—SO I'VE BEEN TOLD
—THE LAMENT OF THE CRUSTY DAMES
—IF YOU WERE I AND I WERE YOU
—THE LIGHT THAT LIES IN GIRLISH EYES
—THE FATAL CURSE OF BEAUTY

1907. *THE HOYDEN*
A musical comedy with book by Cosmo Hamilton, lyrics by Henry Blossom, and starring Elsie Janis in a cast that included Joseph Cawthorn and Mae Murray.
—A SOLITARY FINISH
—THAT'S WHY I NEVER MARRIED
—ON THE PIAZZA
—GRETCHEN
—MY FATHER'S WOODEN LEG
By Joseph Cawthorn and Harry Dillon.
—LOVE'S PRESCRIPTION
By Harry Williams and Egbert VanAlstyne.

—EVERY FELLOW WANTS TO LOVE ME
Lyrics by Raymond Peck.
—I'D LIKE TO LOCK YOUR HEART
—Lyrics by Raymond Peck.
—I'M GROWING FOND OF YOU
Music by John Golden.

1909. *THE SILVER STAR*
A musical comedy with book and lyrics by Harry B. Smith, and starring Adeline Genee in a cast that included Nellie McCoy and Bickel and Watson.
—SLEIGH BELLS MAY BE WEDDING BELLS
—CARNIVAL
—IT MAY BE SO BUT I DOUBT IT
—IF I WERE SANTA CLAUS
—IT'S A LOVING WIFE FOR MINE
—THE COONEY-SPOONEY DANCE
By William Jerome and Jean Schwartz.
—FRANCO-AMERICAN RAGTIME
By William Jerome and Jean Schwartz.
—TO BRING UP A GIRL
Music by Karl Hoschna.
—DANCING THE COTILLION
Music by Raymond Hubbel.
—THEY'RE NOT DOING THAT THIS SEASON
Music by Albert Gumble.
—THE SILVER STAR
Music by Albert Gumble.
—LET GEORGE DO IT
By Edgar Leslie and Al Piantadosi.

John W. Bratton Scores

1900. *HODGE, PODGE & CO.*
A musical comedy with book by George V. Hobart, lyrics by Walter Ford, and presented by a cast headed by Peter F. Dailey, Edward Garvie, William Roderick and Christie MacDonald.
—SPRINGTIME BELLS
—MY SUNFLOWER SUE
—A BILLET DOUX
—A SOLDIER OF LOVE AM I
—I'M A SCION OF THE HOUSE OF HIGHBALL
—MODEST MODEL MAIDENS WE
—YOU'RE ALTOGETHER MODEL GIRLS
—YOU NEVER CAN TELL WHAT A KISS WILL DO
—WHAT A FUNNY STORY
—'E DIDN'T KNOW JUST W'AT TO SAY
—CINDY
By Dave Reed, Jr.
—THE WHITE AND GRAY CADETS
—A PICTURE NO ARTIST CAN PAINT

—SINCE MY LINDA'S IN THE SYN-
   DE-CATE
—I LOVE YOU, BABE, AND YOU
   LOVE ME
—THE TOWN FOLKS WILL BE
   PLEASED
—MY CHARCOAL CHARMER
By Gus Edwards.
—DREAM DAYS OF SEVILLE

1900. *STAR AND GARTER*
A vaudeville-farce with book by J. J.
McNally, lyrics by Walter Ford, and pre-
sented by a cast headed by Marie Cahill,
Otis Harlin, Joseph Coyne, John G.
Sparks and Mons. Agoust and his acro-
batic family.
—I WOULN'T MIND A JOB LIKE
   THAT
—MY HANNAH LADY
—DICKIE THE KING OF THE DUDES
—MY LADY BUG
—EVERY INCH A LADY
By Mathew Woodward and Herman Per-
let.
—GIVE ME BACK MY LIZA
By Dave Reed, Jr.
—THREE THIRTY-THREE IN THE
   MORN
By Dave Reed, Jr.
—AFTER THE SHOW
—AUTO-MO-BILING
By Mathew Woodward.
—WHEN SOUSA LEADS THE BAND.
By Billy Jerome and Frederick V. Bowers.

1901. *THE LIBERTY BELLES*
A musical comedy with book and lyrics
by Harry B. Smith, and presented by a
cast headed by John Slavin, Lotta Faust,
Harry Davenport and Harry Gilfoil.
—A LESSON WITH A FAN
—TO MARRY A MILLIONAIRE
—A LITTLE CHILD LIKE ME
Music by A. Baldwin Sloane.
—JACK O' LANTERN
Music by A. Baldwin Sloane.
—SHOPPING
Music by A. Baldwin Sloane.
—A SPRING HAT
Music by A. Baldwin Sloane.
—A YANKEE TAR
—DE TROP
By Clifton Crawford.
—STARLIGHT
By Clifton Crawford.
—IN FLORIDA
—A GUNNER IN THE NAVY
—ETHIOPIAN ESSENCE
By Aimee Lachaume.

—OH, WHAT A DREAM!
Music by Harry Von Tilzer.

1904. *THE MAN FROM CHINA*
A musical comedy with book and lyrics
by Paul West, and starring Charles A.
Bigelow in a cast that included Stella
Mayhew, Edgar Atchinson-Ely and Billie
Taylor.
—JUST ANOTHER SILLY DAY
—WHAT YOULD YOU DO WITHOUT
   REGGIE?
—LIFE IS TOO SHORT TO BE WAST-
   ING YOUR TIME
—TING TANG KEE
—FIFTY-SEVEN WAYS TO CATCH A
   MAN
—HOW I THOUGHT I LOOKED
—THE BASHFUL MOON
—MAKE BELIEVE
—FOR HE WAS A MARRIED MAN
—FRIGHTENED FAWN
—MY BLACK CLOUD
—FOR GLORY AND FOR LOVE
—THE AMOROUS ESKIMO
—BE A SPY FOR LOVE'S SAKE
—THE HUMAN BAND
—CLORINDA
—COLUMBINE (THE TIMID HUM-
   MING BIRD)
—ONE NICE LITTLE MILLION

1905. *THE PEARL AND THE PUMPKIN*
A musical extravaganza with book and
lyrics by W. W. Denslow and Paul West,
and presented by a cast headed by Gertie
Carlisle, Taylor Granville, Carroll Mc-
Comas, Thomas Whiffen and Harry Mac-
Donough.
—THE FAIRIES' MEETING
—WHO MAKES THE FINEST GINGER-
   BREAD?
—MY PARTY
—JACK O'LANTERN JOE
—SITTING ON THE STARBOARD
   TACK
—STARS ARE SHINING
—COME MY DEAR LOVE
—WHEN THE MOON IS IN THE SKY
—WE'LL HANG TOGETHER
—PIRATES WE
—FOL-DE-IDDLEDY-IDO
—I'M THE DAUGHTER OF ANNIE
   ROONEY
—A STRING OF PEARLS
—FIGHTERS OF FLAME ARE WE
—HONEYMOON HALL
—MY COMBINATION GIRL
—THE PHANTOM SHIP
—THE CANNY CANNER

—LILY WHITE
—MY LITTLE BABY ELEPHANT
—IT IS THE ENGLISH

1908. *BUSTER BROWN*
A musical comedy founded on the Buster Brown cartoon strip, with book by George Newman and George Totten Smith, lyrics by Paul West, and starring Master Gabriel in the title role and George Ali as his dog Tige.
—I'LL BE YOUR HONEY
—GLADYS O'FLYNN
—SUE, SUE I LOVE YOU
—BUSTER'S CHUMS
—RESOLVED
—SWEETHEART SUE
—THE FRENCH MAIDS
—BO-PEEP

1909. *THE NEWLYWEDS AND THEIR BABY*
A musical comedy inspired by the George McManus cartoons, with book by Aaron Hoffman, lyrics by Paul West and A. Seymour Brown, and presented by a cast headed by William Clifton, Fletcher Norton and Flavia Arcaro.
—EVERY BABY IS A SWEET BOUQUET
—LOVING TIME
—SLEEPY LAND
—THE LATEST SENSATION IN GIRLS
—BOOGIE-BOO
—CAN'T YOU SEE I LOVE YOU?
—NAPOLEON

Emil Brugiere Score

1904. *THE BARONESS FIDDLESTICKS*
A musical comedy with book and lyrics by George DeLong, and presented by a cast headed by Anna Fitzhugh.
—COULD YOU BUT KNOW
—HEIGH HO
—SEEING NEW YORK
—ALMA MATER
—LISTEN TO THE NIGHT
—MA DAPHNE SUE
—MR. BUGABOO
—RACHEL O'TOOLE
—WHEN I DROP ROUND
—WHEN YOU LOVE A LITTLE GIRL

Richard Carle Scores

1906. *THE SPRING CHICKEN*
A musical comedy with book and lyrics by the composer, who headed a cast that included Bessie McCoy, Emma Janvier, Adele Rowland and Victor Morley.

—MARCHING
—NO DOUBT YOU LIKE TO CUDDLE UP TO BABY
—ALL THE GIRLS LOVE ME
—WHEN YOU'RE WAITING FOR A CERTAIN GIRL
—A LEMON IN THE GARDEN OF LOVE
—IN SEVILLE
—BARON PAPOUCHE
—I'VE COME ALONG TO PARIS
—BEAUTIFUL SPRING
—I DON'T KNOW BUT I GUESS
—COQUIN de PRINTEMPS

1908. *MARY'S LAMB*
A musical comedy with book and lyrics by the composer, who headed a cast that included Elita Proctor Otis and John Park.
—I IDEALIZE IDA
—LOVE IS ILLUSIVE
—MY MADAGASCAR MAID
—BETSY'S THE BELLE OF THE BATHERS
—IF NO. 1 MET NO. 2
—NEVER BORROW TROUBLE
—LETTERS
Music by Robin Hood Bowers.
—JAMAIS D'LA VIE
—MODEST LITTLE MODEL
—WE'RE HOLLANDAISE

Ivan Caryll Scores

1901. *THE LADIES' PARADISE*
The first musical comedy to be staged at the Metropolitan Opera House, shrine of grand opera, with book and lyrics by George Dance, and presented by a cast that included Queenie Vassar, John Hyams, Alexander Clark, Templar Saxe, Richard Carle and La Torjada and a ballet of two hundred, directed by M. Albertieri.

1901. *THE MESSENGER BOY*
With Lionel Monckton. A musical comedy with book by James T. Tanner and Alfred Murray, lyrics by Adrian Ross and Percy Greenbank, and starring James T. Powers in a cast that included John B. Park, Georgia Caine, May Robson, Jobyna Howland and Flora Zabelle.
—OUR CHARITY BAZAAR
—ASK PAPA
—BRADSHAW
—THE MESSENGER BOY
—ASPIRATIONS
—TARANTELLA
—OFF TO CAIRO

—WASH, WASH, WASH
—HAS ANYBODY SEEN OUR CAT?
—SHELTERED FROM THE NOONDAY
   GLARE
—YOUR OWN
—PANSY
—CAN'T YOU TAKE MY WORD?
—MAISIE
—DERVISH
—THEY ARE ALL AFTER POTT
—TO THE PARIS EXPOSITION
—THE MUMMIES
—THE DIALECT SOUBRETTE

1902. *THE TOREADOR*
   With Lionel Monckton. A musical comedy
   with book by James T. Tanner and
   Harry Nichols, lyrics by Adrian Ross and
   Percy Greenbank, and starring Francis
   Wilson in a cast that included Melville
   Ellis, Christie MacDonald, Adele Richie,
   Queenie Vassar and Maude Raymond.
——WHERE THE GIGANTIC OCEAN
   ATLANTIC
—WE'RE ALL OF US LOVELY AND
   YOUNG
—I'M ROMANTIC
—TOREADOR'S SONG
—WON'T IT BE A LARK?
—EVERYBODY'S AWFULLY GOOD TO
   ME
—IF EVER I MARRY
—MY ZOO
—AWAY TO ESPANA
—THE LANGUAGE OF FLOWERS
—OH, SENOR, PRAY
—HEAR ME, AMELIA
—WITH ALL THE TOWN IN BRIGHT
   ARRAY
—THE GOVERNOR OF VILLAYA
—MY TOREADOR
—THE HALL OF FAME
—KEEP OFF THE GRASS
—ARCHIE
—HERE THEY COME IN GLITTER-
   ING GLORY
—IN THE MOONLIGHT
   By Raymond A. Browne and Theodore
   Morse.

1903. *THE GIRL FROM KAY'S*
   A musical comedy with book and lyrics
   by Owen Hall in which Mary Nash made
   her first stage appearance in a musical
   production, replacing Marie Doro during the show's run and joining a cast that
   included Sam Bernard, Harry Davenport,
   Ernest Lambert, Hattie Williams and
   Elsie Ferguson.
—BRIDE'S SONG

—TIPS
—BONNET SHOP
—MATILDA AND THE BUILDER
—SEMI-DETACHED
—CUSTOMERS FROM KAY'S
—BOB AND ME
—LUCY LINDY LADY
   By Dave Reed, Jr.
—SMILING SAMBO
—I DON'T CARE
—MAKE IT UP
—BIRTHDAY PARTY
—MR. HOGGENHEIMER OF PARK
   LANE
—EGYPT
   By Clare Kummer.
—SUFFICIENCY
   By Clare Kummer.
—MY LITTLE LOVE BIRD
   By Maurice J. Stonehill.

1905. *THE DUCHESS OF DANTZIC*
   A musical comedy based on Sardou's
   "Madame Sans Gene" in which Holbrook
   Blinn and Adrienne Augarde co-starred.
   Book and lyrics by Henry Hamilton.
—THE MIRROR SONG

1905. *THE EARL AND THE GIRL*
   A musical comedy with book by Seymour
   Hicks, lyrics by Percy Greenbank, and
   presented by a cast headed by Eddie Foy,
   Victor Morley, Templar Saxe, Georgia
   Caine, Zelma Rawlston and Amelia Sum-
   merville.
—SPORTING SONG
—LITTLE LADY IN DISTRESS
—SHOPPING
—WHEN THE RIGHT GIRL COMES
   ALONG
—MEDITERRANEAN BLUE
—ONE NIGHT ONLY
—MY SOUTHERN BELLE
—EARL OF STOLE
—I WANT A MAN MADE TO ORDER
   FOR ME
—WON'T YOU CHANGE YOUR NAME?
—GRENADIERS
—HOW'D YOU LIKE TO SPOON WITH
   ME?
   By Edward Laska and Jerome Kern.

1906. *THE LITTLE CHERUB*
   A musical comedy with book and lyrics
   by Owen Hall, and presented by a cast
   headed by Hattie Williams, Tom Wise,
   Winona Winter, John Mayon and Jane
   Blakeley.
—EXPERIENCE
—OLYMPIAN OCTET
—AS A FRIEND

—IT'S THE GIRLS
—DEAR LITTLE GIRLS
—MY WIFE WILL BE MY LADY
—WON'T YOU WALTZ?
—LITTLE WILLIE BROWNE
—THE SUPPER GIRLS
—PIERROT AND CUPID
—CUPID'S RIFLE RANGE
—MY IRISH ROSIE
    By William Jerome and Jean Schwartz.
—THE DOGGIE IN OUR YARD
    By Marie Doro.
—MEET ME AT TWILIGHT
    By J. Clifford Harris and Jerome Kern.
—PLAIN RUSTIC RIDE 'NEATH THE
    SILV'RY MOON
    By Gounard and Jerome Kern.
—UNDER THE LINDEN TREE
    By M. E. Rourke and Jerome Kern.

1907. *THE ORCHID*
    With Lionel Monckton. A musical comedy
    with book by James T. Tanner and
    Joseph W. Herbert, lyrics by Adrian Ross
    and Percy Greenbank, and starring Eddie
    Foy in a cast that included Trixie Fri-
    ganza, Amelia Stone, Maude Fulton, Irene
    Franklin, Melville Ellis, Joseph W. Her-
    bert, William Rock and Grace Studdiford.
—THIS HIGHLY HORTICULTURAL
    COLLEGE
—LADY SECRETARY
—LADIES IN SOCIETY
—OH, MR. REGISTRAR
—A PERFECT LADY
—COLLEGE
—I DON'T WANT THE DARK
—UP AND DOWN, OVER THE TOWN
—ZOO SONG
—LITTLE BLANCHE MARIE
—FAR FROM PERU
—NO WEDDING BELLS FOR ME
    By E. P. Moran, Will Heelan and Sey-
    mour Furth.
—LIZA ANN
—A SHOW GIRL ON BROADWAY
    By Doc Lucia and B. E. Toy.
—COME AROUND ON OUR VERANDA
    By Paul West and Jerome Kern.
—HE GOES TO CHURCH ON SUNDAY
    By Vincent Bryan and E. Ray Goetz.
—I MUST PROPOSE TO YOU
—I DO, I DO
    By Dave Reed, Jr.
—MULBERRY STREET
    By Junie McCree.
—LA PROMENADE ANGLAISE
—DANCE OF THE ORCHID

1908. *THE GIRLS OF GOTTENBURG*
    With Lionel Monckton. A musical comedy

with book and lyrics by George Grossmith
Jr. and L. E. Berman, and presented by
a cast headed by James Blakeley, John E.
Hazzard, Ernest Cossart, Wallace Mc-
Cutcheon, Eddie Garvie and Louise
Dresser.
—A COMMON LITTLE GIRL
—DO YOU KNOW MR. SCHNEIDER?
—STROLLING AND PATROLLING
—I REMEMBER YOU
—I WILL BE WAITING FOR YOU
—QUEENIE WITH HER HAIR IN A
    BRAID
    Music by William T. Francis.
—HERE'S TO THE GIRLS
    Music by Will R. Anderson.
—FRIEDA
    By M. E. Rourke and Jerome Kern.
—I CAN'T SAY YOU'RE THE ONLY
    ONE
    By C. H. Bovill and Jerome Kern.

Frederick Chapin Score

1907. *THE MAID AND THE MILLION-
    AIRE*
    A musical comedy with book and lyrics
    by the composer, and presented by a cast
    that included John C. Hart.
—MY CONEY ISLAND QUEEN
—MY LITTLE GIRLIE

George M. Cohan Scores

1901. *THE GOVERNOR'S SON*
    With a cast headed by Jerry Cohan,
    Helen Cohan, Josephine Cohan and
    George Cohan and his wife, Ethel Levey.
—THE REAL GIRLS
—A WIDOW'S WILE
—A REGULAR WILLIAM GILLETTE
—BEHOLD THE GOVERNOR
—THE STORY OF THE WEDDING
    MARCH
—WINE DIVINE
—TOO MANY MILES FROM BROAD-
    WAY
—THE GOVERNOR'S SON
—OH, MR. MOON
—AND THE MANAGER SAID:
—NEVER BREATHE A WORD OF THIS
    TO MOTHER
—THE QUAKERTOWN CADETS
—LUCY

1903. *RUNNING FOR OFFICE*
    With a cast headed by the Four Cohans
    and Ethel Levey.
—THE FOOTBALL BOYS AND GIRLS
—SWEET POPULARITY

—ROOT FOR RILEY
--THEY ARE HYPNOTIZED
—KID DAYS
—FLIRTATION ON THE BEACH
—IN A ONE-NIGHT STAND
—IF I WERE ONLY MR. MORGAN
—I WANT TO GO TO PAREE, PAPA
—JOHNNY, GET OFF THE CORNER
—I'LL BE THERE IN A PUBLIC
   SQUARE
—THE ELOPEMENT
—REUBENS ON PARADE

1904. *LITTLE JOHNNY JONES*
George M. Cohan's first starring vehicle
in which he played the stage prototype of
Tod Sloan, the American jockey who the
year before had gone to England to ride
for King George. The cast included Jerry
Cohan, Helen Cohan, Ethel Levey, Sam
J. Ryan, Donald Brian, Tom Lewis and
Truly Shattuck.
—THE CECIL IN LONDON TOWN
—THEY'RE ALL MY FRIENDS
—MAM'SELLE FAUCHETTE
—'OP IN MY 'ANSON
—NESTING IN A NEW YORK TREE
—THE YANKEE DOODLE BOY
—OFF TO THE DERBY
—GIRLS OF THE U.S.A.
—SAILORS OF THE ST. HURRAH
—CAPTAIN OF A TEN-DAY BOAT
—GOOD-BYE FLO
—SO LONG, SING SONG
—GOOD OLD CALIFORNIA
—A GIRL I KNOW
—GIVE MY REGARDS TO BROADWAY
—MARCH OF THE FRISCO CHINKS
—IF MR. BOSTON LAWSON HAD HIS
   WAY
—I'M MIGHTY GLAD I'M LIVING
   AND THAT'S ALL
—LIFE'S A FUNNY PROPOSITION
   AFTER ALL

1906. *FORTY-FIVE MINUTES FROM
   BROADWAY*
This musical comedy, which starred Fay
Templeton and elevated Victor Moore to
stardom almost overnight, had the good
citizens of New Rochelle, N.Y., the locale
of the play, up in arms. On the morning
after the premiere, staged on the night of
January 1, an emergency session of the
Chamber of Commerce was called, reso-
lutions were passed calling for a boycott
of the show, and press releases were sent
out to all metropolitan newspapers refut-
ing the "libelous statements" made by
George M. Cohan in the title song to the
effect that there was "not a cafe in the

town" and the male inhabitants had
"whiskers like hay." The cast also in-
cluded Julia Ralph, Marion Singer and
Donald Brian.
—GENTLEMEN OF THE PRESS
—I WANT TO BE A POPULAR MIL-
   LIONAIRE
—MARY'S A GRAND OLD NAME
—FORTY-FIVE MINUTES FROM
   BROADWAY
—SO LONG MARY
—STAND UP AND FIGHT LIKE HELL

1906. *GEORGE WASHINGTON JR.*
With a cast headed by George M. Cohan,
Jerry Cohan, Helen Cohan, Ethel Levey,
Willis P. Sweatman and Truly Shattuck.
—WASHINGTON, HE WAS A WONDER-
   FUL MAN
—I WAS BORN IN VIRGINIA
—*YOU'RE A GRAND OLD FLAG
—I'LL BE THERE WITH BELLS ON
—I'VE NEVER BEEN OVER THERE
—ALL ABOARD FOR BROADWAY
—WEDDING OF THE BLUE AND THE
   GRAY
—IF WASHINGTON SHOULD COME
   TO LIFE TODAY

1907. *THE HONEYMOONERS*
This was a revival of "Running for Of-
fice" with practically a new musical score
and presented by a cast headed by
George M. Cohan, his mother and father,
Jerry and Helen Cohan, and Gertrude
Hoffman.
—LET'S TAKE AN OLD-FASHIONED
   WALK
—I'M A POPULAR MAN
—MAKE A LOT OF NOISE
—THE MUSICAL COMEDY MAID
—KID DAYS
—HONEY BABE
—IN A ONE-NIGHT STAND
—NOTHING NEW BENEATH THE SUN
—I'LL BE THERE IN A PUBLIC
   SQUARE
—MYSTERIOUS MAID
—IF I DIE I'M GOING TO HAVE
   SOME FUN
—STORY OF THE WEDDING MARCH

1907. *THE TALK OF NEW YORK*
Starring Victor Moore, who was sup-
ported by a cast headed by his wife, Em-
ma Littlefield, Gertrude Vanderbilt and
Jack Gardner.
—FOLLOW YOUR UNCLE DUDLEY
—PUT DOWN A BET FOR ME
—MR. BURNS OF NEW ROCHELLE

—WHEN WE ARE M-A DOUBLE R-I-E-D
—BURNING UP THE BOULEVARD
—BUSY LITTLE BROADWAY
—WHEN A FELLOW'S ON THE LEVEL WITH A GIRL THAT'S ON THE SQUARE
—I WANT YOU
—CLAREMONT
—I WANT THE WORLD TO KNOW I LOVE YOU
—UNDER ANY OLD FLAG AT ALL
—DRINK WITH ME
—GEE, AIN'T I GLAD I'M HOME!

1908. *FIFTY MILES FROM BOSTON*
A play with music presented by a cast headed by Edna Wallace Hopper, Lawrence Wheat, George Parsons, James C. Marlowe and Emma Janvier.
—JACK AND JILL
—A SMALL TOWN GIRL
—THE BOYS WHO FIGHT THE FLAMES
—WALTZ WITH ME
—AIN'T IT AWFUL
—HARRIGAN

1908. *THE YANKEE PRINCE*
Presented by a cast headed by the Four Cohans, Jack Gardner, Tom Lewis and Donald Crisp.
—SHOWING THE YANKEES LONDON TOWN
—COME ON DOWN TOWN
—I'M TO MARRY A NOBLEMAN
—THINK IT OVER CAREFULLY
—YANKEE DOODLE'S COME TO TOWN
—SOLDIERS OF THE KING
—I'M STRONG FOR YOU
—I SAY, FLO
—VILLIANS IN THE PLAY
—THE ABC'S OF THE U.S.A.
—M-O-N-E-Y
—TOMMY ATKINS, YOU'RE ALL RIGHT
—COHAN'S RAG BABE
—FROM THE LAND OF DREAMS
—A SONG FOR THE KING

1908. *THE AMERICAN IDEA*
Presented by a cast headed by George Beban, Robert Daly, Trixie Friganza and Gertrude Vanderbilt.
—IN GAY PAREE
—SULLIVAN
—BROTHERS AND SISTERS
—THEY ALL FOLLOW ME
—TOO LONG FROM LONGACRE SQUARE

—WHAT WE'RE SUPPOSED TO BE
—COHAN'S PET NAMES
—THAT'S SOME LOVE
—F-A-M-E
—AMERICAN RAGTIME
—THE GARDEN THAT BLOOMS FOR YOU
—THE BOLD GENDARMES
—WHOOP-LA-LA
—MARCH MILITAIRE

1909. *THE MAN WHO OWNS BROADWAY*
Co-starring Raymond Hitchcock and Flora Zabelle.
—MY DAUGHTER IS WED TO A FRIEND OF MINE
—I'VE ALWAYS BEEN A GOOD OLD SPORT
—I'M IN LOVE WITH ONE OF THE STARS
—WHEN A SERVANT LEARNS A SECRET
—THE MAN WHO OWNS BROADWAY
—YOU'D THINK YOU WERE IN PARIS
—LOVE WILL MAKE OR BREAK A MAN
—THERE'S SOMETHING ABOUT A UNIFORM
—ON A HUNDRED DIFFERENT SHIPS
—I'M ALL O.K. WITH K & E
—A NICE LITTLE PLOT FOR A PLAY
—IN THE WALDORF'S HALLS
—I'LL GO THE ROUTE FOR YOU
—MARCH OF THE KING'S AMAZONS
—WHY THEY MADE HIM KING

Will Marion Cook Scores

1903. *IN DAHOMEY*
A musical comedy with book by J. A. Shipp, lyrics by Paul Lawrence Dunbar and Alex Rogers, and presented by an all-Negro cast headed by Bert Williams, George Walker, Lottie Williams and Ada Overton Walker.
—THE JONAH MAN
—EVERY DARKEY IS KING
—MOLLIE GREEN
—SOCIETY
—EMANCIPATION DAY
—WHEN SOUSA COMES TO COONTOWN
—LEADER OF THE COLORED ARISTOCRACY
—I WANT TO BE A REAL LADY
—CABOCEERS' CHORAL
—DAT GIRL OF MINE

1904. *THE SOUTHERNERS*
A musical comedy with book and lyrics

by Will Mercer and Richard Grant, and
presented by a cast headed by Junie Mc-
Cree, Albert Hart, William Gould and
Eddie Leonard.
—AS THE SUNFLOWER TURNS TO
  THE SUN
—MANDY LOU
—WHERE THE LOTUS BLOSSOMS
  GROW
—DARKTOWN BARBEQUE
—ALLUS DE SAME IN DIXIE
—DAISY DEANE
—DANDY DAN
—SWEET DREAMS, DEAR ONE OF
  THEE
—GOOD EVENIN'
—THE AMOROUS STAR
  By Marie Sutherland.

1906. *ABYSSINIA*
  With Bert Williams. A musical comedy
  with book and lyrics by J. A. Shipp and
  Alex Rogers, and starring Williams and
  Walker in an all-Negro cast.
—ODE TO THE SUN
—JOLLY JUNGLE BOYS
—ODE TO MENELIK
—THE ISLAND OF BY-AND-BY
—WHERE MY FOREFATHERS DIED
—RASTUS JOHNSON, U. S. A.
—HOLIDAY IN THE MARKET
—ANSWERS YOU DON'T EXPECT TO
  GET
—IT'S HARD TO FIND A KING LIKE
  ME
—THE CAPTURE OF YARABOO
—LET IT ALONE
—GOODBYE, ETHIOPIA

1908. *BANDANA LAND*
  A musical comedy with book and lyrics
  by J. A. Shipp and Alex Rogers, and
  presented by a cast headed by Williams
  and Walker, Alex Rogers, Ada Overton
  Walker, Lottie Williams, J. Leubrie Hill,
  J. A. Shipp and Lavinia Rogers.
—CORN SONG
—KINKY
—TAINT GWINE TO BE NO RAIN
—UNTIL THEN
—RED, RED ROSE
—WHEN I WAS SWEET SIXTEEN
—IT'S HARD TO LOVE SOMEBODY
  WHEN SOMEBODY DON'T LOVE
  YOU
—JUST THE SAME
—SOMEWHERE
—LATE HOURS
—I'D RATHER HAVE NOTHIN' ALL
  DE TIME THAN SOMETHIN' FOR
  A LITTLE WHILE

—ETHIOPIA
—BON BON BUDDY
—IN BANDANA LAN'
—SOMEBODY LIED TO ME

Reginald DeKoven Scores

1900. *FOXY QUILLER*
  Book and lyrics by Harry B. Smith, and
  presented by a cast headed by Jerome
  Sykes, Julius Steger, Harry MacDonough
  and Georgia Caine.
—A-HOY! A-HOY!
—THE SWEARING SKIPPER
—WINDING, WINDING
—QUILLER HAS THE BRAIN
—THE VENDETTA
—THE LEGEND OF THE TARANTELLA
—SONG OF THE CHEATING PEDDLER
—POLLY WANT A CRACKER?
—YOUTH IS THE GOLDEN AGE
—SONG OF THE SWORD
—THE WATCHMAN'S RATTLE
—POOR SHEPHERD'S, WE

1901. *THE LITTLE DUCHESS*
  Book and lyrics by Harry B. Smith. A
  Florenz Ziegfeld production that starred
  Anna Held in a cast that included Charles
  A. Bigelow, Joseph Herbert, George
  Marion, Sydney Barraclough, Joe Welch,
  Eva Davenport, Bessie Wynn and a boy
  sporano named Willie Howard at a salary
  of $8 a week. Willie's musical comedy
  debut was highly successful until the show
  played Washington where his voice
  changed one night in the middle of his
  song. After that he was a baritone—and
  "at liberty."
—TAKE ME OUT AND FLOAT ME
—WHAT ARE THE WILD WAVES
  SAYING?
—IN SOCIETY
—THE ONLY GIRL
—BATHING SONG
—FLIRTATION SONG
—THEY TELL ME OF YOU
—MENAGERIE SONG
—CHLOE, I'M WAITING
—MAKE ALLOWANCES FOR LOVE
—THOSE GREAT BIG EYES
—SADIE
  Music by Leo Le Brunn.
—EVERY MORN I BRING THEE
  VIOLETS
  By Ellen Wright and Silvio Hein.
—PRETTY MOLLY SHANNON
  By Gus Ryan and Walter Wolfe.

1902. *MAID MARIAN*
  Book and lyrics by Harry B. Smith. This

was written as a sequel to "Robin Hood," and the cast was headed by Henry Clay Barnabee, W. H. MacDonald, Frank Rushmore, George B. Frothingham, Josephine Bartlett and Grace Van Studdiford.
—ANNABEL WAS THE FAIREST
—THE CELLARER'S TOAST
—SONG OF THE FALCON
—SHERIFF'S SONG
—FORESTER'S SONG
—MADRIGAL
—NEVER IN THE WIDE, WIDE WORLD
—THE MONK AND THE MAGPIE
—SONG OF THE OUTLAW
—SERENADE
—THE MAN AT ARMS
—TELL ME AGAIN SWEETHEART
—SNAKE CHARMER'S SONG
—IF YOU WERE I AND I WERE YOU
—TRUE LOVE IS NOT FOR A DAY
—SONG OF THE CRUSADER
—UNDER THE MISTLETOE BOUGH
—THE COBBLER AND THE FLIES

1903. *THE JERSEY LILY*
Book and lyrics by George B. Hobart. This was Blanche Ring's first starring vehicle, and the cast included Maude Raymond, Gertrude Hoffman, Billy B. Van, Louis Harrison, Billie Taylor and William Cameron.
—WELCOME, THE BRIDE
—THE GINGERBREAD BOY
—PATSY BOLIVAR
—THE NEW COOK
—SOME BEAUTIFUL DAY
—THE UMP-UMP MAN
—OLD GLORY
—THE LILY'S PROMENADE
—SWEETHEART MINE
—MY DEAR OLD NEW JERSEY HOME
—DREAMING
—AURORA
—ROSIE LEE
There were four interpolated numbers in the show, as follows:
—LOOEY
By George V. Hobart and Max Witt.
—ON A CHINESE HONEYMOON
By Max Hoffman.
—'NEATH THY WINDOW, SENORITA
By Max Hoffman.
—BEDELIA
By William Jerome and Jean Schwartz, which was the show-stopper.

1903. *THE RED FEATHER*
Book by Charles Klein, lyrics by Charles Emerson Cook, and presented by a cast

headed by Grace Van Studdiford, Mlle. Elsie De Bere, Olive Celeste and Thomas Q. Seabrooke.
—THE CONSPIRATORS
—THE LITTLE MILLINER
—SONG OF THE GUARD
—RED FEATHER
—TO CALL THEE MINE
—A LESSON IN VERSE
—OUR CABINET
—THE HUMOROUS GHOST
—THE MERRY CAVALIER
—THE TAIL OF THE HIGHBORN ROOSTER
—THE ROSE AND THE BREEZE
—GARDEN OF DREAMS
—A PRINCE OF GOOD FELLOWS
—CARISSIMA
By Arthur Penn.
—THERE'S A LITTLE STREET IN HEAVEN THEY CALL BROADWAY
By James T. Waldon and A. Baldwin Sloane.

1905. *HAPPYLAND*
Book and lyrics by Frederick Ranken, and co-starring Marguerite Clark and DeWolf Hopper.
—BEHOLD, THE KING
—ENTRANCE OF THE TROUBADOURS
—SO THEN, AWAY
—SERENADE FORTUNATUS
—PRETTY MAIDEN
—'TWAS THE ROSE
—MADRIGAL
—SLUMBER ON
—CHORUS OF SHEPHERDS
—ROBIN REDBREAST
—JUST EIGHTEEN YEARS AGO
—MINETTE, MY HUMAN MERMAID
—GIVE ME THY HEART, LOVE
—RING OUT, SWEET BELS

1906. *THE STUDENT KING*
Book by Frederic Ranken, lyrics by Stanislaus Stange, and presented by a cast headed by Lina Abarbanell, Raymond Hitchcock, Eva Fallon and Flavia Arcaro.
—OPPOSITES ARE WE
—THE STUDENT KING
—MY PRETTY TYROLESE
—GIVE ME THY HEART, LOVE
—I TOOK THEM ALL
—MY OLD BASSOON
—HARLEQUIN AND COLUMBINE
—HOW TO WOO
—THE GAY LIEUTENANT
—THE SAME OLD GAME
—SO WE DRINK
—THE JOLLY MILLER

—NUDEL, NUDEL, NUP-NUP

1907. *THE GIRLS OF HOLLAND*
Book and lyrics by Stanislaus Stange, and
with a cast headed by Vera Michelena,
Mary Nash and Harry MacDonough. This
production ran for only fifteen perform-
ances on Broadway but was revived later
as "The Snow Man" with the following
numbers:
—FASCINATION
—ARIELLA
—I WANT YOU FOR MY ALL-TIME
    GIRL
—IN PARADISE
—LOVE ON A SUMMER'S DAY
—PRAY, GO GENTLY
—THE MESSAGE OF THE BELLS
—MY LADY FAIR
—SERENADE D'AMOUR
—SEVEN REASONS WHY
—THE SPANISH GRANDEE

1908. *THE GOLDEN BUTTERFLY*
Book and lyrics by Harry B. Smith, and
with a cast headed by Grace Van Studdi-
ford, Charles Purcell, Louis B. Harrison,
Walter Percival and Gladys Coleman.
—HEROES
—MEMORY'S GARDEN
—THE W A N D E R I N G MINSTREL'S
    SONG
—HEART OF MINE
—ON THE BOULEVARD
—THE RECOGNIZED MAN OF THE
    HOUR
—ORIGINALITY
—THE GOLDEN BUTTERFLY
—IN MOSCOW
—THE HAUNTED CASK
—BELLE OF THE RING
—THE ELF KING

1909. *THE BEAUTY SPOT*
Book and lyrics by Joseph W. Herbert,
and with a cast headed by Marguerite
Clark, Jefferson DeAngelis, George Mac-
Farland and Grace Walton.
—TOUJOURS LA POLITESSE
—DANCE OF THE ABORIGINES
—CREOLE DAYS
—GOO-GOO
—CHICK, CHICK, CHICK
—COO-EE
—HAMMOCK LOVE SONG
—A PRINCE OF BORNEO
—BOYS WILL BE BOYS
—THE CINEMATOGRAPH
—PRETTY PUNCHINELLO

Charles Denee Scores

1900. *LITTLE RED RIDING HOOD*
An extravaganza presented by a cast
headed by Ethel Jackson, Madge Lessing,
Gertrude Carlisle, Amorita, Mayme Geh-
rue and Snitz Edwards. Lyrics by Harrison
Ward.
—PUSSY'S IN THE WELL
—A SOLDIER BOLD
—THE ART OF MAKING LOVE
—THE LEGEND OF THE STORK
—LOVE IS AN INFANT
—LITTLE BOY BLUE COME BLOW
    YOUR HORN
—NELLIE THE MANICURE
—THE PICKANINNY LULLABY
—BOOGIE MAN
—THE SUNSHINE GIRL

1902. *THE DEFENDER*
In this musical comedy with book and
lyrics by Allen Lowe, Blanche Ring made
her first bid for stardom with her ren-
dition of "In The Good Old Summer-
time." The other members of the cast in-
cluded Harry Davenport, Alexander
Clark, Emma Carus and Paula Edwardes.
—HAIL TO THE BARONET
—LIFT THE CUP
—QUEENS OF SOCIETY
—HOUP-LA
—THE LIGHTHOUSE AND THE
    BOATS
—VESPER BELLS
—LOVE IS QUEEN OF THE SEA
—I'LL BE YOUR RAINBOW
—LITTLE FLY
—GOOD NIGHT
—PINKY PANKY POO
—THE MAN WHO HYPNOTIZED Mc-
    CARTHY
—JACK O' LANTERN MAN
—ANGLO-SAXONS OF TODAY
—THE BOYS BEFORE THE MAST
—IN THE GOOD OLD SUMMERTIME
By George "Honey Boy" Evans and Ren
Shields.

Gus Edwards Scores

1905. *WHEN WE WERE FORTY-ONE*
Book and lyrics by Robert B. Smith, and
presented by a cast headed by LaBelle
Dazie, a sensational masked dancer; Harry
Bulger, John McVeigh, Charles H. Prince,
Elsie Janis, Emma Carus and Harry
Meehan.
—SIMPLE SIMON
—UP AND DOWN THE BOARDWALK

—THE MAIDEN OF THE WILD AND
  WOOLLY WEST
—THE ADVANTAGE OF A COLLEGE
  EDUCATION
—MARION THE MAID
—THE MAN WHO LEADS THE BAND
  THAT LEADS THE ARMY
—SWEET KITTY KILLAIRES
—MEET ME UNDER THE WISTARIA
  This song was a plug for the roof garden,
  called the Wistaria Grove, of Hammer-
  stein's New York Theater where the pro-
  duction was staged.

1907. *HIP-HIP-HOORAY*
  Book and lyrics by Edgar Smith, and co-
  starring Weber and Fields in a cast that
  included Harry Tighe, Tom Lewis, Fay
  Tincher, Amelia Stone, Valeska Suratt,
  Bessie Clayton, Charles Ross and Mabel
  Fenton.
—SWEET IVY GREEN
—IN PHILADELPHIA
—ALL I WANT IN THE WIDE, WIDE
  WORLD IS YOU
—I'M A BUSINESS MAN
—COON COLLEGE
—OLD FRIENDS
—WHAT'S THE USE
—WANDER OFF NOWHERE
—FASHION
—HOW'D YOU LIKE TO TAKE ME
  HOME WITH YOU?
—YOU'LL NEVER KNOW WHAT LOVE
  IS TILL I LOVE YOU

1908. *THE MERRY-GO-ROUND*
  Book by Edgar Smith, lyrics by Paul West,
  and presented by a cast that included
  James J. Morton, Mabel Hite, Bobby
  North and Dorothy Jardon.
—BETTY YOU'RE MY ONE BEST BET
—THERE'S NOT A GIRL IN ALL THE
  WIDE   WORLD   THAT   WON'T
  HAVE ME
—IN BOHEMIA WITH YOU
—A TWO-HORSE FELLER IN A ONE-
  HORSE TOWN
—MY LITTLE TAILOR MAID
—I MET HER AT THE METROPOLE
—I WON'T BE HOME FOR DINNER
—WHEN THE MUSIC STARTS TO
  PLAY
—I LIKE THEM JUST LIKE YOU,
  LITTLE GIRL
—HAVE YOU SEEN MY BABY?
—WON'T YOU COME UNDER MY
  MERRY WIDOW HAT?
—ORCHIDS OF THE OPERA
—CAPTAIN OF THE MINEOLA GUARD

—MERRY-GO-ROUND RAG
1908. *SCHOOL DAYS*
  Book by Aaron Hoffman, lyrics by Edward
  Gardenier and Vincent Bryan, and pre-
  sented by a cast that included Gregory
  Kelly, John Hines, Herman Timberg,
  Janet Priest and Joe Keno.
—SCHOOL DAYS
—MAYBE IT'S A BEAR
—FIGHTING KID
—IT TAKES A COP TO COP THE
  GIRLS
—TEDDY-BIRD
—WE'RE GOING TO FIGHT THE IN-
  DIANS
—THE PAPER HAT BRIGADE
—CALENDAR OF LOVE
—SCHOOLMATES
—SEE-SAW
—CAMPBELL SOUP KIDS
—GET ON THE MERRY-GO-ROUND
1909. *BREAKING INTO SOCIETY*
  Book and lyrics by Robert B. Smith, and
  starring the Four Mortons.
—MARRIAGE GAME
—UP AND DOWN THE BOARDWALK
—IF I COULD ONLY LAND A MIL-
  LIONAIRE
—I'M THE BOY
—JOLLY YOURSELF ALONG
—THAT'S WHAT THE PAPERS SAY
—MY SENORITA
—BASHFUL CHAPPIE
—COLUMBIA COLLEEN
—STANDING PAT
—IF WOMEN HAD THEIR WAY
—TING-A-LING PING PONG

Julian Edwards Scores

1900. *PRINCESS CHIC*
  A musical comedy with book and lyrics
  by Kirke LaShelle, and presented by a
  cast headed by Christie MacDonald.
—THE LOVE LIGHT IN YOUR EYES
—WAR IS A BEAUTIFUL JADE
—WEAK AS A WOMAN
—COME LOVE, GO LOVE
—A SOLDIER OF FORTUNE
—THE FOOLISH SWALLOW
—THE WOOD NYMPH
—THE STORY BOOK
1902. *DOLLY VARDEN*
  A musical comedy with book and lyrics
  by Stanislaus Stange, and presented by a
  cast headed by Lulu Glaser and Van
  Rensselaer Wheeler.
—SING MY PRETTY ONE
—MY SHIP'S THE GIRL FOR ME

—DOLLY VARDON
—THE COUNTRY GIRL
—WHAT LOVE MEANS
—WHEN WE MET IN LOVER'S LANE
—THE CANNIBAL MAID
—AN AURAL MISUNDERSTANDING
—LOVEABLE LOVE
—FOR THE BENEFIT OF MAN
—THE NAVY
—THE LAY OF THE JAY
—THE GIRL YOU LOVE
—SONG OF THE SWORD
—BRIDES AND GROOMS

1902. *WHEN JOHNNY COMES MARCH-
    ING HOME*
    A musical comedy with book and lyrics
    by Stanislaus Stange, and presented by a
    cast headed by William G. Stewart, Albert
    McGuckin, Homer Lind, Maude Lam-
    bert, Julia Gifford and Thelma Fair.
—SING, SING, DARKIES, SING
—FAIRYLAND
—WHILE YOU'RE THINKING
—MY OWN UNITED STATES
—KATIE MY SOUTHERN ROSE
—SPRING, SWEET SPRING
—MY HONEYSUCKLE GIRL
—YEARS TOUCH NOT THE HEART
—I COULD WALTZ ON FOREVER
—'TWAS DOWN IN THE GARDEN OF
    EDEN
—JUST MARRY THE GIRL AND BE
    MERRY
—WHEN OUR LIPS IN KISSES MET
—WHO KNOWS?
—THE SWANEE RIVER
—LOVE'S NIGHT
—GOOD DAY, YANKEES
—FLAG OF MY COUNTRY
—BUT THEY DIDN'T
—THE DRUMS

1904. *LOVE'S LOTTERY*
    A musical comedy with book and lyrics
    by Stanislaus Stange, and starring
    Madame Schumann-Heink in a cast that
    included Louise Gunning, John Slavin
    and Wallace Brownlow.
—WHAT ART THOU?
—THE BLARNEY OF KILLARNEY
—THE VILLAGE RECRUITS
—THE HONEYMOON
—THE TEMPTATION
—SWEET THOUGHTS OF HOME
—FOLLOW THE FLAG
—SHE IS THE RIGHT GIRL
—RIGHT FOR YOUR MONEY-O
—SONG OF THE TUB
—BEHOLD OUR LADY GREAT

—HOAX AND COAX
—MY FIRST TRUE LOVE
—CUPID'S A LAD
—KING FORTUNE SMILES TODAY
—LONG FORGOTTEN
—A GLIMPSE OF EDEN
—HOLIDAY JOYS
—IF WE PART

1906. *HIS HONOR THE MAYOR*
    A musical comedy with book and lyrics
    by C. J. Campbell and R. M. Skinner,
    and starring Blanche Ring in a cast that
    included Harry Kelly, Fletcher Norton
    and Fred Walton.
—THE PINK HUSSARS
—MILITARY WILLIE
—WHERE THE WILD VINE CLINGS
—DAISY
—THE GIRL FROM ILLINOIS
—A LITTLE GIRL LIKE ME
—SHE'S ALL MY OWN
—CALL AROUND ON SUNDAY AFTER-
    NOON
—FLOWER SONG
—THE DAINTY MILLINERS
—THE MAYOR OF KANKAKEE
—I'LL TRAVEL THE LINKS WITH
    YOU
—THE LAND YOU LEFT BEHIND
—MARY ANN
—SWEET TOKAY
—MYGAR MAID
—COME TAKE A SKATE WITH ME
    Music by Gus Edwards.
—WALTZ ME AROUND AGAIN WILLIE
    By Will Cobb and Ren Shields.

1907. *THE BELLE OF LONDON TOWN*
    A musical comedy with book and lyrics
    by Stanislaus Stange, and starring Ca-
    mille D'Ardille in a cast that included
    Kathleen Clifford, Giorgio Majeroni and
    Orville Harrold.
—TO DRINK WE HAVE NO FEAR
—THE LIGHT THAT LIES IN WOM-
    EN'S EYES
—MAGICIAN LOVE
—I WAS BORN TO RULE
—I CANNOT WAIT TILL MONDAY
—THEY PICTURED ME LIKE THIS
—LET US GOSSIP OF THE LATEST
    COURT FLIRTATION
—FAIR BEAUTY'S QUEEN
—THE LADY OF SOCIETY
—HINDOO PARADISE
—I SHOULD HAVE BEEN OFFENDED
    IF MY WAIST YOU HADN'T
    SQUEEZED
—WHEN FORTUNE SMILES

—GUARDIANS OF THE HOUSE
—THE LITTLE WEATHER VANE
—DRINK WITH ME THE NIGHT
AWAY
—LOVE'S SECRET
—STILL THE WORLD ROLLS ON

1907. *THE GIRL AND THE GOVERNOR*
A musical comedy with book and lyrics by S. M. Brenner, and starring Jefferson De Angelis.
—DON PASQUALE DE MESQUITA
—I'VE A VERY NASTY TEMPER SO BEWARE
—I WOULD LIKE A FRANK OPINION
—A MUSICAL LOVER I'D BE
—WHO WOULD A BACHELOR BE?
—HAVE YOU HEARD IT TOLD THAT WAY BEFORE?

1908. *THE GAY MUSICIAN*
A musical comedy with book by Edward Siedle, lyrics by Charles Campbell, and presented by a cast that included Joseph C. Miron, Amelia Stone and Walter Percival.
—HAIL TO THE QUEEN OF BEAUTY
—WHAT A DRY WORLD THIS WOULD BE
—IF THE UNEXPECTED HAPPENS
—I HAVE MY DOUBTS
—IT'S A LONG, LONG TIME
—MY DASHING SOLDIER BOY
—WE WON'T DO A THING TO HIS OPERA
—THAT'S HOW I GET TREATED
—THE SAUCY SPARROW
—THE BOX OFFICE TELLS THE STORY
—THAT MELODY
—AT LAST, AT LAST
—DAINTILY, LIGHTLY
—D'UN COQUETTE
—A CUP OF TEA
—I'M NOT AS SIMPLE AS I LOOK
—I WANT TO BE YOUR BLUE-EYED BABY
—COME ALONG, IT'S A TRIFLING AFFAIR
—TAKE THAT

1909. *THE MOTOR GIRL*
A musical comedy with book and lyrics by Charles J. Campbell and Ralph Skinner, and starring Georgia Caine in a cast that included Elizabeth Brice and Ted Lorraine.
—PROSIT
—TROT-I-TY TROT
—WHEN WE WERE TWENTY-ONE

—WILHELMINA
—THE MOTOR GIRL
—OUT IN THE BARNYARD
—ALL THE WORLD LOVES A LOVER
—JUST LIKE THAT
—JUST SUPPOSE YOU LOVED ME
—THE HONOR OF ALTENSTEIN
—FINESSE
—IN PHILADELPHIA
—WHAT CAN A FELLOW DO?
—WHEN I'M A DUCHESS
—BREAD AND CHEESE
—THE BELLE OF THE DAIRY LUNCH
—I'M OLD ENOUGH TO THINK

1909. *THE GIRL AND THE WIZARD*
A musical comedy with book by J. Hartley Manners, lyrics by Robert B. Smith, and starring Kitty Gordon and Sam Bernard in the title roles.
—REVEILLE
—THE LAND OF LOVE
—WHAT WEALTH IS HERE
—SONG OF THE HEART
—THE WEDDING FETE
—HOW CAN YOU TOOT?
By Will Heelan and Seymour Furth.
—I WONDER IF YOU'RE LONELY
By Ned Wayburn and George Dougherty.
—LA BELLE PARISIENNE
By Edward Madden and Louis A. Hirsch.
—MILITARY MARY ANN
By Edward Madden and Louis A. Hirsch.
—THE BLUE LAGOON
By Percival Knight and Jerome Kern.
—FRANZI FRANKENSTEIN
By Percival Knight and Jerome Kern.
—WHEN I SANG TOREADOR
By Melville Gideon.
—OPERA COMIQUE
By Melville Gideon.

Melville Ellis Score

1906. *ABOUT TOWN*
A revue with book and lyrics by Joseph Herbert, and presented by a cast headed by Lew Fields, Joseph Herbert, Harry Fisher, George Beban, Jack Norworth, Vernon Castle, Louise Dresser, Elita Proctor Otis, Edna Wallace Hopper, Gladys Zell, Mae Irwin, Blanche Ring and Peter Dailey.
—THE PICADILLY CRAWL
—I'M A FICKLE MAID
—THE BABY IN THE HOUSE
—THE GIRL IN THE BABY-BLUE TIGHTS
—IN AMSTERDAM

—SEEING THE TOWN IN A YAP
  WAGON
—THE GIBSON GIRL
  Music by Raymond Hubbell.
—GOSSIP
  Music by Raymond Hubbell.
—A FRENCH TONIC
  Music by Raymond Hubbell.
—THERE'S NO ROOM FOR A DEAD
  ONE ON THE GREAT WHITE
  WAY.
  Music by Raymond Hubbell.
—WHEN TOMMY ATKINS MARRIES
  DOLLY GRAY
  By Will Cobb and Gus Edwards.
—I'M SORRY
  By Jack Norworth and Albert VonTilzer.
—THE LEGEND OF THE MOHAVES
  By Gustav Kerker.
—A GIRL FROM NOWHERE
  Music by A. Baldwin Sloane.
—A LITTLE CLASS OF ONE
  By Glen MacDonough and Victor Herbert.

Ludwig Englander Scores

1900. *THE CASINO GIRL*
  With Harry T. MacConnell. A musical
  comedy with book and lyrics by Harry B.
  Smith, and presented by a cast headed by
  Sam Bernard, Virginia Earle, Albert Hart,
  Mabelle Gilman, Irene Bentley, Mayme
  Gehrue and Lotta Faust.
—SLAVE DEALER'S SONG
—SONG OF THE DRUM MAJOR
—MY NEW YORK
—HOW ACTRESSES ARE MADE
—I'LL PUT A TAX ON
—MAM'SELLE
—DOWN DE LOVER'S LANE
  By Will Marion Cook.
—FROM AFRICA
—CHINK! CHINK!
—VARIETY
—THE CASINO GIRL
—SWEET ANNIE MOORE
  By John H. Flynn.

1900. *THE MONKS OF MALABAR*
  A musical comedy with book and lyrics
  by A. Cheever Goodwin, and presented by
  a cast headed by Francis Wilson, Van
  Rensselaer Wheeler, Madge Lessing and
  Clara Palmer.
—DEAR LITTLE FRENCH GRISETTE

1900. *THE CADET GIRL*
  A musical comedy with book and lyrics
  by Harry B. Smith, and presented by a

cast that included Dan Daly, Adele Richie, Bessie Wynn and Christie MacDonald.
—THE DEMON OF THE DEEP
—WHEN A GIRL DOESN'T KNOW
  WHERE SHE IS
—THE CADETS OF ST. CYR
—I ANNEX IT
—IN MY MUSEUM NOW
—CANTINEER OF THE REGIMENT
—VE VAS GERMANS
—THE SPECIAL TRAIN
—WE CANNOT LET YOU GO
—THEY ARE NOTHING BUT GIRLS
—WE ARE THE HEIRESSES
—COME, GENTLE STRANGER
—THE PAVILION OF LOVE
—GOTTET GOT
—BATTALION OF FRANCE

1900. *THE BELLE OF BOHEMIA*
  With Harry T. MacConnell. A musical
  comedy with book and lyrics by Harry B.
  Smith, and presented by a cast headed by
  Sam Bernard, John Hyams, Irene Bentley,
  Anna Laughlin, Trixie Friganza, Marguerite Clark and Virginia Earle.
—STROLLING THROUGH THE RIVER
—MY MOBILE GAL
—BEER, BEAUTIFUL BEER
—NEVER AGAIN
—MATINEE GIRLS
—THE GIRL WHO IS UP-TO-DATE
—ALWAYS MAKE ALLOWANCES FOR
  LOVE
—SHE NEVER LOVED A MAN AS
  MUCH AS THAT
—BE CLEVER
—THE BLUE RIBBON GIRLS
—CHAMPAGNE WALTZ
—FAIRIES' LULLABY
—TELL ME WHEN I SHALL FIND HIM
—BELLE OF BOHEMIA
—HE WAS A MARRIED MAN
—THE LADY IN THE MOON

1901. *THE STROLLERS*
  A musical comedy with book and lyrics
  by Harry B. Smith, and presented by a
  cast headed by Francis Wilson, Eddie
  Foy, Harry Gilfoil, Marie George and
  Irene Bentley.
—GOSSIP CHORUS
—SONG OF THE STROLLERS
—HEAVEN'S BEST GIFT
—HAIL TO THE BRIDEGROOM
—ENGLISH COON SONG
—A LESSON IN FLIRTATION
—THE BOLD HUSSARS
—IN EV'RY AGE

—WHEN THE ORCHESTRA PLAYS
—STROLLERS WE
—I'M TIRED
By William Jerome and Jean Schwartz.

1901. *THE NEW YORKERS*
A musical comedy with book by Glen MacDonough, lyrics by George V. Hobart, and presented by a cast headed by Dan Daly, William Cameron, Virginia Earle, Marguerite Clark and Anna Laughlin.
—CAB, SIR, WANT A CAB?
—RUSSIA THE FATHERLAND
—WHEN YOU SAIL FOR PARIS IN THE SPRING
—STROLLING IN SOCIETY
—KODAK GIRL
—HONOLULU LULU
—TAKE ME BACK TO HERALD SQUARE
—AND THE BAND BEGAN TO PLAY
—OH, FUDGE!
—'IS OLD MAN'S 'AT WON'T FIT 'IM
—THREE WOMEN TO EVERY MAN
—RAGTIME GIRL
—DAT'S ALL
By Will Marion Cook.
—IF I SHOULD SAY GOODBYE

1902. *SALLY IN OUR ALLEY*
A musical comedy with book and lyrics by George V. Hobart, and presented by a cast headed by Marie Cahill, Dan McAvoy, Julius Steger, Joseph W. Herbert, Georgia Caine, Harry Fairleigh and Georgia Kelly.
—COME TAKE A STROLL WITH ME
—WHEN I AM YOURS DEAR
—THE MICROBE IN A KISS
—WHISTLING BILL
—I WANT TO BE A SOLDIER LADY
—YOU AND MY FIANCEE
—ELLEN, ELLEN
—PING PONG, PING
—NORA RYAN
—SPORT, JOKE AND TWO SPOT
—SALLY IN OUR ALLEY
By Henry Carey.
—BILL THE BILL POSTER
—WHEN IT'S ALL GOIN' OUT AND NOTHIN' COMIN' IN
By George Walker and Bert Williams.
—THE GIRLIE WITH THE BABY STARE
By Ernest Hanegan and William H. Penn.
—UNDER THE BAMBOO TREE
By Bob Cole and J. Rosamond Johnson.

1903. *THE JEWEL OF ASIA*
A musical comedy with book and lyrics

by Frederick Ranken and Harry B. Smith, and presented by a cast headed by James T. Powers, William Cameron, Clifton Crawford, Blanche Ring and Harriet Burt.
—I LOVE YOU DOLLY
—PIERRE
—BEGGARS' CHORUS
—PLEASE DON'T MOVE
—WHEN WE SAY WE DO A THING
—TWELVE PRETTY WIVES FROM TURKEY
—THE SAME OLD CROWD
—I AM THE PASHA
—OFF TO TURKEY
—MY HONEY BUNCH
—A WOMAN'S NO MEANS YES
—OH, WHAT'S THE USE?
—OH, THOU ART FAIR
—WANTED: A FLY
—LOVE IS A GAME

1903. *THE OFFICE BOY*
A musical comedy with book and lyrics by Harry B. Smith, and starring Frank Daniels in a cast that included James C. Reany, Sydney Toler, Lawrence Wheat, Walter C. Kelly, Louise Gunning and Eva Tanguay.
—SONG OF THE FIFE AND DRUM
—FOUR BURGLARS
—THE TRIALS OF A SIMPLE MAID
—BOHEMIA
—SIGNS
—A MAIDEN'S HEART
—AFTER BUSINESS HOURS
—PLAIN MAMIE O'HOOLEY
—I'M ON THE WATER WAGON NOW
By Paul West and John W. Bratton.
—I NEVER HAD TO WORK
—THE PROPER WAY TO KISS
—IF I WERE THE BRIDE OF A SOLDIER

1904. *A MADCAP PRINCESS*
An operetta based on Charles Major's novel, "When Knighthood Was In Flower", with book and lyrics by Harry B. Smith, and co-starring Lulu Glaser and William Pruette.
—CAVALIER'S SONG
—LONESOME LITTLE MAID
By Benjamin Hapgood Burt and Alfred Solmon.
—BEAUTIFUL ISLE OF THE SEA
—IF YOU WERE MINE ALONE
—I'M BLUFF KING HAL
—WOMAN RULES THE KING
—KINGS OF THE SEA

—IF I MARRY THE KING OF FRANCE
—LETTER CHANSONETTE

1904. *THE TWO ROSES*
An operetta founded on Oliver Gold-
smith's play "She Stoops To Conquer",
with book and lyrics by Stanislaus Stange,
and presented by a cast headed by Fritzi
Scheff, Louis Harrison and Josephine
Bartlett.
—AIRY MARY
—A SIMPLE DIMPLE
—WHAT MAY A LOVESICK MAIDEN
   DO?
—JUST THREE WORDS
—WHAT'S A KISS?
—THERE'S NOT A THING I WOULD-
   N'T DO
—JACK-IN-THE-BOX
—WHY?
—THE SPIRIT OF MISCHIEF
—ROSE MARIE
—BATTLES OF THE TILES (THE CAT
   DUET)

1905. *THE WHITE CAT*
A Drury Lane spectacle with American-
ized book and lyrics by Harry B. Smith
and William Jerome, and presented by a
cast headed by Helen Lathrop, William
T. Hodge, Maude Lambert, Herbert Cort-
hell and Edgar Atchinson-Ely.
—SAILING AWAY
—GIRLS AND BOYS
—A COURT IS LIKE A CHESSBOARD
—GRAFT
—LET THE TRUMPETS SOUND
—WHERE BROADWAY MEETS FIFTH
   AVENUE
—ANTONIO
—A YEAR AND A DAY
—THE GOLDEN NET
—THE PENANG-OURANG-OUTANG
—CATLAND
Jean Schwartz wrote the music for the
following songs:
—DOWN THE LINE WITH ARABELLA
—MEET ME ON THE FENCE
—MY LADY OF JAPAN
—HIGHLAND MARY
—HENNY KLEIN
—GET THE MONEY
—GOODBYE, MARY DOYLE

**1906. *THE RICH MR. HOGGENHEIM-
ER***
A musical comedy with book and lyrics
by Harry B. Smith, and starring Sam
Bernard in a cast that included Georgia
Caine and Percy Ames.
—FIVE O'CLOCK TEA

—BE DEMURE
—HOMEWARD BOUND
—THE HOMESICK YANKEE
—ANY OLD TIME AT ALL
By William Jerome and Jean Schwartz.
—FOR CHARITY'S SAKE
—CUPID'S AUCTION SALE
—HYACINTH
—THIS WORLD IS A TOY SHOP
—BAGPIPE SERENADE
Music by Jerome Kern.
—DON'T YOU WANT A PAPER DEAR-
   IE?
Music by Jerome Kern.
—POKER LOVE
By Paul West and Jerome Kern.

1907. *THE GAY WHITE WAY*
A revue with book by Sydney Rosenfeld
and J. Clarence Harvey, and presented
by a cast headed by Jefferson DeAngelis,
Maude Raymond, Blanche Ring, Mel-
ville Ellis and Alexander Carr.
—THE GREAT WHITE WAY
—SOMEBODY'S BEEN AROUND HERE
—THE BROADWAY SHOW
—THE SCHOOL OF ACTING
—LE KIC-KING
—MY IRISH GIBSON GIRL
—LAND OF THE BRAVE AND THE
   FREE
—RAIN-IN-THE-FACE
—AREN'T YOU THE GIRL I MET AT
   SHERRY'S?
By E. Ray Goetz and Louis A. Hirsch.
—TIDDLE OM POM
—LOVE'S MERRY-GO-ROUND
—THAT'LL BE ABOUT ALL
By George H. Norton.
—DIXIE DAN
By Will Cobb and Seymour Furth.
—WITHOUT THE GIRL INSIDE
By M. E. Rourke and Jerome Kern.
—CLIMBING THE LADDER OF LOVE

1908. *MISS INNOCENCE*
A musical comedy with book and lyrics
by Harry B. Smith, and starring Anna
Held in a cast that included Charles A.
Bigelow, Emma Janvier, Lillian Lorraine,
Lawrence D'Orsay, Gladys Zell and
Florence Walton.
—AM I A WIFE, WIDOW OR MAID?
—SHINE ON HARVEST MOON
By Jack Norworth and Nora Bayes.
—I'M LEARNING SOMETHING EVERY
   DAY
—YANKIANA RAG
—MARIE, MARIE
—I'VE LOST MY LITTLE BROWN
   BEAR

—WHEN THE BAND BEGINS TO PLAY
—I WONDER WHAT'S THE MATTER
  WITH MY EYES
—WHAT KIND OF A WIFE TO
  CHOOSE
—PERFECTLY TERRIBLE, DEAR
—WE TWO IN AN AEROPLANE
—AFRAID TO GO HOME AT ALL
—THREE WEEKS WITH YOU
—PONY BOY
  By Charles O'Donnell and Bobby Heath.
—MY POST CARD GIRL
  By Addison Burkhardt, Matt Woodward
  and Louis A. Hirsch.
—MY COUSIN CARUS'
  By Edward Madden and Gus Edwards.

Edmund Eysler Scores

1909. *THE LOVE CURE*
  A musical comedy with book and lyrics
  by Oliver Herford, and presented by a
  cast headed by Lina Abarbanell, Eva
  Fallon and Charles J. Ross.
—OH BE JOLLY
—HOW FAIR THE WORLD
—FLIRTATION
—A PRETTY PART FOR ME TO PLAY
—GATHER YE ROSEBUDS
—A TOAST
—CUPID'S MARCH
—FORGET ME NOT
—I'M AN INDIAN
—JUST A PLAY
—MATINEE IDOL
—PEEK-A-BOO
—I WONDER WHAT THE AUDIENCE
  WOULD SAY
—LOVE AND WINE
—WHEN SKIES ARE BRIGHT

1909. *THE DOLLAR PRINCESS*
  A musical comedy with book and lyrics
  by George Grossmith, Jr. and Adrian
  Ross, and starring Valli Valli in a cast
  that included Donald Brian and Percival
  Knight.
—THE DOLLAR PRINCESS
—HIP, HIP, HURRAH
—MY DREAM OF LOVE
—REMINISCENCE
—A SELF-MADE MAIDEN
—TYPEWRITING
—LOVE'S A RACE
—LADY FORTUNE
—INSPECTION
—PARAGRAPHS
—NOT HERE, NOT HERE
  By M. E. Rourke and Jerome Kern.

—A BOAT SAILS ON WEDNESDAY
  Music by Jerome Kern.
—LOVE, LOVE
—TRULY RURAL
—THEN YOU GO

William T. Francis Scores

1900. *THE ROYAL ROGUE*
  A musical comedy with book by Charles
  Klein, lyrics by Grant Stewart, and pre-
  sented by a cast headed by Jefferson De-
  Angelis, Josephine Hall and Eva Daven-
  port.
—WANTED: A COOK IN A RESTAUR-
  ANT
—WHEN I'M MARRIED
—ALL THE WORLD TO ME
—DINNER, DINNER
—DAUGHTERS OF A MINISTER
—DING-DONG-DING
—A WOULD-BE GENERAL
—I'M THE WIDOW GIRODET
—POP, POP, POP

1903. *WHOOP-DEE-DO*
  When this production with book and lyr-
  ics by Edgar Smith closed in the spring
  of 1904, Joe Weber and Lew Fields after
  a theatrical partnership that started in
  1872 decided to go their separate ways,
  and these stars bowed out of the historic
  Weber & Fields' Music Hall: Lillian Rus-
  sell, Peter F. Dailey, Carter DeHaven,
  Al Lewis, Louis Mann and John T. Kelly.
—HOCH, HOCH, HOCH
—THE GOOD OLD U. S. A.
—PAPA WOULDN'T CARE FOR THAT
—ON THE BOULEVARD
—RAGTIME IN EUROPE
—MY GOO-GOO QUEEN
—PARIS ON A MOONLIGHT NIGHT
—IN DREAMLAND
—IF I WERE AN ACTRESS
—MAID OF TIMBUCTOO
  By Bob Cole and J. Rosamond Johnson.

1905. *THE CATCH OF THE SEASON*
  A musical comedy with book by Seymour
  Hicks and Cosmo Hamilton, lyrics by
  Charles H. Taylor, and starring Edna
  May.
—ALL DONE BY KINDNESS
—BACK TO HARROW
—CINDERELLA
—AUF WIEDERSEHN
—SEAWEED
  By Fred Earle.
—CUPID IS THE CAPTAIN OF THE
  ARMY
  By Dave Reed, Jr.

—AROUND THE WORLD
By Grant Stewart and Cassius Freeborn.
—MOLLY O'HALLERAN
By J. Clifford Harris and Jerome Kern.
—RAINING
By J. Clifford Harris and Jerome Kern.
—WON'T YOU KISS ME ONCE BE-
FORE I GO?
Music by Jerome Kern.
1908. *FLUFFY RUFFLES*
In this musical comedy with book by John
J. McNally and lyrics by Wallace Irwin,
Violet Heming made her first Broadway
appearance in a cast headed by John
Bunny, Jack Gardner and Adele Row-
land.
—JANE IS A SUFFRAGETTE
—FLUFFY RUFFLES
—LOOK AT YOU
—EVOLUTION
—I WONDER WHY
—GET YOUR PARTNER FOR THE
BARN DANCE
—WILLIE'S GOT ANOTHER GIRL
NOW
—IN LOVE'S BOUQUET
By E. S. Brill
—TAKE A PUFF-PUFF-PUFF
By Kenneth S. Clark.
Jerome Kern wrote the music for the fol-
lowing songs:
—DINING OUT
Lyrics by George Grossmith.
—SWEETEST GIRL, SILLY BOY, I
LOVE YOU
—LET ME CARRY YOUR PARASOL
Lyrics by C. H. Bovill.
—THERE'S SOMETHING RATHER
ODD ABOUT AUGUSTUS
Lyrics by C. H. Bovill.

Cassius Freeborn Score

1906. *MAM'ZELLE CHAMPAGNE*
This musical revue, a Columbia Univer-
sity varsity show transplanted to the Madison Square Garden roof theater, was
saved from being a one-night flop by
three pistol shots. For on opening night
(June 25th), while the juvenile and the
chorus were singing "I Could Love A
Million Girls", Harry Kendall Thaw
walked over to the table where Stanford
White was sitting and killed the architect. Following the resultant publicity,
the show was a sellout for ten weeks.
Book and lyrics by Edgar Allen Woolf.
—THE LAND OF GOLDEN DREAMS
—GLORIANA

—FASCINATION
—I COULD LOVE A MILLION GIRLS

Seymour Furth Scores

1908. *THE MIMIC WORLD*
With Ben Jerome. A revue with book by
Edgar Smith, lyrics by Edward Madden
and Addison Burkhardt, and presented by
a cast headed by William Bonelli, Roy
Atwell, Dave Lewis, Charles King, Irene
Bentley, Grace Tyson, George Monroe,
Lotta Faust and Vernon Castle.
—ANY OLD NAG AT ALL
—ALL THE STARS AND STRIPES BE-
LONG TO ME
—MADAMOISELLE
—YOUR EYES SAY YES
—WHEN TETRAZINNI SINGS HIGH F
—MARY CAREY
—WHEN JOHNNY COMES MARCHING
HOME FROM COLLEGE
Music by Louis A. Hirsch.
—WOMAN, LOVELY WOMAN
—TWO HEARTS BEAT AS ONE
—I'M NO STINGY ROMEO
—RAGTIME MINSTREL MAN
Music by Louis A. Hirsch.
—PHOEBE SNOW
—CHIP ALONG
—MY LADY WINE
—MISS HOOK OF HOLLAND
—YANKEE PRINCE WALTZ
—MONTE CARLO TOWN
—AMBASSADOR'S MARCH
1908. NEARLY A HERO
A musical comedy with book by Harry B.
Smith, lyrics by Edward B. Claypoole and
Will Heelan, and presented by a cast
headed by Sam Bernard, Elizabeth Brice,
Edgar Norton, Ethel Levey, who was re-
placed by Nora Bayes, and Zelda Sears.
—BRIDGE
—AFTER OFFICE HOURS
—I DON'T WANT TO MARRY YOU
With Edward B. Claypoole.
—MY SAHARA BELL.
With Edward B. Claypoole.
—DON'T YOU EVER TELL I TOLD
YOU
—SINCE MOTHER WAS A GIRL
By Jack Norworth and Albert Von Tilzer.
—I WAS A HERO
By Harry Williams and Egbert Van Al-
styne.
—NOT REALLY
—MARY MY HEATHER QUEEN
—THE QUEEN OF BELLE PAREE
—I WANT A STEAM YACHT

—THE DRAWING LESSON
—WHEN PATRICIA SALOME DANCED
THE DO-DA-PALOME
By Albert Bryan and Harry VonTilzer.
—A SINGER SANG A SONG

Edward German Scores

1903. *A PRINCESS OF KENSINGTON*
An operetta with book and lyrics by Basil
Hood, and presented by a cast headed by
Pauline Frederick, James T. Powers and
Fred Huntley.
—FAIRIES, FAIRIES, COME FORTH
—FROM   WHERE   THE   SCOTCH
MOUNTAINS
—IF WE PASS BEYOND THE PORTALS
—SEVEN O'CLOCK IN THE MORNING
—WHO THAT KNOWS HOW I LOVE
YOU, LOVE
—WE'RE FOUR JOLLY SAILOR MEN
—OH, WHAT IS A WOMAN'S DUTY?
—WE'RE BUTCHERS AND BAKERS
AND CANDLE STICK MAKERS
—TWIN BUTTERFLIES THAT FIT-
FULLY FLY
—NOW HERE'S TO THE 'PRENTICES
—AT THE SEASIDE
—IF LOVE IN A COTTAGE BE ALL
THAT THEY TELL
—TILL THE DAY OF MY MAJORITY
—HIGH AND DRY LET HER LIE
—NUT BROWN ALE
—IF ALL THE STARS WERE MINE
—YARNS
—IF YOU WILL SPARE THE TIME
—SEE A RAINBOW
—FOR WHAT THOU ART
—A GERMAN PRINCE MAY WED ME
SINCE
—IT'S A PRESSING INVITATION
THAT I BRING
—SEVEN O'CLOCK IN THE EVENING
1907. *TOM JONES*
An operetta with book by A. M. Thomp-
son and Robert Courtneidge, lyrics by
Charles M. Taylor, and presented by a
cast headed by Van Rensselaer Wheeler
as Tom Jones, Louise Gunning as Sophia,
William Norris, Gertrude Quinlan and
John Bunny.
—ON A JANUARY MORNING
—WEST COUNTRY LAD
—TODAY MY SPINET
—HERE'S A PARADOX
—HURRY, BUSTLE
—DREAM O' DAY JILL
—YOU HAVE A PRETTY WIT
—A SOLDIER'S SCARLET COAT

—LOVE MAKES THE HEART A GAR-
DEN FAIR
—IF LOVE'S CONTENT
—SAYS A WELL-KNOWN SAW

Harry Girard Score

1907. *THE ALASKAN*
A musical comedy with book and lyrics
by Joseph Blethen and Max Figman, and
starring Gus Weinburg and Richard Car-
roll.
—ARLEE
—BAH, BAH BLACK SHEEP
—ESKIMO
—GOOD, BETTER, BEST
—SHIVER SONG
—THE TROUBLE TREE
—THE FOSSIL MAN
—MOTHER DID
—THE TOTEM POLE
—NAUGHTY LITTLE LADY

John L. Golden Scores

1900. *MISS PRINNT*
A musical comedy with book by George
V. Hobart, lyrics by the composer, and
presented by a cast headed by Marie
Dressler, Jobyna Howland, Charlotte
Walker, Kitty Nugent and Dave Lewis.
1909. *THE CANDY SHOP*
A musical comedy with book by George
V. Hobart, lyrics by the composer, and
presented by a cast headed by Maude
Fulton, Frank Lalor, William Rock and
Louise Dresser.
—I'VE BEEN MARRIED ONCE
—IN VAUDEVILLE
—JUST WE TWO
—NOW THAT I'VE GOT IT, I DON'T
WANT IT
—TO BE CONTINUED IN OUR NEXT
—I'LL FOLLOW YOU
—VIA WIRELESS
—WHEN I MARRY MY MARY IN
MARYLAND
—THE WHITEWASH MAN
—GOOGY OO
—THE SILVERY MOON

Henry Hadley Score

1903. *NANCY BROWN*
A musical comedy with book and lyrics
by Frederick Ranken, and starring Marie
Cahill in a cast that included Edward
Stevens, Albert Parr and George Beban.
—ENTRANCE OF THE BEY

—YOU CAN'T FOOL ALL THE PEO-
PLE ALL THE TIME
—THE RED, WHITE AND BLUE GIRL
—THE GLOW WORM AND THE MOTH
—A LITTLE BIRDIE TOLD ME
—THE KATYDID, THE CRICKET AND
THE FROG
—TWO EYES
—I'M GLAD I'M NOT METHUSALUM
—IT'S A MOST DISAGREEABLE
THING TO DO
—UNDER THE BAMBOO TREE
By Bob Cole and Rosamond Johnson.
—CONGO LOVE SONG
By Bob Cole and Rosamond Johnson.

H. E. Haines Score

1905. *THE BABES AND THE BARON*
A musical comedy with book by A. M.
Thompson and Robert Courteneidge, lyr-
ics by Charles M. Taylor and Robert B.
Smith, and presented by a cast headed by
La Petite Adelaide, Junie McCree, Maude
Lambert, James C. Marlowe and Lillian
Coleman.
—IT'S A JOLLY GOOD THING TO BE
ALIVE
—AN OUTLAW BOLD
—ROBIN HOOD'S ARREST
—I DIDN'T MEAN NO HARM
By J. Fred Helf.
—THE FIREFLY AND THE ROSE
—THE ENGLISH BOW
—COULD YOU LEARN TO LOVE?
By E. Ray Goetz.
—MARCH OF THE TOYS
By Jerome Kern.
—THE MUSIC OF THE BAND
—TAILOR'S DUMMY
—MILO (YOU'RE JUST MY STYLE-O)
By Benjamin Hapgood Burt.
—KNOCK WOOD
By Raymond Hubbell.
—THE LIGHT OF THE HONEYMOON
—IF I BUT DARED
—GEE, BUT THIS IS A LONESOME
TOWN
By Billy Gaston.
—THINK IT OVER
By Alfred E. Aarons.

John T. Hall Score

1908. *THE QUEEN OF THE MOULIN
ROUGE*
A musical comedy with book by Paul
Potter, lyrics by Vincent Bryan, and pre-
sented by a cast headed by Flora Parker,

Carter DeHaven and Frank X. Bushman,
who later changed his first name to
"Francis" and became one of the coun-
try's first screen idols.
—PAINTING PARIS
—THE QUARREL
—SHY LITTLE VIOLET BLUE
—DRILL OF THE COQUETTE CORPS
—TELEGRAPH ME
—QUAT-Z ARTS
—SWEET ROSA POMPETTA
—WHEN I'M ALONE WITH YOU
—TONIGHT'S THE NIGHT
—IN ORCANIA
—PARISIAN TWO-STEP
—THE PLEASURE BRIGADE
—LOVE'S DREAM IS O'ER
—I'VE WAITED LONG FOR THEE
—TAKE THAT OFF, TOO
—THE KICKING POLKA
—DRUMMED OUT
—CLOCK SONG
—LITTLE OLD NEW YORK

Oscar Hammerstein I Score

1903. PUNCH, JUDY & CO.
A musical comedy with book and lyrics
as well as music by the grandfather of
the author-librettist of "Show Boat",
"Oklahoma", "South Pacific" and "The
King And I", and presented by an all-girl
cast headed by Gertrude Hoffman and
Josie Sabel.
—IF I AGAIN WOULD BE A BABY
—THE GIRL IN BLUE
—THERE'S BUT ONE NEW YORK

Joseph Hart Score

1902. *FOXY GRANDPA*
A musical comedy based on the cartoon
strip of the same name, with book by R.
Melville Baker and lyrics by the com-
poser, who headed the cast that included
Carrie DeMar and Clifton Crawford.
—BEFORE AND AFTER TAKING
—MILITARY CHARLEY
—THE STORY OF TWO BAD BOYS
—THE TIGHT ROPE WALKER
—NAPOLI
—THE COUNTRY CLUB
—THE FIRST SUBMARINE BOAT
—DIFFERENT WAYS OF PROPOSING
—THE BATHING LESSON
—FRISA LINDA
—MY CLEMENTINE
—I'M NOT AT LIBERTY TO TELL
—THE BARN DANCE

H. L. Heartz Scores

1901. *MY LADY*
An extravaganza with book and lyrics by
by R. A. Barnet, and presented by a cast
neaded by Charles J. Ross, Clifton Craw-
ford, Lotta Faust and Eva Tanguay.
—SIMPLE LITTLE SISTER MARY
GREEN
By Clifton Crawford.

1902. *THE SHOW GIRL*
With E. W. Corliss. A musical comedy
with book and lyrics by R. A. Barnet and
D. K. Stevens, and presented by a cast
headed by Frank Lalor, Paula Edwardes
and Ferguson and Mack.
—OH SHRINE OF PSYCHE
—THAT'S THE WAY OF A SAILOR
—SOMETIME, PERHAPS
—WE ARE TRYING TO SUPPORT OUR
ONLY MOTHER
—INVITATION TO PIE
—BY-AND-BY
Music by William T. Francis.
—I'M A SIMPLE AUTHOR-MANAGER
—AS THE PRINCE WAKED THE PRIN-
CESS
—THE FAMILY GHOST
—PSYCHE
—CHAMPAGNE AND TERRAPIN, VI-
SION DIVINE
—WHERE JASMINE FLOWERS ARE
TWINING
—REGGIE'S FAMILY TREE
—LOVE IS JUST THE SAME
—LOVER'S LANE
—ADVICE
—IN GAY JAPAN
—ADELINE
—ONE THAT HE LOVES BEST
—KATRINA
—A ROSE AND A LILY

1902. *MISS SIMPLICITY*
A musical comedy with book and lyrics
by R. A. Barnet, and presented by a cast
headed by Frank Daniels, Lawrence
Wheat, William Danforth, Harry Holli-
day, Helen Lord, Grace Belmont and Al-
lene Crater.
—ROSES BEGIN WITH R, LOVE
—THE SUNDAY SCHOOL BOY
—ROSALIE
—OH WHAT A DELIGHT TO BE
DANCING
—LOVE ME LITTLE, LOVE ME LONG
—BABETTE
By Paul West and Benjamin Hapgood
Burt.
—HE DID IT SO POLITELY

—WHEN YOU WERE SHY EIGHTEEN

1904. *THE TENDERFOOT*
A musical comedy with book and lyrics
by Richard Carle, who headed the cast
that included William Rock and Helena
Frederick.
—SOLDIERY
—ADIOS
—FASCINATING VENUS
—THE TORTURED THOMAS CAT
—TEXAS RANGERS
—I'M A PEACEABLE PARTY
—OFF WE GO
—A GAY LOTHARIO
—MY ALAMO LOVE
—WASHING SONG
—MARRIAGE IS A LOTTERY
—A SOLDIER OF FORTUNE
—LOVE IS ELUSIVE
—DANCING

1907. *THE HURDY-GURDY GIRL*
A musical comedy with book and lyrics
by Richard Carle, and presented by a
cast headed by John E. Hazzard, Adele
Rowland, John Ransone, May Boley and
Annie Yeamans.
—HOPE ON
—IN BOHEMIA
—BLUFF
—THE SAUSAGE KING
—MY BUSY DAY
—THE HURDY-GURDY GIRL
—I'M A MISCHIEVOUS GIRL
—THE MODEST MANICURE
—COME LITTLE DEARIE
—FOUR LITTLE FLIRTY GIRLS
—STORIES
—STYLE
—SHE'S THE APPLE OF MY EYE

1909. *THE BOY AND THE GIRL*
With Richard Carle. A musical comedy
with book and lyrics by Richard Carle
and M. E. Rourke, and starring Marie
Dressler and Barney Bernard.
—FICKLE DINNER BELL
—I LEAD AN AWF'LLY LAZY LIFE
—I'M IN A POSITION TO KNOW
—IN YUCATAN
—MY DEARIE DEAR
—NAUGHTY CUPID
—SEDUCTIVE CAROLINE
—WHY ARE ALL THE GIRLS SO HUN-
GRY?
—THE OLD STAGE DOOR

Silvio Hein Scores

1905. *MOONSHINE*
A musical comedy with book by Edward

Milton Royle, lyrics by George V. Hobart, and starring Marie Cahill in a cast that included Clara Palmer, Roy Atwell and George Beban.
—HOW HAPPY THIS CHAPPIE COULD BE
—A HUNDRED YEARS FROM NOW
—DON'T BE WHAT YOU AIN'T
—ROBINSON CRUSOE'S ISLE
—FRIENDSHIP
—I'M LOOKING FOR MY TEN
—IN MY NEW SUBMARINE
—I WANT TO GO BACK TO THE BOULEVARD
—THEY NEVER DO THAT IN OUR SET
—THE MUSICAL GYPSY
—I LIKE YOU VERY MUCH
—FOOLISH
—NAPOLEON BONEPARTE

1906. *MARRYING MARY*
A musical comedy with book by Edward Milton Royle, lyrics by George V. Hobart, and starring Marie Cahill in a cast that included Roy Atwell, William Courtleigh, Eugene Cowles and Virginia Staunton.
—I'M LOOKING FOR A MAN BY THE NAME OF SMITH
—THREE MEN IN A BOAT
—THE LAST ONE IS BEST OF ALL
—GWENDOLYN
—OLD RELIABLE JOKES
—NOAH KNEW A THING OR TWO
—MR. CUPID
—HOTTENTOT LOVE SONG
By Bob Cole and J. Rosamond Johnson.
—HE'S A COUSIN OF MINE
By Cecil Mack and Chris Smith.

1908. *THE BOYS AND BETTY*
A musical comedy with book and lyrics by George V. Hobart, and starring Marie Cahill in a cast that included Edgar Norton, Clara Palmer, Eugene Cowles and Edgar Atchinson-Ely.
—I WANT TO GO TO PARIS
—TAKE PLENTY OF SHOES
—THE TETRAZZINI FAMILY
—AUF WEIDERSEHN
—GIRLS, GIRLS, GIRLS
—A LITTLE FURTHER
—I LOVE TO GO SHOPPING
—THE FOLIES BERGERE
—GEE, BUT YOU LOOK AWFUL GOOD TO ME
—ARAB LOVE SONG
—SHE WAS A DEAR LITTLE GIRL
By Irving Berlin.

Victor Herbert Scores

1900. *THE VICEROY*
Book and lyrics by Harry B. Smith, and presented by The Bostonians.
—HEAR ME
—WE'LL CATCH YOU AT LAST
—TIVOLINI
—THE ROBIN AND THE ROSE
—I'M A LEADER OF SOCIETY
—ALL MEN HAVE TROUBLE OF THEIR OWN
—JUST FOR TODAY
—'NEATH THE BLUE NEAPOLITAN SKIES
—THAT'S MY IDEA OF LOVE

1903. *BABES IN TOYLAND*
Book and lyrics by Glen MacDonough, with a cast headed by William Norris, Mabel Barrison, George W. Denham and Bessie Wynn.
—TOYLAND
—FLORETTA
—THE MOON WILL HELP YOU OUT
—JANE
—NEVER MIND BO-PEEP
—BEFORE AND AFTER
—MARCH OF THE TOYS
—I CAN'T DO THAT SUM
—HE WON'T BE HAPPY TILL HE GETS IT
—GO TO SLEEP, SLUMBER DEEP
—SONG OF THE POET
—THE MILITARY BALL
—HAIL TO CHRISTMAS

1903. *BABETTE*
Book and lyrics by Harry B. Smith, and with a cast headed by Fritzi Scheff, Eugene Cowles and Louis B. Harrison.
—MY HONOR AND MY SWORD
—I'LL BRIBE THE STARS
—MY LADY 'TIS FOR THEE
—WE ARE VERY HIGHLY POLISHED
—BE KIND TO POOR PIERROT
—THERE ONCE WAS AN OWL
—LETTERS
—MADRIGAL
—CLOCK MAKER'S SONG
—MY LADY OF THE MANOR
—WHERE THE FAIREST FLOWERS ARE BLOOMING

1904. *IT HAPPENED IN NORDLAND*
Book and lyrics by Glen MacDonough, with a cast that included Lew Fields, Marie Cahill, Harry Davenport, Joseph Herbert, Harry Fisher, May Robson, Julius Steger, Bessie Clayton and Pauline Frederick.

—BANDANNA LAND
—THE MATINEE GIRL
—BEATRICE BAREFACTS
—SLIPPERY JAMES
—THE MAN MEANT WELL
—MY CATAMARAN
—THE COON BANSHEE
—ABSINTHE FRAPPE
—THE JACK O'LANTERN GIRL
—THE KNOT OF BLUE
—OYANEETAH
—LITTLE CLASS OF ONE
—THE COMMANDRESS-IN-CHIEF

1905. *MISS DOLLY DOLLARS*
Book and lyrics by Harry B. Smith, with a cast headed by Lulu Glaser, Ralph Herz, Carter DeHaven and Elsie Ferguson.
—THE SELF-MADE FAMILY
—DOLLY DOLLARS
—AN EDUCATED FOOL
—THE MOTH AND THE MOON
—LIFE'S A MASQUERADE
—AMERICAN MUSIC
—JUST GET OUT AND WALK
—A WOMAN IS ONLY A WOMAN BUT A GOOD CIGAR IS A SMOKE
—AN AMERICAN HEIRESS
—IT'S ALL IN THE BOOK YOU KNOW
—IT KEEPS ME GUESSING ALL THE TIME

1905. *WONDERLAND*
Book and lyrics by Glen MacDonough, with a cast headed by Sam Chip, Eva Davenport, Lotta Faust and Bessie Wynn.
—HAIL, HAIL HALLOWE'EN
—THE NATURE CLASS
—THE ONLY ONE
—POPULAR PAULINE
—COMPANIONS OF THE BLADE
—JOGRAFREE
—WHEN PERRICO PLAYS
—INDIAN DANCE
—I AND MYSELF AND ME

1905. *MLLE. MODISTE*
Book and lyrics by Henry Blossom, and starring Fritzi Scheff with William Pruette, Walter Percival and Claude Gillingwater in the supporting cast.
—CHARITY BAZAAR
—THE TIME, THE PLACE AND THE GIRL
—LOVE ME, LOVE MY DOG
—KEOKUK KULTURE KLUB
—WHEN THE CAT'S AWAY
—*KISS ME AGAIN
This song was written while the production was in rehearsal, and the title was inspired by a request made by Fritzi Scheff

of Herbert after he had kissed her good night for an osculatory reprise.
—ZE ENGLISH LANGUAGE
—CHORUS OF FOOTMEN
—HATS MAKE THE WOMAN
—I WANT WHAT I WANT WHEN I WANT IT
—IF I WERE ON THE STAGE
—MASCOT OF THE TROOP

1906. *THE RED MILL*
Book and lyrics by Henry Blossom, and starring Montgomery and Stone.
—EV'RY DAY IS LADIES DAY WITH ME
—WHISTLE IT
—YOU NEVER CAN TELL ABOUT A WOMAN
—GOODA-BYE JOHN
Harry Williams and Egbert Van Alstyne should be credited with this song but Victor Herbert, who thought it beneath his dignity to write such a number, refused to permit it to be programmed as an interpolation in his score.
—MOONBEAMS
—THE STREETS OF NEW YORK
—WHEN YOU'RE PRETTY AND THE WORLD IS FAIR
—THE ISLE OF OUR DREAMS
—I WANT YOU TO MARRY ME
—THE LEGEND OF THE MILL
—ALWAYS GO WHILE THE GOIN'S GOOD
—I'M ALWAYS DOING SOMETHING I DON'T WANT TO DO
—BECAUSE YOU'RE YOU

1906. *DREAM CITY* and *MAGIC KNIGHT*
Book and lyrics by Edgar Smith, and with a cast that included Joe Weber, Otis Harlan, William T. Hodge, Maurice Farkoa, Cecilia Loftus and Lillian Blauvelt.
—I DON'T BELIEVE I'LL EVER BE A LADY
—LOVE BY TELEPHONE
—THE RAVENOUS ROOSTER
—I LOVE YOU
—DOWN A SHADY LANE
—THE VOLUNTEER FIREMAN
—AN OPERATIC MAID
—A FARMER'S LIFE
—TA-TA MY DAINTY LITTLE DARLING
—NANCY, I FANCY YOU
—IN VAUDEVILLE
—IMPROVEMENTS
—HANNAH
—A SHY SUBURBAN MAID

1907. *THE TATTOOED MAN*
Book and lyrics by A. C. N. Fowler and Harry B. Smith, with a cast that included Frank Daniels, May Vokes, Sallie Fisher, Harry Clarke and Herbert Waterous.
—THINGS WE ARE SUPPOSED TO KNOW
—OMAR KHAYYAM
—BOYS WILL BE BOYS AND GIRLS WILL BE GIRLS
—HEAR MY SONG OF LOVE
—THE LAND OF DREAMS
—THE LEGEND OF THE DJIN
—THE FLORAL WEDDING
—WATCH THE PROFESSOR
—TAKE THINGS EASY
—NOBODY LOVES ME
—THERE'S JUST ONE GIRL I'D LIKE TO MARRY

1908. *THE ROSE OF ALGERIA*
Book and lyrics by Glen MacDonough, with a cast that included William Pruette, Ida Brooks Hunt, George Marion, Ernest Lambert, Florence Nash, Katherine Howland, William Cameron and Helen Broderick.
—THE BOULE MICH
—THE GREAT WHITE EASIEST WAY
—LOVE IS LIKE A CIGARETTE
—ASK HER WHILE THE BAND IS PLAYING
Lyrics by Vincent Bryan.
—ONLY ONE OF ANYTHING
—LITTLE BIRD OF PARADISE
—BOHEMIA, GOOD-BYE
—THANKSGIVING DAY
—ROSE OF THE WORLD
—YOU'LL FEEL BETTER THEN
—TWILIGHT IN BARAKEESH
—I'LL DREAM OF THEE
—HE WAS A SOLDIER BOY
—THE FOOLISH GARDENER
—IN JAIL
—I'VE BEEN DECORATED

1908. *LITTLE NEMO*
Book and lyrics by Harry B. Smith, with a cast headed by Master Gabriel, Joseph Cawthorn, Billy B. Van, Harry Kelly and Florence Tempest.
—MARCH OF THE VALENTINES
—WHEN CUPID IS THE POSTMAN
—WON'T YOU BE MY VALENTINE?
—THE HEN AND WEATHER VANE
—I WANT TO BE A NAUGHTY GIRL
—THE HAPPY LAND OF ONCE-UPON-A-TIME
—IF I COULD TEACH MY TEDDY BEAR TO DANCE

—WILL-O-THE-WISP
—I GUESS I TALK TOO MUCH
—WHAT FOOLS WE MORTALS BE
—WON'T YOU BE MY PLAYMATE?
—REMEMBER THE OLD CONTINENTALS
—THERE'S NOTHING THE MATTER WITH YOU
—GIVE US A FLEET
—THEY WERE IRISH
—IN HAPPY SLUMBERLAND

1908. *THE PRIMA DONNA*
Book and lyrics by Henry Blossom Jr., starring Fritzi Scheff with St. Claire Bayfield and William J. Harcourt in the supporting cast.
—HERE'S TO MY COMRADE AND ME
—EVERYBODY ELSE'S GIRL LOOKS BETTER THAN MINE
—I'LL BE MARRIED TO THE MUSIC OF A MILITARY BAND
—YOU'D BE SURPRISED
—A SOLDIER'S LOVE
—IF YOU WERE I AND I WERE YOU
—DREAM LOVE

1909. *OLD DUTCH*
Book by Edgar Smith and lyrics by George V. Hobart. Helen Hayes made her debut as a child actress in this production, and the cast was headed by Lew Fields, Alice Dovey, Ada Lewis, John Bunny and Vernon Castle.
—MRS. GRUNDY
—RICH MAN, POOR MAN
—PRETENDING
—I LOVE ZE PARISIENNE
—MY GYPSY SWEETHEART
—I WANT A MAN TO LOVE ME
—ALGY
—YOU DEARIE
—CLIMB, CLIMB
—THAT IS LOVE

Karl Hoschna Score

1908. *THREE TWINS*
Book and lyrics by Otto Harbach. Bessie McCoy achieved stardom and a husband, Richard Harding Davis, durirng the run of this production in which Clifton Crawforrd and Joseph Allen were featured players.
—SUMMER PASTIMES
—OVER THERE
—CUDDLE UP A LITTLE CLOSER, LOVEY MINE
—GOOD NIGHT, SWEETHEART
—BOO-HOO, TEE-HEE
—AT A RECEPTION

—LITTLE MISS UP-TO-DATE
—HYPNOTIC KISS
—THE GIRL UP THERE
—YAMA YAMA MAN
Lyrics by Collin Davis.

Max Hoffman Scores

1903. *ROGERS BROTHERS IN LONDON*
With Melville Ellis. A musical comedy
with book by John J. McNally, lyrics by
George V. Hobart and Ed Gardenier, and
starring Gus and Max Rogers in a cast
that included Lee Harrison, Lillian Cole-
man, Melville Ellis and George Austin
Moore.
—FLOOR WALKERS' SONG
—ON A STARLIGHT NIGHT
—QUEEN OF THE BUNGALOO
—SAY YOU'LL BE A FRIEND OF
MINE
—SIMPLE SUE
—BY THE SYCAMORE TREE
1904. *ROGERS BROTHERS IN PARIS*
A musical comedy with book by John J.
McNally, lyrics by George V. Hobart, and
starring Gus and Max Rogers in a cast
that included George Austin Moore, Fred
Niblo and Josephine Cohan.
—THE STUDENTS' BALL
—SOLDIER BOY
—BELLE OF THE SILVERY NILE
—YANKEE LAND
—McNABB
—SOCIETY
—BY THE OLD OAK TREE
—KINDNESS
—PRETTY POLLY
—THE VILLAGE MAID
1905. *ROGERS BROTHERS IN IRE-
LAND*
A musical comedy with book by John J.
McNally, lyrics by George V. Hobart, and
starring Gus and Max Rogers in a cast
that included Corrine and Josie and Ethel
Intropodi.
—KILLARNEY
—THE IRISH GIRL I LOVE
—MY IRISH MAID
—THE FIRST TIME WE RODE ON
THE CARS
—MIKE DOOLIN'S JAUNTING CAR
—ST. PATRICK'S DAY
—THE SHAMROCK OF ERIN
—THE TOURISTS
—THE BLARNEY STONE
—SO DIFFERENT
—HANNAH DOOLEY
1906. *THE PARISIAN MODEL*
A musical comedy with book and lyrics by

Harry B. Smith, and starring Anna Held
in a cast that included Truly Shattuck,
Charles Bigelow and Gertrude Hoffman.
—BELLS
—KISS, KISS, KISS IF YOU WANT TO
LEARN TO KISS
By Gertrude Hoffman.
—TRYING ON DRESSES
—I'M THE MAN
—A GOWN FOR EACH HOUR OF THE
DAY
—THE AMERICAN GIRL IN PARIS
—ARTISTS AND MODELS
—MA CHERIE
—IN WASHINGTON
—I'D LIKE TO SEE A LITTLE MORE
OF YOU
By Vincent Bryan and Gus Edwards.
—I JUST CAN'T MAKE MY EYES BE-
HAVE
By Will Cobb and Gus Edwards.
—ON SAN FRANCISCO BAY
Lyrics by Vincent Bryan.
—IT'S DELIGHTFUL TO BE MARRIED
By Christine and Scotto.
1907. *ROGERS BROTHERS IN PANAMA*
A musical comedy with book by Aaron
Hoffman and Sylvester Maguire, lyrics by
Edward Madden, and starring Gus and
Max Rogers in a cast that included George
Lydecker, Marion Stanley and Lottie
Greenwood.
—ADORABLE TOREADOR
—SMILE, SMILE, SMILE
—IN PANAMA
—WAY DOWN IN COLON TOWN
—CUPID'S GAY BOUQUET
—UNDER THE JUNGLE MOON

Bernard Holt Score

1904. *GLITTERING GLORIA*
A musical comedy with book and lyrics
by Hugh Morton, and presented by a
cast headed by Cyril Scott, Percy Ames,
Eugene O'Rourke, Adele Richie and
Phyliss Rankin.
—THE HOT HOUSE ON BROADWAY
—MARGATE SANDS
—SAPHIRA
—GLITTERING GLOR-I-A
—TELL ME WHY, WHY, WHY?
—LITTLE MARY
—WHEN I COME OUT OF HERE

Lucius Hosmer Score

1907. *THE ROSE OF THE ALHAMBRA*
A comic opera with book and lyrics by
Charles Emerson Cook, and starring Agnes
Cain Brown in the title role.

—ALL THE KING'S HORSES AND MEN
—THE FALCON
—WEAVING
—GIVE HIM A WELCOME QUITE SPANISH
—LONG LIVE THE KING
—SPLASH! DASH! BANG!
—LOVE'S ETERNAL SONG
—THE PILGRIM OF LOVE
—THE NIGHTINGALE AND THE ROSE
—CASTLES IN SPAIN
—WE'RE THE ROYAL M. D.s
—MANANA
—OH, WON'T YOU SHED A LITTLE TEAR FOR ME?
—THE LAY OF THE LUTE

Joe Howard Scores

1906. *THE DISTRICT LEADER*
Book by Joe Howard, who starred in the production that included Mabel Barrison and Dave Lewis in the cast.
—WON'T YOU BE MY GIRLIE?
—YOU ARE THE SWEETEST GIRL I KNOW
—SO
—MAKE YOUR OWN SUNSHINE
—A HEART TO LET
—WHAT'S THE USE OF DREAMING?

1907. *THE LAND OF NOD*
Book and lyrics by Will Hough and Frank Adams, with a cast headed by Mabel Barrison, William Norris, Knox Wilson, Carrie DeMar and Joe Howard.
—THE BELLE OF BALDHEAD ROW
—WHEN YOU GROW TIRED
—YOU'RE JUST A PAPER DOLL
—DEAR HEART
—SAME OLD MOON
—THE GIRL YOU DREAM ABOUT
—CINDERELLA

1907. *THE TIME, THE PLACE AND THE GIRL*
Book and lyrics by Will Hough and Frank Adams, with a cast headed by Florence Holbrook, Cecil Lean, Olive Vail and Arthur Deagon.
—I DON'T LIKE YOUR FAMILY
—BLOW THE SMOKE AWAY
—DIXIE, I LOVE YOU
—IT'S LONESOME TONIGHT
—THURSDAY IS MY JONAH DAY
—THE WANING HONEYMOON
—DON'T YOU TELL

1907. *THE GIRL QUESTION*
Book and lyrics by Will Hough and Frank Adams, and co-starring Georgie Drew Mendum and Junie McCree.
—THERE IS NO PLACE LIKE HOME

—WHEN EYES LIKE YOURS LOOK INTO EYES LIKE MINE
—IT'S GOOD-BYE, PAL
—THE OLD BUCK AND WING
—I HATE TO WORK ON MONDAY
—OH, GEE! BE SWEET TO ME, KID

1908. *THE FLOWER OF THE RANCH*
Book and lyrics by Will Hough and Frank Adams, and co-starring Mabel Barrison and Joe Howard.
—THAT'S WHAT A FELLOW DOES
—THE PAJAMA AND THE NIGHTIE
—WATCHING THE BLUE SMOKE CURL
—BABY LOU
—CALIFORNIA
—IN THE DAYS OF '49
—MY LOLA MAID
—JUST SAY YOU CARE
—WORRIED

1908. *HONEYMOON TRAIL*
Book and lyrics by Will Hough and Frank Adams, and starring Vera Michelena.
—ONE LITTLE BOY HAD MONEY
—NOTHING TO DO BUT NOTHING
—I'D LIKE TO STEAL THE MOON
—WHEN I FEEL LIKE LOVING
—WHOSE LITTLE GIRL ARE YOU?
—I DON'T WANT A MILLION DOLLARS
—YOU CAN'T BE A FRIEND TO EVERYBODY
—HONEYMOON TRAIL

1909. *THE GODDESS OF LIBERTY*
Book and lyrics by Will Hough and Frank Adams, with a cast headed by May De-Sousa, Frances Demarest and Edward Abels.
—TAXI
—TUMMY-TUMMY-TUM
—DON'T CHOOSE A GIBSON GIRL
—PLEASE KEEP ME YOUNG IN YOUR HEART
—OSKEE WOW WOW!
—THE GODDESS OF LIBERTY
—HERE'S TO YOUR LAST GIRL
—WHERE ARE THEY NOW?
—IF ALL THE MOONS WERE HONEY-MOONS
—LONELY
—THE HAUNTED POOL

1909. *A STUBBORN CINDERELLA*
Book and lyrics by Will Hough and Frank Adams. This was one of two musicals in which John Barrymore ever appeared, being co-starred with Sallie Fisher in a cast that included Charles Prince, Alice Dovey and James Marlowe.

—I LOST MY HEART BUT I DON'T
  CARE
—NONE BUT THE BRAVE DESERVE
  THE FAIR
—I'M IN LOVE WITH ALL THE GIRLS
  I KNOW
—DON'T BE ANYBODY'S MOON BUT
  MINE
—WHAT THE USE?
—IF THEY'D ONLY LEFT POOR
  ADAM'S RIB ALONE
—LOVE ME JUST BECAUSE
—DON'T BE CROSS WITH ME
—DON'T TEACH ME TO SWIM ALONE
—WHEN YOU FIRST KISS THE LAST
  GIRL YOU LOVE

1909. *THE PRINCE OF TONIGHT*
Book and lyrics by Will Hough and Frank
Adams, with Henry Woodruff starred in
a cast that included Sallie Fisher and
Alice Dovey.
—TONIGHT WILL NEVER COME
  AGAIN
—YOU'RE A DEAR OLD WORLD
  AFTER ALL
—EVERYTHING FATHER DID WAS
  RIGHT
—WHEN LOVE IS WAITING ROUND
  THE CORNER
—I DON'T WANT TO MARRY YOUR
  FAMILY
—THE GIRLS THAT CAN NEVER BE
  MINE
—I FELL IN LOVE ON MONDAY
—I CAN'T BE TRUE SO FAR AWAY
—YOU WON'T KNOW ANYBODY
  THERE
—HER EYES ARE BLUE FOR DEAR
  OLD YALE
—FOLLOW THE RAINBOW'S TRAIL
—*I WONDER WHO'S KISSING HER
  NOW
As a result of a court ruling in 1948, Har-
old Orlob is credited with being the co-
composer of this song although he waived
all royalties.

Shafter Howard Score

1906. *HIS MAJESTY*
A musical comedy with book and lyrics
by the composer, and presented by a cast
headed by Blanche Ring, Van Rensselaer
Wheeler, Harry Kelly and Anna Laugh-
lin.
—HIS MAJESTY
—THE MAID FROM BOSTON TOWN
—CONSPIRATORS
—MY OWN

—ARE YOU A SINGLE OR A MARRIED
  MAN?
—FAIRIES' CHORUS
—ISABEL
—THE MAID OF ARCADIE
—SERENADE
—JEMIMA GREEN
—CRAZYISMS

Raymond Hubbell Scores

1903. *THE RUNAWAYS*
Book and lyrics by Addison Burkhardt,
and presented by a cast headed by Edna
Goodrich, Alexander Clark, Van Rensse-
laer Wheeler and Dorothy Dorr, who was
replaced by Fay Templeton during the
New York run of this production.
—PRETTY MAID ADELAIDE
—MISS SUSANNA FROM URBANA
—FOREVER AND A DAY
—THE LAND I LOVE
—MY LITTLE HINDOO BELLE
—IN SWELL SOCIETY
—THE GIRL FROM THE TRACK
—YET I'M THE SAME LITTLE GIRL
—I'M COMING HOME TO DIXIELAND
—A KISS FOR EACH DAY IN THE
  WEEK
—IF I WERE A BRIGHT LITTLE STAR
—IN THE DAYS WHEN KING SOLO-
  MON RULED
—LOVE IS AN AILMENT
—STROLLING
—MY RADIANT FIREFLY
—THE ROSE DANCE
—THE ROOSTER DANCE
—THE MAIDEN AND THE JAY
Music by William Gould.

1905. *FANTANA*
Book and lyrics by Robert B. Smith, and
with Adele Richie, Julia Sanderson, Doug-
las Fairbanks, Jefferson de Angelis and
George Beban heading the cast.
—NORTH, EAST, SOUTH OR WEST
—A LESSON IN ETIQUETTE
—IT'S THE GIRL AND NOT THE
  HORSE THAT WINS THE PRIZE
—THE CAN-CAN VERSUS THE CAKE
  WALK
—DROP IN ON ME AT LUNCHEON
—THE FAREWELL WALTZ
—DARBY AND JOAN
—MY RICKSHAW OF BAMBOO
—HOLD THE LANTERNS HIGH
—LAUGHING LITTLE ALMOND EYES
—THE SECRET
—WHAT WOULD MRS. GRUNDY SAY?
—TAMMANY
By Vincent Bryan and Gus Edwards.

—SONG OF THE PIPE
—THE GIRL AT THE HELM
—THAT'S ART
—JUST MY STYLE
1906. *MEXICANA*
Book by Clara Driscoll, lyrics by Robert
B. Smith, and presented by a cast headed
by Christie Mac Donald, Caro Roma,
Blanche Deyo, Thomas Q. Seabrooke, Jo-
seph Herbert and Edward Martindel
—HOW DO YOU ACCOUNT FOR
THAT?
—UNITED WE STAND
—TAKE CARE SENOR
—HARK TO THE VOICE OF YOUR
LOVER
—THE FICKLE WEATHER VANE
—I AM THE WIZARD OF WALL
STREET
—GRAFT
—WE'VE GOT A LOT TO LEARN
—MAJOR MARJORY
—I'VE HEARD SO MUCH ABOUT YOU
—I WAS JUST SUPPOSING
1906. *MAM'SELLE SALLIE*
Book and lyrics by Harry B. Smith, and
co-starring Katie Barry, the English come-
dienne, and John Slavin.
—THE SWEET GIRL GRADUATE
—EVERY LITTLE OBJECT HAS A HIS-
TORY
—A MILLION
—I'M A LAWYER
—I'D LIKE A SITUATION JUST LIKE
THAT
—LIFE IS A SEE-SAW
—FAREWELL, PROSPERITY
—THESSALY
—HER PORTRAIT
—LA DANCE PARISIENNE
—LOVE MAKES THE WORLD GO
ROUND
—AND I LAUGHED
—YOU NEVER TOLD ME THAT BE-
FORE WE MARRIED
—HURROO, HURRAY AND HURRAH
FOR THAT
—WHISTLE WHEN YOU WALK OUT
1907. *A KNIGHT FOR A DAY*
Book and lyrics by Robert B. Smith, and
presented by a cast headed by Sallie
Fisher, May Vokes, John Slavin and
Percy Bronson.
—THE SWEET GIRL GRADUATES
—MARCELINE'S MEAT SAUCE
—I'D LIKE A SITUATION JUST LIKE
THAT
—WHAT FOOLS WE MORTALS BE
—LIFE IS A SEE-SAW

—MY VERY OWN
—CORSICA
—THE GIRL IN BLUE
—THE BOLD BANDITTI
—HURRAY, HURRAY, HURROO FOR
THAT
—WHISTLE AS YOU WALK OUT
—THE GIRL OF THE GREAT DIVIDE
1906. *THE GIRL AT THE HELM*
Books and lyrics by Robert B. Smith, and
co-starring Cecil Lean and Florence Hol-
brook.
—IN MY LITTLE RUNABOUT
—I DON'T LOVE YOU WELL ENOUGH
FOR THAT
—THE LONG GREEN
—IN WALKED BILL
—THE MAN I MARRY MUST BE A MAN
—ALL I WANT IN THE WIDE, WIDE
WORLD IS YOU
—FISHING IS AN ART
—NOT ALL BUT NEARLY
—YOU'RE ALL THE WORLD TO ME
1909. *THE MIDNIGHT SONS*
Book and lyrics by Glen MacDonough,
and with Harry Fisher, Fritz Williams,
Lotta Faust, George Monroe, Taylor
Holmes, Vernon Castle, Gladys Moore
and Blanche Ring heading the cast.
—HIGH, HIGH, HIGH
—JUST CALL ME BILL
—MY FIREFLY LADY
—THE LITTLE MARY GARDENERS
—THE SOUBRETTE'S SECRET
—MY SIST' TERAZIN
—CINDERELLA AT THE SHOE STORE
—THE BILLIKEN MAN
—THE CYNICAL OWL
—YANKEE HONEYMOON
—EILY RILEY
—LITHOGRAPH LAND
—TRUE BLUE
—CARMEN THE SECOND
1909. *THE AIR KING*
Book and lyrics by Harry B. Smith, and
starring John Slavin in a cast that in-
cluded Josephine Hall and Thomas
Meighan.
—THERE IS NO SUCH THING AS
LUCK
—I'D LIKE TO GO UP IN AN AIRSHIP
—NEWPORT IS WAITING FOR ME
—THE GIRL I USED TO KNOW
—ART WITH A CAPITAL "A"
—I WANT TO BE KISSED BY A MATI-
NEE IDOL
—FAREWELL, PROSPERITY
—I SAVED HIS LIFE
—POLLY

R. Jackson Score
1901. *SWEET MARIE*
A musical comedy with book and lyrics
by W. Brown in which James and John
Russell, the Irish "biddies" of vaudeville,
took a fling in the legitimate field and
headed a cast that included Rhyce
Thomas, Louis Montgomery, Albert La-
Mar, Eleanor Falk, Countess Olga von
Hatzfeldt and Master Gabriel.
—CECELIA AND AMELIA
By Oscar Hammerstein I.

Ben M. Jerome Scores
1903. *THE DARLING OF THE GAL-
LERY GODS*
A musical comedy with book by George
V. Hobart, lyrics by Mathew C. Wood-
ward and John Gilroy, and presented by
a cast that included Junie McCree, Pat
Rooney, Emma Carus and Trixie Friganza.
—KIYOMORI
—MY JAPANESE BABY
—IF YOU EVER WANT A FAVOR
MENTION ME
—HINKY DEE
—OMI OMAI
—IDA BELL
—MOZART LINCOLN
—WATCH ME TONIGHT IN THE
TORCHLIGHT PARADE
—SILVERY MOON
—SIS HOPKINS
—ELLA
—WON'T GO HOME TILL MORNING
—THE MARRIAGE OF THE DAFFODIL
AND THE DAISY
1904. *THE ISLE OF SPICE*
With Paul Schindler. A musical comedy
with book by Allen Lowe, lyrics by
George B. Stoddard, and presented by a
cast headed by Alexander Clark and Her-
bert Cawthorne.
—UNCLE SAM'S MARINES
—MERCENARY MARY
—TOO-HOO
—PEGGY BRADY
—THE GOO-GOO MAN
—FATHER'S ALWAYS TALKING IN
HIS SLEEP
—LITTLE MAID OF NICOBAR
—SILLY SAILORS
—HAIL BOMPOKA
—THE SPORTING KING OF NICOBAR
—STAR OF FATE
—THE WITCHES
—YOU AND I

—KOW TOW
—THE AMBITIOUS ANIMALS

1904. *THE ROYAL CHEF*
A musical comedy with book by Charles
A. Taylor, lyrics by George E. Stoddard,
and starring Dave Lewis in a cast that in-
cluded Joseph Allen, John Park and
Amelia Stone.
—THERE'S A TIDAL WAVE OF
FAMINE MOVING WEST
—IT'S A WAY THAT THEY HAVE IN
CHICAGO
—WHERE OLD GLORY FLOATS
EVERYWHERE
—THE TAIL OF THE TAILLESS FROG
—I'M A LITERARY MILITARY MAN
—LET ME GO BACK
—I'D LIKE TO BREAK INTO SOCIETY
—WOULD YOU IF YOU WERE ME?
—THE HUNGRY CHIMPANZEE
—MYTHICAL ISLE OF OOLONG
—AN ADMIRABLE ADMIRAL
—OLD MOTHER GOOSE
—IN THE MORNING
—WHAT COLOR EYES DO YOU LOVE
BEST?
—LOVE IN A MANGO TREE
—PERHAPS, MAYBE, PERHAPS

1908. *MR. HAMLET OF BROADWAY*
A musical comedy with book by Edgar
Smith, lyrics by Edward Madden, and
starring Eddie Foy in a cast that included
Oscar Ragland, Maude Raymond, Mabel
Baker and Daphne Pollard.
—REGIMENTAL REVIEW
—THAT'S AS FAR AS YOU CAN GO
—THE HORNPIPE RAG
—CHORUS OF BELLHOPS AND PAR-
LOR MAIDS
—THE DUSKY SALOME
—UNDER THE HONEYMOON
—WHEN I WAS A KID LIKE YOU
—THE HYPNOTIC EYE
—WE'VE BEEN TAKEN IN
—IN A SUMMER HOTEL
—WON'T YOU HARMONIZE WITH
ME?
—EVERYTHING DEPENDS ON MONEY
—GOODBYE, MOLLY BROWN
—TELL US WHAT'S THE ROW?
—IN THE GOLDEN DAWN
—A POOR LITTLE GIRL LIKE ME
—NONE OF THEM'S GOT ANYTHING
ON ME
—DANCING IS DELIGHTFUL
—I WANT TO JOIN THE ARMY
—WHEN WE MADE THAT CHARGE
UP BUNKER HILL

J. Rosamond Johnson Scores

1900. *THE BELLE OF BRIDGEPORT*
A farce by Glen MacDonough, co-starring Mae Irwin and Raymond Hitchcock. Lyrics by Bob Cole.
—AIN'T GWINE TO WORK NO MORE
—WHY DON'T THE BAND PLAY?
—I'VE GOT TROUBLES OF MY OWN
—SOUTHERN QUEEN
Other musical numbers in this production were "Dance on Friday Night" by William Jefferson; "Mabel Moore" and "My Dandy Soldier Boy" by Will Accoe; and "Bullfrog Ben" and "Angeline" by Cissie Loftus.

1904. *IN NEWPORT*
Book by John J. McNally, lyrics by Bob Cole and James Weldon Johnson, and presented by a cast headed by Fay Templeton, Peter Dailey, Joe Coyne, Virginia Earle and Lee Harrison.
—SCANDAL
—MARY WAS A MANICURE
—NOBODY BUT YOU
—PEGGY IS A NEW YORKER NOW
—STOCKINGS
—HOW A MONOCLE HELPS THE MIND
—LINDY
—SPIRIT OF THE BANJO

1904. *HUMPTY DUMPTY*
A London Drury Lane spectacle, adapted for the American stage by John J. McNally and produced by Klaw & Erlanger at the New Amsterdam Theater, New York, where it had a run of 132 performances. The lyrics were by Bob Cole, and the cast was headed by Frank Moulan, Maude Lillian Berri, Nellie Daly and John McVeigh.
—MARY FROM TIPPERARY
—THE EGG HAS FALLEN DOWN
—I AM THE KING
—WILL HE EVER SMILE AGAIN?
—THE PUSSY AND THE BOW-WOW
—WE GOT TO FIND THE RING
—MEXICO
—SAMBO AND DINAH
—DOWN IN MULBERRY BEND
—MAN, MAN, MAN
—ON LALAWANA'S SHORE

1907. *THE SHOO-FLY REGIMENT*
Book by Bob Cole, lyrics by James Weldon Johnson, and co-starring Cole and Johnson in an all-colored cast.
—I THINK AN AWFUL LOT OF YOU
—WON'T YOU BE MY LITTLE BROWN BEAR?

—ON THE GAY LUNETA
—DE BO'RD OF EDUCATION
—FLOATING DOWN THE NILE
—THE GHOST OF DEACON BROWN
—IF ADAM HADN'T SEEN THE APPLE TREE
—I'LL ALWAYS LOVE OLD DIXIE
—WHO DO YOU LOVE?
—RUN, BRUDDER RABBIT, RUN
—THERE'S ALWAYS SOMETHING WRONG

1909. *THE RED MOON*
Book and lyrics by Bob Cole, who co-starred with Rosamond Johnson in an all-Negro cast.
—ON THE ROAD TO MONTEREY
—ADA, MA SWEET POTATO
—SAMBO
—AIN'T HAD NO LOVIN' IN A LONG TIME
—I'VE LOST MY TEDDY BEAR
—PATHWAY OF LOVE
—I WANT MY CHICKEN
—MY INDIAN MAID
—LIFE IS A GAME OF CHECKERS
—BIG RED SHAWL
—CUPID WAS AN INDIAN PICKANNINNY
—BLEEDING MOON

1909. *MR. LODE OF KOAL*
Written in collaboration with Bert Williams, who appeared in this production with an all-Negro troupe for the last time before becoming a "Ziegfeld Follies" star. The book and lyrics were by J. A. Shipp and Alex Rogers.
—CAN SONG
—MY OLD MAN
—HARBOR OF LOST DREAMS
—BYGONE DAYS IN DIXIE
—LAMENT
—CHINK-CHINK CHINYMAN
—FETE OF THE VEILED MUGS
—BELIEVE ME
There were two other sonsg in this musical comedy: "Mum's the Word, Mr. Moore" by J. Leubrie Hill and "In Far Off Mandalay" by Al Johns.

Sidney Jones Scores

1900. *SAN TOY*
A comic opera with book by Edward Morton, lyrics by Adrian Ross and Percy Greenbank, and starring James T. Powers in a cast that included Melville Stewart, Wilfred Clarke, George K. Fortesque, Flora Zabelle and Marie Celeste.
—SIX LITTLE WIVES

—A POSY FROM OVER THE SEA
—RHODA AND HER PAGODA
—DOWN BY THE SEA
—A LITTLE BIT OF FUN
—THE MOON
—SAMEE GAMEE
—CHINEE SOJE MAN
—PRIVATE TOMMY ATKINS
By S. Potter.

1904. *MY LADY MOLLY*
A musical comedy with book and lyrics by George H. Jessop, and presented by a cast headed by Vesta Tilley, Sidney Dean, David Torrence, Richard Carroll and Adele Richie.

—A GOOD GIRL
—BALLINASLOE
—OH, I'LL GREET HIM WITH A SMILE
—MERRY MEDIAEVAL MAID
—THERE'S A LITTLE MAID I KNOW
—DON'T WHISTLE SO LOUD
—THERE'S AN EYE

1904. *THE MEDAL AND THE MAID*
A musical comedy with book by Owen Hall, and starring James T. Powers and Emma Carus in a cast that included W. T. Carleton, Ignacio Martinetti and Cyril Scott.

—POLO
—IN MY CURRICULUM
—KATIE AND HER KODAK
—WHO'LL BUY MY FLOWERS?
—A WELL-BRED GIRL
—ANY SORT OF GIRL
—A PRIZE FOR THAT
—FRILLS UPON THEIR PETTICOATS
—MY LOVE I DARE NOT TELL
—I'M GOING TO BE A MARQUIS
—RAIN OR SHINE
—BRIGAND CHIEF
—PUBLICITY
—CONSEQUENCES
—HIDE AND SEEK
—IF GIRLS HAD WINGS
—THE MAN BEHIND
—IN ZANZIBAR
By Will Cobb and Gus Edwards.

Emmerich Kalman Score

1909. *THE GAY HUSSARS*
A musical comedy with book by Maurice Kirby Brown, lyrics by Grant Stewart, and presented by a cast headed by Anna Bussert, Bobby North, Muriel Terry and Florence Reid.

—DREAMING OF LOVE
—THE GAY HUSSARS

—HEART TO HEART
—PLEASE GIVE ME A KISS
—LOVE IS A TRAITOR
—MY FRIEND LEBEL
—OH, SILVER MOON
—SEX DELICIOUS
—A SOLDIER'S LIFE
—VAGRANT FANCIES
—THE ARMY DIRECTORY
—OH, YOU BOLD BAD MEN
—A MISFIT SOLDIER
—SHINE OUT ALL YOU LITTLE STARS
By M. E. Rourke and Jerome Kern.

Gustav Kerker Scores

1901. *THE GIRL FROM UP THERE*
Book and lyrics by Hugh Morton, and starring Edna May in a cast that included Otis Harlan, Harry Kelly, Harry Davenport, Virginia Earle, Edna Aug, Nat Wills, Lawrence Wheat and Montgomery and Stone, each of whom played dual roles.

—DON'T YOU BELIEVE THOSE EYES
—FAIR PHRYNETTE
—I WAS WALKING ROUND THE OCEAN
—SUSIE
—WE'LL NEVER EAT

1902. *THE BILLIONAIRE*
Book and lyrics by Harry B. Smith, and with a cast that included Jerome Sykes in the title role, Julius Steger, Harry Mac-Donough, Harry Kelly, May Robson, Sallie Fisher and Marie Doro.

—TO BE TRULY REFINED
—THE MONEY BURNER
—SUCH A DEAR LITTLE MAN AS YOU
—FOR A SIGHT OF BROADWAY
—THE AGE OF GOLD
—TOAST SONG
—THERE ARE TRICKS TO ALL TRADES

1903. *THE BLONDE IN BLACK*
Book and lyrics by Harry B. Smith, and with a cast headed by Blanche Ring, Harry Conor, Albert Hart and Charles W. Bowers.

—MEN ARE AMBITIOUS
—DON'T OVERDO IT
—THE YANKEE GIRL
—ANY OLD THING
—LOVE ALL THE DAY
—MY IDEAL
—SHE WALKS LIKE THIS
—AWAKE, MA CHILE
—ALTHOUGH I'M SO DEMURE
—COUNTRY BELLES

64 [1900-1910]

—CYNTHIA JONES
—THEY ARE ANGELS WITHOUT WINGS

1903. *WINSOME WINNIE*
Book and lyrics by Frederic Ranken. Paula Edwardes made her debut as a star in a cast that included Julia Sanderson, Jobyna Howland, Helen Redmond and Dick Temple.
—SEE O'ER THE SWELLING TIDE
—THEY'RE LOOKING FOR ME
—I LOVE YOU ONLY
—GOOD OLD DAYS
—EVERYTHING IS BIG IN CHICAGO
—THE BUGLE SOUNDS
—HOLA! HOLA!
—OH, MAIDEN, THOU HAST AN EYE OF BLUE
—THE CROCODILE AND THE MOON
—THE MILLER OF THE ZUYDER ZEE
—THEN HE WENT AWAY
—SING SONG LEE
—I WOULD BE A SOLDIER BOY
—MY WINSOME WINNIE
—HEROES

1906. *THE SOCIAL WHIRL*
Book and lyrics by Charles Daly and Joseph Herbert, and presented by a cast headed by Adele Richie, Mabel Fenton, Maude Raymond, Blanche Deyo, Ada Lewis, Charles J. Ross, Frederic Bond, Joseph Coyne and Elizabeth Brice.
—THE PROFESSION OF A MANICURE
—VI-VI
—OLD MAN MANHATTAN
—A RAINY DAY
—LOVE AMONG THE FREAKS
—JUST KIDS
—RUN AWAY, NAUGHTY MAN
—JUST THE ONE I'M LOOKING FOR
—WE'LL BLOW THE JOLLY HORN
—RACING SONG

1906. *THE TOURISTS*
Book and lyrics by R. H. Burnside, and with a cast headed by Julia Sanderson, Vera Michelena, Grace LaRue and William Pruette.
—DEAR OLD BROADWAY
—IT'S NICE TO HAVE A SWEETHEART
—KEEP ON DOING SOMETHING
—LOVE IS A WONDERFUL THING
—OH, MISTER SUN!
—RUTH, SHE ALWAYS TOLD THE TRUTH
—THAT'S THE TIME
—THEY LIVED TO BE LOVED IN VAIN

—WOULDN'T YOU LIKE TO KNOW?

1907. *THE WHITE HEN*
Book by Roderic C. Penfield, lyrics by Paul West, and with a cast headed by Louise Gunning, Lotta Faust, Louis Mann and Ralph Herz.
—A MAN IS ONLY A MAN
—KEEP COOL
—FOLLOW, FOLLOW
—FISHING
—THE PRIMA DONNA
—WAITING FOR THE BRIDE
—EVERYTHING IS HIGH NOWADAYS
—I'M MARRIED NOW
—THAT'S WHY THE DANUBE'S BLUE
—AT LAST WE'RE ALONE
—VERY WELL THEN
—PRINTEMPS
—SMILE

1907. *FASCINATING FLORA*
Book and lyrics by R. H. Burnside and Joseph Herbert, and starring Adele Richie in a cast that included Ada Lewis, Louis Harrison and Fred Bond.
—I'M GOING TO A PRETTY WEDDING
—IN PARIS
—VARIETY
—ZUYDER ZEE
—I'M A MARVELOUS MUSICIAN
—WHAT WILL HAPPEN THEN?
—OFF TO NEW YORK
—BULLS AND BEARS
—COME ALONG IN, THE WATER'S FINE
—I'D RATHER TWO-STEP THAN WALTZ BILL
By Benjamin Hapgood Burt.
There also were two interpolated numbers in this production by a rising young composer named Jerome Kern:
—THE SUBWAY EXPRESS
With lyrics by James O'Dea.
—BALLOONING

1907. *THE LADY FROM LANE'S*
Book and lyrics by George Broadhurst, and with a cast that included Truly Shattuck, Thomas Wise, Ida Hawley, Walter Percival, Robert Peyton Carter and Percy Bronson.
—DEAR OLD ENGLAND
—THAT REALLY WAS A LOVELY PLACE FOR ME
—TAKE A MAID

Jerome Kern Score

1904. *MR. WIX OF WICKHAM*
The first stage appearance of Julian El-

tinge, the female impersonator, in a cast that included Thelma Fair and Frank Lalor. Lyrics by John H. Wagner.
—ANGLING BY A BABBLING BROOK
—FROM SATURDAY 'TIL MONDAY
—SUSAN
—WAITING FOR YOU

Manuel Klein Scores

1903. *MR. PICKWICK*
A musical comedy with book by Charles Klein, lyrics by Grant Stewart, and starring DeWolf Hopper in a cast that included Marguerite Clark, Louise Gunning and Digby Bell.
—ACTING
—YOU NEVER CAN TELL
—BOYS WILL BE BOYS
—RAINBOW DANCE
—LOVE
—GOLDEN RULES
—SPEAK LOW
—THE PICKWICK CLUB

1905. *A SOCIETY CIRCUS*
Marceline, the French clown, made his American debut in this New York Hippodrome production with book and lyrics by Sydney Rosenfeld.
—MOON DEAR
—TAINTED GOLD
—THE GOOD, KIND, JOLLY MAN
—THE LAUGHING SCHOOL
—SONG OF THE FLOWERS
Music by Gustav Luders.

1906. *PIONEER DAYS and NEPTUNE'S DAUGHTER*
In this New York Hippodrome production, Indians in war paint, cowboys and U. S. cavalrymen staged the opening spectacle, while in the finale, the chorus girls depicted colored fish and disappeared in the water of the huge tank for the first time.
—RED SKY
—HYMN TO THE SUN
—INDIAN WAR SONG
—LUCIA MY ITALIAN MAID

1906. *THE MAN FROM NOW*
A musical comedy with book by Charles Kendrick Bangs, lyrics by Vincent Bryan, and presented by a cast headed by DeWolf Hopper, Marguerite Clark, Grace Cameron, William Cameron and W. L. Romaine.
—IT'S RAH, RAH, RAH
—SCIENCE
—I'M THE COLLEGE PRESIDENT
—WE ARE THE LADDIES
—COME ALONG MY BOYS

—I WILL LOVE YOU FOREVER
—THERE ISN'T ANYTHING THAT CAN'T BE CURED
—WHAT'S THE MATTER WITH OUR TEAM?
—ASTRONOMY
—THE WIRELESS TELEPHONE
—LIQUID AIR
—BRIDGET McCANN
—IN PITY SPARE THEM
—MY GASOLINE MAID
—THE IRRESISTIBLE TUNE
—I WANT TO GO HOME NOW
—DORA
—THE DAINTY MUSIC MAID
—COLLEGE CHUMS
—WHAT SAYS YOUR HEART?

1907. *THE TOP OF THE WORLD*
A musical extravaganza with book by Mark Swan and Anne Caldwell, lyrics by James O'Dea, and presented by a cast headed by Kathleen Clifford, Bessie Franklin, Anna Laughlin, George Monroe and Wellington Cross.
—O'ER THE SNOWS
—BUSY MR. BEE
—RIDDLE-MA-REE
—HOW'D YOU LIKE TO BE MY BOW-WOW-WOW?
—LITTLE BROWN HEN
—THE ONE GIRL
—WHERE FATE SHALL GUIDE
—CUPID AND YOU AND I
—HAIL TO AURORA
—AURORA FROM AURORA, ILLINOIS
—HAND ME A LAUGH
—MY DOLLS
—YANKEE DOODLE YARNS
—IN A SEA-GOING HACK
—GOODBYE, DINAH
—MY SHAGGY OLD POLAR BEAR

1907. *THE AUTO RACE and THE BATTLE OF PORT ARTHUR*
Hagenbeck's Elephants and Margaret Townsend, the "Ice Maiden", shared headline honors with Marceline, the clown, in this New York Hippodrome production in which the Vanderbilt Cup road race provided the opening spectacle while a naval battle in the huge tank rang down the curtain for the finale.
—RIDING IN A MOTOR CAR
—MY STARLIGHT MAID
—THOSE DAYS GONE BY
—SWEET IS THE PERFUME OF SUMMER FLOWERS
—THE FOUR SEASONS

1908. *THE PIED PIPER*
A musical comedy with book and lyrics

by Austin Strong and R. H. Burnside, and presented by a cast headed by Marguerite Clark, DeWolf Hopper, Grace and William Cameron and W. L. Romaine.
—IT'S GOING TO BE A VERY BUSY DAY
—WE TELL HIM JUST WHAT TO DO
—WOMAN'S A WONDERFUL THING
—THE DRESDEN CHINA PLATE
—ADAM AND EVE
—LOVE IS A CURIOUS FEELING
—IT'S THE LITTLE THINGS THAT COUNT IN LIFE
—IT ALL DEPENDS
—IT REALLY WAS A VERY PRETTY STORY
—I SHOULD LIKE TO KNOW THE REASON
—SENTIMENTAL SARAH
—NURSERY RHYMES
—WHOSE LITTLE GIRL ARE YOU?
—WHAT DO YOU THINK OF THAT?

1908. *SPORTING DAYS*
A New York Hippodrome production in which a bird ballet and a battle between airplanes provided the highlights.
—WHEN THE CIRCUS COMES TO TOWN
—ROWING
—GOOD OLD CAMBRIA
—THE RACING GAME
—THE WHOLE YEAR ROUND
—A TOAST TO THE KING OF WAR

1909. *A TRIP TO JAPAN*
This year's New York Hippodrome production with book and lyrics by R. H. Burnside took on an Oriental flavor.
—INSIDE THE EARTH
—EVERY GIRL LOVES A UNIFORM
—FAIR FLOWER OF JAPAN
—MEET ME WHERE THE LANTERNS GLOW
—OUR NAVY'S THE BEST IN THE WORLD

Aimee Lauchaume Score

1901. *THE PRIMA DONNA*
An operetta with book and lyrics by Harry B. Smith, and presented by a cast headed by Lulu Glaser, W. P. Carleton, Herbert Cawthorne, Charles P. Bowers, William Cameron and Mabel Barrison.

Liza Lehman Score

1905. *SERGEANT BRUE*
A musical comedy with book and lyrics by Owen Hall, and starring Frank Daniels in a cast that included Sallie Fisher,

Walter Percival, Lawrence Wheat, Harry MacDonough and Blanche Ring.
—OUR EMPORIUM
—YOUNG MAN IN A SHOP
—A CUP OF TEA
—I'M THE SERGEANT OF POLICE
—HAIL TO THE PICCADILLY HERO
—WE HAVE DINED
—PUT ME IN MY LITTLE CELL
—WELCOME, MR. BRUE
—LET ME SING
—LANCERS
—OH, HELP!
—HAIL TO THE MAGISTRATE
—I WAS BORN ON FRIDAY
—ZOOLOGICAL PARTY
—SWEET ANASTASIA BRADY
—OLD MAN SHEA
By Benjamin Hapgood Burt.
—SATURDAY AFTER TWO
By D. K. Stevens.
—MY IRISH MOLLY-O
By William Jerome and Jean Schwartz.
—DEARIE
By Clare Kummer.

Franz Lehar Score

1907. *THE MERRY WIDOW*
This operetta with book by Victor Leon and Leo Stein and lyrics by Adrian Ross, opened at the New Amsterdam Theater on October 27, 1907 and ran for 416 performances. When Ethel Jackson, who played the title role of Sonia, retired from the cast in March of the following year, she was replaced by Lois Elwell, Lina Abarbanell, Rosemary Glosz, Georgia Caine and Ruby Dale in turn. Donald Brian, who played Prince Danilo, was succeeded by Charles Meakin in August, 1908.
—(I'M HAPPY AT) MAXIM'S
—VILIA
—MERRY WIDOW WALTZ (I LOVE YOU SO)
—LOVELY WOMEN
—SYLVIA
—LOVE IN MY HEART
—GIRLS, GIRLS, GIRLS
—A DUTIFUL WIFE
—IN MARSOVIA
—THE CAVALIER
—OH, SAY NO MORE
—BUTTERFLIES

Maurice Levi Scores

1900. *ROGERS BROTHERS IN CENTRAL PARK*
A musical comedy with book by John J.

McNally, lyrics by J. Cheever Goodwin, and starring Gus and Max Rogers in a cast that included Della Fox, Eugene O'Rourke and Lee Harrison.
—THE MATRIMONIAL AGENT
—THE DUCHESS OF CENTRAL PARK
—WHEN REUBEN COMES TO TOWN
—LINDA, MAH LADY
—IN CENTRAL PARK
—A BOTTLE AND A BIRD
—THE BRAVE HUSSAR
—IS IT YES OR IS IT NO?
—DARKTOWN BARBEQUE
—UP ON THE ROOF
—SALLY
—IF THE CABBY TOLD HALF WHAT HE KNOWS
—RUN, BRUDDER POSSUM, RUN

1901. *ROGERS BROTHERS IN WASHINGTON*
A musical comedy with book by John J. McNally, lyrics by Harry B. Smith, and starring Gus and Max Rogers in a cast that included Charles A. Weinburg, Pat Rooney, James Cherry, Hattie Williams and Nora Bayes.
—THE GIRL OF GREATER NEW YORK
—GET NEXT TO THE MAN WITH A PULL
—IN THE SWIM
—MY EBONY BELLE
—DIPLOMACY
—WATERMELON PARTY
—THE WEDDING OF THE REUBEN AND THE MAID
—THE ELECTRIC LIGHT CADETS
—AT THE PAN-AMERICAN
—MY BUNCO QUEEN
—FROM 1776 TO 1901

1902. *ROGERS BROTHERS AT HARVARD*
A musical comedy with book by John J. McNally, lyrics by J. Cheever Goodwin, and starring Gus and Max Rogers in a cast that included Lee Harrison, Pat Rooney, James Cherry, Hattie Williams and Pauline Frederick, who made her stage debut as a show girl in this production.
—I'M GETTING QUITE AMERICAN YOU KNOW
—ON UPPER BROADWAY AFTER DARK
—MY STARLIGHT QUEEN
—RAINBOWS FOLLOW THE RAIN
—MARY BE WARY
—I'M A LADY
—LINDA LOOK OUT THE WINDOW

1904. *HIGGLEDY-PIGGLEDY*
This was Joe Weber's first Broadway appearance without his old partner, Lew Fields, in a cast that included Anna Held, Marie Dressler, Bonnie Maginn and Charles A. Bigelow. The book and lyrics were by Edgar Smith.
—FOR YOU, HONEY, FOR YOU
—A GREAT BIG GIRL LIKE ME
—MAMA'S BOARDING HOUSE
—BIG INDIAN AND HIS LITTLE MAID
—MISS WATERMELON SWEET
—IN GAY PAREE
—I'M SO LONESOME
—NANCY CLANCY
—THE GAME OF LOVE

1906. *TWIDDLE-TWADDLE*
A revue with book and lyrics by Edgar Smith, and presented by a cast headed by Joe Weber, Charles A. Bigelow, Ernest Lambert, Bonnie Maginn, Marie Dressler and Trixie Friganza.
—A LITTLE BUNCH OF DAISIES
—BUTTERFLIES OF FASHION
—YOU AND THE GIRL YOU LOVE
—LOOKING FOR A SURE THING
—STORIES OF THE STAGE
—I HOPE YOU'LL FORGIVE THESE TEARS
—'TIS HARD TO BE A LADY IN A CASE LIKE THAT
—OH HEIGH-HO
—SYNCOPATED GYPSY MAN
—SOCIETY BIRDS

1908. *THE SOUL KISS*
A musical comedy with book and lyrics by Harry B. Smith in which Mlle. Adeline Genee made her American debut in a cast that included Florence Holbrook, Florence Walton, Ralph Herz, Lee Harrison and Cecil Lean.
—HAPPY DAYS
—MY AFFINITY
—ANY OLD PLACE IN THE WORLD WITH YOU
—THERE WERE ACTORS THEN
—SOUL KISS
—LET'S PRETEND
—I'M THE HUMAN NIGHT KEY OF NEW YORK
—THAT WASN'T ALL
By Addison Burkhardt, Matt Woodward and Louis A. Hirsch.
—WHEN SWALLOWS RETURN IN THE SPRING
—MEET ME AT THE TABARIN
—THE DOLLAR SIGN
—MY DIABALO BEAU

—I WONDER WHERE THEY'LL GO
—I'M GLAD TO GET BACK TO NEW
    YORK
—THOSE COLLEGE YELLS

1908. *ZIEGFELD FOLLIES OF 1908*
This year's cast included Lucy Weston,
Barney Bernard, Nora Bayes, Grace La-
Rue, Harry Watson, George Bickel, Ar-
thur Deagon, Mlle. Dazie, Lee Harrison,
Florence Walton, Mae Murray, Gertrude
Vanderbilt and Rosie Green, mother of
Mitzi Green. Book and lyrics by Harry B.
Smith.
—MOSQUITO SONG
—DUCHESS OF TABLE D'HOTE
—YOU WILL HAVE TO SING AN IR-
    ISH SONG
—THE RAJAH OF BROADWAY
—TITLES
—THE BIG HATS
—NOTHING EVER TROUBLES ME
—NELL BRINKLEY GIRL
—SINCE MOTHER WAS A GIRL
—THE INTERNATIONAL MERRY
    WIDOW
—SOCIETY
—WHEN THE GIRL YOU LOVE IS
    LOVING
By William Jerome and Jean Schwartz.
—TAKE ME ROUND IN A TAXI
By Edgar Selden and Melville Gideon.

1909. *ZIEGFELD FOLLIES OF 1909*
This year's cast was headed by William
Bonelli, Lillian Lorraine, Arthur Deagon,
Nora Bayes, Bessie Clayton, Harry Kelly,
Jack Norworth, Sophie Tucker, Gertrude
Vanderbilt and Eva Tanguay. Book and
lyrics by Harry B. Smith.
—TAKE A TIP FROM VENUS
—LINGER LONGER LINGERIE
—WHAT EVERY WOMAN KNOWS
—I WISH I WAS A BOY AND I WISH
    I WAS A GIRL
—GO AS FAR AS YOU LIKE
—BRINKLEY BATHING GIRLS
—THE PARISIAN TWIST
—LOVE IN THE SPRINGTIME
—THE GREATEST NAVY IN THE
    WORLD
—MY COUSIN CARUS'
By Edward Madden and Gus Edwards.
—COME ON AND PLAY BALL WITH
    ME
By Edward Madden and Gus Edwards.
—UP, UP, UP IN MY AEROPLANE
By Edward Madden and Gus Edwards.
—PLAY THAT FANDANGO RAG
By E. Ray Goetz and Lewis Muir.

—MEXATEXA
By Lewis E. Muir.
—MOVING DAY IN JUNGLE TOWN
By A. Seymour Brown and Nat Ayer.
In the early months of this production,
the following songs by Jack Norworth
and Nora Bayes were introduced:
—MAD OPERA HOUSE
—FALLING STARS
—DEAR OLD FATHER
—BLARNEY
—LET'S GET THE UMPIRE'S GOAT

William Lorraine Scores

1903. *PEGGY FROM PARIS*
A musical comedy with book and lyrics
by George Ade, and presented by a cast
headed by Helen Hale, Josie Sadler,
Georgia Caine, John P. Park and Arthur
Deagon.
—THE JANITOR
—REGULAR LIMITED TRAIN
—TRUE TO THE COLLEGE DAYS
—I LIKE YOU LIL FOR FAIR
—MY EMMALEEN
—GAY FLEURETTE
—HENNY
(The bassoon player "vat played mit
Sousa vunce—but only vunce.")
—HAPPY, HAPPY ILLINOIS
—HIGH-FLUTING MUSIC
—WE ARE THE PRINCIPALS
—ART
—WHEN HE'S NOT NEAR
—IMPORTED YES WE ARE
—OLD FASHIONED SONGS
—THE GIRL WHO COMES FROM THE
    WEST
—WELCOME
—AM I FRENCH ENOUGH FOR YOU?
—I LEFT MY HEART IN DIXIE

1905. *THE PRESS AGENT*
A musical comedy with book and lyrics
by Mark Swan and John P. Wilson, and
presented by a cast headed by Peter F.
Dailey and Frank Lalor.

Gustav Luders Scores

1900. *THE BURGOMASTER*
Book and lyrics by Frank Pixley, and pre-
sented by a cast headed by Raymond
Hitchcock, Henry E. Dixey, Knox Wilson
and Ruth White.
—LOVE CAN'T SAY NO
—GOOD-BYE NEW AMSTERDAM
—JUST KEEP COOL
—NOW WE'RE CIVILIZED

—THE DUTCH CADETS
—I DRINK FROM MY HEART TO YOU
—WE ALWAYS WORK THE PUBLIC
—LAND OF THE MIDNIGHT SUN
—THE LITTLE SOUBRETTE
—MERELY A MATTER OF FORM
—DEAR OLD COLLEGE DAYS
—THE MODERN GLADIATOR
—THE TALE OF A KANGAROO
—THE LIBERTY GIRL
—THE BATHING GIRLS
—WE HAVEN'T DISCOVERED HIM
　　YET
—I LOVE YOU DEAR AND ONLY YOU
—THE ARISTOCRACY
—IF I WERE A HYPNOTIST
—IN GAY PARIS
—REACHING FOR THE CAKE
—PAINTING CHICAGO RED

1902. *KING DODO*
　　Book and lyrics by Frank Pixley, and star-
　　ring Raymond Hitchcock in a cast that in-
　　cluded Arthur Deagon, Eugene O'Rourke
　　and Gertrude Quinlan.
—DRINKING SONG
—LOOK IN THE BOOK AND SEE
—I'LL DO OR DIE
—THE EMINENT DOCTOR FIZZ
—A JOLLY OLD POTENTATE
—I ADORE THEE
—TWO HEARTS MADE ONE
—THE CAT'S QUARTET
—OLD FATHER TIME
—A TRUE BARBARIC SOLDIER
—FOR LOVE I LIVE ALONE
—DIANA
—THAT'S WHAT I'LL DO
—CLAIM THOU THINE OWN
—THE LAD WHO LEADS
—THE TALE OF A BUMBLEBEE

1903. *THE PRINCE OF PILSEN*
　　Book and lyrics by Frank Pixley and
　　starring John E. Ransone in the role of
　　Hans Wagner, the German brewer who
　　asked repeatedly: "Vas you efer in Zin-
　　zinnati?" The cast also included Arthur
　　Donaldson, Edgar Norton and Lillian
　　Coleman.
—THE MODERN PIRATE
—WE KNOW IT'S WRONG TO FLIRT
—WALK, MISTER, WALK
—A SEASON AT THE SHORE
—HAIL TO OUR NOBLE GUEST
—THE MESSAGE OF THE VIOLET
—HEIDELBERG STEIN SONG
—THE WIDOW
—KEEP IT DARK
—PICTURES IN THE SMOKE

—FIELD AND FOREST
—IMAGINATION
—THE AMERICAN GIRL
—THE TALE OF THE SEASHELL
—BACK TO THE BOULVEARDS
—OUR FLORAL QUEEN
—FALL IN

1903. *MAM'SELLE NAPOLEON*
　　Book and lyrics by Joseph W. Herbert,
　　and starring Anna Held in a cast that
　　included Bessie McCoy, Nellie McCoy,
　　Edna Goodrich, Dan McAvoy, Joseph W.
　　Herbert and Fletcher Norton.
—STAGE AND FASHION GO HAND IN
　　HAND
—LIFE IS NOT AN AIRY BUBBLE
—HIT ENORMOUS
—THE LANGUAGE OF LOVE
—FLOWERS, FEATHERS, RIBBONS
　　AND LACES
—THE COCKATOO AND THE CHIM-
　　PANZEE
—I'LL LOVE YOU THEN AS NOW
—THE ART OF STIMULATION
—QUEEN OF THE COMEDIE FRAN-
　　CAISE
—NYMPHS AND THE SATYR
—TOO-WHOO
—LE LION ET LA SOURIS (THE LION
　　AND THE MOUSE)
—LONG LIVE FOLLY
—THE BRAVE SOLDIER BOY
—OUT WITH THE BOYS
—LE RIGEDON
—THE A LA MODE GIRL
—THE GLORY OF FRANCE
—SONG OF THE GRENADIER
—ON TO PARIS

1904. *THE SHO-GUN*
　　Book and lyrics by George Ade, and pre-
　　sented by a cast headed by Christie Mac-
　　Donald, Charles Evans, David Torrence,
　　Edward Martindel and Georgia Caine.
—LITTLE MOOZOO MAY
—LIFE ALL FREE FROM CARE
—THE GIRL JUST OUT
—I AM YOURS TRULY
—ENTRANCE OF FLAI-HA
—SOLDIERS' CHORUS
—THE IRREPRESSIBLE YANK
—MOURNERS' CHORUS
—THE MAN SHE'LL NEVER MEET
—LOVE YOU MUST BE BLIND
—WISTARIA, MY BRIDE
—YOUR HONEYMOON WILL LAST
—HIKE, HIKE (HI-KO, HI-KO)
—FLUTTER LITTLE BIRD
—THE GAMES WE USED TO PLAY

—SHE'S JUST A LITTLE DIFFERENT FROM THE OTHERS THAT I KNOW

1904. *WOODLAND*
A musical fantasy with book and lyrics by Frank Pixley in which all the characters reprented birds. The cast was headed by Harry Bulger, Ida Brooks Hunt, Emma Carus and Helen Hale.
—AT NIGHT, AT NIGHT
—DAINTY LITTLE INGENUE
—TIME IS FLYING
—NO BIRD EVER FLEW SO HIGH HE DIDN'T HAVE TO LIGHT
—BYE-BYE BABY
—PRINCE EAGLE'S ENTRANCE
—WHERE THE HEART IS LIGHT
—CLEAR THE WAY
—YOU NEVER CAN TELL TILL YOU TRY
—THE ROMANCE OF THE BACHELOR BIRD
—SOCIETY
—THE VALLEY OF HOCUS-PO
—SOME DAY WHEN MY DREAMS COME TRUE
—THEY'LL HAVE TO GO
—CHEER UP
—THE MESSAGE OF SPRING
—IF YOU LOVE ME, LINDY, TELL ME SO
—TALE OF THE TURTLE DOVE
—WHEN DUTY CALLS

1907. *THE GRAND MOGUL*
Book and lyrics by Frank Pixley, and with a cast headed by Frank Moulan, Elsa Ryan, Maude Lillian Berri, John Dunsmore and George Austin Moore.
—HONOLULU
—ANNEXATION DAY
—HELP YOURSELF
—I'M THE ONLY ONE OF MY KIND
—ALOHA
—THE LAND WHICH MY HEART CALLS HOME
—MY HULA-HULA GIRL
—THE LOTUS
—THE MILITARY MAN
—CUPID'S PRIVATE CODE
—NESTLE BY MY SIDE
—THE GOOD OLD-FASHIONED WAY
—CHEER UP
—LOVE IS NOT FOR A DAY

1908. *MARCELLE*
Book and lyrics by Frank Pixley, and presented by a cast that included Louise Gunning, Jess Dandy, Herbert Cawthorne and Lawrence Wheat.
—DRINK AND BE MERRY TODAY
—IT'S NOT THE PROPER THING TO DO
—LOVE THE MAGICIAN
—KALAMAZOO
—THE SCHWINDLE CORPS
—MARY AND HER LAMB
—ONCE IN A WHILE
—MY OWN PAREE
—SOMETHING
—THE SOLDIER BOY
—WATCHMEN'S CHORUS
—FORGET IT
—GOOD EVENING
—CUPID SLY LITTLE RASCAL
—THE VOLUNTEERS
—MESSAGE OF THE RED, RED ROSE

1909. *THE FAIR CO-ED*
Book and lyrics by George Ade, and starring Elsie Janis.
—ALMOST
—THE COLLEGE MILITARY
—I'LL DREAM OF THAT SWEET CO-ED
—THE CHAPERONE
—LEAVE IT TO THE BOYS IN THE NAVY
—PLEASE DON'T KEEP ME WAITING
—THE DAY OF THE GAME
—AN ISLE IN THE PHILIPPINES
—A LITTLE GIRL THAT'S WISE

Andre Messager Scores

1905. *VERONIQUE*
A musical comedy with book by Henry Hamilton, lyrics by Lillian Eldee and Percy Greenbank, in which Ruth Vincent starred and Valli Valli and Kitty Gordon made their Broadway debut.
—OUT ON THE BREEZY MORNING AIR
—PLEASE, SIR, WE WANT IF WE MAY
—LIFE IS SHORT, MY DEAR FRIENDS
—BETWEEN US ALL IS O'ER
—NOW THE CARRIAGES ALL ARE WAITING
—AS ALONG THE STREET WE WANDER
—COME DRINK A TOAST
—AT WEDDINGS AS A GENERAL RULE
—WHEN NOT ENGAGED IN FIGHTING
—THE BLOOM OF THE APPLE TREE
—TROT HERE AND THERE
—YOU'RE LAUGHING
—SWEET LIZETTE

—YOU'RE A CHARMING LITTLE MAIDEN
—FAREWELL, I GO
—HUSH, HUSH, SHE'S MEDITATING
—THE GARDEN OF LOVE
—WHILE I'M WAITING
—COME ONE AND ALL
—OH, STRANGE SITUATION
—AH, WELL, WE'LL TRY TO BE PRECISE

1907. *THE LITTLE MICHUS*
A musical comedy with book by Henry Hamilton, lyrics by Percy Greenbank, and presented by a cast headed by Elita Proctor Otis, George Fortesque, Ernest Lambert, Flavio Arcaro and Violet Zell.
—LONG AGO IN ALCALA
Lyrics by F. E. Weatherly and Adrian Ross.
—MISS NOBODY FROM NOWHERE
—IT'S NO USE CRYING FOR THE MOON
—I WOULD LIKE TO BE A GRAND LADY
—LITTLE SISTER
—MY HEART'S A WEATHER GLASS
—MY OLD HOME
—A REGIMENT OF FROCKS AND FRILLS
—THIS LITTLE GIRL AND THAT
—THE SONG OF THE REGIMENT

Lionel Monckton Scores
1904. *THE CINGALEE*
A musical comedy with book by John T. Tanner, lyrics by Adrian Ross and Percy Greenbank, and presented by a cast headed by Martha Carine, Blanche Deyo, Melville Stewart and William Norris.
—PEARL OF SWEET CEYLON
—READING, WRITING, ARITHMETIC
—PEGGY
—WITH A BOO
—SOMETHING DEVILISH WRONG
—MY HEART IS AT YOUR FEET
—TEA, TEA, TEA
—WHITE AND BROWN GIRL
—IN GAY CEYLON
—MY CINNAMON TREE
—I'M A MERRY MAIDEN
—THE CROCODILE
—SHE'S ALL RIGHT
—YOU AND I
—MAKE A FUSS OF ME
—THE COURSE OF TRUE LOVE
—ON THE LAKE
—THE PARAHARA
—THERE'S NOTHING MUCH MORE TO SAY

—THE MONKEYS
—WEDDING MARCH

1909. *KITTY GREY*
With Howard Talbot. A musical comedy with book and lyrics by J. W. Piggot, and presented by a cast headed by Julia Sanderson, Valli Valli, J. P. Huntley and Percival Knight.
—SWEET KITTY
—WELCOME TO HIS MAJESTY
—INCOGNITO
—THE TRACT
—A GENTLEMAN'S GENTLEMAN
—KING HAL'S GIRLS
—MR. SOLDIER
—M'LLE. PIROUTTE
—THE ODE
—JUST GOOD FRIENDS
By M. E. Rourke and Jerome Kern.
—KITTY'S NOT BUILT THAT WAY
—STROLLING, STROLLING IN THE GLOAMING
By Hal Gaze.
—IF A GIRL WANTS YOU
By M. E. Rourke and Jerome Kern.

W. H. Neidlinger Score
1900. *SWEET ANNE PAGE*
A musical comedy with book and lyrics by Louis DeLange and Edgar Smith, and presented by a cast headed by Lulu Glaser, Arthur Donaldson, Josie Intropodi and Alexander Clark.
—BY THE GALLANTS I AM FETED
—SIMPLE LITTLE MAID

A. M. Norden Scores
1904. *AN ENGLISH DAISY*
A musical comedy with book and lyrics by Edgar Smith, and presented by a cast that included Charles A. Bigelow, Templar Saxe, Frank Lalor, Christie MacDonald and Truly Shattuck.
—I'M A LITTLE ENGLISH DAISY
—THE MOON, THE COON AND THE LITTLE OCTAROON
—I ADORE A CERTAIN PARTY
—THE MILITARY MAN
—TO THE END OF THE WORLD TOGETHER
—AT THE MUSIC HALL
—YOU COULDN'T GET ON WITHOUT ME, GIRLS
—WINE, WINE
—SPIN AGAIN
—PREPOSSESSING MAID
—BIG INDIAN CHIEF
By Bob Cole and J. Rosamond Johnson.

1904. *THE WEST POINT CADET*
A musical comedy with book and lyrics by Paul Bilhaud and Alfred Barre, and presented by a cast headed by Della Fox, Clara Palmer, Joseph Herbert and Edward Abeles.
—DREAM SONG
—THE GOOD OLD G. A. R.
—I'LL BE A WEST POINT CADET
—LOVELY LITTLE MARJORIE
—MY LOVE FOREVERMORE
—THOSE DAYS OF LONG AGO
—TWO LITTLE LOVEBIRDS

William F. Peters Score

1905. *THE MAYOR OF TOKIO*
A musical comedy with book and lyrics by Richard Carle, who headed the cast in which Adele Rowland, William Rock and Emma Janvier played supporting roles.
—THE TALE OF A MONKEY
—A TOAST TO THE MOON
—TOKIO
—THE MAYOR OF TOKIO
—PITY MY PITIFUL PLIGHT
—CRUISING HOME
—WHEN THE OCEAN BREEZES BLOW
—JOSIE FROM JOLIET
—BRIDAL SONG
—CONSPIRATORS ARE WE
—WELCOME OLOTO
—CHEER UP EVERYBODY
—COMIC OPERA CAPSULE
—KIDDER'S RECEPTION
—SILVER SEA OF LOVE
—IS MARRIAGE A FAILURE?
—I LIKE YOU
—DANSE BLANCHE ET NOIRE

J. A. Raynes Score

1908. *LONESOME TOWN*
A musical comedy with book and lyrics by Judson D. Brusie, and presented by a cast headed by (C. William) Kolb and (Max M.) Dill with Maude Lambert and Georgia O'Ramey in supporting roles.
—CALIFORNIA SUNRISE
—THE GAME OF GOLF
—THE OLD BARN DANCE
—LANKY YANKEE BOYS IN BLUE
By Edward Madden and Theodore Morse.
—MISSION BELLS
—JUST SOMEONE
By Will R. Anderson.
—THERE'S A BIG CRY BABY IN THE MOON
—WOMEN'S EYES
—WHISTLE WHEN YOU'RE LONELY

—MY CIGARETTE MAID
—WHEN THE MOON PLAYS PEEK-A-BOO
—GEE, BUT THIS IS A LONESOME TOWN
By Billy Gaston.

Alfred G. Robyn Scores

1904. *THE YANKEE CONSUL*
A musical comedy with book and lyrics by Henry M. Blossom, Jr., and starring Raymond Hitchcock in a cast that included William Danforth, John E. Hazzard, Eva Davenport and Flora Zabelle.
—I'D LIKE TO BE A SOLDIER
—AIN'T IT FUNNY WHAT A DIFFERENCE A FEW HOURS MAKE?
—THE HAMMERS GO RAP, RAP, RAP
—MY SAN DOMINGO MAID
—CUPID HAS FOUND MY HEART
—IN THE DAYS OF OLD
—IN OLD NEW YORK
—VIVA THE GAY FIESTA
—OH, GLAD IS THE LIFE OF A SAILOR AT SEA
—THE MOSQUITO AND THE MIDGE
—WE WERE TAUGHT TO WALK DEMURELY
—WE COME FROM PROUD CASTILIAN BLOOD
—GOSSIPS' CHORUS

1907. *PRINCESS BEGGAR*
A musical comedy with book and lyrics by Edward Paulton, and presented by a cast headed by Paula Edwardes, Eddie Garvie, James G. Reaney and Harry MacDonough.
—LOVE, LOVE, LOVE
—WAITING FOR ME
—BEAUTIFUL MAIDENS
—I WANT IT ALL
—I DON'T LOVE YOU
—WOULDN'T YOU LIKE TO LEARN TO LOVE ME?
—MADRIGAL
—ALL HAIL THE QUEEN!
—YOU'RE THE ONLY ONE FOR ME
—HUNTSMAN'S SONG
—ECHO
—RAINING
—ALL THE SAME TO ME
—ELAINE
—CHIMES OF LONG AGO
—A SAD, SAD WORLD
—OH, TELL ME DAISY

1907. *A YANKEE TOURIST*
A musical comedy with book and lyrics by Wallace Irwin, and starring Raymond

Hitchcock in a cast that included Harry West, Wallace Beery, Herbert Cawthorne, Flora Zabelle and Eva Fallon.
—IRISH MEMORIES
—WHEN A GIRL IS BORN TO BE A LADY
—WOULDNT YOU LIKE TO HAVE ME FOR A SWEETHEART?
—GOLDEN SAILS
—THE YANKEE MILLIONAIRE
—COME AND HAVE A SMILE WITH ME
—MY VOLO MAID
—THE TEDDY GIRLS
—SO WHAT'S THE USE?
—RAINBOWS

Paul Rubens Scores

1902. *A COUNTRY GIRL*
With Lionel Monckton. A musical comedy with book by John T. Tanner, lyrics by Adrian Ross, and presented by a cast headed by Minnie Ashley, Melville Stewart, Grace Freeman, Adine Bouvier and William Norris.
—A COUNTRY GIRL
—MY OWN LITTLE GIRLIE
—UNDER THE DEODAR
—CO-YO-HOO, LITTLE GIRLS
—PEACE! PEACE!
—PIXIES
—THE PINK HUNGARIAN BAND
—TRY AGAIN JOHNNIE
—A SAILOR'S LIFE
—MOLLY THE MARCHIONESS
—ME AND MRS. BROWN
—IN THE KING'S NAME, STAND
—I CAN LAUGH, I CAN LOVE

1903. *THREE LITTLE MAIDS*
A musical comedy with book and lyrics by the composer in which Madge Crichton, the English star, made her first American appearance with G. P. Huntley as her vis-a-vis.
—THE GIRL YOU LOVE
—THE MILLER'S DAUGHTER
—MEN
—THAT'S A VERY DIFFERENT THING
—WHAT IS A MAID TO DO?
—SAL
—LOVE YOU'RE A WONDERFUL GAME
—ALGY'S SIMPLY AWFULLY GOOD AT ALGEBRA
—I'LL DREAM OF YOU
—DO I LIKE LOVE!
—MY LITTLE GIRLIE

1906. *MY LADY'S MAID*
A musical comedy with book by R. H. Burnside and lyrics by Percy Greenbank and the composer, in which Madge Crichton starred in an American adaptation of her London success of the previous season, "Lady Madcap".
—PRIMROSE
—MUM'S THE WORD
—MY LADY'S MAID
—I'VE NO PATIENCE WITH A SOLDIER
—A WAY WE HAVE IN THE ARMY
—IT'S HARD TO UNDERSTAND THE LADIES
—A SOLDIER OF MY OWN
—DON'T YOU CARE?
By Joseph E. Miller and Harold Orlob.
—I'D LIKE TO CALL YOU MINE
—IT'S LOVELY WHEN YOUR LOVE LOVES YOU
By E. Ray Goetz.
—ALL I WANT IS YOU
By Paul West and Jerome Kern.

1906. *THE BLUE MOON*
A musical comedy with book by Harold Ellis, lyrics by Percy Greenbank and the composer, and starring James T. Powers in a cast that included Clara Palmer, Grace LaRue, Ethel Jackson, Templar Saxe and Petite Adelaide.
—PIT-A-PAT
—ALL MY GIRLS
—JUGGLAR
—BURMAH GIRL
—I TOLD A FRIEND OF MINE
—OH, BE CAREFUL OF THE CROCODILE
—FAIREST OF THE FAIR
—DON'T YOU THINK IT'S TIME TO MARRY?
By Addison Burkhardt and Gus Edwards.
—DON'T GO IN THE LION'S CAGE TONIGHT
By John Gilroy and E. Ray Goetz.

1907. *THE DAIRY MAIDS*
A musical comedy with book by A. M. Thompson and Robert Courtneidge, lyrics by the composer, and presented by a cast headed by Julia Sanderson, George Gregory, Donald Hall and Eugene O'Rourke.
—I MUST HAVE A LOT OF GIRLS AROUND ME
—HOME AGAIN
—IT'S NAUGHTY TO BE KISSED
—HOW THE WINDS BLOW
—LAZY LAND
—TINKER, TINKER

—POACHING
—HELLO, LITTLE STRANGER
—I WOULD LIKE TO MEET YOUR FATHER
By M. E. Rourke and Jerome Kern.
—I'VE A MILLION REASONS WHY I LOVE YOU
By M. E. Rourke and Jerome Kern.
—MARY McGEE
By M. E. Rourke and Jerome Kern.
—NEVER MARRY A GIRL WITH COLD FEET
By M. E. Rourke and Jerome Kern.
—SANDOW GIRL
—DOWN THE STRAND
—BARCELONA
—OH, MR. BROWN
Music by Harry VonTilzer.
—GOOD NIGHT
—IN THE TWI-TWI-TWILIGHT

1907. *MISS HOOK OF HOLLAND*
A musical comedy with book by Austen Hurgon and the composer, who also contributed the lyrics, and starring Christie MacDonald in a cast that included Tom Wise, Georgia Caine and Florence Nash.
—MISS HOOK
—A LITTLE BIT OF CHEESE
—BOTTLES
—AMSTERDAM
—THE HOUSE THAT HOOK BUILT
—CREAM OF THE SKY
—THE SLEEPY CANAL
—TRA-LA-LA
—FLY AWAY KITE
—THE FLYING DUTCHMAN
—LITTLE MISS WOODEN SHOES
—A PINK PETTY FROM PETER
—SOLDIERS OF THE NETHERLANDS
—I WANT TO BE YOUR WIFE

Jean Schwartz Scores

1904. *PIFF! PAFF!! POUF!!!*
Book by Stanislaus Stange, lyrics by William Jerome, and presented by a cast headed by Eddie Foy, Alice Fisher, John Hyams and Grace Cameron.
—UNDER OUR LOVELY UMBRELLAS
—THE MELANCHOLY SUNBEAM AND THE ROSE
—MARCONI
—I DON'T WANT ANY WURZBURGER
—WE REALLY OUGHT TO BE MARRIED
—UNDER THE GOO-GOO TREE
—DEAR OLD MANHATTAN ISLE
—THE GHOST THAT NEVER WALKED
—MY UNKISSED MAN

—GOOD NIGHT, MY OWN TRUE LOVE
—CORDELIA MALONE
—LOVE, LOVE, LOVE
—LUTI
—I'M SO HAPPY
—DOLLY DIMPLES
—FOR YOU
—RADIUM DANCE
—MARCH OF THE FLAGS

1905. *LIFTING THE LID*
Book by John J. McNally, lyrics by William Jerome, and starring Corrine in a cast that included Fay Templeton, Virginia Earle, Eddie Leonard, Julius Tannen, Louis Harrison, Stella Mayhew and Maude Lambert.
—HOME WITH THE MILK IN THE MORNING
—NOTHING DOING IN THE OLD, OLD TOWN
—ALBANY
—TEXAS DAN
—HOW TO GET IN CENTRAL PARK
—OH MARIE
—MY SYNDI-CATE
There were three interpolated numbers in this production, as follows:
—MAKING EYES
By Harry VonTilzer.
—WHAT YOU WANT AND WHAT YOU GET
By R. A. Brown.
—ROSY
By J. B. Mullen.
Following "Lifting the Lid," an afterpiece, "The Whole Damn Family" was presented with the following songs:
—NOBODY BUT YOU
—TURN OVER
—MY FIRST SMOKE
—I LOVE YOU
—BORNEO
—A MOONLIGHT BUGGY RIDE

1905. *THE HAM TREE*
Book by George V. Hobart and lyrics by William Jerome. The famous blackface comedians, McIntyre and Heath, used this as a starring vehicle for five years with a cast that included Forrest Huff, David Torrence, Jobyna Howland and W. C. Fields, who played the role of Sherlock Baffles and did a travesty on tennis.
—WALKING
—DESDEMONA
—SWEETHEARTS IN EVERY TOWN
—THE MERRY MINSTREL BAND
—GOOD-BYE, SWEET OLD MANHATTAN ISLE

—HONEY, LOVE ME ALL THE TIME
—THE HAM TREE BARBEQUE
—WHEN THE CAT'S AWAY
—ON AN AUTOMOBILE HONEY-
MOON

1905. *FRITZ IN TAMMANY HALL*
Book by John J. McNally, lyrics by Wil-
liam Jerome, and presented by a cast
headed by Joseph Cawthorn, Julius Tan-
nen, Ada Lewis, Melville Ellis, George
Austin Moore and Stella Mayhew.
—IN OLD NEW YORK
—EAST SIDE LIL
—MY SWEET
—WHEN YOU'RE IN LOVE
—IN BAD MAN'S LAND
—MY DEAR LITTLE WISE OLD
BOWERY
—EAST SIDE WALK
—I'M A WOMAN OF IMPORTANCE
—I DON'T WANT A LITTLE CANOE
—YANKEE DOODLE BOODLE
—THE MAN BEHIND THE CLUB
—THE TAMMANY BALL
—THE DEAR OLD FARM
—MY IRISH DAISY
—IN TAMMANY HALL

1905. *A YANKEE CIRCUS ON MARS*
The premiere production at the New York
Hippodrome with book by George V. Hobart and lyrics by Harry Williams, in
which Bessie McCoy and James Cherry
got headline billing, a bankrupt circus was
bought by a Martian envoy and trans-
ported to that distant planet by airship,
and the finale, "The Raiders," recreated
a Civil War battle in which the horses
plunged into the huge tank.
—HOLD YOUR HORSES
—THE BOOGIE MAN
—AURORA BOREALIS
—GET A HORSE
—THE ANIMAL KING
By Manuel Klein.

1907. *LOLA FROM BERLIN*
Book by John J. McNally, lyrics by Wil-
liam Jerome, and starring Lulu Glaser in
a cast that included Gladys Zell and
Ralph Herz.
—MADCHENLIED
—ALTDEUTSCHER LEIBERSREIM
—I THINK OF YOU THE WHOLE
YEAR ROUND
—I'D SOONER BE A HAS-BEEN
—UNTER DEN LINDEN
—BENEATH THE MOON
—JUST HOME FROM COLLEGE
—POOR LITTLE FOOLISH MAN

—SIGNS
—THERE'S NOT ANOTHER GIRLIE
IN THE WORLD LIKE YOU

1909. *IN HAYTI*
Book by John J. McNally, lyrics by Wil-
liam Jerome, and starring McIntyre and
Heath in a cast that included Carl Mc-
Cullough, Adele Rowland and Marion
Stanley.
—THE AMERICAN MONTE CARLO
—CAPTAIN FLO
—CHICKEN
—COME TODDLE ALONG
—EVERYBODY'S RAGTIME CRAZY
—I'D LIKE TO CORRESPOND WITH
YOU
—LOVE ME LIKE ROMEO LOVED
MISS JULIET
—MISTER IZZY ALWAYS BUSY
ROSENSTEIN
—MY HAYTIAN QUEEN
—THE REVOLUTIONARY MAN

A. Baldwin Sloane Scores

1900. *BROADWAY TO TOKIO*
With Reginald de Koven. Book and lyrics
by Louis Harrison and George V. Hobart,
and presented by a cast headed by Fay
Templeton, Josie Sadler, Otis Harlan,
Ignacio Martinetti and Joseph Ott.
—SUSIE MY SUE
—SERPENT OF THE NILE
—LIVE AGAIN
—SALVATION HYMN
—WE'RE A COMIC OPERA COMPANY
—WHEN I'M TRAVELING ON THE
ROAD
—THE LOVELORN LILY
—STORY OF THE DANCE
—DIG YOU DAGOES DIG
—WHEN O'DONAHUE PRESIDED AT
THE GRIP
—THE JOHNNIES OF LONGACRE
SQUARE
—HUNTING FOR A HAPPY LITTLE
HOME IN HARLEM
—NOW I'VE GOT SOME MONEY I'M
COMIN' 'ROUND
Lyrics by Frank Sloane.

1900. *AUNT HANNAH*
Book by Mathew J. Royal, lyrics by Clay
M. Greene, and co-starring John Bunny
and Agnes Findlay.
—MA TIGER LILY
—WHEN THE CAT'S AWAY THE MICE
WILL PLAY
—WHAT'S THE MATTER WITH
HANNAH

—LITTLE BO-PEEP

1900. *A MILLION DOLLARS*
Book and lyrics by Louis Harrison and George V. Hobart, and presented by a cast headed by Joseph Ott, Ignacio Martinetti, Nat Wills, Charles H. Prince and Pat Rooney.
—DIVORCE HUNTERS' CHORUS
—WE ARE THE MEN OF THE LAW
—BARBERS ARE WE
—I AM A MILLIONAIRE
—MARCH OF THE ALLIES
—BELIEVE ME
—McMANUS
—I'M A PRINCE
—PHOEBE, DEAR I LOVE YOU
—HE'S A MAN OF MYSTERY
—ON THE BEACH
—GOOD NIGHT, OH SEA!
—HOOT MON
—THE CHRISTENING
—SIXTEEN TO ONE (GOLD AND SILVER BALLET)

1900. *THE GIDDY THRONG*
A burlesque revue with book by Sydney Rosenfeld, and starring May Yohe, who later became Lady Francis Hope, in a cast that included Louis Harrison, Mabel Fenton, Amelia Summerville, Charles H. Prince, Pat Rooney and Emma Carus.

1901. *THE KING'S CARNIVAL*
Book and lyrics by Sidney Rosenfeld and George V. Hobart, and presented by a cast headed by Charles Prince, Louis Harrison, Mayme Gehrue, Harry Bulger, Emma Carus, Marie Dressler, Adele Richie and Amelia Summerville. This revue was preceded by the ballet, "A Devil's Dream," in which Lilly Collins, Lilly Brink, Laura Lynde and a ballet corps of 200 appeared, and by a vaudeville olio made up of Billy Link, Mayme Gehrue and Johnny Ford, dancers, and Dan McAvoy and Company.
—RAGTIME WILL BE MAH FINISH
—AND THE BAND BEGAN TO PLAY
—IF I HAD A LITTLE BOY TO LOVE ME
—MY SAILOR BOY
—MY EVALINE
Words and music by Mae Anwerda Sloane, the wife of the show's composer.

1902. *THE HALL OF FAME*
With Mae A. Sloane. Book by Sydney Rosenfeld, lyrics by George V. Hobart, and presented by a cast that included Amelia Summerville, Edythe Moyer, Ada Lewis, Charles Prince, Junie McCree,

Louis Harrison, Marie Dressler, Mabelle Gilman, Emma Carus and Alexander Carr.
—NANCY OH MISS NANCY
—HAIL, FAME
—IF I'VE GOT WHAT YOU WANT
—THE WANDERING HERO
—HUNTING SONG
—FOREST LOAFERS
—LOVE IS A JAIL
—MY ANGEMIMA GREEN
—DREAMY EYES
—THE BLACK CAT INN
—ROMANCE AND REALITY
—DARLING LOU
—THE SUNFLOWER AND THE SUN
—MY PAJAMA BEAUTY
—MEET ME WHEN THE SUN GOES DOWN
—THERE IS NO NORTH, THERE IS NO SOUTH

1902. *THE BELLE OF BROADWAY*
A musical comedy with book by William H. Post, lyrics by George V. Hobart, and presented by a cast headed by Thomas Q. Seabrooke, Alexander Clark, Donald Brian, Charles Prince and Amelia Summerville.
—THERE'S A LITTLE STREET IN HEAVEN THEY CALL BROADWAY

1902. *THE MOCKING BIRD*
Book and lyrics by Sydney Rosenfeld, and starring Mabelle Gilman in a cast that included Grace Walton, Edgar Atchison-Ely and Walter Shannon.
—WHAT'S THE MATTER WITH THE MOON TONIGHT?
—SLY MUSETTE
—IN SILENCE
—THE LION AND THE MOUSE
—FRANCE GLORIOUS FRANCE
—JUST A KISS
—IF YOU COULDN'T CHANGE YOUR MIND
—THE RIGADOON
—A STALE WORLD AND A PALE WORLD
—ONE I LOVE THE OTHER I ABHOR
—FROM A DIFFERENT POINT OF VIEW
—A FLASH OF THE SKIPPER'S EYE
—THE KING OF FRANCE
—CARRIED OFF

1903. *THE WIZARD OF OZ*
With Paul Tietjens. Book and lyrics by L. Frank Baum, and starring Montgomery and Stone in a cast that included Anna Laughlin, Grace Kimball and Bessie Wynn.
—NICCOLO'S PICCOLO

—IN MICHIGAN
—CARRIE BARRY
—BALL OF ALL NATIONS
—STAR OF MY NATIVE LAND
Paul Tietjens contributed the following
numbers to this production:
—LIFE IN KANSAS
—ALAS FOR A MAN WITHOUT
BRAINS
—WHEN YOU LOVE, LOVE, LOVE
—POPPY CHORUS
—PHANTOM PATROL
—THE TRAVELER AND THE PIE
—I'VE WAITED IN LOVELAND FOR
YOU
During the run of "The Wizard Of Oz,"
the following songs were interpolated from
time to time:
—ROSALIE
By Will Cobb and Gus Edwards.
—I LOVE ONLY ONE GIRL IN THE
WIDE, WIDE WORLD
By Will Cobb and Gus Edwards.
—POCAHONTAS
By Vincent Bryan and Gus Edwards.
—SAMMY
By James O'Dea and Edward Hutchinson.
—HURRAH FOR BAFFIN'S BAY
By Vincent Bryan and Charles Zimmer-
man.
—FOOTBALL
By Vincent Bryan and Charles Zimmer-
man.

1904. *SERGEANT KITTY*
Book and lyrics by R. H. Burnside, and
starring Virginia Earle and Junie McCree.
—LOVE
—WAR
—WE ARE A GALLANT REGIMENT
—TRUE LOVE LIVES BUT IN OUR
DREAMS
—THE GIRL WE LEFT BEHIND
—THE ONE I LOVE BEST GAVE THAT
TO ME
—LOVE LAUGHS AT LOCKSMITHS
—JUST TAKE THINGS AS THEY
COME
—YOU NEVER KNOW WHAT'S GOING
TO HAPPEN NEXT
—NINON'S FATHER DOESN'T SEEM
TO MIND

1904. *LADY TEAZLE*
An operetta based on "The School For
Scandal" with book and lyrics by John
Kendrick Bangs and Roderic C. Penfield,
and starring Lillian Russell as Lady
Teazle in a cast that included William
Carleton as Sir Peter Teazle, Elsa Ryan

as Maria, Stanley Hawkins as Joseph Sur-
face and Van Rensselaer Wheeler as
Charles Surface.
—THE SMART SET
—THE HYPOCRITE
—YOU MUSTN'T DO THAT IN HIGH
SOCIETY
—THE SCANDAL CLUB
—CHARITY
—LOVE BY PROXY
—WERE I HAPPILY MARRIED
—THE POWER OF THE PRESS
—ROGER DE COVERLY
—THE GAY DIVORCEE
—HERE'S TO A BEAUTIFUL GIRL OF
FIFTEEN
—DEAR OLD LONDON TOWN
—THE CONSCIOUSNESS OF INNO-
CENCE
—THE DAINTY LITTLE MILLINER
—THE WHEREFORE AND THE WHY
—MACARONIS WE
—YOU LIED TO ME
—TITTLE-TATTLE
—WOULD YOU

1905. *THE GINGERBREAD MAN*
Book and lyrics by Frederic Ranken, and
starring Gus Weinberg in a cast that in-
cluded Frankie Bailey and Almyra Forrest.
—THAT AWFUL BOGIE MAN
—EVIL EYE
—MAZIE
—BEAUTIFUL LAND OF BON BON
—JOHN DOUGH
—OLD RAMESES
—NURSERY RHYMES
—MOON SONG
—EVERY LITTLE SOMETHING
—THE GINGERBREAD CADETS

1906. *COMING THRU THE RYE*
Book and lyrics by George V. Hobart, and
presented by a cast that included Dan
McAvoy, Frank Doane, John Park, Riley
Hatch, Alice Fisher and Amelia Stone.
—WHOA, BILL
—WHEN I LOVE
—I LOVE YOU BECAUSE YOU ARE
YOU
—MOTHER PIN A ROSE ON ME
By Bob Adams.
—MY LITTLE CANOE
—I DON'T WANT TO BE A SAILOR
—SPOON TIME
—MY BRONCHO BOY
—THEY ARE WAITING FOR ME
—FIJI
—THE SAND MAN

1906. *SEEING NEW YORK*
Book and lyrics by Joseph Hart and Clifton Crawford, and presented by a cast headed by Clifton Crawford and Carrie and Fleurette DeMar.
—THE ASTOR HOTEL
—TELL THE BAND TO PLAY AN IRISH TUNE
—MY BLUSHING ROSIE
—DIFFERENT GIRLS ON BROADWAY
—GENERAL BINGHAM'S BRIGADE
—THE SHADY SIDE OF BROADWAY
—THE MISFIT FAMILY HOWDY-DO
—I'M NOT PARTICULAR
—MISS DAISY'S GOWN
—THE MIMETIC DOLL

1907. *THE MIMIC AND THE MAID*
Book and lyrics by Allen Lowe, and presented by a cast headed by Gus Weinberg, Harry B. Watson, Dorothy Russell and Hattie Palmer.
—I'M GETTING SO PEEVISH
—HEY THERE BUSTER
—THAT'S ALL I WANT FOR MINE
—SUPERSTITION
—A FISH STORY
—OSCULATION

Alfred Solmon Score

1904. *PARIS BY NIGHT*
A musical comedy with book by Harry Marshall, and starring Ben Welch.
—IN GAY PAREE
—MANDY
—THAT HORRID MOSQUITO
—KING SOLOMON KNEW A THING OR TWO
—THE NAUGHTY SCARECROW
—IN LOVELAND
—KATERERINA
—OH, LOVE DIVINE
—A STUDY IN PINK
—CHANSONETTE
—WINE'S MY ONLY PLEASURE
—MY DEW DROP ROSIE
—TURN THOSE EYES AWAY
—THE GIRL WITH THE CHANGEABLE EYES
—ROAMING WITH THE ROMANS

Frederic Solomon Scores

1901. *THE SLEEPING BEAUTY AND THE BEAST*
With J. M. Glover. A musical extravaganza with book and lyrics by John J. McNally and J. Cheever Goodwin, and presented by a cast headed by Harry Bulger, Charles J. Ross, Joseph Cawthorn,

John Hyams and Viola Gillette.
—FAIRIES WE
—WAS EVER A DAINTIER INFANT SEEN?
—TAKE THY WAY TO EARTH
—CURE OR KILL
—HYGIENE
—MULTI-MILLIONAIRES
—THE ROYAL PAIR ARE OFF TODAY
—THE PRINCESS WE ADORE
—YEARS AGO
—DAY DREAMS
—LET THEM GO
—DROWSILY, DREAMILY
—BANG, BANG, BANG
—RIP VAN WINKLE WAS A LUCKY MAN
By William Jerome and Jean Schwartz.
—TELL ME DUSKY MAIDEN
By Bob Cole and J. Rosamond Johnson.
—COME OUT DINAH ON THE GREEN
By Bob Cole and J. Rosamond Johnson.
—NURSERY RHYMES
By William Jerome and Jean Schwartz.
—IT'S A DREAM THAT NEVER COMES TRUE
—B' GOSH!
—ONWARD
—VIVA LA LIBERTE
—THE OWL AND THE MOON
By Bob Cole and J. Rosamond Johnson.
—TAKE HER AWAY
—BY LOVE UNDYING CROWNED
—FLORA I'M YOUR ADORER
By Vincent Bryan.

1903. *MR. BLUEBEARD*
A musical extravaganza with book by John J. McNally, lyrics by J. Cheever Goodwin, and starring Eddie Foy in a cast that included Dan McAvoy, Flora Parker, Bonnie Maginn, William Danforth, Herbert Cawthorne and Bessie DeVoie.
—COME BUY OUR LUCIOUS FRUIT
—ORIENTAL SLAVES ARE WE
—WE COME FROM DALMACIA
—A MOST UNPOPULAR POTENTATE
—I'M AS GOOD AS I OUGHT TO BE
—THERE'S NOTHING LIKE THE LIFE WE SAILORS LEAD
—READ THE ANSWERS IN THE STARS
By Al Bryan and Nat Vincent.
—I'M A POOR UNHAPPY MAID
By William Jerome and Jean Schwartz.
—HAMLET WAS A MELANCHOLY DANE
By William Jerome and Jean Schwartz.
—MARRIAGE IS SUBLIME
By Al Bryan and Theodore Morse.

—DAYLIGHT IS DAWNING
—SONGBIRD OF MELODY LANE
By Al Bryan and Gus Edwards.
—THE BEER THAT MADE MILWAU-
KEE FAMOUS
By Dan McAvoy.
—IN THE PALE MOONLIGHT
—By Matt Woodword and Billy Jerome.
—WHEN THE C O L O R E D BAND
COMES MARCHING DOWN THE
STREET
By Bob Cole and J. Rosamond Johnson.
—THE OLD WOMAN WHO LIVED IN
A SHOE
By Al Bryan and Theodore Morse.
—LET US BE JOLLY AS LONG AS WE
CAN
—BILLY GREY, U. S. A.
By Will Cobb and Gus Edwards.
—JULIE
By William Jerome and Jean Schwartz.
—THE YANKEE TOURIST GIRL
By William Jerome and Matt Woodward.

John Philip Sousa Scores

1900. *CHRIS AND THE WONDERFUL
LAMP*
Book and lyrics by Glen MacDonough.
Co-starring Edna Wallace Hopper and
Jerome Sykes.
—THE FOURTH OF JULY
—THE PATTER OF THE SHINGLE
—I'M A HIGH-TONED GENII
—WE SENIORS ARE
—THE BOB-O-LINK
—THE COLLEGE OF HOOP-DEE-DOO
—IN POSTERLAND
—ABOVE THE SLIM MINARET
—MAMMA, PAPA
—SWEETHEART OF ALL THE WORDS
OF LOVE
—THE LAMP
—THE PATIENT EGG
—YOUNG TORAH TEP WAS THE BOY
FOR ME
—WHERE IS LOVE?
—HE COULDN'T DO A SINGLE THING
WITHOUT ME
—THE MAN BEHIND THE GUN
1906. *THE FREE LANCE*
Book and lyrics by Harry B. Smith, and
with a cast headed by Joseph Cawthorn,
Albert Hart and Nellie Bergen.
—AH LOVELY ART, WE WORSHIP
AT THY SHRINE
—THREE LOVE STORIES
—LET US GREET WITH JOY PRE-
TENDED

—WE DO IT ALL BY PROXY
—THE GOOSE GIRL
—I AM A POTENTATE
—FRIENDSHIP'S SACRED TOUCH
—IT DEPENDS ON THE HAIR
—LITTLE BAS BLEU
—COME, MY DEAR
—ON TO VICTORY
—THE EMPEROR'S WAR SONG
—THE MYSTERY OF HISTORY
—THE CARRIER PIGEON
—THE LEGEND OF THE SONS OF
SAMSON
—I AM A SALARIED WARRIOR
—CONUNDRUMS
—YOUTH MUST HAVE ITS FLING
—DRUMS ARE BEATING

Johann Strauss Score

1901. *VIENNA LIFE*
An operetta with book and lyrics by Glen
MacDonough, and presented by a cast
headed by Ethel Jackson and Raymond
Hitchcock.

Oscar Straus Scores

1908. *THE WALTZ DREAM*
An operetta with book and lyrics by Jo-
seph W. Herbert, and presented by a cast
headed by Charles Bigelow, Magda Dahl
(replaced by Vera Michelena), Joseph W.
Herbert, Harry Fairleigh, Edward John-
son (replaced by Frank Rushmore), So-
phie Brandt and Josie Sadler.
—KISSING TIME
—PICCOLO
—THE FAMILY'S ANCIENT TREE
—A HUSBAND'S LOVE
—A LESSON IN LOVE
—LIFE IS LOVE AND LAUGHTER
—LOVE CANNOT BE BOUGHT
—A SOLDIER STOLE HER HEART
—SWEETEST MAID OF ALL
—TWO IS PLENTY
—I'D RATHER STAY AT HOME
By C. H. Bovill and Jerome Kern.
—VIENNA
By Adrian Ross and Jerome Kern.
—LOVE'S ROUNDELAY
—WHEN THE SONG OF LOVE IS
HEARD
—I LOVE AND THE WORLD IS MINE
1909. *THE CHOCOLATE SOLDIER*
A musical version of Bernard Shaw's
comedy "The Arms And The Man" with
book and lyrics by Rudolph Bernauer and
Leopold Jacobson, and presented by a

cast headed by Ida Brooks Hunt as Na-
dina, Jack Gardner as Lieut. Brumerli,
William Pruette and Flavio Arcaro.
—THE CHOCOLATE SOLDIER
—COME, HERO MINE
—SYMPATHY
—THE BULGARIANS
—TRA-LA-LA
—THANK THE LORD THE WAR IS
OVER
—FALLING IN LOVE
—FORGIVE, FORGIVE
—THAT WOULD BE LOVELY
—THE LETTER SONG

John Stromberg Scores

1900. *FIDDLE-DEE-DEE*
Book and lyrics by Edgar Smith. For this
production DeWolf Hopper joined the
Weber and Fields cast that included Lil-
lian Russell, Fay Templeton, Bessie Clay-
ton, Bonnie Maginn, Charles J. Ross,
David Warfield and the producer-stars.
Burlesques on "Quo Vadis" and "Ari-
zona" were presented.
—COME ONE, COME ALL AND SEE
THE SIGHTS
—FETCH YOUR BABY HOME
—MY JAPANESE CHERRY BLOSSOM
—THE TIPS OF GAY PAREE
—I SIGH FOR A CHANGE
—COMIC OPERA
—JE NE LA COMPREND PAS
—MY BLUSHING ROSIE
—COME BACK MY HONEY BOY TO
ME
—THE LATEST CURE FOR ENNUI
—THAT'S ABOUT THE SIZE OF IT
—I'M A RESPECTABLE WORKING
GIRL
—BEAUTIFUL ARIZONA
—UNCLE SAM'S BOYS IN BLUE

1901. *HOITY-TOITY*
Book and lyrics by Edgar Smith. During
the run of this production, burlesques on
the following Broadway shows were pre-
sented: "The Message From Mars," "The
Girl and the Judge" and "DuBarry" by
a cast that included Weber and Fields,
DeWolf Hopper, Fritz Williams, Sam
Bernard, John T. Kelly, Lee Harrison,
Lillian Russell, Fay Templeton, Bonnie
Maginn and Bessie Clayton.
—DE PULLMAN PORTER'S BALL
—I'M AN AMERICAN BILLIONAIRE
—AS ON MOONLIT WAVES WE RIDE
—EASY MONEY
—KING KAZOO OF KAKAROO

—MARY BLACK
—POOR LITTLE FLUTTERING
MOTHS
—THE QUEEN OF SOCIETY
—WHEN TWO LITTLE HEARTS ARE
ONE
—THE MINSTREL SHOW
—LOVE A LA MODE
—MA POPPY BELLE
—DOWN THE LINE

1902. *TWIRLY WHIRLY*
Book and lyrics by Edgar Smith and Robert B. Smith. Willie Collier and his wife,
Louise Allen, joined the galaxy of Weber
and Fields' stars for this production, the
cast of which included Lillian Russell, Fay
Templeton, Peter Dailey, Bonnie Mag-
inn, Bessie Clayton and Mabel Barrison,
who was promoted from the chorus to a
speaking part. John Stromberg wrote the
following songs for "Twirly Whirly" be-
fore his death:
—PING PONG
—SUSIE WOOSIE
—DREAM ON DREAM OF ME
—COME DOWN MY EVENING STAR
William T. Francis, who completed the
score and replaced Stromberg in the or-
chestra pit, is credited with the following
numbers:
—ROMEO
—STRIKE OUT McCRACKEN
—IN STAGELAND
—KIT
—THE LONG GREEN
—LITTLE WIDOW BROWN
—I NEVER LOVED A MAN AS MUCH
AS THAT
—MY INTIMATE FRIEND
Lyrics by Wilton Lackeye. Lackeye, who
had written this last named song for Fay
Templeton, thought so well of it that he
recited the lyrics daily at the Lambs Club
throughout the summer, but his pride of
authorship suffered a shock two weeks before "Twirly Whirly" opened when Marie
Cahill introduced a similar song about
"her intimate friend" at the premiere per-
formance of "Sally in Our Alley." Perhaps it was a coincidence but no one ever
could convince Wilton Lackeye of that.

Leslie Stuart Scores

1900. *FLORODORA*
A musical comedy with book and lyrics
by Owen Hall, and presented by a cast
that included R. E. Graham as Gilfain,
Sydney Dean as Abercoed, Fannie John-

stone as Dolores, Edna Wallace Hopper as Lady Holyrood, William Edouin as Tweedle Punch, Cyril Scott as Donegal and the famous Florodora Sextet: Margaret Walker, Marjorie Relyea, Daisy Green, Vaughn Texsmith, Marie L. Wilson and Agnes Wayburn.
—TACT
—SILVER STAR OF LOVE
—QUEEN OF THE PHILIPPINE ISLE
—THE FELLOW WHO MIGHT
—SHADE OF THE PALM
—I WANT TO BE A MILITARY MAN
—TELL ME PRETTY MAIDEN
—PHRENOLOGY
—SOMEBODY
—WHEN I'M A MILLIONAIRE
—COME AND SEE OUR ISLAND
—GALLOPING
—COME, MY DOLORES
—THE CREDIT'S DUE TO ME
—WHEN I LEAVE TOWN
—I WANT TO MARRY A MAN, I DO
—WHEN AN INTERFERING PERSON
—HE LOVES ME, HE LOVES ME NOT
—WILLIE WAS A GAY BOY
—WHEN WE ARE ON THE STAGE
—THE ISLAND OF LOVE

1902. *THE SILVER SLIPPER*
A musical comedy with book by Owen Hall and Clay M. Green, lyrics by W. H. Risque, and presented by a cast that included Edna Wallace Hopper, Josie Sadler, Cyril Scott and Sam Bernard.
—INVITATION TO VENUS
—GLIMPSE
—TONIGHT'S THE NIGHT
—FUN ON A MOTOR
—TWO EYES OF BLUE
—IF I WERE A GIRL INSTEAD
—THE BABY WITH THE DIMPLE AND THE SMILE
—THE DETRIMENTAL MAN
—PING PONG DUET
—COME LITTLE GIRL
—BECAUSE I LOVE YOU DEAR
—FOUR AND TWENTY LITTLE MEN
—CLASS
—MY CELIA
By John Golden and Jerome Kern.

1904. *THE SCHOOL GIRL*
A musical comedy with book and lyrics by Paul Potter and Henry Hamilton, and starring Edna May in a cast that included George Grossmith, Jr.
—A HONEYMOON GIRL
—WHEN I WAS A GIRL
—DAUGHTERS OF THE GUARD

—AMERICAN GIRLS
—BELINDA ON THE TELEPHONE
—NEEDLE IN A HAYSTACK
—AN ENGLISH GIRL
—CALL AROUND AGAIN
—DAYS OF ROMANCE
—MY LITTLE CANOE
—SIMPLER
—JOLLY LITTLE JAPS
—MY COSEY CORNER GIRL
By John W. Bratton.
—ONE OF THE BOYS
Music by Howard Talbot.
—IN BLACK AND WHITE
By Paul West and J. W. Bratton.
—REAL TOWN LADY
Music by Paul Rubens.
—THE ENGLISH CAKE WALK
Music by Paul Rubens.

1906. *THE BELLE OF MAYFAIR*
A musical comedy with book by Charles H. E. Brookfield, lyrics by Cosmo Hamilton, and starring Christie MacDonald in a cast that included Irene Bentley, Bessie Clayton, Valeska Suratt, Jack Gardner, Ignacio Martinetti and Van Rensselaer Wheeler.
—AND THE WEEPING WILLOW WEPT
—COME TO ST. GEORGE'S
—WHY DO THEY CALL ME A GIBSON GIRL?
Lyrics by Leslie Stiles.
—BELLS IN THE MORNING
—EIGHT LITTLE DEBUTANTES ARE WE
—HELLO, COME ALONG, GIRLS
—I AM A MILITARY MAN
—I KNOW A GIRL
—I'M A DUCHESS
—IN GAY MAYFAIR
—MY LITTLE GIRL IS A SHY LITTLE GIRL
—WHAT MAKES THE WOMAN?
—WHERE YOU GO WILL I GO
—SAID I TO MYSELF
—MY LADY FAIR
—WE'VE COME FROM COURT
—A LITTLE GIRL AT THE SWEET SHOP

1909. *HAVANA*
A musical comedy with book by George Goldsmith, Graham Hill and James T. Powers, lyrics by Adrian Ross and George Arthurs, and starring James T. Powers in a cast that included Edith Decker, Eva Davenport, Ernest Lambert, Clara Palmer, William Pruette and Ernest Hare.
—THE YACHT

—MY HUSBAND
—HELLO PEOPLE
—WOULD YOU LIKE TO MOTOR WITH MATER?
—CUPID'S TELEPHONE
—LITTLE MISS QUETTE
—THE SLOPES OF DENMARK HILL
—FILIBUSTER BROWN
—WAY DOWN IN PENSACOLA
—A LITTLE SUPPER FOR TWO
—I'M A CUBAN GIRL

Sir Arthur Sullivan Scores

1900. *THE ROSE OF PERSIA*
An operetta with book and lyrics by Capt. Basil Hood, and presented by a cast headed by Charles Angelo and Ruth Vincent.

1902. *THE EMERALD ISLE*
This light opera with book and lyrics by Capt. Basil Hood was the last one to be written by Sir Arthur Sullivan, who died before its completion, and the score was finished by Edward German. The cast was headed by Jefferson deAngelis and included W. T. Carleton, Helena Frederick, Kate Condon and Amelia Fields.
—HAVE YOU HEARD THE BRAVE NEWS?
—A SAXON STRANGER
—I'M DESCENDED FROM BRIAN BORU
—OF VICEROY'S WE'VE HAD
—IF TO WISH TO APPEAR AS AN IRISH TYPE
—ON THE HEIGHTS OF GLENTANN
—TWO'S COMPANY, THREE'S NONE
—I AM THE LORD LIEUTENANT
—AT AN EARLY STAGE OF LIFE
—OH, SETTING SUN
—THEY'VE COURAGE HIGH
—THAT WE'RE SOLDIERS
—IT IS PAST MY COMPREHENSION
—MANY YEARS AGO
—THEIR FATHERS FOUGHT
(This is an incomplete listing of song titles, since the only program available was mutilated.—The Author.)

Dan Sullivan Score

1907. *MISS POCAHONTAS*
With Augustus Barratt and Carl Willimore. A musical comedy with book and lyrics by R. A. Barnet and R. M. Baker, and presented by a cast headed by Walter Jones, Blanche Deyo, Violet Zell, Lester Allen and Marie Dupois.

—MY LITTLE CARIBOU
—CAPTAIN KIDD

Howard Talbot Scores

1902. *A CHINESE HONEYMOON*
A musical comedy with book and lyrics by George Dance, and starring Thomas Q. Seabrooke in a cast that included William Pruette, Van Rensselaer Wheeler, Adele Richie and Annie Yeamans.
—IN YIANG-YIANG
—ROLY POLY
—A PAPER FAN
—COULD I BUT TELL YOU
—THE EMPEROR HANG CHOW
—A CHINESE HONEYMOON
—THE A-LA GIRL
—NURSERY RHYMES
By William Jerome and Jean Schwartz.
—THE TWIDDLEY BITS
—A ROYAL HONEYMOON
—WITH WEARY HEARTS
—I WANT TO BE A LAIDY
—THE LEADER OF FROCKS AND FRILLS
—WELCOME OFFICIAL MOTHER-IN-LAW
—TID BITS FROM THE PLAYS
—MARTHA SPANKS THE GRAND PIANNER
—MR. DOOLEY
By William Jerome and Jean Schwartz.

1907. *THE GIRL BEHIND THE COUNTER*
A musical comedy with book by Edgar Smith, lyrics by Arthur Anderson, and presented by a cast headed by Lew Fields, Louise Dresser, Lotta Faust, George Beban, Ignacio Martinetti and Vernon Castle.
—WHEN YOU STEAL A KISS OR TWO
By Kenneth S. Clark.
—THE ENTERPRISING FRENCHMAN
—IF YOU'LL WALK WITH ME
—AH! EH! OH!
—SHOPPING
—THE MINSTREL SHOW
—THE BANDBOX GIRL
—WON'T YOU BUY?
—FRIVOLITY
—THE GLOW WORM
By Paul Lincke.
—PASSING BY
—THE CHERRY IN THE GLASS
—NOW I'VE MARRRIED A MILLION-AIRE
—THE WAY OF TRADE
—I WANT TO BE LOVED LIKE A

LEADING LADY
By Paul West and Herman Wade.

1909. *THE BELLE OF BRITTANY*
With Marie Horne. A musical comedy
with book by P. J. Barron and Leedom
Bantock, lyrics by Percy Greenbank, and
presented by a cast headed by Frank
Daniels and Francis Kennedy.
—THE BOIS D'AMOUR
—IT'S TOO LATE NOW
—DAFFODIL TIME
—THE TRYSTING TREE
—I'M NOT A LADY'S MAID
—I MUST GO HOME TONIGHT
—THE STEPPING STONES
—THE DOGGIES AND THE BONE
—THE GIRL WITH THE CLOCKING
ON HER STOCKING
—TWO GIDDY GOATS
—WREATHE THE GOLDEN FLOWERS
—THE BEST BRITTANY
—THE OLD CHATEAU
—LITTLE COUNTRY MICE
—IN THE OVEN
—THE DAWN OF LOVE

Egbert Van Alstyne Score

1909. *A BROKEN IDOL*
Book by Hal Stephens, lyrics by Harry
Williams, and presented by a cast headed
by Alice Yorke, Forrest Huff and Otis
Harlan.
—CURED
—CHINA DOLL
—LOVE MAKES THE WORLD GO
ROUND
—HAPPY DAYS
—THE SIGN OF A HONEYMOON
—POOR OLD DAD IN NEW YORK FOR
THE SUMMER
—YANKEE LAND
—ALABAMA
—UP IN A BALLOON

Harry Von Tilzer Score

1903. *THE FISHER MAIDEN*
Book and lyrics by Arthur Lamb, and
presented by a cast headed by Al Shean,
George A. MacFarlane, Edna Bronson,
Bessie Tannehill, Dorothy Jardon and
Frances Cameron.
—OH, MARJORIE
—LAUGHING SONG
—I'M IN LOVE WITH THE BUGS
—LET THE BAND PLAY
—IN A BEAUTIFUL DISTANT LAND
—WE'RE SECRET SOCIETY MEMBERS
—HE DANGLED ME ON HIS KNEE

—MAYDEE (PRETTY LITTLE SOUTH
SEA ISLAND LADY)
—UNDER THE MULBERRY TREE
—A DAUGHTER OF THE MOON AM I
—THE HIGHLY IMPORTANT FLY
—ROSES FOR THE GIRL I LOVE
—DOWN ON A SOUTH SEA ISLE
—A SAIL ON THE TAIL OF A WHALE
—WHEN YOU GO DOWN TO LONDON
TOWN
—COO-EE, COO-EE
—SECRET SOCIETY

Henry Waller Score

1902. *FAD AND FOLLY*
A musical comedy with book by Safford
Waters and Rupert Hughes, lyrics by
Paul West, and presented by a cast head-
ed by Harry Conor, Richard Lambert,
Blanche Ring and Kathleen Clifford.
—THERE'S A STRANGE FASCINATION
ABOUT THE STAGE
—THE BELLE OF AVENUE A
—SALLY
—I COME FROM SUNNY DIXIE
—WHAT'S IT ALL ABOUT?
—DOING WELL
—TRY, TRY AGAIN
—RUN, BOY, RUN
—MICROBES
—LOVERS' ROOST
By George "Honey Boy" Evans.
—SHE'LL DO
—THE SMOKE GOES UP THE CHIM-
NEY JUST THE SAME
By Frank Chandler.
—SHE READ THE NEW YORK PAPERS
EVERY DAY
Music by John H. Bratton.
—CHANSONETTES
—I'SE BEEN A-LOOKIN' FOR YOU
Music by W. F. Peters.
—MY KIMONA QUEEN
By Henry Blossom and W. F. Peters.

Safford Waters Scores

1902. *TOMMY ROT*
A musical comedy with book by Rupert
Hughes, Joseph Herbert, Paul West and
Kirke LeShelle, lyrics by the composer,
and presented by a cast headed by Flet-
cher Norton, Blanche Ring and Evelyn
Florence Nesbitt.
—HISTORY CLASS
—EVERY DOG MUST HAVE HIS DAY
AND EVERY PUSS HER AFTER-
NOON
—I WANT TO BE ONE OF THE SMART
SET

—THE ONLY THING THAT MAKES LIFE WORTH LIVING
—IN THE PRESS
—THERE'S A STRANGE FASCINATION ABOUT THE STAGE
—SHE USED TO TAKE ME ON HER KNEE
—THE HIT OF THE SEASON
—MIKE McCARTHY'S WAKE
—OH, FOR A GREAT IDEA!
—THE BELLE OF AVENUE A
—AN ACTRESS AND A LADY
—ISLAND OF LOVE
—SALLY
—WHEN THE GIRLS COME BACK TO TOWN
—I COME FROM SUNNY DIXIE
—BOO-RA-BOO

1908. *FUNABASHI*
A musical comedy with book by Irvin Cobb, lyrics by Paul West, Carolyn Wells, Wallace Irwin, Vincent Rose, Ted Snyder and the composer, and presented by a cast headed by Joseph Miron, Walter Percival, Alice Fischer, Vera Michelena, Percy Ames, William Rock and Maude Fulton.
—IN OLD JAPAN
—THE DEAR OLD STORY
—A LITTLE JAPAN LADY
—THE GIRL BEHIND THE MAN BEHIND THE GUN
—HI YAH
—AMBASSADOR OF PEACE
—FOR A GIRL CAN LOVE A SAILOR
—WHEN THERE ISN'T A GIRL ABOUT
—IT'S ONLY A PIECE OF ADVICE
—BOO-RA-BOO
—DIPLOMATS
—FLIRTATION
—I WALKED AROUND
—THE BUTTERFLY AND THE ROSE
—I'VE BEEN DISCHARGED BY THEM ALL
—I'D GUESS YOU
—THE ISLAND OF LOVE
—MY MATRIMONIAL BON BON
—ONE, TWO, THREE—DOWN AND OUT
—HER BAGGAGE WAS CHECKED FOR TROY
—MISS YANKEE DOODLE

Alfred G. Walthall Score

1902. *THE SULTAN OF SULU*
A musical comedy with book and lyrics by George Ade, and presented by a cast headed by Frank Moulan, Templar Saxe,

Maude Lillian Berri and Gertrude Quinlan.
—SALUTE
—THE QUEER LITTLE OSTRICH
—HIKE
—PALM BRANCHES WAVING
—THE PEACHY TEACHER
—SMILING ISLE
—OH, WHAT A BUMP!
—ENGAGED IN A SORT OF WAY
—IF I BUT KNEW
—MY SULU LULU LOU
—TILL THE VOLUNTEERS RETURN
—SLUMBER ON
—R-E-M-O-R-S-E
—IMPERIAL GUARDS' MARCH
—THE OLD JAY BIRD
—SINCE I FIRST MET YOU
—ALWAYS LATE
—ROSABELLA CLANCY
—COME BACK TO MANISTEE
—FOOLISH WEDDING BELLS

Bert Williams Songs

1900. *THE POLICY SHOP*
A comedy with an all-Negro cast headed by Williams and Walker.
—GHOST OF A COON
—WHY DON'T YOU GET A LADY OF YOUR OWN?
—I DON'T LIKE NO CHEAP MAN
—HE'S UP AGAINST THE REAL THING NOW

Isadore Witmark Score

1902. *THE CHAPERONS*
A musical comedy with book and lyrics by Frederick Ranken, and presented by a cast headed by Trixie Friganza, May Boley, Eva Tanguay, Harry Conor, Walter Jones and Joseph C. Miron.
—MY SAMBO
This was Eva Tanguay's first big song hit.
—EGYPT LAND
—IT SEEMS LIKE YESTERDAY
—TALK, TALK, TALK
—BOIS D'BOULOGNE
—IN MY OFFICIAL CAPACITY
—WE'RE ALL GOOD FELLOWS
—SOMEHOW IT MAKES ME THINK OF HOME
—HAPPY WHEN WE EAT
—VIVE LA BOHEMIA

Max S. Witt Score

1905. *THE DUKE OF DULUTH*
A musical comedy with book and lyrics by George Broadhurst, and starring Nat

M. Wills, the tramp comedian.
—THE LAND OF WOT   —ZENEDEE
—THERE'S ONE SWEETHEART I'LL
  NEVER FORGET
—WHILE IN MY SUBMARINE
—MY DAINTY DRESDEN SHEPERDESS
—NICODEMUS   —STRENUOUS
—IF MY MAN COULD DO IT FOR ME
—MY SWEET WILD ROSE
—NO PEACH HANGS TOO HIGH FOR
  HIM THEN   —ROSITA
—THROUGH ALL ETERNITY
—DEATH OR VICTORY   —G.O.P.

E. M. Ziehrer Score

1908. *MLLE. MISCHIEF*
A musical comedy with book and lyrics
by Sydney Rosenfeld, and presented by
a cast headed by Lulu Glaser, Alexander
Clark, W. T. Carleton, Elizabeth Brice
and Josie and Ethel Intropodi.
—THE ARMY CORPS
—LADIES BEWARE
—I DON'T CARE, DO YOU?
—THE JOY DUET   —SWEETHEART
—SHE KNEW A THING OR TWO
—AND OTHER THINGS
—VERILY, MERRILY
—LE COEUR de NINON
—EVERY HOUR BRINGS ITS FLOWER
—A SINGLE DAY —MY OWN VIENNA

Composite Scores

1900. *MADGE SMITH, ATTORNEY*
A farce by Ramsey Morris with songs by
A. Baldwin Sloane, James O'Dea, Ernest
Hogan, Theodore Northrup, Dave Reed,
Jr. and Francis Bryant, and starring Mae
Irwin in a cast that included Ignacio
Martinetti.
—WHY DON'T THE BAND PLAY?
—I'VE GOT TROUBLES OF MY OWN
—I AIN'T GONNA WORK NO MORE
—OUI, OUI MAMOISELLE
—WHEN I'M BY HER SIDE
—I'VE LAID HIM ON THE SHELF
—BULL-FROG BEN
—GIVE ME BACK MY LIZA
—I'M GWINE TO MARRY ANGELINE
—THE TURKEY AND THE TURK
1902. *THE WILD ROSE*
A musical comedy with book by Harry
B. Smith, lyrics by George V. Hobart,
and starring Eddie Foy in a cast that
included Albert Hart, Junie McCree,
Irene Bentley, Marguerite Clark and
Marie Cahill. One of the chorus girls was

Evelyn Nesbitt, who later married Harry
Kendall Thaw and became the *cause
celebre* in the sensational Stanford White
murder.
—I MUST HAVE BEEN SVENGALI IN
  DISGUISE
By Vincent Bryan and Harry Von Tilzer.
—SMILES, SMILES, SMILES.
By William H. Penn.
—THOSE THINGS CANNOT BE EX-
  PLAINED
By Junie McCree and Ben Jerome.
—THE WORLD OF A STAR
Music by Melville Ellis.
—I'M UNLUCKY
By William Jerome and Jean Schwartz.
—NANCY BROWN
By Clifton Crawford.
—MY LITTLE GYPSY MAID
By Paul Lawrence Dunbar and Will
Marion Cook.

1903. *MOTHER GOOSE*
A musical extravaganza with book by
John J. McNally, lyrics by George V.
Hobart, and presented by a cast headed
by Joseph Cawthorn, Harry Bulger, Clif-
ton Crawford, Pat Rooney and Leila Mc-
Intyre.
—RAFFERTY
By Clifton Crawford.
—UNDER THE MISTLETOE BOUGH
By Will Heelan and Fred Helf.
—OUR GOOSE HAS A MINT IN HER
  LITTLE INSIDES
Music by Frederic Solomon.
—WHEN I DO THE HIGHLAND FLING
By Will Heelan and Fred Helf.
—LAUGHING WATER
By Fred Hager and George Totten Smith.
—SOCIAL ECLAT
By Clifton Crawford.
—SWEETER DEN SUGAR CANE
By Billy Johnson.
—GIRLS WILL BE GIRLS AND BOYS
  WILL BE BOYS
Music by Frederic Solomon.
—THE TIME TO LOVE
Music by Frederic Solomon.
—ALWAYS LEAVE 'EM LAUGHIN'
  WHEN YOU SAY GOODBYE
By George M. Cohan.
—I WANT TO HEAR A YANKEE
  DOODLE TUNE
By George M. Cohan.
—WE MARCHED AWAY
Music by Frederic Solomon.
—PANSY FACES
By William H. Penn.

—EVERYBODY'S LOVED BY SOME-
ONE
Music by Frederic Solomon.
—I DON'T WANT TO BE A LADY
By E. H. Glover.
—THE STORY ADAM TOLD TO EVE
By William Jerome and Jean Schwartz.
—THE ROSE OF THE RIVIERA
Music by Frederic Solomon.
—STILL IN THE OLD FRONT LINE
By Mathew Woodward.
1903. *A GIRL FROM DIXIE*
A musical comedy with book and lyrics
by Harry B. Smith, songs by Theodore
Northrup, Ben Jerome, Max Witt, A.
Baldwin Sloane, Will Marion Cook and
Kerry Mills, and presented by a cast that
included Irene Bentley, Arnold Daly, Al-
bert Hart, Charles H. Bowers and Evelyn
Nesbitt.
—DIXIE LAND
—LOVE IN AN ORCHARD
—THE LOVER'S A-B-C
—MARY FROM MARYLAND
—THE DISSIPATED KITTEN
—THE SUNFLOWER AND THE SUN
—WHEN THE MOON COMES OVER
THE HILL
By Bob Cole and J. Rosamond Johnson.
—GLORY   —AN AMERICAN HEIRESS
—BUBBLES   —HAPPY DAYS IN DIXIE
—WAY DOWN SOUTH   —HONEY

1905. *THE ROLLICKING GIRL*
A musical comedy with book and lyrics
by Sydney Rosenfeld, and presented by a
cast headed by Sam Bernard, Harry Fair-
leigh, Hattie Williams, Edna Goodrich.
—TRICKS
By Paul West and John W. Bratton.
—MIRANDA
By Clare Kummer.
—THE INDIANS ALONG BROADWAY
By Benjamin Hapgood Burt.
—WON'T YOU BE MY LOVEY DOVEY?
By E. P. Moran and Seymour Furth.
—MY CABIN DOOR
By Grant Stewart and Tom Lemonier.
—THE GIRL I LEFT IN BOSTON
TOWN
By J. W. Bratton, Douglas and Ernie Ball.
—FRIENDS THAT ARE GOOD AND
TRUE
By Vernon Roy and Edmund Eysler.
—AS WE SWING SWEETHEART
Music by W. T. Francis.
—THE CONTENTED CATERPILLAR
Music by William T. Francis.
—WHEN LOVE BEGINS

Music by William T. Francis.
—THE LIFE OF LOVE
Music by William T. Francis.
—MY LITTLE SUNBEAM SUE
—Music by William T. Francis.
1907. *ZIEGFELD FOLLIES OF 1907*
The premiere of America's most famous
musical revue, staged at the Casino de
Paris, with a cast headed by Harry Wat-
son Jr., George Bickel, Dave Lewis, Grace
LaRue, Charles J. Ross, Emma Carus,
Florence Tempest, Marion Sunshine,
Prince Tokio, Helen Broderick and Mlle.
Dazie. Book by Harry B. Smith.
—POCAHONTAS
By Edgar Selden and Seymour Furth.
—BANDBOX GIRL
—CIGARETTE
By Vincent Bryan, Gertrude Hoffman.
—THE MAN WHO BUILT SUBWAY
—I WANT TO BE A DRUMMER BOY
By Matt Woodward and Silvio Hein.
—REINCARNATION
By Vincent Bryan and E. Ray Goetz.
—IN THE GRAND OLD SANDS
By Will Cobb and Gus Edwards.
—THE GIBSON BATHING GIRLS
By Paul West and Alfred Solmon.
—COME AND FLOAT ME, FREDDIE
DEAR
By Vincent Bryan and E. Ray Goetz.
—I THINK I OUGHTN'T AUTO ANY
MORE
By Vincent Bryan and E. Ray Goetz.
—MISS GINGER OF JAMAICA
By Billy Gaston.
—HANDLE ME WITH CARE
By William Jerome and Jean Schwartz.
—I DON'T WANT AN AUTO
—BUDWEISER'S A FRIEND OF MINE
By Vincent Bryan and Seymour Furth.
—BYE, BYE DEAR OLD BROADWAY
By Will Cobb and Gus Edwards.

Revivals of 1900-1910

1900. *THE VICEROY* with the Bostonians.
1900. *ROBIN HOOD* with the Bostonians.
1900. *THE SERENADE* with the Bostonians.
1902. *ROBIN HOOD* with the Bostonians.
1903. *ERMINE* with Francis Wilson, Jessie
Bartlett Davis and Marguerite Sylva.
1904. *WANG* with DeWolf Hopper, William Pruette and Madge Lessing.
1904. *FATINITZA, GIROFLE-GIROFLA*
and *BOCCACCIO,* all starring Fritzi
Scheff.

1. Gertrude Lawrence (*The King and I*). 2. *South Pacific.*

Richard Rodgers and his lyricist, Oscar Hammerstein II, have enriched post-war years with enduring music, and a newcomer to Broadway, Frank Loesser, gives promise of future greatness.

A Decade of Opulent Revues
(1910-1920)

Just as George M. Cohan, fired by patriotic zeal and the pioneering urge, had raised Old Glory to the top of the musical comedy flagstaff in the 1900s, Florenz Ziegfeld in the second decade of the new century blazed a fresh trail through the tangled wildwood of the Made-in-America revue that led to green and fertile fields of perfection.

There can be no doubt but that the times were made-to-order for the type of entertainment that not only glorified "the glorifier of the American girl" himself but dominated the Broadway theaters where musical shows were staged during this period. It was the era of the Stutz Bear Cat and the Bunny Hug, when the speed cop asked the duster-clad motorist: "Who do you think you are? Barney Oldfield?". The tempo of our national life had quickened and took its beat from the syncopated strains of *Alexander's Ragtime Band*. Father Knickerbocker had discarded the silver-buckled slippers he'd worn to the premiere of *The Beggar's Opera* for dancing shoes in a desire to emulate the latest dance steps introduced by Vernon and Irene Castle, Harry Fox and the Dolly Sisters, Maurice Movet and Florence Walton and Clifton Webb and Mae Murray. And the *Ziegfeld Follies* and other Broadway revues that imitated but never equalled Ziggy's lavish productions matched in speed the accelerated pace of a people who were going places and getting there fast—audiences fed up on comic operas with settings in mythical countries, leisurely waltzes, inevitable Dutch comedians and oriental potentates, and such anaemic jokes as:

Girl: You'd better not cross my father. He's got acute indigestion.

Boy: He's got a cute daughter, too.

A master showman without regard for money and a perfectionist in working out the minutest detail in a production number, Ziegfeld was a connoisseur of color and fabrics as well as of feminine pulchritude, and with Joseph Urban as his scenic designer, struck a new and astounding note in theatrical decor with opulent settings, towering arches and spectacular stairways down which his hand-picked lovelies, trailing ostrich plumes, cloth-of-gold and regal ermine, walked in majestic splendor.

Ziegfeld, who "examined costume material like a virtuoso handling a Stradivarius", according to Eddie Cantor, and whose affection for white, pink and gold amounted to a passion, also had a knowing eye for great but unheralded talent, and his marquee boards during this period carried the names of such brilliant stars as Fanny Brice, Ann Pennington, Marilyn Miller, Bert Williams, W. C. Fields, Eddie Cantor, Will Rogers, Leon Errol and Ed Wynn —all but Williams being newcomers to the Broadway stage.

But Ziegfeld had one vulnerable spot—a poor ear for music, and the songs from the early *Follies* ran a poor second to the sirens and comic skits that were the nucleus of his revues. But this deficiency was corrected later by Louis A. Hirsch, a Johnny-come-lately to the Broadway scene who is credited with three *Follies'* scores during this period; Raymond Hubbell, who contributed the music to five Ziegfeld shows in addition to four New York Hippodrome productions and ten other musicals; and Irving Berlin, whose songs in the 1919 *Follies,* which included *Mandy, A Pretty Girl Is Like A Melody, You Cannot Make Your Shimmy Shake On Tea* and *You'd Be Surprised,* matched the comedians and chorus as box office lure.

In fact, the author-composer of *Alexander's Ragtime Band* became a double-threat man of music during this period—a pop song writer with the versatility to create best-selling tunes for both the stage and the five-and-dime store masses. Teeing off in 1914 with *Watch Your Step,* starring the Castles and the first Broadway musical with an all-syncopated score, Berlin followed through with *Stop, Look and Listen, The Century Girl* and *Dance And Grow Thin* and then introduced a Broadway innovation in *Yip, Yip, Yaphank,* an all-soldier revue he wrote and produced while serving as a sergeant in the U. S. Army and the pattern for his more pretentious *This Is The Army* of World War II.

Although Florenz Ziegfeld was the champ in the musical revue division, he had his challengers, the most ambitious of whom were the Shuberts, who had a KO punch in the person of Al Jolson, whose dynamic personality and ability to sell a song emptied the ticket racks nightly at the Winter Garden, erected on the site of the old Seventh Avenue horse car barns and like the Casino, dedicated to the presentation of musical productions on the night of its gala opening in 1911.

While Jolson owned the stage apron and the runway of this playhouse, the fame of the Winter Garden was not founded on the popularity of the Mammy Singer alone. Here Willie Howard achieved stardom; Fred and Adele Astaire made their Broadway debut in *Over The Top;* Mistinguette, the sweetheart of Paris, and her million-dollar legs had their American premiere; and Gaby Deslys, the darling of a Spanish monarch, got word-of-mouth billing as "chicken a la king".

Neither did all the celebrities on the Shubert payroll score their triumphs on the Winter Garden stage, and one who contributed much to the success of the Winter Garden productions was a young civil engineer from Hungary, who came to this country in 1909 with the idea of spanning our broad rivers with majestic bridges. Instead, he turned to music in order to eat, bridged the years with enduring melodies, and became the most prolific of Broadway musical composers with scores and songs for seventy-nine productions now to his credit. His pay checks were made out to Sigmund Romberg, and in the last six years of the 1910-1920 period alone, he wrote the music for twenty-five productions, including *Dancing Around, Robinson Crusoe Jr.* and *Sinbad,* three shows in which Jolson starred; five *Passing Shows* and two operettas, *The Blue Paradise* and *Maytime.*

Almost as prolific as Romberg during this period was Jerome Kern, who wrote the scores for twenty-one productions, the most notable of which were the highly popular *The Girl From Utah* in which Julia Sanderson sang *They Didn't Believe Me; Very Good Eddie, Oh, Boy* and *Leave It To Jane.* Harry Tierney first crashed the Broadway gate with the music he wrote for *Irene,* which in 1919 shattered the long-run record set by *A Night In Chinatown* in 1893. Rudolf Friml also got off to a flying start with *The Firefly,* but Cole Porter was not as fortunate. His first Broadway musical, *See America First,* only played for two weeks, and its frustrated composer sought to hide his tarnished identity in the ranks of the French Foreign Legion.

At the close of the decade, Florenz Ziegfeld, who had set a new theatrical pace with his *Follies,* faced even stronger competition than that offered by the Winter Garden shows with the birth of two new annual revues: *The Greenwich Village Follies* and *George White's Scandals,* which while lacking the craftsmanship and opulence of the master's productions, introduced far superior songs except when Ziggy entrusted the writing of his music to Irving Berlin.

In this fast-moving era dominated by the fast-moving revue, the graduates of the Viennese school of music trailed in the popularity derby, and while eight of Franz Lehar's operettas were produced on Broadway during this decade, none captivated the American audience as had *The Merry Widow.* Ivan Caryll's *The Pink Lady* in which Hazel Dawn sung *Beautiful Lady* to her own violin accompaniment, Emmerich Kalman's *Sari* and Heinrich Reinhardt's *The Spring Maid* were the only foreign importations that played to consistently packed houses, and while Victor Herbert had four box office successes in *Naughty Marietta, Sweethearts, The Only Girl* and *Eileen* out of a total of fourteen productions, his star had started to wane. He could put as much schmaltz in a valse as Johann Strauss, but he wasn't hep to the pep that made *Swanee* a best-seller at the music counters and marked its composer, George Gershwin, as a man of supreme genius, who was about to take the slattern, jazz, out of the brothels and barrelhouses of New Orleans and transform her into a cultured lady of bewitching charm.

Alfred E. Aarons Score

1910. *THE DEACON AND THE LADY*
The first Broadway appearance of Ed
Wynn in a cast that included Harry
Kelly, Eva Fallon, Fletcher Norton and
Clara Palmer. Book and lyrics by John
Totten Smith.
—DREAMS
—I WANT A WIFE
—MR. TANNHAUSER
—OMAR
—MODEST MAZIE

Felix Albini Scores

1910. *MADAME TROUBADOR*
A musical comedy with book and lyrics
by Joseph Herbert, and presented by a
cast headed by Grace LaRue, Georgia
Caine, Anna Wheaton, Edgar Atchinson-
Ely and Van Rensselaer Wheeler.
—CHIMES NUMBER
—I'LL GO TO GAY PAREE
—OH HOW THAT TAXI GOT ON MY
NERVES
—YESTERDAY AND TODAY
—DON'T BE RASH, RAGE IS BLIND
—MADAME TROUBADOR
—TROU-TROU-BA-BA-TROUBADOUR

1912. *BARON TRENCK*
With Alfred G. Robyn. A comic opera
with book by Henry Blossom, lyrics by
Frederick E. Schrader, and presented by
a cast that included John Slavin, Blanche
Duffield and Ethel Dufre Houston.
—WE'RE BOLD, BAD BANDITS
—CUPID IS A CRUEL MASTER
—MY HEART'S MINE OWN
—WHEN I GET MARRIED
—I'D LIKE TO BE A SOLDIER GAY
—I'M FROM THE COURT OF THE
EMPRESS QUEEN
—TRENCK IS MY NAME
—INCOGNITO
—THIS HANDSOME SOLDIER IS TOO
BOLD
—WITH SONG AND CHEER
—ANGEL, AT LAST I FIND YOU
—IN MERRY, MERRY MAY
—WHEN THE ELVES HOLD MAS-
QUERADE

Will R. Anderson Score

1919. *TAKE IT FROM ME*
A musical comedy with book and lyrics
by Will B. Johnstone, and presented by a
cast headed by Vera Michelena.

—THE CALL OF A COZY LITTLE
HOME
—TAKE IT FROM ME
—GOOD, BAD, BEAUTIFUL BROAD-
WAY
—THE TANGLEFOOT
—I LOVE TO LINGER IN THE LIN-
GERIE
—TOMORROW
—CAMOUFLAGE
—EXPLANATIONS
—LOVE EFFICIENCY
—WHAT MAKES THE TIRED BUSI-
NESS MAN SO TIRED?
—BEWARE
—A PENNY FOR YOUR THOUGHTS
—TO HAVE AND TO HOLD

Harry Auracher Score

1912. *THE PEARL MAIDEN*
A musical comedy with book by Earle C.
Anthony, lyrics by Arthur F. Kales, and
presented by a cast headed by Flora Za-
belle and Jefferson DeAngelis.
—CLOUDLAND
—CORAL ISLE
—I AM LONELY FOR YOU
—IF ONE LITTLE GIRL LOVES ME
—NOTHING SO SOFT EVER HAP-
PENED TO ME
—THE PEARL MAIDEN
—THAT TYPICAL, TOPICAL, TROPI-
CAL TUNE

Anthony Bafunno Scores

1918. *SOMEBODY'S SWEETHEART*
A musical comedy with book and lyrics
by Alonzo Price, and presented by a cast
headed by Walter Scanlon, Eva Fallon
and William Kent.
—VIVA LA TOREADOR
—FOLLOW ME
—GIRL OF MY HEART
—SOMEBODY'S SWEETHEART
—SONG OF THE FIDDLE
—THEN I'LL MARRY YOU
—TWINKLE
—ON WINGS OF DOUBT
—SPAIN
—WHAT SHALL WE SING?
—IS IT YOUR SMILE?
—IN THE OLD FASHIONED WAY
By Arthur Hammerstein and Herbert
Stothart.
—IT GETS THEM ALL
By Arthur Hammerstein and Herbert
Stothart.

Ernest Ball Scores

Chauncey Olcott starred in all the musicals listed below.

1910. *BARRY OF BALLYMORE*
Book and lyrics by Rida Johnson Young.
—*MOTHER MACHREE
—I LOVE THE NAME OF MARY
Lyrics by George Graff.
—IN THE SUNSHINE OF YOUR LOVE
—WILD ROSE
—MY LAND

1912. *ISLE OF DREAMS*
Book and lyrics by Rida Johnson Young.
—THE CALLING OF THE SEA
—ISLE OF DREAMS
—*WHEN IRISH EYES ARE SMILING
Lyrics by Chauncey Olcott and George Graff.
—KATHLEEN AROON

1914. *THE HEART OF PADDY WHACK*
Book and lyrics by Rachel Crothers.
—A BROTH OF A BOY
—THE HEART OF PADDY WHACK
—WHO KNOWS
—IRISH EYES OF BLUE
—A LITTLE BIT OF HEAVEN
Lyrics by J. Keirn Brennan.

1915. *MACUSHLA*
Also billed as "Pulse of My Heart." Book and lyrics by Rida Johnson Young.
—THAT'S HOW THE SHANNON FLOWS
—MACUSHLA ASHORE
—PULSE OF MY HEART
—'TIS AN IRISH GIRL I LOVE AND SHE'S JUST LIKE YOU
—I'LL MISS YOU, OLD IRELAND

Augustus Barratt Scores

1912. *MY BEST GIRL*
With Clifton Crawford, who appeared in this musical comedy with Rita Stanwood. Book by Channing Pollock and lyrics by Rennold Wolf.
—IF THE MORNING AFTER WERE THE NIGHT BEFORE
—I DO LIKE YOUR EYES
—I LOVE MY ART
—I'M SMILING AT THE MOON DAT SMILES AT YOU
—THE LANGUAGE OF LOVER'S SMILES
—MISSIONARY MAIDS
—MR. SCHNOODLE
—A REGULAR ARMY MAN
—SOFT SHOES
—COME TAKE A DANCE WITH ME

—WHEN THE HENRY CLAY COMES STEAMING INTO MOBILE BAY
—I CAN'T DO WITHOUT MEN
—LOVE AND THE AUTOMOBILE
—FOLLOW ME AROUND
By Irving Berlin.
—A TREASURE OF A GIRL
—HOWDY-DO
—DAPHNE
By Billy Jerome and Jean Schwartz.
—MY BEST GIRL

1918. *FANCY FREE*
A musical comedy with book by Dorothy Donnelly and Edgar Smith, lyrics by the composer, and presented by a cast that included Clifton Crawford, Marilyn Miller, Harry Conor and Ed Wynn.
—PRETTY BABY DOLL FROM PAREE
—MODERN GIRLS
—RAT-TAT-A-TAT
—LOVE COMES STEALING
—MAKE UP
—A COCKTAIL OF FLOWERS
—TINKLE-INKLE-INKLE
—WHEN THE MOON SHINES DOWN
—MY BIBLIOPHILE
—SOMEONE HAS YOUR NUMBER
—HELEN, THE MANICURE GIRL
—EVE
By Clifton Crawford.
—A TINY FLAT
—SISTER SUE

1918. *LITTLE SIMPLICITY*
A musical comedy with book and lyrics by Rida Johnson Young, and presented by a cast that included Marjorie Gateson, Walter Catlett, Carl Gantvoort and Mabel Withee.
—DAYS OF YOUTH
—NATIONAL AIRS
—FLOWER SONG
—MY LULU
—YOU DON'T KNOW
—FIRST LOVE
—JUST A LITTLE SUNSHINE
—HUSH, HUSH
—IT'S WORTH WHILE WAITING FOR SOMEONE WORTH WHILE
—MAYBE YOU'LL LOOK GOOD TO ME
—LEARNING TO LOVE
—I CANNOT LEAVE YOU NOW
—SAME OLD WAY
—A VOICE CALLING ME
—BOOMERANG
—FOLLOW THE BOYS
—A MILITARY FOX TROT TUNE
—MY CARAVAN
—WHEN THE WHISTLE BLOWS

94

Bayes and Norworth Score

1911. *LITTLE MISS FIX-IT*
A musical comedy in which Nora Bayes
and Jack Norworth starred. Book by
William J. Hurlburt and additional lyrics
by Harry B. Smith.
—I'VE A GARDEN IN SWEDEN
—FOR MONTHS AND MONTHS
—TURN OFF YOUR LIGHT, MR.
  MOON MAN
—PLEASE GO FIND MY BILLY BOY
—STRAWBERRIES
—THE LITTLE BIT OF IRELAND IN
  NEW YORK
—PARLOR GAMES
—THERE IS A HAPPYLAND
Music by Jerome Kern.
—TURKEY TROT
Music by Jerome Kern and Dave Stamper.
—NO MORE STAYING OUT LATE
With Bert Lee.

William Becker Score

1912. *THE GIRL FROM BRIGHTON*
A musical comedy with book and lyrics
by Aaron Hoffman and Jean C. Havez,
and presented by a cast that included
Henry Lewis and Maude Rockwell.
—THE BRIGHTON BEACH RAG
—SINCE YOU SAID YOU LOVED ME
—THAT ACADEMY RAG
—OH, YOU SILV'RY BELLS
Music by George Botsford.
—MELODY MAN
Music by Les Copeland.
—HONEYMOON DAYS
Music by Les Copeland.
—AFTER VESPERS
By Neil Moret.

Henry Bereny Scores

1911. *LITTLE BOY BLUE*
A musical comedy with book by A. E.
Thomas and Edward Paulton, who also
wrote the lyrics with Ed Madden and
contributed to the score. The cast was
headed by Otis Harlan and Maude Odell.
—ANGUS GORDON DONALD DOUG-
  LAS EWART JOHN McKEE
—THE CRYSTAL BALL
—DETECTIVE SONG
—FLIRT
—IN THE HEART OF THE GOLDEN
  WINE
—LOVE NEVER DIES
—SANDY McDOUGAL

—TWO COCKATOOS
—KISS ME, DEAREST, KISS ME DO
—YOU'RE VERY LIKE YOUR SISTER,
  DEAR
—KING OF THE BOULEVARDS
Music by Paul Rubens.
—I WONDER WHY
By Crane Wilbur and Paul Rubens.

1912. *THE GIRL FROM MONTMAR-
  TRE*
A musical comedy with book and lyrics
by Harry B. and Robert B. Smith, and
starring Hattie Williams in a cast that
included Richard Carle, William Dan-
forth and George Lydecker.
—SOMETHING LIKE THIS
—VIENNA ROLL
—LOVE WILL WIN
—OH, DOCTOR
—IN SPIRIT LAND
—BOHEMIA
Music by Jerome Kern.
—DON'T TURN MY PICTURE TO THE
  WALL
Music by Jerome Kern.
—HOOPLA, FATHER DOESN'T CARE
Music by Jerome Kern.
—I'LL BE WAITING AT THE WIN-
  DOW
Music by Jerome Kern.
—I'VE TAKEN SUCH A FANCY TO
  YOU
Music by Jerome Kern.
—OOO, OOO LENA
—HALF PAST TWO
By Percy Greenbank, Arthur Wimperis
and Howard Talbot.

Irving Berlin Scores

1914. *WATCH YOUR STEP*
A revue with Irene and Vernon Castle,
Frank Tinney, Sallie Fisher, Elizabeth
Murray, Charles King and Elizabeth
Brice.
—OFFICE HOURS
—WHAT IS LOVE?
—MINSTREL PARADE
—AROUND THE TOWN
—THEY FOLLOW ME
—PLAY A SIMPLE MELODY
—SYNCOPATED WALK
—METROPOLITAN NIGHTS
—I LOVE TO HAVE THE BOYS
  AROUND ME
—SETTLE DOWN IN A ONE-HORSE
  TOWN
—CHATTER CHATTER
—MOVE OVER

—SHOW ME HOW TO DO THE FOX
   TROT
—LOOK AT THEM DOING IT!
1915. *STOP! LOOK! LISTEN!*
   A revue with Gaby Deslys, Blossom Seeley,
   Frank Lalor, Doyle and Dixon, Harry
   Fox, Joseph Santley, Marion Davies,
   Florence Tempest, Marion Sunshine and
   Harry Pilcer.
—BLOW YOUR HORN
—GIVE US A CHANCE
—I LOVE TO DANCE
—AND FATHER WANTED ME TO
   LEARN A TRADE
—THE GIRL ON THE MAGAZINE
—I LOVE A PIANO
—THE HULA-HULA
—WHEN I'M OUT WITH YOU
—TAKE OFF A LITTLE BIT
—TEACH ME HOW TO LOVE
—THE LAW MUST BE OBEYED
—WHEN I GET BACK TO THE U. S. A.
—STOP! LOOK! LISTEN
—I'M COMING HOME WITH A SKATE
   ON
—EVERYTHING IN AMERICA IS RAG-
   TIME CRAZY
1916. *THE CENTURY GIRL*
   A revue written in collaboration with
   Victor Herbert in which Hazel Dawn,
   Sam Bernard, Irving Fisher, John Slavin,
   Leon Errol, Elsie Janis, Doyle and Dixon,
   Van and Schenck, Frank Tinney, Lillian
   Tashman and Florence Walton and
   Maurice appeared.
—THE MUSIC LESSON
—YOU'VE GOT ME DOING IT TOO
—THE BROADWAY CHICKEN WALK
—ALICE IN WONDERLAND
—IT TAKES AN IRISHMAN TO MAKE
   LOVE
—ON THE TRAIN OF A WEDDING
   GOWN
1917. *DANCE AND GROW THIN*
   A midnight revue with Van and Schenck,
   Irving Fisher, Leon Errol, Harry Kelly,
   Gertrude Hoffman and Joe Jackson.
—WAY DOWN SOUTH
—MARY BROWN
—BIRDIE
—CINDERELLA LOST HER SLIPPER
—LETTER BOXES
—DANCE AND GROW THIN
1918. *YIP, YIP, YAPHANK*
   A revue presented by a cast of soldiers
   from Camp Upton in which Sgt. Irving
   Berlin sang "Oh, How I Hate To Get Up
   in the Morning" for the first time, and

lightweight champion Benny Leonard, the
camp boxing instructor, appeared in an
exhibition bout. This revue served as the
pattern for the more pretentious "This Is
the Army," written and staged by Irving
Berlin as his contribution to World War
II.
—HELLO, HELLO, HELLO
—BEVO
—WHAT A DIFFERENCE A UNIFORM
   WILL MAKE
—MANDY
—DING DONG
—SOLDIER BOY
—OH, HOW I HATE TO GET UP IN
   THE MORNING
—THE Y. M. C. A.
—WE'RE ON OUR WAY TO FRANCE
1919. *ZIEGFELD FOLLIES OF 1919*
   With a cast that included Eddie Dowling,
   Johnny and Ray Dooley, DeLyle Alda,
   Marilyn Miller, Bert Williams, Eddie Can-
   tor, Van and Schenck, John Steel and the
   Fairbanks Twins.
—MANDY
—THE NEAR FUTURE
—HAREM LIFE
—I'M THE GUY WHO GUARDS THE
   HAREM
—SYNCOPATED COCKTAIL
—A PRETTY GIRL IS LIKE A MELODY
—PROHIBITION
—YOU CANNOT MAKE YOUR SHIM-
   MY SHAKE ON TEA
—I WANT TO SEE A MINSTREL
   SHOW
—WE MADE THE DOUGHNUTS OVER
   THERE
—MY TAMBOURINE GIRL
—*YOU'D BE SURPRISED
—MY BABY'S ARMS
   By Joseph McCarthy and Harry Tierney.
—SWEET SIXTEEN
   By Gene Buck and Dave Stamper.
—TULIP TIME
   By Gene Buck and Dave Stamper.
—THE WORLD IS GOING SHIMMY
   MAD
   By Gene Buck and Dave Stamper.
—WHEN THE MOON SHINES ON THE
   MOONSHINE
   By DeWitt Francis and Robin Hood
   Bowers.

Heinrich Berte Score

1912. *ROSE OF PANAMA*
   A musical comedy with book and lyrics
   by John L. Shine and Sydney Rosenfeld,

and presented by a cast headed by Chapine in the title role, Fay Bainter, Forrest Huff and Mortimer Weldon.
—TIP-A-TOP
—WHEN YOUR FORTUNE HAS FLOWN
—LASSO DUET
—YOU CANNOT BLAME ME FOR MY SPANISH BLOOD
—HE HAS SEDUCED HER
—ISABELLA AND ROMERO
—MAKE A NIGHT OF IT
—LOVE'S FOND DREAM
—THY THOUGHT, MY THOUGHT
—THE DAY OF LOVE
—CUPID'S FLIRTATION
—PRAY TELL ME
—OOLIE GIRL OF PANAMA
By Arthur J. Gillespie, Herman Finck and H. S. Krouse.
—WAITING FOR YOU
By Arthur J. Gillespie and Theodore Norman.

Robin Hood Bowers Scores

1911. *THE RED ROSE*
A musical comedy with book and lyrics by Harry B. and Robert B. Smith, and starring Valeska Suratt in a cast that included Wallace McCutcheon, Alexander Clark, Ernest Lambert, John E. Hazzard and Flavia Arcaro.
—COME ALONG MY CHERIE
—MEN, MEN, MEN
—THE LAND OF THE FREE
—QUEEN OF VANITY FAIR
—I'D LIKE TO GO ON A HONEYMOON WITH YOU
—HAMMOCK SONG
—BOHEMIA
—STUDENTS' GLIDE
—I'M ALL THIN
—BUY, BUY BABY

1911. *A CERTAIN PARTY*
A musical comedy with book and lyrics by Edgar Smith, and starring Mabel Hite in a cast that included John T. Kelly and Mike Donlin, the center fielder for the New York Giants, who took Broadway bows instead of Polo Ground flies.
—I WANT ANOTHER SITUATION JUST LIKE THAT
—LOVE'S WIRELESS TELEPHONE
—GET THE HOOK
—FOGARTY
—THE WALKING DELEGATE
—EMERALD ISLE
—TURKEY TROT

—I WANT A BOY
—YOU'RE GOING TO LOSE YOUR HUSBAND IF YOU DO
By Mabel Hite.

1911. *TEMPTATIONS*
A revue produced at the Folies Bergere by Henry B. Harris and Jesse Lasky, and presented by a cast headed by Elizabeth Goodall, Kathleen Clifford, Ada Lewis, Grace LaRue, Otis Harlan, Laddie Cliff, Ina Claire and Ethel Levey.
—I'LL BE A SISTER TO YOU
—MARCH OF THE TOREADORS
—DOWN THE STRAND
—MARCH OF THE NATIONS
—HE REMINDS ME OF SOMEONE I WANT TO FORGET
Maurice Levi is credited with the music for the following songs:
—HOW'D YOU LIKE TO BE THE SHOE STORE MAN?
—MARCH OF THE NEW YORK CLUBS
The following songs were contributed by Irving Berlin:
—SPANISH LOVE
—I BEG YOUR PARDON, BROADWAY
—KEEP A TAXI WAITING
—ANSWER ME

Jean Briquet Scores

1910. *ALMA, WHERE DO YOU LIVE?*
A musical comedy with book and lyrics by George V. Hobart, and starring Kitty Gordon in a cast that included Ethel Dovey and Charles A. Bigelow.
—ALMA
—BOO-HOO-HOO
—CHILDHOOD DAYS
—DON'T LET THE GIRLIES GET YOU
—SAIL HOME
—ALMA, WHERE DO YOU LIVE?
—KISS ME, MY LOVE
—NEVER MORE
—BOGGIE-BOO
—THE LAND OF BEAUTIFUL DREAMS
—LOVE ME (THE TOM CAT SONG)

1913. *ADELE*
A musical comedy with book and lyrics by Adolph Philipp and Edward Paulton, and presented by a cast that included Hal Forde, William Danforth, Georgia Caine, Alice Yorke and Grace Walton.
—ADELE
—LIKE SWALLOWS FLYING
—IS IT WORTH WHILE?
—CLOSE YOUR EYES
—STRAWBERRIES AND CREAM

—WHEN THE LITTLE BIRDS ARE
SLEEPING
—A HONEYMOON WITH YOU
—MY LONG LOST LOVE LENORE
—YOURS FOR ME AND MINE FOR
YOU
—IT'S A MATTER OF OPINION
—THE CLOCK IS STRIKING TEN
—YESTERDAY
—GAY SOLDIER BOY
—A WASTE OF TIME TO PLAN

1914. *THE MIDNIGHT GIRL*
A musical comedy with book and lyrics
by Adolph Philipp and Edward Paulton,
and presented by a cast headed by Eva
Fallon, Marie Flynn, Margaret Romaine,
George MacFarlane and Harry Delf.
—DECORATIONS
—DOLLY
—BURGLARS
—A LESSON IN LOVE
—LOVE AND VICTORY
—COME BACK TO THE OLD CABARET
—TEN O'CLOCK
—HONEYMOON HALL
—THE MIDNIGHT GIRL
—OH, GUSTAVE!
—A CERTAIN SOMETHING ABOUT
YOU
—WHEN THE BAND BEGINS TO PLAY
—A PLACE TO SPOON
—DEARIE
—THE MIDNIGHT CABARET
—THE PATH TO HONEYMOON LAND
—GOOD NIGHT, LOVE

1915. *THE GIRL WHO SMILES*
A musical comedy with book and lyrics by
Edward A. Paulton and Adolph Philipp,
who also contributed to the score, and
presented by a cast that included William
Danforth, Natalie Ault and Fred Walton.
—TEACH ME TO SMILE
—YOU ARE MY LITTLE CUPID
—A HONEYMOON IN MAY
—YOUR PICTURE
—THE STORY OF THE SPARROW
—MY PAULINE
—WHO IS SHE?
—OH DEAR MARIE
—LET US DANCE
—DANCE ME GOODBYE
—AT LAST UNITED
—THE GIRL WHO SMILES
—LIFE HAS JUST BEGUN

1915. *TWO IS COMPANY*
A musical comedy with book and lyrics
by Adolph Philipp and Edward Paulton,
and presented by a cast headed by Georgia
Caine, May DeSousa, Claude Fleming,

Ralph Nairn and Clarence Harvey.
—A FAMILY QUARREL
—IF YOU KNEW WHAT I KNOW
—AT THE TELEPHONE
—BACK TO LOTUSLAND
—FREE AS AIR
—LA BELLE LULU
—TWO IS COMPANY
—YOU WERE CHARMING
—IN THE LAND OF LORRAINE
—THE FOOTMAN AND THE MAID
—STAMP ENCLOSED
—COME WITH ME TO PAREE
—WE LIKE TO WHIRL
—THE LURE OF THE WALTZ
—I PREFER THE CAT
—FREE
—WHO SAYS SO?

Brown and Gruenberg Score

1919. *ROLY BOLY EYES*
A musical comedy with book and lyrics by
Edgar Allen Woolf, and starring Eddie
Leonard in a cast that included Queenie
Smith.
—WHEN DANCING'S A PROFESSION
—AIN'T IT SWEET?
—BIDDLE-DE-BOO
—THE BLUSHING, GUSHING WIDOW
—A BUNGALOW FOR TWO
—OLD FASHIONED FLOWERS
—WHEN THEY DO THE DIPPY
DOODLUMS
—JUST A GIRL, JUST A BOY
—YOUR VOICE I HEAR
—THAT MINSTREL MAN
—MINSTREL SERENADE
—DREAMY EYES
By Eddie Leonard.
—I WANT A MAN
—ALL WASHED UP
—HARVESTER'S SONG
—WHERE IS SHE?
—IDA, SWEET AS APPLE CIDER
By Eddie Leonard.

James Byrnes Score

1917. *ODDS AND ENDS OF 1917*
A revue with book and lyrics by Bide
Dudley and John Godfrey, and presented
by a cast headed by Lillian Lorraine,
Laura Hamilton, Harry Watson Jr., Paul
Frawley and Jack Norworth.
—THE FURTHER IT IS FROM TIP-
PERARY
—GIVE ME AN OLD-FASHIONED
GIRLIE
—THE VAMPIRE MAID

—WHEN HECTOR WAS A PUP
—WHEN I WAVE MY FLAG
—A LOVELY CROP OF GIRLS
—BRAVO, ANTONIO!
—THE DOVE DANCE
—DEAR OLD BRONX
—FANCY YOU FANCYING ME
    By Nora Bayes and Jack Norworth.
—WHERE DID YOU GET THOSE
    IRISH EYES?
—SISTER SUSIE GLIDE
—MY LADY'S CLOTHES
—WE'VE GOT TO PUT UP WITH IT

Earl Carroll Scores

1916. *SO LONG LETTY*
    A musical comedy with book by Elmer
    Harris and Oliver Morosco, lyrics by the
    composer, and starring Charlotte Green-
    wood in a cast that included May Boley,
    Sidney Grant, Walter Catlett and the
    Cameron Sisters.
—HERE COME THE MARRIED MEN
—TO HEAR YOUR VOICE
—ALL THE COMFORTS OF HOME
—SO LONG LETTY
—CAB-ARABIAN NIGHTS
—THAT RUSHIN' RAG
—ON A BEAUTIFUL BEACH

1917. *CANARY COTTAGE*
    A musical comedy with book by Elmer
    Harris and Oliver Morosco, lyrics by the
    composer, and presented by a cast headed
    by Carl McCullough, Hugh Cameron,
    Charles Ruggles, Dorthy Webb, Herbert
    Corthell and Trixie Friganza.
—SUCH A CHAUFFEUR
—OLD MAN METHUSELAH
—BUT IN THE MORNING
—SYNCOPATED HARP
—IT'S ALWAYS ORANGE DAY IN
    CALIFORNIA
—I NEVER KNEW
—THE MORE I SEE OF MEN THE
    MORE I LOVE MY DOG
—AS LONG AS I HAVE YOU
—FOLLOW THE COOK
—CANARY COTTAGE
—IT RUINED MARC ANTHONY

Harry Carroll Scores

1918. *OH, LOOK!*
    Book by James Montgomery, lyrics by
    Joseph McCarthy, and presented by a cast
    headed by Harry Fox, Genevieve Tobin,
    George Sidney and Clarence Nordstrom.
—I KNOW

—WHEREVER THERE'S MUSIC AND
    BEAUTIFUL GIRLS
—*I'M ALWAYS CHASING RAINBOWS
    Based on Chopin's Fantasie Impromptu
    in C Sharp Minor.
—I THINK SHE'S ABSOLUTELY WON-
    DERFUL
—THESE COLORS WILL NOT RUN
—CHANGEABLE GIRLS
—A KISS FOR CINDERELLA
—I'M JUST A GOOD MAN
—IT'S A LONG WAY TO TIFFANY'S
—WE WILL LIVE FOR LOVE AND
    LOVE ALONE
—SUNKISTLAND
—TYPICAL TROPICAL TUNES

1919. *THE LITTLE BLUE DEVIL*
    Book and lyrics by Harold Atteridge, and
    starring Lillian Lorraine and Bernard
    Granville.
—THE OFFICE BLUES
—HELLO, EVERYBODY
—JUST A KISS
—I'M SO SYMPATHETIC
—SHIMMY-SHAKING LOVE
—THE SECRET SERVICE CLUB
—THE LITTLE BLUE DEVIL
—A STROLLER IN DREAMLAND
—CUCKOO TOWN
—DANCING SHOES
—AUCTION RAG
—THE BUTLER'S FOX-TROT
—PETER PAN
—OMAR KHAYYAM

Ivan Caryll Scores

1910. *OUR MISS GIBBS*
    With Lionel Monckton. A musical comedy
    with book and lyrics by James T. Tanner,
    and presented by a cast headed by Ger-
    trude Vanderbilt, Ernest Lambert, Pauline
    Chase, Bert Leslie and Jean Aylwin.
—MOONSTRUCK
—OUR MISS GIBBS
—HATS
—BETTY'S ADVICE
—CORRECT
—MARY
—BERTIE THE BOUNDER
—I LOVE MacINTOSH
    By George Arthur and Harold Lonsdale.
—COME TINY GOLDFISH TO ME
    By Hugh Marlowe and Jerome Kern.
—EIGHT LITTLE GIRLS
    By M. E. Rourke and Jerome Kern.
—I DON'T WANT TO BE A SISTER
    TO YOU
    By Frederick Day and Jerome Kern.

—WILL YOU SING THIS GLEE WITH ME?
—NOT THAT SORT OF PERSON
—MARCH OF THE FOREIGN COMMIS-SIONERS
—YORKSHIRE
—GENTLEMEN
—DOUGAL
—BEDTIME AT THE ZOO
—OUR FARM
—A LITTLE CHANGE

1911. *MARRIAGE A LA CARTE*
A musical comedy with book and lyrics by C. M. S. McClellan, and presented by a cast headed by Emmy Whelen, Ernest Lambert and Taylor Holmes.
—DID YOU EVER
—WHEN ZIM, ZIM GO THE CYMBALS
—WHAT'S THE USE OF GOING TO BED?
—WALKING ON A WIRE
—OH, ROSALIE
—NO DOUBT I OUGHT TO TRY
—OF ALL HER SEX A PARAGON
—SUCH A BORE!
—TODDLE GO THE GIRLS
—FOR I'M JUST I
—YOU, YOU
—THRIFTY LITTLE MABEL
—CAPTAIN DINKLEPOP
—CASSIE'S NOT A BIT LIKE MOTHER
—SMILE, SMILE, SMILE

1911. *THE PINK LADY*
A musical comedy with book and lyrics by C. H. S. McClellan, and starring Hazel Dawn in a cast that included Florence Walton, Alice Dovey, Frank Lalor and John E. Young.
—BRING ALONG THE CAMERA
—I'M GOING TO BE MARRIED IN JUNE
—WHEN LOVE GOES A-STRAYING
—OH, SO GENTLY
—ON THE SASKATCHEWAN
—THE INTRIGUERS
—DONNY DID, DONNY DIDN'T
—THE KISS WALTZ
—THE DUEL
—THE PARISIAN TWO-STEP
—BEAUTIFUL LADY

1912. *OH, OH DELPHINE*
A musical comedy with book and lyrics by C. M. S. McClellan, and presented by a cast headed by Dorothy Langdon and Frank McIntyre.
—PLEASE TURN YOUR BACKS
—POSING FOR VENUS
—OH, OH DELPHINE
—WHY SHOULDN'T YOU TELL ME THAT?

—POOR BOUCHETTE
—CAN WE FORGET?
—EVERYTHING'S AT HOME EXCEPT YOUR WIFE
—THE VENUS WALTZ
—THEN ALL COME ALONG
—CAPTAIN DINKLEPOP

1913. *THE LITTLE CAFE*
A musical comedy with book and lyrics by C. M. S. McClellan, and starring Hazel Dawn in a cast that included H. P. Huntley and John E. Young.
—I'M A-HUNTING JAGUAR
—I WONDER WHOM I'LL MARRY
—JUST BECAUSE IT'S YOU
—THEY FOUND ME
—THIS GAY PAREE
—THY MOUTH IS A ROSE
—YOU LITTLE CAFE, GOOD DAY
—DO YOU CALL THAT DANCING?
—SERVE THE CAVIAR
—MY PRETTY LITTLE FAMILY OF ONE
—SO I SMILE
—THE BEST QUEEN OF ALL

1914. *THE BELLE OF BOND STREET*
With Lionel Monckton. A musical comedy with book by Owen Hall and Harold Atteridge, lyrics by Adrian Ross and Claude Aveling, and starring Gaby Deslys in a cast that included Sam Bernard, Forrest Huff, Harry Pilcer, Lawrence D'Orsay and Fritzie Von Busing.
—THE BRIDAL BEVY
—AS I CAME DOWN THE AISLE
—WE'VE COME FOR THE LADIES
—THE HAT AND NOT THE GIRL
—THEY SAY I'M FRIVOLOUS
—TOO MANY COOKS
—FLOCTON-ON-SEA
—A HONEYMOON TRIP ALL ALONE
—PIERROTLAND
—PRUNELLA
—HOGGENHEIMER OF PARK AVENUE
—WHO PAID THE RENT FOR MRS. RIP VAN WINKLE WHEN RIP VAN WINKLE WAS AWAY
By Alfred Bryan and Fred Fisher.
—A LITTLE TANGO MAID
By Harold Atteridge and Harry Carroll.
—TANGO DIP
By Harold Atteridge and Harry Carroll.
—MY TURKEY TROTTING BOY
By Harold Atteridge and Harry Carroll.

1914. *CHIN CHIN*
A musical comedy with book by R. H. Burnside and Anne Caldwell, lyrics by Anne Caldwell and James O'Dea, and the final starring appearance of Montgomery

and Stone in a cast that included Belle Story, Tot Qualters, Charles T. Aldrich, Douglas Stevenson, Helen Falconer and the Six Brown Brothers.
—QUAINT TOYS
—SHOPPING THE ORIENT
—THE CHINESE HONEYMOON
—CLIPPEE CHINA CHAPS
—GOODBYE GIRLS, I'M THROUGH
Lyrics by John Golden.
—GO GAR SIG GONG-JUE
—IN AN ORIENTAL WAY
—TEMPLE BELLS
—WEDDING GIFTS OF SILVER
—THE GREY DOVE
—LOVE MOON
—STROLLERS
—IT'S A LONG WAY TO TIPPERARY
By Harry Williams and Joe Judge.

1914. *PAPA'S DARLING*
A musical comedy with book and lyrics by Harry B. Smith, and presented by a cast headed by Alice Dovey, Frank Lalor, Fred Walton and Dorothy Jardon.
—A TOUCH OF SPRING
—A CERTAIN LITTLE WAY OF MY OWN
—EDELWEISS
—EVERYONE IS DANCING MAD
—SPARKLING MOSELLE
—THE LAND OF THE MIDNIGHT SUN
—WHERE SHALL WE GO FOR OUR HONEYMOON?
—WHO CARES?
—DOLORES
—THE POPULAR POP
—OH, THIS LOVE

1917. *JACK O' LANTERN*
A musical comedy with book and lyrics by Anne Caldwell, and starring Fred Stone in a cast that included Charles T. Aldrich, Oscar Ragland, Allene Crater, Helen Falconer, Edna Bates and Violet Zell.
—WAIT TILL THE COWS COME HOME
—COME AND HAVE A SWING WITH ME
—FOLLOW THE GIRLS AROUND
—A SWEETHEART OF MY OWN
—ALONG CAME ANOTHER LITTLE GIRL
Lyrics by Benjamin Hapgood Burt.
—TAKE A TRIP TO CANDYLAND
—THE GIRL'S I'VE MET
Lyrics by Louis Harrison.
—KNIT, KNIT, KNIT
—HEAR THE BELL
—OH, PAPA
—I'LL TAKE YOU BACK TO ITALY
By Irving Berlin.

—THE RECRUITING DOLL
Lyrics by Louis Harrison.

1918. *THE GIRL BEHIND THE GUN*
A musical comedy with book and lyrics by Guy Bolton and P. G. Wodehouse, and starring Wilda Bennett and Donald Brian in a cast that included John E. Hazzard and John E. Young.
—GODSONS AND GODMOTHERS
—THERE'S A LIGHT IN YOUR EYES
—THERE'S LIFE IN THE OLD DOG YET
—BACK TO THE DEAR OLD TRENCHES
—THE GIRL BEHIND THE GUN
—A HAPPY FAMILY
—I LIKE IT, I LIKE IT
—OH, HOW WARM IT IS TODAY
—SOME DAY WAITING WILL END
—I'M TRUE TO THEM ALL (AND THEY'RE JUST AS TRUE TO ME)
—WOMAN HASN'T ANY MERCY ON A MAN
—FLAGS OF THE ALLIES

1918. *THE CANARY*
A musical comedy with book by George Barr and Louis Verneuil, lyrics by P. G. Wodehouse and Anne Caldwell, and starring Julia Sanderson in a cast that included Sam Hardy, Joseph Cawthorn, Louis Harrison and Doyle and Dixon.
—JULIE AND HER JOHNNIES
—THAT'S WHAT MEN ARE FOR
—THOUSANDS OF YEARS AGO
—THE HAUNTING HONEYMOON
—ONLY IN DREAMS
Lyrics by Harry B. Smith.
—OH, DOCTOR
Music by Harry Tierney.
—LOVE ME IN THE SPRING
By Richard Fechheimer and William B. Kernell.
—JAZZ MARIMBA
Music by Harry Tierney.
—OH PROMISE ME YOU'LL WRITE HIM TODAY
By Edward Clarke and Jerome Kern.
—TAKE A CHANCE LITTLE GIRL AND LEARN TO DANCE
By Harry B. Smith and Jerome Kern.
—THIS IS THE TIME
By Clifton Crawford.
—IT'S THE LITTLE BIT OF IRISH
By Irving Berlin.
—THAT LITTLE GERMAN BAND
By Benjamin Hapgood Burt.

George M. Cohan Scores

1911. *THE LITTLE MILLIONAIRE*

Jerry J. and Helen Cohan made their last Broadway appearance in this musical comedy with George M. Cohan, Tom Lewis, George Parsons and Donald Crisp heading the cast.
—NEW YORKERS
—THE LITTLE MILLIONAIRE
—WE DO ALL THE DIRTY WORK
—DRILL OF THE SEVENTH
—ANY PLACE THE OLD FLAG FLIES
—THE MUSICAL MOON
—OH, YOU WONDERFUL GIRL
—BARNUM HAD THE RIGHT IDEA
—THE DANCING WEDDING

1914. *HELLO, BROADWAY*
Starring George M. Cohan in a cast that included William Collier, Tom Dingle, Louise Dresser, Peggy Wood, Florence Moore and Lawrence Wheat.
—IT PAYS TO ADVERTISE
—MY MIRACLE MAN
—PYGMALION ROSE
—HELLO, BROADWAY
—LOOK OUT FOR MR. WU
—I WANTED TO COME TO BROADWAY
—SNEAKY STEPS
—BROADWAY TIPPERARY
—THOSE IRVING BERLIN MELODIES
—HIPPODROME FOLKS
—BARNUM & BAILEY RAG
—THAT OLD FASHIONED CAKE WALK
—JESSE JAMES GLIDE
—DOWN BY THE ERIE CANAL
—MY FLAG

1916. *THE COHAN REVUE OF 1916*
Presented by a cast headed by John Boles, Harry Bulger, Elizabeth Murray, Fred Santley, Harry Delf, Richard Carle, Valli Valli, Charles Winninger and Little Billie.
—HE CAN CURE YOU OF LOVE
—CRYING JANE
—THE FAIR AND WARMER COCKTAIL
—IT'S A LONG WAY FROM BROADWAY TO EDINBORO TOWN
—ALONE AT LAST
—YOU CAN TELL THAT I'M IRISH
—BUSY, BUSY, BUSY
—MY MUSICAL COMEDY MAID
—GABY
—RUNNING AROUND WITH CHORUS GIRLS
—YOUNG AMERICA
—JULIA, DONALD AND JOE
This was a travesty in song on Julia Sanderson, Donald Brian and Joseph Cawthorn, who had scored a phenomenal hit in "The Girl From Utah."

—THOSE SOUSA MELODIES
—ZIEGFELD RAG
—THAT FRISCO MELODY

1917. *COHAN REVUE OF 1918*
George M. Cohan collaborated with Irving Berlin on the score of this production, the cast of which was headed by Nora Bayes, Charles Winninger, Irving Fisher and Fred Santley.
—POLLY, PRETTY POLLY WITH A PAST
With Irving Berlin.
—WHEN ZIEGFELD'S FOLLIES HIT THE TOWN
—OUR ACROBATIC MELODRAMATIC HOME
—SPANISH
—THE EYES OF YOUTH SEE THE TRUTH
—ALL DRESSED UP IN A TAILORMADE
—THE POTASH AND PERLMUTTER BALL
—THEIR HEARTS ARE OVER HERE
Irving Berlin wrote the following songs for this production:
—SHOW ME THE WAY
—A MAN IS ONLY A MAN
—KING OF BROADWAY
—WEDDING OF WORDS AND MUSIC
—A BAD CHINAMAN FROM SHANGHAI
—DOWN WHERE THE JACK O' LANTERNS GROW
In addition, Nora Bayes introduced the following interpolated songs:
—WHO DO YOU LOVE?
By Ed Moran and James Brockman.
—REGRETFUL BLUES
By Grant Clarke and Cliff Hess.

1918. *THE VOICE OF McCONNELL*
A muscial drama that brought Chauncey Olcott, the great Irish tenor, out of retirement and back in the Broadway spotlight once more.
—YOU CAN'T DENY YOU'RE IRISH
—IRELAND THE LAND OF MY DREAMS
—I AM TRUE TO THEM ALL
—WHEN I LOOK IN YOUR EYES MAVOURNEEN

1919. *THE ROYAL VAGABOND*
Cohan wrote the score for this cloak-and-dagger musical comedy with Anselm Goetzl, the book and lyrics of which were by William Cary Duncan. The cast included Tessa Kosta, Fred Santley, Gladys Zell, Dorothy Dickson and Earl Hyson.
—OPERA, COMIC OPERA
By George M. Cohan.

—LOVE OF MINE
—HERE COME THE SOLDIERS
By George M. Cohan.
—DEMOCRACY
—WHERE THE CHERRY BLOSSOMS
FALL (LOVE IS LOVE)
—ROYALTY
With lyrics by George M. Cohan.
—WHAT YOU DON'T KNOW WON'T
HURT YOU
—MESSENGER
With lyrics by George M. Cohan.
—IN A KINGDOM OF OUR OWN
By George M. Cohan.
—GOOD-BYE BARGRAVIA
By George M. Cohan.
Harry Tierney and Joseph McCarthy also
contributed these two songs to this pro-
duction:
—A WEE BIT OF LACE
—CHARMING

Charles Cuvillier Scores

1914. *THE LILAC DOMINO*
A musical comedy with book by Harry B.
Smith, lyrics by Robert B. Smith, and
starring Eleanor Painter in a cast that in-
cluded Wilfred Douthitt and John E
Hazzard.
—LADIES DAY
—LET THE MUSIC PLAY
—THE LILAC DOMINO
—WHAT IS DONE YOU CAN NEVER
UNDO
—WHERE LOVE IS WAITING
—I CALL YOU BACK TO ME
By Wilfred Douthitt and Ellen Tuckfield.
1916. *FLORA BELLA*
With Milton Schwartzwald. An operetta
with book by Cosmo Hamilton and Dor-
othy Donnelly, lyrics by Percy Waxman,
and starring Lena Abarbanell in a cast
that included Charles Purcell.
—GOOD DAY, GOOD NIGHT
—BLOSSOM OF MY OWN
—IT WAS VERY HARD TO BRING
UP FATHER
—YOUNG MAN TAKE A TIP FROM
ME
—LOVE IS A DANCE
—ON TO PETROGRAD!
—HAIL TO THE GOLDEN CALF
—WE'LL DANCE TILL DAWN OF DAY
—HYPNOTIZING
—ADAM
—CAT, YOU CAN'T LEAVE MICE
ALONE
—FLORA BELLA
Lyrics by Earl Carroll.

—GIVE ME ALL OF YOU
Lyrics by Earl Carroll.
—YOU'RE THE GIRL
Lyrics by Victor Schertzinger.
—CREEP, CREEP, THE WORLD'S
ASLEEP

Walter Damrosch Score

1912. *THE DOVE OF PEACE*
A musical comedy with book and lyrics
by Wallace Irwin, and presented by a cast
headed by Arthur Deagon, Frank Pol-
lock, Alice Yorke and Ernest Torrence.
—EMPTY HOURS OF SUMMER
CHATTER
—MARK HIS BRIGHT AND FLASHING
EYE
—WHAT LIPS ARE MADE FOR
—DOVE OF PEACE
—STEP BY STEP
—BLOOD IS THICKER THAN WATER
—YOU SHOW SOME SURPRISE
—CAKE WALK
—OH THANK YOU KINDLY, MY
PRETTY DEARS
—WAS EVER A MAID OF SPAIN
—THE BRAG AND THE BLUSTER
—YOUR EYES HAVE TOLD ME AND
MY HEART HAS HEARD
—PRINCE OF MY DREAMS
—BEHOLD THE DOVE
—OH, THE WORLD OF PEACE!
—PRE-HISTORIC MAN
—THE CAVEMAN AND THE CAVE-
WOMAN
—PROMISE ME TOMORROW YOU
WILL AGAIN LOVE ME
—WOMAN, HOW DARE YOU!
—FAR IS THE MANGO ISLAND
—MARCH OF THE MILITANT SUF-
FRAGETTES
—AT LAST HAS DOWN-TRODDEN
WOMAN
—PRISONERS, STAND UP
—AS LONG AS MAN LOVES WOMAN
—TWO LITTLE CANNIBAL LADIES

Herman Darewski Songs

1918. *THE BETTER 'OLE*
A comedy of the trenches in World War
I with book by Capt. Bruce Brainsfather
and Capt. Arthur Elliott, in which the
following songs were introduced with
lyrics by Percival Knight. The cast was
headed by Mr. and Mrs. Charles Coburn
and Charles McNaughton.
—TOMMY
—THAT TRIP ACROSS THE RHINE

—CARRYING ON
—WHEN YOU LOOK IN THE HEART
  OF A ROSE
By Florence Methven.
—SHE'S VENUS DE MILO TO ME
By Peter Bernard and Oliver DeGerde.
—WE WISH WE WAS IN BLIGHTY
—JE SUIS QUE VOUS ETES GENTIL
—A REGIMENT OF OUR OWN

Leon DeCosta Score

1919. *FIFTY-FIFTY LTD.*
A musical comedy with book by Margaret
Mitchell and William Lennox, lyrics by
the composer, and presented by a cast
headed by Gertrude Vanderbilt, Herbert
Corthell and John Slavin.
—EVERY LITTLE GIRL HAS A WAY
  OF HER OWN
—THE GIMMIES
—HONEY BUNCH
—MY MIGHT-HAVE-BEEN
—NANETTE
—SILENCE OF LOVE
—SPOOKY NIGHTS
—WON'T YOU CUDDLE UP A LITTLE
  CLOSER?
—IS IT THE GIRL OR IS IT THE
  GOWN?
—THE MAGIC PLACE
—MAKE A WISH
—NERVES
—ME AND MY DOG
—THAT WAS WONDERFUL
—SO LONG—GOODBYE
—A LITTLE BIT OF JAZZ

Reginald DeKoven Scores

1911. *THE WEDDING TRIP*
Book by Fred DeGresac, lyrics by Harry
B. Smith, and starring Christine Nielson.
—SOLDIER'S SONG
—THE LOVE WALTZ
—FLIRTATION
—MARIE
—THE MIRACULOUS CURE
—FOND LOVE
—THE SEASHELL TELEPHONE
—LE BEAU SABREUR
—THE GENTLEMANLY BRIGAND
—MODERN BANDITTI
1913. *HER LITTLE HIGHNESS*
Book and lyrics by Channing Pollack and
Rennold Wolf, and with a cast headed by
Mitzi Hajos, Wallace McCutcheon and
Mae Murray.
—PRACTICAL PATRIOTS
—WHEN YOU'RE SWEET SIXTEEN

—A SELF-MADE MAN
—MY FAIRY PRINCE
—MARY ANN
—C. O. D.
—COME ALONG
—TELL ME
—ONE LITTLE GIRL
—WHEN THE LANDLORD COMES
  KNOCKING AT THE DOOR
—ETIQUETTE
—TO THE LADIES
—DRINK AND BE MERRY

Harry Delf Score

1918. *SOME NIGHT*
A musical comedy with book and lyrics
by the composer, and presented by a cast
headed by Roma June, Forrest Winant
and James C. Marlowe.
—ALONE IN A GREAT BIG WORLD
—SEND ME A GIRL
—SOMETHING THAT MONEY CAN'T
  BUY
—WITH THE BOY I LOVE
—BY THE WINDOW I'LL BE WAITING
  FOR YOU
—I'LL KEEP YOU HERE ALL NIGHT
—ONCE UPON A TIME
—SOME DAY, SOMEHOW, SOME-
  WHERE
—LOOK BEFORE YOU LEAP
—WE AIN'T GOT NO LUCK

Frank Dossert Score

1910. *A SKYLARK*
A musical comedy with book and lyrics
by William B. Harris Jr., and presented
by a cast headed by May DeSousa, John
Slavin and Gertrude Vanderbilt.
—THE CHICKEN AND THE FROG
—THE GALLUS OLD GODDESSS OF
  GREECE
—GOODBYE YANKEE DOODLE
—I JUST CAN'T WAIT
—I'M LOOKING FOR A LITTLE GIRL
  WHO'S LOOKING FOR A MAN
—IN PRAISE OF THE JOLLY TAR
—JUST BECAUSE I'M ME
—MARCH OF THE GODS
—OH, WE KNOW
—TUCK ME IN A TAXICAB
—WEDDING BELLS
—WHEN LOVE IS THERE
—ANYTIME AT ALL
—MY OWN BOTANICAL GARDEN
—OH, MR. JUPITER
—WHEN THE BLOOM IS ON THE
  BOTTLE

Gus Edwards Score

1910. *ZIEGFELD FOLLIES OF 1910*
Book and lyrics by Harry B. Smith. Fanny
Brice and Bert Williams made their first
"Follies" appearance in this edition of
this annual revue in a cast that included
Harry Watson, George Bickel, Lillian Lor-
raine, Bobby North and Grace Tyson.
—LOOK ME OVER CAREFULLY
—SWEET KITTY BELLAIRES
—KIDLAND
—A WOMAN'S DREAM
—DON'T TAKE A GIRL DOWN TO
  CONEY
—THE CHICKEN THIEF MAN
—THE COCK OF THE WALK
—MISTER EARTH AND HIS COMET
  LOVE
—WALTZING LIEUTENANT
—NIX ON THE CONCERTINA, LENA

Julian Edwards Score

1910. *MOLLY MAY*
A musical comedy with book and lyrics
by Walter Browne, and presented by a
cast that included Grace LaRue, Eva
Fallon and Sydney Grant.
—LOVE COMES TO STAY
—THE MERRY MODEL'S BALL
—ART WITH A CAPITAL A
—MOLLY MAY
—MY FACE IS MY FORTUNE
—POOR LITTLE LONELY KID
—THE BAGPIPES

Leo Edwards Score

1910. *THE MERRY WHIRL*
A revue with book by Don Roth, lyrics
by Ed Ray, and presented by a cast that
included James C. Morton, Frank F.
Moore, Mildred Elaine and Rita Red-
mond.
—YANKEE DOODLE GIRL
—THE MAN WITH THE MONEY
—LIMA BEAN
—LA BELLE FRANCAISE
—HAVANA BAY
—I'LL BE THERE WITH YOU
—WHEN I'M ALONE I'M LONESOME
—PLAY, PLAY, PLAY
—A MODEL OF FASHION AM I
—RING THE WEDDING BELLS
—WHEN I WALTZ WITH YOU
—THE PARIS PUSH
—STRIKE UP A BAGPIPE TUNE

Ludwig Englander Score

1914. *MADAME MOSELLE*
A musical comedy with book and lyrics
by Edward A. Paulton, and presented by
a cast headed by Ralph Herz, Olga Roll-
er, Josie Intropodi, Ernest Lambert and
William Pruette.
—EVERYBODY KNOWS MADAME MO-
  SELLE
—STUDENTS OF ART ARE WE
—WHAT ARE WE GOING TO DO
  ABOUT IT?
—IS THAT ALL?
—THE MODEL
—TELL ME THE FRENCH WORD FOR
  SQUEEZE ME
—IN CONSTANTINOPLE
—ROSIE FROM PALERMO
—BACK OUT WHILE THE BACKING
  IS GOOD
—BY TUMNA'S ROLLING WATERS
—DING, DONG
—I'LL BE THERE
—IF I SHOULD LOSE MY ONLY GIRL
By William P. Chase.

Edmund Eysler Scores

1911. *VERA VIOLETTA*
A star is born at the New York Winter
Garden—and his name was Al Jolson.
The cast also included Mae West, Barney
Bernard, Billie Taylor, Melville Ellis,
Gaby Deslys, Stella Mayhew, the Gordon
Brothers and Annette Kellerman in the
aquatic revue, "Undine", by Manuel
Klein.
—PAREE, GAY PAREE
—OLGA FROM THE VOLGA
—MY LOU
—VERA VIOLETTA
—FIFTY-SEVEN WAYS TO WIN A
  MAN
—I WONDER IF IT'S TRUE
—COME BACK TO ME
—THAT HAUNTING MELODY
By George M. Cohan.
—RUM TUM TIDDLE
By Billy Jerome and Jean Schwartz.
—THE GABY GLIDE
By Harry Pilcer and Louis A. Hirsch.
—ANGELINE FROM THE OPERA
  COMIQUE
By Mel Gideon and Louis A. Hirsch.
—COME AND DANCE WITH ME
By Mel Gideon and Louis A. Hirsch.
—I'VE HEARD THAT BEFORE
By Mel Gideon and Louis A. Hirsch.

—WHEN YOU HEAR LOVE'S HELLO
By E. Ray Goetz and Louis A. Hirsch.

1912. *THE WOMAN HATERS*
A musical comedy with book and lyrics
by George V. Hobart, and presented by
a cast headed by Sallie Fisher, Joseph
Santley and Dolly Castles.
—LOVE IS THE JOY OF LIVING
—WOMAN HATERS CLUB HYMN
—IT WAS MARIE
—LITTLE GIRL COME BACK TO ME
—HE WILL TAKE ME TO HIS HEART
—THE LETTERS THAT NEVER WERE
WRITTEN
—THE RACING QUARTET
—LOVE'S ALPHABET
—THE JAG OF JOY

1914. *THE LAUGHING HUSBAND*
A musical comedy with book and lyrics
by Arthur Wimperis, and presented by a
cast headed by Fred Walton, William
Norris, Frances Demarest and Roy At-
well.
—LITTLE MISS UNDERSTOOD
—GO TO PARIS OR VIENNA
—FORBIDDEN FRUIT
—IN BEAUTIFUL ITALIANO
—LIZETTE
—A HEART WILL FALL
—WINE SONG
—AWAY FROM THEE
—SINCE GRANDPA LEARNED TO
TANGO
—SILKEN SCREEN
—MARITAL MALIGNITY
—TELEPHONE DUET
—BOUGHT AND PAID FOR
By H. B. Smith and Jerome Kern.
—LOVE IS LIKE A VIOLIN
By H. B. Smith and Jerome Kern.
—TAKE A STEP WITH ME
By H. B. Smith and Jerome Kern.
—YOU'RE HERE AND I'M HERE
By H. B. Smith and Jerome Kern.

Leo Fall Scores

1910. *THE GIRL IN THE TRAIN*
A musical comedy with book and lyrics
by Harry B. Smith, and presented by a
cast headed by Vera Michelena, Claude
Gillingwater and James Reaney.
—YOU MUST BE MINE DEAR
—I'M FANCY FREE
—FOLLOW ME
—THAT'S WHY LOTS OF PEOPLE
MARRY
—THE GIRL IN THE TRAIN
—GONDA WALTZES

—A RAGTIME TABLE D'HOTE
By Carter DeHaven.

1911. *THE SIREN*
A musical comedy with book and lyrics
by Harry B. Smith, and starring Julia
Sanderson and Donald Brian in a cast
that included Frank Moulan.
—LITTLE GIRLS BEWARE
—COUNTRY LIFE, FARMING LIFE
—WALLFLOWER
—SHE IS THE ONE GIRL
—ANCESTORS BOLD
—THE DONKEY
—OH DO STEP THE TWO-STEP
Music by Howard Talbot.
—FOLLOW ME AROUND
By Adrian Ross and Jerome Kern.
—MAID FROM MONTBIJOU
By M. E. Rourke and Jerome Kern.
—I WANT TO SING IN OPERA
By David, Arthurs and Jerome Kern.
—MY HEART I CANNOT GIVE YOU
By Matt Woodward and Jerome Kern.

1913. *THE DOLL GIRL*
A musical comedy with book and lyrics
by Harry B. Smith, and starring Hattie
Williams in a cast that included Richard
Carle and Charles McNaughton.
—NOW AND THEN
—WHAT DO YOU SAY, DOLLY DEAR?
—BRITTANY
—PAPA
—YOU'RE SO FASCINATING
—ROSALILLA OF SEVILLA
—I'M GOING AWAY
—SERENADE
—WHEN YOU'RE ON THE STAGE
—SILLY TALES
—IN THE MOVIES
—IT IS I
—THAT RAGTIME DINNER BAND
By Wilfred Chandler and Will Haines.
—THAT'S LOVE WITH A CAPITAL L
By Christiné.
—COME ON OVER HERE
—I LITTLE THING LIKE A KISS
—IF WE WERE ON OUR HONEY-
MOON
Music by Jerome Kern.
—WILL IT ALL END IN SMOKE?
Music by Jerome Kern.

1913. *LIEBER AUGUSTIN*
A musical comedy with book and lyrics
by Edgar Smith, and presented by a cast
headed by DeWolf Hopper, George Mac-
farlane, Roszika Dolly and May DeSousa.
—ANNA, WHAT'S WRONG WITH
YOU?
—MISS CAPRICE

—LIEBER AUGUSTIN
—CLEMENTINE
—DO YOU LOVE ME BEST?
—WEDDING BELLS
—IF YOU WERE MINE
—THE TRUTH MUST COME OUT SOME DAY
—LOOK IN HER EYES
By M. E. Rourke and Jerome Kern.
—I'M THE PATSY BOLIVAR OF ALL THE WORLD
By Dick Temple.
—WHY DO THEY ALL MAKE LOVE TO ME?
By Dick Temple.

Hugo Felix Scores

1912. *TANTALIZING TOMMY*
A musical comedy with book by Michael Morton and Paul Gavault, lyrics by Adrian Ross, and presented by a cast headed by Elizabeth Brice.
—IRISH STEW
—TANTALIZING TOMMY
—YOU DON'T KNOW
—ZIZI
—I AM A TOM-BOY
—A TANDEM
—JUST LIKE YOU
—OH, GO AWAY
—FAIRY BELLS
—CUPID'S CAR
—TIK SONG
—THIS AND THAT AND THE OTHER

1916. *POM-POM*
A musical comedy with book and lyrics by Anne Caldwell, and starring Mitzi Hajos.
—EVELYN
—KISS ME
—POM-POM
—COME AND CUDDLE ME
—ONLY ONE HOUR
—ZIM-ZIM
—SHE'S GONE
—THE ARMY OF CROOKS
—I'M UNLUCKY
—MR. LOVE
—SHIPS IN THE NIGHT
—THE CIRCUS IN THE MOON
—YOU SHALL NOT GO
—IN THE DARK
—MON DESIR

Score by Herman Finck

1915. *AROUND THE MAP*
A musical comedy with book and lyrics by C. M. S. McClellan, and presented

by a cast headed by William Norris, Bob Adams, Georgia O'Ramey, Louise Groody and Jacqueline Bonheur.
—I'M THE BOOM BOOM BOOMER
—I DON'T KNOW HER NAME YET
—HERE COMES TOOTSIE
—I'M MADAME KAPINSKI
—LAZY LULU
—LITTLE MAUDE ISN'T MEANT FOR YOU
—WHEN THE RIGHT GIRL COMES ALONG
—GOODNESS, AREN'T YOU GLAD?
—IT'S A VERY FINE WORLD
—LET US STAY WHERE THE CROWD IS
—DOLLY DEAR
—THE DEAR OLD FIGHTING DAYS
—SOME GIRL HAS GOT TO DARN HIS SOCKS
—TAKE ME ON A JOY RIDE
—THERE'S ONLY ONE THING A COON CAN DO
Music by Louis A. Hirsch.
—KATIE CLANCY
Music by Louis A. Hirsch..
—BILLIE THE BLUBBER
Music by Louis A. Hirsch.

Alfred Francis Score

1918. *THE LOVE MILL*
A musical comedy with book and lyrics by Earl Carroll, and presented by a cast headed by Harry Tighe, Victor Morley, Grace Fisher and Clarence Nordstrom.
—I MAY LOOK STRONG BUT I'M FAR FROM HEALTHY
—IT'S THE WOMEN
—WHEN YOU FEEL A LITTLE LONGING IN YOUR HEART
—THE LOVE MILL
—EVERY FLOWER HAS A MELODY
—FOLLOW MAMA'S ADVICE
—I LOVED HIM FOR HE LOVED THE LOVE THAT I LOVED
—IN THE STATE OF MATRIMONY
—PRSEAPRODENSKY
—WATCH THE THINGS YOU EAT
—WHY CAN'T IT ALL BE A DREAM?
—DOWN THE BRIDLE PATH OF LOVE
—WHERE THOSE COTTON BLOSSOMS GROW
—A SEASICK BUCCANEER
—Q. T. U. C. I. M. 4 U. (CUTEY, YOU SEE I'M FOR YOU)

Malvin F. Franklin Score

1919. *A LONELY ROMEO*

With Robin Hood Bowers. A musical comedy with book by Harry B. Smith and Lew Fields, lyrics by Robert B. Smith, and presented by a cast headed by Lew Fields, Herbert Fields, Alan Hale and Frances Cameron.
—CANDY JAG
—DON'T DO ANYTHING TILL YOU HEAR FROM ME
—I WANT A LONELY ROMEO
—INFLUENZA BLUES
—SWEETS TO THE SWEET
—UNDERNEATH A BIG UMBRELLA
—WILL O' THE WISP
The following songs were credited to Robin Hood Bowers:
—YOU NEVER CAN TELL
—WAIT FOR ME
—SAVE A LITTLE DAYLIGHT FOR ME
—ONE I LOVE, TWO I LOVE
—JOLLY ME
—I GUESS I'M MORE LIKE MOTHER THAN LIKE FATHER
By Ray Egan and Richard Whiting.
—ANY OLD PLACE WITH YOU
By Lorenz Hart and Richard Rodgers.

Harold Fraser-Simpson Score

1918. *THE MAID OF THE MOUNTAINS*
A musical comedy with book by Frederick Lonsdale, lyrics by Harry Graham, and presented by a cast headed by Sidonie Espero in the title role, William Courtenay, William Danforth, John Steele and Gertrude Hamilton.
—FRIENDS HAVE TO PART
—LIVE FOR TODAY
—MY LIFE IS LOVE
—FAREWELL
—DIVIDING THE SPOILS
—THOUGH CURS MAY QUAIL
—WE'RE GATHERED HERE
—FOR MANY A YEAR
—LOVE WILL FIND A WAY
—DIRTY WORK
—A PARADISE FOR TWO
—I DON'T CARE
—HUSBANDS AND WIVES
—WHEN EACH DAY
—GOOD PEOPLE GATHER ROUND
—WHEN YOU'RE IN LOVE
—OVER THERE AND OVER HERE
—WAITING FOR YOU
By Marcus C. Connelly and Gitz-Rice.

Anatole Friedland Scores

1911. *THE WIFE HUNTERS*

With Malvin Franklin. A musical comedy with book by Edgar Allen Woolf, lyrics by David Kemper, and presented by a cast headed by Emma Carus, Dorothy Brenner, Edith Decker and Arthur Conrad.
—LOVE WAVES
—FOLLETTE
—GIRLS KEEP YOUR FIGURES
—HAVANA MADE
—THE PICNIC CLUB
—HONEYLAND
—IN YOUR ARMS
—MAMMY JINNY
—LET'S TAKE HIM HOME IN TRIUMPH
—THE WAVE CREST WALTZ
—ON THE AVENUE
—THE WALTZ OF THE WILD
—LEONORA
—LITTLE DANCING JUMPING JIGGER

1912. *BROADWAY TO PARIS*
With Max Hoffman. A revue with book by George Bronson Howard, lyrics by Harold Atteridge, and presented by a cast headed by George Austin Moore, Marion Sunshine, George Bickel, James C. Morton, Gertrude Hoffman, Maurice and Florence Walton, Louise Dresser, Irene Bordoni and Doyle and Dixon.
—PAREE'S A BRANCH OF BROADWAY
—THE EYE THAT NEVER SLEEPS
—SEND ME A FELLOW
—COME TO ME CHIMPANZEE
—THE GERTRUDE HOFFMAN GLIDE
—EVERYBODY LOVES A CHICKEN
—LIFE IS A GAME OF CHANCE
—MR. YANKEE DOODLE
—THE GARDEN OF GIRLS
—I'LL FIND A BOY, I'LL FIND A GIRL
—ROLLER RINKING
—YOU'RE THE KIND OF A GIRL FOR ME
By Grant Clarke, Edgar Leslie and Jean Schwartz.
—TAKE ME TO THAT SWANEE SHORE
By L. Wolfe Gilbert and Lewis Muir.
—THE MERRY MERRY MAIDS OF THE OLD FRONT ROW
—MILESTONES
—RIDE ME AROUND WITH YOU DEARIE
—THE RAGTIME BOXING MATCH

Rudolf Friml Scores

1912. *THE FIREFLY*
Book and lyrics by Otto Harbach, and starring Emma Trentini in a cast that

included Ray Atwell, Audrey Maple and Craig Campbell.
—A TRIP TO BERMUDA
—HE SAYS YES—SHE SAYS NO
—CALL ME UNCLE
—LOVE IS LIKE A FIREFLY
—SOMETHING
—GIANNINA MIA
—IN SAPPHIRE SEAS
—TOMMY ATKINS ON DRESS PARADE
—SYMPATHY
—A WOMAN'S SMILE
—DE TROP
—BEAUTIFUL SHIP FROM TOYLAND
—WHEN A MAID COMES KNOCKING AT YOUR HEART
—AN AMERICAN BEAUTY ROSE
—THE LATEST THING FROM PARIS
—KISS ME AND 'TIS DAY

1913. *HIGH JINKS*
Book and lyrics by Leo Ditrichstein and Otto Harbach, and starring Elaine Hammerstein in a cast that included Ignatti Martinetti, Tom Lewis and Elizabeth Murray.
—SOMETHING SEEMS TINGLE-ING-ELING
—JIM
—IS THIS LOVE AT LAST?
—I'M THROUGH WITH ROAMING ROMEOS
—CHI-CHI
—NOT NOW BUT LATER
—I KNOW YOUR HUSBAND VERY WELL
—COME HITHER EYES
—THE BUBBLE
—WHEN SAMMY SANG THE MARSEILLAISE
—DIXIANA RISE
—HIGH JINKS
—ALL ABOARD FOR DIXIELAND
By Jack Yellen and George L. Cobb.

1915. *THE PEASANT GIRL*
Book by Edgar Smith, lyrics by Herbert Reynolds and Harold Atteridge, and starring Emma Trentini in a cast that included Clifton Crawford, Ernest Hare and John Charles Thomas.
—AND DREAMS COME TRUE
—LISTEN, DEAR (THE BEST WALTZ OF ALL)
—HEART OF A ROSE
—WHEN ONE YOU LOVE
—THE FLAME OF LOVE
—WANDA
—LOVE IS LIKE A BUTTERFLY
—KNOCK, KNOCK—NOBODY HOME

1915. *KATINKA*
Book and lyrics by Otto Harbach, and co-starring Adele Rowland and Franklyn Ardell.
—IN VIENNA
—KATINKA
—ONE WHO WILL UNDERSTAND
—IN A HURRY
—RACKETY-COO
—STAMBOUL
—YOUR PHOTO
—THE WEEKLY WEDDING
—THE WALKING MUSIC STORE
—MY PARADISE
—I CAN TELL BY THE WAY YOU DANCE, DEAR
—I WANT ALL THE WORLD TO KNOW
—SKIDISKISCATCH
—I WANT TO MARRY A MALE QUARTET
—ALLAH'S HOLIDAY

1917. *YOU'RE IN LOVE*
Book and lyrics by Otto Harbach and Edward Clark, and presented by a cast headed by Carl McCullough, Clarence Nordstrom and May Thompson.
—MARRIED LIFE
—YOU'RE IN LOVE
—KEEP OFF THE GRASS
—HE WILL UNDERSTAND
—BUCK UP
—THINGS YOU MUST NOT DO
—SNATCHED FROM THE CRADLE
—BE SURE IT'S LIGHT
—A YEAR IS A LONG, LONG TIME
—LOVE LAND
—THE MUSICAL SNORE
—I AM ONLY DREAMING
—THAT'S THE ONLY PLACE WHERE OUR FLAG SHALL FLY
—BOOLA BOO

1917. *KITTY DARLIN'*
A musical play based on David Belasco's "Sweet Kitty Bellairs," with book and lyrics by P. G. Wodehouse and starring Alice Nielson.
—DEAR BATH
—THE BLARNEY STONE
—SWING SONG
—KITTY DARLIN'
—AM I TO BLAME?
—I'D DO THE SAME
—YOU'LL SEE
—THE SWORD OF MY FATHER
—WHEN SHE GIVES HIM A SHAMROCK BLOOM
—THE MAID AND THE VALET
—NOAH

—PEGGY'S LEG
—JUST WE TWO
—THE DAWN OF LOVE
—SPREAD THE NEWS
—DEAR OLD DUBLIN

1918. *SOMETIME*
Book and lyrics by Rida Johnson Young, and presented by a cast headed by Ed Wynn, Mae West and Francine Larrimore.
—ANY KIND OF MAN
—BABY DOLL
—BEAUTIFUL NIGHT
—SOMETIME
—DEARIE
—KEEP ON SMILING
—NO ONE BUT YOU
—OH ARGENTINE
—PICKING PEACHES
—SPANISH MAID
—THE TUNE YOU CAN'T FORGET

1918. *GLORIANNA*
Book and lyrics by Catherine Chisholm Cushing, and starring Eleanor Painter in a cast that included Ralph Whitehead and Alexander Clark.
—THE DANCING LESSON
—FROCKS AND FRILLS
—JUST A LITTLE LAUGHTER
—NENETTE AND RIN TIN TIN
—WHEN A GIRL
—SPEAK FOR YOURSELF, JOHN
—LOVE, LOVE, LOVE
—TOODLE-OO
—CHIANTI
—MY CLIMBING ROSE
—THE BEST MAN NEVER GETS THE WORST OF IT
—CRYSTAL BALL
—TEA IN THE ORIENT
—EVERYDAY WILL BE SUNDAY WHEN THE TOWN GOES DRY

1919. *TUMBLE INN*
Book and lyrics by Otto Harbach, and presented by a cast headed by Peggy O'Neil, Zelda Sears, Johnny Ford, Herbert Corthell and Charles Ruggles.
—I'VE TOLD MY LOVE
—LIMBO LAND
—A LITTLE CHICKEN FIT FOR OLD BROADWAY
—THE THOUGHTS I WROTE ON THE LEAVES OF MY HEART
—THE TROUSSEAU BALL
—THE WEDDING BLUES
—WON'T YOU HELP ME OUT?
—YOU'LL DO IT ALL OVER AGAIN
—TROUSSEAU WALTZ

—GOWNS SOFT AND CLINGY
—SNUGGLE AND DREAM
—THE LAUGH
—VALSE AU L'AIR

1919. *THE LITTLE WHOOPER*
Book by Otto Harbach, lyrics by Bide Dudley, and with Vivienne Segal and Sydney Grant heading the cast.
—OH YOU MAJOR SCALES
—TWINKLE LITTLE STAR
—OH WHAT A LITTLE WHOOPER
—ROUND THE CORNER
—I HAVE A DATE
—IT CAN'T BE WRONG
—IT'S GREAT TO BE MARRIED
—I'VE GOT TO LEAVE YOU
—I'M LONELY WHEN I'M ALONE
—THE KISS
—SNAP YOUR FINGERS
—IF YOU GO I'LL DIE
—WE MAY MEET AGAIN
—YOU'LL DREAM AND I'LL DREAM
—THERE'S ONLY ONE THING TO DO
—LET IT BE SOON
—GOOD MORNING ALL

M. Louis Ganne Score

1910. *HANS THE FLUTE PLAYER*
A musical fantasy, inspired by "The Pied Piper of Hamlin", with book by Maurice Vaucaire and Georges Mitchell, lyrics by A. St. John Brennan, and presented by a cast headed by Georges Chadal and Olive Ulrich.
—HANS
—I COME FROM AFAR
—SONG OF THE FLUTE
—YOU CAN NEVER KNOW SIR

Charles J. Gebest Scores

1911. *THE RED WIDOW*
A musical comedy with book by Channing Pollock, lyrics by Rennold Wolf, and presented by a cast headed by Raymond Hitchcock and Gertrude Vanderbilt.
—I'LL NEVER LOOK AT A PRETTY GIRL AGAIN
—WHEN WOMAN IS THE QUESTION
—YOU CAN'T PAY THE LANDLORD WITH LOVE
—NEVER MIND SINGING JUST DANCE, MY DEAR
—I LOVE LOVE
—WE WILL GO GO TO GO-GO

1914. *THE BEAUTY SHOP*
A musical comedy with book by Channing Pollock, lyrics by Renold Wolf, and

presented by a cast headed by Tessa Kosta, Raymond Hitchcock, Marion Sunshine, Joseph Herbert and George Romaine.
—WHEN YOU HEAR THAT UMPAH-UMPAH IN THE BAND
—LONGING MY DEARIE FOR YOU
—MY TANGO QUEEN
—THE WAY A WOMAN WANTS TO LOVE A MAN
—WE'LL GO TO THE CABARET
—FISHING YARNS
—OLD DOCTOR BUDD
—I WANT TO LOOK LIKE LILLIAN RUSSELL
—AMERICAN TOURISTS
—COME ALONG
—'TWAS IN SEPTEMBER
By Benjamin Hapgood Burt and Silvio Hein.
—ALL DRESSED UP AND NO PLACE TO GO
By Benjamin Hapgood Burt and Silvio Hein.

George Gershwin Scores

1919. *LA-LA LUCILLE*
Book by Fred Jackson, lyrics by B. G. DeSylva and Arthur Jackson, and co-starring Jack Hazzard and Janet Velie.
—WHEN YOU LIVE IN A FURNISHED FLAT
—THE BEST OF EVERYTHING
—FROM NOW ON
—MONEY, MONEY, MONEY
—TEE-OODLE-UM-BUM-BO
—I LOVE TO BE LOVED BY YOU
—IT'S GREAT TO BE IN LOVE
—THERE'S MORE TO A KISS THAN THE SOUND
—SOMEHOW IT SELDOM COMES TRUE
—THE TEN COMMANDMENTS OF LOVE
—NOBODY BUT YOU
—THE LOVE OF A WIFE

1919. *MORRIS GEST'S MIDNIGHT WHIRL*
A revue presented by a cast headed by Helen Shipman, Bernard Granville, Bessie McCoy Davis and the Rath Brothers. Lyrics by Irving Caesar and John Henry Mears.
—I'LL SHOW YOU A WONDERFUL WORLD
—THE LEAGUE OF NATIONS DEPEND ON BEAUTIFUL CLOTHES
—BABY DOLLS

—LET CUTIE CUT YOUR CUTICLE
—DOUGHNUT SONG
—LIMEHOUSE NIGHTS
—POPPYLAND

Jean Gilbert Scores

1912. *MODEST SUZANNE*
A musical comedy with book and lyrics by Harry B. and Robert B. Smith, and presented by a cast headed by Sallie Fisher, Lawrence Wheat and Ernest Torrence.
—SUZANNE, SUZANNE
—CONFIDENCE
—VIRTUE IS ITS OWN REWARD
—A MODEL MARRIED PAIR
—PARIS
—ALL THE WORLD LOVES A LOVER
—FATHER AND SON
—THE RETURN
—THE TANGALANGO TAP
By Grant Clarke and Jean Schwartz.
—I WOULD LIKE TO SEE THE PEACHES
By Harry Ralph and Jean Schwartz.

1914. *QUEEN OF THE MOVIES*
A musical comedy with book and lyrics by Glen MacDonough, and presented by a cast headed by Valli Valli, Alice Dovey and Frank Moulan.
—PARDON ME IF I STUTTER
—WHO IS TO KNOW?
—FORGIVE AND FORGET
—OH, CECELIA
—GIRLS RUN ALONG
—CUTIE
—WHEN THE MOON SLYLY WINKS IN THE NIGHT
—WHISTLE
Music by Leslie Stuart.
—FOLLOW THE CROWD
By Irving Berlin.

E. Ray Goetz Scores

1913. *ALL ABOARD*
With Malvin Franklin. A revue with book by Mark Swan, lyrics by the composer, and presented by a cast headed by Lew Fields, Lawrence D'Orsay, Zoe Barnett, Carter De Haven, Flora Parker, George Monroe and Will Philbrick.
—CUBIST GIRL
—GOODBYE POOR OLD MANHATTAN
—IN MY GARDEN OF EDEN FOR TWO
—LOVE IS JUST THE SAME OLD GAME IN EVERY LAND
—MR. BROADWAY, U. S. A.
—THE RAGTIME YODELING MAN

—TULIP TIME
—UNDER THE CHINA MOON
—ASIA
By John Lindsay.
—SERAFINA
By Joaquin Valverde.

1913. *THE PLEASURE SEEKERS*
A revue with book by Edgar Smith, lyrics by the composer, and presented by a cast headed by Harry Cooper, Bobby North, Dorothy Jardon, Max Rogers, William Montgomery and Florence Moore.
—MY AVERNE ROSE
With Bert Grant.
—I'VE GOT A LITTLE CHALET IN THE VALLEY
With Bert Grant.
—GIVE ME SOMETHING IN A UNIFORM OF BLUE
—LOVE ME TO A VIENNESE MELODY
—SWITZERLAND
—THE ALPINE GIRL
—SIT DOWN YOU'RE ROCKING THE BOAT
—LEVI IS A GRAND OLD NAME
—FOLLOW THE MIDNIGHT GIRL
—DON'T BLAME IT ALL ON BROADWAY
By Joe Young, Harry Williams and Bert Grant.
—THEY WERE ON THEIR HONEYMOON
—HE'D HAVE TO GET UNDER, GET OUT AND GET UNDER (TO FIX UP HIS AUTOMOBILE)
By Grant Clarke, Edgar Leslie and Maurice Abrahams.
—THERE'S A LOT OF PRETTY LITTLE THINGS IN PARIS

1917. *HITCHY-KOO*
This was the premiere production of this annual revue with book and lyrics by Harry Grattan and Glen MacDonough, and starring Raymond Hitchcock in a cast that included Irene Bordoni, William Rock, Grace LaRue, Frances White, Leon Errol and George Monroe.
—CHINESE LETTER SONG
—DRIVING HOME WITH ANGELINE
—THE PILL BOX REVUE
—WHEN YOU'VE PICKED YOUR BASKET OF PEACHES
—THE ISLE OF LOST ROMANCE
—DREAMY PARISIAN TUNE
—IF YOU WERE HERE
—IT'S EASIER TO KISS THAN TALK
—LADY OF THE SEA
—I WISH I WAS A BIG SKYROCKET
—SIX TIMES SIX IS THIRTY-SIX
By Bert Hanlon and William White.
—I'D LIKE TO BE A MONKEY IN THE ZOO
By Bert Hanlon and William White.
—M-I-S-S-I-S-S-I-P-P-I
Music by Harry Tierney.
—I MAY BE GONE FOR A LONG, LONG TIME
By Lew Brown and Albert VonTilzer.

1917. *WORDS AND MUSIC*
A revue with book by Raymond Hitchcock, lyrics by the composer, and presented by a cast headed by Wellington Cross, Marion Davies, Elizabeth Brice, Richard Carle, Edna Aug and William, Ray and Gordon Dooley.
—CHRISTMASTIDE LOVE
Music by Willy White.
—EVERYTHING LOOKS ROSY AND BRIGHT
—GINGER
—HANDLE ME WITH CARE
Music by Jean Schwartz.
—MY BROADWAY BUTTERFLY
Music by Willy White.
—RAG DOLL
Music by Willy White.
—STOP YOUR CAMOUFLAGING WITH ME
Music by Jean Schwartz.
—THEY'LL BE WHISTLING IT ALL OVER TOWN
Music by Jean Schwartz.
—LADY ROMANCE
—IT'S ALL RIGHT IF YOU'RE IN LOVE
—I MAY STAY AWAY A LITTLE LONGER
—NEW YORK, WHAT'S BECOME OF YOU?
—IF YOU HAVEN'T ANSWERED NO
—WALK DOWN THE AISLE WITH ME

John Golden Scores

1912. *OVER THE RIVER*
A musical comedy with book by George V. Hobart and H. A. DuSochet, lyrics by the composer, and presented by a cast headed by Eddie Foy, Lillian Lorraine, Mae Busch, Peggy Wood and Maurice and Walton.
—THE DAY WE CELEBRATE
—MEXICO
—WHEN THERE'S NO LIGHT AT ALL
—COONTOWN QUARTET
—RING-A-TING-A-LING ON THE TELEPHONE

—THE RAGGETY MAN
—EDNA MAY
—CHOP STICK RAG
—LOCK-STEP, TWO-STEP SLIDE
—NEW YORK ISN'T SUCH A BAD OLD
  TOWN
By Billy Jerome and Jean Schwartz.
—THE MAURICE RAG
By William H. Penn.
—THE BROADWAY CABARET
By E. J. Griffin and Charles N. Grant.
1916. *GO TO IT*
A musical version of Charles H. Hoyt's
"A Milk White Flag" by Anne Caldwell
and John E. Hazzard, and presented by
a cast headed by Percival Knight, Ger-
trude Vanderbilt, Helen Bond and Wel-
lington Cross.
—LADIES DAY
—KISS YOUR SOLDIER BOY
—COME ALONG GIRLS
—GIRLS IF YOU EVER GET MAR-
  RIED
—EVERY LITTLE WHILE
—EXTRA!
—LANGUANAY
—DOESN'T ANYBODY WANT ME?
—LOVE ME JUST A LITTLE BIT
—A LITTLE WORLD OF OUR OWN
—WHEN YOU'RE IN LOVE YOU'LL
  KNOW
Music by Jerome Kern.
—THERE'S SOMETHING ABOUT YOU
—KEEP ME FROM FALLING ASLEEP
—YOU'RE THE GIRL THAT SETS ME
  STUTTERING
—GO TO IT
Music by Raymond Hubbell and Max
Darewski.
—WHERE'S THE LITTLE BOY FOR
  ME?
By Schuyler Greene and Charles N. Grant.
—LITTLE BY LITTLE AND BIT BY
  BIT
By Schuyler Green and Worten David.

Alfred Goodman Score

1919. *LINGER LONGER LETTY*
A musical comedy with book by Anne
Nichols, lyrics by Bernard Grosman and
Oliver Morosco, and starring Charlotte
Greenwood in a cast that included Olin
Howard.
—SSH-SSH-SSH
—DID YOU, MY BOY, DID YOU?
—LET'S PRETEND
—PARISIENNE MECHANICAL MAR-
  VELS

—MOVEMENTS
—TWO TO ONE
—A TWENTIETH CENTURY LULLABY
—CLIMBING THE LADDER OF LOVE
—LINGER LONGER LETTY
—SLOW TOWN IS JAZZ TOWN NOW
—OH BY JINGO, OH BY GEE
By Lew Brown and Albert VonTilzer.

Bruno Granichstaedten Score

1912. *THE ROSE MAID*
With Anslem Goetzl. A musical comedy
with book by Harry B. Smith and Ray-
mond Peck, lyrics by Harry B. Smith, and
starring Gallagher and Shean in a cast
that included Edith Decker and J. H.
Duffey.
—TWO LITTLE HEARTS
—THE COURSE OF TRUE LOVE
—LIBERTY HALL
—TELEPHONE
—THE HAPPY FAMILY
—LOST A HEART
—MONEY TALKS
—MOON, LOVELY MOON
—ONE WALTZ, ONLY ONE WALTZ
—ROSES BLOOM FOR LOVERS
—SWEETHEARTS, WIVES AND GOOD
  FELLOWS
—WHEN TWO HEARTS BEAT TO-
  GETHER
—THE HEIRESSES
Music by Robin Hood Bowers.
—TIP YOUR HAT TO THE AMERICAN
  MILLIONAIRESS
—SOLDIERS OF BOHEMIA
Music by Robin Hood Bowers.
—THE AMERICAN HEIRESS
—I LIVE FOR YOU ALONE
—NOW HIS CHOICE WE SEE

Bert Grant Score

1916. *STEP THIS WAY*
A musical comedy with book by Edgar
Smith, lyrics by E. Ray Goetz, and pre-
sented by a cast headed by Lew Fields,
Alice Fisher, John Charles Thomas, Er-
nest Torrence, Gladys Clark and Lew
Brice.
—KEEP UP THE PACE
—ROMANY
—HEART OF THE GOLDEN WEST
—BY THE SAD LUANA SHORE
—STEP THIS WAY
—YOU OUGHT TO GO TO PARIS
—WHEN YOU STEP OFF AT CAIRO,
  ILLINOIS
—LOVE ME AT TWILIGHT

—WON'T YOU BUY?
—ALL FOR YOU
—IF I KNOCK THE "L" OUT OF
  KELLY
Lyrics by Sam Lewis and Joe Young.
I'VE GOT A SWEET TOOTH BOTH-
ERING ME
By Irving Berlin.

Charles N. Grant Songs

1916. *BROADWAY AND BUTTERMILK*
A comedy by Willard Mack with songs,
and presented by a cast headed by
Blanche Ring, Charles Withers and
Charles Walton. Lyrics by Schuyler
Greene.
—GIRLS IF YOU EVER GET MARRIED
—PICKIN' 'EM UP AND LAYIN' 'EM
  DOWN
—I HAVE ALWAYS BEEN THE PATSY
Music by Dave Stamper.

Silvio Hein Scores

1910. *THE YANKEE GIRL*
A musical comedy with book and lyrics
by George V. Hobart, and starring
Blanche Ring in a cast that included
Harry Gilfoil, Dorothy Jardon, William
Halliday and Charles Winninger.
—THE YANKEE GIRL
—TOP OF THE MORNING
—HYPNOTIZING RAG
—WHERE'S MAMA?
—LOUISIANA ELIZABETH
—MAID OF SEVILLA
—ALL, ALL ALONE
—I'LL MAKE A RING AROUND ROSIE
—WHOOP DADDY OODEN DOODEN
  DAY
—NORA MALONE
—I'VE GOT RINGS ON MY FINGERS
  AND BELLS ON MY TOES
By Weston, Barnes and Maurice Scott.

1910. *A MATINEE IDOL*
A musical comedy with book by Armand
Barnard, lyrics by E. Ray Goetz and Sey-
mour Brown, and presented by a cast
headed by Louise Dresser, Joseph Sant-
ley and DeWolf Hopper.
—EXERCISE
—A YANKEE ROMEO
—LOVING WAYS
—AUTOGRAPHS
—THE DANCING BANSHEE
—I'LL ALWAYS LOVE YOU DEAR
—MISS BODDLE AND HER POODLE
—NONSENSE

—HYPNOTIC WALTZ
—LITTLE LADY IN THE MOON
—IF YOU COULD ONLY SEE YOUR-
  SELF AS OTHER PEOPLE DO
—TAKE A LOOK AT ME NOW
—I WANT TO WED A JOCKEY BOY
—LET ME BUILD A NEST FOR YOU

1910. *JUDY FORGOT*
A musical comedy with book and lyrics
by Avery Hopwood, and presented by a
cast headed by Truly Shattuck, Joseph
Santley and Marie Cahill.
—STUDENTS' SERENADE
—THE QUARREL
—SONG OF THE HONEYMOON
—GOOD MO'NIN' JUDGE
—MY SOLDIER BOY
—THE STAR FACTORY
—GIVE ME ALL THE FLOWERS
—JUDY TWO-STEP
—WHOOP-LA
—DREAM, DREAM MAN
—WOMEN'S EYES
—THINKY THINKY THINK
—MY TOREADOR
—THE SOCIETY CIRCUS
—TURKISH LOVE SONG

1913. *WHEN DREAMS COME TRUE*
A musical comedy with book and lyrics
by Philip Bartholomae, and presented by
a cast that included Joseph Santley, Am-
elia Summerville, Anna Wheaton and
Mae Vokes.
—AMERICA
—BEAUTIFUL BOUNDING SEA
—DEAR WORLD
—WHEN DREAMS COME TRUE
—YOU, D-E-A-R, YOU
—LOVE IS SUCH A FUNNY LITTLE
  FEELING
—COME ON, ALL TOGETHER
—THE OK TWO-STEP
—WHO'S THE LITTLE GIRL?
—THERE AIN'T NO HARM IN WHAT
  YOU DO
—THE BOY WITH THE VIOLIN
—COME ALONG TO THE MOVIES
—LAUGHING WATER RIPPLE
—MINNIE, HA HA
—IT'S GREAT TO BE A WONDERFUL
  DETECTIVE
—THE TOWN THAT GROWS WHERE
  THE HARLEM FLOWS
—WHEN THE CLOCK STRIKES ONE

1914. *MISS DAISY*
A musical comedy with book and lyrics
by Philip Bartholomae, and presented by
a cast headed by Anna Wheaton, Mae

Murray, Charles Murray, Allen Kearns and John Boyle.
—DREAM, OH DREAM
—WON'T YOU DANCE?
—I ADORE THE AMERICAN GIRL
—I LOVE YOU, DEAR, I LOVE YOU
—IF YOU PROPOSE TO PROPOSE
—MY QUEEN BEE
—TEA LEAVES
—WEAVE FROM YOUR LOOMS
—YOUTH
—YOU CAN'T STOP ME FROM THINKING
—THE RACE OF LIFE
—CHEER UP
—YOU WERE MADE FOR LOVE
—GENTLE MOON
—SHADOWS
—KISSING
—CHERRIES ARE RIPE
—LITTLE GIRL WHAT HAVE YOU DONE TO ME?
—PIERROT'S BALL

1915. *ALL OVER TOWN*
A musical comedy with book by Joseph Santley, lyrics by Harry B. Smith, and presented by a cast headed by Joseph Santley, Walter Jones and Blanche Deyo.
—TALK, TALK, TALK
—I CANNOT TAKE A STEP TOO FAR
—I CAN'T FORGET YOUR EYES
—DON'T TEMPT ME
—NO ONE'S TO BLAME BUT YOU
—ANY OLD PLACE WHERE I HAVE A GOOD TIME
—TODDLE ALL OVER TOWN
—IT'S A GAME OF POLO
—MY MOVING PICTURE MAN
—SOME LITTLE BUG WILL FIND YOU SOME DAY
By Roy Atwell and Benjamin Hapgood Burt.

1917. *FURS AND FRILLS*
A musical comedy with book and lyrics by Edward Clark, and presented by a cast that included Ruby Norton, Ernest Torrence and Frances Demarest.
—DOES POLLY WANT WALLY?
—A SHORT FAREWELL IS BEST
—THE YULETIDE SPIRIT
—ALWAYS TAKE MOTHER'S ADVICE
—FURS AND FRILLS
—IT'S EASY TO LIE TO YOUR HUSBAND
—THIS IS SURE MY LUCKY DAY
—HEART OF MY HEART
—WHEN MY WIFE RETURNS

—YOU CAN'T TAKE IT WITH YOU WHEN YOU DIE
—MAKE YOURSELVES AT HOME
—THE TALE OF A COAT

1917. *FLO FLO*
A musical comedy with book and lyrics by Fred DeGresac and Edward Paulton, and starring Vera Michelena.
—A WONDERFUL CREATURE
—THERE'S ONLY ONE LITTLE GIRL
—BUSINESS IS BUSINESS
—GOODBYE HAPPY DAYS
—IN SPAIN
—LINGERIE
—WHEN A SMALL TOWN GIRL MEETS A SMALL TOWN BOY
—WOULD YOU SAY NO?
—IF IT WASN'T FOR MY WIFE AND FAMILY
—I DON'T SEE WHAT YOU SEE IN ME
—THAT'S THE KIND OF A BOY FOR ME
—DON'T TRUST THEM
—THE ZIEGFELD GIRL
—SARAH FROM SAHARA
Music by Hugo Frey.

1918. *HE DIDN'T WANT TO DO IT*
A musical comedy with book and lyrics by George Broadhurst, and presented by a cast headed by Ernest Torrence, Helen Shipman and Ned Sparks.
—WHAT MOTHER USED TO SAY TO ME
—WHAT WOULD YOU DO IN A CASE LIKE THAT?
—THE SONG OF THE TREES
—I'M DYING TO DANCE WITH OSCAR
—EVERYONE HE SWEAR AT THE WAITER
—I'M ONLY A GIRL FROM THE CITY
—THE SONG OF THE WORLD
—IT'S THE SCOTCH
—NOTHING ESCAPES ME
—THE SPIRIT OF THE CARNIVAL
—I'M FOND OF THE GIRLS
—YOU'RE THE ONLY ONE FOR ME

Victor Herbert Scores

1910. *NAUGHTY MARIETTA*
Book and lyrics by Rida Johnson Young, and co-starring Emma Trentini and Orville Harrold.
—TRAMP, TRAMP, TRAMP ALONG THE HIGHWAY
—DREAM MELODY
—DANCE OF THE MARIONETTES

—IT'S PRETTY SOFT FOR SIMON
—I'M FALLING IN LOVE WITH SOME-
    ONE
—ITALIAN STREET SONG
—CONVENT MAIDS
—'NEATH THE SOUTHERN MOON
—SAN DOMINGO GIRL
—NAUGHTY MARIETTA
—*AH SWEET MYSTERY OF LIFE
—SWEET BYE-AND-BYE
—IF I WERE ANYBODY ELSE BUT ME
—ALL I CRAVE IS MORE OF LIFE

1911. *WHEN SWEET SIXTEEN*
    Book and lyrics by George V. Hobart, and
    with William Norris, Roy Purviance and
    Josie Intropodi.
—WILD ROSE
—THERE ONCE WAS A PRINCE
—ROSALIND
—FAIRYLAND
—THERE'S MONEY IN GRAFT
—OH, THOSE BOYS!
—THEY FOLLOW ME EVERYWHERE
—MY TOAST TO YOU
—A MAN'S A MAN FOR A' THAT
—PEOPLE WILL TALK
—MAH HONEYLOVE

1911. *THE DUCHESS*
    Book and lyrics by Joseph Herbert and
    Harry B. Smith, and co-starring Fritzi
    Scheff and John E. Hazzard.
—GIRLIE LAND
—SALLY
—THE CORYPHEE
—UPSI-DAISY
—THE LAND OF THE SULTAN'S
    DREAMS
—ISN'T IT NASTY OF PAPA?
—WHAT'S THE USE OF MOONLIGHT?
—IF I SHALL DREAM OF YOU
—I'M SUCH A ROMANTIC GIRL
—CUPID TELL ME WHY
—THERE'S A SOUL MATE

1911. *THE ENCHANTRESS*
    Book by Fred DeGresac and lyrics by
    Harry B. Smith, starring Kitty Gordon.
—GOLD FISH SONG (COME, LITTLE
    FISHES)
—WHEN THE RIGHT MAN SINGS
    TRA-LA-LA
—THAT PRETTY LITTLE SONG
—TO THE LAND OF MY OWN RO-
    MANCE
—ART IS CALLING FOR ME (I WANT
    TO BE A PRIMA DONNA)
—I'VE BEEN LOOKING FOR A PER-
    FECT MAN
—ONE WORD FROM YOU
—THEY ALL LOOK GOOD WHEN

THEY'RE FAR AWAY

1912. *THE LADY OF THE SLIPPER*
    Book by Lawrence McCarthy and Anne
    Caldwell, lyrics by James O'Dea, and with
    a cast that included Elsie Janis, Mont-
    gomery and Stone, James Reaney, Peggy
    Wood and Vernon Castle.
—AT THE BAL MASQUE
—ENTRANCE OF CINDERELLA
—CAT DUET
—THE PRINCESS OF FAR-AWAY
—A LITTLE GIRL AT HOME
—GAMES OF HALLOWE'EN
—PUT YOUR BEST FOOT FORWARD,
    LITTLE GIRL
—LIKE A REAL, REAL MAN
—BAGDAD
—JUST LOVE ME ALL THE TIME
—JUST YOU AND I IN DREAMLAND

1913. *SWEETHEARTS*
    Book by Harry B. Smith and Fred De-
    Gresac, lyrics by Robert B. Smith, and
    with a cast headed by Christie MacDonald
    and Tom MacNaughton.
—CRICKET ON THE HEARTH
—IRON, IRON, IRON
—WHILE ON PARADE
—THERE IS MAGIC IN A SMILE
—MOTHER GOOSE
—THE ANGELUS
—PILGRIMS OF LOVE
—EVERY LOVER MUST MEET HIS
    FATE
—SWEETHEARTS
—THE IVY AND THE OAK
—I DON'T KNOW HOW I DO IT BUT
    I DO
—IN THE CONVENT THEY NEVER
    TAUGHT ME THAT
—GAME OF LOVE
—JEANETTE AND HER LITTLE
    WOODEN SHOES
—I MIGHT BE YOUR ONCE-IN-A-
    WHILE
—PRETTY AS A PICTURE
—WELCOMING THE BRIDE
—TO THE LAND OF MY OWN
    ROMANCE

1913. *THE MADCAP DUCHESS*
    Book and lyrics by David Stevens and
    Justin Huntley McCarthy, and starring
    Ann Swinburne with Peggy Wood and
    Glenn Hall in the supporting cast.
—THE SUN IS A-SLANT
—AURORA BLUSHING ROSILY
—LOVE AND I ARE PLAYING
—THE DEUCE YOUNG MAN
—TWEEDLEDUM AND TWEEDLEDEE
—OH, UP! IT'S UP!

—LOVE IS A STORY THAT'S OLD
—THAT IS ART
—TO PARIS
—NOW IS THE SOUTH WIND BLOW-
  ING
—BABETTE OF BEAUJOLAIS
—GODDESS OF MINE
—WINGED LOVE
—FAR UP THE HILL
—DO YOU KNOW?

1914. *THE ONLY GIRL*
  Book and lyrics by Henry Blossom Jr. and
  with a cast that included Adele Rowland,
  Wilda Bennett, Thurston Hall, Jed Prouty
  and Ernest Torrence.
—BE HAPPY BOYS TONIGHT
—WHEN YOU'RE AWAY
—PERSONALITY
—TELL IT ALL OVER AGAIN
—YOU'RE THE ONLY GIRL FOR ME
—HERE'S TO THE LAND WE LOVE,
  BOYS!
—EQUAL RIGHTS
—YOU HAVE TO HAVE A PART
—THE MORE I SEE OF OTHERS,
  THE BETTER I LIKE YOU
—HERE'S HOW
—WHEN YOU'RE WEARING THE BALL
  AND CHAIN

1914. *THE DEBUTANTE*
  Book and lyrics by Harry B. and Robert
  B. Smith, and with a cast headed by Hazel
  Dawn and William Danforth.
—LOVE IS A BATTLE
—MARRIED LIFE
—PROFESSOR CUPID
—ALL FOR THE SAKE OF A GIRL
—THE GOLDEN AGE
—THE LOVE OF THE LORLEI
—PEGGY'S A CREATURE OF MOODS
—NEVER MENTION LOVE WHEN
  WE'RE ALONE
—WHEN I PLAYED CARMEN
—THE BAKER'S BOY AND THE CHIM-
  NEY-SWEEP
—THE CUBIST OPERA
—CALL AROUND AGAIN
—THE WILL-O-THE-WISP
—THE DANCING LESSON
—THE FACE BEHIND THE MASK
—FATE
—THE SPRINGTIME OF LIFE IS FAIR-
  EST

1915. *PRINCESS PAT*
  Book and lyrics by Henry Blossom Jr, and
  with a cast that included Eleanor Painter,
  Sam Hardy, Alexander Clark, Eva Fallon,
  Al Shean and Doris Kenyon.
—I WISH I WAS AN ISLAND IN AN

OCEAN OF GIRLS
—I'D LIKE TO BE A QUITTER
—IN A LITTLE WORLD FOR TWO
—TWO LAUGHING IRISH EYES
—LOVE IS THE BEST OF ALL
—ESTELLITA
—THERE'S A MESSAGE OF LOVE IN
  YOUR EYES
—NEAPOLITAN LOVE SONG
—ALLIES
—ALL FOR YOU
—FOR BETTER OR FOR WORSE
—I NEED AFFECTION
—MAKE HIM GUESS
—THE SHOES OF HUSBAND NO. 1
  ARE WORN BY NO. 2

1917. *EILEEN*
  Book and lyrics by Henry Blossom, and
  co-starring Walter Scanlon and Grace
  Breen.
  This production was originally titled
  Hearts Of Erin, but while it was in re-
  hearsal for a Toronto opening, the theater
  burned down and the scenery and cos-
  tumes were destroyed. Victor Herbert
  claimed the fire was an act of arson in
  protest against his anti-English feelings.
  So the producers played safe and changed
  the title to *Eileen* for the New York pre-
  miere.
—ERIN SLANTHOGAL GO BRAGH
—LIFE'S A GAME AT BEST
—I'D LOVE TO BE A LADY
—FREE TRADE AND A MISTY MOON
—WHEN LOVE AWAKES
—IF EVE HAD LEFT THE APPLE ON
  THE BOUGH
—TOO-RE-LOO-RE
—CUPID, THE CUNNIN PANDEEN
—STARS AND ROSEBUDS
—EILEEN ALLANA ASTHORE
—IN ERIN'S ISLE
—MY LITTLE IRISH ROSE
—THINE ALONE
—THE IRISH HAVE A GREAT DAY
  TONIGHT
—WHEN SHALL I AGAIN SEE IRE-
  LAND?
—WHEN IRELAND STANDS AMONG
  THE NATIONS OF THE WORLD
—DINY'S SERENADE
—GLAD, TRIUMPHANT HOUR
—MY GOOD FRIENDS OF ERIN'S ISLE

1917. *HER REGIMENT*
  Book and lyrics by William LeBaron, and
  with a cast headed by Donald Brian and
  Frank Moulan.
—SOMEDAY
—OH, MY!

—AS THE YEARS ROLL BY
—IF THINGS WERE WHAT THEY SEEM
—'TWIXT LOVE AND DUTY
—SOLDIER MEN
—AMERICAN SERENADE
—ART SONG
—VIVE LA FRANCE
—NERVES
—SUPERLATIVE LOVE
—THE GIRL BEHIND THE GUN
—A LITTLE FARM IN NORMANDY

1919. *THE VELVET LADY*
Book by Fred Jackson, lyrics by Henry Blossom, and with a cast headed by Ernest Torrence, Georgia O'Ramey, Jed Prouty, Eddie Dowling and Fay Marbe.
—THERE'S NOTHING TOO FINE FOR THE FINEST
—SPOOKY-OOKUM
—I'VE DANCED TO BEAT THE BAND
—LOGIC
—LIFE AND LOVE
—FAIR HONEYMOON
—WHAT A POSITION FOR ME
—DANCING AT THE WEDDING

1919. *ANGEL FACE*
Book and lyrics by Harry B. and Robert B. Smith, and with John E. Young and Jack Donahue featured in the cast.
—EVERYBODY'S CRAZY HALF THE TIME
—THOSE SINCE-I-MET-YOU DAYS
—I MIGHT BE YOUR ONCE-IN-A-WHILE
—CALL IT A DAY
—BYE BYE, BABY
—I DON'T WANT TO GO HOME
—SOMEONE LIKE YOU
—MY IDEA OF SOMETHING TO GO HOME TO
—HOW DO YOU GET THAT WAY?
—TIP YOUR HAT TO HATTIE

Richard Herendeen Score

1916. *YVETTE*
A musical comedy with book by Benjamin Thorpe Gilbert, lyrics by the composer, and starring Chapine in the title role.
—WIMMENS
—LOVE'S SERENADE
—ST. CYR MARCH
—LOVE HOLDS SWAY
—SOME GIRLS
—TICK-TOCK
—I WANT ALL THE BOYS
—I LOVE YOU SO
—THE GALLOPING MAJOR

—JUST ONE MORE KISS
—SUMMER NIGHT
—AMERICAN BEAUTIES
—WONDERFUL KISS
—SOMEONE JUST LIKE YOU
—SILLY ASS
—SINCE I MET YOU
—A MODERN MELODY

Richard Heuberger Score

1912. *THE OPERA BALL*
A musical comedy with book and lyrics by Clare Kummer and Sydney Rosenfeld, and presented by a cast that included Marie Cahill and George Lydecker.
—WE HAVE ONLY ONE LIFE TO LIVE
—PARIS IS A SPOT SO FAIR
—WHAT ARE WE COMING TO?
—I WANT A LITTLE LOVIN' SOMETIME
By Chris Smith.
—SERGEANT PHILIP OF THE LANCERS
—LADY WITH THE TWINKLING FEET
—LET US FIND A CHARMING RENDEZVOUS
—THROUGH DELIGHT DAY AND NIGHT
—NEVER AGAIN
—FOLLY
—LISTEN TO ME
—KISS AND BE FRIENDS

B. C. Hilliam Score

1919. *BUDDIES*
A musical comedy with book by George V. Hobart, lyrics by the composer, and presented by a cast headed by Peggy Wood, Donald Brian and Roland Young.
—MY BUDDIES
—FAIRY TALES
—MY INDISPENSABLE GIRL
—HELLO HOME
—PLEASE LEARN TO LOVE
—TO BE TOGETHER IS THE THING
—THE HOME THEY LOVE SO DEAR
—DARLING ONE
—I NEVER REALIZED
By Cole Porter and Melville Gideon.

Louis A. Hirsch Scores

1910. *HE CAME FROM MILWAUKEE*
With Ben Jerome. Book by Mark Swan, lyrics by Edward B. Madden, and presented by a cast headed by Adele Rowland, Winona Winter, Amelia Summerville, Sam Bernard and Louis Harrison.

—IN GYPSY LAND
—WHEN WE ARE MARRIED TO YOU AND ME
—LOVE IS LIKE A RED, RED ROSE
—LENA
—MERRY WEDDING BELLS
—COME BACK TO BOHEMIA
—CONSEQUENCES
—ZINGA ZULA MAN
—TIE A RED RIBBON ON ME
—SENTIMENTAL MOON
—THERE'S AN AEROPLANE AIR ABOUT YOU
—THE CORONATION

1911. *REVUE OF REVUES*
With Melville J. Gideon. Book by Edgar Smith, Jean Havez and Leo Donnelly. Lyrics by Havez, Donnelly and Harold Atteridge. Gaby Deslys, the girl friend of King Alphonso of Spain, made her American debut in this production in a cast that included Harry Jolson (Al's brother), Ernest Hare, Frank Tinney, Maude Raymond, Lydia Berry and Dorothy Jardon.
—VISIT LOONEY PARK
—BOXING BOYS
—THE CARMEN GIRL
—ON THE CONGO
—PITTSBURGH, PA.
—BOARDWALK CRAWL
—TWENTY YEARS AGO
—THE MINSTREL BAND
—ORIENTAL EYES
—SOUSA'S MARCHES
—TONI CAPONI
—TRA-LA-LI

1912. *THE PASSING SHOW OF 1912*
With Earl Carroll. This was the premiere production in this series of annual Winter Garden revues, with book and lyrics by Harold Atteridge and starring Eugene and Willie Howard in a cast that included Jobyna Howland, Harry Fox, Anna Wheaton, Ernest Hare, Sydney Grant, Charlotte Greenwood, Trixie Friganza and Adelaide and Hughes.
—WE'VE BEEN TO EUROPE
—THERE YOU HAVE NEW YORK TOWN
—HANDY ANDY
—THE PIRATES AND THE QUAKER GIRL
—THE WEDDING GLIDE
—IDA
—MODERN LOVE
—GIRLISH LAUGHTER
—WHEN WAS THERE EVER A NIGHT LIKE THIS?

—ALL THE WORLD IS MADLY PRANCING
—THE BACCHANAL RAG
—A POLICEMAN'S LOT IS A HAPPY ONE
—YOU NEVER COULD TELL WE WERE MARRIED
—MY REUBEN GIRLIE
—IT'S ALL OVER NOW
—IN 2010
—THE KANGAROO HOP
—COHEN'S BAND
—ALWAYS TOGETHER
—THE PHILADELPHIA DRAG
By Harold Orlob.
—THE RAGTIME JOCKEY MAN
By Irving Berlin.

1915. *THE ZIEGFELD FOLLIES OF 1915*
With Dave Stamper. Book and lyrics by Channing Pollock, Rennold Wolf and Gene Buck. W. C. Fields made his "Follies" debut in a cast that included Ann Pennington, Mae Murray, Bert Williams, Bernard Granville, George White, Ina Claire, Leon Errol, Carl Randall and Ed Wynn, who got a clout over the head with a billiard cue from Fields one night for stealing laughs.
—MY ZEBRA LADY FAIR
—MY RADIUM GIRL
—HELLO, FRISCO, HELLO
—WE'LL BUILD A LITTLE HOME IN THE U. S. A.
—I CAN'T DO WITHOUT GIRLS
—I'LL BE SANTA CLAUS TO YOU
—MARIE ODILE
—A GIRL FOR EVERY MONTH IN THE YEAR
—ORIENTAL LOVE
—I'M NEUTRAL
—IN THE EVENING
—HOLD ME IN YOUR LOVING ARMS
—MIDNIGHT FROLIC GLIDE

1916. *ZIEGFELD FOLLIES OF 1916*
Book and lyrics by George V. Hobart and Gene Buck. Presented by a cast headed by Emma Haig, William Rock, Carl Randall, Francis White, Tot Qualters, Bernard Granville, Don Barclay, Ina Claire, Sam Hardy, Bert Williams, Allyn King, Marion Davies, Ann Pennington, Lilyan Tashman, W. C. Fields and Fanny Brice.
—I LEFT HER ON THE BEACH AT HONOLULU
—GOODBYE, DEAR OLD BACHELOR DAYS
—I WANT THAT STAR
—STOP AND GO
—BEAUTIFUL ISLAND OF GIRLS

[1910-1920] 119

—SIX LITTLE WIVES OF THE KING
In addition to the above songs, the follow-
ing numbers were interpolated in this pro-
duction.
—MY LADY OF THE NILE
—HAVE A HEART
—WHEN LIGHTS ARE LOW
—AIN'T IT FUNNY WHAT A DIFFER-
ENCE A FEW DRINKS MAKE?
Music by Jerome Kern.
—SOMNABULISTIC TUNE
By Dave Stamper.
—I'VE SAVED ALL MY LOVIN' FOR
YOU
By Dave Stamper.
—NIJINSKY
By Dave Stamper.
—I'VE SAID GOODBYE TO BROAD-
WAY
By Dave Stamper.
—THERE'S RAGTIME IN THE AIR
By Dave Stamper.

1916. *MY HOME TOWN GIRL*
Book and lyrics by Frank Stammers, and
starring Leila McIntyre and John Hyams.
—TONIGHT AT TEN
—HELLO, DOROTHY MAY
—BOY OF MINE I'LL WAIT FOR YOU
—THOUSANDS OF GIRLIES
—TILL YOU BELONG TO ME
—MY HOME TOWN
—MY CIGARETTE
—PERFUME OF LOVE
—TAKE A LITTLE KISS
—WHEN I FOUND YOU
—THE FORTUNE TELLING MAN

1917. *THE GRASS WIDOW*
Book and lyrics by Channing Pollock and
Rennold Wolf, and presented by a cast
headed by George Marion, Natalie Ault,
Victor Morley and Howard Marsh.
—SOUP
—C. D. Q.
—DANCE WITH ME?
—SONG OF LOVE
—FAREWELL (LETTER SONG)
—YOU CAN'T BE A HUSBAND TODAY
—THE GRASS WIDOW
—SOMEWHERE THERE'S SOMEONE
FOR ME
—JUST YOU AND ME
—ALL THE GIRLS HAVE GOT A
FRIEND IN ME

1917. *GOING UP*
A musical comedy based on James Montgomery's play, "The Aviator," with book
and lyrics by Otto Harbach and presented
by a cast headed by Frank Craven, Ruth

Donnelly, Donald Meek and Marion Sun-
shine.
—I'LL BET YOU
—I WANT A DETERMINED BOY
—IF YOU LOOK IN HER EYES
—GOING UP
—WHEN THE CURTAIN FALLS
—THE TOUCH OF A WOMAN'S HAND
—THERE'S A BRAND NEW HERO
—DO IT FOR ME
—THE TINKLE TOE
—UP, DOWN, LEFT, RIGHT
—HERE'S TO THE TWO OF YOU
—KISS ME

1918. *THE RAINBOW GIRL*
Book and lyrics by Rennold Wolf, and
presented by a cast headed by Ethel Del-
mar, Laura Hamilton and Billy B. Van.
—MY RAINBOW GIRL
—WON'T SOME NICE BOY MARRY
ME?
—JUST YOU ALONE
—ALIMONY BLUES
—IN A MONTH OR TWO
—WE FEAR YOU WILL NOT DO, LADY
WETHERELL
—LET'S GO DOWN TO THE SHOP
—LOVE'S EVER NEW
—MISTER DRUMMER MAN
—I WONDER
—SOON WE'LL BE UPON THE SCREEN
—BEAUTIFUL LADY
—I'LL THINK OF YOU

1918. *ZIEGFELD FOLLIES OF 1918*
Book and lyrics by Rennold Wolf and Gene
Buck. Marilyn Miller made her debut as
a "Follies" star in a cast that included
Eddie Cantor, Harry Kelly, Allyn King,
Ann Pennington, W. C. Fields, Lillian
Lorraine and the Fairbanks Twins.
—ANY OLD TIME AT ALL
—GARDEN OF YOUR DREAMS
—STARLIGHT
—SYNCOPATED TUNE
—WHEN I'M LOOKING AT YOU
—MINE WAS A MARRIAGE OF CON-
VENIENCE
—I WANT TO LEARN TO JAZZ DANCE
—I'LL PIN MY MEDAL ON THE GIRL
I LEFT BEHIND
By Irving Berlin.
—BLUE DEVILS OF FRANCE
By Irving Berlin.
—SHIP BUILDING SONG

1918. *OH, MY DEAR!*
Book and lyrics by Guy Bolton and P. G.
Wodehouse, and starring Ivy Sawyer and
Joseph Santley in a cast that included Roy
Atwell.

120

[1910-1920]

—CITY OF DREAMS
—I LOVE A MUSICAL COMEDY SHOW
—I WONDER WHETHER I'VE LOVED
  YOU ALL MY LIFE
—YOU NEVER KNOW
—NOW AND THEN BUT NOT ALL
  THE TIME
—I SHALL BE ALL RIGHT NOW
—ASK DAD
—COME WHERE NATURE CALLS
—PHOEBE SNOW
—GO LITTLE BOAT
  By Jerome Kern.
—TRY AGAIN
—CHILDHOOD DAYS
—I'LL ASK NO MORE
—IF THEY EVER PARTED ME FROM
  YOU
—IT SORTA MAKES A FELLOW STOP
  AND THINK
1919. SEE-SAW
  Book and lyrics by Earl Derr Biggers, and
  presented by a cast headed by Elizabeth
  Hines, Guy Robertson, Dorothea McKaye
  and Frank Carter.
—THE HAPPIEST MOMENT I'VE EVER
  KNOWN
—SEE-SAW
—WHEN TWO HEARTS DISCOVER
—A WORLD FULL OF GIRLS
—GOODBYE, HELLO
—WHEN YOU DANCE
—SENORITA
—PEEP-PEEP
—YOU'LL HAVE TO FIND OUT
—WON'T YOU COME AND JOIN THE
  NAVY?
—I JUST WANT JAZZ

Max Hoffman Score

1910. THE YOUNG TURK
  A musical comedy with book by Aaron
  Hoffman, lyrics by Harry Williams, and
  presented by a cast headed by Max Rog-
  ers, Fred Bowers and Mae Murray.
—I'LL BE HAPPY TOO
—I THOUGHT I WANTED OPERA
—THE PARISIAN GLIDE
—PROPOSALS
—THE SWORD IS MY SWEETHEART
  TRUE
—THOSE DEAR OLD WEDDING BELLS
—UNDER THE ORIENTAL MOON

Victor Hollander Scores

1912. THE CHARITY GIRL
  A musical comedy with book and lyrics
  by Edward Peple, and presented by a

cast headed by Blossom Seeley, Ralph
Herz and Miller and Lyles.
—THE BELLE OF THE BEACH
—COME, COME (THE CRADLE OF
  OUR HEARTS)
—I WANT A GIRL THAT'S ALL
—THE MAGIC KISS
—YUM-YUM TIME
—CHAMPAGNE
—RAGTIME DANCING MAN
  By Ed Rogers and Abel Baer.
—THE GHETTO GLIDE
  Music by Hollis Victor.
—THOSE RAGTME MELODIES
  By Gene Hodgkins.
1915. A MODERN EVE
  With Jean Gilbert. A musical comedy
  with book by Will Hough, lyrics by Ben-
  jamin Hapgood Burt, and presented by a
  cast headed by William Norris, Alexander
  Clark, Ernest Glendinning, Leila Hughes
  and Georgia Drew Mendum.
—THE SONG OF THE SIRENS
—THAT'S THE LESSON I'M TEACH-
  ING TO YOU
—WHEN LOVE COMES STEALING IN
—WHEN THE MADAME GOES AWAY
—GOODBYE EVERYBODY
—WON'T YOU SMILE?
—IS THE GIRL YOU MARRY STILL
  THE GIRL YOU LOVE?
—A QUIET EVENING AT HOME
  Music by Ben Jerome.
—KEEP MOVING
  Music by Otto Motzan.
—EXCUSE ME
—CERTAINLY
—I'D LOVE TO DANCE THROUGH
  LIFE WITH YOU
  By H. B. Smith and Jerome Kern.
—WAITING FOR YOU
  By H. B. Smith and Jerome Kern.

Karl Hoschna Scores

1910. KATY DID
  Book and lyrics by William C. Duncan
  and Frank Smithson, and starring Flor-
  ence May.
—SAVE UP YOUR KISSES FOR A
  RAINY DAY
—IN THE SWIM
—I JOHN, TAKE THEE, MILTILDA
—KATY DID
—THAT'S THE WAY WE DO IT OUT
  IN KANSAS
—COME CLOSER
—OUT WITH THE OWL
—NIGHT TIME
  By Louis Weslyn and Felix Arndt.

1910. *BRIGHT EYES*
Book by Charles Dickson, lyrics by Otto Harbach, and starring Florence Holbrook and Cecil Lean.
—ON WITH THE REHEARSAL
—TOM BOY, TOM BOY
—FOR YOU, BRIGHT EYES
—CHEER UP, MY HONEY
—THE MOOD YOU'RE IN
—GOOD OLD DAYS OF YORE
—THAT'S THE LIFE OF A STABLE BOY
—THE MAN ON THE BOX
—IF ONLY YOU WOULD TAKE A TIP FROM ME
—THE LINES IN MOLLY'S HANDS
—MRS. CASEY
—HE'S A FAN, FAN, FAN

1910. *MADAME SHERRY*
Book and lyrics by Otto Harbach, and starring Lina Abarbanell in a cast that included Frances Demarest, Ralph Herz, Elizabeth Murray and Jack Gardner.
—AESTHETIC DANCING
—THEOPHILUS
—EVERY LITTLE MOVEMENT
—THE KISS YOU GAVE
—UNCLE SAYS I MUSN'T, SO I WON'T
—BIRTH OF THE BUTTERFLY
—THE SMILE SHE MEANS FOR ME
—THE LOVE DANCE
—WON'T SOMEONE TAKE ME HOME?
—THE OTHER FELLOW
—I'M ALL RIGHT
—THE BIRTH OF PASSION
—OFF FOR A SAIL
—PUT YOUR ARMS AROUND ME, HONEY
—I WANT TO PLAY HOUSE WITH YOU
—WE ARE ONLY POOR WEAK MORTALS
During the run of this production, Elizabeth Murray sang the following interpolated numbers:
—DUBLIN RAG
By Harold Atteridge and Phil Schwartz.
—LOADING UP THE MANDY LEE
By Stanley Murphy and Henry I. Marshall.

1911. *JUMPING JUPITER*
Book and lyrics by Richard Carle and Sydney Rosenfeld, and presented by a cast headed by Richard Carle, Edna Wallace Hopper, Ina Claire and Jeanne Eagles, who made her Broadway debut in this production and achieved stardom eleven years later as Sadie Thompson in "Rain."
—IT ALL GOES UP IN SMOKE
—THE MAIL MAN
—ANGELO
—MEET ME TONIGHT AT 9
—THE REST OF THE WEEK SHE'S MINE
—NOTHING
—I LIKE TO HAVE A FLOCK OF MEN AROUND ME
—FASCINATION
—PET OF THE FAMILY
—THANK YOU, KIND SIR
—ROSA ROSANA
—KISS ME
—GEOGRAPHY
—SNUGGLE
—I'M AWFULLY AFRAID OF GIRLS
—IT CAN'T BE DID
—ONLY A MAN
—POSSUM RAG
—THE WEDDING MARCH

1911. *DR. DE LUXE*
Book and lyrics by Otto Harbach, and with Lillian Berry, Ernest Truex, Ralph Herz and William Pruette.
—MAMA'S LITTLE PET
—A MAN OF THE WORLD
—THE ACCENT MAKES NO DIFFERENCE IN THE LANGUAGE OF LOVE
—WAR IS HELL, BUT OH YOU JEALOUSY
—WHAT YOU WANT AND WHAT YOU GET
—THAT WILL KEEP HIM TRUE TO YOU
—FOR EVERY BOY THAT'S LONELY THERE'S A GIRL LONELY TOO
—THE FAMILY BRAWL
—THAT'S THE WAY TO TREAT A LITTLE DOGGIE
—NO ONE BUT YOU
—WHAT'S THE USE OF SAYING NO
—HIDE AND SEEK
—WHEN THE OLD TOP HUMMED
—THE HARUM-SCARUM
—LOVE'S A ROSE
—SKELETONS IN THE CLOSET

1911. *THE GIRL OF MY DREAMS*
Book by Wilbur Nesbit, lyrics by Otto Harbach, and starring Leila McIntyre and John Hyams in a cast that included Harry Clark and Anna Laughlin.
—BACHELOR DAYS
—BELLES OF THE TALLY-HO BOARDING SCHOOL
—I'M READY TO QUIT AND BE GOOD
—QUAKER TALK
—THE GIRL WHO WOULDN'T SPOON

—THE LETTER YOU SHOULDN'T HAVE SENT
—STORY OF A MARIONETTE
—SOMETHING VERY MYSTERIOUS
—SAUCE FOR THE GANDER IS SAUCE FOR THE GOOSE
—GIRL OF MY DREAMS
—EVERY GIRLIE LOVES ME BUT THE GIRL I LOVE
—DEAR LITTLE GAMES OF GUESSING
—OOH! MAYBE IT'S A ROBBER
—DOCTOR TINKLE TINKER

1911. *THE FASCINATING WIDOW*
Book and lyrics by Otto Harbach, and starring Julian Eltinge in a cast that included Winona Winter, Natalia Ault and Eddie Garvie.
—PUT YOUR ARMS AROUND ME
—THE FASCINATING WIDOW
—DON'T TAKE YOUR BEAU TO THE SEASHORE
—YOU BUILT A FIRE DOWN IN MY HEART
—LOVE IS THE THEME OF MY DREAM
—THE RAGTIME COLLEGE GIRL
—VALSE JULIAN
—DON'T YOU MAKE A NOISE
—I'M TO BE A BLUSHING BRIDE

1912. *THE WALL STREET GIRL*
Book by Margaret Mayo and Edgar Selwyn, lyrics by Benjamin H. Burt. A gum-chewing cowboy, who left the 101 Ranch to twirl a lasso in vaudeville, made his musical comedy debut in this production. His name was Will Rogers. Other members of the cast, then far more famous, were Blanche Ring, Charles Winninger and Wellington Cross.
—I WANT A REGULAR MAN
—ON THE QUIET
—DEEDLE-DUM-DEE
—LOVE IS A PECULIARITY
By Joseph McCarthy and Al Piantadosi.
—I SHOULD HAVE BEEN BORN A BOY
By A. Seymour Brown and Nat D. Ayer.
—THE INDIAN RAG
By A. Seymour Brown and Nat D. Ayer.
—YOU'RE SOME GIRL
By A. Seymour Brown and Nat D. Ayer.
—WHISTLE IT
By Billy Jerome and Jean Schwartz.
—I NEVER KNEW WHAT EYES COULD DO
By Stanley Murphy and Henry I. Marshall.
—SPOONEY LAND
By Ed Madden and M. J. Fitzpatrick.

Raymond Hubbell Scores

1910. *THE JOLLY BACHELORS*
Book and lyrics by Glen MacDonough, and co-starring Nora Bayes and Jack Norworth in a cast that included Billie Taylor, Elizabeth Brice, Gertrude Vanderbilt, Nat Fields, Stella Mayhew and Josie Sadler.
—TAX THE BACHELORS
—ROSA ROSETTA
—THE RED CROSS GIRL
—THE LUNCHEON LINE
—HAS ANYBODY HERE SEEN KELLY?
By C. W. Murphy, Will Letters and W. J. McKenna.
—PLEASE, OH, PLEASE
—LANGUAGE OF SIGNS
—WHAT AM I GOING TO DO TO MAKE YOU LOVE ME
—STOP THAT RAG
By Irving Berlin.
—FRESHIE, OH, FRESHIE
—THE SINGLE BIRD
—WE'UNS FROM DIXIE
—SAVANNAH
—THE AIRSHIP JOYRIDE
—YOUNG AMERICA
Words and music by Jack Norworth and Nora Bayes.
—COME ALONG MY MANDY
Words and music by Jack Norworth and Nora Bayes.

1910. *THE BACHELOR BELLES*
Book and lyrics by Harry B. Smith, and starring Adeline Genee in a cast that included Frank Lalor, Eva Fallon and Mae Murray.
—TRYING IT ON
—A POPULAR GIRL
—IT'S STYLE THAT MAKES THE GIRL
—SHE TRIMMED THEM ALL SO NICELY
—THE BACHELOR BELLES
—WHY DON'T YOU BE NICE TO SOME NICE FELLOW?
—I'M DYING FOR YOU
—EVERYBODY BRUSHES BY
—SONG OF THE FASHIONS
—IN VANITY FAIR
—KISSES AT AUCTION
—IF I JUST THINK OF HER
—YOU'VE BEEN KISSING THE BLARNEY STONE
—WHAT HAS BECOME OF THE GIRL I USED TO KNOW?
—ROSES AND BUTTERFLIES
—THE SUMMER GIRL
—GIVE US A RAGTIME TUNE
—THOSE WERE THE HAPPY DAYS
—CARMENITA

Al Jolson (*Robinson Crusoe*); Eddie Cantor (*Make It Snappy.*)

1911. *THE NEVER HOMES*
Book by Glen MacDonough, lyrics by E.
Ray Goetz, and presented by a cast head-
ed by George Monroe, Jess Dandy, Joseph
Santley, Bessie Clifford and Helen Hayes.
—TONIGHT'S THE NIGHT
—THERE'S A GIRL IN HAVANA
Music by A. Baldwin Sloane.
—TAKE ME ALONG WITH YOU,
  DEARIE
—I'M ALL FOR YOU
—FIRE BELLES
—THE FIRE LADIES' BALL
—THE KISS BURGLAR
—THAT SPOOKY TUNE
Music by A. Baldwin Sloane.
—GOOD MORNING, JUDGE
—FIRST LOVE DAYS
—THE BASEBALL GIRL
—HERE WE ARE SCRUBBING
—JUST A BIT OF LINGERIE

1911. *THE THREE ROMEOS*
Book and lyrics by R. H. Burnside, and
with Peggy Wood, Georgie Caine, William
Danforth and Fritz Williams.
—ALONG BROADWAY
—ANABELLA JEROME
—DIVORCE
—HE'S CRAZY
—IT'S NICE TO HAVE SOMEONE TO
  LOVE LIKE YOU
—MOONLIGHT
—EXPERIENCE
—OH, ROMEO
—THAT'S BETWEEN YOU AND ME
—SHE DIDN'T SEEM TO CARE
—MARY ANN, WHERE ARE YOU?
—I'VE BEEN LOOKING FOR A GIRL
  LIKE YOU
—HUMPTY DUMPTY

1911. *ZIEGFELD FOLLIES OF 1911*
With Maurice Levi. Book and lyrics by
George V. Hobart. With Bessie McCoy
Davis, Leon Errol, George White, the
Dolly Sisters, Bert Williams, Harry Wat-
son and Fanny Brice.
—NEW YORK
—THE WIDOW WOOD
—BE MY LITTLE BABY BUMBLEBEE
By Stanley Murphy and Henry Marshall.
—THE GIRL IN PINK
—IMITATION RAG
—TAKE CARE, LITTLE GIRL
—TEXAS TOMMY
—MY BEAUTIFUL LADY
—WOODMAN, WOODMAN, SPARE
  THAT TREE
By Irving Berlin.
—EPRAHAM
By Irving Berlin.

—THAT'S HARMONY
By Grant Clarke and Bert Williams.

1912. *ZIEGFELD FOLLIES OF 1912*
Book and lyrics by Harry B. Smith. The
cast was headed by Leon Errol, Harry
Watson, Bernard Granville, Bert Williams,
Lillian Lorraine and Rae Samuels.
—HURRY, LITTLE CHILDREN
—YOU MIGHT AS WELL STAY ON
  BROADWAY
—ROMANTIC GIRL
—YOU GOTTA KEEP GOIN'
—MOTHER DOESN'T KNOW
—THE BROADWAY GLIDE
—IN A PRETTY LITTLE COTTAGE
—SOCIETY CIRCUS PARADE
—GOOD OLD CIRCUS BAND
—IN A PRETTY LITTLE WHITE
  HOUSE OF OUR OWN
By Blanche Merrill and Leo Edwards.
—DIP, DIP, DIP
—BEAUTIFUL, BEAUTIFUL GIRLS
—ROW, ROW, ROW
By William Jerome and Jimmy Monaco.
—DADDY HAS A SWEETHEART AND
  MOTHER IS HER NAME
By Gene Buck and Dave Stamper.

1912. *THE MAN FROM COOK'S*
Book and lyrics by Henry Blossom, and
with Flavio Arcaro, Walter Percival and
Fred Walton heading the cast.
—ALL FOR YOU
—GIRL OF CHANCE
—A LITTLE WORLD FOR TWO
—NAPOLI
—PERHAPS
—TRAVELOGUE
—YOU AND I
—WE CAN'T DO WITHOUT MEN
—A LITTLE POT OF TEA
—WHY IS A GIRL? DO YOU KNOW?
—A WOMAN'S WORK IS NEVER DONE
—THE LITTLE TIN SOLDIER AND
  THE LITTLE RAG DOLL

1912. *A WINSOME WIDOW*
A musical comedy founded on Charles
H. Hoyt's "A Trip to Chinatown," and
presented by a cast headed by Harry
Kelly, Charles J. Ross, Charles King,
Leon Errol, Kathleen Clifford, Elizabeth
Brice, Frank Tinney, the Dolly Sisters,
Mae West and Jack Clifford.
—TEACH ME EVERYTHING YOU
  KNOW
—YOU'RE A REGULAR GIRL
—THEY MEAN MORE
—I TAKE AFTER DAD
—POUSSE CAFE
—PICCOLO
—SONGS OF YESTERDAY

—THE FRISCO
—COULD YOU LOVE A GIRL LIKE
  ME?
—FASCINATING GIRL
—I NEVER KNEW WHAT EYES
  COULD BE
By Stanley Murphy and Henry Marshall.
—STRING A RING OF ROSES
By Billy Jerome and Jean Schwartz.
1913. *ZIEGFELD FOLLIES OF 1913*
Book and lyrics by George V. Hobart.
Ann Pennington made her "Follies" debut
in this production in a cast that included
Nat Wills, Leon Errol, Frank Tinney and
Elizabeth Brice.
—YOU MUST HAVE EXPERIENCE
—KATIE ROONEY
—NEW YORK, WHAT'S THE MATTER
  WITH YOU?
—GOING THERE
—THE RAGTIME SUFFRAGETTE
—IF A TABLE AT RECTOR'S COULD
  TALK
—PANAMA
—HELLO, HONEY
—SLEEP TIME, MY HONEY
—YOU'RE SOME GIRL
—ISLE D'AMOUR
By Earl Carroll and Leo Edwards.
—NEVER TOO OLD TO LOVE
Gene Buck and Dave Stamper contributed
the following numbers to the score:
—JUST YOU AND I AND THE MOON
—EVERYBODY SOMETIME MUST
  LOVE SOMEBODY
—WITHOUT YOU
1914. *ZIEGFELD FOLLIES OF 1914*
With Dave Stamper. Book by George V.
Hobart, lyrics by Gene Buck, and Ed
Wynn making his Follies' debut in a cast
headed by Vera Michelena, Ann Pen-
nington, Gertrude Vanderbilt, Arthur
Deagon, Leon Errol and Bert Williams.
—BE CAREFUL WHAT YOU DO
—I'M A STATESMAN
—I'VE GOT HIM NOW
—THE HURDY-GURDY MAN
—I'M CURED
—BECAUSE I CAN'T TANGO
—RAGTIME REGIMENT
—THE LONE STAR GIRL
—THE FUTURIST GIRL
—SAVE YOUR LOVE FOR ME
—UNDERNEATH THE JAPANESE
  MOON
—GOOD NIGHT
—NIGHT LIFE IN OLD MANHATTAN
—NOBODY SEEMS TO CARE
—TANGORILLA

—PRUNELLA MINE
—NOTHING TO WEAR
—MY LITTLE PET CHICKEN
—THERE'S SOMETHING IN THE AIR
  IN SPRINGTIME
—AT THE BALL THAT'S ALL
By J. Leubrie Hill.
—ROCK ME IN A CRADLE OF LOVE
By J. Leubrie Hill.
1915. *FADS AND FANCIES*
Book and lyrics by Glen MacDonough,
and presented by a cast headed by Frank
Moulan, Tom MacNaughton, Madge Les-
sing, Leo Carrillo and Laura Hamilton.
—COME ACROSS
—I'M SEEKING A THRILL
—LOVE ME, LOVE MY DOG
—IT'S HEAVEN TO BOHEME
—HONEY
—I'M STILL SINGLE
—I'M LONELY FOR ONLY ONE
—MARY ANN O'SAN
—THE HUNT BALL
—MUSIC WITH MEALS
—WE'LL TAKE CARE OF YOU HERE
—THOSE GIRLS OF LONG AGO
—THEY DO YOU MUCH BETTER AT
  HOME
—NEVER AGAIN
—ALIMONY ALLEY
—THE YUCCA TANGO
1915. *HIP HIP HOORAY*
Book by R. H. Burnside, lyrics by John
Golden, and with Arthur Deagon, Belle
Storey, Nat Wills, Toto and John Philip
Sousa and his band being headlined in
this New York Hippodrome production.
—HIP, HIP, HOORAY
—FOR THE HONOR OF THE FLAG
—THE LADDER OF ROSES
—MY CUTIE DOLL
—MY FOX TROT WEDDING DAY
—THE WEDDING OF JACK AND JILL
—I'D RATHER BE A LAMP POST ON
  OLD BROADWAY
By Benjamin Hapgood Burt.
—MY LAND, MY FLAG
By Marcus C. Connelly and Zoel J. Par-
anteau.
—CHIN CHIN (OPEN YOUR HEART
  AND LET ME IN)
By A. Seymour Brown.
—SAN SAN SOO (IN A SAMPAN FOR
  TWO)
By Percy Edgar and Alfred J. Lawrence.
1916. *THE BIG SHOW*
Book by R. H. Burnside, lyrics by John
Golden, and with Toto, the clown, and
Pavlowa, the dancer, sharing headline

honors in this New York Hippodrome production.
—HIPPODROME STREET PARADE
—HELLO, I'VE BEEN LOOKING FOR YOU
—*POOR BUTTERFLY
Sung by Haru Onuki and the Elm City Four.
—WE'LL STAND BY OUR COUNTRY
—COME ON DOWN TO RAGTIME TOWN
—THE GOOD SHIP HONEYMOON
—QUEEN OF THE LAND OF SNOW
—MY SKATING GIRL
1917. *ZIEGFELD FOLLIES OF 1917*
With Dave Stamper and a patriotic finale by Victor Herbert. Book and lyrics by George V. Hobart and Gene Buck, with Will Rogers and Eddie Cantor making their Follies debut in a cast that included Irving Fisher, Walter Catlett, Lillian Tashman, W. C. Fields, Bert Williams, the Fairbanks Twins, Dorothy Dickson and Carl Hyson, Fanny Brice, Allyn King and Peggy Hopkins.
—MY ARABIAN MAID
—BEAUTIFUL GARDEN OF GIRLS
—THE POTATO BUG
—HELLO, DEARIE
—JUST YOU AND ME
—CHU, CHIN, CHOW
—JEALOUS MOON
—HOME, SWEET, HOME
By Ring Lardner.
—UNHAPPY
By Henry Creamer and J. Turner Layton.
—BECAUSE YOU'RE JUST YOU
Music by Jerome Kern.
—CAN'T YOU HEAR YOUR COUNTRY CALLING?
Music by Victor Herbert.
—THAT'S THE KIND OF BABY FOR ME
By Alfred Harrison and Jack Egan.
—MODERN MAIDEN'S PRAYER
By Ballard MacDonald and James Hanley.
1917. *CHEER UP*
Book by R. H. Burnside, lyrics by John Golden, and with Nat Wills, the tramp comic, and Harry Houdini, the magician, getting top New York Hippodrome billing.
—MELODY LAND
—BEAUTIFUL QUEEN OF THE NILE
—MY BRIDAL ROSE
—CHEER UP, LIZA
—JOY TOWN
—WON'T YOU FOLLOW ME THERE?
—WHAT A WONDERFUL MATE YOU'LL BE

—ONE, TWO, THREE
—THE BLUSHING BRIDE AND GROOM
Lyrics by William Jerome.
—WHEN OLD NEW YORK GOES DRY
By Benjamin Hapgood Burt.
1918. *THE KISS BURGLAR*
Book and lyrics by Glen MacDonough, and presented by a cast headed by Fay Bainter, Janet Velie and Armand Kalisz.
—HE LOVED ME, HE LOVES ME NOT
—A LITTLE CLASS OF ONE
—SINCE I MET WONDERFUL YOU
—ONE DAY
—THE MANTLEPIECE TRAGEDY
—THE SHIMMERING, GLIMMERING NILE
—I WANT TO LEARN TO DANCE
—THE GIRL I CAN'T FORGET
—BECAUSE YOU DO NOT KNOW
—THE LITTLE BLACK SHEEP
—THE ROSE
—YOUR KISS IS CHAMPAGNE
1919. *HAPPY DAYS*
Book and lyrics by R. H. Burnside. A New York Hippodrome show that featured Belle Story, Happy Jack Lambert and the Hanneford Family in a circus riding act.
—LET'S GO TO FAIRYLAND
—JAZZ TIME CITY
—BE A PARTY AT THE PARTY TONIGHT
—LOVE IS VERY WONDERFUL
—DON'T YOU REMEMBER THOSE SCHOOL DAYS?
—HAPPY DAYS
—LIFE'S A RACE
—THE STATELY AMERICAN ROSE
—THE MARRIAGE OF THE LILY AND THE ROSE
—MY SING SONG GIRL
—SOMEWHERE THERE'S SOME GIRL
—I FOUND THE GIRL I'VE BEEN LOOKING FOR
—BEAUTIFUL GOLDEN LAND
1919. *AMONG THE GIRLS*
Book by Roi Cooper Megrue and Henry Blossom, lyrics by Henry Blossom and Glen MacDonough, and starring Percival Knight.
—LADIES' DAY
—I'M A HUMAN POUSSE CAFE
—I WANT TO GO BACK TO WAR
—SAYONARA
—I'M MARRIED, I'M SINGLE, I'M DIVORCED, I'M IN LOVE
—YOUR CIGARETTE
—THE OVERSEAS GIRL

—TELL ME TONIGHT
—IN DREAMS ALONE
—M-O-N-E-Y
—COME ON, JIM
—KING SOLOMON
—THE NIGHT HAS A THOUSAND EYES
—WE HEAD FOR LITTLE OLD NEW YORK TOMORROW
—THE CAMOUFLAGE CLUTCH
1919. *MISS MILLIONS*
Book and lyrics by R. H. Burnside and starring Valli Valli.
—DON'T SAY GOODBYE
—DREAMS
—THE FARMER'S DAUGHTER
—IF YOU'LL JUST WAIT A LITTLE WHILE
—I KNOW THAT I'M IN LOVE
—MARY

Victor Jacobi Scores

1913. *THE MARRIAGE MARKET*
A musical comedy with book by Gladys Unger, lyrics by Adrian Ross and Arthur Anderson, and presented by a cast headed by Donald Brian.
—JOY BELLS
—OH, COULD I FIND THE WOMAN
—THE MIDDY
—ALL THE GIRLS LOVE A SAILOR MAN
—COME NESTLE IN MY ARMS
—AMERICAN COURTSHIP
—THE GOLDEN DAY OF LOVE
—HAND-IN-HAND
—LOVE OF MINE
—I DON'T BELIEVE IN FAIRIES NOW
By Paul Rubens.
—THE ONE I LOVE
—I'M NOT A SILLY BILLY
By Paul Rubens.
—VERY LITTLE TIME FOR LOVING NOWADAYS
Music by Pedro de Zulueta.
—BOYS
By M. E. Rourke and Edwin Burch.
—THE FUTURIST WHIRL
By M. E. Rourke and Edwin Burch.
—A LITTLE BIT OF SILK
By M. E. Rourke and Jerome Kern.
—I'VE GOT MONEY IN THE BANK
By M. E. Rourke and Jerome Kern.
—I'M LOOKING FOR AN IRISH HUSBAND
By M. E. Rourke and Jerome Kern.
—MENDOCINO STROLL
By Donald Brian.

1916. *SYBIL*
A musical comedy with book and lyrics by Harry Graham and Harry B. Smith, and starring Julia Sanderson in a cast that included Donald Brian and Joseph Cawthorn.
—GOOD ADVICE
—TWO CAN PLAY THAT GAME
—WHEN CUPID CALLS
—FOLLOWING THE DRUM
—LOVE MAY BE A MYSTERY
—SYBIL
—AT A GRAND HOTEL
—LETTER DUET
—THE COLONEL OF THE CRIMSON HUSSARS
—A CUP OF TEA
—LIFT YOUR EYES TO MINE
—GIRLS YOU ARE SUCH WONDERFUL THINGS
—I LIKE THE BOYS
—I CAN DANCE WITH ANYONE BUT MY WIFE
By Joseph Cawthorn and John Golden.
1917. *RAMBLER ROSE*
A musical comedy with book and lyrics by Harry B. Smith, and starring Julia Sanderson in a cast that included Joseph Cawthorn and Walter Smith.
—THE LAND OF THE MIDNIGHT SUN
—JUST A LITTLE BIT OF LOVE
—DREAM, DREAM
—BUNDLE OF NERVES
—I KNOW NOW
—COME TO GYPSY LAND
—ONE LOOK, ONE WORD
—RAMBLER ROSE
—SMILE A LITTLE SMILE FOR ME
—I MIGHT SAY YES
—BUT NOT FOR YOU
—WHENEVER I THINK OF YOU
By Schuyler Greene and Charles N. Grant.
—POOR LITTLE RICH GIRL'S DOG
By Irving Berlin.
1919. *APPLE BLOSSOMS*
With Fritz Kreisler. A musical comedy with book and lyrics by William LeBaron, and presented by a cast headed by Fred and Adele Astaire, Wilda Bennett, John Charles Thomas and Roy Atwell.
—LITTLE GIRLS, GOODBYE
—YOU ARE FREE
—BROTHERS
—I'LL BE TRUE TO YOU
—ON THE BANKS OF THE BRONX
—WHEN THE WEDDING BELLS ARE RINGING
Fritz Kreisler wrote the music for the following songs:

—I'M IN LOVE
—LETTER SONG
—WHO CAN TELL?
—A GIRL, A MAN, A NIGHT, A DANCE
—NANCY'S FAREWELL
—THE SECOND VIOLIN
—STAR OF LOVE
—MARRIAGE KNOT

Georges Jarno Score

1910. *THE GIRL AND THE KAISER*
A musical comedy with book and lyrics by Leonard Liebling, and presented by a cast headed by William Bonelli, Lulu Glaser, Flavia Arcaro and Harry Conor.
—CRADLED IN THY ARMS
—OH, KAISER, DEAR KAISER
—A TAILOR MAN
—MUSIC OF THE VIOLS
—BUTTERFLY, BUTTERFLY
—ONLY A GYPSY MAID
—LAUGHING AND HAPPY AM I
—FREE ETIQUETTE
—AT COURT
—WITH A GLANCE DEMURE
—MINE FOR EVERMORE

J. Rosamond Johnson Score

1911. *HELLO PARIS*
Book by William LeBaron and lyrics by J. Leubrie Hill. When produced by Henry B. Harris and Jesse L. Lasky at the Follies Bergere, now the Fulton Theater, New York, this revue was advertised as "the first cabaret in America," with a first-act curtain at 11:15 and a 1 a.m. finale. The cast was headed by Harry Pilcer, James J. Morton, Zeke Colvan, Minerva Coverdale and Nita Allen.
—HELLO PARIS
—LOOK ME OVER
—THAT AEROPLANE RAG
—LOVING MOON
—YOU'RE THE NICEST LITTLE GIRL I EVER KNEW
—FASCINATION WALTZ
—THE SIBERIAN WHIRL
—SENTIMENTAL TOMMY
By E. Ray Goetz and A. Baldwin Sloan.
—THE FRISCO FRIZZ
By Collin Davis and Ned Wayburn.

Tom Johnstone Scores

1911. *BETSY*
A musical comedy with book by Kellett Chambers, lyrics by Will Johnstone, and presented by a cast headed by Grace LaRue and Hassard Short.

—COMPOSING
—THE FIRST GRAY HAIR
—SNOOP, SNOOP
—THE DAY BEFORE THE MORNING AFTER
—DREAM LOVE
—LAUGHTER AND LOVE
—ARISTOCRACY
—ONLY A VOICE
—THERE CAME A VISION
—LOVE'S CONQUEST

1912. *MISS PRINCESS*
A musical comedy with book by Frank Mandel, lyrics by Will Johnstone, and starring Lina Abarbanell in a cast that included Robert Warwick.
—ALL AGREE ON A PRETTY GIRL
—AY-OOMPS
—HUMPTY DUMPTY
—I WANT TO BE THE LAST TO KISS YOU
—A LITTLE RED BOOK AND A FIVE-CENT BAG
Lyrics by H. E. Russell.
—TEMPERMENTAL DANCES
—WHEN I PROPOSE
—THE WIRELESS WAY
—QUEEN THOU ART
—COME MY SWEETHEART
Music by Joseph Strauss.
—IT MIGHT HAVE BEEN

1918. *FIDDLERS THREE*
A musical comedy with book by William Cary Duncan, lyrics by Will Johnstone, and presented by a cast headed by Louise Groody, Josie Intropodi and Hal Skelly.
—WHEN THE FIDDLE BOWS BEGIN TO FLY
—ONE HOUR SWEETHEART WITH YOU
—PROUD LITTLE PAGES
—CAN IT BE LOVE AT LAST?
—DON'T YOU THINK YOU'LL MISS ME
—AS THE FLITTING SWALLOWS FLY
—LOVE OF A DAY
—FOR LOVE

Score by Charles Jule

1919. *OH, WHAT A GIRL*
With Jacques Presburg. A musical comedy with book by Edgar Smith, lyrics by Ed Clark, and presented by a cast headed by Harry Kelly, Frank Fay, Hazel Kirke and Sam Ash.
—OH, WHAT A GIRL
—MUSICAL POKER GAME
—GIMME
—OH THAT SHIMMY!

—PRINCE CHARMING
—GET HIM UP
—DAINTY LITTLE GIRL
—BREEZE IN THE TREES
—COULD YOU TEACH ME?
—SUCH A BABY
—WHEN IT COMES TO LOVING GIRLS I'M WAY AHEAD OF THE TIMES
By Murray Kissen, Joe Burnes and Jack Glogan.

Emmerich Kalman Scores

1914. *SARI*
A musical comedy with book and lyrics by C. C. S. Cushing and E. P. Heath, and starring Mitzi Hajos in a cast that included Van Rensselaer Wheeler and Harry Davenport.
—STOP IT, STOP IT
—TIME, OH TIME
—MARRY ME
—PICK A HUSBAND
—PARIS? OH MY! YES DEAR
—LOVE HAS WINGS
—HA-ZA-ZA
—TRIUMPHANT YOUTH
—WITH LOWERED HEAD
—FOLLOW ME
—THERE'S NO PLACE LIKE HOME WITH YOU
—MY FAITHFUL STRADIVARI
—SOFTLY THROUGH THE SUMMER NIGHT
—LONG LIVE THE KING
—*LOVE'S OWN SWEET SONG
—THE CONTEST

1916. *MISS SPRINGTIME*
A musical comedy with book and lyrics by Guy Bolton, and presented by a cast headed by Georgia O'Ramey, John E. Hazzard, George MacFarlane, Elsie Alder and Jed Prouty.
—SUNRISE
—THIS IS THE EXISTENCE
—ONCE UPON A TIME
—A BID FOR SYMPATHY
—THE LOVE MONOPOLY
—A VERY GOOD GIRL ON SUNDAY
—SOMEONE
—THE GARDEN OF ROMANCE
—A COUNTRY MOUSE
—THROW ME A ROSE
Lyrics by P. G. Wodehouse and Herbert Reynolds.
—WHEN YOU'RE ALL FULL OF TALK
By P. G. Wodehouse and Jerome Kern.
—MY CASTLE IN THE AIR
By P. G. Wodehouse and Jerome Kern.

—SATURDAY NIGHT
By P. Herbert Reynolds and Jerome Kern.

1917. *THE RIVIERA GIRL*
A musical comedy with book and lyrics by Guy Bolton and P. G. Wodehouse, and starring Wilda Bennett in a cast that included Sam Hardy and Eugene Lockhart.
—HALF A MARRIED MAN
—JUST A VOICE TO CALL ME DEAR
—LIFE'S A TALE
—THE LILT OF A GYPSY STRAIN
—MAN, MAN, MAN
—THERE'LL NEVER BE ANOTHER GIRL LIKE DAISY
—SOMETIMES I FEEL JUST LIKE GRANDMA
—THE FALL OF MAN
—WHY DON'T YOU HAND IT TO ME?
—GYPSY BRING YOUR FIDDLE
—WILL YOU FORGET?
Music by Jerome Kern.
—LET'S BUILD A LITTLE BUNGALOW IN QUOGUE
Music by Jerome Kern.

Gustav Kerker Score

1911. *TWO LITTLE BRIDES*
Book and lyrics by Arthur Anderson, James T. Powers and Harold Atteridge, and starring James T. Powers in a cast that included Leila Hughes, Flavia Arcaro and Frances Cameron.
—SNOWDROPS AND THE SPRING
—THE LETTER
—BUZZ ON LITTLE BUSY BEE
—KISS ME AGAIN, BEBE
—OH, HONORKA
—ARE WE WIDOWS, WIVES OR WHAT?
—SO AWAY WITH SORROW
—I LIKE ALL THE GIRLS
—WAITING FOR ME
—SOMEHOW, SOMETIME, S O M E-WHERE
—A WALTZ WITHOUT A KISS
—WHAT ABOUT IT?

Jerome Kern Scores

1910. *THE KING OF CADONIA*
A musical comedy with book by Frederick Lonsdale, lyrics by M. E. Rourke, and starring Marguerite Clark in a cast that included William Norris.
—CATAMARANG
Lyrics by Percival Knight.
—COME ALONG PRETTY GIRL
—COO-OO, COO-OO

—EVERY GIRL I KNOW
Lyrics by Percival Knight.
—LENA, LENA
—MOTHER AND FATHER
—BLUE BULGARIAN BAND
—HIPPOPOTAMUS
1911. *LA BELLE PAREE*
With Frank Tours. A musical comedy
with book by Edgar Smith, lyrics by Ed-
ward Madden, and presented by a cast
headed by Kitty Gordon, Stella Mayhew,
Mitzi Hajos, Mlle. Dazie, Al Jolson and
Tempest and Sunshine.
—LOOK ME OVER DEARIE
—THE GOBLIN'S GLIDE
—I'M THE HUMAN BRUSH
—PARIS IS A PARADISE FOR COONS
—SING TRAVATORE
—THE EDINBORO WIGGLE
—THAT'S ALL RIGHT FOR McGILLI-
GAN
1912. *THE RED PETTICOAT*
Book by Rida Johnson Young, lyrics by
Paul West, and presented by a cast headed
by William Pruett and Helen Lowell.
—SHE'S MY GIRL
—I WONDER
—THE CORRESPONDENCE SCHOOL
—LITTLE GOLDEN MAID
—OH, YOU BEAUTIFUL SPRING
—WHERE DID THE BIRD HEAR
THAT?
—MY PEACHES AND CREAM
—THE RAGTIME RESTAURANT
—A PRISONER OF LOVE
—WALK, WALK, WALK
—OO-OO-OO
—SINCE THE DAYS OF GRANDMAMA
—THE JOY OF THAT KISS
—THE WALTZ TIME GIRL
1913. *OH, I SAY*
Book by Sidney Blow and Douglas Hoare,
lyrics by Harry B. Smith, and presented
by a cast headed by Joseph Herbert, Nellie
King, Walter Jones, Alice Yorke, Welling-
ton Cross and Clara Palmer.
—HOW DO YOU DO
—SUZANNA
—I KNOW AND SHE KNOWS
—WELL, THIS IS JOLLY
—EACH PEARL A THOUGHT
—ALONE AT LAST
—THE OLD CLARINET
—A WOMAN'S HEART
—KATY-DID
—I CAN'T FORGET YOUR EYES
—A WIFIE OF YOUR OWN
1914. *THE GIRL FROM UTAH*
While Paul Rubens and Sydney Jones are

credited with the score of this production,
Jerome Kern's songs dominated the show,
which had book and lyrics by James T.
Tanner and starred Julia Sanderson, Don-
ald Brian and Joseph Cawthorn.
—SAME SORT OF GIRL
—YOU NEVER CAN TELL
—WHY DON'T THEY DANCE THE
POLKA ANY MORE?
—LAND OF LET'S PRETEND
—THEY DIDN'T BELIEVE ME
Lyrics by Herbert Raynolds.
—ALICE IN WONDERLAND
—WE'LL TAKE CARE OF YOU ALL
—AT THE TANGO TEA
Paul Reubens and Sydney Jones contribut-
ed the following songs:
—FLORRIE THE FLAPPER
—GILBERT THE FILBERT
—THE GIRL IN THE CLODS AND
SHAWL
1915. *90 IN THE SHADE*
Book and lyrics by Guy Bolton and Clare
Kummer, and presented by a cast headed
by Richard Carle, Marie Cahill, Otis Har-
lan, Victor Morley and Pedro de Cordoba.
—WHERE'S THE GIRL FOR ME?
—JOLLY GOOD FELLOW
—LONELY IN TOWN
Words and music by Clare Kummer.
—I'VE BEEN ABOUT A BIT
—RICH MAN, POOR MAN
—A REGULAR GUY
—HUMAN NATURE
—WHISTLING DAN
—A PACKAGE OF SEEDS
—MY LADY'S DRESS
—FOOLISHNESS
—PETER PAN
—THE TRIANGLE
—WONDERFUL DAYS
—MY MINDANAO CHOCOLATE SOL-
DIER
1915. *NOBODY HOME*
Book and lyrics by Guy Bolton and Paul
Rubens, and presented by a cast that in-
cluded Maude Odell, Alice Dovey, George
Lydecker and Adele Rowland.
—WHY TAKE A SANDWICH TO A
BANQUET?
—YOU KNOW THAT I KNOW
—CUPID AT THE PLAZA
—IN ARCADY
—THE MAGIC MELODY
—TEN LITTLE BRIDESMAIDS
—BED, WONDERFUL BED
—ANOTHER LITTLE GIRL
—ANY OLD NIGHT IS A WONDERFUL
NIGHT

—THE SAN FRANCISCO FAIR
1915. *COUSIN LUCY*
Book by Charles Klein, lyrics by Schuyler Green, and starring Julian Eltinge in a cast that included Leo Donnelly, Jane Oaker and Olive Tell.
—THOSE COME HITHER EYES
—MAM'SELLE LUCETTE
By Edward Madden and Percy Wenrich.
—TWO HEADS ARE BETTER THAN ONE
—SOCIETY
—KEEP GOING
1915. *MISS INFORMATION*
Book and lyrics by Paul Dickey and Charles W. Goddard, and starring Elsie Janis in a cast that included Irene Bordoni, Melville Ellis and Maurice Faroka.
—BANKS OF WYE
—A LITTLE LOVE BUT NOT FOR ME
—SOME SORT OF SOMEBODY
—THE MIX-UP RAG
—CONSTANT LOVER
By Arthur Wimperis and Herman Finck.
—TWO BIG EYES
By Cole Porter.
1915. *VERY GOOD EDDIE*
Book by Philip Bartholomae and Guy Bolton, lyrics by Schuyler Green, and presented by a cast headed by Alice Dovey, Helen Raymond, Ada Lewis, Oscar Shaw, John E. Hazzard and Ernest Truex.
—WE'RE ON OUR WAY
—SAME OLD GAME
—SOME SORT OF SOMEONE ALL THE TIME
—ISN'T IT GREAT TO BE MARRIED?
—WEDDING BELLS ARE CALLING ME
—ON THE SHORES OF LE LEI WI
—IF I FIND THE GIRL
—WHEN YOU WEAR A 13 COLLAR
—OLD BOY NEUTRAL
—BABES IN THE WOODS
—THE FASHION SHOW
—I WISH I HAD A MILLION IN THE BANK
—NODDING ROSES
—OLD BILL BAKER
Lyrics by Ring Lardner.
—I'VE GOT TO DANCE
1917. *HAVE A HEART*
Book and lyrics by Guy Bolton and P. G. Wodehouse, and presented by a cast that included Flavia Arcaro, Louise Dresser, Billy B. Van and Thurston Hall.
—SHOP
—I'M SO BUSY
—HAVE A HEART
Lyrics by Gene Buck.

—AND I'M ALL ALONE
—I'M HERE, LITTLE GIRL, I'M HERE
—BRIGHT LIGHTS
—THE ROAD THAT LIES BEFORE
—HONEYMOON INN
—SAMARKAND
—COME OUT OF THE KITCHEN
—MY WIFE, MY MAN
—YOU SAID SOMETHING
—NAPOLEON
—PETER PAN
—POLLY BELIEVED IN PREPAREDNESS
—LOOK IN HIS EYES
—DAISY
—THEY ALL LOOK ALIKE
1917. *LOVE O' MIKE*
Book by Thomas Sydney, lyrics by Harry B. Smith, and starring Peggy Wood in a cast that included Luella Gear, George Hassell and Clifton Webb.
—DRIFT WITH ME
—HOW WAS I TO KNOW?
—IT WASN'T YOUR FAULT
—DON'T TEMPT ME
—WE'LL SEE
—IT CAN'T BE DONE
—I WONDER WHY
—MOO COW
—LIFE'S A DANCE
—WHO CARES
—HOOT MAN
—THE BABY VAMPIRE
—IT'S IN THE BOOK
—SIMPLE LITTLE TUNE
1917: *OH, BOY!*
Book and lyrics by Guy Bolton and P. G. Wodehouse, and presented by a cast headed by Marion Davies, Anna Wheaton, Edna May Oliver, Hal Forde, Tom Powers and Justine Johnstone.
—LET'S MAKE A NIGHT OF IT
—YOU NEVER KNEW ABOUT ME
—A PACKAGE OF SEEDS
—AN OLD-FASHIONED WIFE
—A PAL LIKE YOU
—TILL THE CLOUDS ROLL BY
—A LITTLE BIT OF RIBBON
—THE FIRST DAY OF MAY
—KOO-LA-LOO
—ROLLED INTO ONE
—OH, DADDY, PLEASE
—NESTING TIME IN FLATBUSH
—WORDS ARE NOT NEEDED
—FLUBBY DUB THE CAVE MAN
—I NEVER KNEW ABOUT YOU
—AIN'T IT A GRAND AND GLORIOUS FEELING?
—BE A LITTLE SUNBEAM
—EVERY DAY

1917. *LEAVE IT TO JANE*
A musical version of George Ade's "The College Widow," with book and lyrics by Guy Bolton and P. G. Wodehouse, and presented by a cast that was headed by Oscar Shaw, Georgia O'Ramey and Edith Hallor.
—A PEACH OF A LIFE
—WAIT TILL TOMORROW
—JUST YOU WATCH MY STEP
—LEAVE IT TO JANE
—THE SIREN'S SONG
—THERE IT IS AGAIN
—CLEOPATTERER
—THE CRICKETS ARE CALLING
—SIR GALAHAD
—THE SUN SHINES BRIGHTER
—I'M GOING TO FIND A GIRL
—A GREAT BIG LAND
—WHAT I'M LONGING TO SAY

1917. *MISS 1917*
Book and lyrics by Guy Bolton and P. G. Wodehouse. A revue with an all-star cast that included Lew Fields, Vivienne Segal, Charles King, Emma Haig, Peggy Hopkins, Bessie McCoy Davis, Van and Schenck, Irene Castle, Bert Savoy, Joe Brennan, Cleo Mayfield, Tot Qualters, Lilyan Tashman, Pauline Hall, George White and Ann Pennington. While this show was being readied for Broadway, George Gershwin served as rehearsal pianist.
—GO LITTLE BOAT
—THE LAND WHERE THE GOOD SONGS GO
—TELL ME ALL YOUR TROUBLES CUTIE
—WE'RE CROOKS
—I'M THE OLD MAN IN THE MOON
—A PICTURE I WANT TO SEE
—PEACHES
—PALM BEACH DIP
Music by Harry Tierney.

1918. *OH, LADY! LADY!*
Book and lyrics by Guy Bolton and P. G. Wodehouse, and presented by a cast headed by Vivienne Segal, Janet Velie and Carl Randall.
—I'M TO BE MARRIED TODAY
—NOT YET
—DO IT NOW
—OUR LITTLE NEST
—LITTLE SHIPS COME SAILING HOME
—OH, LADY! LADY!
—YOU FOUND ME, I FOUND YOU
—MOON SONG
—WAITING AROUND THE CORNER

—THE SUN STARTS TO SHINE AGAIN
—GREENWICH VILLAGE
—A PICTURE I HAD TO SEE
—IT'S A HARD, HARD WORLD FOR A MAN

1918. *TOOT-TOOT*
Book by Edgar Allen Woolf, lyrics by Berton Braley, and presented by a cast that included Flora Zabelle, Louise Groody and William Kent.
—TOOT-TOOT
—QUARREL AND PART
—RUNAWAY COLTS
—KAN THE KAISER
—EVERY GIRL IN ALL AMERICA
—A SHOWER OF RICE
—IT'S GREEK TO ME
—LET'S GO
—THE LAST LONG MILE
—WHEN YOU WAKE UP DANCING
—GIRLIE
—SMOKE
—YOU'RE SO CUTE, SOLDIER BOY
Music by Anatol Friedland.
—IT'S IMMATERIAL TO ME
—IF YOU ONLY CARE ENOUGH
—I WILL KNIT A SUIT OF DREAMS
—HONEYMOON LAND

1918. *ROCK-A-BYE BABY*
Book by Edgar Allen Woolf and Margaret Mayo, lyrics by Herbert Reynolds, and presented by a cast headed by Carl Hyson, Dorothy Dickson, Frank Morgan, Walter Jones and Louise Dresser.
—HURRY NOW
—MOTORING ALONG THE OLD POST ROAD
—A KETTLE IS SINGING
—I BELIEVE ALL THEY SAID
—I NEVER THOUGHT
—ONE, TWO, THREE
—THE BIG SPRING DRIVE
—THERE'S NO BETTER USE FOR TIME THAN KISSING
—LITTLE TUNE GO AWAY
—STITCHING, STITCHING
—ROCK-A-BYE, BABY DEAR
—ACCORDING TO DR. HOLT
—MY OWN LIGHT INFANTRY
—I CAN TRUST MYSELF WITH A LOT OF GIRLS

1918. *HEAD OVER HEELS*
Book and lyrics by Edgar Allen Woolf and starring Mitzi in a cast that included Joe Keno, Boyd Marshall and Edward Sells.
—WITH TYPE A-TICKING
—TODAY IS SPRING
—ANY GIRL
—MITZI'S LULLABY

—THE BIG SHOW
—MOMENTS OF THE DANCE
—HEAD OVER HEELS
—VORDEVEELE
—ME
—ALL THE WORLD IS SWAYING
—THE CHARITY BAZAAR
—EVERY BEE HAS A BUD OF HIS
OWN
—LADIES HAVE A CARE
—I WAS LONELY
—FUNNY LITTLE SOMETHING
—LET US BUILD A LITTLE NEST
1919. *SHE'S A GOOD FELLOW*
Book and lyrics by Anne Caldwell, and
starring Ivy Sawyer and Joe Santley in
a cast that included Rosetta and Vivian
Duncan.
—SOME PARTY
—THE NAVY FOXTROT MAN
—FIRST ROSE OF SUMMER
—A HAPPY WEDDING DAY
—JUBILO
—FAITH, HOPE AND CHARITY
—TEACHER, TEACHER
—THE BULLFROG PATROL
—OH, YOU BEAUTIFUL PERSON
—SNIP, SNIP, SNAP
—I WANT A LITTLE GOB
—THE BUMBLE BEE
—LETTER SONG
—GINGER TOWN
—JUST A LITTLE LINE

William Kernell Score

1919. *ELSIE JANIS AND HER GANG*
A revue staged by Elsie Janis on her re-
turn from France where she entertained
American doughboys during World War
I, and presented by an all-soldier cast
with the exception of Elsie Janis and Eva
LeGallienne, who made her stage debut
in this production. Lyrics by Richard
Fechheimer, and additional songs by B.
C. Hilliam and Elsie Janis.
—AH OUI
—JUST A LITTLE TOUCH OF PARIS
—LET'S GO
—SOMEWHERE IN AMERICA
—GEE BUT IT'S GREAT TO MEET A
GIRL FROM HOME
—IN THE LATIN QUARTER
—IT'S MY TEMPERMENT
—SONGS WE SANG
—I LOVE THEM ALL JUST A LITTLE
BIT
—JUST A LITTLE AFTER TAPS
—WHEN I TOOK MY JAZZ BAND TO
THE FATHERLAND

Manuel Klein Scores

1910. *THE INTERNATIONAL CUP* and
THE BALLET OF NIAGARA
A New York Hippodrome production with
book by R. H. Burnside, lyrics by the com-
poser, and starring Albertina Rausch.
—THE FIGHTING REGIMENT
—HAIL THE HERO OF TODAY
—TAKE A TRIP TO THE SEASIDE
—LOVING AND YACHTING
—THE SONG OF EVERY NATION
—THE NORTH AND SOUTH OF TO-
DAY
—MAIDS OF NIAGARA
—LOVE IS LIKE A RAINBOW
1911. *AROUND THE WORLD*
Marcelaine, the French clown, was the
star of this New York Hippodrome pro-
duction with book by Carroll Fleming
and lyrics by the composer.
—MY OLD TOWN
—IT'S A LONG LANE THAT HAS NO
TURNING
1912. *UNDER MANY FLAGS*
A New York Hippodrome production with
book by Carl Fleming.
—THE DEAR LITTLE WHITE HOUSE
—TEMPLE BELLS
—SCOTLAND FOREVER
—EVERY NATION HAS A FLOWER
—HOME IS WHERE THE HEART IS
—YOUNGSTERS OF THE NAVY
—PRETTY LITTLE MAIDEN ON THE
SCREEN
—SWEETHEART
—LET'S GO WALKING
1913. *AMERICA*
John P. Wilson provided the book for this
New York Hippodrome production.
—DARK EYES ARE NOW A-SHININ'
FOR YOU
—THE GIRL IN THE GINGHAM GOWN
—HIPPODROME TANGO
—MERRY LITTLE CHOP, CHOP, CHOP
—ON A SUMMER AFTERNOON
—RAGTIME IN THE AIR
—EVERYBODY LOVES A SOLDIER
—FLOWER BELLS
—LOLA, FAIREST DAUGHTER OF
PANAMA
1913. *HOP O' MY THUMB*
A musical comedy with book and lyrics
by Sidney Rosenfeld, and starring De-
Wolf Hopper in a cast that included Eva
Fallon, Flavia Arcaro and Texas Guinan.
—COME AND WATCH THE MOON
WITH ME
—RUN ALONG MR. OGRE MAN

—NO DAMAGED GOODS
—TAKE A LITTLE PERFUME
—THOSE DAYS OF LONG AGO
—THE DATE TREE
—LADIES IT'S REALLY ALARMING
1914. *WARS OF THE WORLD*
A New York Hippodrome production.
—THE SEER
—WHEN YOU COME HOME AGAIN
   JOHNNY
—UNDER A GAY SOMBRERO
—BABY EYES
—DEAR OLD HENLEY
—IN SIAM
—YOU'RE JUST THE ONE I WAITED
   FOR

Score by Walter Kollo

1913. *THE GIRL ON THE FILM*
With Albert Sirmay. A musical comedy
with book by James T. Tanner, lyrics by
Adrian Ross, and presented by a cast
headed by Emmy Wehlen, George Gross-
mith and Madeline Seymour.
—OH, OH, OH
—SONG OF THE MILL
—WON'T YOU COME AND WALTZ
   WITH ME?
—IN BOND STREET
—DOWN BY THE COUNTRYSIDE
—CORRESPONDENCE
—I'VE HEARD THAT TALE BEFORE
—YOU DON'T SEE IT BUT IT'S
   THERE
—ON THE GROUND
—AH CHE VEDO
—OH, IF YOU WERE A GIRL
—GIVE ME SOMETHING IN A UNI-
   FORM
By Percy Greenbank and Paul Rubens.

Franz Lehar Scores

1911. *GYPSY LOVE*
An operetta with book and lyrics by
Harry B. and Robert B. Smith, and star-
ring Marguerita Sylva in a cast that in-
cluded Arthur Albro, Carl Hayden, Fran-
ces Demarest and George Bickel.
—GYPSY LOVE
—BABY DUET
—I WILL GIVE YOU ALL FOR LOVE
—LESSONS IN LOVE
—LOVE IS LIKE THE ROSE
—THE MELODY OF LOVE
—DELAYING THE STORM
—THE LAND OF FANCY
—WEDDING GUESTS
—LOVE'S SORCERY

—WHEN I'M WALTZING WITH YOU
—MATRIMONY
1912. *THE COUNT OF LUXEMBOURG*
An operetta with book by Glen Mac-
Donough, lyrics by Adrian Ross and Basil
Hood, and presented by a cast headed by
Ann Swinburne, Frank Moulan, Fred
Walton and George Monroe.
—SAY NOT LOVE IS A DREAM
—ARE YOU GOING TO DANCE?
—COUSINS OF THE CZAR
—ROOTSIE-TOOTSIE
—CARNIVAL
—MAKE THE MOST OF CARNIVAL
—LAND OF MAKE BELIEVE
—LOVE SPATS
—COUNT OF LUXEMBOURG
—I AM IN LOVE
—HAIL ANGELE, OUR NIGHTINGALE
—DAY DREAMS
—IN SOCIETY
—THE WEDDING MARCH
1912. *EVA*
An operetta with book and lyrics by
Glen MacDonough, and presented by a
cast that included Sallie Fisher, Wallace
McCutcheon and Walter Percival.
—LOVE IS A PILGRIM
—DREAMING OF YOU
—STARLIGHT GUARDS
—JOY AND GLASS
—VOICE OF PARIS
—THE UP-TO-DATE TROUBADOR
—THE QUARREL
—CINDERELLA
—ON THE DAY I MARRY
—THE IMP OF MONTMARTRE
1913. *THE MAN WITH THREE WIVES*
An operetta with book and lyrics by
Paul M. Potter, Harold Atteridge and
Agnes Morgan, and presented by a cast
headed by Cleo Mayfield, Alice Yorke,
Charlotte Greenwood, Cecil Lean and
Sydney Grant.
—KISSES THAT I HAVE MISSED
—LOVE'S FAIRY TALES
—ROSE OF YESTERDAY
—THERE'S ALWAYS A GIRL WHO'S
   WAITING
—THE VALE OF DREAMING
—WHEN YOU'RE TRAVELING
—TOOTSIE-WOOTSIE
—MAN IS FAITHFUL TILL HE'S
   CAUGHT
—VENGEANCE
—PARIS, OH FESTIVE LAND
—LULLABY
—WOMEN OF TEMPERAMENT
—TO LONDON

—ALL IN A LITTLE DANCE
—TALE OF THE JEALOUS CAT
Music by Al W. Brown.
—HELLO, HELLO
—WE ARE FREE
—CUPID'S SOLDIERS
1914. *MAIDS OF ATHENS*
An operetta with book and lyrics by
Carolyn Wells, and presented by a cast
headed by Leila Hughes and Elbert
Fretwell.
—LIFE IS LONELY
—BID ME FORGET
—BRIGANDS' CHORUS
—WALTZ, YOU SIREN OF MELODY
—WHEN THE HEART IS YOUNG
—AH YES, I AM IN LOVE
—THE GIRL HE COULDN'T KISS
—NURSE, NURSE, NURSE
—HEAVENLY LADIES
—ROSIE
By Frederick Norton.
—OUR GLORIOUS STRIPES AND
STARS
Music by Paul Kerr.
—ONE OR ANOTHER
Music by Oscar Haase.
—THE CLEVER DETECTIVE
Music by Charles J. Anditzer.
1915. *ALONE AT LAST*
An operetta with book by Edgar Smith
and Joseph W. Herbert, lyrics by Mathew
C. Woodward, and presented by a cast
headed by Elizabeth Goodhall, Madame
Namara, Jose Collins, Roy Atwell and
John Charles Thomas.
—PRETTY EDELWEISS
—BRIGHT MORNING STAR
—NATURE DIVINE
—OH MY DARLING TILLIE
—NOT NOW BUT BY THE MOON
—VICT'RY TO THE BOLD
—ONLY HE WHO HAS LOVE
—PEASANT WEDDING PARTY
—THY HEART MY PRIZE
—PICNIC IN THE SKY
Music by Gaetano Merola.
—ONE IN THE GAME OF LOVE
—WALTZ ENTRANCING
—SOME LITTLE BUG IS GOING TO
FIND YOU SOME DAY
By Benjamin Hapgood Burt, Roy Atwell
and Silvio Hein.
—SCANDALS IN THE AIR
—WE DON'T KNOW WHY WE LOVE
1917. *THE STAR GAZER*
An operetta with book by Cosmo Hamil-
ton, lyrics by Mathew C. Woodward, and
presented by a cast headed by Elizabeth

Goodhall, John Charles Thomas, John T.
Murray and Jennetta Mathven.
—AS A BUTTERFLY SIPS THE ROSES
—MY HEART IS LIKE A BIRD IN MAY
—WHEN YOU ARE MINE ALL MINE
—IF A BACHELOR SHOULD FALL IN
LOVE
—YOU, YOU, YOU
—A BACHELOR'S BUTTON
—DRINK SOME TEA
—WHILE WE ARE ASLEEP
—WE LOVED AND WE LOST
—GOODBYE
—TWINKLE, TWINKLE
—YOU MY SWEETHEART WILL HAVE
TO BE
—IF YOU ONLY KNEW
—WON'T YOU COME UP TO THE
TABLE?
—RHYMING FOR A DANCE
—STAR GAZER
—BUT YOU ALONE

Hans Linne Score
1912. *MAMMA'S BABY BOY*
With Will H. Becker. A musical comedy
with book and lyrics by Junie McCree,
who appeared in a cast that included
Anna Laughlin, Grace Tyson and Albert
Hart.
—BACK FROM THIRTY-SIX TO
TWENTY-NINE
—CAPITAL H
—WHITE LIES, BLACK LIES
—THE WHITE MAN'S HOPE
—TIME HAS CHANGED SO MANY
CUSTOMS IN THE LAST DECADE
—CECELIA
—LONEGAN
—IF THE MAN IN THE MOON
WOULD SPEAK

Gustav Luders Scores
1910. *THE OLD TOWN*
Book and lyrics by George Ade. Peggy
Wood made her New York debut in this
starring vehicle for Montgomery and
Stone.
—THE MAN WHO WILL NOT LOVE
BACK
—QUEEN OF THE ONE-RING SHOW
—THE NOOVO RICHE
—ELECTRIC SIGNS
—WHEN I WOULD THINK OF YOU
—WHAT MAN DARE SAY (MY TRU-
ANT HEART)
—WEAK LITTLE WOMEN
—KEEP YOUR WHIP IN YOUR HAND

—MY JAPANEE
—MINNESOTA
By Thomas T. Railey and Alfred Robyn.
—A POPULAR SONG
By Thomas T. Railey and Alfred Robyn.
—TRAVEL, TRAVEL, LITTLE STAR
By Vincent Bryan and Arthur Pryor.
1912. *THE GYPSY*
Book and lyrics by Frank Pixley, and
with a cast headed by John Hazzard, Vio-
let Seaton and Eleanor Kent.
—WHAT ELSE CAN A GYPSY DO
—SING A SONG OF SIXPENCE
—DISAPPEAR
—DAFFY
—GEMS OF THE NIGHT
—FLIRTING
—THE TALE OF THE TADPOLE
—GYPSY ROVER
—THE GYPSY'S GOOD NIGHT
—THE CHAPERONE
—ISN'T IT DELICIOUS
—I LOVE YOU AS YOU ARE
—EVERY YEAR IS LEAP YEAR
—WE KNOW, SWEETHEART, WE
KNOW
—TRAIL ALONG
—THE GIRL I CAN'T FORGET
—AUF WIEDERSEHEN
1913. *SOMEWHERE ELSE*
Book and lyrics by Avery Hopwood, and
with a cast headed by Elene Leska, Tay-
lor Holmes and Will Philbrick.
—FATHER
—SOMEBODY'S EYES
—TWINKLE, TWINKLE LITTLE STAR
—IF I KISSED YOU
—I JUST WANT SOMEONE TO LOVE
ME
—THE LAY OF THE EGG
—THE SONG OF THE ROSEBUD
—LOOK OUT FOR THE STRANGE
YOUNG MAN
—HOW DO YOU DO
—IT'S STRICTLY NICE

Milton Lusk Score

1914. *THE DANCING DUCHESS*
A musical comedy with book and lyrics
by C. V. Kerr and R. H. Burnside, and
presented by a cast headed by Dorothy
Jardon, Leila McIntyre, John Hyams,
Ada Lewis, Harry Davenport and Otis
Harlan.
—WE'RE OFF FOR BUDAPEST
—ON WITH THE DANCE
—THE BUMBLE BEE AND THE BUT-
TERFLY

—DANUBE SO BLUE
—I'M LOOKING FOR A GIRL LIKE
VENUS
—I'VE BEEN LOOKING FOR YOU
—THAT'S THE WAY TO WIN A GIRL
—WITH JOY THAT IS ECSTATICAL
—THE TANGO BREAKFAST
—LOVE IS A SUMMER'S MORNING
—THAT'S THE KIND OF A MAN YOU
OUGHT TO MARRY
—CELESTINE
—EVERYBODY'S HAPPY IN VIENNA
—FOL-DE-ROL-LOL
—THE SONG OF SONGS
—NAY, NAY PAULINE
—DO YOU LIKE ME? I LIKE YOU
—THE RAGTIME WHIRL

Lionel Monckton Scores

1910. *THE ARCADIANS*
A musical comedy with book by Mark
Ambient and A. M. Thompson, lyrics by
Arthur Wimperis, and presented by a cast
headed by Julia Sanderson, Grace Studdi-
ford, Frank Moulan and Percival Knight.
—MY MATER
—FICKLE FORTUNE
—PIPES OF PAN
—SWEET SIMPLICATUS
—ARCADIA IS EVER YOUNG
—BRING ME A ROSE
—I LIKE LONDON
—THE JOY OF LIFE
—THE GIRL WITH THE BROGUE
—CHARMING WEATHER
—TRUTH IS SO BEAUTIFUL
1911. *THE QUAKER GIRL*
A musical comedy with book by James
T. Tanner, lyrics by Adrian Ross and
Percy Greenbank, and presented by a
cast headed by Ina Claire, Olga Petrova,
Percival Knight, Clifton Crawford and
Lawrence Eddinger.
—TAKE A STEP
—A BAD BOY AND A GOOD GIRL
—COME TO THE BALL
—A RUNAWAY MATCH
—TONY FROM AMERICA
—GET AWAY, I'M A MARRIED MAN
—TIPTOE
—JUST AS FATHER USED TO DO
—OR THEREABOUTS
—ON REVIENT de CHANTILLY
—I WANT TO TELL YOU SOMETHING
By Clifton Crawford.
—BARBIZON
—QUAKER MEETING
—WONDERFUL

1919. *GOOD MORNING, JUDGE*
A musical comedy with book by Frederick Thompson, lyrics by Adrian Ross and Percy Greenbank, and presented by a cast headed by Molly and Charles King and George Hassell.
—A GAME THAT ENDS WITH A KISS
—THAT HAS NOTHING TO DO WITH YOU
—MAKE HAY
—SWINGING DOORS
—OH THAT WE TWO WERE MAYING
—SPORTING BOYS
—MIDNIGHT CABARET
—PANSY DAY
—I'M THE BOY (AND I'M THE GIRL)
By B. G. DeSylva and Louis Silvers.
—DINKY DOODLE DICKY
Music by Howard Talbot.
—I AM SO YOUNG AND YOU ARE SO BEAUTIFUL
By Alfred Bryan, Irving Caesar and George Gershwin.
—THERE'S MORE TO A KISS THAN THE X-X-X
By Irving Caesar and George Gershwin.

Kenneth Murchison Score
1919. *COME TO BOHEMIA*
A musical comedy with book and lyrics by George S. Chappell, and presented by a cast headed by Natalie Ault, William Danforth, Walter Percival, Fritz Williams and Ada Mae Weeks.
—THE BIG BRASS BAND
—COME TO BOHEMIA
—DEEP IN THE HEART
—A MATTER OF BUSINESS
—THE OLD STAGE DOOR
—THE ROSE'S STORY
—STICKTITE
—THE THREE ARTS
—FRIENDSHIP
—SHE DOESN'T EXIST AT ALL
By Glen MacDonough and Raymond Hubbell.
—WHEN SOMEBODY ISN'T THERE
By Glen MacDonough and Raymond Hubbell.
—ON THE SHIMMERING, GLIMMERING NILE
By Glen MacDonough and Raymond Hubbell.
—IN PORTLAND
By Glen MacDonough and Raymond Hubbell.

John L. Nelson Score
1919. *COME ALONG*

A musical comedy with book by Bide Dudley, lyrics by the composer, and presented by a cast that included Harry Tighe, Paul Frawley, Allen Kearns and Marjorie Pringle.
—YANKEE LAND
—IN HER LITTLE BLUE BONNET WITH RED RIBBONS ON IT SHE'S SALVATION NELL
—MOTHER DEAR
—THOUGHTS
—ROLLIN' DE BONES FROM COBLENZ TO THE RHINE
—LONG, LONG TIME
—GAS
—WHEN YOU ARE HAPPY
—WHEN THEY'RE BEAUTIFUL
—CUCKOO
—K. P.
—CUPID
—BUT YOU CAN'T BELIEVE THEM
By Blanche Merrill.
—MY SOUTH AMERICAN MAID
By Neal Harper.
—OH, MR. MAN
By Neal Harper.

Frederick Norton Score
1917. *CHU CHIN CHOW*
A musical extravaganza that kept up London's morale during World War I, and presented in this country by a cast headed by Tyrone Power, Tessa Kosta, Florence Reed and Henry Dixon. Book and lyrics by Oscar Asche.
—CLEOPATRA'S NILE
—JAVANESE DANCE
—ANY TIME IS KISSING TIME
—MAHUBAH
—COBBLER'S SONG
—CARRALINE
—ROBBER'S MARCH

Harry B. Olsen Score
1917. *GOOD NIGHT, PAUL*
A musical comedy with book and lyrics by Roland Oliver and Charles Dickson, and presented by a cast headed by Ralph Herz, Elizabeth Murray, Frank Lalor, Audrey Maple and Burrell Bardaretto.
—GOWNS
—EENIE-WEENIE
—THE WORLD IS ALL WRONG
—MARY ANN O'SHEA
—CONSTANCY
—FLATTERY
—SERENADE
—I'VE GIVEN MY HEART TO YOU DEAR

--LOVEY DOVEY
—PURITY
—I LIKE YOU
—GOOD NIGHT, PAUL
—SAILING AWAY ON THE HENRY
    CLAY
By Gus Kahn and Egbert VanAlstyne.

Harold Orlob Scores

1914. *THE RED CANARY*
A musical comedy with book and lyrics
by William LeBaron and Tom Johnstone,
lyrics by Will B. Johnstone, and presented
by a cast headed by Adele Rowland,
Leila Hughes and T. Roy Barnes.
—FRIEND CHAMPAGNE
—I LIKE YOU A WHOLE LOT MORE
    NOW
—I'M SO WEARY
—THE GLOBE-TROTTER
—THE CALL OF LOVE
—SOMETHING NEW

1915. *NED WAYBURN'S TOWN TOPICS*
A revue with book and lyrics by Harry B.
and Robert B. Smith and Thomas Gray,
and presented by a cast headed by Lew
Hearns, Blossom Seeley, Clifton Craw-
ford, Trixie Friganza, Vera Michelena,
Wellington Cross, Will Rogers and Ade-
laide and Hughes.
—I'LL KEEP THE ROSES BLOOMING
    FOR YOU
—IN TIME OF PEACE PREPARE FOR
    WAR
—THE KEYSTONE GLIDE
—MARIONETTES
—MELODY OF THE CENTURY
—THE OLD ARE GETTING YOUNGER
    EVERY DAY
—THE OSKALOOSA PETS
—PUT IT OVER
—RIFF-RAFF RAFFERTY
—SUBWAY LOVE
—TAKE IT FROM ME
—WAKE UP, IT'S CAKE WALK DAY
—WHAT YOU ARE AND WHAT YOU
    WANT TO BE
—YOU HAVE GOT THE STYLE
—COTTON BLOSSOM
—SERENADE
—AN OLD-FASHIONED GROOM AND
    AN UP-TO-DATE BRIDE
—PLANTATION DAYS
By Bobby Jones and Billy Morrissey.

1918. *LISTEN LESTER*
A musical comedy with book and lyrics
by Harry L. Cort and George E. Stoddard, and presented by a cast headed by

Mary Milburn, Eddie Garvie, Johnny
Dooley, Clifton Webb, Ada Mae Weeks,
Ada Lewis and Gertrude Vanderbilt.
—I WAS A VERY GOOD BABY IN THE
    DAYTIME
—I'D LOVE TO
—WHEN THE SHADOWS FALL
—WHO WAS THE LAST GIRL (YOU
    CALLED BY HER FIRST NAME)?
—SHOW A LITTLE SOMETHING NEW
—WHEN THINGS COME YOUR WAY
—FEATHER YOUR NEST
—WAITING FOR YOU
—TWO IS COMPANY
—FOR A GIRL LIKE YOU
—SWEET STUFF
—SEE HER FIRST

1919. *NOTHING BUT LOVE*
A musical comedy with book and lyrics
by Frank Stammers, and presented by a
cast that included Marion Sunshine, Don-
ald Meek, Andrew Tombes, Robert Wool-
sey, Ruby Norton and Clarence Nord-
strom.
—I'LL REMEMBER YOU
—WHEN I WALK OUT WITH YOU
—WONDERFUL MAN
—ASK THE STARS
—MOONBEAMS
—BEWARE
—SOME OTHER TIME
—DAWN
—THE STOP WALTZ
—IT'S NOT WHAT YOU SAY
—AT THE SHORE

1919. *JUST A MINUTE*
A musical comedy with book and lyrics
by Harry L. Cort and George E. Stod-
dard, and presented by a cast headed by
Wellington Cross, Mabel Withee and
Johnny Hines.
—MELODY
—BECAUSE YOU'RE DIFFERENT
—I'M GOING TO BE LONESOME
—SOME OTHER GIRL
—WONDERFUL DAY
—NO BIRDIE EVER FLEW SO HIGH
—ROLL ME
—GRANDFATHER'S CLOCK
—JUST IMAGINE
—TO MAKE THEM FALL
—I'LL SAY I WILL
—THE GIRL I WANT TO CALL MY
    WIFE
—OVER AND OVER AGAIN

Nat Osborne Score

1918. *ATTA BOY*
A revue produced and presented by the

soldiers of the Aberdeen Proving Grounds, Maryland. Frank Tinney headed the cast, Ballard MacDonald provided the lyrics, and Arthur Gutman collaborated on the songs.
—ELEPHANT SKID
—HOLD ME IN YOUR ARMS
—I LOVE HER AND SHE LOVES ME
—STROLLING 'ROUND THE CAMP WITH MARY
—THE MAGIC IN YOU BIG BLUE EYES
—THE RAGTIME WEDDING
—THE WORST IS YET TO COME
—THE STARS IN OUR SERVICE FLAG

Zoel Parenteau Scores

1916. *THE AMBER EXPRESS*
With Robert Planquette. A musical comedy with book and lyrics by Marc Connelly and Robert B. Smith, and presented by a cast headed by Emma Janvier and Frank Lalor.
—KING CARNIVAL
—WITH MILITANT STRIDE
—CANNONADING EYES
—THEY CAN'T RUN OFF THE REELS TOO FAST FOR ME
—GOSSIP
—YOU'RE A HERO
—THE SERENADE
—MELODY WILL KEEP YOU YOUNG
—PALACE OR COT
—THERE'S NOTHING SO UNCERTAIN AS A DEAD SURE THING
—'APPY 'OLIDAY
—DON'T LOSE YOUR WAY, LITTLE BOY
—IT'S THE ONLY ONE FOR ME
—A KISS AFFECTS ME MOST OF ALL
—LOVE FLIES EVERYWHERE
—SOMEWHERE A RAINBOW LIES
—THERE'S ALWAYS ONE YOU CAN'T FORGET
—OPEN YOUR HEART TO LOVE
—CHINESE FOX TROT

1918. *FOLLOW THE GIRL*
A musical comedy with book and lyrics by Henry Blossom, and presented by a cast headed by William Danforth, Jobyna Howland, Walter Catlett and George Bickel.
—DADDY DEAR
—DON'T LOSE YOUR WAY
—NO MATTER WHAT OR WHERE
—ON OUR LITTLE MERRY-GO-ROUND

—UNDER THE HONEYMOON
—I LIKE THE BOYS
—WINE, WOMEN AND JAZZ
—EVER BY YOUR SIDE
By Harold Atteridge and Sigmund Romberg.
—HONEYMOON LAND
By Harold Atteridge and Sigmund Romberg.
—EVERYTHING IS ROSY NOW
By Harold Atteridge and Sigmund Romberg.

William F. Peters Scores

1911. *MISS JACK*
A musical comedy with book and lyrics by Mark Swan, and presented by a cast headed by Bothwell Browne, Olive Ulrich, Ernest F. Young and Hazel Cox.
—THE ENGLISH LANGUAGE
—FENCING GIRL
—GOODBYE, LITTLE GIRL
—IF YOU COULD FANCY ME
—OLD DEACON PETTIGUE
—THE SERPENT OF THE NILE
—SLUMBERTOWN
—SONG OF THE SKYLARK
—THAT'S PECULIAR, ISN'T IT?
—THERE REALLY ISN'T ANY MORE TO TELL
—THERE IS NO PLACE FOR A GOOD LITTLE GIRL
—VISIONS OF LOVE

1913. *IOLE*
A musical comedy with book and lyrics by Robert W. Chambers, and presented by a cast headed by Frank Lalor.
—BACK TO NATURE
—IF DREAMS COME TRUE
—COMES AN EXQUISITE SITUATION
—TO RENT, TO LET
—THINK OF THAT
—TIME IS FLYING
—LIKE A SHEPHERDESS
—NUDE DESCENDING A STAIRCASE
—AND THAT IS ALL
—TAKE IT FROM ME
—IOLE
—NONE BUT THE BRAVE DESERVE THE FAIR
—OH WHAT'S THE USE?
—AMO
—I WONDER WHY
—PRETTY LITTLE PEGGY
—OH PRECIOUS THOUGHT
—WHY DO YOU THINK I LOVE YOU SO?

140   **[1910-1920]**

Robert Planquette Score

1911. *THE PARADISE OF MAHOMET*
A musical comedy with book and lyrics by Harry B. and Robert B. Smith, and presented by a cast headed by Harry MacDonald and Grace VanStuddiford.
—WHEN HIS EYES LOOK INTO MINE
—THE SUN SHINES ON MY WEDDING DAY
—THOSE EYES
—I'VE GOT TO GIVE HER HER OWN WAY
—LOOK OUT, LOOK OUT, LOOK OUT!
—THERE'S SOMETHING ABOUT YOU THAT APPEALS TO ME
—GYPSY SONG
—LIFE ORIENTAL
—THE JOYS OF LOVE
—I HAVE FOUND THEM ALL
—I CAN'T GET ENOUGH
—Y. M. D.
—MY IDEA OF PARADISE
—FORGIVE AND FORGET
—THE ROSE OF THE ORIENT
—WHEN THE CAT COMES BACK

Cole Porter Scores

1916. *SEE AMERICA FIRST*
Book by T. Lawrason Riggs, and presented by a cast headed by Clifton Webb, Red Eagle, Jeanne Cartier, Leo Gordon and Felix Adler.
—BUY HER A BOX AT THE OPERA
—EVER AND EVER YOURS
—I'VE A SHOOTING BOX IN SCOTLAND
—I'VE AN AWFUL LOT TO LEARN
—THE LANGUAGE OF FLOWERS
—LIMA
—OH BRIGHT FAIR DREAM
—PITY ME PLEASE
—PRITHEE COME
—SEE AMERICA FIRST
—SLOW SINKS THE SUN
—SOMETHING'S GOT TO BE DONE
—WHEN I USED TO LEAD THE BALLET

1919. *HITCHY-KOO OF 1919*
Book by Raymond Hitchcock, who starred in this revue that had a cast that included Charles Howard, Florence O'Denishawn and Joe Cook.
—PAGLIACCI
—WHEN BLACK SALLIE SINGS PAGLIACCI
—I INTRODUCED—
—HITCHY'S GARDEN OF ROSES

—WHEN I HAD A UNIFORM ON
—I'VE GOT SOMEBODY WAITING
—PETER PIPER
—THE SEA IS CALLING
—I'M AN ANESTHETIC DANCER
—MY COZY LITTLE CORNER IN THE RITZ
—AN OLD-FASHIONED GARDEN
—BRING ME BACK MY BUTTERFLY
—A LITTLE BEAR
By Sally J. Farnum and Neysa McMein.

Heinrich Reinhardt Scores

1910. *THE SPRING MAID*
A musical comedy with book and lyrics by Harry B. and Robert B. Smith, and presented by a cast headed by Christie MacDonald and Tom MacNaughton.
—IF YOU WANT A GIRL
—HOW I LOVE A PRETTY FACE
—FOUNTAIN FAY PROTECTIVE INSTITUTE
—ON THE TRACK
—TWO LITTLE LOVE BIRDS
—THE FOUNTAIN FAY
—DAY DREAMS (VISIONS OF BLISS)
—CARLSBAD MARCH
—HUNGARIA
—THE LOVING CUP
Music by Robin Hood Bowers.

1913. *THE PURPLE ROAD*
With William Frederick Peters. A musical comedy with book and lyrics by Fred DeGresac and William Cary Duncan, and presented by a cast headed by Valli Valli, Clifton Webb, Eva Fallon, Janet Beecher, Elita Proctor Otis and Edward Martindel.
—WHEN SOMEONE MARRIES ME
—MARCH OF THE BRIDEGROOMS
—I AM ALL ALONE
—A HIT IN PARIS
—FEED ME WITH LOVE
—THE LOVE SPELL
—DIPLOMACY
—DEAR LITTLE PAGES
—THE MYSTERIOUS KISS
—IN THE VALLEY OF BEAUTIFUL DREAMS
—PRETTY LITTLE CHICHIS
—THE REAPER'S CHORUS
—HE IS GONE
—IRRESISTIBLE

Aladar Renyi Score

1914. *SUZI*
A musical comedy with book and lyrics by Otto Harbach, and presented by a

cast headed by Tom MacNaughton, Jose
Collins and Lew Hearn.
—I LOVE YOU MARINA
—I'LL NOT LET LOVE DISPARAGE
   MARRIAGE
—OH, FASCINATING NIGHT
—HEAVEN MEASURED YOU FOR ME
—IT THRILLS, IT THRILLS
—THE BRAVE HUSSAR
—LIFE IS A GARDEN
—SECRETS
—MARINA
—THE MATCH MAKERS
—THE OCEAN, THE OCEAN
—'TWAS IN A GARDEN
—VENUS CALLS AND I'LL OBEY
—SUZI, I'M TICKING LOVE TAPS
   Music by Max Perschk.
—THE BEST TOAST OF ALL
   Music by Franz Lehar.
—TEENIE-EENIE-WEENIE
   Music by Paul Lincke.

Alfred J. Robyn Scores

1912. *ALL FOR THE LADIES*
   A musical comedy with book and lyrics
   by Henry Blossom, and starring Adele
   Richie in a cast that included Sam Ber-
   nard.
—I'D LIKE A GIRL LIKE YOU TO
   LIKE ME
—IN DREAMS ALONE
—IT'S PERMISSIBLE
—SUNDAY DRESS PARADE
—WOMEN, WOMEN!
—IF YOU LOVE ME, MARRY ME
—WHAT A CHANGE
—CUPID IS A CRUEL MASTER
—IF I WERE ONLY A MAN
—PARIS, PARIS

1914. *PRETTY MRS. SMITH*
   A musical comedy with book by Elmer
   Harris and Oliver Morosco, lyrics by
   Earl Carroll, and starring Fritzi Scheff in
   a cast that included Charlotte Greenwood,
   Sydney Grant, Charles Purcell and James
   Gleason.
—DRUCILLA
—MY DREAM OF DREAMS
—PRETTY MRS. SMITH
—LONG, LEAN, LANKY LETTY
   By Sydney Grant.
—MISSISSIPPI YOU'RE A GRAND OLD
   GIRL
   By Gould and Ashlyn.
—THE BENSONHURST GAVOTTE
—THE PLAIN OL' NAME OF SMITH

—LOVE HAS COME TO LIVE IN OUR
   HOUSE
—LET BYGONES BE BYGONES
—DAWN IN FLORIDA
1913. *A GLIMPSE OF THE GREAT
   WHITE WAY*
   A vaudeville-revue with book and lyrics
   by Henry Blossom, and presented by a
   cast headed by Frances Demarest, Sam
   Bernard and Forrest Huff. In the one-
   act finale, "The Modeste's Shop", the
   following songs were introduced:
—WHAT A CHANGE
—IF I WERE ONLY A MAN
—I'LL MARRY HIM FOR LOVE
—PERMISSIBLE

Sigmund Romberg Scores

1914. *THE WHIRL OF THE WORLD*
   Book and lyrics by Harold Atteridge, and
   presented by a cast headed by Eugene and
   Willie Howard, Ralph Herz, Bernard
   Granville, Lillian Lorraine, Roszika Dolly
   and Walter C. Kelly.
—COME ON IN, THE DANCIN'S FINE
—A BROADWAY IN PAREE
—NOBODY WAS IN LOVE WITH ME
—THE WHIRL OF THE WORLD
—A DANCING ROMEO
—LIFE'S A DRESS PARADE
—HELLO, LITTLE MISS U. S. A.
—TWENTIETH CENTURY RAG
—THE NOBLE CAUSE OF ART
—WE FORGOT THE NUMBER OF THE
   HOUSE
—ALL ABOARD
—RAGTIME PINAFORE
—HOW DO YOU DO—GOOD-BYE
—EVERYBODY MEANS IT WHEN
   THEY SAY GOOD-BYE
—A LOVELY TRIP
—I'LL COME BACK TO YOU
—EARLY HOURS OF THE MORN
—GOOD-BYE, LONDON TOWN
—OH, ALLAH
—MY CLEOPATRA GIRL
—RAGTIME ARABIAN NIGHTS
1914. *DANCING AROUND*
   With Harry Carroll. Book and lyrics by
   Harold Atteridge, and presented by a cast
   that included Al Jolson, James Doyle,
   Harland Dixon, Bernard Granville, Lucy
   Weston, Georgia O'Ramey and Melville
   Ellis.
—THE ARMY CLUB
—WHEN TOMMY ATKINS SMILES AT
   ALL THE GIRLS
—NEVER TRUST A SOLDIER MAN

—MY RAINBOW BEAU
—I WAS BORN ON THE ISLE OF MAN
—THERE'S SOMETHING ABOUT YOU
—MY LADY OF THE TELEPHONE
By Jean Gilbert.
—THE CALL OF THE COLORS
—SOMEBODY'S DANCING WITH MY
GIRL
—THE AFTERNOON TEA
—SEEKING FOR SIGFRIED
—A FASHION SLAVE
—VENETIA
—HE IS SWEET, HE IS GOOD
—THE SHUFFLING SHIVEREE
—WHEN AN ENGLISHMAN MARRIES
A PARISIAN
—I WANT TO BE IN NORFOLK
—OH, YOU JOHN
—IT'S A LONG WAY TO TIPPERARY
By Harry Williams and Joe Judge.
—OH, TENNESSEE, I HEAR YOU
CALLING ME
By Jeff Godfrey and Harry Robe.

1914. *THE PASSING SHOW OF 1914*
Book and lyrics by Harold Atteridge, and
the musical comedy debut of Marilyn
Miller in a cast that included Frances
Demarest, George Monroe, Lew Brice,
Bernard Granville, José Collins and Nat
Nazzaro Jr.
—OMAR KHAYYAM
—WORKING FOR THE PICTURES
—THE MAUDE ADAMS OF THE
SCREEN
—THE MIDNIGHT GIRL AT THE MID-
NIGHT CABARET
—THE SARI DANCE
—KITTY McKAY
—DREAMS OF THE PAST
—EUGENIC GIRLS
—THE GIRL OF TODAY
—ON A MODERN WEDDING DAY
—BOHEMIAN RAG
—THE SLOPING PATH
—DON'T HESITATE WITH ME
—GOOD OLD LEVEE DAYS
—THE GRAPE DANCE
—YOU CAN'T GO WRONG WITH US
—CALIFORNIA
Harry Carroll contributed the following
songs to this production:
—THE MOVING PICTURE GLIDE
—IN FRISCO TOWN
—THE EAGLE ROCK
—YOU'RE JUST A LITTLE BETTER
THAN THE ONE I THOUGHT WAS
BEST

1915. *HANDS UP*
With A. Ray Goetz. Book and lyrics by

Edgar Smith, and presented by a cast that
included George Hassell, Alice Dovey,
Maurice and Florence Walton, Bobby
North, Ralph Herz, Irene Franklin, Bur-
ton Green and Will Rogers.
—CUTE LITTLE SUMMERTIME
—THE BEST LITTLE SWEETHEART
OF ALL
—ESMERALDA
—GINGER
—PIRATE'S RAG
—TIFFANY GIRL
—CLING A LITTLE CLOSER
—ORANGE BLOSSOM TIME IN SAN
JOSE
—POPULAR RAG
—SING SING TANGO TEA
—THE LEVEE ALONG BROADWAY
—TING-A-LING
—COME ON IN, THE WATER'S FINE
—HOW DO YOU DO—GOOD-BYE
—I'M SIMPLY CRAZY OVER YOU
By William Jerome, E. Ray Goetz and
Jean Schwartz.

1915. *MAID IN AMERICA*
With Harry Carroll. Book and lyrics by
Harold Atteridge, and presented by a cast
that included Harry Carroll, Blossom See-
ley, Harry Fox, Lew Brice, Hal Forde,
Nora Bayes, Joe Jackson, Mlle. Dazie,
Yansci Dolly and Yvette.
—HAVE A RESTAURANT OF YOUR
OWN
—THE GIRLIE FROM THE CABARET
—SISTER SUSIE STARTED SYNCOPA-
TION
—IT'S ALL FOR YOU
—TIMES SQUARE ARGUMENTS
—GARDEN OF PARADISE
—OH, THOSE DAYS
—I'M LOOKING FOR SOMEONE'S
HEART
—CASTLES IN THE AIR
—WHEN GRANDMA WAS A GIRL
—DANCING AROUND THE U. S. A.
—DIANA
—EVERYBODY'S MOVING UP TOWN
—MANHATTAN MAD
—MADE IN THE U. S. A.
By Harry Carroll.
—HERE'S A BALE OF COTTON FOR
YOU
By Harry Carroll.
—THERE WAS A TIME
By Harry Carroll.
—THERE'S A LITTLE BIT OF EVERY-
THING ON BROADWAY
By Leo Edwards.
—THE STOLEN MELODY
By Phil Schwartz and Nora Bayes.

1915. *THE BLUE PARADISE*
With Edmund Eysler. Book and lyrics by Edgar Smith, and presented by a cast headed by Cecil Lean, Cleo Mayfield, Vivienne Segal, Ted Lorraine and Frances Demarest.
—HERE'S TO YOU, MY SPARKLING WINE
—AUF WIEDERSEHEN
—I'M DREAMING OF A WONDERFUL NIGHT
—I'M FROM CHICAGO
—JUST WIN A PRETTY WIDOW
—MY MODEL GIRL
—ONE STEP INTO LOVE
—TO PARADISE WE'LL GAILY TRIP
—VIENNA, VIENNA
—WALTZ OF THE SEASON
—TOAST TO A WOMAN'S EYES
—VIENNA, HOW D'YE DO?
—WE WISH YOU A PLEASANT JOURNEY
—THERE'S ONLY ONE WHO RULES MY HOUSE
—THE TUNE THEY CROON IN THE U. S. A.
By Cecil Lean.
—OLD BLUE PARADISE
—I HAD A DAY
1915. *A WORLD OF PLEASURE*
Book and lyrics by Harold Atteridge, and presented by a cast that included Kitty Gordon, Stella Mayhew, Clifton Crawford, Lew Holtz and the Mosconi Brothers.
—THE GOOD FELLOWS' CLUB
—FIFTH AVENUE
—THE EMPLOYMENT AGENCY
—IN THE WAR AGAINST MEN
—MISS INNOVATION
—GIRLIES ARE OUT OF MY LIFE
—I'LL MAKE YOU LIKE THE TOWN
—I COULD GO HOME TO A GIRLIE LIKE YOU
—SYNCOPATION
—AT THE TOY SHOP
—REMINISCENT ROSY-POSY
—THE MELTING POT
—THE RAGTIME PIPE OF PAN
—IN ARABY
—GIRL OF THE FAN
—TAKE ME HOME WITH YOU
—FASCINATION
—THE GREATEST BATTLE SONG OF ALL
—RAGTIME CARNIVAL
—THE JIGAREE
1915. *RUGGLES OF RED GAP*
A comedy with music, founded on Harry

Leon Wilson's Saturday Evening Post story, by Harrison Rhodes, with lyrics by Harold Atteridge and starring Ralph Herz in a cast that included Louise Closer Hale, George Hassell and Jobyna Howland.
—BEWARE OF LOVE
—EVERYBODY HUM WITH ME
—THE IMP OF MONTMARTRE
—SING ME A SONG OF LOVE
—WHEN THE COLORED REGIMENT GOES OFF TO WAR

1916. *ROBINSON CRUSOE, JR.*
With James Hanley. Book and lyrics by Harold Atteridge and Edgar Smith, and starring Al Jolson in a cast that included Kitty Doner, Lawrence D'Orsay, Helen Shipman and Barry Lupino.
—SIMPLE LIFE
—YOU'LL HAVE TO GALLOP SOME
—WHEN YOU'RE STARRING IN THE MOVIES
—DANCE A LITTLE MORE
—PRETTY LITTLE MAYFLOWER GIRL
—HAPPY HOTTENTOTS
—MY VOODOO LADY
—DON'T BE A SAILOR
—SAILOR'S FLING
—MY PIRATE LADY
—ROBINSON CRUSOE
—SPINNING A YARN
By John Golden.
—HUNTER'S FOX TROT TRAIL
—MINSTREL DAYS
—YOU'RE A DOG GONE DANGEROUS GIRL
By Grant Clarke and Jimmy Monaco.

1916. *THE PASSING SHOW OF 1916*
With Otto Motzan. Book and lyrics by Harold Atteridge, and presented by a cast headed by Fred Walton, Stella Hoban, Frances Demarest, Ed Wynn, Herman Timberg, Jack Boyle, Will Philbrick, the Ford Sisters, James Hussey, Mack and Swor and Florence Moore.
—THE CRAZY DANCE
—LET CUPID IN
—THE MAKING OF A GIRL
By George Gershwin.
—RAGGING THE APACHE
—RAGTIME CALESTHENICS
—ROMEO AND JULIET
—SO THIS IS PARIS
By Harry Tierney.
—SWEET AND PRETTY

1916. *THE GIRL FROM BRAZIL*
With Robert Winterburg. Book and lyrics

by Edgar Smith, and presented by a cast headed by Maude Odell, Hal Forde, George Hassell and Frances Demarest.
—CHILDHOOD DAYS
—LIKE THE FJORDS OF SCANDINA-VIA
—THE FINANCIAL VIKING
—I WANT TO BE A ROMEO
—STOLEN KISSES
—DARLING, I LOVE YOU SO
—IVY AND OAK
—THE RIGHT BRAZILIAN GIRL
—COME BACK SWEET DREAM
—OH YOU LOVELY LADIES
—HEART TO HEART
—A BACHELOR BOY AND GIRL
—SKI-ING
—BACCAROLE
—SENORITA

1916. *THE SHOW OF WONDERS*
With Otto Motzan and Herman Timberg. Book and lyrics by Harold Atteridge, and presented by a cast that included John T. Murray, Willie and Eugene Howard, Ernest Hare, George Monroe, Tom Lewis, McIntyre and Heath, Lew Clayton, Sam White, Walter C. Kelly and Marilyn Miller.
—BACK TO NATURE
—WEDDING BELLS
—WHEN PAVLOVA STARTS BUCK AND WINGING
—GIRLS PREPARE
—BRING YOUR KISSES TO ME
—ANGELS
—ALADDIN
—THE GIRL ON THE SQUARE
—LOUISIANA
By Harry Tierney.
—PAJAMA GIRLIES
—GET A GIRLIE
—NAUGHTY, NAUGHTY, NAUGHTY
By Nat Vincent.
—WEDDING BY THE SEA
—DIABOLO
—THE ZOO STEP
—LOVE IS LIKE A BUBBLE

1916. *FOLLOW ME*
Book by Felix Doerman and Leo Ascher, lyrics by Robert B. Smith, and starring Anna Held in a cast that included Harry Tighe.
—WE ALWAYS TAKE THEM HOME
—TWO HAPPY TADPOLES
—WHEN A MAN IS SINGLE
—A TETE-A-TETE WITH YOU
—FOLLOW ME
—THE GIRLS ARE GETTING WISER
—ADAM WAS THE ONLY LOVER

—THE VIOLIN SONG
—A LITTLE BIT OF NONSENSE
—I AM TRUE TO THEM ALL
—WHEN THE GIRLS GROW OLDER THEY GROW A LITTLE BOLDER
By Sam Lewis, Joe Young and Jean Schwartz.
—SINBAD WAS IN BAD ALL THE TIME
By Stanley Murphy and Harry Carroll.
—OH, JOHNNY, OH!
By Ed Rose and Abe Olman.
There were three interpolated numbers by Alfred Bryan and Harry Tierney, as follows:
—I WANT TO BE GOOD BUT MY EYES WON'T LET ME.
—MILADY'S TOILETTE SET
—IT'S A CUTE LITTLE WAY OF MY OWN

1916. *HER SOLDIER BOY*
With Emmerich Kalman. Book and lyrics by Rida Johnson Young, and presented by a cast headed by Adele Rowland, Louise Galloway, Clifton Crawford and John Charles Thomas.
—MOTHER
—ALL ALONE IN A CITY FULL OF GIRLS
—AMSTERDAM
—HE'S COMING HOME
—HISTORY
—HOME AGAIN
—THE LONELY PRINCESS
—SLAVERY
—SONG OF HOME
—I'D BE HAPPY ANYWHERE WITH YOU
—SMILE, SMILE, SMILE
—GOLDEN SUNSHINE
—THE KISS WALTZ
—MILITARY STAMP

1917. *THE PASSING SHOW OF 1917*
With Otto Motzan. Book and lyrics by Harold Atteridge, and presented by a cast that included Burton Green, Irene Franklin, Zeke Colvan, Yvette Rugel, Johnny Dooley, Tom Lewis, DeWolf Hopper, Jefferson de Angeles, Marie Nordstrom and Franklyn Batie.
—FATHER KNICKERBOCKER
—THE PASSING SHOW
—SAME OLD SONG
—WON'T YOU WRITE TO ME
—FASTER AND FASTER
—AMERICA'S FIGHTING JACK
—MEET ME AT THE STATION
By Sam Lewis, Joe Young and Ted Snyder.

—I'VE GOT A LITTLE BIT OF SCOTCH IN ME
—DANCING FAMILY
—PIERROT
—MY BEDOUIN GIRL
—THE GOLDEN WEST
—I'LL BE A COLLEGE BOY'S DEAR
—UNDER THE WILLOW TREE
—MY YOKOHOMA GIRL
—WON'T YOU BE MY DADDY
—THE LANGUAGE OF THE FAN
—A TABLE FOR TWO
—THE CHORUS GIRL
—THE TELEPHONE GIRL
—THAT PEACH-A-REENO, PHIL-I-PEENO DANCE
—RING OUT LIBERTY
1917. *MY LADY'S GLOVE*
With Oscar Straus. Book and lyrics by Edward A. Paulton and Edgar Smith, and starring Vivienne Segal in a cast that included Charles Purcell and Charles Mc-Naughton.
—OFFICERS OF THE 25TH.
—KEEP REPEATING IT
—I HATE TO LEAVE THE BOYS
—FOOLISH LITTLE MAIDEN I
—THE FICKLE SET
—I'M MADLY IN LOVE WITH A DREAM GIRL
—AMOROUS ROSE
—DO BUY SOME CANDY, SIR
—SECRECY
—I MEAN TO BE MARRIED AS SOON AS I CAN
—PRUDENCE HAS FLED
—SINCE TODAY OUR COLONEL'S MATING
—NO MORE GIRLS FOR ME
—ANTICIPATION
—LOOK BEFORE YOU LEAP
1917. *MAYTIME*
Book and lyrics by Rida Johnson Young and Cyrus Wood, and presented by a cast headed by Peggy Wood, Charles Purcell and William Norris.
—IN OUR LITTLE HOME SWEET HOME
—IT'S A WINDY DAY AT THE BATTERY
—GYPSY SONG
—WILL YOU REMEMBER (SWEETHEART)?
—JUMP JIM CROW
—THE ROAD TO PARADISE
—REMINISCENCE
—SELLING GOWNS
—DANCING WILL KEEP YOU YOUNG
—ONLY ONE GIRL FOR ME

1917. *DOING OUR BIT*
With Herman Timberg. Book and lyrics by Harold Atteridge, and presented by a cast that included James J. Corbett, Ada Lewis, Herman Timberg, Ed Wynn, Frank Tinney, Sam Ash, Henry Lewis and Vivian and Rosetta Duncan.
—ORANGE BLOSSOMS
—MISTER RAG AND I
—OH YOU SWEETIES
—DOING MY BIT
—A LOVING DADDY
—EGYPTIAN RAG
—NOTHING ON TODAY
—LET HER GO
—THE PHANTOM OF YOUR SMILE
—THE FASHION SHOW
—FIESTA
—DANCE, DANCE, DANCE
—SALLY DOWN OUR ALLEY
—FOR THE SAKE OF HUMANITY
—OLD-FASHIONED GIRLS
—FINE FEATHERS
—I MAY BE SMALL BUT I HAVE BIG IDEAS
—PERFECT JEWELS
—ROSES
—HELLO, MISS TANGO
1917. *OVER THE TOP*
With Herman Timberg. Book and lyrics by Philip Bartholomae, and starring Justine Johnstone in a cast that included Joe Laurie, Vivian Oakfield, T. Roy Barnes, Ted Lorraine, Mary Eaton and Fred and Adele Astaire, who made their Broadway debut in this revue.
—FROCK AND FRILLS
—MY RAINBOW GIRL
—THE GIRL FOR ME
—POSTERLAND
—THAT AIRSHIP OF MINE
—GREENWICH VILLAGE BELLE
—OH GALATEA
—THE GOLDEN PHEASANT
—ALGERIAN GIRL
—WHERE IS THE LANGUAGE TO TELL?
—JUSTINE JOHNSTONE RAG
1918. *SINBAD*
Book and lyrics by Harold Atteridge, and starring Al Jolson in a cast that included Lawrence D'Orsay, Edgar Atchinson-Ely, Forrest Huff and Kitty Doner.
—ON CUPID'S GREEN
—A LITTLE BIT OF EVERY NATIONALITY
—OUR ANCESTORS
—A THOUSAND AND ONE ARABIAN NIGHTS

—WHERE DO YOU GET THOSE GUYS?
—BEAUTY AND THE BEAST
—BAGDAD
—THE RAG LAD OF BAGDAD
—A NIGHT IN THE ORIENT
—I HAIL FROM CAIRO
—LOVE AHOY!
—BEDALUMBO
—ISLE OF YOUTH
—I'LL TELL THE WORLD
—IT'S WONDERFUL
—RAZ-MA-TAZ
—SWANEE
By Irving Caesar and George Gershwin.
—DIXIE ROSE
By Irving Caesar, B. G. DeSylva and George Gershwin.
—ROCK-A-BYE YOUR BABY TO A DIXIE MELODY
By Joe Young, Sam Lewis and Jean Schwartz.
—HELLO CENTRAL GIVE ME NO MAN'S LAND
By Joe Young, Sam Lewis and Jean Schwartz.
—MAMMY
By Irving Caesar and Walter Donaldson.
—BY THE HONEYSUCKLE VINE
By B. G. DeSylva and Al Jolson.
—CHLOE
By B. G. DeSylva and Al Jolson.
—I GAVE HER THAT
By B. G. DeSylva and Al Jolson.
—THEY CAN'T FOOL ME
By B. G. DeSylva and Al Jolson.

1918. *THE PASSING SHOW OF 1918*
With Jean Schwartz. Book and lyrics by Harold Atteridge, and presented by a cast that included Sam White, Lew Clayton, Fred and Adele Astaire, Charles Ruggles, Frank Fay, Eugene and Willie Howard, Nita Naldi and George Hassell.
—OH YOU VAMPIRE GIRLS
—DRESS, DRESS, DRESS
—I CAN'T MAKE MY FEET BEHAVE
—WAR STAMPS
—MY BABY-TALKING GIRL
—GO WEST, YOUNG GIRL
—TROMBONE JAZZ
—SQUAB FARM
—THE SHIMMY SISTERS
—I'LL MAKE AN ANGEL OUT OF YOU
—BRING ON THE GIRLS
—TWIT, TWIT, TWIT
—MY HOLIDAY GIRL
—QUICK SERVICE
—GALLI CURCI RAG

—SMILES
By J. Will Callahan and Lee J. Roberts.
—MY DUCHESS OF LONG AGO

1918. *THE MELTING OF MOLLY*
Book by Marie Thompson Davies and Edgar Smith, lyrics by Cyrus Wood, and presented by a cast headed by Charles Purcell, Gladys Walton and Ted Lorraine.
—DANCING SCHOOL
—DARLING
—REMINISCENCE
—BILLS
—DEAR OLD GOWN
—JAZZ—HOW I LOVE IT
—LODGER
—JAZZ ALL YOUR TROUBLES AWAY
—OH DOCTOR, DOCTOR
—YOU WIN
—FLOATING DOWN A MOONLIGHT STREAM
—YOU REMEMBER ME
—BRIDESMAIDS
—WEDDING BY PROXY
—I WANT MY HUSBAND WHEN I WED

1919. *THE PASSING SHOW OF 1919*
With Jean Schwartz. Book and lyrics by Harold Atteridge, and presented by a cast that included Blanche Ring, Charles Winninger, Walter Woolf, James Barton, Lon Hascall, Avon Comedy Four and George and Dick Raft.
—WINE BALLET
—SEVEN AGES OF WOMEN
—MOLLY MALONE
—TUMBLE INN
—GOOD-BYE
—IN SALEM
—THERE'S MISCHIEF IN YOUR EYES
—THE ROAD TO DESTINY
—DREAM FLORENCE
—NEAPOLITAN JAZZ
—ORIENT
—THE KING'S FAVORITE
—SHIMMY LA EGYPTIAN
—WATER LILY
—SUMMERTIME AT THE WINTER GARDEN
—AMERICA'S POPULAR TUNE
—LOVE BOAT
—MISS UNRULY
—SING SONG GIRL
—LOVABLE MOON
—HOCKEY

1919. *MONTE CRISTO, JR.*
With Jean Schwartz. Book and lyrics by Harold Atteridge, and presented by a cast that included Charles Purcell, Ralph Herz, Chic Sale, Adelaide and Hughes,

Tom Lewis, Sam Ash, William and Gordon Dooley and the Watson Sisters.
—JUST MY TYPE
—SENTIMENTAL KNIGHTS
—FIJI
—BROADWAY BUTTERFLY
—THE MILITARY GLIDE
—STEPPING OUT TONIGHT
—MONTE CRISTO
—MARSEILLES
—A GIRL IN EVERY PORT
—FESTIVE NIGHTS
—POCAHONTAS
—EMPIRE DAYS
—SUGAR BABY
—INDOOR SPORTS
—SAHARA
By Alfred Bryan and Jean Schwartz.
—WOMEN AND LIGHT
By Earl Carroll.

Paul Rubens Scores

1911. *THE BALKAN PRINCESS*
A musical comedy with book by Frank Curzon and Frederick Lonsdale, lyrics by the composer and Arthur Wimperis, and with Christine Nielson and Louise Gunning alternating in the title role in a cast that included Robert Warwick, Herbert Corthell and Alice Brady in the role of Rose Marie—her stage debut.
—HOLIDAYS
—I CHAR
—I LIKE YOU ALL
—LOVE AND LAUGHTER
—LADY AND GENTLEMAN
—IT'S A HARD LIFE
—WONDERFUL WORLD
—DEAR DELIGHTFUL WOMEN
—DON'T LET'S MEET AGAIN
—THE OPERA BALL
—DREAMING
—A MAN'S A MAN
—THE SUNSHINE OF SPRINGTIME

1913. *THE SUNSHINE GIRL*
A musical comedy with book by Cecil Raleigh and the composer, who also collaborated with Arthur Wimperis on the lyrics, and starring Julia Sanderson in a cast that included Vernon Castle, Joseph Cawthorn and Tom Lewis.
—HERE'S TO LOVE
—LADIES
—LITTLE GIRL MIND HOW YOU GO
—ARGENTINE TANGO
—JOSEPHINE
—GET A MOVE ON
—YOU AND I
—KITCHEN RANGE

—NUTS
—TINY TOUCH
—THE BUTLER
—GOODBYE TO FLIRTATION
—YOU CAN'T PLAY EVERY INSTRUMENT IN THE BAND
By Joseph Cawthorn and John Golden.
—WHO'S THE BOSS?
—MISS BLUSH
—IN YOUR DEFENSE
—I'VE BEEN TO AMERICA

1914. *TONIGHT'S THE NIGHT*
A musical comedy with book by Fred Thompson, lyrics by the composer, and starring Emmy Wehlen.
—WHEN THE BOYS COME HOME TO TEA
—TOO PARTICULAR
—YOU MUST NOT FLIRT WITH ME
—THE ONLY WAY
—LAND AND WATER
—TONIGHT'S THE NIGHT
—ROUND THE CORNER
—I'D LIKE TO BRING MY MOTHER
—I'M A MILLIONAIRE
—BOOTS AND SHOES
—DANCING MAD
—STARS
—PINK AND WHITE
—I COULD LOVE YOU IF I TRIED

1916. *BETTY*
A musical comedy with book by Gladys Unger and Frederick Lonsdale, lyrics by Adrian Ross, Percy Greenbank and the composer, and starring Raymond Hitchcock in a cast that included Joseph Santley, Marion Davies and Ivy Sawyer.
—HIGH LIFE DOWN STAIRS
—THE DUCHESS OF DREAMS
—DANCE WITH ME
—I FEEL SO HAPPY
—ON A SATURDAY AFTERNOON
—I LOVE THE GIRLS
—CINDERELLA
—WE'VE GOT SOME WORK TO DO
—I'M JOTTE, THE DRESSMAKER
—THE LITTLE HARLEQUIN
—IF IT WERE TRUE
Music by Ernest Steffan.
—HERE COMES THE GROOM
By Benjamin Hapgood Burt.
—EYES HAVE A LANGUAGE OF THEIR OWN
By Benjamin Hapgood Burt and Silvio Hein.
—SOMETIME
By William Jerome and Harry Tierney.
—WHEN I WAS TWENTY-ONE
By Edgar Leslie and Jean Schwartz.

William Schroeder Scores

1914. *LADY LUXURY*
A musical comedy with book and lyrics by Rida Johnson Young, and presented by a cast headed by Ina Claire, Forrest Huff and Harry Conor.
—DREAM ON, MY PRINCESS
—WHISTLE WHEN YOU WANT ME
—I'LL TAKE YOU ALL
—DON'T YOU REALLY THINK I'LL DO?
—PICK-PICK-PICKANINNY
—IT'S WRITTEN IN THE BOOK OF DESTINY
—KISS ME ONCE MORE
—LONGING FOR YOU
—THAT RAG-TAG DANCE
—THOSE AWFUL TATTLE-TALES
—HI THERE, BUDDY
—POSTER DANCE
—WHEN I SING IN GRAND OPERA

1917. *HIS LITTLE WIDOWS*
A musical comedy with book by Rida Johnson Young, lyrics by William Cary Duncan, and presented by a cast that included Flora Parker, Alma Pickard, Julia Ralph, Harry Tighe, Frank Lalor and Carter DeHaven.
—THAT CREEPY, WEEPY FEELING
—I WANT 'EM ALL
—IF IT SHOULD BE YOU
—PLEASE DON'T BE A SISTER TO ME
—MY LOVE IS A SECRET
—TEACH ME TO LOVE IN MEXICO
—I NEED SOMEONE'S LOVE
—IN CABARET LAND
—OH, YOU GIRLS
—A WIFE FOR EVERY DAY IN THE WEEK
—WHEN THE ANIMALS ARE GONE
By Thomas J. Gray and Malvin Franklin.
—SALT LAKE CITY
By Benjamin Hapgood Burt and Silvio Hein.
—OUR WEDDING DAY
By Ballard MacDonald and James F. Hanley.
—I WANT TO BE LOVED A LITTLE BY A LOT OF LITTLE BOYS
By Arthur Jackson and James Hanley.

1919. *BIFF! BANG!*
A revue written and acted by sailors from the Naval Training Station with book and lyrics by Phillip Dunning, Robert Cohen and William Isreal.
—COME ALONG WITH ME
—I LOVE THEM WHEN THEY'RE WILD

—I'VE A CORNER IN MY HEART FOR YOU
—LOVE
—LOVE IN A PERSIAN GARDEN
—THAT GYPSY RAG
—WE'RE GOING ACROSS

Jean Schwartz Scores

1910. *UP AND DOWN BROADWAY*
Book by Edgar Smith and lyrics by William Jerome. Irving Berlin was featured with his partner, Ted Snyder, in the revue, the cast of which was headed by Eddie Foy, Ernest Hare, Emma Carus, Anna Wheaton and Adelaide and Hughes.
—THE MILITARY GLIDE
—DREAMY FANDANGO TUNE
—I WANT A LOT OF GIRLS
—I'M THE LILY
—CHINATOWN, MY CHINATOWN
—THE PRETTY LITTLE GIRL INSIDE
—EVERYBODY IS BAGPIPE CRAZY
—COME DOWN TO EARTH
—I'M THE GHOST OF KELLY
—OH, THAT BEAUTIFUL RAG
By Irving Berlin and Ted Snyder.
—SWEET ITALIAN LOVE
By Irving Berlin and Ted Snyder.

1913. *THE HONEYMOON EXPRESS*
Book by Joseph W. Herbert, lyrics by Harold Atteridge, and a revue in which Al Jolson and Gaby Deslys headed the following cast: Harry Fox, Harry Pilcer, Melville Ellis, Ada Lewis, Fanny Brice, Doyle and Dixon and Yancsi Dolly.
—THAT'S THE LIFE FOR ME
—THE MOVING MAN
—WHEN THE HONEYMOON STOPS SHINING
—SYNCOPATIA LAND
—YOU CALL THE NEXT LOVE THE FIRST
—I WANT THE STROLLING GOOD
—RAGTIME EXPRESS
—THAT GAL OF MINE
—UPON THE HUDSON SHORE
—COCA-COLA BELLE
—THE SAME ONE THEY PICKED FOR ME
—I WANT A TOY SOLDIER MAN
—A LITTLE CABARET AT HOME
—MY RAGGYDORE
—WHEN GABY DID THE GABY GLIDE
—GOODBYE BOYS
By A. B. Sterling, William Jerome and Harry Von Tilzer.

1913. *THE PASSING SHOW OF 1913*
With Albert W. Brown. Book and lyrics by Harold Atteridge. The cast was headed

by Herbert Corthell, Carter De Haven, Wellington Cross, May Boley, Lew Brice, Charles King, Sydney Grant, Bessie Clayton, John Charles Thomas, Charlotte Greenwood, Sadie Burt, George Whiting and Mlle. Anne Dancrey, of the "Folies Bergere" of Paris.
—FLORODORA SLIDE
—MY IRISH ROMEO
—RAGGING THE NURSERY RHYMES
By Albert W. Brown.
—REFLECTIONS
—WON'T YOU COME INTO MY PLAY-HOUSE
—HOW DO DO
—IF YOU DON'T LOVE ME WHY DO YOU HANG AROUND?
—OH, YOU TANGO
—BALTIMORE
By Andy Razaf.
—WHEN I WANT TO SETTLE DOWN
—MY CINDERELLA GIRL
—LE PARADIS DE MOHAMET
—IT WON'T BE THE SAME OLD BROADWAY
—GOOD OLD-FASHIONED CAKE-WALK
—DANCE OF THE PERFUME
—THE BUTTERFLY AND THE ROSE
—CHIFFONS FROUS FROUS
—I'M LOOKING FOR A SWEETHEART
—STRONGHEART
—HIGH LIGHTS
—ON THE BOAT
—EAST NORTH G.A.R. SOUTH WEST
—THE WHITE HOUSE GLIDE
—LOVE ME WHILE THE LOVING'S GOOD
By Stanley Murphy and Harry Von Tilzer.
—TANGO FOOTED MONKEY
—WENCH DANCE
—ZATUMA
—INAUGURATION DAY

1914. *WHEN CLAUDIA SMILES*
Book and lyrics by Anne Caldwell, and presented by a cast that included Blanche Ring, Harry Conor and Charles Winninger.
—GRAND OLD LIFE
—I'VE GOT EVERYTHING I WANT BUT YOU
—THE FLOWER GARDEN BALL
—IF THEY'D ONLY MOVE OLD IRE-LAND OVER HERE
—DINAH
By Stanley Murphy and Henry Marshall.
—DEAR OLD PET
—EVERYBODY SOMETIME MUST LOVE SOMEONE

—YOU'RE MY BOY
—WHY IS THE OCEAN SO NEAR THE SHORE?
By Arthur Weinberg and Clarence Jones.
—THE BOYS ALL FALL FOR ME
—LET US DANCE THE BOSTON

1919. *HELLO, ALEXANDER*
Book by Edgar Smith and Emily Young, lyrics by Alfred Bryan, and starring McIntyre and Heath in a cast that included Johnny Burke, Eva Puck, Dan Quinlan, Lou Clayton, Sam White and Gilda Gray.
—TWO LIPS IN GEORGIA
—YOU'RE LIVING RIGHT NEXT DOOR TO HEAVEN WHEN YOU LIVE IN DIXIELAND
—JUNO, MY HONEYMOON GIRL
—WHEN THESE MASON-DIXON MINSTRELS HIT THE TOWN
—SHIMMYING EVERYWHERE
—THOSE DIXIE MELODIES

1919. *SHUBERT'S GAIETIES OF 1919*
A revue with book by Edgar Smith, lyrics by Alfred Bryan, and presented by a cast headed by Henry Lewis, Irving Fisher, Ted Lorraine, Gladys Walton, George Jessel and Gilda Gray, who was replaced by Sophie Tucker during the run of this production.
—CHERRY BLOSSOM LANE
—COSY CORNER
—FREEDOM OF THE C's
—LAMP OF LOVE
—MY TIGER GIRL
—PLEASE DON'T TAKE AWAY THE GIRLS
—RAINBOW BALL
—MILITARY DECORATION DAY
—BABY VAMPIRE
—COAT O' MINE
—A MAID LIKE YOU
—VAMP A LITTLE LADY
—THE GIRL YOU MARRY
—CRAZY QUILT
—BEAUTIFUL AMERICAN GIRL
—EVERYBODY SHIMMIES NOW
—BOY BLUE

A. Baldwin Sloane Scores

1910. *TILLIE'S NIGHTMARE*
Book and lyrics by Edgar Smith, and starring Marie Dressler.
—HEAVEN WILL PROTECT THE WORKING GIRL
—ON BROADWAY AT NIGHT
—THERE HE GOES
—THERE GOES ANOTHER ONE
—SHOPPING

—EVERY PRETTY GIRL
—THE SHOPPING GLIDE
—I WANT TO BRING YOU A RING
—KIND MOON MAN
—SPOOK DANCE
—BEE-BE
—WHAT I COULD DO ON THE STAGE
—LIFE IS WHAT YOU MAKE IT
—WHITE LIGHT LANE
1910. *THE SUMMER WIDOWERS*
Book and lyrics by Glen MacDonough, and presented by a cast headed by Lew Fields, Willis P. Sweatham, Fritz Williams, Burton Green, Irene Franklin, Vernon Castle, Ada Lewis, Alice Dovey and Helen Hayes.
—ON THE BOARDWALK
—WE'LL GO TO A MINSTREL SHOW
—CALCIUM MOON
—FLYING HIGH
—THERE'S NO PLACE LIKE HOME BOYS WHEN YOUR WIFE HAS GONE AWAY
—I KNEW HER WHEN
—WE'RE LOOKING FOR SOMETHING IN PEACHES
—GEE BUT I'D LIKE TO FURNISH A FLAT FOR YOU
—OH YOU SUMMERTIME ROMEO
—COME TAKE A DIP IN THE SEA WITH ME
—MISS DENNETT
—THE LADY USHERS' BALL
—THOSE WERE THE HAPPY DAYS
—REDHEAD
By Irene Franklin and Burton Green.
—THE SAHARA TWINS
—MUSCOVITE
1910. *PRINCE OF BOHEMIA*
Book by J. Hartley Manners, lyrics by E. Ray Goetz, and starring Christie MacDonald and Andrew Mack.
—SHANNON BELLS
—CUPID'S WIRELESS TELEGRAPH
—SENTIMENTAL TOMMY
—A YANKEE BOHEMIA
—DOLLARS AND DEBUTANTES
—JUST SAY YOU'LL BE A FRIEND OF MINE
—LOVESICK
—JUST A BIT OF BLARNEY
—VERSES FROM HOME
—HI SPY
1911. *THE HEN-PECKS*
Book by Glen MacDonough, lyrics by E. Ray Goetz, and starring Lew Fields in a cast that included Sam Watson, Gertrude Quinlan, Vernon Castle and Blossom Seeley.

—LITTLE ITALY
—JUST TELL ME WITH YOUR EYES
—WHITE LIGHT ALLEY
—DON'T FORGET THE BEAU YOU LEFT BEHIND
—TRY THIS ON YOUR PIANNY ANNIE
—TODDLING THE TODALO
—IT'S THE SKIRT
—JUNE
—HAIL TO THE BRIDE
—NEXT
—THE MANICURE GIRL
Music by Jerome Kern.
—IT'S NOT THE TRICK ITSELF BUT THE TRICKY WAY IT'S DONE
—HE'S THE WONDER OF THEM ALL
—WINE MAID DIVINE
1911. *LO*
Book by O. Henry, lyrics by Franklin P. Adams, and starring John E. Young. While this musical comedy never made Broadway but closed after playing one-night stands in Illinois and Wisconsin, it is included in this anthology because it is O. Henry's only venture in the theater although several of his short stories were made the basis for stage and screen plays.
—LOVE IS ALL THAT MATTERS
—YOU MAY ALWAYS BE MY SWEETHEART
—LITTLE OLD MAIN STREET FOR MINE
—IN YUCATAN
—IT'S THE LITTLE THINGS THAT COUNT
—STATUE SONG
—SNAPSHOTS
—DEAR YANKEE MAID
—LET US SING
—NEVER FORGET YOUR PARENTS
—WHILE STROLLING THROUGH THE FOREST
—CARAMBA
—TAMMANY ON PARADE
1912. *HOKEY-POKEY*
The reunion of Weber and Fields after an 8-year separation in a burlesque-revue with book and lyrics by E. Ray Goetz and Edgar Smith. The cast included Willie Collier, John T. Kelly, George Beban, Lillian Russell, Fay Templeton, Frankie Bailey, Ada Lewis and Bessie Clayton. The opening overture consisted of a medley of John Stromberg's songs from earlier Weber and Fields shows, and "Bunty Pulls the Strings" was burlesqued.
—LA BELLE PAREE
—THE MINSTREL PARADE
—THE SINGER AND THE SONG

—THE GARDEN OF YESTERDAY
—ON THE STAGE
—SENORITA
—ROSIE
—IF IT WASN'T FOR THE IRISH AND
   THE JEWS
By William Jerome and Jean Schwartz.
—THE ISLAND OF ROSES AND LOVE
By Neil Moret.
—ALEXANDER'S BAGPIPE BAND
By Irving Berlin.
1912. *HANKY-PANKY*
Book by Edgar Smith, lyrics by E. Ray
Goetz, and presented by a cast headed by
Bobby North, Max Rogers, Harry Cooper,
Carter DeHaven, William Montgomery,
Florence Moore and Christine Nielson.
—WHEN THE EDELWEISS IS BLOOM-
   ING
—OPERA BURLEQUE
By Irving Berlin.
—THE LYRE BIRD AND THE JAY
—ROSE OF PARAMID LAND
—THE DOLLAR BILL'S THE FLAG
   THAT RULES THE WORLD
—TENNIS
—THE RAGTIME FLAG
—COLLEGE DAYS
—MEET ME AT THE STAGE DOOR
   TONIGHT
—DIXIE LOVE
—THE MILLION DOLLAR BALL
—THE HANKY-PANKY GLIDE
—OH YOU CIRCUS DAY
By Edith Maada Lessing and Jimmy Mo-
naco.
—ON THE MISSISSIPPI
By Ballard MacDonald and Harry Carroll.
1912. *ROLY-POLY*
Book by Edgar Smith and lyrics by E.
Ray Goetz. The gala reopening on No-
vember 21st of Weber & Fields Music
Hall with a cast headed by Weber and
Fields, Jack Norworth, Nora Bayes, Frank
Daniels, Marie Dressler, Bessie Clayton
and Hazel Kirke.
—AT GAY RAATENBAD
—DEAR OLD HEIDELBERG
—I'M A LONESOME ROMEO
—THE PRIMA DONNAS
—WAY DOWN IN CUBA
By Jack Norworth and Nora Bayes.
—IN MY BIRCH CANOE (WITH EMMY
   LOU)
—STEINLAND
—I CANNOT DRINK THE OLD
   DRINKS
—NOBODY KNOWS WHAT WE GIRLS
   GO THROUGH

—WHEN I'M WALTZING
—THE BROOKLYN BURGLAR'S BALL
—PINKERTON DETECTIVE MOON
By Jack Norworth and Nora Bayes.
—WHEN IT'S APPLE BLOSSOM TIME
   IN NORMANDY
By Mellor, Gifford and Trevor.
1912. *THE SUN DODGERS*
A musical comedy with book by Edgar
Smith, lyrics by E. Ray Goetz, and pre-
sented by a cast headed by Bessie Wynn,
George Monroe, Nan Brennan, Harry
Clark and Harold Crane.
—DOWN IN THE OLD RATHSKELLAR
—RAG ME AROUND
—SONG OF THE COCKTAIL
—YOU'RE MY BABY
—GINGER
—WHEN YOU SAID HOW DO YOU DO
—GARDEN OF FLOWERS
—EVERY FLOWER HAS A MELODY
—MARRY A SUNSHINE GIRL
—THE NIGHT BRIGADE
—GOOD MORNING
—TWO HEADS ARE BETTER THAN
   ONE
—SOCIETY
—DIXIE LOVE
—WHAT HAPPENED TO MARY
—AT THE AUTOMAT
—AT THE PICTURE SHOW
—1918. *LADIES FIRST*
Book and lyrics by Harry B. Smith, and
starring Nora Bayes in a cast that in-
cluded William Kent, Irving Fisher and
Clarence Nordstrom.
—DRINK OUT THE OLD DRINKS
—WHAT COULD BE SWEETER THAN
   YOU?
—THE TEA PARTY
—HERE COMES THE BRIDE
—WHAT MEN CAN DO
—ON TO VICTORY
—WHAT A GIRL CAN DO
By Bert Kalmar and Harry Ruby.
—JUST LIKE A GYPSY
By Seymour Simons and Nora Bayes.
—JUST THE TWO OF US
By Seymour Simons and Nora Bayes.
1919. *THE GREENWICH VILLAGE
   FOLLIES*
The premiere production of this annual
revue with book by Philip Bartholomae,
lyrics by Arthur Swanstrom and J. Mur-
ray Anderson, and presented by a cast
that included Bessie McCoy Davis, Harry
Delf and Ted Lewis and his band.
—I'VE A SWEETHEART IN EACH
   STAR

—RED AS THE ROSE
—MY LITTLE JAVANESE
—MESSAGE OF THE CAMEO
—MY MARIONETTE
—I WANT A DADDY WHO WILL
  ROCK ME TO SLEEP
—I'M ASHAMED TO LOOK THE
  MOON IN THE FACE
—THE STOLEN MELODY

John Philip Sousa Score

1913. *THE AMERICAN MAID*
Book and lyrics by Leonard Liebling. This
production, which starred Louise Gunning
and featured "The Battle of Santiago" as
a spectacular finale, revived most of the
songs from "The Glass Blowers." Sousa,
however, wrote the following new numbers for this comic opera:
—MOST OMNISCIENT MAID
—CHEER UP, ANNABEL
—WITH PLEASURE
—SWEETHEART
—FROM MAINE TO OREGON

Dave Stamper Scores

1918. *ZIEGFELD'S 9 O'CLOCK FROLIC*
Presented by a cast headed by Delyle Al-
da, Bert Williams, Georgie Price, Bee
Palmer, Fanny Brice, Lillian Lorraine and
Lillian Leitzell, the circus aerialist. Lyrics
by Gene Buck.
—AFTER THE FIRST OF JULY
—WON'T YOU PLAY THE GAME?
—LET ME SHIMMY AND I'M SATIS-
  FIED
—HERE COME THE YANKS
—TIPPERARY MARY
—IT'S ALL OVER OVER THERE
—I LOVE TO LINGER WITH YOU
—YOU'RE SO PRETTY
—KISSES
—EVERY GIRLIE DID HER BIT
1919. *ZIEGFELD'S MIDNIGHT
  FROLICS*
Presented by a cast headed by Frances
White, Fanny Brice, Chic Sale, Ted Lew-
is, W. C. Fields, Allyn King and Savoy
and Brennan. Lyrics by Gene Buck.
—BY PIGEON POST
—TIPPERARY MARY
—SHANGHAI
—ROSE OF WASHINGTON SQUARE
By Ballard MacDonald and James Han-
ley.
—BABY
By Gus Kahn and Egbert Van Alstyne.

—IT'S NOBODY'S BUSINESS BUT MY
  OWN
By Will Skidmore and Marshall Walker.

Leslie Stuart Scores

1911. *PEGGY*
A musical comedy with book by Charles
Grossmith, Jr., lyrics by C. H. Bovill, and
presented by a cast headed by Florence
Walton, Tom Dingle, Alva York and John
W. Ransone.
—JULIET AND ROMEO
—LADIES BEWARE
—WHISTLE AND THE GIRLS COME
  AROUND
—GO AWAY, LITTLE GIRL, GO BACK
  TO SCHOOL
—I BEG YOUR PARDON
—THE LASS WITH THE LASSO
—DANCE FASCINATION
—MR. EDISON
—ANY OLD TUNE AT ALL
1911. *THE SLIM PRINCESS*
A comedy with book and lyrics by Henry
Blossom, and starring Elsie Janis in a
cast that included Queenie Vassar, Eliz-
abeth Brice, Charles King, Joseph Caw-
thorn and Wallace McCutcheon.
—QUEEN OF MY DREAMS
—CADDIES' SONG
—BLESS YOU EVER LOVING LITTLE
  HEART
—FOR I LOVE ONLY YOU
By Elsie Janis and Herman Darewski.
—A SOLDIER'S LIFE
By John P. Wilson and Alfred G. Robyn.
—MY YANKEE DOODLE GIRL

Johann Strauss Score

1912. *THE MERRY COUNTESS*
An operetta, based on the score of "Die
Fledermaus", with book by Gladys Unger,
lyrics by Arthur Anderson, and presented
by a cast headed by Fritzi Von Busing,
Maurice Farkoa, Forrest Huff and the
Dolly Sisters. In addition to untitled num-
bers, the following songs were in the
score:
—HOMELAND
—JUST THAT YOU ARE YOU
—LETTER SONG
—MUST WE SAY GOODBYE?
By Joseph H. McKeon and Arthur Gut-
man.
—THE TANGO DANCE
By Melville Ellis.
—JAIL BIRDS
By Melville Ellis.

Oscar Straus Score

1913. *MY LITTLE FRIEND*

A musical comedy with book and lyrics by Harry B. and Robert B. Smith, and presented by a cast headed by Leila Hughes, Fred Walton, William Pruette and Louis Harrison.

—LOVE THE WORLD OVER IS MUCH THE SAME
—MY LITTLE FRIEND
—NO JOURNEY'S TOO FAR FOR A LOVER
—WHAT YOU NEVER KNOW
—WHEN I WAS YOUNG

Deems Taylor Score

1910. *THE ECHO*

A musical comedy with book and lyrics by William LeBaron, and presented by a cast headed by Rose and Jenny Dolly, Eva Fallon, Georgia Drew Mendum, Bessie McCoy, George White and John E. Hazzard.

—HEIGH-HO
—TOO-RAL-I-OO-RAL-I-AY
—I WANT TO BE A SOLDIER BOY
—IT'S NEVER TOO LATE TO LEARN
—MY GUIDING STAR
    By James R. Brewers Jr. and Edward B. Claypoole.
—YOU'RE JUST THE GIRLIE I ADORE
    By A. Seymour Brown and Nat Ayer.
—THE YANKEE DOODLE GUARDS.
    By DeWitt Coleman and John Golden.
—I DON'T WANT TO BE A SOLDIER BOY
    By George V. Hobart and Karl Hoschna.
—FRENCH FANDANGO
    By John Golden and Christiné.
—WHISTLE WHEN YOU'RE LONELY
    By M. E. Rourke and Jerome Kern.

Harry Tierney Score

1919. *IRENE*

Book by James Montgomery, lyrics by Joseph McCarthy, and starring Edith Day and Walter Regan.

—HOBBIES
—ALICE BLUE GOWN
—CASTLE OF DREAMS
—THE TALK OF THE TOWN
—TO BE WORTHY OF YOU
—WE'RE GETTING AWAY WITH IT
—IRENE
—TO LOVE YOU
—SKYROCKET
—THE LAST PART OF ANY PARTY
—THERE'S SOMETHING IN THE AIR

Frank Tours Score

1918. *GIRL O' MINE*

A musical comedy with book and lyrics by Philip Bartholomae, and presented by a cast headed by Carl Hyson, Dorothy Dickson, Edna Wallace Hopper, Marie Nordstrom and Frank Fay.

—THE WINNING RACE
—THE WOMAN PAYS
—I LIKE TO PLAY WITH BOYS
—SHRUG YOUR SHOULDERS
—EVERY CLOUD IS SILVER-LINED
—RUG, SNUG
—CHANGING STYLES
—SATURDAY NIGHT
—THE BIRDIES IN THE TREES
—LOVE IS JUST A FAIRY TALE
—NOT SO FAST
—OMAR KHAYYAM, THE POET
—TODAY IS THE DAY
—GIRL O' MINE

Joaquin Valverde Score

1917. *THE LAND OF JOY*

A Spanish-American revue adapted by Ruth Boyd Ober, and presented by a cast of Spanish singers and dancers.

—BOLERO
—SONG OF THE GUITARS
—ZINGARA DANCE
—CAN THIS BE LOVE?
—LOVE IS VERY DIFFERENT
—COME WITH ME
—OFF TO SPAIN
—ALBAES
—HOLY WEEK WALTZ
—OH MY DARLING
—TAMBOURINE DANCE
—THERE'S A CHAPTER
—I KNOW NEW YORK, U.S.A.
—YO TE QUIERO

Egbert VanAlstyne Score

1910. *GIRLIES*

Book by George V. Hobart, lyrics by Harry Williams, and with Maude Raymond, Joseph Cawthorn, Ernest Truex and Jed Prouty featured members of the cast.

—UP IN MY AEROPLANE
—THAT'S GOOD
—LIFE IS JUST A MERRY-GO-ROUND
—LOVELIGHT
—YOU WILL READ IT IN THE PAPERS EVERY DAY
—WHO ARE YOU WITH TONIGHT?
—THE BULLFROG AND THE DOVE
—WHY BE A HERO?

—BABY TALK
—RING ME UP IN THE MORNING
—BARBER SHOP CHORD
—HONOLULU RAG

Armand Vecsey Score

1919. *THE ROSE OF CHINA*
A musical comedy with book by Guy Bolton, lyrics by P. G. Wodehouse, and presented by a cast headed by Oscar Shaw, Frank McIntyre, Jane Richardson and Cecil Cunningham.
—HYMN TO THE SUN
—THE LEGEND OF THE TEA TREE
—ROMEO AND JULIET
—PROPOSALS
—WHEN YOU ARE IN CHINA
—LOVE IS A WONDERFUL FEELING
—SPIRIT OF THE DRUM
—LOVELY LADIES
—COLLEGE SPIRIT
—BUNNY DEAR
—YESTERDAY
—DOWN ON THE BANKS OF SUBWAY
—OUR CHINESE BUNGALOW
—NEVER MORE   —YALE

Oreste Vessela Score

1916. *THE ROAD TO MANDALAY*
A musical comedy with book by William H. Post, lyrics by William McKenna, and presented by a cast headed by Hazel Kirke, Robert Corthell, Frank Pollock and Stanley Ridges.
—TOURISTS
—SAIL AWAY
—LOOKING FOR A GIRL MY SIZE
—YOU'LL FIND THE PARTY ISN'T THERE
—HEART OF MY HEART
—ARRIVAL OF THE BOOM
—IMAGINATION
—MOONLIGHT GAVOTTE
—FATHER'S WHISKERS
—BRIGHT DAY DAWNING
—TILL YOU TRY
—BACK TO PARIS
—SEE AMERICA FIRST
—FIREFLY
—OCEAN OF DREAMS
—THE ROAD TO MANDALAY
Lyrics by Jack Appleton.
—SHADOWS

The albums listed below were available on September 15, 1951, refer to 78 rpm recor

ROSE MARIE. (Score by Rudolf Friml)
RCA Victor WK-15. Marion Bell, Charles Fredericks, Christina Lind and the Guild Choristers with Al Goodman's orchestra.
Columbia MM-1005. Dorothy Kirsten and Nelson Eddy with chorus and orchestra.

ST. LOUIS WOMAN. (Score by Harold Arlen)
Capitol CE-28. Ruby Hill, Rex Ingram, Pearl Bailey and members of original cast.

SEVENTEEN. (Score by Walter Kent)
RCA Victor OC-4. Ann Crowley, Ken Nelson, Ellen McCown, Dick Kallman and cast.

SHOW BOAT. (Score by Jerome Kern)
Decca A-619. Bing Crosby, Lee Wiley, Kenny Baker, Frances Langford and Tony Martin.
Columbia ML-4058 (33⅓ rpm). Jan Clayton, Carol Bruce, Colette Lyons, Helen Dowdy, Charles Fredericks and Kenneth Spencer with chorus and orchestra.

SING OUT SWEET LAND. (Music based mainly on folk songs.)
Decca A-404. Al Drake, Burl Ives, Alma Kaye, Osterwald, J. McCauley and J. Hall.

SOUTH PACIFIC. (Score by Richard Rodgers)
Decca A-714. Bing Crosby, Danny Kaye, Evelyn Knight and Ella Fitzgerald with chorus.
Columbia MM-850. Mary Martin, Ezio Pinza and other members of the original cast.
RCA Victor K-18. Sandra Deel, Thelma Carpenter, Jimmy Carroll, Dickinson Eastham, the Guild Choristers and Al Goodman's orchestra.
Capitol CD-162. Margaret Whiting, Peggy Lee and Gordon MacRae with Dave Barbour.

STREET SCENE. (Score by Kurt Weill)
Columbia MM-683. Anne Jeffreys, Polyna Staska, Brian Sullivan and other members of the original Broadway cast with chorus and orchestra.

STUDENT PRINCE, THE. (Score by Sigmund Romberg)
Columbia MM-724. Risé Stevens and Nelson Eddy with chorus and orchestra.
Columbia C-134. Marek Weber orchestra and chorus.

SWEETHEARTS. (Score by Victor Herbert)
RCA Victor K-6. Frances Greer, Christine Lind, Jimmy Carroll. Earl Wrightson and the Guild Choristers with Al Goodman's orchestra.

THIS IS THE ARMY. (Score by Irving Berlin)
Decca A-340. Irving Berlin, Ezra Stone, Stuart Churchill, Phillip Truex, Julie Oshins, Earl Oxford, James Cross, Robert Shanley with other members of the original cast.

Albert Von Tilzer Score

1911. *THE HAPPIEST NIGHT OF HIS LIFE*
Book and lyrics by Junie McCree and Sydney Rosenfeld, and with a cast headed by Gertrude Vanderbilt, Emma Littlefield, Victor Moore and Junie McCree.
—OH, WHAT A BEAUTIFUL MORNING
—WE ARE LAUGHING WIDOWS
—BECAUSE IT CAN'T SIT DOWN
—NEW YORK AND CHICAGO
—THE HAPPIEST NIGHT OF HIS LIFE
—THERE'S ONE BORN EVERY MINUTE
—HURRY, BOYS
—I'M JUST ONE OF MY TEENS
—NECTAR FOR THE GODS
—A JOY RIDE
—BLIND MAN'S BUFF
—THINGS LEFT UNSAID
—THE FIDDLER MUST BE PAID
—WHAT A DIFFERENCE WHEN YOU'RE MARRIED
—THE LITTLE CHURCH AROUND THE CORNER
—TWENTY-FOUR HOURS OF LOVE

Harry Von Tilzer Score

1910. *THE KISSING GIRL*
Book by Stanislaus Stange, lyrics by Vincent Bryan, and starring Amelia Stone in a cast that included Olive Vail, John Park, Mort Lorenz and Joseph Miron.
—HUNTER'S HOLIDAY
—THE SCHUETZEN CORPS
—GOOD OLD GERMAN BEER
—WHEN YOU KISS THE ONE YOU LOVE
—MAJOR GENERAL PUMPERNICKEL
—MY SOLDIER BOY
—COME LITTLE GIRL AND DANCE WITH ME
—THE HAIR OF THE DOG THAT BIT YOU
—ON THE B, ON THE BOU, ON THE BOULEVARD
—LOVE IS LIKE A ROSE
—A LITTLE BAND OF GOLD

Percy Weinrich Score

1914. *CRINOLINE GIRL*
Book by Otto Harbach, lyrics by Julian Eltinge, and starring this female impersonator in cast that included Jeanne Eagles.
—IN MY DREAMS OF YOU
—GAME OF EYES

—WHEN MARTHA WAS A GIRL
—THAT TEMPTING TANGO

Richard Whiting Scores

1919. *TOOT SWEET*
A postwar revue with lyrics by Ray Egan, and presented by a cast headed by Elizabeth Brice, May Boley, Clarence Nordstrom, Lon Haskell and Will Morrissey.
—AMERICA'S ANSWER
—CHARGE OF THE SONG BRIGADE
—ROSE OF VERDUN
—JUST AROUND THE CORNER
—BLIGHTY BOUND
—ELEPHANT SKID
—EYES OF THE ARMY
—GIVE HIM BACK HIS JOB
—SALVATION SAL
—TOOT SWEET

1919. *GEORGE WHITE'S SCANDALS*
This was the premiere production of this annual revue with book and lyrics by George White and Arthur Jackson, and presented by a cast headed by Ann Pennington, Yvette Rugel, Ona Munson, George White, George Bickel and Lou Holtz.
—LAND OF HEART'S DESIRE
—UP ABOVE THE STARS
—I'LL BE THERE
—GIRLS ARE LIKE THE WEATHER TO ME
—STEP THIS WAY
—PEACOCK ALLEY
—GIRLS IN MY ADDRESS BOOK
—BROADWAY BELLES

Richard Winterberg Score

1919. *THE LADY IN RED*
A musical comedy with book and lyrics by Anne Caldwell, and starring Adele Rowland in a cast that included Donald MacDonald.
—PRETTY LITTLE GIRLS LIKE YOU
—FAMILY FACES
—CHINA DRAGON BLUES
By Irving Caesar and Walter Donaldson.
—PLAY ME THAT TUNE
By Irving Caesar and Walter Donaldson.
—BEAUTIFUL LADY IN RED
—MY OWN CALIFORNIA
—WALTZ OF MY HEART'S DESIRE
—CUPID NEVER WROTE THE ALPHABET
By Arthurs and David.
—MR. LOVE WILL GET YOU YET
Music by Jean Gilbert.
—SHIPS IN THE NIGHT
—I CAN'T FORGET YOUR EYES

—WHERE IS THE GIRL FOR ME?
By Harry B. Smith and Jerome Kern.
—SOMETHING ABOUT LOVE
By Louis M. Paley and George Gershwin.
—I'D RATHER DANCE HERE THAN
  HEREAFTER
—I WANT SOMEBODY
—A LITTLE BIT OF SCOTCH
—I WANT TO BE LIKE CLEO

Carl Woess Score

1916. *MOLLY O'*
A musical comedy with book and lyrics
by Harry B. and Robert B. Smith, and
presented by a cast that included John
E. Young, Tom Lewis, Josie Intropodi,
Elizabeth Hines, Grace Field and Donald
MacDonald.
—THE GIRL THAT WINS MY HEART
—ANNA OF HAVANA
—MARRY ME AND SEE
—WHEN THE RIGHT GIRL COMES
  ALONG
—LITTLE WOMEN—LOVE IS AN ART
—WHEN FORTUNE SMILES
—THE VOICE OF LOVE
—ONE WAY OF DOING IT
—ISN'T THAT LIKE A MAN!
—AESOP WAS A VERY MORAL MAN
—CHAMPAGNE AND LAUGHTER

E. M. Ziehrer Score

1911. *THE KISS WALTZ*
With Jerome Kern. A musical comedy
with book by Edgar Smith, lyrics by
Mathew Woodward, and starring Adele
Rowland.
—NOW'S THE TIME
—THE WALTZ LESSON
—O'ER THE BLUE WATERS
—TODALO
—THE KISS WALTZ
—OH, YOU GIRLS
Jerome Kern contributed music for the
following numbers:
—FAN ME WITH A MOVEMENT SLOW
—LOVE IS LIKE A LITTLE RUBBER
  BAND
—LOVE'S CHARMING ART
—TA-TA LITTLE GIRL

Composite Scores

1911. *HELL and GABY*
These two one-act plays—the first by Rennold Wolf and the second by Harry B.
and Robert B. Smith—were presented by
a cast headed by Ada Lewis, Otis Harlan,

Kathleen Clifford, Taylor Holmes, Lad-
die Cliff and Ethel Levey. In the musical
production "Gaby", the following songs
were introduced.
—HOW'D YOU LIKE TO BE THE
  SHOE STORE MAN?
Music by Robin Hood Bowers.
—ANSWER ME
By Irving Berlin.
—DON'T STOP MR. JENKINSON
By Laddie Cliff.
—I BEG YOUR PARDON BROADWAY
By Vincent Bryan, Irving Berlin and Ted
Snyder.
—DOWN THE STRAND

1912. *THE WHIRL OF SOCIETY*
A revue with book by Harrison Rhodes,
lyrics by Harold Atteridge, and presented
by a cast headed by Billie Taylor, Gaby
Deslys, Al Jolson, Barney Bernard, Stella
Mayhew, Blossom Seeley, Ernest Hare,
Melville Ellis and George White.
—WHEN WAS THERE EVER A NIGHT
  LIKE THIS?
—MY SUMURAN GIRL
Music by Louis A. Hirsch.
—HOW DO YOU DO, MISS RAGTIME
Music by Louis A. Hirsch.
—ON THE MISSISSIPPI
By Ballard MacDonald, Arthur Fields and
Harry Carroll.
—BILLY'S MELODY
By L. Wolfe Gilbert and Joe Cooper.
—FOUR O'CLOCK TEA
—FOL-DE-ROL
—I'M SAVING MY KISSES
—HOW DO YOU KNOW?
—I WANT SOMETHING NEW TO
  PLAY WITH
—THE COTILLION
—CINDERELLA WALTZ
—COME BACK TO ME

1915. *THE PASSING SHOW OF 1915*
A revue with book by Harold Atteridge,
songs by J. Leurbie Hill, Leo Edwards
and William F. Peters, and presented by
a cast headed by Marilyn Miller, Frances
Demarest, John Charles Thomas, John
Boles, John T. Murray, Daphne Pollard,
Willie and Eugene Howard, George Mon-
roe and Ernest Hare.
—SPRINGTIME IN THE COUNTRY
—FIRST LOVE IS THE BEST LOVE OF
  ALL
—EVERY SMALL TOWN GIRLIE HAS
  A BIG TOWN WAY
—I WILL FOLLOW HER
—THERE'S SOMETHING MISSING IN
  THE MOVIES

—SHOPPING
—THE MIDNIGHT CAKEWALK BALL
—MY TROMBONE MAN
—I DON'T LIKE THE SEA
—BROADWAY SAM
—AMERICA FIRST
—PEASANT GIRL
—THE SPANISH FANDANGO
—MY TRILBY MAID
—GAMBLE ON ME
—MY BROTHER BILL
—THE SHAKESPEARIAN RAG
—FLOWER OF MY HEART
—SUMMER SPORTS
—ANY OLD TIME WITH YOU
—PANAMA-PACIFIC DRAG
—THE PRIMROSE PATH

1918. *EVERYTHING*
A musical spectacle staged at the New York Hippodrome with a book by R. H. Burnside, lyrics by John Golden, and an all-star cast that included Belle Story, Charles T. Aldrich, Houdini, Tom Brown's Saxophone Band, Bert Levy and DeWolf Hopper. While John Philip Sousa is credited with the score of this production, he wrote only the incidental music, all the song numbers being interpolations by the following authors and composers.
—THE CIRCUS IS COMING TO TOWN
By Irving Berlin.
—COME ALONG TO TOYLAND
By Irving Berlin.
—A RAINBOW FROM THE U.S.A.
By William Jerome, Jack Mahoney and Percy Wenrich.
—ON ATLANTIC BEACH
By Joseph McCarthy and Harry Tierney.
—HONKY TONK TOWN
By Joseph McCarthy and Harry Tierney.
—SUNSHINE ALLEY
By John Golden and William Daly.
—COME TO THE LAND OF ROMANCE
By John Golden and William Daly.
—ROLL ALONG
By John Golden and William Daly.
—YOU'RE THE VERY GIRL I'VE LOOKED FOR
By John Golden and William Daly.
—I LIKE NEW YORK
By John Golden and James Tate.
—FOLLOW THE FLAG
By R. T. Burnside and Raymond Hubbell.

1918. *HITCHY-KOO OF 1918*
A revue with book and lyrics by Glen MacDonough and E. Ray Goetz, and starring Raymond Hitchcock in a cast that included Irene Bordoni in her Amer-

ican premiere, Leon Errol, George Austin Moore, Ray Dooley, Emma Haig and Florence O'Denishawn.
—LILY OF LONGACRE SQUARE
Music by Raymond Hubbell.
—RESURRECTION RAG
Music by Raymond Hubbell.
—HERE COME THE YANKS WITH THE TANKS
By Ned Wayburn and Harold Orlob.
—HOW CAN YOU TELL?
By Ned Wayburn and Harold Orlob.
—UNDERNEATH A PARASOL
By Ned Wayburn and Harold Orlob.
—COME DANCE WITH ME
By Ned Wayburn.
—TWILIGHT NIGHT
By Ned Wayburn.
—JAZZ-MA-TAZZ
By Ned Wayburn.
—WHERE DO THEY COME FROM?
Music by Fred Herendeen.
—YOU-OO JUST YOU
By Irving Caesar and George Gershwin.
—SAN SEBASTIAN'S SHORES
Music by Harry Carroll.
—SAY HITCHY-KOO, THAT'S ALL
By S. D. Mitchell and Willy White.

1918. *LET'S GO*
A revue presented by a cast that included William Rock, Frances White, Beatrice Herford and Bobby Edwards.
—THE LAND OF YESTERYEAR
By E. Ray Goetz.
—KITCHENER GIRL
—By V. M. Lezard and Cecil Kellaway.
—I NEVER TRAVEL ROUND WITHOUT A JAZZ BAND
By Richard Fechheimer and William Kernell.
—THE NEWSPAPER GIRL
—SINCE DADDY'S GONE AWAY
—DICTIONARY SONG
—WHY CAN'T A GIRL BE A SOLDIER?
—FLOWER GARDEN BALL
—I'M ONLY A POOR LITTLE KID

Revivals of 1910-20

1912. FORTY-FIVE MINUTES FROM BROADWAY with Sallie Fisher, Lawrence Wheat, George M. Cohan and George Parsons.
1912. ROBIN HOOD with Pauline Hall and George Frothingham.
1913. MLLE. MODISTE with Fritzi Scheff, Peggy Wood and Claude Gillingwater.
1913. ROB ROY with Jefferson DeAngelis, Herbert Waterous and Bessie Abbott.

Songs from Sigmund Romberg's *The Student Prince* and *Blossom Time*, Rudolf Friml's *Rose Marie* and Jerome Kern's *Sunny* and *Sally* were big sellers during Broadway's Golden Decade.

The Golden Decade (1920-1930)

Broadway and show business are lousy with pet superstitions, and always have been. Charles Hoyt, for example, clung to the notion that the indefinite article was his personal talisman and produced only plays whose titles began with the letter A. Florenz Ziegfeld regarded as unfailing tokens of good luck the miniature ivory elephants he collected. And Jerome Kern found during the Turbulent Twenties that the capital letter S stood for smooth sailing and superlative success as far as he was concerned.

While Jerome Kern was far too practical a man to believe in lucky charms, these pertinent facts can't be overlooked: His first smash hit during this decade of lethal booze and bullets was *Sally* in which Marilyn Miller became the darling of Broadway. Five years later, in 1925, he again hit the jackpot with *Sunny.* And in 1927, *Show Boat* carried him into the snug harbor reserved only for those composers who write truly enduring music. Add to these three signal successes, each of which had a Broadway run in excess of 500 performances, two other starting-with-S productions, *Stepping Stones* and *Sweet Adeline,* and you find that the letter S glows like a neon light in Jerome Kern's success story.

Although Jerome Kern reached towering heights during the decade that lionized Babe Ruth, Jack Dempsey and Red Grange, it would be unjust to say that he dominated this era of champions as George M. Cohan did the 1900s and Florenz Ziegfeld the 1910s, for this was Broadway's Golden Age of great and lasting music to which composers other than Kern contributed much.

Sigmund Romberg matched Kern's Broadway long-run record with three musicals that passed the 500-performance mark: *Blossom Time, The Student Prince* and *The New Moon,* and added for good measure the music for *My Maryland* and *The Desert Song* in a ten-year period in which his name appeared on the scores of twenty-five productions.

Rudolf Friml also entered the golden circle to which only the composers of 500-performance shows are eligible with *Rose Marie* and *The Vagabond King.* Harry Tierney was credited with the memorable *Kid Boots* and *Rio Rita,* produced by Florenz Ziegfeld with the magic touch that gave alluring lustre to his *Follies.* Irving Berlin gained new laurels from the songs he wrote for his *Music Box Revues,* produced at his new Music Box Theater, a playhouse with the warmth and charm of a Berlin ballad. And Victor Herbert's reign as the king of light opera composers ended on a high note, *A Kiss In The Dark* from *Orange Blossoms,* written shortly before death rang down the final curtain on a highly brilliant and fruitful career.

But the Old Guard of Broadway had to open ranks for a company of new recruits, soundly schooled in music and well armed with ability.

George Gershwin quickened the pulse beats of Father Knickerbocker with the songs he wrote for three *George White's Scandals* and six outstanding musical comedies: *Lady Be Good, Tip Toes, Oh, Kay, Funny Face, Treasure Girl* and *Show Girl*—songs that delighted a jazzy generation of short-skirted, shingle-bobbed flappers and their flask-toting escorts.

Richard Rodgers and his lyricist, Larry Hart, came out with a "lucky seven" in the Broadway crap game, and demonstrated with the songs they wrote for *Dearest Enemy, The Girl Friend, Peggy Ann, The Connecticut Yankee, Present Arms, Spring Is Here* and *Heads Up* an affinity for collaboration that had had no equal since the days of Gilbert and Sullivan.

Vincent Youmans made the lights of the Great White Way brighter with the music he wrote for *Wildflower, Hit The Deck, Great Day* and *No. No Nanette.* Cole Porter, now a wealthy playboy of Paris, atoned for his first Broadway flop, *See America First,* with the sophisticated lyrics and sprightly music he created for *Paris,* starring Irene Bordoni; *Fifty Million Frenchmen* and *Wake Up And Dream.* And Buddy DeSylva, Lew Brown and Ray Henderson, graduates of the pop song school, earned *magna cum laude* degrees in the stage musical college with the scores they fashioned for *Good News,* a 551-performance sellout; *Manhattan Mary, Hold Everything* and *Follow Through* in addition to replacing George Gershwin on George White's *Scandals'* payroll.

In these come-easy, go-easy years when even charwomen and panhandlers were playing the stock market, peanuts often were parlayed into bankrolls that dwarfed in size those the top rum-runners carried, and the biggest long shot to come through was *Shuffle Along,* rescued from the Jersey sticks by a $10,000 guarantee that netted the angel $1,000,000 during the 504-performance run of this Negro revue that skyrocketed Florence Mills to stardom.

It's Getting Awful Dark On Broadway, a sign of the theatrical trend set to music and sung by the shimmy-shaking Gilda Gray in the 1922 *Ziegfeld Follies,* was due for a reprise seven years later when the *Blackbirds Of 1928* bettered the long-run record of *Shuffle Along,* and in 1929, *Hot Chocolates,* with music by Fats Waller, made it three of a kind—and all black aces.

There were other innovations during this decade that made Broadway sit up and take notice. Out of Greenwich Village, haven of the intelligensia, came the *Grand Street Follies* to poke fun at Queen Marie and other front page celebrities, ridicule the whacky customs of an era that produced flagpole sitters and marathon dancers, and bring out of obscurity Albert Carroll, Jessica Dragonette and Jimmy Cagney, then a hoofer without a trace of menace in his voice.

The First Little Show set the pattern for the intimate revue and changed Libby Holman from a torch singer in a side street speakeasy into a Broadway star. The *Chauve Souris,* imported from Moscow via Paris, was a far better ambassador of good will than Molotov or Jacob Malik, and charmed American audiences with the folk songs and dances of a kindly, friendly people not yet in thralldom to Joe Stalin. And Beatrice Lillie and Gertrude Lawrence, co-stars of *Andre Charlot's Revue,* found Broadway as warm in its welcome as was London's West End.

Earl Carroll caught the revue fever, and staged the first of his annual *Vanities* in 1923. Ed Wynn wrote and produced three shows—*Ed Wynn's Carnival, The Grab Bag* and *The Perfect Fool*—in which to display his ludicrous costumes and zany inventions. The names of Joe Cook, Bill Robinson, Clark and McCullough, Harry Richman, Ruth Etting, Helen Morgan, Clara Bow and Jimmy Durante appeared on Broadway marquee boards for the first time. And Oscar Hammerstein II renounced the study of law to follow in the footsteps of his illustrious grandfather, Oscar the I, and seven years after writing his first libretto, shared with Jerome Kern the plaudits given *Show Boat.*

Although George M. Cohan took his final curtain call as a song-and-dance man in the *Merry Malones* in 1927 and produced his last musical, *Billie,* a year later, there was no dearth of theatrical producers on Broadway during a decade when practically everybody seemed to have the Midas touch or were out to get it. Even the bootleggers muscled in on the Shuberts' territory, primarily to curry favor with their molls—chorus girls and speakeasy thrushes with a yen to see their names in lights.

In fact, no decade before or since sponsored as many musicals as did the 1920s—a total in excess of 400, not counting the revivals, and twelve hitting the 500-or-better continuous performance mark. Moreover, this record was set in the face of competition from two fronts—the movies and newborn commercial radio, which offered entertainment at bargain prices or for free, respectively. The movies already had killed the road show, and with the advent of the sound track late in 1927, coupled with the stock market crash of 1929, Broadway's Golden Age came to an abrupt close.

Panic replaced prosperity overnight, Shubert Alley became a wailing wall, the trucks from Cain's warehouse worked on an around-the-clock schedule, and only the Santa Fe Chief and other west-bound trains profited from the Broadway debacle. Most of the songwriters and the stage stars who had popularized their songs suddenly became imbued with the spirit of the Forty-niners and were "off to Californi-ay with their press books on their knees."

Milton Agar Scores

1920. *WHAT'S IN A NAME?*
Book by John Murray Anderson, lyrics by
Jack Yellen, and presented by a cast head-
ed by James J. Corbett, Billy B. Van,
Marie Gaspar and Herb Williams.
—A YOUNG MAN'S FANCY
—RAP-TAP-A-TAP
—IN FAIR JAPAN
—THAT REMINISCENT MELODY
—MY BRIDAL VEIL
—WHAT'S IN A NAME?
—STRIKE
—VALLEY OF DREAMS
—THE JEWELS OF PANDORA
—STAGE DOOR BLUES
—WITHOUT KISSING LOVE ISN'T
  LOVE

1922. *ZIG-ZAG*
A revue starring Bessie McCoy Davis on
the road and featuring Cecil Lean and
Cleo Mayfield on Broadway. Lyrics by
Jack Yellen.
—ZIG ZAG
—TELL ME WHO LOOKS GOOD TO
  YOU
—STEPPIN' SCHOOL
—MOONBEAM TRAIL
—CRINOLINE
—CAVEMAN DAYS
—JINGLE BELLS
—EVERY LITTLE BIT
—CARTOON TOWN
—SHANTY DEBUTANTES' BALL

1923. *TED LEWIS FROLIC*
A revue starring Ted Lewis with a book
by Bugs Baer and William K. Wells and
lyrics by Jack Yellen.
—CHANGE YOUR STEP
—BACK HOME
—BEYOND THE MOONBEAM TRAIL
—TWINKLE, TWINKLE LITTLE STAR
—BEAUTIFUL GIRLS (YOU HAVE
  THE WORLD AT YOUR FEET)
—TIC TOC
—PAISLEY SHAWL
—STRUTTIN' SCHOOL

1928. *RAIN OR SHINE*
With Owen Murphy. Book by James Glea-
son and Maurice Marks, lyrics by Jack
Yellen, and starring Joe Cook in a cast
that included Tom Howard, Warren Hull,
Joe Lyons and Nancy Welford.
—GLAD TIDINGS
—CIRCUS DAYS
—SO WOULD I
—ADD A LITTLE WIGGLE
—RAIN OR SHINE

—PIERROT AND PIERRETTE
—OH, BABY!
—ROUSTABOUT SONG
—FALLING STAR
—FEELIN' GOOD
—FOREVER AND EVER
—WHO'S GONNA GET YOU?

1929. *MURRAY ANDERSON'S ALMA-
NAC*
A revue by John Murray Anderson, lyrics
by Jack Yellen, and presented by a cast
headed by Jimmy Savo, Roy Atwell, Fred
Keating, Trixie Friganza, Eleanor Shaler
and Helen Thompson.
—TINKLE, TINKLE
—I CAN'T REMEMBER THE WORDS
—THE HAPPY ENDING
—THE NEW YORKER
—EDUCATE YOUR FEET
—SONG OF THE NIGHTINGALE
Henry Sullivan is credited with the follow-
ing songs in this production:
—I MAY BE WRONG (BUT I THINK
  YOU'RE WONDERFUL)
Lyrics by Harry Ruskin.
—BUILDERS OF DREAMS
Lyrics by Clifford Orr.
—SAME OLD MOON
—Lyrics by Clifford Orr.
—THE POLKA DOT
Lyrics by Clifford Orr.

Harry Akst Score

1927. *ARTISTS AND MODELS OF 1927*
With Maurice Rubens. Lyrics by Benny
Davis, Ted Lewis, Jack Osterman and J.
Keirn Brennan, and presented by a cast
headed by Florence Moore, Gladys Whea-
ton, Margie Evans, Ted Lewis, Jack
Osterman and Jack Pearl.
—I'LL BE YOUR ARTIST AND YOU'LL
  BE MY MODEL
—OH, LADY!
—BANGAWAY ISLE
—THE REIMS CATHEDRAL
—WHAT WOMEN AND MEN WILL
  WEAR
—START THE BAND
—BRACELETS

Harry Archer Scores

1923. *LITTLE JESSE JAMES*
A musical comedy with book and lyrics
by Harlan Thompson, and presented by a
cast headed by Allen Kearns, Mariam
Hopkins, Jay Velie, Nan Halperin and
Frances Upton.
—I LOVE YOU

—COME ON, LET'S STEP, STEP AROUND
—LITTLE JESSE JAMES
—MY HOME TOWN IN KANSAS
—SUCH IS LIFE
—SUPPOSE I'D NEVER MET YOU
—FROM BROADWAY TO MAIN STREET
—A QUIET AFTERNOON
—KNOCKING BOOKWORMS
—LITTLE JACK HORNER

1924. *MY GIRL*
A musical comedy with book and lyrics by Harlan Thompson, and presented by a cast that included Jane Taylor, Russell Mack, Harry Puck and Frances Upton.
—BEFORE THE DAWN
—DESERT ISLE
—(WHEN A FELLOW LIKE ME LIKES) A GIRL LIKE YOU
—RAINBOW OF JAZZ
—A SOLO ON A DRUM
—YOU AND I
—YOU WOMEN

1924. *PARADISE ALLEY*
With Carle Carlton and A. Otvos. A musical comedy with book by Ed Clarke and Charles Bell, lyrics by Howard Johnson, and presented by a cast headed by Ida May Chadwick, Helen Shipman, Charles Derickson and George Bickel.
—CHIMES
—ALWAYS LOOK FOR A RAINBOW
—ANY OLD ALLEY IS PARADISE ALLEY
—HAPPINESS
—PARADISE ALLEY
—TELL ME TRULY
—PUT ON THE RITZ
Music by Irving Bibo.

1925. *MERRY, MERRY*
A musical comedy with book and lyrics by Harlan Thompson, and presented by a cast headed by Harry Puck, Marie Saxon and William Frawley.
—EVERY LITTLE NOTE
—I WAS BLUE
—IT MUST BE LOVE
—LITTLE GIRL
—MY OWN
—PIERROT WALTZ
—POOR PIERROT
—THE SPANISH MICK
—STEP, STEP SISTERS
—WE WERE A WOW
—WHAT A LIFE
—YOU'RE THE ONE
—BUBBLING OVER WITH JOY

By Henry Waller, R. P. Weston and Bert Lee.
—BUT I DO SAY SO
By Henry Waller, R. P. Weston and Bert Lee.

Abel Baer Score

1927. *LADY DO*
Book by Jack McClelland and Albert Cowles, lyrics by Joe Young and Sam Lewis, and presented by a cast headed by Nancy Welford, Karyl Norman, Francis Upton and Lew Hearn.
—BUDDY ROSE
—LIVE TODAY
—PARIS TAUGHT ME ZIS
—DREAMY MONTMARTRE
—DOUBLE FIFTH AVENUE
—YOU CAN'T BE A SHY BABY
—LADY DO
– OH SOLE MIA WHOSE SOUL ARE YOU?
—LITTLE MISS SMALL TOWN
—SNAP INTO IT
—TOO BLUE
—IN THE LONG RUN
—IN MY CASTLE IN SORENTO
—THIS IS MY WEDDING DAY
—JIGGLE YOUR FEET

Irving Berlin Scores

1921. *THE MUSIC BOX REVUE*
This rang up the first curtain at the new Music Box Theater with a cast that included Irving Berlin, Willie Collier, Sam Bernard, Joe Santley, Ivy Sawyer, Wilda Bennett, Florence Moore, Paul Frawley and Emma Haig.
—DANCING THE SEASONS AWAY
—BEHIND THE FAN
—IN A COZY KITCHENETTE APARTMENT
—MY BEN ALI HAGGIN GIRL
—SAY IT WITH MUSIC
—EVERYBODY STEP
—I'M A DUMB BELL
—SCHOOL HOUSE BLUES
—THEY CALL IT DANCING
—THE LEGEND OF THE PEARLS

1922. *THE MUSIC BOX REVUE OF 1922*
A production in which William Gaxton made his musical comedy debut in a cast that included Grace LaRue, Charlotte Greenwood, John Steel, the Fairbanks Twins and Clark and McCullough.
—TAKE A LITTLE WIFE
—DANCE YOUR TROUBLES AWAY
—PORCELAIN MAID

—THREE CHEERS FOR THE RED, WHITE AND BLUE
—DADDY LONG LEGS
—CRINOLINE DAYS
—PACK UP YOUR SINS AND GO TO THE DEVIL
—WILL SHE COME FROM THE EAST?
—MY DIAMOND HORSESHOE OF GIRLS
—TOO MANY BOYS
—BRING ON THE PEPPER
—LADY OF THE EVENING

1923. *THE MUSIC BOX REVUE OF 1923*
A production in which Robert Benchley made his first stage appearance, giving his "Treasurer's Report," in a cast that included Frank Tinney, Joseph Santley, John Steel, Phil Baker, Solly Ward, Florence Moore, Grace Moore, Ivy Sawyer, Florence O'Denishawn and Brox Sisters.
—WHEN YOU WALKED OUT SOMEBODY ELSE WALKED RIGHT IN
—TELL ME A BEDTIME STORY
—YOUR HAT AND MY HAT
—AN ORANGE GROVE IN CALIFORNIA
—MAID OF MESH
—CLIMBING THE SCALE
—LITTLE BUTTERFLY
—LEARN TO DO THE STRUT
—WALTZ OF LONG AGO

1924. *THE MUSIC BOX REVUE OF 1924*
With a cast that included Clark and McCullough, Oscar Shaw, Carl Randall, Tamara, Fanny Brice, Grace Moore, Claire Luce and the Brox Sisters.
—WHERE IS MY LITTLE OLD NEW YORK?
—SIXTEEN, SWEET SIXTEEN
—TOKIO BLUES
—A COUPLE OF SENSELESS CENSORS
—DON'T SEND ME BACK
—WHO
—TELL HER IN SPRINGTIME
—WILD CATS
—UNLUCKY IN LOVE
—LISTENING
—THE CALL OF THE SOUTH
—BANDANNA BALL
—COME ALONG WITH ALICE
—I WANT TO BE A BALLET DANCER
—ROCK-A-BYE BABY
—IN THE SHADE OF A SHELTERING TREE

1925. *THE COCOANUTS*
A revue with Janet Velie, Frances Williams and the Four Marx Brothers: Julius (Groucho), Herbert (Zeppo), Arthur (Harpo) and Leonard (Chico).

—FAMILY REPUTATION
—LUCKY BOY
—WHY AM I A HIT WITH THE LADIES?
—A LITTLE BUNGALOW
—FLORIDA BY THE SEA
—MONKEY DOODLE-DOO
—FIVE O'CLOCK TEA
—THEY'RE BLAMING THE CHARLESTON
—WE SHOULD CARE
—MINSTREL DAYS
—THE TALE OF A SHIRT

1927. *THE ZIEGFELD FOLLIES OF 1927*
With a cast that included Eddie Cantor, Harry McNaughton, Franklyn Bauer, Dan Healy, Claire Luce, Ruth Etting, Frances Upton, Irene Delroy and the Brox Sisters.
—SHAKING THE BLUES AWAY
—I WANT TO BE GLORIFIED
—RIBBONS AND BOWS
—MAYBE IT'S YOU
—RAINBOW OF GIRLS
—IT'S UP TO THE BAND
—JIMMY
—THE JUNGLE JINGLE
—LEARN TO SING A LOVE SONG
—TICKLIN' THE IVORIES

Robin Hood Bowers Score

1927. *OH, ERNEST!*
A musical comedy with book and lyrics by Francis DeWitt, and presented by a cast that included Harry McNaughton, Hal Forde, Marjorie Gateson, Dorothy Dilley and Vivian Marlowe.
—GIVE ME SOMEONE JUST LIKE YOU
—LET'S PRETEND
—TEA
—FEELING WONDERFUL
—ON THE BEACH
—OVER THE GARDEN WALL
—TRUE TO TWO
—TAKEN BY SURPRISE
—POLLYANNA
—DON'T SCOLD
—THERE'S TROUBLE
—CUPID'S COLLEGE
—IT'S ALL RIGHT WITH ME
—JUST A LITTLE STRANGER
—SHAKE A LITTLE SHOE
—WHAT'S A GIRL TO DO

Martin Broones Score

1927. *RUFUS LeMAIRE'S AFFAIRS*
A revue with book and lyrics by Ballard

MacDonald and Andy Rice, and presented by a cast headed by Ted Lewis, Lester Allen, John Price Jones, William Halligan, Lon Hascall, Charlotte Greenwood, Beth Beri, Peggy Fears, Mary Lewis and Bobbe Arnst.
—WAH WAH
—LILY
Music by Harry Warren.
—HOT STEPS
—I CAN'T GET OVER A GIRL LIKE YOU LOVING A BOY LIKE ME
—MINSTREL DAYS
—MEXICO
—LAND OF BROKEN DREAMS
—MORNING GLORIES
—DANCING BY MOONLIGHT
—TRAVEL ON

Shep Camp Score

1927. *HALF A WIDOW*
A musical comedy with book and lyrics by Harry B. Smith and Frank Dupree, and presented by a cast that included Gertrude Lang, Alfred Young and Benny Ruben.
—UNDER THE MIDNIGHT MOON
—IT'S GREAT TO BE A DOUGHBOY IN THE ARMY
—LONGING FOR YOU
—TELL ME AGAIN
—LET'S LAUGH AND FORGET
—I WONDER IF SHE'LL REMEMBER
—AMERICA
—STEP, STEP, STEP
—A THOUSAND TIMES
—SOLDIER BOY
—I DON'T WANT TO BE A SOLDIER
—BABETTE'S WEDDING DAY
—YOU'RE A WONDERFUL GIRL
—I'M THROUGH WITH WAR
—SPANISH LOVE
—FRANCE WILL NOT FORGET
By Gordon Johnstone and Geoffrey O'Hara.

Carle Carlton Score

1927. *LACE PETTICOAT*
With Emil Gerstenberger. A musical comedy with book by Stewart St. Clair, and presented by a cast headed by Vivian Hart, Tom Burke, Stella Mayhew, James C. Morton and Dick Powell.
—WATCH THE BIRDIES
—RENITA REINETTE
—SOUTH WIND IS CALLING
—A BOY IN A BLUE UNIFORM
—DEAR, DEAR DEPARTED

—CREOLE CRAWL
—HAVE YOU FORGOTTEN?
—THE ROSE ARIA
—CARNIVAL OF ROSES
—THE HEART IS FREE
—THE ENGAGEMENT RING
Lyrics by Howard Johnstone.
—LITTLE LACE PETTICOAT

Monte Carlo and Alma Sanders Scores

1921. *TANGERINE*
A musical comedy with book by Phil Bartholomae and Guy Bolton, lyrics by Howard Johnstone, and presented by a cast that included Julia Sanderson, Frank Crumit and Joseph Cawthorn.
—IN OUR MOUNTAIN BOWER
—ISLE OF TANGERINE
—IT'S GREAT TO BE MARRIED AND LEAD A SINGLE LIFE
—SWEET LADY
Music by Dave Zoob.
—LISTEN TO ME
—CIVILIZATION
—GIVE ME YOUR LOVE
—LOVE IS A BUSINESS
—MULTIPLIED BY SIX
—THE SPICE OF LOVE
—THE VOICE AT THE END OF THE LINE
—SHE WAS VERY DEAR TO ME
—WE'LL NEVER GROW OLD
—TROPIC VAMPS
—MULTIPLIED BY EIGHT
—THERE'S A SUNBEAM FOR EVERY DROP OF RAIN
—LORDS OF CREATION
Music by Jean Schwartz.
—MAN IS THE LORD OF IT ALL
Music by Jean Schwartz.
1924. *THE CHIFFON GIRL*
A musical comedy with book by George Murray, and presented by a cast that included Eleanor Painter and Joseph Lertoira.
—JUST ONE ROSE
—MY TONITA
—THE RAINDROP AND THE ROSE
—WE'RE SWEETHEARTS
—DID YOU COME BACK?
—MIA CARA
—TILL THE END OF TIME
—NEW YORK LIFE
—DUST CHASERS
—WHEN THE SUN GOES DOWN
—NINETEEN HUNDRED AND EIGHT
—THE KIND OF A GIRL FOR ME

—THE CHIFFON GIRL
—LITTLE DEVILS
—CAFE BOHEME
—MAYBE YES OR NO
—CUDDLE UP TO ME
1924. *PRINCESS APRIL*
A musical comedy with book by William
Cary Duncan and Lewis Allen Brown, and
starring Tessa Kosta in a cast that in-
cluded Nathaniel Wagner.
—WE'RE ALL IN THE SWIM
—ONE-PIECE BLUES
—DREAMY EYES
—SOCIETY
—SWEETHEART OF MINE
—DUMB-BELLS MAY BE FOOLISH
—SCANDAL
—AN IRISH ROSE FOR ME
—CHAMPAGNE
—PAGE A MAN FOR ME
—WHEN KNIGHTS WERE BOLD
—THE LOVE CLOCK
—TANTALIZING APRIL
—STRING 'EM ALONG
1924. *BYE, BYE BARBARA*
A musical comedy with book and lyrics by
Sidney Toler and Alonzo Price, and pre-
sented by a cast headed by Janet Velie
and Jack Hazzard.
—CHINA
—LIVE FOR TODAY
—CURIOSITY
—KISS INVENTION
—BO-PEEP
—QUAINT LITTLE HOUSE FOR TWO
—GEE, YOU MUST BE IN LOVE
—BYE, BYE BARBARA
—HARMONY
—PAS SEUL
—AMUSING MYSELF
—AS KIPLING SAYS: ("I LEARNED
ABOUT WOMEN FROM HER")
By Benjamin Hapgood Burt.
—SITTIN' IN CLOVER
—WHY DON'T YOU LEAVE THE
SHIEK ALONE?
1925. *OH, OH NURSE!*
A musical comedy with book by George
A. Stoddard, and presented by a cast
that included Gertrude Vanderbilt, John
Price Jones and Don Barclay.
—SHOW A LITTLE PEP
—LOVE WILL KEEP US YOUNG
—YOU MAY HAVE PLANTED MANY A
LILY
—WAY OUT IN RAINBOW LAND
—CLEOPATRA
—WHO BITES THE HOLES IN

SCHWEISTER CHEESE?
—KEEP A KISS FOR ME
—PIERRE
—GOOD NIGHT MY LADY LOVE
—I'LL GIVE THE WORLD TO KNOW
—MY HEART'S FOR SALE
—IS IT ANY WONDER?
—BUTTER-AND-EGG BABY
—THE NEWLYWED EXPRESS
—NO, I WON'T!
—SHOOTING STARS

Earl Carroll Scores
1923. *EARL CARROLL'S VANITIES OF
1923*
This was the first production of this an-
nual revue, and with Joe Cook, Bernard
Granville, Dorothy Knapp and Peggy
Hopkins Joyce heading the cast.
—THE BAND PLAYS HOME SWEET
HOME
—PRETTY PEGGY
—A GIRL IS LIKE SUNSHINE
By Roy Turk and William Daly.
—LAUGH WHILE YOU'RE DANCING
AROUND
By Roy Turk, William Daly and Carroll.
—CRETONNE GIRL
—GET IN A BATHING SUIT
—GIRLS WERE MADE FOR DANCING
—WHOA PAGLIACCI
—FINE FEATHERS
—MR. WAGNER'S WEDDING MARCH
1924. *EARL CARROLL'S VANITIES OF
1924*
A revue in which Joe Cook, Sophie Tuck-
er and Desiree Tabor headed the cast.
—IN THE SOUTH OF FRANCE
—TIDDLE LEE TOT
—OVER THE RADIO
—GET THEM ALL OVER AT ONCE
—SHADOWLAND
—TWELVE LITTLE HEELS
—ON A CHRISTMAS NIGHT
—PERFUME

Harry Carroll Score
1921. *ZIEGFELD'S 9 OCLOCK FROLIC*
Presented by a cast headed by Oscar
Shaw, the Fairbanks Twins, Anna Wheat-
on and Princess White Deer. Lyrics by
Ballard MacDonald.
—THE LITTLE LOVE MILL
—I'M GONNA DO IT IF I LIKE IT
By Irving Berlin and Harry Akst.
—TWO QUACK QUAKERS
By Herman Hupfeld.

—PAINTED BUTTERFLY
—LITTLE RED BOOK
  Music by Dave Stamper.
—ZIEGFELD'S PAPER DOLLIES
—WHEN SUNDAY COMES AROUND
—ICY SWITZERLAND

Ivan Caryll Scores

1920. *KISSING TIME*
  A musical comedy with book by George
  V. Hobart, lyrics by Philander Johnson,
  Irving Caesar and Clifford Grey, and pre-
  sented by a cast headed by Edith Talia-
  ferro, Paul Frawley and Frank Norris.
—BILL AND COO
—MIMI, THE BELLS ARE RINGING
—WEE, WEE MARIE
  By Fred Fisher.
—KISSING TIME
—DO YOU RECALL?
—SOME DAY WAITING WILL END
—IT'S THE NICEST SORT OF FEEL-
  ING
  Music by John Daly.
—KEEP A FOX TROT FOR ME
—KIKERIKEE
—TEMPORARY WIVES
—AN ABSOLUTE DON OF A JUAN
—LOVE'S TELEPHONE
—SO LONG AS THE WORLD GOES
  ROUND
—MIMI JAZZ
—KISSIMEE
—ABSOLUTELY CERTAIN

1920. *TIP TOP*
  A musical comedy with book and lyrics by
  R. H. Burnside and Anne Caldwell, and
  starring Fred Stone in a cast that includ-
  ed Vivian and Rosetta Duncan, Pauline
  Hall, Violet Zell, Helen Rich, Oscar Rag-
  land and the Six Brown Brothers.
—THE GIRL WHO KEEPS ME GUESS-
  ING
—I WANT A LILY
—I'LL SAY I LOVE YOU
—THE LANTERN OF LOVE
—FEATHER YOUR NEST
—WONDERFUL GIRL, WONDERFUL
  BOY
—WHEN SHALL WE MEET AGAIN?
—THE GIRL I NEVER MET
—I DON'T BELONG ON A FARM
  By Dorothy Clark and Arthur Swanstrom.
—BABY SISTER BLUES
  By Henry I. Marshall and the Duncan
  Sisters.

Ida H. Chamberlain Score

1927. *ENCHANTED ISLE*
  A musical comedy with book and lyrics
  by the composer, and presented by a cast
  headed by Marga Waldron and Greek
  Evans.
—CLOSE IN YOUR ARMS
—DREAM GIRL
—JULIANNE
—HACIENDA GARDEN
—JAZZ
—BUSINESS IS BUSINESS
—WHOA, GAL!
—CALIFORNIA
—ENCHANTED ISLE
—LOVE THOUGHT GARDEN
—COWBOY POTENTATE
—WHAT A JAMBOREE!
—VOICE OF THE SIERRAS
—DREAM BOAT
—ROULETTE
—DOWN TO THE SEA
—COULD I FORGET

Phil Charig Scores

1927. *YES, YES YVETTE*
  With Ben Jerome. A musical comedy with
  book by James Montgomery and William
  Cary Duncan, lyrics by Irving Caesar, and
  presented by a cast that included Jeanette
  MacDonald, Jack Whiting and Charles
  Winninger.
—DO YOU LOVE AS I LOVE?
—I'M A LITTLE BIT FONDER OF YOU
—MY LADY
—JUST PACK UP YOUR BLUES AND
  SMILE
—SIX O'CLOCK
—YOU OR NOBODY
—FOR DAYS AND DAYS
—MAYBE I WILL

1927. *JUST FANCY*
  With Joseph Meyer. A musical comedy
  with book by Joseph Santley and Gertrude
  Purcell, lyrics by Leo Robin, and pre-
  sented by a cast that included Mrs. Thom-
  as Whiffen, Peggy O'Neill, Ivy Sawyer,
  Joseph Santley, Eric Blore and Raymond
  Hitchcock.
—COO-COO
—TWO LOVING ARMS
—SHAKE, BROTHER
—SUNDAY BEAU
—YOU CAME ALONG
—HUMPTY DUMPTY
—A MILLION GIRLS TOO MANY

By Arthur Wimperis and Herman Darewski.

1929. *POLLY*
With Herbert Stothart. A musical comedy
with book by Guy Bolton and George
Middleton, lyrics by Irving Caesar, and
presented by a cast headed by Lucy Mon-
roe, John Huntley, Rosa June, Harry K.
Morton and Fred Allen.
—COMME CI, COMME CA
—HEEL AND TOE
—ON WITH THE DANCE
—POLLY
—SWEET LIAR
—WHEN A FELLOW MEETS A FLAP-
    PER ON BROADWAY
—THE ABADABA NIGHT CLUB
—LOTTA TIME FOR SUE
—LITTLE BO-PEEP
—NOBODY WANTS ME
—POLO
—LIFE IS LOVE
—SOMETHING SPANISH IN YOUR
    EYES
—SING A SONG IN THE RAIN
By Douglas Furber, Irving Caesar and
Harry Rosenthal.
—ALL THE WORLD IS LOVING
By Hugo Felix, Margaret May and Au-
drey Kennedy.

George M. Cohan Scores

1922. *LITTLE NELLY KELLY*
Presented by a cast headed by Elizabeth
Hines, Charles King and Arthur Deagon.
—OVER THE PHONE
—ALL IN THE WEARING
—GIRLS FROM DeVERE'S
—DANCING MY WORRIES AWAY
—LITTLE NELLIE KELLY I LOVE
    YOU
—WHEN YOU DO THE HINKY DEE
—SOMETHING'S GOT TO BE DONE
—THE NAME OF KELLY
—THE BUSY BEES OF DeVERE'S
—THE DANCING DETECTIVE
—THEY'RE ALL MY BOYS
—YOU REMIND ME OF MY MOTHER
—THE GREAT NEW YORK POLICE
—THE MYSTERY PLAY
—TILL MY LUCK COMES ROLLING
    ALONG
—THE VOICE IN MY HEART

1923. *THE RISE OF ROSIE O'REILLY*
Presented by a cast that included Mary
Lawlor, Virginia O'Brien, Jack McGow-
an and Bobby Watson.
—I NEVER MET A GIRL LIKE YOU

—BORN AND BRED IN BROOKLYN
—MY GANG
—THE ARRIVAL OF SOCIETY
—IN THE SLUMS OF THE TOWN
—SOMETHING'S HAPPENED TO
    ROSIE
—POOR OLD WORLD
—STAGE SOCIETY
—ALL NIGHT LONG
—LOVE DREAMS
—JUST ACT NATURAL
—WHEN JUNE COMES ALONG WITH
    A SONG
—AT MADAME REGAY'S
—ON A HOLIDAY
—LET'S YOU AND I SAY GOOD-BYE
—THE RING TO THE NAME OF ROSIE
—KEEP A-COUNTIN' EIGHT
—TWO GIRLS FROM THE CHORUS
—NOTHING LIKE A DARNED GOOD
    CRY
—THE ITALIAN WHIRLWIND
—THE MARATHON STEP
—GATHERING

1927. *THE MERRY MALONES*
George M. Cohan took his final curtain
call as a song-and-dance man in this pro-
duction, the cast of which included Polly
Walker and Allan Edwards.
—TALK ABOUT A BUSY LITTLE
    HOUSEWIFE
—LIKE A WANDERING MINSTREL
—FLIRTATION WALTZ
—SON OF A BILLIONAIRE
—MOLLY MALONE
—THE HONOR OF THE FAMILY
—A FEELING IN YOUR HEART
—THE BRONX EXPRESS
—A NIGHT OF MASQUERADE
—BEHIND THE MASK
—WE'VE HAD A GRAND OLD TIME
—CHARMING
—WE'VE GOT HIM
—A BUSY LITTLE CENTER
—OUR OWN WAY OF GOING ALONG
—EASTER PARADE
—ROSES UNDERSTAND
—GIP-GIP
—GOD'S GOOD TO THE IRISH
—BLUE SKIES, GRAY SKIES
—LIKE A LITTLE LADYLIKE LADY
    LIKE YOU

1928. *BILLIE*
This was George M. Cohan's last muscial
production, an adaptation of his comedy
"Broadway Jones," in which June O'Dea,
Polly Walker and Joseph Wagstaff were
featured.

—NEW YORK
—COME TO ST. THOMAS
—HAPPY
—BILLIE
—GO HOME EV'RY ONCE IN A
  WHILE
—THOSE WONDERFUL FRIENDS
—THE CAUSE OF THE SITUATION
—EVERY BOY IN TOWN'S MY SWEET-
  HEART
—THEY FALL IN LOVE
—WHERE WERE YOU, WHERE WAS I?
—THE JONES' FAMILY FRIENDS
—I'M A ONE-GIRL MAN
—PERSONALITY
—BLUFF
—THE TWO OF US

Con Conrad Scores

1924. *MOONLIGHT*
Book by William LeBaron, lyrics by W.
B. Friedlander, and presented by a cast
headed by Allyn King, Ernest Glendin-
ning and Maxine Brown. Later Julia San-
derson and Frank Crumit took over the
leading roles.
—FAIR WEATHER FRIENDS
—THE DAFFYDILL
—IF I WERE OF THE HOI POLLOI
—FOREVER
—HOW CAN A LADY BE CERTAIN?
—AREN'T WE ALL?
—SAY IT AGAIN
—ON SUCH A NIGHT
—JAPANESE GIRL
—SOUTH SEA ISLAND GIRL
—IN A BUNGALOW
—TURN ON THE POPULAR MOON
—HOW DO I KNOW HE LOVES ME?
—THE PASSING OF THE NIGHT
—DON'T PUT ME OUT OF YOUR
  HEART
—DANCING
—HONEYMOON BLUES

1925. *MERCENARY MARY*
With William B. Friedlander. Book and
lyrics by Isabel Leighton and Friedlander,
and presented by a cast that included Al-
len Kearns, Madeline Fairbanks, Sam
Hearn and Winnie Baldwin.
—OVER A GARDEN WALL
—JUST YOU AND I AND THE BABY
—CHARLESTON MAD
—HONEY I'M IN LOVE
—THEY STILL LOOK GOOD
—TOMORROW
—COME ON ALONG
—MERCENARY MARY
—BEAUTIFUL BABY

—CHASTE WOMAN
—CHERCHEZ LA FEMME
—EVERYTHING'S GOING TO BE ALL
  RIGHT
1925. *THE COMIC SUPPLEMENT*
With Henry Souvaine. Book and lyrics by
J. P. McEvoy, and starring W. C. Fields
in a cast that included Ray Dooley, Clar-
ence Nordstrom and Brooke Johns.
—SUNDAY POIPERS
—ON THE BEACHES
—KISSING
—CAFETERIA CHOW
—GOO-GOO-GOO
—LITTLE TWO BY FOUR
—JUNGLE JOY
Henry Souvaine is credited with the fol-
lowing numbers:
—THE COP AND THE NURSE
—LOVIN' YOU
—MARRIAGE LICENSE
—BY THE SIDE OF THE ROAD
1926. *KITTY'S KISSES*
Book by Philip Bartholomae and Otto
Harbach, lyrics by Gus Kahn, and pre-
sented by a cast that included Dorothy
Dilley, John Boles and Nick Long, Jr.
—WALKIN' THE TRACK
—CHOO-CHOO LOVE
—KITTY'S KISSES
—I LOVE TO DANCE
—THINKING OF YOU
—I'M IN LOVE
—TWO FELLOWS AND A GIRL
—BOUNCE ME
—I'M A LITTLE TOO OLD TO DANCE
—MISTER AND MISSUS
—EARLY IN THE MORNING
—I DON'T WANT HIM
—NEEDLES
—DON'T DO THAT
—STEPPING ON THE BLUES
—CRYSTAL BALL
1926. *AMERICANA*
With Henry Souvaine. Book and lyrics by
J. P. McEvoy and presented by a cast
that included Roy Atwell, Lew Brice,
Charles Butterworth, Betty Compton and
Helen Morgan, who made her first stage
appearance perched on a piano.
—RIVERSIDE BUS
—TABLOID PAPERS
—THANKS AWFUL
Lyrics by Sam Lewis and Joe Young.
—SUNNY DISPOSISH
By Ira Gershwin and Phil Charig.
—DREAMING
Music by Henry Souvaine.

—NOBODY WANTS ME
Music by Henry Souvaine.
—LOST BARBER SHOP CHORD
By Ira and George Gershwin.
—KOSHER KLEAGLE
Music by Phil Charig.
—BLOWING THE BLUES AWAY
By Ira Gershwin and Phil Charig.
—WHY DO YOU ROLL THOSE EYES?
By Morris Ryskind and Phil Charig.

J. Fred Coots Scores

1922. *SALLY, IRENE AND MARY*
A musical comedy with book by Eddie
Dowling and Cyrus Wood, lyrics by Ray-
mond Klages, and starring Eddie Dowling
in a cast that included Edna Moon, Jean
Brown and Kitty Flynn in the title roles.
—KID DAYS
—TIME WILL TELL
—PALS
—STAGE DOOR JOHNNIES
—I WONDER WHY
—DO YOU REMEMBER?
—HOW I MISSED YOU, MARY
—WHEN THE RIGHT BOY COMES
ALONG
—OUR HOME, SWEET HOME
—PEACOCK ALLEY
—SOMETHING IN HERE
—OPPORTUNITY
—WE ARE WAITING
—WEDDING TIME
1925. *ARTISTS AND MODELS OF 1925*
With Al Goodman and Maurice Rubens.
Book by Harold Atteridge and Harry
Wagstaff Gribble, lyrics by Clifford Grey,
and presented by a cast headed by Walter
Woolf, Billy B. Van, Phil Baker, Jay Bren-
nan, Herbert Corthell and Frances Wil-
liams.
—MAID OF THE MILKY WAY
—CELLINI'S DREAM
—TAKE A LITTLE BABY HOME WITH
YOU
—MOTHERS OF THE WORLD
—FOLLOW YOUR STAR
—THE MAGIC GARDEN OF LOVE
—ORIENTAL MEMORIES
1925. *JUNE DAYS*
Book by Harry Wagstaff Gribble and
Cyrus Wood, lyrics by Clifford Grey, and
presented by a cast headed by Elizabeth
Hines, Jay C. Flippen, Roy Royston and
Millie James.
—REMEMBERING YOU
—ALL I WANT IS LOVE
By Hal Dyson and James Kendis.

—WHY IS LOVE?
—JUNE DAYS
Music by Stephen Jones.
1925. *GAY PAREE*
With Al Goodman and Maurice Rubens.
Book by Harold Atteridge, lyrics by Clif-
ford Grey, and presented by a cast that
included Chic Sale, Billy B. Van, Jack
Haley and Winnie Lightner.
—A STUDY IN LEGS
—A VISION OF HASSAN
—EVERY GIRL MUST HAVE A
LITTLE BULL
—WONDERFUL GIRL
—VENETIAN NIGHTS
—BABY'S BABY GRAND
—WEDGEWOOD MAID
—FLORIDA MAMMY
—TODDLE TROT
—BAMBOO BABIES
By Ballard MacDonald, Joe Meyer and
James Hanley.
—GIVE ME THE RAIN
By Lester Allen, Henry Creamer and
Maurice Rubens.
—MY SUGAR PLUM
By B. G. DeSylva and Joe Meyer.
1926. *THE MERRY WORLD*
A revue with lyrics by Clifford Grey, and
presented by a cast headed by Alexander
Gray, Evelyn Herbert and Grace Hayes.
—GOLDEN GATES OF HAPPINESS
—WHISPERING TREES
Lyrics by Herbert Reynolds.
—WHY SHOULD WE BE WASTING
TIME?
—DON'T FALL IN LOVE WITH ME
—DEAUVILLE
—SUNDAY
—I FELL HEAD OVER HEELS IN
LOVE
By Donovan Parsons and Pat Thayer.
1926. *A NIGHT IN PARIS*
With Maurice Rubens. Book by Harold
Atteridge, lyrics by Clifford Grey, and pre-
sented by a cast that included Jack Oster-
mann, Jack Pearl, Norma Terris and
Yvonne George.
—SERGEANT'S DREAM
—POSTER GIRL
—ZULU
—THE NEWPORT GLIDE
—IN CHINATOWN IN FRISCO
—IN THE GARDENS OF THE KING
—POWDER PUFF
—LOUISIANA
—THEY SATISFY
—DANCE MAD
—WEDDING DAY

1927. *WHITE LIGHTS*
Book by Leo Donnelly and Paul Gerard Smith, lyrics by Al Dubin, and presented by a cast that included Rosalie Claire, Sam Ash, Jimmy Steiger, Tammany Young, Florence Parker and Leo Donnelly.
—I'LL KEEP ON DREAMING OF YOU
—AN EYEFUL OF YOU
—DON'T THROW ME DOWN
—SITTING IN THE SUN
—WHITE LIGHTS
—ROMANY ROVER
—TAPPING THE TOE
—SHOW GIRL
—BETTER TIMES ARE COMING
By Dolph Singer and Jimmy Stegler.

1929. *SONS O' GUNS*
A musical comedy with book by Fred Thompson and Jack Donahue, lyrics by Benny Davis and Arthur Swanstrom, and starring Jack Donahue and Lily Damita in a cast that included William Frawley.
—THE YOUNGER SET
—MAY I SAY "I LOVE YOU"?
—I'M THAT WAY OVER YOU
—WE'LL BE THERE
—THE CAN-CANOLA
—WHY?
—CROSS YOUR FINGERS
—RED HOT AND BLUE RHYTHM
—OVER HERE
—IT'S YOU I LOVE
—LET'S MERGE
—SENTIMENTAL MELODY
—THERE'S A RAINBOW ON THE WAY
—THE VICTORY PARADE

William Cortelyou Score
1927. *KISS ME*
A musical comedy with book and lyrics by Max Simon and Derick Wulff, and presented by a cast headed by Desiree Ellinger, Fred Santley and Ralph Whitehead.
—I HAVE SOMETHING NICE FOR YOU
—KISS ME
—POOLS OF LOVE
—ROSE OF IRAN
—SLEEPING BEAUTY'S DREAM
—ARAB MAID WITH MIDNIGHT EYES
—YOU IN YOUR ROOM, I IN MINE
—TWO IS COMPANY
—WELCOME HOME
—IF YOU'LL ONLY SAY YES
—DODO
—ALWAYS ANOTHER GIRL

Noel Coward Scores
1928. *THIS YEAR OF GRACE*
A musical play with book and lyrics by the composer, and presented by a cast headed by Beatrice Lillie, Noel Coward and G. P. Huntley.
—A ROOM WITH A VIEW
—CABALLERO
—DANCE LITTLE LADY
—MARY MAKE-BELIEVE
—TEACH ME TO DANCE LIKE GRANDMA
—TRY TO LEARN TO LOVE
—WORLD WEARY
—THIS YEAR OF GRACE
—LORELEI

1929. *BITTER SWEET*
A musical play with book and lyrics by the composer, and presented by a cast that included Evelyn Laye, Gerald Nodin and Peggy Wood.
—THE CALL OF LIFE
—IF YOU COULD COME WITH ME
—I'LL SEE YOU AGAIN
—WHAT IS LOVE?
—LADIES OF THE TOWN
—IF LOVE WERE ALL
—EVERMORE AND A DAY
—TOKAY
—KISS ME
—ZIGEUNER
—GREEN CARNATION

Charles Cucillier Score
1920. *AFGAR*
A musical play with book by Frederick Thompson and Worten David, lyrics by Douglas Furber, and presented by a cast that included Alice Delysia, Lupino Lane, Irving Beebe and W. H. Rawlins.
—DEAR LONELY LOVER
—GIVE THE DEVIL HIS DUE
—LIVE FOR LOVE
—ROSE OF SEVILLE
—SUNSHINE VALLEY
—EYES OF BLUE
—WHY DON'T YOU?
By Joseph McCarthy and Harry Tierney.
—WHERE ART THOU, ROMEO?
By Joseph McCarthy and Harry Tierney.
—I HATE THE LOVELY WOMEN
By Joseph McCarthy and Harry Tierney.
—CARESSES
—By Jimmy Monaco.

Ford Dabney Score
1927. *RANG TANG*
A musical comedy with book by Kaj Gynt,

lyrics by Jo Trent, and starring Miller and Lyles in an all-Negro cast.
—BROWN
—COME TO AFRICA
—SIX LITTLE WIVES
—EE YAH
—PAY ME
—HARLEM
—EVERYBODY SHOUT
—JUBILEE
—IN MONKEYLAND
—JUNGLE ROSE
—KING AND QUEEN
—RANG TANG
—SAMMY AND TOPSY
—SAMMY'S BANJO
—SOME DAY
—SWEET EVENING BREEZE
—VOODOO
—ZULU FIFTH AVENUE

Max Darewski Songs

1923. *HAMMERSTEIN'S NINE OCLOCK REVUE*
A revue with book by Harold Simpson and Morris Harvey, and presented by a cast of English music hall stars. Lyrics by Graham John.
—SHADOW MAN
—SNOW BALL SONG

Leon DeCosta Score

1926. *THE BLONDE SINNER*
A musical comedy with book and lyrics by the composer, and starring Enid Markey in a cast that included Ralph Bunker and Marjorie Gateson.
—BYE, BYE BABY
—DON'T YOU CHEAT
—LIPS
—THE WHISPERING SONG
—OH, WHAT A PLAYMATE YOU'D MAKE
—IF YOU SAID WHAT YOU THOUGHT
—MAN IS A MISTAKE

Lucien Denni Score

1926. *HAPPY GO LUCKY*
A musical comedy with book and lyrics by Helena Phillip Evans and Gwynne Denni, and presented by a cast headed by Taylor Holmes, Nydia D'Arnell, Jack Squire and Lina Abarbanell.
—CHOOSE YOUR FLOWERS
—HAPPY MELODY
—HOW ARE YOU, LADY LOVE?
—LOVE THOUGHTS
—SING A LITTLE SONG

—WHEN I MAKE A MILLION FOR YOU
—CINDERELLA
By Clifford Grey and James Hanley.
—TINKER TAILOR
By Desmond Carter and James Hanley.

Harry Delf Score

1923. *SUN SHOWERS*
A musical comedy with book and lyrics by the composer, and presented by a cast that included Tom Dingle, Douglas Stevenson, Allyn King and the author-composer.
—EVERY ONE IS BEAUTIFUL IN SOMEONE'S EYES
—WHAT'S WORTH HAVING IS WORTH WAITING FOR
—ON A MOONLIGHT NIGHT
—THE JOY OF LIVING
—IF THE OLD FOLKS COULD SEE US NOW
—HE LOVES ME
—HOW DO YOU DOODLE?
—I'M THE GREENWICH VILLAGE CHAMBERMAID
—OH, PROFESSOR!
—IN THE MORNING
—EACH LITTLE JACK
—SPEAK WITHOUT COMPUNCTION
—YOURS TRULY
—CLIP THE COUPONS

Harry Denny Score

1927. *FOOTLIGHTS*
A revue with book by Roland Oliver, and presented by a cast that included J. Kent Thurber, Louis Sorin, Ruth Wheeler, Ellalee Ruby, Jack Wilson and Hazel Dean.
—LOVE-O-LOVE
—SURE SIGN YOU REALLY LOVE ME
—CHAMPAGNE
—THE DUCK CALLS IT LUCK
—FOOTLIGHT WALK
—COLLEGE PALS
—JUST WHEN I THOUGHT I HAD YOU ALL TO MYSELF
With Joe Fletcher.
—GYPSY SWEETHEART
By Francis Wheeler, Irving Kahal and Ted Snyder.
—I ADORE YOU
By Ballard MacDonald and Rene Mercier.
—SAHARA MOON
With Dave Ringle.
—YOU CAN'T WALK BACK FROM AN AEROPLANE
By Irving Bibo and W. B. Friedlander.

Walter Donaldson Scores

1926. *SWEETHEART TIME*
With Joe Meyer. Book by Harry B. Smith, lyrics by Ballard MacDonald and Irving Caesar, and starring Mary Milburn and Eddie Buzzell.
—ONE WAY STREET
—MARIAN
—TWO BY FOUR
—ACTIONS SPEAK LOUDER THAN WORDS
—WHO LOVES YOU AS I DO?
By Joe Meyer.
—SWEETHEART TIME
By Joe Meyer.
—A GIRL IN YOUR ARMS
By Jay Gorney.

1928. *WHOOPEE*
Book by William Anthony McGuire, lyrics by Gus Kahn, and starring Eddie Cantor in a cast that included Ruth Etting, Ethel Shutta, Gladys Glad, Paul Gregory, Tamara Geva, Chief Caupolican and George Olsen and his orchestra.
—IT'S A BEAUTIFUL DAY TODAY
—HERE'S TO THE GIRLS OF MY HEART
—I'M BRINGING A RED, RED ROSE
—GYPSY JOE
—MAKING WHOOPEE
—GO GET 'EM
—UNTIL YOU GET SOMEBODY ELSE
—TAPS
—COME WEST, LITTLE GIRL, COME WEST
—WHERE THE SUNSET MEETS THE SEA
—STETSON
—SONG OF THE SETTING SUN
—LOVE IS THE MOUNTAIN
—RED MAMA
—WE'LL KEEP ON CARING
—HALLOWE'EN TONIGHT
—MY BABY JUST CARES FOR ME
—MY BLACKBIRDS ARE BLUEBIRDS NOW
—LOVE ME OR LEAVE ME
—HALLOWE'EN WHOOPEE BALL

Duncan Sisters Score

1924. *TOPSY AND EVA*
A musical version of "Uncle Tom's Cabin" with book by Catherine Chisholm Cushing and lyrics by the composers, who starred in a cast that included Harriet Hoctor, Frederic Santley and Basil Ruysdael.
—I NEVER HAD A MAMMY

—REMEMB'RING
—DO-RA-ME
—PLANTATION MELODIES
—GIVE ME YOUR HEART AND GIVE ME YOUR HAND
—UM-UM-DA-DA
—THE MOON AM SHININ'
—THE LAND OF LONG AGO
—IN THE AUTUMN
—JUST IN LOVE WITH YOU
—SIGHIN'
—BIRD DANCE
—WE'LL DANCE THROUGH LIFE TOGETHER
—WEDDING PROCESSION

Gus Edwards Score

1923. *SUNBONNET SUE*
Book and lyrics by Robert B. Smith, and starring Fred Hildebrand and Olga Cook in a cast that included Chester Fredericks and Helen Lynd.
—SUNBONNET SUE
—'MEMBER WHEN
—SHINNY ON YOUR OWN SIDE
—LOVE IS A GARDEN OF ROSES
—I'M GOING TO MEET MINNIE TONIGHT
—DOWN WHERE THE BLUEBELLS GROW
—SAME OLD SUNBONNET SUE
—BABIES A LA MODE
—THE KID IS CLEVER
—SCHOOL DAYS ARE OVER
—OVER THE GARDEN WALL

Vivian Ellis Score

1925. *BY THE WAY*
An English revue starring Jack Hulburt. Lyrics by Graham John.
—SUMMER'S HERE
—GATHER ROSES WHILE YOU MAY
—WHAT DO YOU SEE IN DANCING?
—MY CASTLE IN SPAIN
By Isham Jones.
—NOTHING EVER HAPPENS TO ME
By Ronald Jean and Philip Braham.
—HIGH STREET AFRICA
By Clark, Trevor and Lynton.
—I'VE FOUND THE BLUEBIRD
By Leo Robin and Richard Myers.
—LOOKING AROUND
By Leo Robin and Richard Myers.
—OH, HOW I'VE WAITED FOR YOU
By Carle Carlton and Nat Ayer.

Max Ewing Scores

1927. *GRAND STREET FOLLIES OF 1927*

A Neighborhood Playhouse revue with book and lyrics by Agnes Morgan, and presented by a cast headed by Dorothy Sands and Albert Carroll.
—IF YOU HAVEN'T GOT IT
—SILVER APRON STRINGS
—UNACCUSTOMED AS I AM—
Lyrics by Albert Carroll.
—STARS WITH STRIPES
Lyrics by Dorothy Sands and Marc Loebell.
—THREE LITTLE MAIDS FROM BROADWAY TOWN
—DON'T ASK HER ANOTHER
—THE NAUGHTY NINETIES
—MANY OLD FRIENDS

1928. *GRAND STREET FOLLIES OF 1928*
With Lily Hyland and Serge Walter. An intimate revue with book and lyrics by Agnes Morgan, and presented by a cast that included James Cagney, Albert Carroll and Dorothy Sands.
—BRINY BLUES
—HUSKY, DUSKY ANNABEL
—JUST A LITTLE LOVE SONG
—SOME ONE TO ADMIRE, SOME ONE TO ADORE

Leo Fall Score

1924. *MADAME POMPADOUR*
A musical comedy with book and lyrics by Clare Kummer, and presented by a cast headed by Wilda Bennett, Frederick Lewis, John Quinlan and Louis Harrison.
—CARNIVAL TIME
—LOVE ME NOW
—BY THE LIGHT OF THE MOON
—IF I WERE KING
—LOVE'S SENTRY
—TELL ME WHAT YOUR EYES WERE MADE FOR
—MADAME POMPADOUR
—OH, JOSEPH!
—TWO LITTLE BIRDS
Lyrics by Harry Graham.
—ONE, TWO AND ONE, TWO, THREE
—SERENADE
—MAGIC MOMENTS
—I'LL BE YOUR SOLDIER
—MUSIC OF THE DRUM
Lyrics by Harry Graham.

Fanchon and Marco Score

1921. *SUNKIST*
A musical extravaganza, first staged on the Pacific coast, and presented by a cast

starring the composers in a cast that included Donald Kerr, Muriel Stryker, Jack Squire and Eva Clark.
—BRAGGING SONG
—MY SWEETIE'S SMILE
—THE LOVE A GYPSY KNOWS
—THEY CALL ME POLLYANNA
—THE I DONNO WHAT
—I WANT TO MEET YOU SOME DAY IN CALIFORNIA
—A PRETTY DANCE IS LIKE A VIOLIN

Hugo Felix Scores

1920. *LASSIE*
A musical comedy with book and lyrics by Catherine Chisholm Cushing, and presented by a cast that included Tessa Kosta, Carl Hyson and Dorothy Dickson.
—BONNIE SWEET KITTY
—BOO-HOO
—CROODLIN' DOO
—DILLY-DALLY-O
—FAIRY WHISPERS
—ECHO
—PIPER OF DUNDEE
—LASSIE
—LOVELY CORALS

1920. *THE SWEETHEART SHOP*
A musical comedy with book and lyrics by Anne Caldwell, and presented by a cast that included Helen Ford, Dan Healy and William K. Morton.
—SWEETHEART SHOP
—RING THOSE JUNE BELLS
—I WANT TO BE A BRIDE
—IS THERE ANY LITTLE THING I CAN DO?
—THE ROAD OF LOVE
—MY CARAVAN
—WAITIN' FOR THE SUN TO COME OUT
By Irving Caesar and George Gershwin.
—DERE MABEL
By Irving Caesar and George Gershwin.
—WE'RE PALS
By Irving Caesar and George Gershwin.

1922. *MARJOLAINE*
A musical comedy with book by Catherine Chisholm Cushing, lyrics by Brian Hooker, and presented by a cast that included Peggy Wood, Mary Hay and Irving Beebe.
—CUDDLE UP TOGETHER (MY OLD BROWN COAT)
—MARJORLAINE
—OH LOVE OF MINE!
—RIVER OF DREAMS

—I WANT YOU
—DON'T
—HERE AWAY, THERE AWAY
—WONDERLAND
—NESTING PLACE
By John H. Mears and Ernest Golden.

1924. *PEG-O'-MY-DREAMS*
A musical comedy with book by J. Hartley Manners, lyrics by Anne Caldwell, and presented by a cast that included Susanne Keener, Roy Royston and G. P. Huntley.
—A RAINBOW WAITING FOR YOU
—LOVE'S YOUNG DREAM
—PEG-O'-MY-DREAMS
—A DAINTY NOSEGAY
—ALL ALONE
—ROSE IN THE SNOW
—HAVEN'T WE MET BEFORE?
—THE GAP IN THE HEDGE
—LILY BELL POLKA
—HER BRIGHT SMILE
—DOOR MATS
—SHY LITTLE IRISH SMILE
—MOSCOW BELLES
—LOVE IS LIKE A BUTTERFLY
—L'HEURE BLEU
—RIGHT-O

Percy E. Fletcher Score

1920. *MECCA*
An operetta with book and lyrics by Oscar Asche, and presented by a cast headed by Orville R. Cadwell.
—A FOOL THERE WAS
—HAST THOU BEEN TO MECCA?
—IN THE DANCE
—MY KING OF LOVE
—WHEN LOVE KNOCKED UPON THE DOOR
—LOVE IN MY BREAST
—MECCA
—CHINAMAN'S SONG

Alexander Fogarty Score

1929. *CAPE COD FOLLIES*
A revue with book and lyrics by Stewart Baird, and presented by a cast that included Lloyd Nolan.
—THAT'S WHY WE MISBEHAVE
Lyrics by Edith Lois and Urana Clarke.
—THAT'S THE TIME WHEN I MISS YOU
Lyrics by Seymour Morris.
—CLUTCHING AT SHADOWS
Lyrics by Seymour Morris.
—WONDERING WHO
—THAT OLD HOOKED RUG

—IN A CAPE COD GARDEN
—LOOKING AT LIFE THROUGH A RAINBOW
By Walter Craig and Kenneth Burton.

W. B. Friedlander Scores

1920. *FRIVOLITIES OF 1920*
A revue with sketches and lyrics by William Anthony McGuire, and presented by a cast that included Irene Delroy and Henry Lewis.
—ARABY
—CUDDLE-UDDLE
—PEACHIE
—By Jack Yellen and Al Gumble.
—WHAT IS LOVE?
—THE FARMETTES
—IN PEACOCK ALLEY
—MILITARY MARCHES
—ON A MOONLIGHT NIGHT
—JAZZ UP JASPER
By Tom Johnstone and Harry Auracher.

1920. *PITTER PATTER*
A musical comedy with book by Will Hough, lyrics by the composer, and presented by a cast that included John Price Jones, Jack Squire, William Kent, Helen Bolton and Mildred Keats.
—BAGDAD ON THE SUBWAY
—I'VE SAVED A WALTZ FOR YOU
—PITTER PATTER
—SEND FOR ME
—SINCE YOU CAME INTO MY LIFE
—THE WEDDING BLUES
—YOU NEVER CAN TELL
—JAZZING IT UP IN HAVANA
—MEET YOUR TRUE LOVE HALF-WAY

Cliff Friend Scores

1927. *PIGGY*
With Ludwig Englander. A musical comedy with book by Harry B. Smith, lyrics by Lew Brown, and presented by a cast headed by Sam Bernard, Harry McNaughton, Brooke Johns and Wanda Lyons.
—I NEED A LITTLE BIT, YOU NEED A LITTLE BIT
—I WANTA GO VOOM VOOM
—IT JUST HAD TO HAPPEN
—IT'S EASY TO SAY HELLO
—A LITTLE CHANGE OF ATMOSPHERE
—THE MUSIC OF A LITTLE RIPPLING STREAM
—OH, BABY!
—WHEN
—DIDN'T IT?

—DING DONG DELL

1929. *GEORGE WHITE'S SCANDALS OF 1929*
A revue with book by W. K. Wells and George White, and presented by a cast that included George White, Willie and Eugene Howard, Frances Williams, Mitchell and Durante and the Elm City Four.
—BIGGER AND BETTER THAN EVER
—SITTING IN THE SUN
—BOTTOMS UP
—YOU ARE MY DAY DREAM
—DROP YOUR KERCHIEF
—LOVE BIRDS
—EIGHTEEN DAYS AGO
By DeSylva, Brown and Henderson.
—STEP BY STEP, MILE BY MILE I'M MARCHING HOME TO YOU
By Al Lewis, Al Sherman and Abner Silver.

Rudolf Friml Scores

1921. *JUNE LOVE*
Book by Otto Harbach and W. H. Post, lyrics by Brian Hooker, and presented by a cast headed by Elsa Adler, Johnny Dooley, W. B. Davidson and Clarence Nordstrom.
—RUNAWAY LITTLE GIRL
—DEAR LOVE MY LOVE
—KEEP YOUR EYE ON THE BALL
—I'M NOT IN LOVE WITH YOU
—BE CAREFUL
—SOMEBODY LIKE YOU
—JUNE LOVE
—THE FLAPPER AND THE VAMP
—DON'T KEEP CALLING ME DEARIE

1922. *THE BLUE KITTEN*
Book and lyrics by William Cary Duncan and Otto Harbach, and presented by a cast headed by Joseph Cawthorn, Lillian Lorraine, Robert Woolsey and Marion Sunshine.
—LE MINET BLEU (The Blue Kitten)
—I COULD DO A LOT FOR YOU
—TACT
—CUTIE
—I FOUND A BUD AMONG THE ROSES
—HER LOVE IS ALWAYS THE SAME
—WHERE THE HONEYMOON ALONE CAN SEE
—THE BEST I GET IS THE WORST OF IT
—A TWELVE O'CLOCK GIRL IN A NINE O'CLOCK TOWN
—SMOKE RINGS
—BLUE KITTEN BLUES

—SWEET AS YOU CAN BE
—WHEN I WALTZ WITH YOU

1923. *CINDERS*
Book and lyrics by Edward Clark, and starring Queenie Smith in a cast that included Walter Regan and George Bancroft.
—ONE GOOD TIME
—GET TOGETHER
—YOU GOT WHAT GETS 'EM
—I'M SIMPLY MAD ABOUT THE BOYS
—YOU AND I
—THE ARGENTINE ARANGO
—HAWAIIAN SHORES
—YOU REMIND ME OF SOMEONE
—THE FASHION PARADE
—THREE THOUSAND YEARS AGO
—GRANDMA'S DAY
—FLAME OF LOVE
—LA FAVORITE
—MOONLIGHT ON THE WATERS
—CINDERS
—THE BELLES OF THE BRONX
—RAGS IS ROYAL RAIMENTS

1924. *ROSE MARIE*
Book and lyrics by Otto Harbach and Oscar Hammerstein II, and presented by a cast headed by Mary Ellis, Dennis King, Arthur Deagon and Edward Hawley.
—HARD-BOILED HERMAN
—ROSE MARIE
—SONG OF THE MOUNTIES
—LAK JEEM
—*INDIAN LOVE CALL
—PRETTY THINGS
—WHY SHOULDN'T WE?
Music by Herbert Stothart.
—TOTEM TOM-TOM
—ONLY A KISS
—ONE MAN WOMAN
—THE DOOR OF MY DREAMS

1925. *THE VAGABOND KING*
Book and lyrics by Brian Hooker and W. H. Post, and presented by a cast headed by Carolyn Thomson and Dennis King.
—SONG OF THE VAGABONDS
—LOVE FOR SALE
—HUGUETTE WALTZ
—A FLAGON OF WINE
—TOMORROW
—ONLY A ROSE
—THE HUNTING SONG
—LOVE ME TONIGHT
—SOME DAY
—SONG OF VICTORY

1926. *NO FOOLIN'*
Book and lyrics by J. P. McEvoy, Gene

Buck and Irving Caesar, and presented by a cast headed by James Barton, Charles King, Irving Fisher, Bugs Baer, Moran and Mack, Ray Dooley, Beth Berri, Polly Walker, Peggy Fears, Clare Boothe Luce and Greta Nissen.

—WE'RE CLEANING UP BROADWAY
—I WANT A GIRL TO CALL MY OWN
—FLORIDA, THE MOON AND YOU
—GENTLEMEN PREFER BLONDES
—WASN'T IT NICE?

For this revue James Hanley composed the following songs:

—WHEN THE SHAKER PLAYS A COCKTAIL TUNE
—HONEY, BE MINE
—POOR LITTLE MARIE
—NO FOOLIN'
—EVERY LITTLE THING YOU DO
—NIZE BABY
—DON'T DO THE CHARLESTON

1926. *THE WILD ROSE*
Book and lyrics by Otto Harbach and Oscar Hammerstein II, and presented by a cast headed by Desiree Ellinger, Joseph Santley and Lew Fields.

—RIVIERA
—LOVELY LADY
—HER EYES ARE BROWN
—LOVE ME, DON'T YOU?
—IT WAS FATE
—THE WILD ROSE
—LADY OF THE ROSE
—L'HEURE D'OR (ONE GOLDEN HOUR)
—A LITTLE KINGDOM OF OUR OWN
—WON'T YOU COME ACROSS?
—CORONATION

1927. *WHITE EAGLE*
Book and lyrics by Brian Hooker and W. H. Post. An operetta based on the play "The Squaw Man," with Marion Keeler and Allan Pryor heading the cast.

—GATHER THE ROSE
—GIVE ME ONE HOUR
—REGIMENTAL SONG
—SMILE, DARN YOU, SMILE
—SILVER WING
—ALONE (MY LOVER)

1928. *THE THREE MUSKETEERS*
Book by William Anthony McGuire, lyrics by Clifford Grey and P. G. Wodehouse, and presented by a cast headed by Vivienne Segal, Harriet Hoctor, Dennis King and Lester Allen.

—SUMMERTIME
—ALL FOR ONE AND ONE FOR ALL
—THE HE FOR ME

—GASCONY
—HEART OF MINE
—VESPER BELL
—DREAMS
—MARCH OF THE MUSKETEERS
—THE COLONEL AND THE MAJOR
—LOVE IS THE SUN
—YOUR EYES
—PAGES
—GOSSIPS
—WELCOME TO THE QUEEN
—WITH RED WINE
—MA BELLE
—A KISS BEFORE I GO
—MY SWORD
—QUEEN OF MY HEART
—EVERY LITTLE WHILE

Harold G. Frost Score

1924. *KEEP KOOL*
A revue with book and lyrics by Paul Gerard Smith, and presented by a cast headed by Johnny Dooley, Charles King, Lou Hascall and Hazel Dawn.

—BY THE SHALIMAR
—CALICOQUETTE
—DANDELION TIME
—DAWN WILL COME
—PAINTED ROSE
—HOW YOU GONNA KEEP COOL?
—OUT WHERE THE PAVEMENT ENDS

Seymour Furth Score

1925. *BRINGING UP FATHER*
A musical comedy, based on the George McManus cartoon strip, with Danny Simons playing Jiggs and Beatrice Harlowe his wife Maggie. Book by Nat Leroy, lyrics by R. F. Carroll, with Leo Edwards getting an assist in writing the score.

—WHEN IT GETS DARK
—WE HOPE TO MAKE A HIT
—PLAY ME A BAGPIPE TUNE
—THE GIRLS OF NEW YORK
—THE GAINESBORO GLIDE
—THE MERRY-GO-ROUND
—MOONLIGHT
—POPPY, THE DREAM GIRL
—MY LADY'S FAN
—WEDDING CHIMES
—WHEN DAD WAS TWENTY-ONE
—ON OUR WAY TO SPAIN

Clarence Gaskill Scores

1922. *FRANK FAY'S FABLES*
A revue with lyrics by the composer and Jimmy Duffy, and presented by a cast

178 [1920-1930]

headed by Frank Fay, Bernard Granville, Helen Groody and Olga Steck.

—FABLES, DON'T BELIEVE THEIR FABLES
—TWO ARE ONE
—YOU NEED TWO SOULS WITH BUT ONE THOUGHT
—IT'S A POP, POP, POPULAR SONG
—THAT SWANEE RIVER MELODY

1925. *EARL CARROLL'S VANITIES OF 1925*
A revue with book by Earl Carroll, lyrics by the composer, and presented by a cast headed by Julius Tannen, Ted Healy, Wallace McCutcheon, Dave Chassen and Jessica Dragonette.

—THIS IS A NIGHT CLUB
—ONE, TWO, THREE, FOUR
—HOT OFF THE OVEN
—A KISS IN THE MOONLIGHT
—SENTIMENTAL SALLY
—THINKING OF YOU
—PONIES ON PARADE
—C-H-A-R-L-E-S-T-O-N
—COFFEE POT
—VENETIAN NIGHTS
—THE DRILL
—YES AND NO
—THE COLOR BALLET
—BOTTLE OF CANADA DRY
—LONESOME
—ADVANCEMENT
—THE BIRD BALLET
—POT POURRI
—I'M THE MAJOR BOZO
—HE'S A STEW
—THE NORTHWEST MOUNTED POLICE
—SHAKE YOURSELF OUT OF HERE
—HUGS AND KISSES
By Ray Klages and Louis Alter.
—PANGO PANGO MAID
By Fred Phillips and Irving Bibo.
—SOMEBODY'S CRAZY ABOUT YOU
By Owen Murphy and Jay Gorney.

Lewis Gensler Scores

1922. *QUEEN O' HEARTS*
A musical comedy with book and lyrics by Frank Mandel and Oscar Hammerstein II, and presented by a cast headed by Norma Terris, Nora Bayes, Harry Richman and Max Hoffman, Jr.

—DING DONG DING
—DREAMING ALONE
—TOM-TOM
—YOU NEED SOMEONE, SOMEONE NEEDS YOU
—QUEEN OF HEARTS

—ALL YEAR AROUND WITH YOU
By Herman Frink.
—DEAR LITTLE GIRLIE
Music by Nora Bayes.
—THAT'S THAT
By Nora Bayes, Harry Richman and Dudley Wilkinson.
—LOVE'S BAROMETER
By Philip Rodway, Tom Townson and Harry Rushworth.
—THE COAL SCUTTLE BONNET
By Philip Rodway, Tom Townson and Harry Rushworth.

1924. *BE YOURSELF*
With Milton Schwartzwald. A musical comedy with book by George S. Kaufman and Marc Connelly, lyrics by Ira Gershwin, and starring Queenie Smith and Jack Donahue in a cast that included Georgia Caine.

—THE DECENT THING TO DO
—COOKING BREAKFAST FOR THE ONE I LOVE
By Billy Rose and Henry Tobias.
—I CAME HERE
—A LITTLE BIT OF THIS
—MY ROAD
—UH-UH
—BONGA BOO
Lyrics by Owen Murphy and Jay Gorney.
—BE YOURSELF
—THE WRONG THING AT THE RIGHT TIME
—RAIN
—HIGH IN THE HILLS
—A GOOD HAND ORGAN AND A SIDEWALK'S ALL WE NEED
—GRANDMA'S A FLAPPER TOO
—DO IT NOW

1925. *CAPTAIN JINKS*
A musical comedy with book by Frank Mandel and Lawrence Schwab, lyrics by B. G. DeSylva, and presented by a cast headed by Joe E. Brown, Louise Brown, Marion Sunshine and J. Harold Murray.

—PALS
—SO THIS IS THE STATES
—STRICTLY BUSINESS
—YOU NEED A MAN SUZANNE
—OH, HOW I HATE WOMEN!
—AT THE PARTY
—THE NEW GAME
—AIN'T LOVE WONDERFUL?
—FOND OF YOU
—I DO
—KIKI
—THE ONLY ONE FOR ME
—SEA LEGS
—YOU-MUST-COME-OVER BLUES

1926. *QUEEN HIGH*
A musical comedy with book and lyrics by Lawrence Schwab and B. G. DeSylva, and presented by a cast that included Mary Lawlor, Luella Gear, Charles Ruggles, Frank McIntyre and Clarence Nordstrom.
—GENTLEMEN PREFER BLONDES
—CROSS YOUR HEART
—EVERYTHING WILL HAPPEN FOR THE BEST
—YOU'LL NEVER KNOW
—WHO'LL MEND A BROKEN HEART?
—IT PAYS TO ADVERTISE
—OH WHAT A LOVELY DAY!
—QUEEN HIGH
—THE WEAKER SEX
—DON'T FORGET
Music by James F. Hanley.
—BEAUTIFUL BABY
Music by James F. Hanley.
—MY LADY
By Frank Crumit and Ben Jerome.
—TWO MILLION SURPLUS WOMEN
By Bernard Green.
—BROTHER JUST LAUGH IT OFF
By E. Y. Harburg, Arthur Schwartz and Ralph Rainger.
—I'M AFRAID OF YOU
By Ed Eliscu, Arthur Schwartz and Ralph Rainger.
—SEEMS TO ME
By Dick Howard and Ralph Rainger
1928. *UPS-A-DAISY*
A musical comedy with book and lyrics by Clifford Grey and Robert A. Simon, and presented by a cast headed by Marie Saxon, Luella Gear, William Kent, Bob Hope (who played a butler) and Roy Royston.
—HOT
—OH-HOW-I-MISS-YOU BLUES
—UPS-A-DAISY
—WILL YOU REMEMBER, WILL YOU FORGET?
—OH HOW HAPPY WE'LL BE
—A GREAT LITTLE GUY
—I'VE GOT A BABY
—DESIRE UNDER THE ALPS
—SWEET ONE
—SWEETEST OF ALL THE ROSES

Charles George Score
1922. *GO EASY MABEL*
A musical comedy with book and lyrics by the composer, and presented by a cast headed by Will J. Deming, Estelle Winwood and Ethel Levey.
—ETHEL LEVEY'S SMILE SONG
—GO EASY MABEL
—HONEY I LOVE YOU
—LOVE IS KING

George Gershwin Scores
1920. *GEORGE WHITE'S SCANDALS OF 1920*
Book by Andy Rice and George White, lyrics by Arthur Jackson, and starring Ann Pennington in a cast that included Ethel Delmar, Lou Holtz, Lester Allen, Jack Rose and George (Doctor) Rockwell.
—MY LADY
—EVERYBODY SWAT THE PROFITEER
—ON MY MIND THE WHOLE NIGHT LONG
—SCANDAL WALK
—COME ON AND KISS ME
—I LOVE THE OLD SONGS
—IDLE DREAMS
1920. *BROADWAY BREVITIES OF 1920*
Book by Blair Traynor and Archie Gottler, lyrics by Arthur Jackson, and presented by a cast that included George LaMaire, the producer; Eddie Cantor, Bert Williams and Hal Van Rensellaer.
—I LOVE TO DANCE
—LOVE HONOR AND OH BABY
—SPANISH LOVE
—LOVE ME WHILE THE SNOWFLAKES FALL
—LU-LU
—BEAUTIFUL FACES NEED BEAUTIFUL CLOTHES
By Irving Berlin.
—I'M A DANCING FOOL
—WON'T YOU LET ME TAKE A PICTURE OF YOU?
—WE'VE GOT THE STAGE DOOR BLUES
By Bert Kalmer and Harry Ruby.
1921. *GEORGE WHITE'S SCANDALS OF 1921*
Book by "Bugs" Baer and George White, lyrics by Arthur Jackson, and presented by a cast headed by George White, Ann Pennington, Lester Allen, George Bickel, Aunt Jemima, Charles King, Lou Holtz, Harry Rose and Bert Gordon.
—I LOVE YOU
—SOUTH SEA ISLES
—WHERE EAST MEETS WEST
—DRIFTING ALONG WITH THE TIDE
—JUST A BABY
—MOTHER EVE
By Ballard MacDonald and James Hanley.

1921. *A DANGEROUS MAID*
Book by Charles W. Bell, lyrics by Arthur Jackson, and presented by a cast headed by Vinton Freedley, Juliette Day and Amelia Bingham.
—ANYTHING FOR YOU
—JUST TO KNOW YOU ARE MINE
—BOY WANTED
—THE SIMPLE LIFE
—THE SIRENS
—DANCING SHOES
—TRUE LOVE
—SOME RAIN MUST FALL

1922. *GEORGE WHITE'S SCANDALS OF 1922*
Book by George White, W. C. Fields and Andy Rice, lyrics by E. Ray Goetz and B. G. DeSylva, and presented by a cast headed by George White, Lester Allen, W. C. Fields, Winnie Lightner, Jack McGowan, Franklyn Ardell, Jay Velie, Ed Wynn and Paul Whiteman's band.
—SHE HANGS OUT IN OUR ALLEY
—LITTLE CINDERELATIVES
—I FOUND A FOUR-LEAF CLOVER
—I CAN TELL WHERE THEY'RE FROM WHEN THEY DANCE
—I'LL BUILD A STAIRWAY TO PARADISE
—JUST A TINY CUP OF TEA
—WHERE IS THE MAN OF MY DREAMS?
—MY HEART WILL SAIL ACROSS THE SEA
—THE MOTH FOR MY FLAME
—THE GRAB BAG
—ARGENTINA

1922. *OUR NELL*
A musical "mellerdramer" by A. E. Thomas and Brian Hooker, and starring Mr. and Mrs. Jimmy Barry.
—INNOCENT INGENUE BABY
—WALKING HOME WITH ANGELINE
—BYE-AND-BYE
—MY OLD NEW ENGLAND HOME

1923. *GEORGE WHITE'S SCANDALS OF 1923*
Book by George White and William K. Wells, lyrics by E. Ray Goetz, B. G. DeSylva and Ballard MacDonald, and presented by a cast that included Johnny Dooley, Lester Allen, Tom Patricola, Winnie Lightner and Margaret Breen.
—LITTLE SCANDAL DOLLS
—YOU AND I (IN OLD VERSAILLES)
—KATINKA
—LOLA LO
—THERE IS NOTHING TOO GOOD FOR YOU

—LET'S BE LONESOME TOGETHER
—LIFE OF A ROSE
—LOOK IN THE LOOKING GLASS
—WHERE IS SHE?
—LAUGH YOUR CARES AWAY
—THROW HER IN HIGH
—ON THE BEACH AT HOW'VE YOU BEEN
—THE GOLD DIGGER
By James Hanley.
—STINGO STUNGO
By Lew Brown and James Hanley.

1924. *GEORGE WHITE'S SCANDALS OF 1924*
Book by George White and William K. Wells, lyrics by B. G. DeSylva, and presented by a cast headed by Lester Allen, Will Mahoney, Tom Patricola and Winnie Lightner.
—I NEED A GARDEN
—NIGHT TIME IN ARABY
—YEAR AFTER YEAR WE'RE TOGETHER
—SOMEBODY LOVES ME
—TUNE IN TO STATION J O Y
—MAH JONGG
—ROSE OF MADRID
—KONGO KATE
—I'M GOING BACK

1924. *LADY BE GOOD*
Book by Guy Bolton and Fred Thompson, lyrics by Ira Gershwin, and starring Fred and Adele Astaire in a cast that included Walter Catlett and Cliff Edwards.
—HANG ON TO ME
—A WONDERFUL PARTY
—THE END OF A STRING
—WE'RE HERE BECAUSE
—SO AM I
—FASCINATING RHYTHM
—OH, LADY BE GOOD
—LINGER IN THE LOBBY
—THE HALF OF IT DEARIE BLUES
—JUANITA
—LITTLE JAZZ BIRD
—CARNIVAL
—SWISS MISS
—THE MAN I LOVE

1924. *SWEET LITTLE DEVIL*
Book by Frank Mandel and Lawrence Schwab, lyrics by B. G. DeSylva, and presented by a cast that included Constance Binney, Irving Beebe and Marjorie Gateson.
—STRIKE, STRIKE, STRIKE
—LUCKY
—VIRGINIA, DON'T GO TOO FAR
—SOMEONE WHO BELIEVES IN YOU
—JIJIBO

—QUITE A PARTY
—UNDER A ONE-MAN TOP
—SUPPOSING
—HEY, HEY, LET 'ER GO
—HOORAY FOR THE U.S.A.
—SWEET LITTLE DEVIL
—THE MATRIMONIAL HANDICAP
—PEPITA

1925. *TELL ME MORE*
Book by Fred Thompson and William K. Wells, lyrics by Ira Gershwin and B. G. DeSylva, and presented by a cast that included Alexander Gray, Phyllis Cleveland, Emma Haig and Lou Holtz.
—TELL ME MORE
—MR. AND MRS. SIPKIN
—THREE TIMES A DAY
—WHEN THE DEBBIES GO BY
—WHY DO I LOVE YOU?
—KICKIN' THE CLOUDS AWAY
—LOVE IS IN THE AIR
—MY FAIR LADY
—IN SARDINIA
—BABY
—UKULELE LORELEI
—OH, SO LA MI

1925. *TIP-TOES*
Book by Guy Bolton and Fred Thompson, lyrics by Ira Gershwin, and starring Jeanette MacDonald in a cast that included Robert Halliday, Harry Watson, Queenie Smith and Allen Kearns.
—WAITING FOR THE TRAIN
—NICE BABY
—LOOKING FOR A BOY
—LADY LUCK
—WHEN DO WE DANCE?
—THESE CHARMING PEOPLE
—THAT CERTAIN FEELING
—SWEET AND LOW DOWN
—OUR LITTLE CAPTAIN
—IT'S A GREAT LITTLE WORLD
—NIGHTY NIGHT
—TIP-TOES

1925. *SONG OF THE FLAME*
With Herbert Stothart. Book and lyrics by Otto Harbach and Oscar Hammerstein II, and starring Tessa Kosta in a cast that included Guy Robertson and Greek Evans.
—FAR AWAY
—SONG OF THE FLAME
—WOMAN'S WORK IS NEVER DONE
—GREAT BIG BEAR
—COSSACK LOVE SONG (DON'T FORGET ME)
—MIDNIGHT BELLS
—TARTAR

—YOU MAY WANDER AWAY
—VODKA
—YOU ARE YOU

1926. *OH, KAY*
Book by Guy Bolton and P. G. Wodehouse, lyrics by Ira Gershwin, and presented by a cast that included Betty Compton, Gerald Oliver Smith, Harland Dixon, Victor Moore, Oscar Shaw, Gertrude Lawrence and the Fairbanks Twins.
—THE WOMAN'S TOUCH
—DON'T ASK
—DEAR LITTLE GIRL
—MAYBE
—CLAP YO' HANDS
—DO-DO-DO
—BRIDE AND GROOM
—SOMEONE TO WATCH OVER ME
—FIDGETY FEET
—HEAVEN ON EARTH
—OH, KAY

1927. *FUNNY FACE*
Book by Paul Gerard Smith and Fred Thompson, lyrics by Ira Gershwin, and presented by a cast headed by Betty Compton, Adele and Fred Astaire, William Kent, Victor Moore and Allen Kearns.
—BIRTHDAY PARTY
—ONCE
—'SWONDERFUL
—FUNNY FACE
—HIGH HAT
—LET'S KISS AND MAKE UP
—IN THE SWIM
—HE LOVES AND SHE LOVES
—TELL THE DOC
—MY ONE AND ONLY
—This also was published as "What Are We Gonna Do.?
—SING A LITTLE SONG
—THE BABBITT AND THE BROMIDE
—DANCE ALONE WITH YOU
—THE WORLD IS MINE

1928. *TREASURE GIRL*
Book by Vincent Lawrence and Fred Thompson, lyrics by Ira Gershwin, and presented by a cast headed by Clifton Webb, Ferris Hartman, Mary Hay, Gertrude Lawrence, Walter Catlett and Paul Frawley.
—SKULL AND BONES
—I'VE GOT A CRUSH ON YOU
—OH, SO NICE
—ACCORDING TO MR. GRIMES
—A PLACE IN THE COUNTRY
—K-RAZY FOR YOU
—I DON'T THINK I'LL FALL IN LOVE TODAY

—GOT A RAINBOW
—I'VE GOT A FEELIN' I'M FALLIN'
—WHAT CAUSES THAT?
—WHAT ARE WE HERE FOR?
—WHERE'S THE BOY?—HERE'S THE GIRL
1929. *SHOW GIRL*
Book by J. P. McEvoy and William Anthony McGuire, lyrics by Ira Gershwin and Gus Kahn, and presented by a cast that included Jimmy Durante, Joseph Macauley, Eddie Foy Jr., Frank McHugh, Lou Clayton, Eddie Jackson, Ruby Keeler, Barbara Newberry and Harriet Hoctor.
—HAPPY BIRTHDAY
—MY SUNDAY FELLA
—HOW COULD I FORGET?
—CAN BROADWAY DO WITHOUT ME?
By Jimmy Durante.
—LOLITA
—DO WHAT YOU DO
—SPAIN
—ONE MAN
—SO ARE YOU
—I MUST BE HOME BY TWELVE O'CLOCK
—BLACK AND WHITE
—JIMMY THE WELL-DRESSED MAN
By Jimmy Durante.
—HARLEM SERENADE
—HOME BLUES
—BROADWAY MY STREET
—I UPS TO HIM
By Jimmy Durante.
—FOLLOW THE MINSTREL BAND
—LIZA

Melville Gideon Score

1928. *THE OPTIMISTS*
A revue with sketches and lyrics by Clifford Grey, George Newman and Austin Melford, and presented by a cast headed by Bobby Watson, Luella Gear, Eleanor Powell, George Hassell and the composer.
—AMAPU
Lyrics by Edward Knoblock.
—(I PROMISE I'LL BE) PRACTICALLY TRUE TO YOU
—LITTLE LACQUER LADY
Lyrics by Clifford Seyler.
—SPARE A LITTLE LOVE
—BOW-WOW
—ROLLING STONES
—I MADE THEM STEP
—DREAMY DAYS
—TO THE RACES

—THREE LITTLE SCHOOL GIRLS
—LONDON TOWN
—IF I GAVE YOU A ROSE
By Granville English.
—WE ALL PLAY THE GRAND PIANO

Jean Gilbert Scores

1926. *KATJA, THE DANCER*
A musical comedy with book by Frederick Lonsdale, lyrics by Harry Graham and Clifford Grey, and presented by a cast headed by Lillian Davies and Allan Pryor.
—JUST FOR A NIGHT
Lyrics by Maurice Rubens.
—IF YOU CARE
—BACK TO MY HEART
By Percy Greenbank and Vernon Duke.
—TRY A LITTLE KISS
By Percy Greenbank, Arthur Wimperis and Vernon Duke.
—LEANDER
—THOSE EYES SO TENDER
—WHEN LOVE'S IN THE AIR
—CRUEL CHIEF
—DANCE WITH YOU
—ALL THE WORLD LOVES A LOVER
—I FELL HEAD OVER HEELS IN LOVE
—NIGHT BIRDS
—IN JAIL
—OH, WOE IS ME
—CONGRATULATIONS
1928. *THE RED ROBE*
A musical comedy with book and lyrics by Harry B. Smith, and presented by a cast headed by Violet Carson and Walter Woolf.
—HOME OF MINE
—IF I COULD FORGET
—OH, HOW THE GIRLS ADORE ME!
—A SOLDIER OF FORTUNE
—WHERE THE BANNERS LEAD
—YOU AND I ARE PASSERSBY
—WINGS OF ROMANCE
—BELIEVE IN ME
1929. *THE STREET SINGER*
With Nicholas Kempner and Sammy Timberg. A musical comedy with book by Cyrus Wood and Edgar Smith, lyrics by Graham John, and presented by a cast that included Queenie Smith, Guy Robertson, Harry K. Morton and Cesar Romero.
—JUMPING JIMMINY
—YOU NEVER CAN TELL
—WATER
—WHEN EVERYTHING IS HUNKY-DORY
—THE GIRL THAT I ADORE

—SOMEBODY QUITE LIKE YOU
—I AM
—YOU
—LADY OF THE MOON
—OH, THEODORE; OH, ELMER
—SOMETHING WRONG WITH ME
—DOWN WHERE THE DAISIES GROW
—I MIGHT HAVE KNOWN I LOVED YOU
—YOU MADE ME HAPPY TODAY

E. Ray Goetz Score

1920. *AS YOU WERE*
A musical with book by Arthur Wimperis, lyrics by Vincent Bryan, and presented by a cast that included Sam Bernard, Irene Bordoni, Clifton Webb and Hugh Cameron.
—IF YOU COULD CARE
—WHO ATE NAPOLEONS WITH JOSEPHINE WHEN NAPOLEON WAS AWAY?
—WHEN YOU'RE DANCIN' IN YOUR NIGHTIE ON THE LAWN
—FOLLOW MR. WATTEAU
By Arthur Wimperis, Herman Darewski and E. Ray Goetz.
—HELEN OF TROY
By Arthur Wimperis, Herman Darewski and E. Ray Goetz.
—IF YOU'LL SAY IT WITH FLOWERS
—LIVE FOR ALL YOU'RE WORTH
—NINON WAS A NAUGHTY GIRL
—ON THE BOSOM OF THE SLEEPY NILE
With Howard Smith.
—TWO BITS OF GRACE
—UNDER GRECIAN SKIES
—WASHINGTON SQUARE
By Melville Gideon, E. Ray Goetz and Cole Porter.

Anslem Goetzl Score

1921. *THE ROSE GIRL*
A musical comedy with book and lyrics by William LeBaron and William Cary Duncan, and presented by a cast headed by Mabel Withee, Charles Purcell and May Boley.
—BABY'S CANDY SHOP
—THAT ONE SWEET HOUR WITH YOU
—IF YOU KEEP THEM WONDERING
—THAT'S HOW I FEEL ABOUT YOU
—DEAR LITTLE ROSE GIRL
—WHEN OUR SUNDAYS ARE BLUE
—THERE COMES A SOMEDAY

—GIRL, YOU'VE NEVER BEEN KISSED!
—I'M ALWAYS THINKING OF YOU
—IN THE HEART OF MY CRIMSON ROSE
—COME ON, GIRLS, LET'S GO
—MY OLD NEW JERSEY HOME
By Ballard MacDonald and Nat Vincent.

Lieut. Gitz-Rice Scores

1921. *PRINCESS VIRTUE*
With B. C. Hilliam, who also collaborated on the book and lyrics, and presented by a cast headed by Tessa Kosta, Frank Moulan and Bradford Kirkbride.
—DEAR SWEET EYES
—SMOKE RINGS
—WHEN I MET LOVE
—EIGHT LITTLE NOBODYS
—THE MODERN VILLAGE BLACKSMITH
—THERE'S SOMETHING IRRESISTIBLE ABOUT ME
—PRINCESS VIRTUE
—SEEING PARIS
—PERFECT SONG OF LOVE
—VOICES OF YOUTH
—WHILE MY WIFE'S AWAY
—CLOTHES
—RED RIDING HOOD
—MOONLIGHT
—BACCHANALE
—TODDLING ALONG

1926. *NIX-NAX OF 1926*
A revue with sketches by Paul Porter and Matt Kennedy, lyrics by Roger Gray, and presented by a cast headed by Nancy Gibbs, Lieut. Gitz-Rice, Fred Santley and Nat Nazzaro, Jr.
—EVERYTHING IS HIGH YELLOW NOW
—FOR A GIRL LIKE YOU
Lyrics by Joe Goodwin.
—I HAVE FORGOTTEN YOU ALMOST
Lyrics by Anna Fitziu.
—WHEN THE SUN KISSED THE ROSE GOOD NIGHT
Lyrics by Paul Porter.
—WITHOUT THE ONE YOU LOVE
Music by Warren Janssen.
—OH, DADDY!

Alfred Goodman Scores

1920. *CINDERELLA ON BROADWAY*
With Bert Grant. A musical comedy with book and lyrics by Harold Atteridge, and presented by a cast headed by Al Sexton,

Georgie Price, Jessica Brown, John T. Murray and Al Shean.
—CINDY
—ANY LITTLE MELODY
—PHANTOM LOVES
—JUST LIKE THE HOUSE THAT JACK BUILT
—LAND BEYOND THE CANDLELIGHT
—PRIMROSE WAY
—WHISTLE AND I'LL COME TO YOU
—WHY DON'T YOU GET A SWEETIE?

1921. *THE WHIRL OF NEW YORK*
With Lew Pollack. A modernized version of "The Belle of New York" with Mlle. Adelaide, J. Harold Murray, John T. Murray, Louis Mann, and Joe Smith and Charles Dale. Book and lyrics by Edgar Smith.
—I KNOW THAT I'M IN LOVE
—MOLLY ON THE TROLLEY
—GEE, I WISH I HAD A GIRL LIKE YOU
—JUST ONE GOOD TIME
—THE QUEEN OF MUSICAL COMEDY
—DANCING FOOLS
—TEACH ME HOW TO KISS
—FROM FAR COHOES
—LITTLE BABY
—FOLLOW ON
—MANDALAY
—THE BELLE OF NEW YORK
—TIFFIN, TIFFIN
—DANCE, DANCE, DANCE
—WHISTLING IT ALL OVER TOWN
—WHEN WE ARE MARRIED
—THE PURITY BRIGADIERS
—I DO SO, THERE!
—LA BELLE PARISIENNE
—TAKE ME DOWN TO CONEY

1922. *THE PASSING SHOW OF 1922*
A revue with book and lyrics by Harold Atteridge and Jack Stanley, and presented by a cast that included Willie and Eugene Howard, Janet Adair, George Hassell, Sam Ash, Mlle. Alcorn, Nat Nazzaro Jr. and Fred Allen, who made his Broadway debut in this production.
—THE PASSING SHOW
—CIRCUS DAYS
—MY COAL BLACK MAMMY
—MY DIAMOND GIRLS
—PRINCE OF WALES
—ORPHANS OF THE STORM
—LOVE OF LONG AGO
—I CAME, I SAW, I FELL
—RADIANCE
—ELEANOR

—POOR J'EN-AI-MARRE
—IN ITALY
—AMERICAN JAZZ
—DO YOU, DON'T YOU, WILL YOU, WON'T YOU LOVE ME
By George P. Little.
—DON'T STOP PLAYING IT
By Jack Denny and Billy Baskette.
—CAROLINA IN THE MORNING
By Gus Kahn and Walter Donaldson.

1922. *THE LADY IN ERMINE*
With Jean Gilbert. A musical comedy with book by Cyrus Wood and Frederick Lonsdale, lyrics by Harry Graham and Cyrus Wood, and starring Wilda Bennett and Walter Woolf.
—LADY IN ERMINE
—WHEN HEARTS ARE YOUNG (IN SPRINGTIME)
Music by Sigmund Romberg.
—DEAR OLD LAND OF MINE
—MARIANNA
—LITTLE BOY
—CHILDHOOD DAYS
—HOW FIERCELY YOU DANCE
—ESPANOLE
—PLAY WITH FIRE
—MEN GROW OLDER
—CATCH A BUTTERFLY
—FOLLOW YOU ALL OVER THE WORLD

1923. *DEW DROP IN*
A musical comedy with book by Walter DeLeon and Edward Delany Dunn, lyrics by Cyrus Wood, and presented by a cast headed by James Barton, Harry Clark and Mabel Withee.
—IF THERE WERE NOT ANY MEN
—GOODBYE FOREVER
—PRETTY ANKLE
—PORTER! PORTER!
—THE STRUTTINGEST STRUTTER
—A GIRL MAY AS WELL MARRY WELL
—THE PRIMROSE PATH
—MOONLIGHT WALTZ
—YOU CAN'T EXPERIMENT ON ME
—I'M A FLAPPER
—WE TWO
With Rudolf Friml.
—M. T. POCKET BLUES
By Eli Dawson, Lewis Michelson and Victor Olivier.
—LADY
By McElbert Moore, Jean Schwartz and J. Fred Coots.

Frank Grey Scores

1922. *SUE DEAR*
A musical comedy with book by Bide Dudley and C. S. Mactayne, lyrics by Bide Dudley, and presented by a cast headed by Olga Steck, Bradford Kirkbride and Bobby O'Neil.
—DA, DA, DADDY DEAR
—PIDGIE WIDGIE
—THAT SAMPSON AND DELILAH MELODY
—SMILE AND FORGET
—LOVE'S CORPORATION
—MY LITTLE FULL-BLOWN ROSE
—LOVER'S LANE WITH YOU
—LADY LINGERIE
—THE LOVE SHIP

1926. *THE MATINEE GIRL*
A musical comedy with book and lyrics by McElbert Moore and Bide Dudley, and presented by a cast that included Olga Steck, James Hamilton and Jack Squire.
—LIKE-A-ME LIKE-A-YOU
—ONLY ONE
—AT THE MATINEE
—MASH NOTES
—JOY RIDE
—THE ONE YOU LOVE
—WHEN MY SHIP COMES IN
—JUMPING JACK
—HIS SPANISH GUITAR
—HOLDING HANDS
—HAVANOLA ROLL
—WAITING ALL THE TIME FOR YOU
—A LITTLE BIT OF SPANISH
—THE BIGGEST THING IN MY LIFE
—DO I, DEAR? I DO

1927. *HAPPY*
A musical comedy with book by Vincent Lawrence and McElbert Moore, lyrics by Earle Crooker and McElbert Moore, and presented by a cast headed by Frederick Santley, Percy Helton and Madelene Fairbanks.
—HAPPY
—LORELEI
—MAD ABOUT YOU
—SUNNY SIDE OF YOU
—THROUGH THE NIGHT
—PLASTIC SURGERY
—CHECK YOUR TROUBLES
—IF YOU'LL PUT UP WITH ME
—THE SERPENTINE
—THE YOUNGER GENERATION
—ONE GOOD FRIEND
—HERE'S TO YOU, JACK

—HITTING ON HIGH
—BLACK SHEEP
—WHICH SHALL IT BE?

Jay Gorney Scores

1924. *TOP HOLE*
Book by Eugene Conrad and George Dill, lyrics by Owen Murphy, and presented by a cast headed by Clare Stratton and Ernest Glendinning.
—WE RAN AWAY FROM SCHOOL
—EVERY SILKEN LADY HAS A TOUCH OF CALICO
—DANCE YOUR WAY TO PARADISE
—"YOU MUST COME OVER" EYES
—IN CALIFORNIA
—IS IT ANY WONDER
—THE GIRLS
—THE MUSIC OF AN IRISH SONC
—THEN YOU'RE IN LOVE
Robert Braine is credited with the following numbers:
—GOLF
—LOVE IS A SANDMAN
—WINGS OF LOVE

1924. *VOGUES OF 1924*
With Herbert Stothart. Book by Fred Thompson, lyrics by Clifford Grey, and presented by a cast headed by Odette Myrtil, May Boley, J. Harold Murray, Jimmy Savo and Fred Allen.
—HUSH, LOOK AWAY
—MEDICOS
—DRESSING
—KATINKA
—THE SPIELMAN
—WHEN THE PIPER PLAYS
—THREE LITTLE MAIDS
—PIERROT
—RAIN
—THE BELLE OF THE BALL
—LAUGH AND PLAY
—STAR OF DESTINY
—ELDORADO
—THAT'S THE TUNE
—LEGEND OF THE SHIRT
—THE BELLE OF TODAY

1927. *MERRY-GO-ROUND*
With Henry Souvaine. Book and lyrics by Morrie Ryskind and Howard Dietz, and presented by a cast headed by Marie Cahill, Libby Holman, Willie Collier, Don Barclay and Etienne Girardot.
—GABRIEL IS BLOWING HIS HORN
—HOGAN'S ALLEY
—YES GIRL
—WHAT D'YA SAY?

—NEW YORK TOWN
—TAMPA
—LET'S BE HAPPY NOW
—SENTIMENTAL SILLY

1929. *EARL CARROLL'S SKETCH BOOK*
Book by Earl Carroll, lyrics by E. Y. Harburg, and presented by a cast headed by Will Mahoney, William Demarest, George Givot, Dorothy Britton, Patsy Kelly, Dorothy Carroll and the Three Sailors.
—LEGS, LEGS, LEGS
—KINDA CUTE
—LIKE ME LESS LOVE ME MORE
—CRASHING THE GOLDEN GATES
—PAPA LIKES A HOT PAPOOSE
—DON'T HANG YOUR DREAMS ON A RAINBOW
By Irving Kahal and Arnold Johnson.
—YOU BEAUTIFUL SO-AND-SO
By Billy Rose and Ted Snyder.
—MY SUNNY SOUTH
By Abner Silver.
—FOR SOMEONE I LOVE
By Benny Davis and Ted Snyder.
—SONG OF THE MOONBEAMS
By Harry and Charles Tobias and Vincent Rose.
—FASCINATING YOU
By Harry and Charles Tobias and Vincent Rose.
—RHYTHM OF THE WAVES
By Harry and Charles Tobias and Vincent Rose.

Arthur Gutman Score

1921. *SUZETTE*
A musical comedy with book and lyrics by Roy Dixon, and presented by a cast headed by Marie Astroba, Frank Lalor, John Cherry and James R. Marshall.
—NO! NO!
—OH, WAITER
—DREAMS OF TOMORROW
—A MODERN DIPLOMAT
—SUZETTE
—GYPSY ROSE
—A FOREST LEGEND
—BAGDAD
—HONEY-LOVE-MOON
—SATURDAY EVENING POST
—SWEETHEART

Karl Hajos Scores

1925. *NATJA*
An operetta, based on Tschaikowsky's melodies, with book and lyrics by Harry

B. Smith, and presented by a cast headed by Mary Mellish, Madeline Collins, George Reimherr and Alexander Clark.
—SHALL I TELL HIM?
—I HEAR LOVE CALL ME
—THE MAGIC OF MOONLIGHT AND LOVE
—THERE IS A GARDEN IN LOVELAND
—UPS AND DOWNS
—HONOR AND GLORY
—COMRADE, YOU HAVE A CHANCE HERE
—STAR OF GLORY
—YOU'LL HAVE TO GUESS
—MARCH ON
—EYES THAT HAUNT ME
—REMINISCENCE

1928. *WHITE LILACS*
An operetta, based on Frederic Chopin's melodies, with book by Harry B. Smith, lyrics by J. Keirn Brennan, and starring Odelle Myrtil in a cast that included Guy Robertson and DeWolf Hopper.
—DON'T GO TOO FAR GIRLS
—FAR AWAY AND LONG AGO
—I LOVE YOU AND I ADORE YOU
—MELODIES WITHIN MY HEART
—ADORABLE YOU
By David Goldberg and Maurice Rubens.
—CASTLE OF LOVE
Music by Sammy Timberg.
—LONELY HEART
—WHITE LILACS

Morris Hamilton Score

1926. *EARL CARROLL'S VANITIES OF 1926*
With sketches by Stanley Rauh and William A. Grey, lyrics by Grace Henry, and presented by a cast headed by Julius Tannen, Harry Delf, Moran and Mack, Charles Dale, Joe Smith, Yvette Rugel and Dorothy Knapp.
—COOL 'EM OFF
—GATES OF MADRID
—HERE AM I
—LADY OF THE VEIL
—LEGIONNAIRES
—MELODY MAKERS
—MORE THAN ENOUGH
—TWILIGHT
—VANITY
—VERY, VERY, VERY

James T. Hanley Scores

1920. *JIM JAM JEMS*
A musical with book and lyrics by Harry L. Cort and George E. Stoddard, and

presented by a cast that included Ada
Mae Weeks, Joe E. Brown, Frank Fay,
Harry Langdon, Ned Sparks and the King
Sisters.
—FROM YOUR HEART TO MINE
—I'VE ALWAYS BEEN FOND OF
  BABIES
—THE MAGIC KISS
—RAGGEDY ANN
—SWEET LITTLE STRANGER
—WHEN THE RIGHT LITTLE GIRL
  COMES ALONG
—EVERYBODY BUT ME
Lyrics by Joe Goodwin.

1922. *PINS AND NEEDLES*
A revue from the Gaiety Theater, London
with lyrics by Ballard MacDonald, Irving
Caesar and Rupert Hazel, and starring
Harry Pilcer and Edith Kelly Gould.
—AH, AH, AH
—ALL PULL TOGETHER
—SOUTH SEA SWEETHEART
Music by Maurice Yvain.
—NO ONE ELSE BUT THAT GIRL OF
  MINE
Music by George Gershwin.
—PICCADILLY WALK
By Arthur Riscoe and Edward Horan.
—LOVE SPANS THE WORLD
—OFF WE GO
—THE LITTLE TIN SOLDIER AND
  THE LITTLE RAG DOLL
—I'LL BUILD A HOME IN THE
  JUNGLE
—MELANCHOLY BLUES
—SLOW MOVIES
—THE GYPSY WARNED ME
—THE SYNCOPATED MINUET
—THE HOLLOW OF MY HAND

1922. *SPICE OF 1922*
A revue with book by Jack Lait, and
presented by a cast headed by Alman
Kaliz, Nan Halperin, Valeska Suratt,
Georgie Price, Sam Hearn and Flavia
Arcaro.
—DREAMS FOR SALE
—I'M IN LOVE WITH YOU
—A LITTLE SIDE STREET IN PAREE
—OLD FASHIONED CAKE WALK
—TWO LITTLE WOODEN SHOES
—WAY DOWN YONDER IN NEW OR-
  LEANS
By Henry Creamer and Turner Layton.
—YANKEE DOODLE BLUES
By Irving Caesar, B. G. DeSylva and
George Gershwin.
—BACK NUMBERS IN MY LITTLE
  RED BOOK

Music by J. Fred Coots.
—ANGEL CHILD
By Benny Davis, Georgie Price and Ab-
ner Silver.

1926. *HONEYMOON LANE*
A musical comedy with book and lyrics
by Eddie Dowling in which Kate Smith
made her stage debut in the role of Tiny
Little. The cast included Florence O'Den-
ishawn, Pauline Mason and Eddie Dowl-
ing.
—(A LITTLE WHITE HOUSE AT THE
  END OF) HONEYMOON LANE
Lyrics by Irving Caesar.
—DREAMS FOR SALE
—JERSEY WALK
—MARY DEAR
—HALF A MOON IS BETTER THAN
  NO MOON
—HEAD OVER HEELS IN LOVE
—CHORUS-PICKIN' TIME ON BROAD-
  WAY
—HALLOWEEN
—GEE, BUT I'D LIKE TO BE BAD
—WHAT DO YOU SAY WE STEAL
  AWAY?
—MARCHING ON TO HOLLYWOOD

1927. *SIDEWALKS OF NEW YORK*
In this musical comedy with book and
lyrics by Eddie Dowling, Jim Thornton,
songwriter and vaudeville headliner at the
turn of the century, Barney Fagin, the or-
iginator of the cake walk, and Josephine
Sabel, the soubrette who made "Hot Time
In The Old Town Tonight" famous, had
a chance to relive their nights of former
glory. The cast included Ray Dooley, Ed-
die Dowling, Fisk O'Hara, Charles Dale,
Joe Smith, Ruby Keeler and Bob Hope
in a "bit" part.
—PLAYGROUND IN THE SKY
—WHEREVER YOU ARE
—GOLDFISH GLIDE
—HEADING FOR HARLEM
—JUST A LITTLE SMILE FROM YOU
—THE YOUNGER SET
—WAY DOWN TOWN
—CONFIRMATION DAY
—NOTHING CAN EVER HAPPEN IN
  NEW YORK
—OH, FOR THE LIFE OF A COWBOY
—SIDEWALKS OF NEW YORK
By J. W. Blake and C. B. Lawlor.
—LITTLE BUM
—SPRINGTIME OF LONG AGO
—WE'RE THE GRLS YOU CAN'T FOR-
  GET

Ben Harris Score

1923. *HOW COME*
With Henry Creamer and Will Vodery.
Book by Eddie Hunter, who headed a
cast that included Nina Hunter, Alice
Brown and Chappy Chappelle.
—CHARLESTON CUTOUT
—E-GYPSY ANN
—LOVE WILL BRING YOU HAPPINESS
—SWEETHEART, FAREWELL
—PRETTY MALINDA
—CERTAINLY IS THE TRUTH
—GOODNIGHT, BROTHER GREEN
—SYNCOPATED STRAIN
—BANDANA ANNA
—PICKANINNY VAMP
—DINAH
—IN MY DIXIE DREAMLAND
—WHEN I'M BLUE
—I DIDN'T GRIEVE OVER DANIEL
—KEEP THE MAN YOU'VE GOT
—COUNT YOUR MONEY

Franke Harling Score

1926. *DEEP RIVER*
A musical play with book and lyrics by
Lawrence Stallings, and presented by a
cast headed by Jules Bludsoe, Luis Aber-
ni, Lottice Howell and Roberto Ardelli.
—ASHES AND FIRE
—CHEROKEE ROSE
—DE OLD CLAY ROAD
—DEEP RIVER
—DIS IS DE DAY
—LOVE LASTS A DAY
—SERENADE CREOLE
—TWO LITTLE STARS

Silvio Hein Scores

1920. *LOOK WHO'S HERE*
A musical comedy with book by Frank
Mandel, lyrics by Edward Paulton, and
presented by a cast headed by Cleo May-
field and Cecil Lean.
—MY NIGHT IN VENICE
—IF I HAD ONLY MET YOU DEAR
—I KNOW AND YOU KNOW
—BUBBLES
—LOVE, LOVE, LOVE
—I WONDER WHAT SHE'S THINKING
OF NOW
—LOVE NEVER CHANGES
—GIVE ME A COZY LITTLE CORNER
—LOOK WHO'S HERE
—THE TURK HAD THE RIGHT IDEA
—I CANNOT UNDERSTAND
—WHEN A WIFE GETS FAT

—BELLHOP BLUES
By Frank Goodman and Al Piantadosi.
—SOME WONDERFUL SORT OF PER-
SON
By Schuyler Green and George Gershwin.

1920. *THE GIRL FROM HOME*
A musical comedy, based on Richard
Harding Davis' novel and play "The Dic-
tator", with book and lyrics by Frank
Craven, who starred in a cast that in-
cluded Gladys Caldwell, Marion Sunshine
and Flora Zabelle.
—DON'T SAY GOODBYE
—MARIMA
—OCEAN BLUES
—SOMETIME
—WIRELESS HEART
—NINE LITTLE MISSIONARIES

1922. *SOME PARTY*
With Gustav Kerker and Percy Wenrich.
A revue with book and lyrics by R. H.
Burnside, and presented by a cast headed
by DeWolf Hopper, Jefferson DeAngelis
and Lew Dockstader.
—KEEP ON BUILDING CASTLES IN
THE AIR
—MINSTREL DAYS
By Percy Wenrich.
—BELLS OF THE SEA
By Albert Solman.
—IN YAMA YAMA LAND
By Henry Creamer and Turner Layton.
—IN ROSE TIME
By Mary Earl.
—RUSTIC ANN
By Percy Wenrich.

Ray Henderson Scores

1925. *GEORGE WHITE'S SCANDALS
OF 1925*
Book by George White and William K.
Wells, lyrics by Lew Brown and Buddy
DeSylva, and presented by a cast that in-
cluded Helen Morgan, Tom Patricola,
Harry Fox, Gordon Dooley and Miller
and Lyles.
—THE WHOSIS WHATSIS
—ROSETIME
—I WANT A LOVEABLE BABY
—FLY BUTTERFLY
—EVEN AS YOU AND I
—ROOM ENOUGH FOR ME
—SAY IT WITH SABLE
—THE GIRL OF TOMORROW
—LOVELY LADY
—WHAT A WORLD THIS WOULD BE
—BEWARE OF THE GIRL WITH A
FAN

1926. *GEORGE WHITE'S SCANDALS OF 1926*
Book by George White and William K. Wells, lyrics by Lew Brown and Buddy DeSylva, and presented by a cast headed by Ann Pennington, Frances Williams, Harry Richman, Willie and Eugene Howard, Tom Patricola, McCarthy Sisters and the Fairbanks Twins.
—TALENT IS WHAT THE PUBLIC WANTS
—THIS IS MY LUCKY DAY
—TWEET-TWEET
—LADY FAIR
—WALKING DOGS AROUND
—BLACK BOTTOM
—BIRTH OF THE BLUES
—SEVILLA
—DAVID AND LENORE
—THE GIRL IS YOU (THE BOY IS ME)
—MY JEWELS
—TWENTY YEARS AGO
—ARE YOU SATISFIED?

1927. *GOOD NEWS*
Book by Lawrence Schwab and Buddy DeSylva, lyrics by Lew Brown and Buddy DeSylva, and presented by a cast headed by Joseph Santley, replaced by John Price Jones during the play's run; Mary Lawlor, Zelma O'Neal and George Olsen and his band.
—A LADY'S MAN
—FLAMING YOUTH
—HAPPY DAYS
—JUST IMAGINE
—THE BEST THINGS IN LIFE ARE FRE
—ON THE CAMPUS
—VARSITY DRAG
—BABY! WHAT?
—LUCKY IN LOVE
—GIRLS OF PI BETA PHI
—GOOD NEWS
—IN THE MEANTIME

1927. *MANHATTAN MARY*
Book by George White and William K. Wells, lyrics by Lew Brown and Buddy DeSylva, and starring Ed Wynn in a cast that included Harlan Dixon, Ona Munson, George White, Lou Holtz and Paul Frawley.
—BROADWAY (THE HEART OF THE WORLD)
—HUDSON DUSTER
—MANHATTAN MARY
—THE FIVE-STEP
—NOTHING BUT LOVE
—IT WON'T BE LONG NOW

—MY BLUEBIRD'S HOME AGAIN

1928. *GEORGE WHITE'S SCANDALS OF 1928*
Book by George White and William K. Wells, lyrics by Lew Brown and Buddy DeSylva, and starring Willie and Eugene Howard in a cast that included Harry Richman, Tom Patricola, Ann Pennington, Frances Williams and Arnold Johnson's Orchestra.
—NOT AS GOOD AS LAST YEAR
—SECOND CHILDHOOD
—AN OLD FASHIONED GIRL
—PICKIN' COTTON
—A REAL AMERICAN TUNE
—WHERE YOU CARVED YOUR NAME
—WHAT D'YA SAY?
—ORIGIN OF THE TAP DANCE
—BUMS
—STARS, STARS SHINING BRIGHT

1928. *HOLD EVERYTHING*
Book by John McGowan and Buddy DeSylva, lyrics by Lew Brown and Buddy DeSylva, and presented by a cast headed by Ona Munson, Betty Compton, Jack Whiting, Bert Lahr and Victor Moore.
—YOU'RE THE CREAM IN MY COFFEE
—DON'T HOLD EVERYTHING
—WE'RE CALLING ON MR. BROOKS
—AN OUTDOOR MAN FOR MY INDOOR SPORTS
—FOOTWORK
—WHEN I LOVE I LOVE
—TOO GOOD TO BE TRUE
—TO KNOW YOU IS TO LOVE YOU
—FOR SWEET CHARITY'S SAKE
—GENEALOGY
—OH GOSH
—IT'S ALL OVER BUT THE SHOUTING

1929. *FOLLOW THROUGH*
Book by Lawrence Schwab, lyrics by Lew Brown and Buddy DeSylva, and presented by a cast that included Irene Delroy, Zelma O'Neal, Jack Haley, Eleanor Powell, Madeline Cameron and John Barker.
—BUTTON UP YOUR OVERCOAT
—I WANT TO BE BAD
—YOU WOULDN'T FOOL ME WOULD YOU?
—MY LUCKY STAR
—THE DARING GIBSON GIRL
—THE 1908 LIFE
—IT'S A GREAT SPORT
—HE'S A MAN'S MAN
—THEN I'LL HAVE TIME FOR YOU
—MARRIED MEN AND SINGLE MEN
—IF THERE WERE NO MORE YOU

—I COULD GIVE UP ANYTHING BUT
  YOU
—FOLLOW THROUGH

Victor Herbert Scores

1920. *MY GOLDEN GIRL*
Book and lyrics by Frederic Arthur Kummer, and with a cast headed by Victor Morley, Marie Carroll, Ned Sparks and Edna May Oliver.
—I WANT YOU
—MY GOLDEN GIRL
—A LITTLE NEST FOR TWO
—DARBY AND JOAN
—RAGTIME TERPSICHORE
—OH DAY IN JUNE!
—I'D LIKE A HONEYMOON WITH
  YOU
—IF WE HAD MET BEFORE
—NAME THE DAY
—IN VENICE
—SHOOTING STAR
—A SONG WITHOUT (MANY) WORDS

1920. *OUI MADAME*
Book by J. M. Wright, lyrics by Robert B. Smith, and with a cast headed by Georgia O'Ramey, Glenn Anders and Harry Kelly.
—HE WANTED TO GO AND HE WENT
—IF I SAW MUCH OF YOU
—MY DAY HAS COME
—OVER THE GARDEN WALL
—PLAY ME SOMETHING I CAN
  DANCE TO
—WHEN YOU KNOW ME BETTER
—THE WOOING OF THE VIOLIN
—WHERE WERE YOU?
—EVERY HOUR AWAY FROM YOU IS
  SIXTY MINUTES LOST
—IF THAT'S NOT LOVE WHAT DO
  YOU CALL IT?
—OUI MADAME
—WHEN YOU AND I WERE TAD-
  POLES
—SUCH A HAPPY FAMILY
—THE GIRL WHO KEEPS YOU WAIT-
  ING
—A GIRL WHO CAN LOVE
—THE TABLE D'HOTE CABARET

1920. *THE GIRL IN THE SPOTLIGHT*
Book and lyrics by Richard Bruce, and with a cast headed by Mary Milburn, Johnny Dooley and Hal Skelly.
—CATCH 'EM YOUNG, TREAT 'EM
  ROUGH, TELL 'EM NOTHING
—I LOVE THE GROUND YOU WALK
  ON
—IT WOULD HAPPEN ANYWAY

—I CANNOT SLEEP WITHOUT
  DREAMING OF YOU
—I'LL BE THERE
—THERE'S A TENDER LOOK IN YOUR
  EYE
—SOMEWHERE I KNOW THERE'S A
  GIRL FOR ME

1922. *ORANGE BLOSSOMS*
Book by Fred deGresac, lyrics by B. G. DeSylva, and with a cast headed by Queenie Smith, Edith Day, Jack Whiting and Hal Skelly.
—A KISS IN THE DARK
—WAY OUT WEST IN JERSEY
—THEN COMES THE DAWNING
—THIS TIME IT'S LOVE
—LEGEND OF THE GLOW WORM
—LONELY NEST
—A DREAM OF ORANGE BLOSSOMS

1924. *DREAM GIRL*
Book and lyrics by Rida Johnson Young and Harold Atteridge, and with a cast headed by Fay Bainter, Walter Woolf and Billy B. Van.
—MAKING A VENUS
—ALL YEAR 'ROUND
—DANCING AROUND
—OLD SONGS
—MAIDEN LET ME IN
—STOP, LOOK AND LISTEN
—BROAD HIGHWAY
—MY HERO
—I WANT TO GO HOME
—BUBBLES
—SAXOPHONE MAN
—GYPSY LIFE
—MAKE LOVE IN THE MORNING
—AT THE RAINBOW'S END
—IF SOMEBODY ONLY WOULD FIND
  ME
—DREAM GIRL

Donald Heywood Score

1927. *AFRICANA*
A revue with book and lyrics by the composer, and starring Ethel Waters in an all-Negro cast.
—BLACK CARGO
—BUGLE BLUES
—WEARY FEET
—HERE COMES MY SHOWBOAT
—THE CAKE WALK STRUT
—TIME AIN'T VERY LONG
—SMILE
—SHINE 'EM UP
—CLORINDA
—AFRICANA STOMP

—I'M COMING VIRGINIA
With Will Marion Cook.

Louis A. Hirsch Scores

1920. *MARY*
Book and lyrics by Otto Harbach and
Frank Mandel, and starring Janet Velie
and Jack McGowan.
—THAT MAY HAVE SATISFIED
GRANDMA
—DOWN ON THE OLD KANSAS FARM
—ANYTHING YOU WANT TO DO,
DEAR
—EVERY TIME I MEET A LADY
—TOM TOM TODDLE
—LOVE NEST
—MARY
—WHEN A WOMAN EXITS LAUGHING
—DON'T FALL UNTIL YOU'VE SEEN
THEM ALL
—WAITING
—FLIRTATION DANCE
—MONEY, MONEY, MONEY
—WE'LL GIVE A WONDERFUL PARTY

1921. *THE O'BRIEN GIRL*
Book and lyrics by Otto Harbach and
Frank Mandel, and presented by a cast
headed by Elizabeth Hines, Truman Stan-
ley, Ada Mae Weeks and Georgia Caine.
—CURIOSITY
—GIVE, GIVE
—I'LL TREAT YOU LIKE A SISTER
—I WONDER HOW I EVER PASSED
YOU BY?
—INDIAN PRANCE
—LEARN TO SMILE
—MY LITTLE CANOE
—I'M SO EXCITED
—THE CONVERSATION STEP
—MURDER
—THE O'BRIEN GIRL
—PARTNERS
—TO KEEP YOU IN YOUR SEATS

1922. *GREENWICH VILLAGE FOLLIES
OF 1922*
Book and lyrics by George V. Hobart,
John Murray Anderson and Irving Caesar,
and presented by a cast headed by John
Hazzard, Savoy and Brennan, Carl Ran-
dall and Lucille Chalfonte.
—BEAUTIFUL GIRLS
By Bert Kalmar and Harry Ruby.
—YOU ARE MY RAIN-BEAU
—CINDERELLA BLUES
—NIGHTINGALE, BRING ME A ROSE
—A KISS FROM A RED-HEADED MISS
—SIXTY SECONDS EVERY MINUTE I
DREAM OF YOU

—A CHAUVE-SOURIS OF OUR OWN
—GOOD-BYE TO DEAR OLD ALASKA
—GEORGETTE
By Lew Brown and Ray Henderson.
—GREENWICH VILLAGE NIGHTS

1922. *ZIEGFELD FOLLIES OF 1922*
Book and lyrics by Ring Lardner, Ralph
Spence and Gene Buck. Gilda Gray made
her "Follies" debut in a cast that included
Will Rogers, Evelyn Law, Lulu McCon-
nell, Mary Eaton, Gallagher and Shean,
and Olsen and Johnson.
—HELLO, HELLO, HELLO
—MY MELODY
—'NEATH THE SOUTH SEA MOON
WITH YOU
—RAMBLER ROSE
—THROW ME A KISS
—SUNNY SOUTH
—IT'S GETTING AWFUL DARK ON
OLD BROADWAY
By Dave Stamper.
—BRING ON THE GIRLS
By Dave Stamper.
—LISTENING ON THE RADIO
By Dave Stamper.
—SONGS I CAN'T FORGET
By Dave Stamper.
—FLAPPERS
By Dave Stamper.
—WEAVING MY DREAM
By Victor Herbert.
—MR. GALLAGHER AND MR. SHEAN
By Gallagher and Shean and Ernest Ball.
—OH GEE, OH GOSH, OH GOLLY, I'M
IN LOVE
By Olsen and Johnson and Ernest Breuer.

1923. *GREENWICH VILLAGE FOLLIES
OF 1923*
With Con Conrad. Book and lyrics by
John Murray Anderson and Irving Caesar,
and presented by a cast headed by Tom
Howard, Sammy White, The Mandells,
Daphne Pollard, Eva Puck, Ruth Urban
and Irene Delroy.
—LOVEY
—KAMA'S GARDEN
—BUSTLE
—COCK-A-DOODLE-DOO
—SEEING STARS
—GOLDEN TRAIL
—THE BARCAROLE
—RAISIN' THE ROOF
—DANCING STEP CHILD
—JUST A BIT OF HEAVEN IN YOUR
SMILE

1924. *BETTY LEE*
With Con Conrad. A musical comedy
based on the Paul Armstrong-Rex Beach

play, "Going Some," with book and lyrics
by Otto Harbach and Irving Caesar, and
presented by a cast that included Gloria
Foy, Hal Skelly, and Joe E. Brown.
—ALONG THE RIO GRANDE
—LITTLE PONY OF MINE
—SWEET CACTUS ROSE
—ATHLETIC BOY
—MONTEREY
—THE DAILY DOZEN
—THEY ALWAYS RUN A LITTLE
    FASTER
—SWEET ARABIAN DREAMS
—GIVE HIM YOUR SYMPATHY
—BABY BE GOOD

Raymond Hubbell Scores

1920. *GOOD TIMES*
Book and lyrics by R. H. Burnside, and
starring Joe Jackson, the tramp cyclist, in
a New York Hippodrome production in
which the disappearing diving girls pro-
vided a spectacular finale.
—YOUTH AND TRUTH
—WAKE UP, FATHER TIME
—THE LAND I LOVE
—THE WEDDING OF THE DANCING
    DOLL
—HANDS UP
—JUST LIKE A ROSE
—HELLO, IMAGINATION
—I WANT TO SHOW YOU COLOR-
    LAND
—SING A SERENADE
—WELCOME TRUTH
—TRUTH REIGNS SUPREME
—YOU CAN'T BEAT THE LUCK OF
    THE IRISH

1921. *SONNY*
Book and lyrics by George V. Hobart,
and with Carl Randall, Ernest Glenden-
ning and Emma Dunn as featured mem-
bers of the cast.
—I'M IN LOVE, DEAR
—DREAM
—SONNY
—MY CHUM
—PEACHES
—HOMETOWN BLUES

1922. *BETTER TIMES*
Book and lyrics by R. H. Burnside. Long
Tack Sam, Powers' elephants and Marce-
line, the French clown, were the headline
attractions in this New York Hippodrome
production.
—AN UP-TO-DATE TUNE
—BETTER TIMES
—BLOWING BUBBLES ALL DAY LONG

—GRAND OPERA BALL
—MY GOLDEN DREAM SHIP
—PEACH BLOSSOM TIME
—TALE OF A FAN

1922. *THE ELUSIVE LADY*
Book and lyrics by Glen MacDonough,
and starring Julian Eltinge.
—DESERT LOVE
—HEART O' ME
—WHEN YOU'RE ASLEEP IN YOUR
    BED AT NIGHT
—I'LL BREAK THE HEARTS OF MEN
    WHO BREAK THE BANK AT
    MONTE CARLO
—A TUNE LIKE YOU
—FASCINATION
—VIOLIN AND CELLO
—A CUTE LITTLE BEAUT FROM
    BUTTE, MONTANA

1927. *YOURS TRULY*
Book by Clyde North, lyrics by Anne
Caldwell, and presented with a cast head-
ed by Irene Dunne and Leon Errol.
—FOLLOW THE GUIDE
—MAYFAIR
—SHUFFLIN' BILL
—LOOK AT THE WORLD AND SMILE
—SOMEBODY ELSE
—THE GUNMAN
—THE LOTUS FLOWER
—QUIT KIDDIN'
—MARY HAS A LITTLE FAIR
—DON'T SHAKE MY TREE
—I WANT A PAL
—YOURS TRULY
—JADE
—HIGH YALLER
—DAWN OF DREAMS

1927. *THE GIRL FROM COOK'S*
Book and lyrics by R. H. Burnside.
—I'M IN LOVE, IT'S A WONDERFUL
    FEELING
—LOVE IS ALWAYS JUST WHAT IT
    SEEMS
—THE ROAD TO HAPPINESS
—STELLA
—YOU TELL HIM

1928. *THREE CHEERS*
Book and lyrics by R. H. Burnside and
Anne Caldwell. Fred Stone planned to
make this musical his Broadway farewell,
but during the rehearsals, he was taken
ill and Will Rogers substituted for him in
a cast that included Dorothy Stone, Patsy
Kelly and Allan Edwards.
—THE AMERICANS ARE HERE
—LADY LUCK
—MAYBE THIS IS LOVE

—IT'S AN OLD SPANISH CUSTOM
—BECAUSE YOU'RE BEAUTIFUL
—BOBBY AND ME
—THE SILVER TREE
—GEE IT'S GREAT TO BE ALIVE
—PUTTING ON THE RITZ
—TWO BOYS
—HAPPY HOBOES
—BRIDE BELLS
—POMPANOLA
By Buddy DeSylva, Lew Brown and Ray Henderson.

Victor Jacobi Score

1920. *THE HALF MOON*
An operetta with book and lyrics by William LeBaron, and presented by a cast headed by Edna May Oliver, Ivy Sawyer, Joseph Cawthorn, Oscar Shaw and Joseph Santley.
—DEEP IN YOUR EYES
—THE HALF MOON
—DAYS THAT USED TO BE
—LITTLE BOOK
—GIRLS ALONG FIFTH AVENUE
—THE DANCING BAND
—WHEN YOU SMILE
—WHAT IS THE MATTER WITH WOMEN?

Maurice Jacquet Score

1929. *THE SILVER SWAN*
An operetta with book and lyrics by William S. Brady and Alonzo Price, and starring Lina Abarbanell in a cast that included Edward Nell, Jr., Vivian Hart and Alice McKenzie.
—THE BRAVE AND THE FAIR
—THE DANGEROUS AGE
—MEMORIES
—PRETTY GIRLS AND ROSES
—PETER AND THE CHORUS GIRLS
—CIGARETTE
—I LOVE YOU, I ADORE YOU
—A LONELY ROAD
—LOVE LETTERS
—LIFE IS JUST A MERRY-GO-ROUND
—TILL I MET YOU

Werner Janssen Scores

1921. *LOVE DREAMS*
A musical comedy with book by Anne Nichols, lyrics by Oliver Morosco, and presented by a cast headed by Vera Michelena and Tom Powers.
—ANY TIME IS LOVE TIME
—LOVE DREAMS

—I'M JUST LOOKING FOR A LONE-SOME GIRL WHO'S LOOKING FOR A LONESOME BOY
—KNIGHTS OF THE TABLE
—MY DREAM OF LOVE IS YOU
—PITY ME
—REPUTATION
—THE TODDLE TOP WHIRL
—WHERE SMOKE RINGS GO

1922. *LETTY PEPPER*
A musical comedy with book by George V. Hobart, lyrics by Leo Wood and Irving Bibo, and starring Charlotte Greenwood.
—BLUE BIRD BLUES
—COO-EE-DOO
—I LOVE A DANCER
—LAVENDER AND LACE
—YOU'RE LIKE A RAY OF SUNSHINE
—EVERY LITTLE MISS MUST HAVE A MISTER
—LANKY LETTY PEPPER
—SITTIN' PRETTY
—YOU TEACH ME
By Ballard MacDonald and James Hanley.

1923. *LADY BUTTERFLY*
A musical comedy with book and lyrics by Clifford Grey, and presented by a cast headed by Florenz Ames, Allen Kearns and Marjorie Gateson.
—MY COTTAGE IN SUNSHINE LANE
—WONDERFUL YOU
—SWAY WITH ME
—WALTZ TIME
—LADY BUTTERFLY
—KISS TIME
—SOON WE'LL BE UPON THE SEA
—GIRLS I HAVE MET
—DOLL'S HOUSE
—SAILORS SAIL AWAY
—BEAUTIFUL LOVE
—MAN OVERBOARD!
—BY THE GARDEN WALL
—THE BAD MAN WALK
—GOOD EVENING, GOOD NIGHT
—THE CHASE
—THE BOOZE OF AULD LANG SYNE

1929. *BOOM! BOOM!*
A musical comedy with book by Fanny Todd Mitchell, lyrics by Mann Holiner and J. Keirn Brennan, and presented by a cast headed by Jeanette MacDonald, Stanley Riggs and Frank McIntyre.
—BLOW THE BLUES AWAY
—SHAKE HIGH, SHAKE LOW
—WHAT A GIRL!

—WHAT COULD I DO?
—ON THE TOP
—BE THAT WAY
—JUST A BIG-HEARTED MAN
—NINA
—HE'S JUST MY IDEAL
—PICK 'EM UP AND LAY 'EM DOWN
—WE'RE GOING TO MAKE BOOM-
BOOM

Freddie Johnson Score

1925. *LUCKY SAMBO*
A musical with book and lyrics by Porter
Grainger and the composer, and pre-
sented by an all-Negro cast.
—HAPPY
—STOP
—JUNE
—DON'T FORGET BANDANA DAYS
—ANYBODY'S MAN WILL BE MY MAN
—AUNT JEMIMA, I'M COMING HOME
—CHARLEY FROM THAT CHARLES-
TON DANCING SCHOOL
—IF YOU CAN'T BRING IT YOU'VE
GOT TO SEND IT
—STROLLING
—DREARY, DREARY, RAINY DAYS
—HAVIN' A WONDERFUL TIME
—ALEXANDER'S WEDDING DAY
—TAKE HIM TO JAIL
—ALWAYS ON THE JOB
—LEGOMANIA
—SINGING NURSES
—DANDY DAN
—LOVE ME WHILE YOU'RE GONE
—PORTEROLOGY
—KEEP A DIGGIN'
—RUNNIN'
—MIDNIGHT CABARET
—NOT SO LONG AGO

James P. Johnson Scores

1923. *RUNNING WILD*
A muscial comedy with book by F. E.
Miller and A. L. Lyles, lyrics by Cecil
Mack, and starring the librettists in an
all-Negro cast.
—CHARLESTON
—OLD-FASHIONED LOVE
—WATCHING THE CLOCK
By Jo Trent and Porter Grainger.
—EASY GOIN' MAN
By Turner Layton and Darl MacBoyle.
—LOVE BUG
—OPEN YOUR HEART
—GINGER BROWN
—HEART-BREAKIN' JOE
By Jo Trent and Porter Grainger.

1929. *MESSIN' AROUND*
An all-Negro revue with lyrics by Perry
Bradford.
—YOUR LOVE IS ALL I CRAVE
—HARLEM TOWN
—SKIDDLE-DE-SCOW
—GET AWAY FROM MY WINDOW
—SHOUT ON
—I DON'T LOVE NOBODY
—ROUSTABOUTS
—MISSISSIPPI MOON
—MISSISSIPPI
—PUT YOUR MIND RIGHT ON IT
—SORRY
—MESSIN' AROUND

Tom Johnstone Scores

1922. *UP IN THE CLOUDS*
A musical comedy with book and lyrics
by Will B. Johnstone, and starring Grace
Moore in a cast that included Hal Van-
Rensallear and Skeets Gallagher.
—THE MOVIE LESSON
—LOOK-A-LOOK
—FRIENDS
—IT'S A GREAT LIFE IF YOU DON'T
WEAKEN
—UP IN THE CLOUDS
—THE LAST GIRL IS THE BEST GIRL
—JEAN
—THE GIRL I MARRY
—NOBODY KNOWS
—BETSY ROSS
—RUM-TUM-TIDDLE
—HAPPINESS

1923. *MOLLY DARLING*
A musical comedy with book by Otto
Harbach and William Cary Duncan, lyrics
by Phil Cook, and presented by a cast
headed by Mary Milburn, Jack Donahue,
Billy Taylor and Billie Taylor.
—DEAR LITTLE GAD-ABOUT
—MELLOW MOON
—MELODY DREAMS
—MOLLY DARLING
—SOME ONE
—SYNCOPATE
—YOU KNOW WHAT TO DO

1924. *PLAIN JANE*
A musical comedy with book by Phil
Cook and McElbert Moore, lyrics by Phil
Cook, and presented by a cast headed by
Lorraine Manville, Charles McNaughton,
Dan Healy, Jay Gould and Joe Laurie, Jr.
—DON'T TAKE YOUR TROUBLES TO
BED
—IF FLOWERS COULD SPEAK
—PLAIN JANE

—ALONG THE ROAD TO LOVE
—WHAT'S NEW?
—WINNING THE PRIZE
—HAND IN HAND
—WHEN YOUR HEART'S IN THE RING
—I LOVE A FIGHT
—PUTTIN' ON THE RITZ
—PROVERBS
—BENEATH THE STARS
—A PLAYHOUSE PLANNED FOR YOU
—COME ON FEET, LET'S GO
—TRICKS OF THE TRADE
—WHEN THE WHISTLE BLOWS

1924. *I'LL SAY SHE IS*
The Four Marx Brothers—Herbert, Leonard, Julius and Arthur—desert big time vaudeville for a flyer in musical comedy. The book and lyrics were by Will B. Johnstone.
—ONLY YOU
—WHEN SHADOWS FALL
—I'M SAVING FOR A RAINY DAY
—WONDERFUL NILE
—DO IT
—PRETTY GIRL
—GIVE ME A THRILL
—BREAK INTO YOUR HEART
—SAN TOY
—WALL STREET BLUES
—GLIMPSES OF THE MOON

1925. *WHEN YOU SMILE*
A musical comedy with book by Jack Alicoate and the composer, lyrics by Phil Cook, and presented by a cast that included Carol Joyce, Jack Whiting, Imogene Coca and Ray Raymond.
—WHEN YOU SMILE
—WONDERFUL YESTERDAY
—OH WHAT A GIRL!
—JUNE
—SPANISH MOON
—NAUGHTY EYES
—ONE LITTLE GIRL
—LET'S HAVE A GOOD TIME
—GEE, WE GET ALONG!
—ALL WORK AND NO PLAY
—KEEP THEM GUESSING
—KEEP ON BUILDING CASTLES
—LET'S DANCE AND MAKE UP
—WONDERFUL RHYTHM
—BUY AN EXTRA
—SHE LOVES ME

1927. *THE GIRL FROM CHILD'S*
A musical comedy with book by Archie Colby and Al Jackson, lyrics by Phil Cook, and presented by a cast headed by Ann Milburn, Virginia Watson, Thomas

Mann and Irving Fisher.
—LITTLE MISS NOBODY
—YOU'RE A PERFECT LITTLE LADY
—THE HOUSE THAT JAZZ BUILT
—ONLY A PAPER ROSE
—A QUIET LIFE AT CHILD'S
—SOCIETY SNOBS
—HIGH HATS
—TWITTER
—I'LL DO ALL MY DANCING WITH ONE GIRL
—NECKIN' TIME IN GREAT NECK
—THE CHARITY BALL
—MARY

Stephen Jones Score

1923. *POPPY*
With Arthur Samuels. A musical comedy with book and lyrics by Dorothy Donnelly, and starring W. C. Fields in a cast that included Madge Kennedy, Luella Gear, Robert Woolsey and Alan Edwards.
—WHAT DO YOU DO SUNDAYS MARY?
—HANG YOUR SORROWS IN THE SUN
—SOMEONE WILL MAKE YOU SMILE
By Irving Caesar and Rudolph Sieczynski
—ALIBI BABY
Lyrics by Howard Dietz (his first published song) and music by Arthur Samuels.
—MARY
Lyrics by Irving Caesar.
—A PICNIC PARTY WITH YOU
—TWO MAKE A HOME
—WHEN YOU ARE IN MY ARMS

Joe Jordan Score

1929. *DEEP HARLEM*
An all-Negro revue with book by Whitney and Homer Tutt, and lyrics by Homer Tutt and Henry Creamer.
—DEEP HARLEM
—POSSUM TROT
—OLD TIME REEL
—I LOVE YOU MORE
—WHY
—SNAKE DANCE
—SLAVE SHIP

Edmund Joseph Score

1927. *POLLY OF HOLLYWOOD*
A musical comedy with book and lyrics by Will Morrissey, who also collaborated on the score, and presented by a cast headed by Midge Miller.

—COMPANY MANNERS
—TEXAS STOMP
—WANTING YOU
—MIDNIGHT DADDY
—POLLY OF HOLLYWOOD
—A NEW KIND OF RHYTHM

Roger Wolfe Kahn Scores

1928. *HERE'S HOWE*
A musical comedy with book by Frederick
Thompson and Paul Gerard Smith, lyrics
by Irving Caesar, and presented by a cast
headed by Irene Delroy, Allen Kearns,
Eric Blore and William Frawley.
—LIFE AS A TWOSOME
—ON MY MIND A NEW LOVE
—CRAZY RHYTHM
Music by Joseph Meyer.
—IMAGINATION
Music by Joseph Meyer.
—DISMAL WHISTLE
—BEAUTY IN THE MOVIES
—I'D RATHER DANCE HERE THAN
HEREAFTER
—HERE'S HOWE
—BOSTON POST ROAD

1928. *AMERICANA OF 1928*
A revue with book by J. P. McAvoy,
lyrics by Irving Caesar, and presented by
a cast that included J. Rosamond John-
son, Baby Banks and John Hamilton.
—AMERI-CAN-CAN
—HE'S MINE
—HOT PANTS
—NO PLACE LIKE HOME
—YOUNG BLACK JOE
—WILD OAT JOE
—MY KINDA LOVE
By Jo Trent and Louis Alter.
—IF I LOVE AGAIN
By John Murray and Ben Oakland.
—LIFE AS A TWOSOME

Emmerich Kalman Scores

1922. *THE YANKEE PRINCESS*
A musical comedy with book by William
LeBaron, lyrics by B. G. DeSylva, and
presented by a cast headed by Vivienne
Segal, Thorpe Bates, Vivian Oakland and
John P. Murray.
—STARS OF THE STAGE
—I'LL DANCE MY WAY INTO YOUR
HEART
—A HUSBAND'S ONLY A HUSBAND
—FRIENDSHIP
—EYES SO DARK AND LURING
—CAN IT BE THAT I'M IN LOVE?

—LOVE THE WIFE OF YOUR
NEIGHBOR
—FORBIDDEN FRUIT
—I STILL CAN DREAM
—IN THE STARLIGHT
—MY BAJADERE
—ROSES LOVELY ROSES

1926. *COUNTESS MARITZA*
A musical comedy with book and lyrics
by Harry B. Smith, and presented by a
cast that included Yvonne D'Arle, Walter
Woolf, Carl Randall and Harry K. Mor-
ton.
—HOLA, FOLLOW, FOLLOW ME
—COME AT THE CALL OF LOVE
—I'LL KEEP ON DREAMING
—LOVE HAS FOUND MY HEART
Music by Al Goodman.
—THE ONE I'M LOOKING FOR
—IN THE DAYS GONE BY
—MAKE UP YOUR MIND
—THE MUSIC THRILLS ME
—GOLDEN DREAMS
—DON'T TEMPT ME
—WHO AM I?
—WHY IS THE WORLD SO CHANGED
TODAY?
—BROWN-EYED GIRL
—PLAY, GYPSIES, DANCE GYPSIES

1927. *THE CIRCUS PRINCESS*
A musical comedy with book and lyrics by
Harry B. Smith, and presented by a cast
headed by Desiree Tabor, Guy Robertson,
Gloria Foy, Ted Doner, George Bickel
and Poodles Hanneford and his family of
bareback riders.
—BRAVO, BRAVO
—THERE'S SOMETHING ABOUT YOU
—THE SAME OLD LOVE SONGS
—I DARE TO SPEAK OF LOVE TO
YOU
—JOY BELLS
—THE HUSSARS' SONG
—DEAR EYES THAT HAUNT ME
—WE TWO SHALL MEET AGAIN
—I DREAM OF YOUR EYES
—BUT WHO CARES?
—GIRLS? I AM TRUE TO THEM ALL
—I LIKE THE BOYS
—WHAT D'YA SAY?
By Ray Klages, Jesse Greer and Kalman.
—GUARDED
—WAITERS
—I'LL BE WAITING

1927. *GOLDEN DAWN*
With Herbert Stothart. A musical drama,
inspired by the best-selling novel "Trader
Horn," with book and lyrics by Otto Har-

bach and Oscar Hammerstein II, and presented by a cast headed by Marguerita Sylva, Louise Hunter, Robert Chisholm and Paul Gregory.

—WE TWO
—WHEN I CRACK MY WHIP
—CONSOLATION
—MY BWANNA
—HERE IN THE DARK
—AFRICA
—JUNGLE SHADOWS

Jerome Kern Scores

1920. *THE NIGHT BOAT*
Book and lyrics by Anne Caldwell, and presented by a cast headed by Louise Groody, John E. Hazzard, Hal Skelly and Wellington Cross.

—SOME FINE DAY
—WHOSE BABY ARE YOU?
—LEFT ALL ALONE AGAIN BLUES
—GOOD NIGHT BOAT
—I'D LIKE A LIGHTHOUSE
—CATSKILLS, HELLO
—DON'T YOU WANT TO TAKE ME?
—I LOVE THE LASSIES (I LOVE THEM ALL)
—A HEART FOR SALE
—GIRLS ARE LIKE A RAINBOW
—BOB WHITE
—MY SPANISH ROSE
Music by José Padilla.
—RIP VAN WINKLE AND HIS LITTLE MEN

1920. *HITCHY-KOO OF 1920*
Book and lyrics by Glen MacDonough and Anne Caldwell, and starring Raymond Hitchcock in a cast that included Julia Sanderson, G. P. Huntley, Florence O'Denisshawn, Grace Moore, Bobby Connelly and Mosconi Brothers.

—CHICK CHICK CHICK
—MILLINERY MANNEQUIN
—I AM DAGUERRE
—OLD FASHIONED DANCES
—SWEETIE
—DING-DONG, IT'S KISSING TIME
—MOON OF LOVE
—CANAJOHARIE
—BUGGY RIDING
—OLD NEW YORK
—WE'LL MAKE A BET
—I WANT TO MARRY
—TREASURE ISLAND
—BRING 'EM BACK
—THE STAR OF HITCHY-KOO

1920. *SALLY*
Book by Guy Bolton, lyrics by Clifford

Grey and B. G. DeSylva, and starring Marilyn Miller in a cast that included Mary Hay, Delores, Walter Catlett, Leon Errol and Irving Fisher.

—ON WITH THE DANCE
—YOU CAN'T KEEP A GOOD GIRL DOWN
—*LOOK FOR THE SILVER LINING
—SALLY
—WILD ROSE
—THE SCHNITZKA KOMISSKA
—WHIP-POOR-WILL
—THE LITTLE CHURCH AROUND THE CORNER
—THE SOCIAL GAME
—LORELEI

1921. *GOOD MORNING, DEARIE*
Book and lyrics by Anne Caldwell, and starring Louise Groody in a cast that included Oscar Shaw, Harlan Dixon and William Kent.

—EVERY GIRL
—WAY DOWN TOWN
—ROSE-MARIE
—DIDN'T YOU BELIEVE?
—THE TEDDY TODDLE
—BLUE DANUBE BLUES
—EASY PICKIN'S
—MELICAN PAPA
—NIAGARA FALLS
—KA-LU-A
—GOOD MORNING, DEARIE
—SING SONG GIRL

1922. *THE BUNCH AND JUDY*
Book by Hugh Ford and Anne Caldwell, lyrics by Anne Caldwell, and starring Fred and Adele Astaire in a cast that included Johnny Dooley, Ray Dooley, Grace Hayes and the Six Brown Brothers.

—THE NAUGHTY NOBLEMAN
—PALE VENETIAN MOON
—PEACH GIRL
—MORNING GLORY
—LOVELY LASSIE
—EVERY DAY IN EVERY WAY
—TIMES SQUARE
—HOW DO YOU DO, KATINKA
—HAVE-YOU-FORGOTTEN-ME BLUES
—HOT DOG

1923. *STEPPING STONES*
Book and lyrics by W. C. Burnside and Anne Caldwell, and starring Fred Stone in a cast that included Jack Whiting, Dorothy Stone, Allene Stone and Dorothy Herbert.

—LITTLE ANGEL CAKE
—BECAUSE YOU LOVE THE SINGER
—EVERYBODY CALLS ME LITTLE RED RIDING HOOD

—WONDERFUL DAD
—PIE
—BABBLING BABETTE
—IN LOVE WITH LOVE
—OUR LOVELY ROSE
—ONCE IN A BLUE MOON
—RAGGEDY ANN
—DEAR LITTLE PETER PAN
—STEPPING STONES

1924. *SITTING PRETTY*
Book and lyrics by Guy Bolton and P. G.
Wodehouse, and starring Queenie Smith
in a cast that included Frank McIntyre,
Dwight Frye, Gertrude Bryan and Ru-
dolph Cameron.
—IS NOT THIS A LOVELY SPOT?
—WORRIES
—MR. AND MRS. ROVER
—BONGO ON THE CONGO
—THERE ISN'T ONE GIRL
—A YEAR FROM TODAY
—SHUFFLING SAM
—THE POLKA DOT
—DAYS GONE BY
—ALL YOU NEED IS A GIRL
—DEAR OLD FASHIONED PRISON OF
  MINE
—ON A DESERT ISLAND
—ENCHANTED TRAIN
—SHADOW OF THE MOON
—SITTING PRETTY
—TULIP TIME IN SING SING

1924. *DEAR SIR*
Book by Edgar Selwyn, lyrics by Howard
Dietz, and starring Genevieve Tobin and
Oscar Shaw with Walter Catlett featured.
—GRAB A GIRL
—WHAT'S THE USE
—I WANT TO BE THERE
—A MORMON LIFE
—DANCING TIME
—TO THE FAIR
—MY HOUSEBOAT ON THE HARLEM
—ALL LANES MUST REACH A TURN-
  ING
Music by Arthur Schwartz.
—SEVEN DAYS
—IF YOU THINK IT'S LOVE YOU'RE
  RIGHT
—WEEPING WILLOW TREE

1925. *SUNNY*
Book and lyrics by Otto Harbach and
Oscar Hammerstein II, and starring Mari-
lyn Miller and Jack Donahue in a cast
that included Mary Hay, Cliff Edwards,
Joseph Cawthorn, Clifton Webb and Paul
Frawley.
—SUNNY

—WHO?
—SO'S YOU'RE OLD MAN
—LET'S SAY GOODNIGHT TILL IT'S
  MORNING
—D'YA LOVE ME?
—THE WEDDING KNELL
—TOO LITTLE LOVEBIRDS
—WHEN WE GET OUR DIVORCE
—SUNSHINE
—STROLLING OR WHAT HAVE YOU
—MAGNOLIA IN THE WOODS
—BE STILL MY HEART
—DREAM A DREAM
—I'LL SAY TO YOU AND YOU'LL SAY
  TO ME
—I'M MOVING AWAY
—I WAS ALONE
—JUST A LITTLE THING CALLED
  RHYTHM

1925. *THE CITY CHAP*
A musical comedy based on Winchell
Smith's "The Fortune Hunter" with book
by James Montgomery, lyrics by Anne
Caldwell, and starring Skeet Gallagher in
a cast that included Irene Dunne and
Phyllis Cleveland.
—LIKE THE NYMPHS OF SPRING
—THE GO-GETTER
—JOURNEY'S END
—SYMPATHETIC
—HE'S THE TYPE
—THE CITY CHAP
—I'M HEAD OVER HEELS IN LOVE
—FOUNTAIN OF YOUTH
—A PILL A DAY
—WALKING HOME WITH JOSIE
—SARATOGA
—NO ONE KNOWS
—WHEN L FELL IN LOVE
—SUCCESS

1926. *CRISS CROSS*
Book by Otto Harbach, lyrics by Anne
Caldwell, and starring Dorothy and Fred
Stone in a cast that included Lucy Mon-
roe and Oscar Ragland.
—HYDROPHOBIA BLUES
—INDIGNATION MEETING
—CINDERELLA GIRL
—SHE'S ON HER WAY
—FLAP-A-DOODLE
—THAT LITTLE SOMETHING
—IN ARABY WITH YOU
—DEAR ALGERIAN LAND
—DREAMING OF ALLAH
—ROSE OF DELIGHT
—I LOVE MY LITTLE SUSIE
—THE ALI BABA BABIES
—BREAD AND BUTTER

—KISS A FOUR LEAF CLOVER
—YOU WILL, WON'T YOU?

1927. *SHOW BOAT*
Book and lyrics by Oscar Hammerstein II, and presented by a cast that included Charles Winninger, Aunt Jemima, Edna May Oliver, Eva Puck, Sammy White, Helen Morgan, Howard Marsh, Norma Terris, Eleanor Shaw and Jules Bludsoe.
—COTTON BLOSSOM
—MAKE BELIEVE
—*OL' MAN RIVER
—CAN'T HELP LOVIN' DAT' MAN
—LIFE ON THE WICKED STAGE
—TILL GOOD LUCK COMES MY WAY
—YOU ARE LOVE
—AT THE FAIR
—WHY DO I LOVE YOU?
—IN DAHOMEY
—HEY; FELLER
—I MIGHT FALL BACK ON YOU
—BILL
Lyrics by P. G. Wodehouse.
—GOOD-BYE MY LADY LOVE
By Joe Howard.
For the revival of "Show Boat" in 1945, Jerome Kern wrote his last song:
—NOBODY ELSE BUT ME

1929. *SWEET ADELINE*
Book and lyrics by Oscar Hammerstein II, and presented by a cast headed by Helen Morgan, Irene Franklin, Charles Butterworth, Max Hoffman, Jr., Robert Chisholm, Caryl Bergman, James Thornton and George White's Girl Band.
—PLAY US A POLKA DOT
—'TWAS NOT SO LONG AGO
—MY HUSBAND'S FIRST WIFE
—HERE AM I
—FIRST MATE MARTIN
—SPRING IS HERE
—OUT OF THE BLUE
—NAUGHTY BOY
—ORIENTAL MOON
—MOLLIE O'DONAHUE
—WHY WAS I BORN?
—WINTER IN CENTRAL PARK
—THE SUN ABOUT TO RISE
—SOME GIRL ON YOUR MIND
—DON'T EVER LEAVE ME
—WE WERE SO YOUNG
—INDESTRUCTIBLE KATE
By Irene Franklin and Jerry Jarnagin.
—LONELY FEET
—SHE'S DOING IT ALL FOR THE BABY

William B. Kernell Score

1926. *HELLO, LOLA*
A musical comedy, based on Booth Tarkington's "Seventeen," with book and lyrics by Dorothy Donnelly, and presented by a cast headed by Wyn Richmond, Edythe Baker and Jay C. Flippen.
—IN THE DARK
—MY BABY TALK LADY
—SWINGING ON THE GATE
—BREAD, BUTTER AND SUGAR
—THE SUMMERTIME
—LULLABY
—MY BROTHER WILLIE
—HELLO, COUSIN LOLA
—FIVE FOOT TWO
—WATER, WATER WILDFLOWERS
—STEP ON THE GASOLINE
—THAT CERTAIN PARTY
—I KNOW SOMETHING
—LITTLE BOY BLUE
—BRAU BRAE NIGHT
—KEEP IT UP
—SOPHIE
—DON'T STOP

I. B. Kornblum Score

1921. *BLUE EYES*
A musical comedy with book by LeRoy Clemons and Leo Gordon, lyrics by Z. Meyers, and presented by a cast that included Ray Raymond, Lew Fields, Mollie King and Delyla Alda.
—BLUE EYES
—JUST SUPPOSE
—TAKE ME TO HEAVEN
—WHEN GRAMERCY SQUARE WAS UP TOWN
—WITHOUT A GIRL LIKE YOU
—IN ZE PARK
—WHEN GENTLEMEN DISAGREE
—WANTING YOU
By Irving Caesar and George Gershwin.
—BABY WALK
—DANGER AHEAD
—SO LONG JAZZ

Charles Kunneke Scores

1923. *CAROLINE*
A musical comedy with book and lyrics by Harry B. Smith, and presented by a cast that included Tessa Kosta and J. Harold Murray.
—I'M ONLY A PILGRIM
—MAN IN THE MOON
—SWEETHEART
—SHOULDER ARMS

—WILL-O'-WISP
—YOUR FORTUNE
—PAY THE PIPER
—LAND OF ROMANCE
—CAROLINE
Music by Al Goodman.
—WAY DOWN SOUTH
Music by Al Goodman.
—ARGENTINE
Music by Al Goodman.

1925. *MAYFLOWERS*
A musical comedy with book and lyrics by Clifford Grey, and starring Ivy Sawyer and Joseph Santley in a cast that included Robert Woolsey.
—SEVEN DAYS
—MAYFLOWER I LOVE YOU
By Pat Thayer, J. Fred Coots and Maurice Rubens.
—PUT YOUR TROUBLES IN A CANDY BOX
Music by J. Fred Coots.
—THE ROAD OF DREAMS
By Pat Thayer, J. Fred Coots and Maurice Rubens.
—TAKE A LITTLE WALK
Music by J. Fred Coots and Maurice Rubens.
—WHOA, EMMA
—HOW DO YOU DO, HOW DO YOU DO
—THE GRECIAN BEND
—PLAY ME A NEW TUNE
Music by Maurice Rubens and J. Fred Coots.
—FOOLISH WIVES
—OH, SAM
—THE REGIMENT LOVES THE GIRLS
—GOOD NIGHT LADIES
—WOMAN
—THE WEDDING REHEARSAL
—DOWN ON A COUNTRY FARM

Paul Lannin Score

1922. *FOR GOODNESS SAKE*
With William Daly. A musical comedy with book by Fred Jackson, lyrics by Arthur Jackson, and presented by a cast headed by Fred and Adele Astaire, John E. Hazzard, Helen Ford and Marjorie Gateson.
—OH GEE, OH GOSH, I LOVE YOU
—ALL MY LIFE
—EVERY DAY
—FRENCH PASTRY WALK
—FOR GOODNESS SAKE
—THE WHICHNESS OF THE WHATNESS

—SOMEONE
Music by George Gershwin.
—TRA-LA-LA
Music by George Gershwin.
—TWILIGHT
—ALL TO MYSELF
—HUBBY
—WHEN YOU'RE IN ROME
—THE GREATEST TEAM OF ALL
—WHEN SOMEBODY CARES
—IN THE DAYS OF WILD ROMANCE

Ring Lardner Songs

1920. *JUNE MOON*
For this comedy about Tin Pan Alley's songwriters, which was presented by a cast headed by Norman Foster, Linda Watkins, Jean Dixon, Lee Patrick, Harry Rosenthal and Florence D. Rice, Lardner and his co-librettist, George S. Kaufman, wrote the following songs:
—JUNE MOON
—MONTANA MOON

Turner Layton Scores

1920. *THREE SHOWERS*
A musical comedy with book by William Cary Duncan, lyrics by Henry Creamer, and presented by a cast that included Anna Wheaton and Paul Frawley.
—WHERE IS THE LOVE?
—THERE'S A WAY OUT
—DANCING TUMBLE-DOWN
—OPEN YOUR HEART
—IT MUST BE LOVE
—HOW WONDERFUL YOU ARE
—ONE OF THE BOYS
—LOVE ME, SWEETHEART MINE
—YOU MAY BE THE WORLD TO YOUR MOTHER
—IT'S ALWAYS THE FAULT OF THE MEN
—THE OLD LOVE IS THE TRUE LOVE
—HE RAISED EVERYBODY'S RENT BUT KATIE'S
—BABY LAMB
—I'LL HAVE MY WAY
—PUSSY FOOT
—B IS THE NOTE

1922. *STRUT MISS LIZZIE*
An all-Negro revue with lyrics by Henry Creamer and presented by a cast that included Creamer and Layton, Hamtree Harrison, Alice Brown, Cora Green and Grace Rector.
—ARGENTINA

—BEWARE OF THE CHICKENS
—BUZZ MIRANDY
—I'M NOBODY'S GIRL
—IN YAMA
—BROTHER-IN-LAW DAN
—I LOVE SWEET ANGELINE
—MANDY
—BREAKIN' THE LEG

Harold A. Levy Scores

1920. *LADY BILLY*
A musical comedy with book and lyrics by Zelda Sears, and presented by a cast headed by Mitzi, Sydney Greenstreet and Boyd Marshall.
—GOODBYE, GOODBYE
—COME TO ARCADY WITH ME
—JUST PLANT A KISS
—THE LEGEND
—LOVE COMES LIKE A BUTTERFLY
—THE TUNE THEY PLAY
—THAT'S ALL HE WANTS
—GREENWICH VILLAGE
—THE FUTURIST RAG
—THE WORM'S REVENGE
—HISTORIC HUZZIES
—IF

1922. *THE CLINGING VINE*
A musical comedy with book and lyrics by Zelda Sears, and presented by a cast headed by Peggy Wood, Irene Dunne and Nathaniel Wagner.
—A LITTLE BIT OF PAINT
—GRANDMA
—HOMEMADE HAPPINESS
—LOVE NEEDS NO SINGLE WORD
—ONCE UPON A TIME
—ROUMANIA
—LADY LUCK
—SPRING FEVER
—AGE OF INNOCENCE
—THE CLINGING VINE
—CUPID
—SERENADE

1924. *MAGNOLIA LADY*
A musical comedy with book and lyrics by Anne Caldwell, and presented by a cast headed by Ruth Chatteron, Muriel Stryker, Skeets Gallagher, Ralph Forbes and Minor Watson.
—THE FRENCH LESSON
—MOON MAN
—MY HEART'S IN THE SUNNY SOUTH
—THE OLD RED GATE
—TIGER LILY LOU
—ON THE WASHINGTON TRAIN
—THREE LITTLE GIRLS

—I WILL BE GOOD
—WHEN WHITEMAN STARTS TO PLAY
—THE MAGIC HOUR
—LIZA JANE
—WHEN THE BELL GOES TING-A-LING-LING
—A LA GASTRONOME
—PHANTOMS OF THE BALLROOM

1926. *RAINBOW ROSE*
With Owen Murphy. A musical comedy with book and lyrics by Walter DeLeon and Owen Murphy, and presented by a cast that included Jack Squire, Jack Whiting, Louise Galloway and Marguerite Walker.
—FIRST, LAST AND ONLY
—IF YOU WERE SOMEONE ELSE
—LET'S RUN AWAY AND GET MARRIED
—SOMETHING SEEMS TO TELL ME I'M IN LOVE
—RAINBOW
Lyrics by Zelda Sears.
—ALL THE TIME
With Anita Owen.
—WHEN THE HURDY GURDY PLAYS

1927. *AIN'T LOVE GRAND*
With Dave Stamper. A musical comedy with book by Gladys Unger and Cyrus Wood, lyrics by Cyrus Wood, and presented by a cast headed by Edna Leedom and Donald Brian.
—HEY, HEY
—LOVELY LADY
—AT THE BARBECUE
—BOY FRIENDS
—MAKE BELIEVE YOU'RE HAPPY
—NEW TULSA BLUES
Music by Bennie Moten.
—THE LOST STEP
—BREAKFAST IN BED
—IN FRANCE
—I WANT A GOOD TIME
—JUST SAY THE WORD

Gene Lockhart Songs

1926. *BUNK OF 1926*
A revue by Gene Lockhart and Percy Waxman, and presented by a cast that included Gene Lockhart and Carol Joyce.
—CUDDLE UP
Music by Robert Armbuster.
—THE MILKY WAY

Jimmy McHugh Scores

1928. *BLACKBIRDS OF 1928*
Book and lyrics by Dorothy Fields, and

presented by an all-Negro cast headed by Adelaide Hall, Aida Ward and Bill Robinson.

—*I CAN'T GIVE YOU ANYTHING BUT LOVE (BABY)

Dorothy Fields and Jimmy MmHugh had the score completed for "Blackbirds of 1928" except for one song. It couldn't be just an ordinary production number since the spot to be filled called for a smash tune. They racked their brains for days for an idea but drew nothing but blanks. Then one evening, while walking down Fifth Avenue, they noticed a young couple window-shopping in front of Tiffany's. It was obvious they didn't belong to the carriage trade to which Tiffany catered, but bought what jewelry they could afford at Woolworth's. As the songwriters drew nearer, they heard the young man say: "Gee, honey, I'd like to get you a sparkler like dat, but right now, I can't give you nothin' but love!"

Then and there, the team of Fields and McHugh broke all speed records in getting to a Steinway, and inside of an hour, they completed the smash song for which they had been searching.

—DIGA-DIGA-DOO
—I MUST HAVE THAT MAN
—PORGY
—HERE COMES MY BLACKBIRD
—SHUFFLE YOUR FEET AND ROLL ALONG
—DOIN' THE NEW LOW-DOWN
—BANDANNA BABIES
—DIXIE
—THE CALL OF THE SOUTH
—MAGNOLIA'S WEDDING DAY

1928. HELLO DADDY
Book by Herbert Fields, lyrics by Dorothy Fields, and starring Lew Fields in a cast that included Betty Starbuck, Mary Lawlor, Allen Kearns and George Hassell.

—THREE LITTLE MAIDS FROM SCHOOL
—I WANT PLENTY OF YOU
—FUTURISTIC RHYTHM
—LET'S SIT AND TALK ABOUT YOU
—MY LADY'S FAN
—YOUR DISPOSITION IS MINE
—IN A GREAT BIG WAY
—MAYBE MEANS YES
—AS LONG AS WE'RE IN LOVE
—OUT WHERE THE BLUES BEGIN

J. L. McManus Score
1920. IT'S UP TO YOU

A musical comedy with book by Augustine McHugh and Douglas Leavitt, lyrics by Edward Paulton and Harry Clarke, and presented by a cast that included Charles King, Betty Pierce and Ruth Mary Lockwood.

—BEE-DEEDLE-DEE-DUM-DAY
—THE ORIENTAL BLUES
—HAVANA
—FIREFLY
—EVERY TIME I SEE YOU DEAR
Music by Manuel Klein.
—I WANT A HOME
Music by Manuel Klein.
—SOMEONE CONSOLE ME
Music by Manuel Klein.

Marcus and Martin Score
1929. BAMBOOLA
Book and lyrics by D. Frank Marcus, and presented by a cast that included Billy Cortez, Brevard Burnett, Revella Hughes, Dusty Andrews and Isabel Washington.

—EVENIN'
—ACE OF SPADES
—DIXIE VAGABOND
—RUB-A-DUB YOUR RABBIT'S FOOT
—THE WAY TO DO BAMBOOLA
—SOMEBODY LIKE ME
—TAILOR-MADE BABIES
—AFRICAN WHOOPEE
—TAMPICO TUNE
—SONG OF HARLEM
—SHOUTIN' SINNERS
—ANNA
—HOT PATOOTIE WEDDING NIGHT

George Meyers Score
1924. DIXIE TO BROADWAY
With Arthur Johnston. Book by Walter DeLeon, Tom Howard, Lew Leslie and Sidney Lazarus. Lyrics by Roy Turk and Grant Clarke. Starring Florence Mills in an all-Negro cast that included Hamtree Harrison and Shelton Brooks.

—MANDY, MAKE UP YOUR MIND
—I'M A LITTLE BLACKBIRD LOOKING FOR A BLUEBIRD
—DIXIE DREAMS
—JAZZTIME CAME FROM THE SOUTH
—RED HOT HANNAH FROM SAVANNAH
—JUNGLETOWN HAS MOVED TO DIXIELAND

Joseph Meyer Scores

1925. *BIG BOY*
A musical comedy with book by Harold
Atteridge, lyrics by B. G. DeSylva, and
starring Al Jolson in a cast that included
Ralph Whitehead, Franklyn Batie, Flo
Lewis and Edythe Baker.
—*CALIFORNIA HERE I COME
—AS LONG AS I'VE GOT MY MAMMY
—BORN AND BRED IN OLD KEN-
    TUCKY
—DANCE FROM DOWN YONDER
—HELLO LUCKY
—IT ALL DEPENDS ON YOU
By B. G. DeSylva, Lew Brown and Ray
Henderson.
—MIAMI
By B. G. DeSylva, Al Jolson and Con
Conrad.
—NOBODY BUT FANNY
By B. G. DeSylva, Al Jolson and Con
Conrad.
—WHO WAS CHASING PAUL RE-
    VERE?
With Lewis Sensler.
—KEEP SMILING AT TROUBLE
By Al Jolson, B. G. DeSylva and Lewis
Gensler.
—LACKAWANNA
By B. G. DeSylva, James Hanley and Jo-
seph Meyer.

1929. *LADY FINGERS*
Book by Eddie Buzzell, lyrics by Edward
Eliscu, and presented by a cast headed by
Eddie Buzzell, John Price Jones, Louise
Brown and Ruth Gordon.
—THERE'S SOMETHING IN THAT
—ALL ABOARD
—YOU'RE PERFECT
—THE LIFE OF A NURSE
—AN OPEN BOOK
—I LOVE YOU MORE THAN YESTER-
    DAY
—SING "BOOM"
—FOLLOW MASTER
—GA-GA
—MY WEDDING
—SHAH! RISE THE DUST

Jimmy Monaco Score

1927. *HARRY DELMAR'S REVELS*
Book by William K. Wells, lyrics by Billy
Rose and Ballard MacDonald, and with
Frank Fay, Bert Lahr, Jeanne Hackett
and Patsy Kelly heading the cast.
—I LOVE A MAN IN A UNIFORM
—MY RAINBOW

—SAY IT WITH A SOLITAIRE
—IF YOU HAVE TROUBLES LAUGH
    THEM AWAY
—JIGABOO JIG
—IRRESISTIBLE YOU

Carey Morgan Score

1921. *GREENWICH VILLAGE FOLLIES
OF 1921*
Book and lyrics by John Murray Anderson
and Arthur Swanstrom, and presented by
a cast headed by Irene Franklin, Ted
Lewis, Peggy Hope and Donald Kerr.
—I'M UP IN THE AIR WITH YOU
—SNOW FLAKE
—BANG, BANG, BANG
—THE HAUNTED VIOLIN
—THE LAST WALTZ
—WHEN DREAMS COME TRUE
—DOWN THE OLD CHURCH AISLE
By Ray Perkins.
—EASIN' ALONG
By Irving Bibo and Thomas Morris.
—TOODLE-DEE-DOO
By Sidney Mitchell, Ernie Golden and Phil
Baker.
—SUNDOWN BRINGS BACK MEMO-
    RIES OF YOU
By Al Dubin, Paul Cunningham and
Charles Edmonds.
—I WANT A PICTURE OF YOU
Music by Percy Wenrich.

Will Morrissey Scores

1920. *BUZZIN' AROUND*
A musical with book and lyrics by the
composer and Edward Madden, and pre-
sented by a cast that included Elizabeth
Brice, Will Morrissey and Ernest F.
Young.
—POOR WINTER GARDEN GIRL
—BUZZIN' AROUND
—CHING-A-LING FLING
—GOOD NIGHT DEAR, DON'T BE
    LONELY
—I'LL BE JUST THE SAME
—VOULEZ-VOUS
—PIP? TOOT TOOT
—O-I-L SPELLS OIL
—EVERY NATION HAS A BROADWAY
    OF ITS OWN
—HOW COULD SHE LOVE ME LIKE
    THAT?

1923. *THE NEWCOMERS*
A musical comedy with book by the composer and Joe Burrowes, and presented by
a cast that included Frank Gaby, Al

Fields, Florence Stone and Grace Masters.
—COVERED WAGON DAYS
—DOWN ON PANGO PANGO BAY
—THE ULTRA PEACOCK STRUT
—WASHINGTON SQUARE
—WHEN I THINK OF YOU
—SUN AND RAIN
—CALIFORNIA SUNSHINE
—TEACH ME TO DANCE
—TAKE THIS LITTLE ROSEBUD
—MOTHER, ME AND THE FLAG
—FORGIVE US

Owen Murphy Score

1922. *RED PEPPER*
With Albert Gumble. A musical comedy with book by Edgar Smith and Emily Young, lyrics by Howard E. Rogers and Owen Murphy, and starring McIntyre and Heath.
—DREAMY HOLLOW
—IT MUST BE YOU
—LEVEE LAND
—SENORA
—STRUT YOUR STUFF

Richard Myers Scores

1926. *BUBBLING OVER*
A musical comedy with book by Clifford Grey, lyrics by Leo Robin, and starring Cecil Lean and Cleo Mayfield.
—BREEZIN' ALONG
—BUBBLING OVER
—CRADLE SNATCHER
—I'M A ONE-MAN GIRL
—IT'S ALL RIGHT WITH ME
—SAY IT WITH A UKE
—SHAKE ME AND WAKE ME
—SNAP-OUT-OF-IT BLUES
—TRUE TO TWO

1927. *ALLEZ-OOP*
A revue with book by J. P. McEvoy, lyrics by Leo Robin, and presented by a cast that included Charles Butterworth, Victor Moore, Charles Haskell, Bobby Watson, Alan Moran, Esther Howard, Evelyn Bennett, Madeline Fairbanks and the George Sisters.
—BLOW HOT AND HEAVY
With Phil Charig.
—RED CAP PORTER BLUES
By Eleanor Johnson and Benton Overstreet.
—WHERE HAVE YOU BEEN ALL MY LIFE?
—PULL YOURSELF TOGETHER

1928. *HELLO YOURSELF*
A musical comedy with book by Walter DeLeon, lyrics by Leo Robin, and featuring Fred Waring and his Pennsylvanians in a cast that included Lucy Monroe.
—WE MIGHT PLAY TIDDLE DE WINKS
—HELLO YOURSELF
—THE DAILY DOZEN
—TIRED OF IT ALL
—BOBBY'S NIGHTMARE
—I WANT THE WORLD TO KNOW
—SAY THAT YOU LOVE ME
—TRUE BLUE
—YOU'VE GOT A WAY WITH YOU

Alfred Nathan Score

1927. *THE MANHATTERS*
A revue with book and lyrics by Aline Erlanger and George Oppenheimer, and presented by a cast that included Raymond Knight, Mary Marsh, Eleanor Shaler and Aida Ward.
—CLOSE YOUR EYES
—NIGGER HEAVEN BLUES
—OFF TO SEE NEW YORK
—UP ON HIGH
—WHAT WE PICK UP
—LOVE'S OLD SWEET SONG
—I WANT TO SING AT TWILIGHT
—TOO BAD
—EVERY ANIMAL HAS ITS MATE
—SAILOR BOY
—MAMMY

Jacques Offenbach Score

1925. *THE LOVE SONG*
An operetta with book and lyrics by Harry B. Smith, and presented by a cast that included Allan Pryor, Evelyn Herbert and Dorothy Francis.
—DAYS GO BY
—TELL ME NOT
—LOVE WILL FIND YOU SOME DAY
Music by Ed Kunneke.
—HE WRITES A SONG
—ONLY A DREAM
—YES OR NO
—YOU WILL FORGET
Music by Ed Kunneke.
—IS IT LOVE?

Harold Orlob Scores

1923. *GINGER*
A musical comedy with book and lyrics by H. I. Phillips, and presented by a cast that included Letta Corder and Walter Douglas.

—DON'T FORGET
—TEACH ME HOW
—THAT OUGHT TO COUNT FOR
  SOMETHING
—GINGER
—LOVE'S ART
—DON'T JUDGE A GIRL BY HER
  NAME
—TAKE A CHANCE
—BEFORE YOU TAKE A MAN
—MOUNTAIN MOON
—BEWARE
—IF I EVER GET UP MY IRISH
—HE FAILED TO UNDERWRITE A
  HAPPY HOME
—MATING TIME
—PRETTY GIRL

1927. *TALK ABOUT GIRLS*
  With Stephen Jones. Book by William
  Cary Duncan and Daniel Kusell, lyrics
  by Irving Caesar, and presented by a cast
  headed by Frances Upton, Jane Taylor,
  Russell Mack and Andrew Tombes.
—A LONELY GIRL
—MAYBE I WILL
—TALK ABOUT GIRLS
—IN CENTRAL PARK
—COME TO LOWER FALLS
—THE ONLY BOY
—HOME TOWN
—HEEL AND TOE
—IN TWOS
—SEX APPEAL
—THAT'S MY MAN
—NINETEEN TWENTY-SEVEN
—ONE BOY'S ENOUGH FOR ME

Will Ortman Score

1925. *HOLKA POLKA*
  Book by Bert Kalmer and Harry Ruby,
  lyrics by Gus Kahn, and presented by a
  cast headed by Patti Harrold, Robert Hal-
  liday and Orville Harrold.
—IN A LITTLE WHILE
  Lyrics by Ray Egan.
—HOLKA POLKA
—FAIRY TALE
—WHEN LOVE IS NEAR
—THIS IS MY DANCE
—GOOD FELLOW DAYS
—CHIMES OF THE CHAPEL
—HOME OF MY HEART

Zoel Parenteau Songs

1921. *KIKI*
  In this David Belasco drama starring Lenore Ulric, these two songs were introduced in the cabaret scene.

—SOME DAY I'LL FIND YOU
  Lyrics by Schuyler Green.
—KIKI (MY WILD, WILD ROSE)
  Lyrics by Schuyler Green.

Edward Paula Score

1929. *WOOF! WOOF!*
  Book by Estelle Hunt, Sam Summers and
  Cyrus Wood, lyrics by Eddie Brandt, and
  presented by a cast that included Louise
  Brown, Eddie Nelson, Jack Squire and
  Al Sexton.
—I MEAN WHAT I SAY
—THAT CERTAIN THING
—WON'T I DO?
—I LIKE IT
—I'LL TAKE CARE OF YOU
—TREE TOP TODDLE
—YOU'RE ALL THE WORLD TO ME
—SATANIC STRUT
—A TRIP AROUND THE WORLD
—A GIRL LIKE YOU
—FAIR WEATHER
—TOPPLE DOWN
—LAY YOUR BETS

Maceo Pinkard Scores

1922. *LIZA*
  A musical comedy with book by Irvin
  C. Miller, lyrics by Nat Vincent and
  Pinkard, and presented by an all-Negro
  cast headed by Irvin C. Miller.
—I'VE GOT THOSE RUNNING WILD
  BLUES
—LIZA
—LOVE ME
—PLANNING
—MY OLD MAN
—TAG DAY
—PLEASURE
—I'M THE SHERIFF
—I'M GWINE TO TALK
—THAT BROWNSKIN FLAPPER
—JUST A BARBER SHOP CHORD
—ON THE MOONLIT SWANEE
—ESSENCE
—FORGET YOUR TROUBLES
—THE CHARLESTON DANCE
—DANDY
—MY CREOLE GIRL
—DON'T BE BLUE

1929. *PANSY*
  A musical comedy with book by Alex
  Belledna, lyrics by the composer, and pre-
  sented by an all-Negro cast headed by
  Pearl McCormick in the title role, Bessie
  Smith and the Cole Brothers.
—IT'S COMMENCEMENT DAY

—BREAKIN' THE RHYTHM
—PANSY
—CAMPUS WALK
—I'D BE HAPPY
—GETTIN' TOGETHER
—SHAKE A LEG
—IF THE BLUES DON'T GET YOU
—A STRANGER INTERLUDE
—A BOUQUET OF FOND MEMORIES

Muriel Pollock Score

1929. *PLEASURE BOUND*
A musical comedy with book by Harold
Atteridge, lyrics by Max and Nat Lief,
and presented by a cast headed by Phil
Baker, Jack Pearl, Shaw and Lee, Aileen
Stanley, Grace Brinkley and Yolanda and
Tito.
—WE LOVE TO GO TO WORK
—WHEN YOU ARE NEAR
—IN YOUR ARMS
—WE'LL GET ALONG
—TWO WISE MEN FROM THE EAST
—PEP UP
—PARISIAN FASHION PARADE
—WHY DO YOU TEASE ME?
—PARK AVENUE STRUT
By Moe Jaffe, Phil Baker and Maurice
Rubens.
—JUST SUPPOSE
By Sid Silvers, Moe Jaffe, Phil Baker and
Maurice Rubens.
—SWEET LITTLE MANNIKIN DOLL
By John Muldowney, Phil Baker and
Maurice Rubens.

Cole Porter Scores

1924. *GREENWICH VILLAGE FOLLIES
OF 1924*
Book by Irving Caesar and John Murray
Anderson, and presented by a cast headed
by the Dolly Sisters, Moran and Mack,
Bobbe Arnst and Vincent Lopez.
—SYNCOPATED PIPES OF PAN
—I'M IN LOVE AGAIN
—LIEBESTRAUM
—LET EVERY DAY BE A HOLIDAY
—BOM-BOM-BEEDLE-UM-BO
By Owen Murphy and Jay Gorney.
—WHEN EVENING SHADOWS FALL
By Owen Murphy and Jay Gorney.
—ZULU LOU
By Owen Murphy and Jay Gorney.
—THE GARDEN OF USED TO BE
By Owen Murphy and Jay Gorney.
—DO A LITTLE THIS, DO A LITTLE
THAT
By Benton Ley and Lee David.

1928. *PARIS*
With E. Ray Goetz. Book by Martin
Brown, and presented by a cast headed
by Irene Bordoni, Albert Margetson, Lou-
ise Closer Hale and Irving Aaronson's
Commanders.
—LET'S MISBEHAVE
—BABES IN THE WOOD
—DON'T LOOK AT ME THAT WAY
—VIVIENNE
—HEAVEN HOP
—LET'S DO IT (LET'S FALL IN LOVE)
—THE LAND OF GOING TO BE
By E. Ray Goetz and Walter Kollo.
—PARIS
By E. Ray Goetz and Louis Alter.

1929. *FIFTY MILLION FRENCHMEN*
Book by Herbert Fields, and presented by
a cast headed by William Gaxton, Gene-
vieve Tobin, Jack Thompson, Betty Comp-
ton and Helen Broderick.
—A TOAST TO VOLSTEAD
—YOU DO SOMETHING TO ME
—THE AMERICAN EXPRESS
—YOU'VE GOT THAT THING
—FIND ME A PRIMITIVE MAN
—WHERE WOULD YOU GET YOUR
COAT?
—DO YOU WANT TO SEE PARIS?
—AT LONGCHAMPS TODAY
—THE HEAVEN OF HARLEM
—WHY SHOULDN'T I HAVE YOU?
—IT ISN'T DONE
—TALE OF THE OYSTER
—PAREE, WHAT DID YOU DO TO
ME?
—YOU DON'T KNOW PARIS
—I'M UNLUCKY IN GAMBLING
—I WORSHIP YOU

1929. *WAKE UP AND DREAM*
Book by J. H. Turner, and starring Jack
Buchanan in a cast that included Tilly
Losch and Jessie Mathews.
—WHAT IS THIS THING CALLED
LOVE?
—SHE'S SUCH A COMFORT TO ME
By Douglas Furber, Donovan Parsons and
Arthur Schwartz.
—ONLY A SCHOOL GIRL
—FANCY OUR MEETING
By Douglas Furber, Phil Charig and Joe
Meyer.
—WHICH IS THE RIGHT LIFE?
—I'M A GIGOLO

Hugo Reisenfeld Score

1920. *BETTY BE GOOD*
A musical comedy with book and lyrics

by Harry B. Smith, and presented by a cast headed by Frank Crumit and Josephine Whittell.
—LET'S PRETEND WE'RE FREE
—WHERE SHALL WE GO?
—TELL ME, DAISY
—BETTY BE GOOD
—YOU MUST BE GOOD GIRLS
—KEEP THE LOVE LAMP BURNING
—KEEP THEM GUESSING
—'TIS IN VAIN
—LISTEN TO MY HEART BEAT
—THE END OF A PERFECT NIGHT
—I'D LIKE TO TAKE YOU AWAY
—MOONLIGHT DANCE
—TEMPTATION
—SAME OLD STARS

C. Luckyeth Roberts Scores

1923. *GO-GO*
A musical with book by Harry L. Cort and George E. Stoddard, lyrics by Alex Rogers, and presented by a cast headed by Josephine Stevens, Don Barclay and Bernard Granville.
—NEW YORK TOWN
—GOODBYE HONEY FALLS
—HAVE YOU ANY LITTLE THING
—ANY OLD TIME AT ALL
—I'M SCARED OF YOU
—ROSETIME AND YOU
—THE MAILMAN MUST BE MAD AT ME
—STRUTTING THE BLUES AWAY
—DOGGONE WHIPPOORWILL
—UNO
—STRUT
—HONEY
—A WONDERFUL DANCE
—MO'LASSES
—INDIAN MOON
—ISABEL
—LOLLY-PAPA
—ANY OLD MAN'S DARLING
—GO-GO BUG
—PAT YOUR FEET

1923. *CHARLIE*
A musical with book by Harry L. Cort and George E. Stoddard, lyrics by Alex Rogers, and presented by an all-Negro cast.
—LONESOME LONGING BLUES
—COMPLAINING

1926. *MY MAGNOLIA*
Book by Eddie Hunter, lyrics by Alex Rogers, and presented by an all-Negro cast headed by Eddie Hunter.
—MAGNOLIA
—BABY MINE

—SWEET POPOPPER
—AT YOUR SERVICE
—SHAKE YOUR DUSTER
—PAY DAY
—HARD TIMES
—SPEND IT
—JAZZLAND BALL
—LAUGH YOUR BLUES AWAY
—GALLOPIN' DOMINOES
—HEADIN' SOUTH
—MERRY CHRISTMAS
—STRUTTING TIME
—OUR CHILD
—GEE CHEE
—SUNDOWN SERENADE
—PARADE OF THE CHRISTMAS DINNER
—BABY WANTS
—THE OOF DAH MAN

Armand Robi Score

1924. *FLOSSIE*
A musical comedy with book by the composer, lyrics and additional songs by Ralph Murphey, and presented by a cast that included Doris Duncan, Alice Cavanaugh and Sydney Grant.
—THE FIRST IS LAST
—WALLA WALLA
—WHEN THINGS GO WRONG
—I WANT TO BE A SANTA CLAUS
—FLOSSIE
—I'M IN WONDERFUL
—NOW IS THE TIME
—THAT'S IN MY LINE
—POOGIE-WOO
—'FRAID CAT
Music by Harold Lewis.
—BLIND MAN'S BUFF
—JUST ANOTHER NEW STEP
Music by Harold Lewis.
—THE BATTLE CRY OF FREEDOM

J. Russell Robinson Score

1922. *PLANTATION REVUE*
Book by Lew Leslie, lyrics by Roy Turk, and starring Florence Mills in a cast that included Shelton Brooks, Chappy Chappelle and Will Vodery's band.
—HAWAIIAN NIGHT IN DIXIELAND
—BUGLE CALL BLUES
—OLD BLACK JOE
—ROBERT E. LEE
—SWANEE RIVER
—I WANT TO BE VAMPED IN GEORGIA
—GYPSY BLUES
—SOUTHLAND

—MANDY
—MINSTRELS ON PARADE
—YOU'VE STILL GOT THAT THRILL
—PANGO PANGO
—HE USED TO BE YOUR MAN BUT
HE'S MY MAN NOW
By Robert Kelley.

Richard Rodgers Scores

1925. *GARRICK GAIETIES*
Lyrics by Lorenz Hart, and presented by a cast that included Sterling Holloway, Romney Brent, Betty Starbuck, Elizabeth Holman and Philip Loeb, with Richard Rodgers directing the orchestra.
—ROMANTIC YOU AND SENTIMENTAL ME
—MANHATTAN
—DO YOU LOVE ME?
—ON WITH THE DANCE
—GILDING THE GUILD

1925. *DEAREST ENEMY*
Book by Herbert Fields, lyrics by Lorenz Hart, and co-starring Helen Hart and Charles Purcell.
—HEIGH-HO, LACKADAY
—WAR IS WAR
—I BEG YOUR PARDON
—CHEERIO
—BYE AND BYE
—HERE IN MY ARMS
—FULL BLOWN ROSES
—THE HERMITS
—I'D LIKE TO HIDE IT
—WHERE THE HUDSON RIVER FLOWS
—OLD ENOUGH TO LOVE
—SWEET PETER
—HERE'S A KISS

1926. *GARRICK GAIETIES*
Lyrics by Lorenz Hart, and presented by a cast that included Philip Loeb, Sterling Holloway, Bobbie Perkins, Jack Edwards, Betty Starbuck and Lester Cole.
—MOUNTAIN GREENERY
—GIGOLO
—WHAT'S THE USE OF TALKING?
—ALLEZ-UP

1926. *THE GIRL FRIEND*
Book by Herbert Fields, lyrics by Lorenz Hart, and co-starring Eva Puck and Sam White.
—HEY, HEY
—THE SIMPLE LIFE
—THE GIRL FRIEND
—GOOD-BYE LENNY
—THE BLUE ROOM

—CABARETS
—WHY DO I?
—THE DAMSEL THAT DONE ALL THE DIRT
—HE'S A WINNER
—TOWN HALL TONIGHT
—GOOD FELLOW MINE
—SLEEPYHEAD (CREOLE CROONING SONG)
—I'D LIKE TO TAKE YOU HOME
—WHAT IS IT?

1926. *PEGGY-ANN*
Book by Herbert Fields, lyrics by Lorenz Hart, and presented by a cast headed by Helen Ford, Lulu McConnell, Betty Starbuck and Lester Cole.
—HELLO
—A TREE IN THE PARK
—HOWDY, BROADWAY
—A LITTLE BIRDIE TOLD ME
—CHARMING, CHARMING
—WHERE'S THAT RAINBOW THEY TALK ABOUT?
—IN HIS ARMS
—CHUCK IT
—HAVANA
—MAYBE IT'S ME
—GIVE THIS LITTLE GIRL A HAND

1926. *BETSY*
Book by Irving Caesar and David Freedman, lyrics by Lorenz Hart, and starring Belle Baker in a cast that included Al Shean, Jimmy Hussey, Dan Healy, Bobbie Perkins, Evelyn Law, Allen Kearns and Borrah Minnevitch and His Harmonica Rascals.
—THE KITZEL ENGAGEMENT
—MY MISSUS
—STONEWALL MOSKOWITZ MARCH
—ONE OF US SHOULD BE TWO
—SING
—IN OUR PARLOR ON THE THIRD FLOOR BACK
—THIS FUNNY WORLD
—FOLLOW ON
—CRADLE OF THE DEEP
—IF I WERE YOU
—LEAVE IT TO LEVY
—BIRDS ON HIGH
—SHUFFLE
—BLUE SKIES
Words and music by Irving Berlin, and introduced for the first time by Belle Baker in this production.
—TALES OF HOFFMAN
By Irving Caesar and Al Segal.

1927. *A CONNECTICUT YANKEE*
Book by Herbert Fields, lyrics by Lorenz

Hart, and presented by a cast headed by William Gaxton, William Norris, Nana Bryant and Constance Carpenter.
—A LADY'S HOME COMPANION
—MY HEART STOOD STILL
Written after a wild taxi ride through the streets of Paris, and inspired by the remark of a girl companion who exclaimed as the cab took off: "Gee, my heart stood still!"
—THOU SWELL
—ON A DESERT ISLE WITH THEE
—NOTHING'S WRONG
—I FEEL AT HOME WITH YOU
—EVELYN, WHAT DO YOU SAY?

1928. *PRESENT ARMS*
Book by Herbert Fields, lyrics by Lorenz Hart, and starring Charles King in a cast that included Florence LeBreton and Joyce Barbour.
—TELL IT TO THE MARINES
—YOU TOOK ADVANTAGE OF ME
This was the favorite song of the Prince of Wales while he was courting Wallie Simpson. One night in a London night club he asked Morton Downey to sing it nine times. In the light of subsequent events, culminating in his relinquishment of the British throne for "the woman I love," the title was truly prophetic.
—DID I HEAR YOU SAYING "I LOVE YOU?"
—A KISS FOR CINDERELLA
—IS IT THE UNIFORM?
—CRAZY ELBOWS
—DOWN BY THE SEA
—I'M A FOOL FOR YOU
—BLUE OCEAN BLUES
—HAWAII
—KOHALA WELCOME

1928. *SHE'S MY BABY*
Book by Bert Kalmer and Harry Ruby, lyrics by Lorenz Hart, and starring Beatrice Lillie in a cast that included Irene Dunne, Clifton Webb and Jack Whiting.
—THIS GOES UP
—MY LUCKY STAR
—YOU'RE WHAT I NEED
—TRY AGAIN TOMORROW
—HERE SHE COMES
—THE SWALLOWS
—WHEN I GO UPON THE STAGE
—SMART PEOPLE
—CAMERA SHOT
—WHERE CAN THE BABY BE?
—A LITTLE HOUSE IN SOHO
—A BABY'S BEST FRIEND
—IF I WERE YOU

—I NEED SOME COOLING OFF

1928. *CHEE-CHEE*
Book by Herbert Fields, lyrics by Lorenz Hart, and presented by a cast headed by Betty Starbuck, Helen Ford, George Hassell and William Williams.
—I MUST LOVE YOU
—DEAR, OH DEAR
—MOON OF MY DELIGHT
—BETTER BE GOOD TO ME
—THE TARTAR SONG
—SINGING A LOVE SONG

1929. *SPRING IS HERE*
Book by Owen Davis, lyrics by Lorenz Hart, and starring Lillian Taiz in a cast that included Glenn Hunter and Charles Ruggles.
—SPRING IS HERE
—YOURS SINCERELY
—YOU NEVER SAY YES
—WITH A SONG IN MY HEART
—BABY'S AWAKE NOW
—RED HOT TRUMPET
—WHAT A GIRL
—RICH MAN, POOR MAN
—WHY CAN'T I?

1929. *HEADS UP*
Book by John McGowan and Paul Gerard Smith, lyrics by Lorenz Hart, and presented by a cast headed by Barbara Newberry, Janet Velie, Jack Whiting, Victor Moore and Ray Bolger.
—YOU'VE GOT TO SURRENDER
—PLAY BOY
—MOTHER GROWS YOUNGER
—WHY DO YOU SUPPOSE?
—ME FOR YOU (MOLLY AND JERRY)
—ONGSAY AND ANCEDAY
—IT MUST BE HEAVEN
—MY MAN IS ON THE MAKE
—THE LASS WHO LOVED A SAILOR
—A SHIP WITHOUT A SAIL
—KNEES

Sigmund Romberg Scores

1920. *THE MAGIC MELODY*
Book and lyrics by Frederic Arnold Kummer, and starring Charles Purcell and Fay Marbe.
—TWO IS COMPANY, THREE'S A CROWD
—LIPS, LIPS, LIPS
—LOVE MAKES THE WORLD GO ROUND
—DREAM GIRL GIVE BACK MY DREAMS TO ME
—ONCE UPON A TIME

—THE MELODY OF THE DANCE
—DOWN BY THE NILE
—GIANIA
—THE LITTLE CHURCH AROUND
THE CORNER
—I AM THE PASHA
—NIGHT OF LOVE
—WE ARE THE FIXERS
—WE TAKE IT, JUST TAKE IT FROM
YOU

1920. *POOR LITTLE RITZ GIRL*
With Richard Rodgers. Book by Herbert
Fields, lyrics by Lorenz Hart, and present-
ed by a cast headed by Lulu McConnell,
Charles Purcell, Florence Webber and
Andrew Tombes.
—POOR LITTLE RITZ GIRL
—PRETTY MING TOY
—I LOVE TO SAY HELLO
—WHEN I FOUND YOU
—MY VIOLIN
—IN THE LAND OF YESTERDAY
—THE PHANTOM WALTZ
—THE BOMBAY BOMBASHAY
Richard Rodgers is credited with the fol-
lowing songs in this production:
—MARY QUEEN OF SCOTS
—LOVE WILL CALL
—YOU CAN'T FOOL YOUR HEART
—WHAT HAPPENED NOBODY KNOWS
—ALL YOU NEED TO BE A STAR
—LOVE IS INTENSE IN TENTS
—THE DAISY AND THE LARK

1921. *LOVE BIRDS*
Book and lyrics by Edgar Allen Woolf
and Ballard MacDonald, and starring
Marion Bent and Pat Rooney in a cast
that included Elizabeth Murray, Elizabeth
Hines, Tom Dingle and Vincent Lopez.
—LET'S PRETEND
—A GIRL LIKE GRANDMA
—I LOVE TO GO SWIMMIN' WITH
WIMMIN'
—FAT, FAT FATIMA
—A LITTLE DREAM THAT LOST ITS
WAY
—IS IT SO HARD TO GUESS?
—WHEN THE CAT'S AWAY
—TROUSSEAU INCOMPLETE
—IN BOKARA MISS O'HARA
—CAN MACY DO WITHOUT ME?
—TWO LITTLE LOVE BIRDS
—LOVE WILL ALWAYS FIND A WAY
—CARNIVAL NIGHT

1921. *BOMBO*
Book and lyrics by Harold Atteridge, and
starring Al Jolson in a cast that included
Janet Adair and Forrest Huff.

—LIFE IS A GAMBLE
—ANY PLACE WITH YOU
—IN THE LAND OF THERE
—JIMMY VALENTINE AND SHER-
LOCK HOLMES
—GINNY GINNY SHORE
—THE GLOBE TROT
—THE NEXT GIRL I SEE
—IN OLD GRANADA
—JAZZA-DA-DADA
—NO ONE LOVES A CLOWN
—ROSE OF SPAIN
—I'M GLAD I'M SPANISH
—IN A CURIO SHOP
—WAIT UNTIL MY SHIP COMES IN
—MY GUIDING STAR
—A GIRL HAS A SAILOR IN EVERY
PORT
—BYLO BAY
—THROUGH THE MIST
—WETONA
—THREE LITTLE VAMPIRES
—THE LAST DANCE? THAT'S OUT
—MORNING WILL COME
Music by Con Conrad.
—DON'T CRY SWANEE
Music by Con Conrad.
—DON'T SEND YOUR WIFE TO THE
COUNTRY
Music by Con Conrad.
—THAT BARBER IN SEVILLE
Music by Con Conrad.
—OH, HOW SHE CAN DANCE
By Cliff Friend.
—SOME BEAUTIFUL MORNING
By Cliff Friend.
—LET THE LITTLE JOY BELLS RING
By Cliff Friend.

1921. *BLOSSOM TIME*
An operetta with book and lyrics by
Dorothy Donnelly based upon the life
and music of Franz Schubert with Olga
Cook as Mitzi, Bertram Peacock as Franz
Schubert and Howard Marsh as Franz.
—MELODY TRISTE
—THREE LITTLE MAIDS
—THE SERENADE
—(THIS IS MY) SONG OF LOVE
Based on Schubert's "Unfinished Sym-
phony."
—MY SPRINGTIME THOU ART
—LOVE IS A RIDDLE
—LET ME AWAKE
—TELL ME DAISY
—ONLY ONE LOVE EVER FILLS THE
HEART
—ONCE TO EVERY HEART
—LONELY HEARTS (PEACE TO MY
LONELY HEART)

1922. *THE ROSE OF STAMBOUL*
   With Leo Fall. Book and lyrics by Harold
Atteridge, and starring Tessa Kosta in a
cast that included Marion Greene and
James Barton.
—THE LADIES FROM THE CULTUR-
ED WEST
—MY HEART IS CALLING
—LOVEY DOVE
—A BLUE BOOK OF GIRLS
—ROSE OF STAMBOUL
—DING-A-LING
—WITH PAPERS DULY SIGNED
—WHY DO THEY DIE AT THE END
OF A CLASSICAL DANCE?
—THE LOVE TEST
—MAZUMA

1922. *THE BLUSHING BRIDE*
   Book and lyrics by Cyrus Wood, and star-
ring Cecil Lean and Cleo Mayfield.
—BAD LITTLE BOY AND GOOD
LITTLE GIRL
—LOVE'S HIGHWAY
—GOOD-BYE, ROSY-POSY
—JUST A REGULAR GIRL
—MISTER AND MISSUS
—SPRINGTIME IS THE TIME FOR
LOVING

1922. *SPRINGTIME OF YOUTH*
   With Walter Kollo. Book and lyrics by
Mathew C. Woodward and Cyrus Wood,
and presented by a cast that included
Grace Hamilton, Olga Steck, J. Harold
Murray and George MacFarlane.
—LOVE WHILE YOU MAY
—LOVE FINDS A WAY
—A SAILOR'S BRIDE
—STARLIGHT OF HOPE
—SI, SI, SENOR
—JUST LIKE A DOLL
—BUT IN BRAZIL
—YOUTH IN SPRING
—OUR BUSY NEEDLES FLY
—WON'T YOU TAKE ME TO PARIS
—SOMEWHERE IN LOVE'S GARDEN
   Walter Kollo is credited with the follow-
ing songs:
—I KNEW 'TWOULD BE SO
—BEST OF FRIENDS

1923. *THE PASSING SHOW OF 1923*
   With Jean Schwartz. Book and lyrics by
Harold Atteridge, and presented by a
cast that included George Hassell, Walter
Woolf, Roy Cummings, George Jessel,
Helen Shipman, Phil Baker, Nat Nazzaro
Jr., and Alex Morrison, who was then the
champion trick shot maker of golf.
—KISSABLE LIPS
—MY GABY DOLL

—GO INTO YOUR DANCE
—THE LIFE OF A ROSE
—BEAUTIFUL AND DAMNED
—GOLFING BLUES
—MY DUTCH LADY
—YOUR OTHER SIDE
—MY LITTLE LOTUS FLOWER
—AUX ARMES
—MY RAINBOW
—BIRDS OF PLUMAGE
—STEP ON IT

1923. *THE DANCING GIRL*
   With George Gershwin. Book and lyrics
by Harold Atteridge and Irving Caesar,
and starring Trini in a cast that included
Marie Dressler, Cyril Scott, Ted and Kitty
Doner, Nat Nazzaro Jr., and Jack Pearl.
—LUCKY IN LOVE
—ANY LITTLE GIRL WILL FALL
—HAIL U. S. A.
—WHAT HAVE YOU TO DECLARE?
—THE BOWERY OF TODAY
—MY LOVE BOUQUET
—I'M A DEVIL WITH THE LADIES
—I'VE BEEN WANTING YOU
—VERSAILLES
—THAT ROMANCE OF MINE
—PLAY ME A TUNE
—VENETIAN
   George Gershwin is credited with the
following songs in this production:
—THAT AMERICAN BOY OF MINE
—CUDDLE ME AS WE DANCE
—WHY AM I SAD?
—PANGO PANGO

1924.*INNOCENT EYES*
   With Jean Schwartz. Book by Harold At-
teridge and lyrics by Harold Atteridge
and Tot Seymour. Mistinguette, the dar-
ling of Paris, made her American pre-
miere in this production in a cast that
included Cleo Mayfield, Cecil Lean, Lew
Hearn and Ted Doner.
—I'M FOR YOU
—LA JAVA
—I'M FED UP
—ON THE Q. T.
—ON BROADWAY
—ORGANDY DAYS
—GARDEN OF LOVE

1924. *MARJORIE*
   With Herbert Stothart. Book by Fred
Thompson and Clifford Grey, lyrics by
Harold Atteridge, and presented by a
cast headed by Jack Squires, Skeets Gal-
lagher, Elizabeth Hines and Ethel Shutta.
—LISTENING TO THE RADIO
—BRINDLE'S FARM
—SONG OF LOVE

—HAPPY ENDING
—GOOD THINGS AND BAD THINGS
—TWILIGHT ROSE
—GO AWAY GIRLS GO AWAY
—LEADING MAN
—NATURE
—SUPER SHEIK
—WHAT DO YOU SAY?
—SHUFFLE YOUR TROUBLES AWAY

1924. *THE PASSING SHOW OF 1924*
With Jean Schwartz. Book and lyrics by Harold Atteridge, and presented by a cast that included James Barton, George Hassel, Allen Tryor, Jack Rose, Harry Mc-Naughton, Lulu McConnell and Olga Cook.
—JOY AND GLOOM
—GOLD, SILVER AND GREEN
—EVERYBODY DANCE
—WHEN KNIGHTHOOD WAS IN FLOWER
—DUBINOLA
—NOTHING NAUGHTIE IN A NIGHTIE
—SOCIETY BLUES

1924. *ANNIE DEAR*
With Clare Kummer, who also wrote the book and lyrics, and starring Billie Burke in a cast that included Ernest Truex, Marion Green and Bobby Watson.
—TWILLY OF FIFTH AVENUE
—THE ONLY GIRL
—ONE MAN IS LIKE ANOTHER
—WHISPER TO ME
—LOUWANNA
—SOMEONE, SOMEWHERE, SOME-DAY
—BERTIE
—PLAY FOR THE LOVE OF THE PLAY
By Joseph McCarthy and Harry Tierney. Clare Kummer is credited with the following numbers:
—ANNIE DEAR
—COME TO MY PARTY
—OFF TO WIMBLEMERE
—IN LOVE AGAIN
—HELP, HELP, HELP
—GYPSY BRIDE

1924. *ARTISTS AND MODELS*
With J. Fred Coots. Book by Harry Wagstaff Gribble, lyrics by Sam Coslow and Clifford Grey, and starring Trini in a cast that included Frank Gaby and Mabel Wither.
—WHAT A VILLAGE GIRL SHOULD KNOW
—TOMORROW'S ANOTHER DAY
—ALWAYS THE SAME

—WHAT A BEAUTIFUL FACE WILL DO
—OFF TO GREENWICH VILLAGE
—I LOVE TO DANCE WHEN I HEAR A MARCH
—PULL YOUR STRINGS
—SHOES
—MODEL DODDLE
—WHO'S THE LUCKY FELLOW?
—DANCING COLORS
—BEHIND MY LADY'S FAN
—MEDITERRANEAN NIGHTS
—RIVIERA ROSE

1924. *THE STUDENT PRINCE*
Book and lyrics by Dorothy Donnelly, and presented by a cast headed by Howard Marsh, Ilsa Marvenga, George Hassell and Roberta Beatty.
—BY OUR BEARING SO SEDATE
—GOLDEN DAYS
—TO THE INN WE'RE MARCHING
—DRINKING SONG
—WELCOME TO HEIDELBERG
—DEEP IN MY HEART, DEAR
—SERENADE
—I'VE NEVER HEARD ABOUT LOVE
—STUDENT LIFE
—JUST WE TWO
—WHAT MEMORIES
—SING A LITTLE SONG
—COME BOYS, BE GAY, BOYS
—BIRDS ARE WINGING
—COME ANSWER TO OUR CALL
—THE FLAG THAT FLIES ABOVE US

1925. *LOUIS THE 14TH*
Book and lyrics by Arthur Wimperis, and starring Leon Errol in a cast that included Ethel Shutta and Evelyn Law.
—MARKET DAY
—WAYSIDE FLOWER
—REGIMENTAL BAND
—TAKING A WIFE
—THE LITTLE BLUE PIG
—PEP
—RIN-TIN-TIN
—THE MAJOR DOMO
—FOLLOW THE RAJAH
—I'M HAROLD, I'M HAROLD
—MOON FLOWER
—VAMP YOUR MAN
—EDELWEISS
—HOMELAND
—MY LITTLE PEACH
—MY FIRST LOVE LETTER
—SWEETHEART OF MINE
—TRUE HEARTS

1925. *PRINCESS FLAVIA*
An operetta based on "The Prisoner of Zenda" with book and lyrics by Harry B.

Smith and starring Evelyn Herbert in a cast that included Henry Welchman.
—YES OR NO
—ON COMRADES
—MARIONETTES
—WHAT CARE I?
—CONVENT BELLS ARE RINGING
—I DARE NOT LOVE YOU
—BY THIS TOKEN
—DANCE WITH ME
—TWILIGHT VOICES
—ONLY ONE
—I LOVE THEM ALL
—IN RURITANA

1926. *THE DESERT SONG*
Book and lyrics by Otto Harbach, Frank Mandel and Oscar Hammerstein II, and co-starring Vivienne Segal and Robert Halliday in a cast that included Eddie Buzzell.
—SONG OF THE RIFFS
—MARGOT
—I'LL BE A BOUYANT GIRL
—FRENCH MARCHING SONG
—WHY DID WE MARRY SOLDIERS?
—ROMANCE
—THEN YOU WILL KNOW
—I WANT A KISS
—IT
—DESERT SONG
—SONG OF THE BRASS KEY
—ONE GOOD MAN GONE WRONG
—LET LOVE GO
—ONE FLOWER GROWS ALONE IN YOUR GARDEN
—ONE ALONE

1927. *CHERRY BLOSSOMS*
Book and lyrics by Harry B. Smith, and co-starring Desiree Ellinger and Howard Marsh.
—I'LL PEEK-A-BOO YOU
—IF YOU THINK WHAT I THINK
—FEAST OF THE LANTERNS
—HAPPY RICKSHAW MAN
—I WANT TO BE THERE
—ROMANCE
—I'VE WAITED FOR YOU
—MY OWN WILLOW TREE
—SOME DAY
—TELL ME CIGARETTE
—WAIT AND SEE
—'NEATH THE CHERRY BLOSSOM MOON

1927. *MY MARYLAND*
Book and lyrics by Dorothy Donnelly, and starring Evelyn Herbert and Nathaniel Wagner.
—STROLLING WITH THE ONE I

LOVE THE BEST
—MISTER CUPID
—WON'T YOU MARRY ME?
—YOUR LAND AND MY LAND
—THE SAME SILVER MOON
—THE MOCKING BIRD
—STRAWBERRY JAM
—MEXICO
—SOMETHING OLD, SOMETHING NEW
—OLD JOHN BARLEYCORN
—SONG OF VICTORY
—KER-CHOO
—MOTHER
—BOYS IN GRAY
—THE BONNIE BLUE FLAG
—HAIL STONEWALL JACKSON

1927. *MY PRINCESS*
Book and lyrics by Dorothy Donnelly, and presented by a cast headed by Hope Hampton, Leonard Creeley and Donald Meek.
—GIGOLO
—I WONDER WHY?
—FOLLOW THE SUN TO THE SOUTH
—WHEN I WAS A GIRL LIKE YOU
—HERE'S HOW
—DEAR GIRLS, GOOD-BYE
—EVIVA
—OUR BRIDAL NIGHT
—MY PASSION FLOWER

1927. *THE LOVE CALL*
A musical version of the play, "Arizona," with book by Edward Locke, lyrics by Harry B. Smith, and presented by a cast headed by Berna Dean, John Barker and Volez and Volanda.
—TONY, TONY, TONY
—WHEN I TAKE YOU ALL TO LONDON
—BONITA
—EYES THAT LOVE
—GOOD PALS
—I LIVE I DIE FOR YOU
—THIS LOVE
—IF THAT'S WHAT YOU WANT
—THE RANGER'S SONG
—THE LARK
—I AM CAPTURED
—HEAR THE TRUMPET CALL
—YOU APPEAL TO ME
—FIESTA
—SPANISH LOVE
—MY LITTLE NEST OF HEAVENLY BLUE
By Sigmund Spaeth and Franz Lehar.

1928. *ROSALIE*
With George Gershwin. Book by William Anthony McGuire, lyrics by Ira Gersh-

win and P. G. Wodehouse, and presented
by a cast headed by Marilyn Miller,
Gladys Glad, Bobbe Arnst, Frank Mor-
gan and Jack Donahue.
—HERE THEY ARE
—ENTRANCE OF THE HUSSARS
—HUSSAR MARCH
—THE KING CAN DO NO WRONG
—WEST POINT BUGLE
—WEST POINT MARCH
—KINGDOM OF DREAMS
—EVERYBODY KNOWS I LOVE SOME-
BODY
—FOLLOW THE DRUMS
George Gershwin contributed the follow-
ing songs to this production:
—SHOW ME THE TOWN
—SAY SO
—LET ME BE A FRIEND TO YOU
—OH GEE, OH JOY
—NEW YORK SERENADE
—HOW LONG HAS THIS BEEN GOING
ON?
—YANKEE DOODLE RHYTHM
1928. *THE NEW MOON*
Book and lyrics by Lawrence Schwab,
Frank Mandel and Oscar Hammerstein
II, and starring Evelyn Herbert and
Robert Halliday.
—MARIANNE
—THE GIRL ON THE PROW
—GORGEOUS ALEXANDER
—TAVERN SONG
—SOFTLY AS IN A MORNING SUN-
RISE
—STOUT-HEARTED MEN
—ONE KISS
—WANTING YOU
—FUNNY LITTLE SAILOR MAN
—LOVE IS QUITE A SIMPLE THING
—TRY HER OUT AT DANCING
—LOVER COME BACK TO ME

G. Romilli Score

1929. *FIORETTA*
A musical comedy with book by Earl
Carroll and Charlton Andrews, lyrics by
the composer, and presented by a cast
headed by Dorothy Knapp, Leon Errol,
Fanny Brice, Jay Brennan, Lionel Atwill
and George Houston.
—PIERROT AND PIERRETTE
—ALONE WITH YOU
—CARNIVAL OF VENICE
—CORONATION OF THE QUEEN
—WICKED OLD VILLAGE OF VENICE
—WEDDING OF FIORETTA
—CHANT OF THE MONKS

—IN MY GONDOLA
—MY HEART BELONGS TO YOU
—ROSES OF RED
—FIORETTA
—BLADE OF MINE
By Grace Henry and George Bagby.
—CARISSIMA
Lyrics by Grace Henry.
—DREAM BOAT
By Grace Henry, Jo Trent and George
Bagby.

Leon Rosebrook Score

1920.*SILKS AND SATINS*
A musical comedy with book by Thomas
Duggan, lyrics by Louis Weslyn, and pre-
sented by a cast headed by Thomas Dug-
gan, Jay Regan, Aileen Stanley and Wil-
liam Rock.
—AROUND THE TOWN
—MIDSUMMER MAIDEN
—MY ROSE OF MEMORY
—NANKING BLUES
—STEP ALONG WITM ME
—SUNDAY'S CHILD
—WAS MRS. MACBETH REALLY
SLEEPING WHEN SHE TOOK
THAT FAMOUS WALK?
—I WANT TO BE SOMEBODY'S BABY
By Jesse Greer and Ed Smalle.
—THIS IS THE END OF ME NOW
—By Ray Egan and Henry I. Marshall.
—I'M JUST A SENTRY
By Arthur Freed and Oliver G. Wallace.
—THAT COLORED JAZZBORAY
By Arthur Freed and Oliver G. Wallace.

Walter Rosemont Score

1923. *BATTLING BUTTLER*
A musical comedy with book and lyrics
by Ballard MacDonald, and presented by
a cast headed by Charles Ruggles, Wil-
liam Kent, Marie Saxon, Jack Squire and
Francis Halliday.
—IF EVERY DAY WAS SUNDAY
—APPLES, BANANAS AND YOU
—TWO LITTLE PALS
—WILL YOU MARRY ME?
—TINKLE TUNE
—YOU'RE SO SWEET
Music by Joseph Meyer.
—AS WE LEAVE THE YEARS BEHIND
Music by Joseph Meyer.
—IN THE SPRING
Music by Adorjan Otvos.
—DANCING HONEYMOON
By Philip Braham.

Charles Rosoff Score

1927. *JUDY*
A musical comedy with book by Mark Swan, lyrics by Leo Robin, and presented by a cast headed by Queenie Smith and Charles Purcell.
—JUDY, WHO D'YA LOVE?
—PRETTY LITTLE STRANGER
—START STOMPIN'
—WEAR YOUR SUNDAY SMILE
—POOR CINDERELLA
—HOBOHEMIA
—HARD TO GET ALONG WITH
—LOOKING FOR A THRILL
—WHAT A WHALE OF A DIFFERENCE A WOMAN CAN MAKE
—WHEN GENTLEMEN GREW WHISKERS AND LADIES GREW OLD
—SIX LITTLE CINDERELLAS
—CURFEW SHALL NOT RING TONIGHT

Maurice Rubens Scores

1926. *GREAT TEMPTATIONS*
A revue with book by Harold Atteridge, lyrics by Clifford Grey, and presented by a cast that included Hazel Dawn, Miller and Lyles, Florenz Ames, Jay C. Flippen and Jack Benny, who made his Broadway debut in this production.
—BEAUTY IS VANITY
—TEMPTATION STRUT
—LOVE BIRDS
Music by Kenneth Burton.
—WHITE ROSE, RED ROSE
Music by R. Moretti.
—VALENCIA
Music by Jose Padilla.
—THE ATLANTIC CITY GIRL
—NEVER SAY THE WORLD WAS MEANT TO CRY
—ANY STEP
—THE SPIDER WEB
—THE SESQUECENTENIAL BABY
—THE GUARDS OF FANTASY
—QUERIDA
—THE GARDEN OF MEMORIES
—DANCING TOWN
—THE CHEVALIER OF THE HIGHWAY

1928. *THE MADCAP*
A musical comedy with book by Gertrude Purcell and Gladys Unger, lyrics by Clifford Grey, and presented by a cast headed by Mitzi, Harry Puck and Arthur Treacher.
—STOP! GO!

—BUY YOUR WAY
—OLD ENOUGH TO MARRY
—I WANT TO TELL A STORY
—WHAT HAS MADE THE MOVIES?
—HONEYMOON BLUES
—WHY CAN'T IT HAPPEN TO ME?
—ODLE-DE-O DO, "I DO"
—ME, THE MOONLIGHT AND ME
—BIRDIES
—MY BEST PAL
—STEP-TO-PARIS BLUES

1928. *GREENWICH VILLAGE FOLLIES OF 1928.*
Book by Harold Atteridge, lyrics by Nat and Max Lief, and presented by a cast headed by Doc Rockwell, Jans and Whalen, Bobby Watson, Grace LaRue, Shiela Barrett, Benny Fields and Blossom Seeley.
—DOWN AT THE VILLAGE
—PADLOCK YOUR BLUES
—GOLDEN GATE
—LITTLE BOY'S BLUE
—SLAVES OF BROADWAY
—HIGH, HIGH UP IN THE CLOUDS
—DIRTY DIG
—GET YOUR MAN
Music by Ray Perkins.
—WHO'S THE BOY?
Music by Ray Perkins.
—THE SUBWAY SUN
Music by Ray Perkins.
—WHAT'S THE REASON?
—BROOKLYN HEIGHTS
Music by Ray Perkins.

1929. *MUSIC IN MAY*
With Emil Berte. A musical comedy with book by Fanny Todd Mitchell, lyrics by Keirn Brennan, and presented by a cast headed by Gertrude Lang, Greek Evans and Bartlett Simmons.
—EVERY MONTH IS MAY
—I'M IN LOVE
—UNTO MY HEART
—GLORY OF SPRING
—HIGH, HIGH, HIGH
—I FOUND A FRIEND
—I'D LIKE TO LOVE THEM ALL
—LIPS THAT LAUGH AT LOVE
—NO OTHER LOVE WAS MEANT FOR ME
—THERE'S LOVE IN THE HEART I HOLD

1929. *A NIGHT IN VENICE*
With Lee Davis, A musical comedy with book and lyrics by J. Keirn Brennan and Moe Jaffe, and presented by a cast headed by Ted Healy, Laura Lee and the Dodge Sisters.
—I'M FOR YOU, YOU'RE FOR ME

—ONE NIGHT OF LOVE
—SLIDING DOWN A SILVER CLOUD
—LOOSE ANKLES
—CELLINI'S PLATE
—THE ONE GIRL
  Music by Vincent Youmans.
—LIDO SHORES
—THE STORK DON'T COME AROUND
  NO MORE
—THE LEGEND OF LEDA
—TONDELAYO
—THE "IT" IN ITALY
—THE MISTINGUETTE FAN
—LITTLE OLD DREAMY NEW YORK

1929. *BROADWAY NIGHTS*
  With Sammy Timberg and Lee Davis. *A*
  revue with book by Edgar Smith, lyrics
  by Moe Jaffe and J. Keirn Brennan, and
  presented by a cast headed by Doc Rock-
  well, Frank Gabby, Odette Myrtil and
  Laura Lee.
—BABY DOLL DANCE
—WHY DON'T WE?
—THE RIGHT MAN
—YOUR BROADWAY AND MINE
—STRANDED IN A ONE-HORSE TOWN
—HEART OF A ROSE
—ARABIAN NIGHTS
—LOBSTER CRAWL
—COME HIT YOUR BABY

Harry Ruby Scores

1923. *HELEN OF TROY, NEW YORK*
  Book by Marc Connelly and George Kauf-
  man, lyrics by Bert Kalmar, and presented
  by a cast that included Roy Atwell, Tom
  Lewis, Paul Frawley, Helen Ford and
  Queenie Smith.
—UP ON YOUR TOES
—CRY BABY
—HELEN OF TROY, NEW YORK
—I LIKE A BIG TOWN
—HAPPY ENDING
—WHAT THE GIRLS WILL WEAR
—WHAT MAKES A BUSINESS MAN
  TIRED
—ADVERTISING
—IF I NEVER SEE YOU AGAIN
—NIJIGO NOVGO GLIDE
—IT WAS MEANT TO BE
—A LITTLE BIT OF JAZZ

1924. *NO OTHER GIRL*
  Book by Aaron Hoffman, lyrics by Bert
  Kalmar, and starring Helen Ford and
  Eddie Buzzell.
—A PLEASANT GREETING
—MOLLY
—THE BEST IN THE TRADE

—AFTER THE CURFEW RINGS
—NO OTHER GIRL
—DOING THE TOWN
—KEEP THE PARTY GOING
—I KNOW THAT I LOVE YOU
—HONDURAS
—THE CORNER OF MY MIND
—IT'S THE DANCER YOU LOVE
—I WOULD RATHER DANCE A WALTZ
—LOOK OUT FOR US, BROADWAY
—YOU FLEW AWAY FROM THE NEST
—DAY DREAMS

1926. *THE RAMBLERS*
  Book by Guy Bolton, Harry Ruby and
  Bert Kalmar, lyrics by Bert Kalmar, and
  starring Bobby Clark and Paul McCul-
  lough in a cast that included Jack Whit-
  ing, Georgia O'Ramey and Marie Saxon.
—ALL ALONE MONDAY
—LIKE YOU DO
—ALMA MATER
—JUST ONE KISS
—ANY LITTLE TUNE
—CALIFORNIA SKIES
—YOU SMILED AT ME
—YOU MUST, WE WON'T
—GOOD-BYE
—THE MOVIE BALL

1927. *LUCKY*
  With Jerome Kern. Book by Otto Har-
  bach, lyrics by Bert Kalmar, and pre-
  sented by a cast that included Joseph
  Santley, Skeet Gallagher, Walter Catlett,
  Ivy Sawyer, Ruby Keeler, Mary Eaton
  and Paul Whiteman and his orchestra.
—DANCING THE DEVIL AWAY
—THE SAME OLD MOON
—CINGALESE GIRLS
—THAT LITTLE SOMETHING
—WHEN THE BO TREE BLOSSOMS
  Jerome Kern contributed the following
  songs:
—PEARL OF BROADWAY
—LUCKY
—THE TREASURE HUNT
—WITHOUT THINKING OF YOU
—THE PEARL OF CEYLON

1927. *FIVE O'CLOCK GIRL*
  Book by Guy Bolton and Fred Thomp-
  son, lyrics by Bert Kalmar ,and starring
  Mary Eaton and Oscar Shaw in a cast
  that included Shaw and Lee.
—UP IN THE CLOUDS
—THINKING OF YOU
—I'M ONE LITTLE PARTY
—WE WANT YOU
—HAPPY GO LUCKY
—ANY LITTLE THING

—FOLLOWING IN FATHER'S FOOT-
STEPS
—LONESOME ROMEOS
—WHO DID?
—SOCIETY LADDER
—TELL THE WORLD I'M THROUGH

1928. *GOOD BOY*
Book by Henry Myers, Otto Harbach and
Oscar Hammerstein II, lyrics by Bert
Kalmar, and presented by a cast that in-
cluded Effie Shannon, Sam Hearn, Charles
Butterworth, Eddie Buzzell, Dan Healy,
Helen Kane and Borroh Minnewitch.
—I WANNA BE LOVED BY YOU
—DOWN IN ARKANSAS
—GOOD BOY
—THE VOICE OF THE CITY
—SOME SWEET SOMEONE
—I HAVE MY MOMENTS
—DON'T BE LIKE THAT
—LET'S GIVE A CHEER
—NINA
—GOOD BOY WEDDING MARCH
—YOU'RE THE ONE
By Otto Harbach and Arthur Schwartz.

1928. *ANIMAL CRACKERS*
Book by George S. Kaufman and Morrie
Ryskind, lyrics by Bert Kalmar, and star-
ing the Four Marx Brothers in a cast
that included Bobbie Perkins.
—NEWS
—HOORAY FOR CAPTAIN SPALDING
—WHO'S BEEN LISTENING TO MY
HEART?
—THE LONG ISLAND LOW-DOWN
—GO PLACES AND DO THINGS
—WATCHING THE CLOUDS ROLL BY
—WHEN THINGS ARE BRIGHT AND
ROSY
—COOL OFF
—MUSKETEERS

Arthur Samuels Score

1922. *THE FORTY-NINERS*
A revue with book by George Kaufman
and Marc Connelly, and presented by a
cast that included May Irwin, Roland
Young and Albert Carroll. The following
songs provided the score for a parody on
the Viennese operas, "The Love Girl," by
Franklin P. Adams:
—CAN THIS BE LOVE?
—YOU NEVER CAN TELL ABOUT
LOVE
—LOVE, LOVE, LOVE
—MY GARDEN OF LOVE
—OH LOVE ME NOW
—THE LOVE I BEAR THEE

—LOVE ME FOREVER
—IN LOVE WITH YOU
—WHEN LOVE COMES TRIP, TRIP,
TRIPPING
—JUST LOVE
In addition, the following songs were in-
troduced in this revue:
—WHERE CREDIT IS DUE
Music by Lewis Gensler.
—THE ALLEGORICAL BLUES
By Morrie Ryskind and Lewis Gensler.
—THE POWER OF LIGHT
By Arthur Dietz and Morrie Ryskind.

Walter G. Samuels Score

1929. *NED WAYBURN'S GAMBOLS*
A revue with a cast that included Charles
Irwin, Roger Gray, Lew Hearn, Fuzzy
Knight and Libby Holman. Lyrics by
Morrie Ryskind.
—CRESCENT MOON
—THE CHURCH AROUND THE COR-
NER
—I BRING MY GIRLS ALONG
—IN THE DAYS GONE BY
—SWEET OLD FASHIONED WALTZ
—WHAT IS THE GOOD?
—SAVANNAH STOMP
—THE SUN WILL SHINE
Music by Arthur Schwartz.
—INDIAN PRAYER
—THE PALM BEACH WALK
—GYPSY DAYS
Music by Arthur Schwartz.
—THE SHADES OF MINSTRELSY

Charles M. Schwab Score

1926. *BARE FACTS OF 1926*
A revue with book by Stuart Hamill and
lyrics by Henry Myers.
—NICE GIRL
—STAND UP ON YOUR FEET AND
DANCE
—TRIANGLE BLUES
—WON'T YOU TELL ME?
—TEA TIME
—TREAT 'EM ROUGH

Arthur Schwartz Score

1929. *FIRST LITTLE SHOW*
This cut the pattern for the intimate revue, and had its genesis in a series of
Sunday night concerts staged by James
B. Pond and Tom Weatherly at the Selwyn Theater, New York. With the exception of Clifton Webb, the cast as-
sembled by Dwight Deere Wiman, the

producer, was made up of comparative
unknowns that included Fred Allen, who
had shown comic possibilities in a Broad-
way flop *Rainbow;* Libby Holman, a torch
singer recruited from Tony's speakeasy,
Peggy Conklin and Bettina Hall, while
Ralph Rainger and Adam Carroll were
featured at dual pianos in the orchestra
pit. Book and lyrics by Howard Dietz.
—I GUESS I'LL HAVE TO CHANGE
  MY PLAN
—MAN ABOUT TOWN
—GET UP ON A NEW ROUTINE
—I'VE MADE A HABIT OF YOU
—LITTLE OLD NEW YORK
—SONG OF THE RIVETER
  Lyrics by Lew Levenson.
—WHAT EVERY LITTLE GIRL
  SHOULD KNOW
  Lyrics by Henry Mears.
—THE THEME SONG
—OR WHAT HAVE YOU
  By Grace Henry and Morris Hamilton.
—MOANIN' LOW
  By Howard Dietz and Ralph Rainger.
—CAN'T WE BE FRIENDS?
  By Paul James, the pseudonym of a New
  York banker, James Warburg, and his
  wife, Kay Swift.
—CAUGHT IN THE RAIN
  By Howard Dietz and Henry Sullivan.
—A HUT IN HOBOKEN
  By Herman Hupfeld.
—STICK TO YOUR DANCING MABEL
  By Charlotte Kent.

Jean Schwartz Score

1920. *CENTURY REVUE*
  Book by Howard E. Rogers, lyrics by Al-
  fred Bryan, and presented by a cast
  headed by Walter Woolf, Mlle. Madelon,
  Milo and Vivienne Oakland.
—MILLIONS OF TUNES
—SHINE ON, LITTLE SON
—MARCELLE
—KEEP YOUR WEIGHT DOWN
—BOTTLE UP A PRETTY GIRL
—THE SPHINX
—HOLD ME

1920. *MIDNIGHT ROUNDERS OF 1920*
  Book by Howard E. Rogers, lyrics by Al-
  fred Bryan, and presented by a cast
  headed by Walter Woolf, Mlle. Madelon
  La Varre, Ted Lorraine, Gladys Walton,
  Lew Hearn, Harry Kelly, Vivienne Oak-
  land and Tot Qualters.
—WHO CARES
  Music by Leo Edwards.

—ROMANTIC BLUES
—CLOCK SONG
—THE RAG DOLL
—JE NE COMPRENDS PAS
—MANSION OF ROSES
—HEART BREAKERS
—A MOUTHFUL OF KISSES
—THE SWING
—BEAUTY IS LIKE A ROSE
—JOSEPHINE
—THREE LITTLE MARYS
—WHISPER IN MY EAR
—HEAVENLY BODY
—LA VEDA
—WILLIAM TELL IT TO ME
—BEAUTIFUL SHOULDERS
—LADY OF THE CAMEO
—THE CENTERY PROMENADE

1921. *MIDNIGHT ROUNDERS OF 1921*
  With Lew Pollack. A revue with book by
  Harold Atteridge, lyrics by Alfred Bryan,
  and presented by a cast headed by Eddie
  Cantor and Jane Green.
—ANGELS, WE CALL THEM MOTH-
  ERS DOWN HERE
—I'D LOVE TO BE IN IRELAND
—THE LADIES MAN
—SCANDANAVIA
—DAPPER DAN
—MY SUNNY TENNESSEE
  By Bert Kalmar, Herman Ruby and Harry
  Ruby.
—GEORGIA ROSE
  By Alex Sullivan, Jimmy Flynn and
  Harry Rosenthal.
—IF YOU KNEW
  By Eddie Cantor, Harry Tobias and
  James Blyler.
—MAMA, MAMA, PAPA'S GOT A LOT
  OF LOVIN' ALL SAVED UP FOR
  YOU
  By Cliff Friend.
—LET YOUR CONSCIENCE BE YOUR
  GUIDE
  By Cliff Friend.

1921. *THE PASSING SHOW OF 1921*
  Book and lyrics by Harold Atteridge, and
  starring Eugene and Willie Howard in a
  cast that included Marie Dressler, Harry
  Watson, Janet Adair and J. Harold Mur-
  ray.
—HELLO MISS KNICKERBOCKER
—IN LITTLE OLD NEW YORK
—WHEN THERE'S NO ONE TO LOVE
—THE CHARM SCHOOL
—A RATTLING GOOD TIME
—SILKS AND SATINS
—BROADWAY IN SAHARA
—YOU MAY BE A BAD MAN

—MY WIFE
—TA VOO
—THE LADY OF THE LAMP
—I'M ORIENTAL
—DREAM FANTASIES
—BEAUTIFUL FACES
—SMILING SAM
—TIP TOP TOREADOR
—RUBYIATS FROM THE RUBYIAT
—SWEETEST MELODY
—THE DANCING BLUES
—BECKY FROM BABYLON
By Abner Silver.

1922. *MAKE IT SNAPPY*
Book and lyrics by Harold Atteridge, and with a cast headed by Eddie Cantor, Lew Hearn, J. Harold Murray, Nan Halperin, Georgia Hale and Tot Qualters.
—BLOSSOM TIME
—GOOD-BYE MAIN STREET
—WHEN THE WEDDING CHIMES ARE RINGING
—TO MAKE THEM BEAUTIFUL LADIES
—BOUQUET OF GIRLS
—I LEARNED ABOUT WOMEN FROM HER
—HUMORESQUIMOS
—THE FLAPPER
—MY CASTILLIAN GIRL
—WON'T YOU BUY A FLOWER?
—HOOTCH RYTHM
—LOVEABLE EYES
—FRAGONARD GIRL
—DESERT ROSE
—THE SHIEK
—THE BUTTERFLY AND THE WHEEL
—LAMPLIGHT LAND

1923. *TOPICS OF 1923*
With Al Goodman. Book and lyrics by Harold Atteridge and Harry Wagstaff Gribble, and with a cast headed by Alice Delysia, Jay Gould, Jack Pearl, Harry McNaughton, Nat Nazzaro Jr. and Ethel Shutta.
—OH, ALICE
—WHEN YOU LOVE
—THE FLOWERS OF EVIL
—QUEENS OF LONG AGO
—GOOD QUEEN BESS
—A BEAUTIFUL EVENING
—RIN TIN TIN
—THE JAZZ WEDDING
—LOTUS FLOWER
—DOING THE APACHE
—LEGEND OF THE WOODLAND
—YANKEE DOODLE OO-LA-LA

1923. *ARTISTS AND MODELS OF 1923*
This production was based on a revue

staged by the Illustrators Society of New York, to which James Montgomery Flagg, Rube Goldberg, Clare Briggs, Fontaine Fox, H. T. Webster and Harry Hershfield were contributors. Harold Atteridge whipped the production into shape for Broadway, and Al Goodman collaborated with Schwartz on the score. The cast was headed by Frank Fay, Grace Hamilton, Harry Kelly, Etta Pillard and Bob Nelson.
—SOMEHOW
—JOHNNY
—CARMENCITA
—FLOWER OF THE WOODLAND
—MUSIC OF LOVE

1927. *A NIGHT IN SPAIN*
Book by Harold Atteridge, lyrics by Vincent Bryan, and presented by a cast headed by Phil Baker, Sid Silvers, Ted and Betty Healy, Jay Brennan, Helen Kane, Grace Hayes and Marion Harris.
—ARGENTINE
—INTERNATIONAL VAMP
—DE DUM DUM
—THE SKY GIRL
—PROMENADE THE ESPANADE
—MY ROSE OF SPAIN
—COLUMBUS AND ISABELLA
—HOT, HOT HONEY
—A SPANISH SHAWL
—THE NOCTURNE
—THE CURFEW WALK
—BAMBAZOOLA
—A MILLION EYES

1928. *SUNNY DAYS*
Book and lyrics by Clifford Grey and William Cary Duncan, and with a cast headed by Jeanette MacDonald, Frank McIntyre, Billy B. Van, Carl Randall and Lynn Overman.
—A BELLE, A BEAU AND A BOUTONNIERE
—ONE SUNNY DAY
—GINETTE
—I'LL BE SMILING
—REALLY AND TRULY
—I'VE GOT TO BE GOOD
—HANG YOUR HAT ON THE MOON
—SO DO I
—THE GIRLS BRIGADE
—ORANGE BLOSSOMS
—TRAMPLE YOUR TROUBLES

Kenyon Scott Score
1929. *A NOBLE ROGUE*
A musical comedy with book and lyrics by the composer, and presented by a cast headed by Robert Rhodes as the pirate Jean LaFitte and Marguerite Zender.

Madelyn Sheppard Score

1922. *JUST BECAUSE*

A musical comedy with book and lyrics by Anne Wayne O'Ryan and Helen S. Woodruff, and presented by a cast headed by Queenie Smith, Frank Moulan and Charles Trowbridge.

—DAY DREAM BAY
—I'LL NAME MY DOLLY FOR YOU
—JUST BECAUSE
—OH, THOSE JAZZING TOES
—LOVE, JUST SIMPLY LOVE
—OH, DAD
—CHOP STICKS
—ORPHANS' DRILL
—PEP UP YOUR STEP
—THE LINE IS BUSY
—IT'S HARD TO BE A LADY
—WIDOW'S BLUES
—DAISY TELL ME TRULY
—ELOPING
—THE ASSOCIATED PRESS

Manning Sherwin Score

1926. *BAD HABITS OF 1926*

A revue presented by a cast that included Robert Montgomery. Lyrics by Arthur Herzog.

—WOULD-JA?
—ARE YOU DOWN HEARTED?
—WHEN
—GONE-AWAY BLUES
—STATION L-O-V-E
—THE FUNERAL OF THE CHARLESTON
—MANHATTAN TRANSFER
—GEISHA GIRL
—LET ME BE MYSELF
—KEEP YOUR SHIRT ON
—THE LIFE GUARDS
—THE STUDENT ROBIN HOOD OF PILSEN
  By Perry Ivins and Randall Thompson.

Seymour Simons Score

1920. *HER FAMILY TREE*

A musical comedy by Al Weeks and Bugs Baer, and starring Nora Bayes in a cast that included the Randall Sisters, Julius Tannen, Donald Sawyer and Frank Morgan.

—AS WE SOW SO SHALL WE REAP
—THE GOLD-DIGGERS
—I LOVE YOU
—LOVE HAS COME MY WAY
—NO OTHER GIRL
—OUIJA BOARD

—WHEN CUPID FLIES AWAY
—IN THE LAND WHERE TOMORROWS BEGIN
—WHY WORRY?

Sissle and Blake Scores

1921. *SHUFFLE ALONG*

A musical comedy with book by Miller and Lyles, who headed an all-Negro cast that included Florence Mills and Noble Sissle.

—BANDANA DAYS
—I'M CRAVING FOR THAT KIND OF LOVE
—I'M JUST WILD ABOUT HARRY
—IF YOU'VE NEVER BEEN VAMPED BY A BROWNSKIN
—GOOD NIGHT, MY ANGELINE
—HONEYSUCKLE TIME
—GYPSY BLUES
—BALTIMORE BUZZIN' SONG
—LOVE WILL FIND A WAY

1923. *ELSIE*

A musical comedy with book by Charles W. Bell, and presented by a cast headed by Marguerite Zender, Stanley Ridges and Vinton Freedley.

—A REGULAR GUY
—HEARTS IN TUNE
—MY CRINOLINE GIRL
—I'D LIKE TO WALK WITH A PAL LIKE YOU
—BABY BUNTING
—SAND FLOWERS
—EVERYBODY'S STRUTTIN' NOW
—THUNDERSTORM JAZZ
  Monte Carlo and Alma Sanders contributed the following songs:
—ONE DAY IN MAY
—ELSIE
—HONEYMOON HOME
—THE FIREFLY
—CLOUDS OF LOVE

1924. *CHOCOLATE DANDIES*

A revue with book by Noble Sissle and Lew Payton, both of whom appeared with Valada Snow in an all-Negro cast.

—DIXIE MOON
—JESSAMINE LANE
—MANDA
—SLAVE OF LOVE
—THERE'S NO PLACE AS GRAND AS BANDANALAND
—MAMMY'S CHOC'LATE CULLUD CHILE
—HAVE A GOOD TIME EVERYBODY
—JAZZTIME BABY
—I'LL FIND MY LOVE IN D-I-X-I-E

—DUMB LUCK
—JUMP STEADY
—A JOCKEY'S LIFE FOR ME
—I LOST MY HEAD ALL OVER YOU
By Spencer Williams.
—AIN'T GOT NO WORRY (LONG AS
YOU'RE MY BABY)
By Spencer Williams.
—THE SONS OF OLD BLACK JOE
—LAND OF DANCING PICKANINNIES
—ALL THE WRONGS YOU DONE ME
—TAKE DOWN DIS LETTER
—CHOCOLATE DANDIES

A. Baldwin Sloane Scores

1920. *GREENWICH VILLAGE FOLLIES
OF 1920*
Book by Thomas J. Gray, lyrics by Arthur
Swanstrom and J. Murray Anderson, and
presented by a cast headed by Frank
Crumit, Jay Brennan, Bert Savoy, Howard Marsh and Harriet Gimble.
—THE NAKED TRUTH
—PERFUME OF LOVE
—COME TO BOHEMIA
—I'LL BE YOUR VALENTINE
—AT THE KRAZY KAT'S BALL
—JUST SWEET SIXTEEN
—TSIN
—MURDER IN MY HEART
—SONG OF THE SAMOVAR
—TAM
—SNAP YOUR FINGERS AT CARE
By B. G. DeSylva and Louis Silvers.
—I'M A LONESOME LITTLE RAIN-
DROP (WAITING FOR A PLACE
TO FALL)
By Joe Goodwin, Murray Roth and James
Hanley.

1925. *CHINA ROSE*
Book and lyrics by Harry L. Cort and
George E. Stoddard, and starring Olga
Steck in a cast that included J. Harold
Murray and Jefferson deAngelis.
—SUN WORSHIP
—SOLDIERS TRUE
—MAIDENS FAIR
—CHINESE POTENTATE
—BAMBOO BUNGALOW
—I'M HI I'M LOW
—CHINA ROSE
—I'M ALL ALONE
—WHO AM I THINKING OF
—I LIKE THE GIRLS
—THROUGH THE BAMBOO
—CHINESE LANTERN MAN
—HOME
—CHINA BOOGY MAN

—JUST A KISS
—HAIL THE BRIDEGROOM
—TOMORROW
—THE GREAT WHITE WAY IN CHINA
—I'M NO BUTTERFLY
—CALLING YOU MY OWN
—WHY DO THEY MAKE THEM SO
BEAUTIFUL?
—HAPPY BRIDE

Ted Snyder Score

1923. *FASHIONS OF 1924*
A revue with Arnold Daly, Jimmy Hussey,
Edith Taliaferro and Marie Nordstrom.
Lyrics by H. B. Smith.
—ONE MORE WALTZ
—A LITTLE BIT OF LOVE
—OH, JOE
Lyrics by Harry DeCosta.
—MISS WHOZISS AND MISTER
WHATCHANAME

Dave Stamper Scores

1920. *ZIEGFELD GIRLS OF 1920*
Also known as "Ziegfeld's 9 O'clock Re-
vue" with Allyn King, John Price Jones,
Fanny Brice, Lillian Lorraine and W. C.
Fields. Lyrics by Gene Buck.
—WHERE ARE THE PLAYS OF YES-
TERDAY?
—WE ARE THE MAIDS OF THE MER-
RY MERRY
—I'M CRAZY ABOUT SOMEBODY
—EVERY TELEPHONE
—DON'T YOU REMEMBER ME?
—WHEN GRANDPA WAS A BOY
—WONDERFUL GIRL
—EMANCIPATION DAY
—ORCHARD OF GIRLS
Lyrics by Rennold Wolf.
—YOU KNOW WHAT I MEAN
—MY ROSARY OF MELODIES
—METROPOLITAN LADIES
By Irving Berlin.
—MY MAN
By Channing Pollock and Maurice Yvain.
—THE WINTER BEACHES
—OUIJA
—SPIRITUALISTIC JAZZ
—DANCE DREAM

1920. *ZIEGFELD MIDNIGHT FROLIC*
Presented by a cast that included Frisco,
Allyn King, W. C. Fields, Fanny Brice,
John Price Jones, Lillian Lorraine and
Carl Randall. Lyrics by Gene Buck.
—SHANGHAI
—DEAREST

—LIFE IS A GAMBOL
—I'LL SEE YOU IN C-U-B-A
By Irving Berlin.
—ROSE OF WASHINGTON SQUARE
By Ballard MacDonald and James F. Hanley.
—BEAUTIFUL BIRDS
—THE WORLD IS GOING SHIMMY MAD

1921. *ZIEGFELD'S MIDNIGHT FROLIC*
With Will Rogers, Leon Errol, Carl Randall, Carlotta Ryan and Gloria Foy. Lyrics by Gene Buck.
—COME ON, LET'S GO
—VIOLET RAY
—DAY DREAMS
By Mathew Woodward and Robert King.
—IT TAKES A GOOD MAN TO DO THAT
By Jack Bayha and Chris Smith.

1923. *ZIEGFELD FOLLIES OF 1923*
Paul Whiteman and his band received headline billing as a Follies' attraction along with Eddie Cantor, Brooke Johns, Bert Wheeler, Hap Ward, Lew Hearn, Harlan Dixon, Fanny Brice and Betty Wheeler. Lyrics by Gene Buck.
—GLORIFYING THE GIRLS
—KAYO TORTONI
—I WONDER HOW THEY GET THAT WAY
—THAT BROADWAY INDIAN OF MINE
—SHAKE YOUR FEET
—LITTLE OLD NEW YORK
—I'M BUGS OVER YOU
—SWANEE RIVER BLUES
—TAKE, OH TAKE THOSE LIPS AWAY
By Joseph McCarthy and Harry Tierney.
—THAT OLD FASHIONED GARDEN OF MINE
Music by Victor Herbert.
—I'D LOVE TO WALTZ THROUGH LIFE WITH YOU
Music by Victor Herbert.
—LADY OF THE LANTERN
Music by Victor Herbert.

1927. *TAKE THE AIR*
Book by Anne Caldwell, lyrics by Gene Buck, and presented by a cast headed by Trini, Will Mahoney, Dorothy Dilley, Greek Evans and York and King.
—MAYBE I'LL BABY YOU
—WINGS
—WE'LL HAVE A NEW HOME IN THE MORNING
—ALL I WANT IS A LULLABY
—JUST LIKE A WILD, WILD, ROSE

—ON A PONY FOR TWO
—HAM AND EGGS IN THE MORNING
By Al Dubin, Con Conrad and Abner Silver.

1927. *LOVELY LADY*
With Harold E. Levey. A musical comedy with book and lyrics by Gladys Unger and Cyrus Wood and presented by a cast that included Edna Leedom and Guy Robertson.
—AIN'T LOVE GRAND
—LOVELY LADY
—MAKE BELIEVE YOU'RE HAPPY
—THE LOST STEP
—AT THE BARBECUE
—I COULD LOVE A GIRL LIKE YOU
—IF YOU ONLY KNEW
—YESTERDAY
—TRIOLEE-TRIOLAY
By Arthur Wimperis and Jean and Robert Gilbert.

Herbert P. Stothart Scores

1920. *ALWAYS YOU*
A musical comedy with book and lyrics by Oscar Hammerstein II, and presented by a cast that included Helen Ford, Walter Scanlon and Ralph Herz.
—ALWAYS YOU
—THE VOICE OF BAGDAD
—I NEVER MISS
—A WONDERFUL WAR
—SAME OLD PLACES
—SYNCOPATED HEART
—SOME BIG SOMETHING
—HEYWOOD'S HARLEM HELLIONS
—MY POUSSE CAFE
—WOMAN
—I'LL SAY SO
—PASSING THROUGH
—DRIFTING
—THE TIRED BUSINESS MAN

1920. *TICKLE ME*
A musical comedy with book and lyrics by Otto Harbach, Frank Mandel and Oscar Hammerstein II, and presented by a cast headed by Louise Allen, Allen Kearns and Frank Tinney.
—IF A WISH COULD MAKE IT SO
—INDIA RUBBER
—TICKLE ME
—UNTIL YOU SAY GOODBYE
—WE'VE GOT SOMETHING
—COME ACROSS
—FAMOUS YOU AND SIMPLE ME
—LITTLE HINDOO MAN

1920. *JIMMY*
A musical comedy with book by Otto

Harbach, lyrics by Frank Mandel, Otto Harbach and Oscar Hammerstein II, and presented by a cast headed by Francis White, Harry Delf, Ben Welch and Howard Truesdale.
—BABY DREAMS
—CUTE LITTLE TWO BY FOUR
—JIMMY
—BELOW THE MACY-GIMBEL LINE
—ALL THAT I WANT
—CARLOTTI'S
—I WISH I WAS A QUEEN
—SHE ALONE COULD UNDERSTAND
—TOODLE OODLE UM
—IT ISN'T HARD TO DO
—A LITTLE PLATE OF SOUP
—JUST A SMILE
—DO, RE, ME
—SOME PEOPLE MAKE ME SICK
1922. *DAFFY DILL*
A musical comedy with book and lyrics by Guy Bolton and Oscar Hammerstein II, and presented by a cast headed by Marion Sunshine, Georgia O'Ramey, Frank Tinney and Guy Robertson.
—DOCTOR
—ONE FLOWER THAT BLOOMS FOR YOU
—TWO LITTLE RUBY RINGS
—DAFFY DILL
—I'LL BUILD A BUNGALOW
—MY BOY FRIEND
—TARTAR
—PRINCE CHARMING
—YOU CAN'T LOSE ME
—LET'S PLAY HOOKEY
—KINDERGARTEN BLUES
—I'M FRESH FROM THE COUNTRY
—A COACHMAN'S HEART
—FAIR ENOUGH
—MY LITTLE REDSKIN
—CHINKY CHINK
—CAPTAIN KIDD'S KIDS

Johann Strauss Score
1929. *A WONDERFUL NIGHT*
An operetta with book and lyrics by Fanny Todd Mitchell, and presented by a cast headed by Peggy Udell, Archie Leach and Allan Rogers. In addition to several untitled numbers, including two duets and two trios, the following songs comprised the score:
—TWO IN LOVE
—GIRLS MUST LIVE
—LETTER SONG
—CHACUN A SON GOUT

—LAUGHING SONG
—CZARDAS

Oscar Straus Scores
1921. *THE LAST WALTZ*
An operetta with book and lyrics by Harold Atteridge and Edward Delancy Dunn, and presented by a cast headed by Eleanor Painter, Gladys Walton, Ted Lorraine, James Barton and Walter Woolf.
—HAIL TO OUR GENERAL
—LIVE FOR TODAY
—CHARMING LADIES
—MY HEART IS WAKING
—ROSES OUT OF REACH
—THE LAST WALTZ
—REMINISCENCE
—LADIES' CHOICE
—OO-LA-LA
—BRING HIM MY LOVE THOUGHTS
—THE WHIP IN HAND
—A BABY IN LOVE
By Al Goodman and R. Benatzky.
—THE NEXT DANCE WITH YOU
By Al Goodman and Louis Friedman.
—NOW FADES MY GOLDEN LOVE DREAM
1926. *NAUGHTY RIQUETTE*
An operetta with book and lyrics by Harry B. Smith, and presented by a cast headed by Mitzi, Alexander Gray and Stanley Lupino.
—IN ARMENIA
—MAKE BELIEVE YOU'RE MINE
—I MAY
With Maurice Rubens and Kendall Burgess.
—NAUGHTY RIQUETTE
With Maurice Rubens and Kendall Burgess.
—SOMEONE
Music by Maurice Rubens and Al Goodman.
—ME
—SOMEHOW I'D RATHER BE GOOD
—YOU MIGHT SAY YES TODAY
—TWO ARE COMPANY
—WHAT GREAT MEN CANNOT DO
—ALCAZAR

Milton Suskind Score
1925. *FLORIDA GIRL*
A musical comedy with book and lyrics by Paul Potter, Benjamin Hapgood Burt and William A. Grew, and presented by a cast headed by Vivienne Segal, Lester Allen, Irving Beebe and the Ritz Brothers.

—TRAVEL, TRAVEL, TRAVEL
—DANCE OF THE PORTERS
—ORANGES
—THE COLLEGIANS
—LADY OF MY HEART
—SKIPPER
—SMILE ON
—INTO SOCIETY
—DAPHNE
—BEAUTIFUL SEA
—OH, YOU!
—TROUBLE
—CHINKY CHINA CHARLESTON
—AS A TROUBADOR
—VENETIAN SKIES

Harry Tierney Scores

1921. *THE BROADWAY WHIRL*
Book and lyrics by Joseph McCarthy, Richard Carle, B. G. DeSylva and John Henry Mears, and presented by a cast that was headed by Richard Carle, Blanche Ring, Charles Winninger, Winona Winter, Jay Gould and the Janet Sisters.
—FROM THE PLAZA TO MADISON SQUARE
—BUTTON ME UP THE BACK
—STAND UP AND SING FOR YOUR FATHER
By Ray Perkins.
—WOOD ALCOHOL BLUES
By J. Hershkowitz and E. S. S. Huntington.
—OH BABE
By Frost and Klickman.
—THREE LITTLE MAIDS
—OH DEARIE
—ALL GIRLS ARE LIKE A RAINBOW
—LET CUTIE CUT YOUR CUTICLE
—CAREFREE CAIRO TOWN
By Thomas and Wyman.
—THE BROADWAY WHIRL

1922. *UP SHE GOES*
Book by Frank Craven, lyrics by Joseph McCarthy, and starring Gloria Foy and Donald Brian.
—THE VISITORS
—TAKES A HEAP OF LOVE
—JOURNEY'S END
—LET'S KISS AND MAKE UP
—NEARING THE DAY
—BOB ABOUT A BIT
—TYUP
—ROOFTREE
—LADY LUCK SMILE ON ME
—WE'LL DO THE RIVIERA

—SETTLE DOWN, TRAVEL ROUND
—UP WITH THE STARS
—UP SHE GOES

1922. *GLORY*
Book by James Montgomery, lyrics by Joseph McCarthy and James Dyrenforth, and presented by a cast headed by Patti Harrold, Helen Groody, Flo Irwin, Jack Clifford and Walter Ryan.
—SAW MILL RIVER ROAD
—A LITTLE WHITE HOUSE WITH GREEN BLINDS
—MOTHER'S WEDDING DRESS
—THE UPPER CRUST
—WE'VE GOT TO BUILD
—WHEN THE CURFEW RINGS AT NINE
By Al W. Brown.
—POPULARITY
—POST OFFICE
—THE SAME OLD STORY
—GLORY
By Maurice DePackh.
—THE MOON WAS GOOD ENOUGH FOR DAD AND MOTHER
By Maurice De Packh.
—THE GOODLY LITTLE THINGS WE DO
By Maurice DePackh.
—THE TENOR MARRIED THE SOPRANO AND THE ALTO MARRIED THE BASS
By Maurice DePackh.

1923. *KID BOOTS*
Book by William Anthony McGuire and Otto Harbach, lyrics by Joseph McCarthy, and starring Eddie Cantor in a cast that included Ethelind Terry, Beth Berri, Mary Eaton, Harlan Dixon and George Olsen and his band.
—A DAY AT THE CLUB
—IF YOUR HEART'S IN THE GAME
—KEEP YOUR EYE ON THE BALL
—THE SAME OLD WAY
—SOME ONE LOVES YOU AFTER ALL
—GOT TO HAVE MORE
—POLLY PUT THE KETTLE ON
—LETS DO AND SAY WE DIDN'T
—IN THE SWIM
—THE OLD LAKE TRAIL
—ON WITH THE GAME
—BET ON THE ONE YOU FANCY
—I'M IN MY GLORY
—A PLAY-FAIR MAN
—WIN FOR ME
—THE CAKE EATERS' BALL
—THE COCOANUTS BALL
—WHEN THE COCOANUTS CALL

1924. *ZIEGFELD FOLLIES OF 1924*
With lyrics by Gene Buck and Joseph McCarthy, and presented by a cast that included Will Rogers, Brandon Tynon, Irving Fisher, Tom Lewis, Vivienne Segal, Lupino Lane, Ann Pennington, Lina Basquette, Evelyn Law, W. C. Fields, Ray Dooley, George Olsen and his band and Tiller London Dancing Girls.
—ADORING YOU
—ALL PEPPED UP
—THE OLD TOWN BAND
—THE BEAUTY CONTEST
With Victor Herbert.
—I'D LIKE TO PUT YOU IN A BIG GLASS CAGE AND LOOK AT YOU ALL DAY
—THE WIDE OPEN SPACES
By Dave Stamper.
—LONELY LITTLE MELODY
By Dave Stamper.
—BIMINY
By Dave Stamper.
—MONTMARTRE
By Raymond Hubbell.
—A NIGHT IN JUNE
By Raymond Hubbell.
—YOU'RE MY HAPPY ENDING
By James Hanley.

1927. *RIO RITA*
Book and lyrics by Guy Bolton and Fred Thompson, and presented by a cast that included Ethelind Terry, J. Harold Murray, Bert Wheeler, Vincent Serrano and Walter Catlett.
—SIESTA TIME
—THE JINGLE DANCE
—THE TAMBOURINE DANCE
—THE BEST LITTLE LOVER IN TOWN
—SWEETHEARTS
—RIVER SONG
—ARE YOU THERE?
—RIO RITA
—SONG OF THE RANGER
—THE SPANISH SHAWL
—THE CHARRO DANCE
—THE KINKAJOU
—IF YOU'RE IN LOVE YOU'LL WALTZ
—MOONLIGHT BALLET
—OUT ON THE LOOSE
—I CAN SPEAK ESPANOL
—FOLLOWING THE SUN AROUND
—THE JUMPING BEAN
—MOONSHINE
—YOU'RE ALWAYS IN MY ARMS BUT ONLY IN MY DREAMS

1928. *CROSS MY HEART*
Book by Daniel Kussell, lyrics by Joseph McCarthy, and presented by a cast headed by Bobby Watson, Lulu McConnell, Mary Lawlor, Clarence Nordstrom, and Edgar Fairchild and Ralph Rainger with their Brunswick recording orchestra.
—DREAM SWEETHEART
—HOT SANDS
—RIGHT OUT OF HEAVEN AND INTO MY ARMS
—STEP UP AND PEP UP THE PARTY
—SOLD
—SALAAMING THE RAJAH
—IN THE GARDENS OF NOR-ED-EEN
—COME ALONG SUNSHINE
—SUCH IS FAME
—LADY WHIP-POOR-WILL
—GOOD DAYS AND BAD DAYS
—THANKS FOR A DARN NICE TIME

Herman Timberg Score

1920. *TICK-TACK-TOE*
A musical comedy with book and lyrics by the composer, who also appeared in a cast that included Jay Gould, Pearl Eaton and Flo Lewis.
—A DOUBLE ORDER OF CHICKEN
—CHINESE-AMERICAN RAG
—TAKE ME BACK TO PHILADELPHIA, PA.
—A LESSON IN LOVE
—SHIMMY ALL THE BLUES AWAY
—PLAYING FOR THE GIRL
—GIRLS, GIRLS, GIRLS
—TELL ME KIND SPIRIT
—WHERE'S MY SWEET AND PRETTY MAN?
—DANCE MAD
—I'D LIKE TO KNOW WHY I FELL IN LOVE WITH YOU
—HOPPY POPPY GIRL
—LOVE IS A GAME OF CARDS
—MY MANICURE MAIDS
—THE DARDANELLA BLUES
By Fred Fisher and John S. Black.

Vincent Valentini Score

1928. *PARISIANA*
A Continental revue with book and lyrics by the composer, and presented by a cast that included Beth Miller and Olive May.
—HELP THE GIRLIES ALONG
—KEEP ON DANCING
—MAYBE
—WHEN YOU SAY "NO" TO LOVE
—LEVEE LOU

—KEEP IT UNDER YOUR HAT
—WHO WOULDN'T?
—WHAT'S BECOME OF THE BOWERY?
—THE GHOST OF OLD BLACK JOE
—IN A GONDOLA WITH YOU
—GOLLIWOG
—THEY'RE HOT NOW UP IN ICE-
LAND
—PEEPIN' TOMMY
—PAREE HAS THE FEVER NOW

Armand Vecsey Scores

1922. *THE HOTEL MOUSE*
With Ivan Caryll. A musical comedy with
book by Guy Bolton, lyrics by Clifford
Grey, and presented by a cast headed by
Frances White and Taylor Holmes.
—I'LL DREAM OF YOU
—LITTLE MOTHER
—WHY DO THE GIRLS?
—NEARLY TRUE TO YOU
—ROMANCE
—OOZEY-WOOZEY
—MAURICETTE
—ONE TOUCH OF LOVING
—RHYMING
—WHERE LANTERNS GLEAM
—EVERYTHING I DO GOES WRONG
—ROUND ON THE END AND HIGH IN
THE MIDDLE
By Al Bryan and Ned Hanlon.

1927. *THE NIGHTINGALE*
An operetta inspired by Jenny Lind's
American tour, with book by Guy Bolton,
lyrics by P. G. Wodehouse, and starring
Eleanor Painter as Jenny Lind, Tom
Wise as P. T. Barnum, Stanley Lupino
and Ralph Errolle.
—BREAKFAST IN BED
—ENOUGH IS ENOUGH
—MAY MOON
—ONCE IN SEPTEMBER
—TWO LITTLE SHIPS
—WHEN I MET YOU
—JOSEPHINE
—HOMELAND
—HE DOES'NT KNOW
—FAIRYLAND
—SANTA CLAUS
—COMING THROUGH THE RYE

Albert Von Tilzer Scores

1920. *HONEY GIRL*
A muscial comedy based on Henry Blossom's "Checkers" with a book by Edward
Clark and lyrics by Neville Fleeson. The
cast was headed by Lynn Overman,

George McKay, Louise Meyers and Edna
Bates.
—SHOPPING
—A SMALL TOWN GIRL
—I'M LOSING MY HEART TO SOME-
ONE
—IT'S A VERY SIMPLE MATTER
—ANYTHING YOU LIKE
—CLOSE TO YOUR HEART
—RACING BLUES
—CAN I FIND A TOREADOR?
—I'D PLACE A BET
—YOU'RE JUST THE BOY FOR ME
—WHY WORRY?
—I'M TRYING
—MYLTIL AND TYLTIL (THE BLUE-
BIRD SONG)
—I LOVE TO FOX-TROT
—I'M THE FELLOW

1922. *THE GINGHAM GIRL*
Book by Daniel Kussell, lyrics by Neville
Fleeson, and starring Eddie Buzzell in a
cast that included Helen Ford, Louise Al-
len and Walter Jones.
—THE DOWN EAST FLAPPER
—THE TWINKLE IN YOUR EYE
—YOU MUST LEARN THE LATEST
DANCES
—AS LONG AS I HAVE YOU
—THE 42d STREET AND BROADWAY
STRUT
—DOWN GREENWICH VILLAGE WAY
—TELL HER WHILE THE WALTZ IS
PLAYING
—THE WONDERFUL THING WE CALL
LOVE
—LIBBY
—SWEET COOKIE
—NEWLYWEDS
—LOVE AND KISSES

1923. *ADRIENNE*
Book and lyrics by A. Seymour Brown,
and with a cast headed by Vivienne Segal,
Billy B. Van and Richard Carle.
—LIVE WHILE YOU'RE HERE
—SWEETHEART OF MYSTERY
—HINDOO HOP
—LOVE IS ALL
—AS LONG AS THE WIFE DOESN'T
KNOW
—CHEER UP
—SING SING
—JUST A PRETTY LITTLE HOME
—KING SOLOMON
—WHERE THE GANGES FLOW
—DANCE WITH ME

1927. *BYE BYE, BONNIE*
Book and lyrics by Louis Simon and Bide
Dudley. During the out-of-town tryouts

of this musical comedy, Fritzi Scheff and Frances White were featured but when the production reached Broadway, they were replaced by Laine Blaire and Dorothy Burgess in a cast that included George Hale and William Frawley.

—HAVE YOU USED SOFT SOAP?
—PROMISE NOT TO STAND ME UP AGAIN
—OUT OF TOWN BUYERS
—LOOK IN YOUR ENGAGEMENT BOOK
—YOU AND I LOVE YOU AND ME
—JUST ACROSS THE RIVER FROM QUEENS
—BYE BYE, BONNIE
—I LIKE TO MAKE IT COZY
—TOODLE-OO
—WHEN YOU GET TO CONGRESS
—LOVIN'S OFF MY MIND
—TAMPICO TAP

Dan Walker Songs

1924. *GRAND STREET FOLLIES OF 1924-25*
The first of a series of intimate revues staged at the Neighborhood Playhouse with book by Agner Morgan, incidental music by Lily Hyland, and presented by a cast that included Albert Carroll and Aline MacMahon.

—BROADWAY MAMMY BLUES
—GLORY, GLORY, GLORY (I WANT TO BE GLORIFIED)

"Fats" Waller Scores

1928. *KEEP SHUFFLIN'*
With J. C. Johnson. An all-Negro revue with lyrics by Henry Creamer and Andy Razaf, and with sketches by Miller and Lyles, who headed the cast. Fats Waller and Jimmy Johnson, dual pianists, and Jazzbo Smith on the trumpet were in the orchestra pit.

—HOW JAZZ WAS BORN
—CHOC'LATE BAR
—LABOR DAY PARADE
—KEEP SHUFFLIN'
—EVERYBODY'S HAPPY IN JIMTOWN
—WILLOW TREE

1929. *HOT CHOCOLATES*
With Harry Brooks. An all-Negro revue with book and lyrics by Andy Razaf, and presented by a cast headed by Jazzlips Richardson, Jimmy Baskette, Eddie Green, Baby Cox, Thelma and Paul Morres, Edith Wilson, Margaret Simms and the Jubilee Singers.

—AIN'T MISBEHAVIN'
—THAT RHYTHM MAN
—WHAT DID I DO TO BE SO BLACK AND BLUE?
—PICKANINNY LAND
—SONG OF THE COTTON FIELDS
—SWEET SAVANNAH SUE
—SAY IT WITH YOUR FEET
—DIXIE CINDERELLA
—CAN'T WE GET TOGETHER?
—REDSKINLAND
—OFF-TIME

Percy Wenrich Scores

1921. *THE RIGHT GIRL*
Book and lyrics by Raymond Peck, and presented by a cast headed by Helen Montrose, Robert Woolsey and Charles Purcell.

—COCKTAIL HOUR
—THINGS I LEARNED IN JERSEY
—YOU'LL GET NOTHING FROM ME
—GIRLS ARE ALL AROUND ME
—WE WERE MADE TO LOVE
—OLD FLAMES
—THE ROCKING CHAIR FLEET
—A GIRL IN YOUR ARMS
—LOVE'S LITTLE JOURNEY
—HARMONY
—LOOK FOR THE GIRL
—ALADDIN
—THE RIGHT GIRL

1926. *CASTLES IN THE AIR*
Book and lyrics by Raymond Peck, and presented by a cast headed by Vivienne Segal, J. Harold Murray and Bernard Granville.

—LOVE'S REFRAIN
—I DON'T BLAME 'EM
—LANTERN OF LOVE
—THE SINGER'S CAREER, HA! HA!
—THE OTHER FELLOW'S GIRL
—IF YOU ARE IN LOVE WITH A GIRL
—THE FIRST KISS OF LOVE
—I WOULD LIKE TO FONDLE YOU
—THE RAINBOW OF YOUR SMILE
—LATVIAN FOLK SONG
—BABY
—LAND OF ROMANCE
—LATVIA
—MY LIPS, MY LOVE, MY SOUL
—GIRLS AND THE GIMMIES
—LOVE RULES THE WORLD

Clarence Williams Scores

1927. *BOTTOMLAND*
Book and lyrics by the composer, and

presented by a all-Negro cast headed by
Eva Taylor.

—ANYTIME
—DANCING GIRL
—I'M GOING TO TAKE MY BIMBO
BACK TO BAMBO
—SHOOTIN' THE PISTOL
Lyrics by Chris Smith.
—STEAMBOAT DAYS
—WHEN I MARCH IN APRIL WITH
MAY
By Gerald and Spencer Williams.
—YOU'RE THE ONLY ONE THAT I
LOVE
Music by Len Gray.
—COME ON HOME
By Donald Heywood.

Spencer Williams Score

1921. *PUT AND TAKE*
A revue with book by Irvin C. Miller,
and presented by a cast that included
Hamtree Harrington and Cora Green.
—WEDDING DAY IN GEORGIA
—STOP AND REST AWHILE
—DOG
—WEDDING BELLS
—JUNE LOVE
—SNAG 'EM BLUES
—SEPARATION BLUES
—PUT AND TAKE
—CREOLE GAL
—CHOCOLATE BROWN
—GEORGIA ROSE
—OLD TIME BLUES
—BROADWAY DOWN IN DIXIELAND
By Bernie Barber.

Ed Wynn Scores

1920. *ED WYNN'S CARNIVAL*
A revue starring Ed Wynn in a cast that
included Marion Davies.
—COME ALONG
—MY LOG FIRE GIRL
—SPHINX OF THE DESERT
—IN OLD JAPAN
Lyrics by Alfred Bryan.
—ROSE OF SPAIN
By Fred Fisher, Tom Brown, Billy Faz-
ioli and Ray Miller.
—UNDERNEATH THE DIXIE MOON
By Ray Miller, Ray Klages and Billy
Fazioli.
—IN THE SPRINGTIME
By Jack Maloy.
—IT MUST BE YOU
By Bobby Jones and Con Conrad.

—OO, I'D LOVE TO BE LOVED BY
YOU
By Louis M. Paley and George Gershwin.

1921. *THE PERFECT FOOL*
A revue with book and lyrics by the com-
poser-comedian, who headed a cast that
included Janet Velie and Guy Robertson.
—DAISY
—A DOLL HOUSE
Lyrics by Harry Richman and Lou Davis.
—TYPEWRITER SONG
—VISIONS THAT PASS IN THE NIGHT
—GIRLS PRETTY GIRLS
—OLD HOME WEEK IN MAINE
—SHE LOVES ME, SHE LOVES ME
NOT
—MY LOG CABIN HOME
By Irving Caesar, B. G. DeSylva and
George Gershwin.
—SWEETHEART WILL YOU ANSWER
YES?
By James Brennan, Al Wilson and Rolf
Piquet.

1924. *THE GRAB BAG*
A revue starring Ed Wynn in a cast that
included Jay Velie, Shaw and Lee, Mar-
ion Fairbanks and Janet Adair.
—A CHORUS GIRL'S SONG
—THE HEART OF MY ROSE
—I WANT A HOME
—WHAT DID ANNIE LAURIE PROM-
ISE?
—SOMETIMES YOU WILL, SOME-
TIMES YOU WON'T
By Henry Creamer and James Hanley.
—FLAME OF LOVE

Vincent Youmans Scores

1921. *TWO LITTLE GIRLS IN BLUE*
With Paul Lannin. Book by Fred Jackson,
lyrics by Arthur Francis, and starring
Madeline and Marion Fairbanks in a
cast that included Evelyn Law, Emma
Janvier, Oscar Shaw and Fred Santley.
—WE'RE OFF ON A WONDERFUL
TRIP
—WONDERFUL U. S. A.
—WHEN I'M WITH THE GIRLS
—TWO LITTLE GIRLS IN BLUE
—THE SILLY SEASON
—OH ME, OH MY, OH YOU
—YOU STARTED SOMETHING WHEN
YOU CAME ALONG
—WE'RE OFF FOR INDIA
—HERE, STEWARD
—THE GYPSY TRAIL
Music by Paul Lannin.
—DOLLY

—WHO'S WHO ARE YOU?
—JUST LIKE YOU
  Music by Paul Lannin.
—THERE'S SOMETHING ABOUT ME
  THEY LIKE
—RICE AND SHOES
—SHE'S INNOCENT
—HONEYMOON
  Music by Paul Lannin.
—I'M TICKLED SILLY
—ORIENTA
1923. *MARY JANE McKANE*
  With Herbert Stothart. Book and lyrics
  by William Cary Duncan and Oscar Hem-
  merstein II, and presented by a cast head-
  ed by Mary Hay, Hal Skelley and Stanley
  Ridges.
—THE RUMBLE OF THE SUBWAY
—SPEED
—NOT IN BUSINESS HOURS
—MY BOY AND I
—YOU'RE NEVER TOO OLD TO
  LEARN
—TOODLE-OO
—DOWN WHERE THE MORTGAGES
  GROW
—TIME-CLOCK SLAVES
—LAUGH IT OFF
—JUST LOOK AROUND
—THE FLANNEL PETTICOAT GIRL
—THISTLEDOWN
—MARY JANE McKANE
1923. *WILDFLOWER*
  With Herbert Stothart. Book and lyrics by
  Otto Harbach and Oscar Hammerstein
  II, and starring Edith Day and Guy
  Robertson.
—I LOVE YOU, I LOVE YOU, I LOVE
  YOU
—SOME LIKE TO HUNT
—WILDFLOWER
—BAMBALINA
—I'LL COLLABORATE WITH YOU
—APRIL BLOSSOM
—THE BEST DANCE I'VE HAD TO-
  NIGHT
—'COURSE I WILL
—CASINO
—YOU CAN'T BLAME A GIRL FOR
  DREAMING
—GOOD-BYE, LITTLE ROSEBUD
—THE WORLD'S WORST WOMAN
—YOU CAN'T ALWAYS FIND AN-
  OTHER PARTNER
1924. *LOLLYPOP*
  Book and lyrics by Zelda Sears, and pre-
  sented by a cast headed by Ada May,
  Harry Puck, Nick Long Jr. and Gloria
  Dawn.

—DEEP IN MY HEART
—GOING ROWING
—HONEY BUN
—TAKE A LITTLE ONE-STEP
—TIE A STRING AROUND YOUR
  FINGER
—LOVE IN A COTTAGE
—TIME AND A HALF FOR OVERTIME
—WHEN WE ARE MARRIED
—AN ORPHAN IS THE GIRL FOR ME
—BOO KOO
1925. *A NIGHT OUT*
  Book by George Grossmith and Arthur
  Miller, lyrics by Clifford Grey and Irving
  Caesar, and presented by Edward Lauril-
  lard's London Company.
—HOTEL NEVER TELL
—BIRD ON THE WING
—SOMETIMES I'M HAPPY
—BOLSHEVIK LOVE
—SO THIS IS KISSING
—I'VE GOT THE DAY OFF TODAY
—A HAPPY FAMILY
—IT'S A LONG DAY AT OUR HOTEL
—READY—WOULD YOU BELIEVE IT?
—THE POLICE
—WAITING FOR SOMETHING
—CARNIVAL
—HAPPY
1925. *NO, NO, NANETTE*
  Book by Otto Harbach and Frank Man-
  del, lyrics by Otto Harbach and Irving
  Caesar, and starring Louise Groody in a
  cast that included Mary Lawlor, Well-
  ington Cross and Charles Winninger.
—THE CALL OF THE SEA
—TOO MANY RINGS AROUND ROSIE
—I'M WAITING FOR YOU
—I WANT TO BE HAPPY
—NO, NO, NANETTE
—THE DEAP BLUE SEA
—MY DOCTOR
—FIGHT FOR ME
—*TEA FOR TWO
—YOU CAN DANCE WITH ANY GIRL
—HELLO, HELLO TELEPHONE
  GIRLIE
—WHO'S THE WHO?
—PAY DAY PAULINE
1926. *OH, PLEASE*
  Book and lyrics by Anne Caldwell and
  Otto Harbach, and staring Beatrice Lillie
  in a cast that included Charles Winninger
  and Helen Broderick.
—HOMELY BUT CLEAN
—SAPPY SHOW IN TOWN
—NICODEMUS
—I'LL STEAL A STAR

—I KNOW THAT YOU KNOW
—WONDERFUL GIRL
—LOVE ME
—I CAN'T BE HAPPY
—THE GIRLS OF THE OLD BRIGADE
1927. *HIT THE DECK*
Book by Herbert Fields, lyrics by Clifford
Grey and Leo Robin, and presented by a
cast headed by Louise Groody, Stella
Mayhew, Charles King, Bobbie Perkins
and Roger Gray.
—JOIN THE NAVY
—WHAT'S A KISS AMONG FRIENDS?
—HARBOR OF MY HEART
—SHORE LEAVE
—LUCKY BIRD
—LOOLOO
—NOTHING COULD BE SWEETER
—SOMETIMES I'M HAPPY
—HALLELUJAH
—IF HE'LL COME BACK TO ME
1928. *RAINBOW*
A musical comedy with book by Lawrence
Stallings, lyrics by Oscar Hammerstein II,
and presented by a cast headed by Libby
Holman, Charles Ruggles, Allan Pryor
and Harlan Dixon.
—HAY, STRAW
—WHO AM I THAT YOU SHOULD
CARE FOR ME?
Lyrics by Gus Kahn.
—I LIKE YOU AS YOU ARE
—I WANT A MAN
—THE ONE GIRL
1929. *GREAT DAY*
Book by William Cary Duncan and John
Wells, lyrics by Billy Rose, and presented
by a cast headed by Mayo Methot, Allan
Pryor, Walter C. Kelly and Miller and
Lyles.
—DOES IT PAY TO BE A LADY?
—I LIKE WHAT YOU LIKE
—HAPPY BECAUSE I'M IN LOVE
—GREAT DAY
—ONE LOVE
—SI SI SENOR
—OPEN UP YOUR HEART
—THE WEDDING BELLS RING ON
—MORE THAN YOU KNOW
—PLAY THE GAME
—SWEET AS SUGAR CANE
—WITHOUT A SONG
—SCARECROWS

Maurice Yvain Scores

1923. *ONE KISS*
A musical comedy with book and lyrics
by Clare Kummer, and presented by a

cast headed by Louise Groody, Oscar
Shaw, John E. Hazzard and John Price
Jones.
—JUST A LITTLE LOVE
—THERE ARE SOMETHINGS WE CAN
NEVER FORGET
—YOUR LIPS
—ONE KISS
—UP THERE
—WHEN WE ARE MARRIED
—DON'T BE A POOR RELATION
—A LITTLE BIT OF LACE
—GENTLEMEN
—IS THAT SO?
—IN MY DAY
—LONDON TOWN
1929. *LUCKEE GIRL*
With Maurice Rubens. A musical com-
edy with book by Gertrude Purcell, lyrics
by Max and Nat Lief, and presented by a
cast headed by Irene Dunne, Irving Fish-
er, Frank Lalor and Harry Puck.
—A FLAT IN MONTMARTRE
With Lew Pollack.
—IN OUR LITTLE STUDIO
With Lew Pollack.
—FRIENDS AND LOVERS
—I'LL TAKE YOU TO THE COUNTRY
—MAGIC MELODY
—COME ON AND MAKE WHOOPEE
By Mann Holiner and Werner Janssen.
—I'M GLAD I FELL FOR YOU
By Douglas Furber, R. P. Watson, Bert
Lee and Phil Charig.
—UNDER THE STAR WHERE I WAS
BORN
By Adolph Philipp.
—LUCKY GIRL
Music by Phil Charig.
—WHEN I SET EYES ON YOU
Music by Phil Charig.

Efrem Zimbalist Score

1920. *HONEYDEW*
A musical comedy with book and lyrics
by Joseph W. Herbert, and presented by
a cast headed by Ethelind Terry, Hal
Forde, John Park and Sam Ash.
—A CUP OF TEA
—DROP ME A LINE
—BELIEVE ME, BELOVED
—THE BUG SONG
—MARRY FOR WEALTH
—THE MORALS OF A SAILORMAN
—MORNING GLORY
—OH HOW I LONG FOR SOMEONE
—THE SOUND OF THE SOUND AT
LARCHMONT BAY

Composite Scores

1920. *ZIEGFELD FOLLIES OF 1920*
Charles Winninger made his Follies debut in a cast that included Ray Dooley, John Steel, Delyle Alda, Van and Schenck, Fanny Brice, W. C. Fields, Bernard Granville, Carl Randall and Art Hickman's orchestra.
—THEY'RE SO HARD TO KEEP WHEN THEY'RE BEAUTIFUL
By Joseph McCarthy and Harry Tierney.
—SUNSHINE AND SHADOWS
By Gene Buck and Dave Stamper.
—WHEN THE RIGHT ONE COMES ALONG
By Gene Buck and Victor Herbert.
—I'M A VAMP FROM EAST BROADWAY
By Bert Kalmar, Harry Ruby and Irving Berlin.
—GIRLS OF MY DREAMS
By Irving Berlin.
—ANY PLACE WOULD BE WONDERFUL WITH YOU
By Gene Buck and Dave Stamper.
—MARY AND DOUG
By Gene Buck and Dave Stamper.
—WHERE DO THE MOSQUITOS GO?
By Joseph McCarthy and Harry Tierney.
—BELLS
By Irving Berlin.
—THE LEG OF NATIONS
By Irving Berlin.
—I WAS A FLORODORA BABY
By Ballard MacDonald and Harry Carroll.
—CHINESE FIRECRACKERS
By Irving Berlin.
—THE LOVE BOAT
By Gene Buck and Victor Herbert.
—SYNCOPATED VAMP
By Irving Berlin.
—TELL ME LITTLE GYPSY
By Irving Berlin.
—ALL SHE'D SAY WAS "UM HUM".
By King Zany, Van and Schenck.
—SMART LITTLE FELLER STOCK UP YOUR CELLAR
By Grant Clarke and Milton Agar.

1921. *PASSING SHOW OF 1921*
A revue with book and lyrics by Harold Atteridge, and presented by a cast headed by Willie and Eugene Howard, Marie Dressler, Harry Watson, Janet Adair and J. Harold Murray.
—WONDERFUL KID
By Willie Howard, Sidney Clare and Lew Pollack.

—I'M ORIENTAL
Music by Lew Pollack.
—DANCE OFF THE BLUES
Music by Lew Pollack.
—KENTUCKY BLUES
Music by Clarence Gaskill.
—UNDERNEATH HAWAIIAN SKIES
Music by Fred Rose.
—THE SWEETEST MELODY
By Abner Silver.
—CHARM SCHOOL
By Al Bryan and Jean Schwartz.
—THE DREAM OF MY LAST WALTZ WITH YOU
By Gus Kahn, Charles Drury and George Raft.
—IN LITTLE OLD NEW YORK
By Harold Atteridge and Jean Schwartz.
—LET'S HAVE A RATTLING GOOD TIME
By Al Bryan and Jean Schwartz.
—MY LADY OF THE LAMP
Music by Lew Pollack.
—TA-HOO
Music by Jean Schwartz.
—WHEN THERE'S NO ONE TO LOVE
Music by Jean Schwartz.
—WHERE IS THE BEAUTIFUL FACE?
Music by Lew Pollack.
—I WISH I HAD A GIRL LIKE YOU
By Cliff Friend.
—IF YOU HAVE A GIRL WHO LOVES YOU (LEAVE THE OTHER GIRLS ALONE)
By Cliff Friend.
—I WAS BORN IN MICHIGAN
By Alex Gerber and Malvin Franklin.
—HOW IS IT BY YOU? BY ME IT'S FINE
By Ray Perkins and John W. Bratton.

1921. *SNAPSHOTS OF 1921*
A revue presented by a cast that included Nora Bayes, Lew Fields, DeWolf Hopper, Lulu McConnell, Alan Edwards, Delyle Alda, Ernest Lambert and Gilda Gray.
—EVERY GIRLIE WANTS TO BE A SALLY
By Alex Gerber and Malvin Franklin.
—SATURDAY
By Sidney Mitchell and Harry Brooks.
—DAB-DERRO
By Alex Gerber and Malvin Franklin.
—BEAUTIFUL FEATHERS MAKE BEAUTIFUL BIRDS
By E. Ray Goetz and George Meyers.
—ON THE BRIM OF HER OLD-FASHIONED BONNET
By E. Ray Goetz and George Gershwin.

232

—BABY DOLLIE WALK
By Con Conrad.
—MEMORIES
By Bert Kalman and Harry Ruby.
—THE BAMBOULA
By E. Ray Goetz and Jose Padilla.
—FUTURISTIC MELODY
By E. Ray Goetz and George Gershwin.
—YOKOHAMA LULLABY
By Grant Clarke and Jimmy Monaco.
—MOTHER, DIXIE, THE FLAG AND
YOU
By E. Ray Goetz and George Meyers.
—AMBITION
By Morrie Ryskind and Lewis Gensler.
—SENTENCE ME FOR LIFE
By Morrie Ryskind and Lewis Gensler.
—CHINISH
By Morrie Ryskind and Lewis Gensler.
1921. *ZIEGFELD FOLLIES OF 1921*
This year's edition of the Follies was
staged at the Globe Theater with a cast
that included Raymond Hitchcock, Fanny
Brice, Van and Schenck, Ray Dooley,
Florence O'Denishawn, W. C. Fields, John
Clarke, Mary Eaton, Mary Milburn and
Vera Michelena.
—STRUT MISS LIZZY
—PRINCESS OF MY DREAMS
By Gene Buck and Victor Herbert.
—LEGEND OF THE CYCLAMEN TREE
By Gene Buck and Victor Herbert.
—SECOND-HAND ROSE
By Grant Clarke and James Hanley.
—BRING BACK MY BLUSHING ROSE
By Gene Buck and Rudolf Friml.
—PLYMOUTH ROCK
By Channing Pollock and Dave Stamper.
—SCOTCH LASSIE
By Blanche Merrill and Leo Edwards.
—RAGGEDY RAG
By Gene Buck and Dave Stamper.
—COME BACK TO OUR ALLEY SALLY
By Gene Buck and Dave Stamper.
—OUR HOME TOWN
By Ballard MacDonald and Harry Carroll.
—MY MAN
By Channing Pollock and Maurice Yvain.
—FOUR LITTLE GIRLS WITH A FU-
TURE AND FOUR LITTLE GIRLS
WITH A PAST
By B. G. DeSylva and Rudolf Friml.
—SOMEDAY THE SUN WILL SHINE
—NOW I KNOW
By Grant Clarke and Jimmy Monaco.
—ALLAY-OOP
By Ballard MacDonald and James Hanley.
—EVERY TIME I HEAR A BAND PLAY
By Gene Buck and Rudolf Friml.

—IN KHORASSAN
By Gene Buck and Victor Herbert.
—YOU MUST COME OVER
By B. G. DeSylva and Jerome Kern.
1922. *CHAUVE SOURIS*
A Russian song-and-dance revue with M.
Nikita Balieff as master of ceremonies,
and presented by a troupe of singers and
dancers from the Bat Theater of Moscow.
During the two-year run of this produc-
tion on Broadway, the program was
changed from time to time, and the fol-
lowing songs introduced:
—ANUSKA
By Steiner and Virag.
—CHAUVE SOURIS
By Eugene Platzman.
—CHINESE BILLIKENS
By Daly Paskman and Alexei Archangel-
sky.
—DEAR NIGHTINGALE
By Daly Paskman and Aliabick.
—DARK EYES
By A. Salami.
—GRIEF
By Daly Paskman, based on a melody by
Chopin.
—KATINKA
By Czaroulch and Alexei Archangelsky.
—NIGHT IDYL
By Daly Paskman and Alexei Archangel-
sky.
—PASSING REGIMENT
By Leigh and Strauss.
—VOLGA BOAT SONG
By Daly Paskman and Alexei Archangel-
sky.
—PIERROT'S MOONLIGHT SERE-
NADE
By Daly Paskman.
—SPARKLING WINE
By Daly Paskman.
—THREE HUNTSMEN
By Daly Paskman.
—'TWAS IN THE MONTH OF MAY
By Brian Hooker and Walter Kollo.
—PORCELAINE DE SAXE
By Frank Waller.
—PARADE OF THE WOODEN SOL-
DIERS
By Ballard MacDonald and Leon Jessel.
—MARLBOROUGH GOES TO THE
WARS
—THE EVENING BELLS
—THE KING ORDERS THE DRUMS
TO BE BEATEN
—THE CLOWN
—THE JAPANESE BOX
—THE RUSSIAN TOYS

—THE MINUET
When the Chauve Souris came back to
New York City in 1925 for a return en-
gagement, many of the songs listed above
were repeated and the following new
numbers added:
—STENKA RAZIN
—THE RENDEZVOUS OF LOVE
—LOVE IN THE RANKS
—SICILANA
—YOU OUGHTA HEAR OLAF LAUGH
By L. Wolfe Gilbert and Abel Baer.
—IN A LITTLE FRENCH CAFE
By Mitchell Parish and Sammy Fain.
—I MISS MY SWISS
By L. Wolfe Gilbert and Abel Baer.

1922 *RAYMOND HITCHCOCK'S PIN-
WHEEL*
An intimate revue with Raymond Hitch-
cock, Frank Fay and Eva Clark.
—SILVER STARS
By Percy Wenrich.
—MY LADY OF THE FAN
By Earl Carroll.
—OH SAY, OH SUE
By Irving Caesar and Joseph Meyer.

1922. *THE FRENCH DOLL*
A comedy by A. E. Thomas, starring
Irene Bordoni, who introduced the fol-
lowing songs:
—DO IT AGAIN
By B. G. DeSylva and George Gershwin.
—GEE, BUT I HATE TO GO HOME
ALONE
By Joe Goodwin and James Hanley.
—YOU DON'T HAVE TO DO AS I DO
By E. Ray Goetz, Hugh E. Wright and
Paul Rubens.
—WHEN EYES MEET EYES (WHEN
LIPS MEET LIPS)
By Will Cobb and Gus Edwards.

1923. *LITTLE MISS BLUEBEARD*
A comedy by Avery Hopwood, starring
Irene Bordoni and featuring Eric Blore,
in which the following songs were intro-
duced:
—SO THIS IS LOVE
By E. Ray Goetz.
—THE GONDOLA AND THE GIRL
By E. Ray Goetz and Paul Rubens.
—WHO'LL BUY MY VIOLETS?
By E. Ray Goetz and Jose Padilla.
—I WON'T SAY I WILL, I WON'T SAY
I WON'T
By Ira Gershwin, B. G. DeSylva and
George Gershwin.

1923. *JACK AND JILL*
A musical comedy with book by Frederic

Isham and Otto Harbach, and presented
by a cast headed by Brooke Johns, Beth
Berri, Georgia O'Ramey, Clifton Webb
and Ann Pennington.
—DANCING IN THE DARK
By Oliver Deerin and Muriel Pollock.
—I LOVE, THOU LOVEST
By John Murray Anderson and Augustus
Barratt.
—I WANT A PRETTY GIRL
Music by William Daly.
—NO OTHER EYES
By John Murray Anderson and Augustus
Barratt.
—VOODOO MAN
By Otto Harbach and Alfred Newman.
—HOPING
By Irving Caesar and William Daly.
—IT'S THE NICEST SORT OF FEEL-
ING
By Irving Caesar and William Daly.

1923. *NIFTIES OF 1923*
A revue with book by Sam Bernard and
Willie Collier, who headed a cast that
included Frank Crumit, Van and Schenck,
Hazel Dawn, Ray Dooley and Helen Brod-
erick.
—AT HALF PAST SEVEN
By B. G. DeSylva and George Gershwin.
—NASHVILLE NIGHTINGALE
By Irving Caesar and George Gershwin.
—LITTLE MISS BLUEBIRD
By Arthur Jackson, B. G. DeSylva and
George Gershwin.
—I WON'T SAY I WILL
By Arthur Jackson, B. G. DeSylva and
George Gershwin.
—SUNSHINE TRAIL
By Arthur Jackson and George Gershwin.
—LITTLE BROWN ROAD
By Frank Crumit.
—FABRIC OF DREAMS
By Arthur Francis, B. G. DeSylva and
Raymond Hubbell.
—ARE YOU HERE, MAGGIE MOONEY,
ARE YOU HERE?
By Worton David and C. W. Murphy.
—AN OLD TIME TUNE
By Van and Schenck.
—WHERE ARE THE OLD PALS OF
YESTERDAY?
By Van and Schenck.
—IF YOU'LL MARRY US WE'LL
STROLL BY THE BABBLING
BROOK
By Bert Kalmar and Harry Ruby.
—THAT BRAN' NEW GIRL OF MINE
By Van and Schenck, Benny Davis and
Harry Akst.

1924. *ANDRE CHARLOT'S REVUE OF 1924*
A revue with a cast that included Beatrice Lillie, Sam Hardy, Gertrude Lawrence and Herbert Mundin.
—HOW D'YOU DO
By Eric Blore, Ronald Jeans and Philip Braham.
—THERE ARE TIMES
By Ronald Jeans and Philip Braham.
—PARISIAN PIERROT
By Noel Coward.
—I WAS MEANT FOR YOU
By Noble Sissle and Eubie Blake.
—I DON'T KNOW
By Ronald Jeans and Philip Braham.
—CIGARETTE LAND
By R. P. Weston and Bert Lee.
—THERE'S LIFE IN THE OLD GIRL YET
By Noel Coward.
—I MIGHT
By Ronald Jeans and Philip Braham.
—MARCH WITH ME
By Douglas Furber and Ivor Novello.
—LIMEHOUSE BLUES
By Douglas Furber and Philip Braham.
—NIGHT MAY HAVE ITS SADNESS
By Collie Knox and Ivor Novello.

1924. *ROUND THE TOWN*
A revue with book by Herman Mankiewicz and S. Jay Kaufman, and presented by a cast headed by Julius Tannen, Heywood Broun, Harry Fox, Jay Velie, Jack Haley, Irene Delroy and Janet Velie.
—LIZA JANE
By Ned Wever and Alfred Nathan.
—POOR LITTLE WALLFLOWER
By Ned Wever and Alfred Nathan.
—IF ONE OF US WAS YOU DEAR
By S. Jay Kaufman and Jay Velie.
—IT'S GOOD FOR YOU TO EXERCISE YOUR MIND
By Dorothy Parker and Arthur H. Samuels.
—CHIQUITA
By Walter Donaldson.
—I WONDER WHY THE GLOW-WORM WINKS HIS EYES AT ME?
By Oscar Hammerstein II and Herbert Stothart.
—SAVE A KISS FOR RAINY WEATHER
By Richard H. Whiting.

1924. *HASSARD SHORT'S RITZ REVUE*
Presented by a cast headed by Raymond Hitchcock, Hal Forde, Jay Brennan, Charlotte Greenwood and Madeline Fairbanks.

—BROADWAY BOUDOIR
By Anne Caldwell and Frank Tours.
—FROM COTTAGE TO SUBWAY
By Kenneth and Roy Webb.
—THE LITTLE BLACK CAT
By Anne Caldwell and Raymond Hitchcock.
—HELLO GIRLS
By Roger Gray and Werner Janssen.
—SPRINGTIME
By Kenneth and Roy Webb.
—I WANT TO BELONG
By Owen Murphy and Jay Gorney.
—SUN GIRL
By Anne Caldwell and Frank Tours.
—DANCING BLUES
By Franke Harling.
—UKING THE UKE
By Franke Harling.
—CRYSTAL WEDDING DAY
By Anne Caldwell and Frank Tours.
—THE RED LADIES
By Kenneth and Roy Webb.
—A PERFECT DAY
By Harry Raskin, May Tally and Martin Broones.
—TOO TALL
By Harry Raskin, May Tally and Martin Broones.
—BEEDLE-UM-BEE
By Eric Valentine, William Gaston and Martin Broones.
—THE WANDERER
By Jay Gorney, Tom Burke and Owen Murphy.
—SCANDAL AND A CUP OF TEA
By Kenneth and Roy Webb.
—WHEN YOU AND I WERE DANCING
By Graham John and H. M. Tennent.
—WHAT THE MEN WILL WEAR
By Kenneth and Roy Webb.
—MONSIEUR BEAUCAIRE
By Anne Caldwell and Frank Tours.

1925. *ANDRE CHARLOT'S REVUE OF 1925*
A revue with a cast headed by Gertrude Lawrence and Jack Buchanan.
—A CUP OF COFFEE, A SANDWICH AND YOU
By Billy Rose, Al Dubin and Joseph Meyer.
—GIGOLETTE
By Irving Caesar and Franz Lehar.
—MENDER OF BROKEN DREAMS
By John W. Bratton.
—THE ANIMALS CAME IN TWO BY TWO
By Philip Braham.

—MONA WHEN SHE TAPS ON HER CORONA
By Clifford Seyler and Jara Benes.

—LOVE'S LOTTERY
By Billy Mayerl and Gene Paul.

—THE BALLAD SINGER
By Leonard Henry and H. B. Hedley.

—HE'S RELIABLE
By Laddie Cliff, Leonard Henry and H. B. Hedley.

—OXFORD BAGS
By Arthur Wimperis and Philip Braham.

—THOSE WERE THE DAYS
By Ronald Jeans and Philip Braham.

—MOUSE, MOUSE
By Hilda Brighton and Muriel Lillie.

—BABY BLUES
By Ronald Jeans and Ivor Novello.

—BE CAREFUL WHAT YOU DO
By Reginald Arkell and Geoffrey Gwyther.

1925. *GREENWICH VILLAGE FOLLIES OF 1925*
The cast for this year's edition of the John Murray Anderson revue was headed by Tom Howard, Frank McIntyre, Sam Hearn, Florence Moore and Irene Delroy. Lyrics by Owen Murphy and Irving Caesar.

—GARDEN OF USED-TO-BE
Music by Jay Gorney.

—WHEN EVENING SHADOWS FALL
Music by Jay Gorney.

—I AM IN LOVE AGAIN
Lyrics and music by Cole Porter.

—HAPPY PRINCE
By Irving Caesar, John Murray Anderson and Willy Engel-Berger.

—GO SOUTH
Music by Richard Myers.

—LADY OF THE SNOW
Music by Harold Levey.

—YOU HAVE ME, I HAVE YOU
Music by Harold Levey.

1925. *PUZZLES OF 1925*
A revue with book by Elsie Janis, who headlined a cast that included Jimmy Hussey, Walter Pidgeon and Helen Broderick.

—DO-I-OR-DON'T-I BLUES
By Elsie Janis.

—THE DOO DAB
By Bert Kalmar and Harry Ruby.

—JE VOUS AIME

—TITANIA
by Billy Rose, and presented by a cast
By William C. Duncan and Leo Daniderff.

—YOU'VE GOT TO DANCE
By Elsie Janis.

—LOOK WHO'S HERE
By Raymond Klages and Ken Whitmer.

1925. *SKY HIGH*
A musical comedy with book and lyrics by Harold Atteridge and Harry Graham, and presented by a cast headed by Willie Howard.

—BARBER OF SEVILLE
By Clifford Grey and Maurice Rubens.

—GIVE YOUR HEART IN JUNETIME
Music by Victor Herbert.

—TRIM THEM ALL BUT THE ONE YOU LOVE
By Carleton Kelsey and Maurice Rubens.

FIRST ME, THEN YOU
By H. M. Tennent and Eric Little.

—IN MY GARDEN
By Adrian Ross and Harry Rosenthal.

—JAPANESE DOLL
By Adrian Ross and Harry Rosenthal.

—UNDER THE PALM
By Adrian Ross and Harry Rosenthal.

—KEEP ON CROONING A TUNE
By Sammy Fain, Irving Weill and Jimmy McHugh.

—TIMBUCTOO
By Eric Little and H. M. Tennent.

1925. *ZIEGFELD FOLLIES OF 1925*
This was a continuation of the 1924 revue with new sketches by J. P. McEvoy, Will Rogers and W. C. Fields, and the following new songs:

—EVERYONE KNOWS WHAT JAZZ IS
By Gene Buck and Werner Janssen.

—TODDLE ALONG
By Gene Buck and Werner Janssen.

—I'D LIKE TO CORRAL A GAL
By Gene Buck and Raymond Hubbell.

—EVER LOVIN' BEE
By Gene Buck and Dave Stamper.

—SETTLE DOWN IN A ONE-HORSE TOWN
By Gene Buck and Werner Janssen.

—TITANIA
By Gene Buck and Leo Daniderff.

—BERTIE
By Clifford Grey and Sigmund Romberg.
Ethel Shutta joined the summer edition of this year's Follies, and the following new songs were added to the score:

—HOME AGAIN
By Gene Buck and Raymond Hubbell.

—SYNCOPATING BABY
By Gene Buck and Dave Stamper.

—TONDELEYO
By Gene Buck and Dave Stamper.

—IN THE SHADE OF THE ALAMO
By Gene Buck and Raymond Hubbell.

—EDDIE, BE GOOD
By Gene Buck and Dave Stamper.

—I'D LIKE TO BE A GARDENER IN A GARDEN OF GIRLS
By Gene Buck and Raymond Hubbell.

1926. *GRAND STREET FOLLIES OF 1927*
A Neighborhood Playhouse revue presented by a cast that included Albert Carroll and Jessica Dragonette.

—A LITTLE IGLOO FOR TWO
By Agnes Morgan and Arthur Schwartz.

—IF YOU KNOW WHAT I MEAN
By Theodore Goodwin, Albert Carroll and Arthur Schwartz.

—POLAR BEAR STRUT
By Agnes Morgan and Arthur Schwartz.

—UNCLE TOM'S CABIN
By Agnes Morgan and Arthur Schwartz.

—FIXED FOR LIFE
By Agnes Morgan and Randall Thompson.

—THE BOOSTER'S SONG OF THE FAR NORTH
By Agnes Morgan and Randall Thompson.

—AURORY BORY ALICE
By Agnes Morgan and Lily Hyland.

—TAXI DRIVER'S LAMENT
By Agnes Morgan and Randall Thompson.

—THE DISCONTENTED BANDITS
By Agnes Morgan and Lily Hyland.

—BEATRICE LILLIE BALLAD
By Agnes Morgan and Randall Thompson.

—MY ICY FLOE
By Agnes Morgan and Randall Thompson.

—SKATING BALLET
By Lily Hyland.

—REINDEER DANCE
By Lily Hyland.

—ICE MAZURKA
By Randall Thompson.

—THE ESKIMO BLUES
By Robert Simon and Walter Haenschen.

1927. *A LA CARTE*
A revue with book by George Kelly, and presented by a cast headed by Charles Irwin, Jay Velie, Little Billy, York and King, Harriet Hoctor and Bobbe Arnst.

—BABY'S BLUE
By Herman Hupfeld.

—GIVE TROUBLE THE AIR
By Leo Robin and Louis Alter.

—THE CALINDA
By Herman Hupfeld.

—BOO JOOM BOO JOOM
By Herman Hupfeld.

—WHEN THE MOON IS HIGH
By Harry Steinberg and John McLaughlin.

—I'M STEPPING OUT WITH LULU
By Henry Creamer and J. C. Johnson.

—SORT OF LONESOME
By Herman Hupfeld.

1927. *THE NEW YORKERS*
A revue with book by Jo Swerling and lyrics by Henry Myers. Arthur Schwartz is credited with the following songs:

—NINETY-NINE PERCENT PURE

—I CAN'T GET INTO THE QUOTA

—SELF-EXPRESSION

—HERE COMES THE PRINCE OF WALES

—HE WHO GETS SLAPPED

—FLOATING THROUGH THE AIR

—ROMANY

—A SONG ABOUT LOVE

—INDIAN CHANT
The following songs are credited to Edgar Fairchild:

—BURN 'EM UP

—NOTHING LEFT BUT DREAMS

—OLD FASHIONED BALLET

—PRETTY LITTLE SO-AND-SO

—A SIDE STREET OFF BROADWAY
These songs were written by Charles M. Schwab:

—TRIANGLE

—HOW TO WELCOME HOME YOUR HUBBY

—SLOW RIVER

—WORDS AND MUSIC

1927. *PADLOCKS OF 1927*
A revue with book by Paul Gerard Smith and Ballard MacDonald, music by Henry Tobias, Lee David and Jesse Greer, lyrics by Billy Rose, and presented by a cast headed by Texas Guinan, Lillian Roth, Helen Shipman, Frances Healy, Jans and Whalen, Jay C. Flippen and George Raft.

—TEXAS

—HERE I AM

—IF I HAD A LOVER

—SUMMERTIME

—THE TAP-TAP

—STRING ALONG WITH TEXAS

—HOT HEELS

—THAT STUPID MELODY

—TOM-TOM

1928. *EARL CARROLL'S VANITIES OF 1928*
A revue with book by Earl Carrol, and presented by a cast headed by W. C. Fields, Joe Frisco, Gordon Dooley, Ray Dooley, Dorothy Knapp, Lillian Roth and Vincent Lopez and his band.

—SAY IT WITH GIRLS
By Grace Henry and Morris Hamilton.

—PRETTY GIRL
By Grace Henry and Morris Hamilton.
—ROSE OF THE WORLD
By Grace Henry and Morris Hamilton.
—FLUTTERBY BABY
By Grace Henry and Morris Hamilton.
—WHEELS
By Grace Henry and Morris Hamilton.
—GETTING THE BEAUTIFUL GIRLS
By Ned Washington and Michael Cleary.
—MY ARMS ARE WIDE OPEN
By Ned Washington and Michael Cleary.
—YOU ALONE
By Jean Herbert and Bernard Malten.
—VANITEASER
By Paul Jones and Michael Cleary.
—RAQUEL
By George Whiting and Joseph Burke.
—ONCE IN A LIFETIME
By Raymond Klages and Jesse Greer.
—BLUE SHADOWS
By Raymond Klages and Louis Alter.
—OH, HOW HE CAN LOVE!
By Lillian Roth and Herb Magidson.
—WATCH MY BABY WALK
By Jo Trent and Peter DeRose.
—PAINTING A VANITIES' GIRL
By Ernie Golden.
—I'M FLYING HIGH
By Jack LeSoir, Roy Doll and Abner Silver.

1928. *SAY WHEN*
A musical comedy with book by Calvin Brown, and presented by a cast headed by Dorothy Fitzgibbons, Bartlett Simmons and Alison Skipworth.
—ONE STEP TO HEAVEN
By Ray Klages and Jesse Greer.
—HOW ABOUT IT?
By Ray Klages and Jesse Greer.
—TABLE FOR TWO
—CHEERIO
By James J. Walker and Jesse Greer.
—NO ROOM FOR ANYBODY IN MY HEART BUT YOU
By Nat and Max Lief and Ray Perkins.
—IN MY LOVE BOAT
By Nat and Max Lief and Countess de Segonzac.
—MY ONE GIRL
By W. Franke Harling.
—GIVE ME A NIGHT
By W. Franke Harling.

1929. *KEEP IT CLEAN*
A musical comedy with book by Jimmy Duffy and Will Morrissey, and presented by a cast headed by Will Morrissey and Midge Miller.

—H-O-K-U-M
—DOING THE HOT-CHA-CHA
By Lester Lee.
—ALL I NEED IS SOMEONE LIKE YOU
By Charles Tobias and Harry Archer.
—I SEE YOU BUT WHAT DO YOU SEE IN ME?
By Jack Murray and Lester Lee.
—JUST A LITTLE BLUE FOR YOU
By James Hanley.
—BROADWAY MAMMY
By Jimmy Duffy and Clarence Gaskill.
—SOMEONE TO LOVE YOU
Music by Harry Archer.

REVIVALS OF 1920-30

1929. SWEETHEARTS with Gladys Baxter and Charles Massinger.
1929. MLLE. MODISTE with Fritzi Scheff and Dick Powell.
1929. NAUGHTY MARIETTA with Ilse Marvenga and Dick Powell.
1929. THE FORTUNE TELLER with Tessa Kosta and Roy Cropper.
1929. ROBIN HOOD with Roy Cropper, William Danforth, Greek Evans and Olga Steck.
1929. THE MERRY WIDOW with Beppe DeVries, Evan Thomas, Roy Cropper and Dick Powell.
1929. BABES IN TOYLAND with Betty Byron, Frank Gallagher and Barry Lupino.

Minstrel Shows of 1900

1904. *LEW DOCKSTADER'S MINSTRELS,* headed by Lew Dockstader, Neil O'Brien, Manuel Romaine, Eddie Leonard, Tommy Hyde and Johnny King.
1906. *LEW DOCKSTADER'S MINSTRELS,* headed by Lew Dockstader, Eddie Leonard, Neil O'Brien, Johnny King, Johnny Dove, Reese Prosser, Manuel Romaine and the Foley Brothers.
1908. *COHAN & HARRIS MINSTRELS,* headed by George "Honey Boy" Evans, Eddie Leonard, Julian Eltinge, George Thatcher, Johnny King, and Waterbury Brothers and Tenney.
1909. *COHAN & HARRIS MINSTRELS,* headed by Vaughn Comfort, Johnny King, Will Oakland and George "Honey Boy" Evans.

While *Brother Can You Spare a Dime?* was the theme song of the Depression years, the Cole Porter and George Gershwin songs put musical sunshine in the nation's loud speakers.

The Lean Decade (1930-1940)

At first, Broadway couldn't believe its own eyes. Hadn't Herbert Hoover pledged "a chicken in every pot"? Weren't the Democrats chanting *Happy Days Are Here Again?* It just couldn't last—the blank marquee boards, the half-filled theaters, the blues wailed nightly by the operators of the cut-rate ticket agencies. But old Apple Mary, her territory invaded and her monopoly broken by a host of rival apple venders, knew the Depression was the real McCoy. And despite the phoney optimism and the passing-the-graveyard whistling, the lean years did last for a decade, and Broadway never was to be quite the same again.

There were evidences of a changing theatrical age on every hand. The loud speaker carried the seductive voice of Rudy Vallee into millions of homes—and for free. The magic of sound lured to the movie houses, which offered Garbo with glassware and Crosby with crockery, both the masses and the carriage trade that had paid tribute to Flo Ziegfeld's lovelies in hard cash at the box office. And many of the stage doors through which the great of Broadway had passed soon were to be closed forever.

Dynamite blasts first sounded the doom of these historic portals in 1930 when the walls of the Casino, early shrine of the Broadway musical, came tumbling down to provide a site for a ready-to-wear clothing factory—a transition from glamour to garments. And this was only the beginning.

More than a third of the sixty-eight legitimate playhouses of which Broadway boasted in 1930 gradually disappeared from the fold. In the four-year span between 1930 and 1934 alone, twelve theaters were converted to what is known in Broadway parlance as "grind houses", and such hallowed landmarks as the New Amsterdam, the Sam H. Harris, the Eltinge, the Selwyn and the George M. Cohan, once the scenes of epochal first nights, offered a continuous showing of second- and third-run films around the clock.

Twelve more legitimate theaters were converted into movie houses or radio studios between 1935 and the outbreak of World War II, and another, the New York Hippodrome, was razed in 1940 to provide room for a parking lot. But this spacious playhouse, famous for aquatic spectacles and eye-filling tableaux, had a glorious end. The songs that rang down the final curtain were by Rodgers and Hart, and the last production bore the title of *Jumbo*.

While the lights of Broadway did not shine as brightly as they had during the Terrific Twenties, the quality of the musical comedies and revues staged during the Troubled Thirties did not suffer from the Depression blight, and although most producers were willing to settle for a 200-performance run, two productions zoomed to stratospheric heights of popularity—*Pins And*

Needles, staged by the New York Garment Workers Union, which ran for 1108 performances, and *Hellz-a-poppin*, starring Olsen and Johnson, which hit 1404 performances and proved the closest runner-up to *Tobacco Road*, a non-musical that set the all-time endurance record at close to five years.

In addition to writing the music for two of his biggest successes, *Girl Crazy* and *Strike Up The Band*, during this period, George Gershwin reached supreme heights before his untimely death in 1937 with *Of Thee I Sing*, the first musical to be awarded the Pulitzer Prize, and *Porgy and Bess*, a folk opera as bewitching as it was sincere in depicting the Negro as he really is.

Neither did Irving Berlin let Broadway down, and contributed music to two highly successful revues: *Face The Music* in which *Let's Have Another Cup of Coffee*, sung by a party of socialites in Child's, gave the Depression a rib-tickling "sunshine song", and *As Thousands Cheer*, which elevated Ethel Waters to stardom and put *Heat Wave* and *Easter Parade* on the best-selling-song list.

Before deserting Broadway for a permanent home in Hollywood, Jerome Kern added to his towering stature as a composer with the scores he wrote for *The Cat And The Fiddle* and *Roberta*, while Vincent Youmans closed his Broadway career by providing *Through The Years* with memorable music.

Richard Rodgers and Larry Hart were among the most prolific songwriters of the decade with nine Broadway productions, three of which, *I'd Rather Be Right*, *I Married An Angel* and *Babes In Arms*, fell just short of the 300-performance mark, with *Too Many Girls* and *Jumbo* each being responsible for better than 200 final curtain calls.

During this period, Cole Porter moved into the Broadway king row with four out of eight productions that played better than 200 performances: *The Gay Divorcee*, *Anything Goes*, *Leave It To Me* and *DuBarry Was A Lady*, with *Red, White And Blue* close up in total box office receipts. Three of these musicals put a star on the dressing room door of Ethel Merman, and the Cole Porter scores of the 1930s included such enduring hits as *Night and Day*, *Blow Gabriel Blow*, *I Get A Kick Out Of You*, *You're The Top*, *Begin The Beguine*, *Just One Of Those Things*, *It's De-lovely* and *My Heart Belongs To Daddy*, the latter introducing Mary Martin to Broadway and theatrical fame.

Of the comparative newcomers to Broadway, Arthur Schwartz, a practicing barrister who decided he'd rather write the country's songs than interpret the country's laws, and his librettist-lyricist, Howard Dietz, were the most prolific and successful with *Three's A Crowd*, *The Band Wagon*, *Flying Colors*, *Revenge With Music*, *At Home Abroad* and *Stars In Your Eyes*. Two European expatriates also thrilled to the applause of Broadway for the first time in the 1930s, Vernon Duke, a White Russian who couldn't see eye-to-eye with

Communism, making his American debut with scores for *Walk A Little Faster* and two *Ziegfeld Follies,* while Kurt Weill, fleeing from the wrath of Hitler, made an initial payment on the debt he owed the land of his adoption with the *September Song* and other *Knickerbocker Holiday* numbers.

Florenz Ziegfeld, always in hock even when there were SRO signs in front of the theaters where his productions were playing, was plagued and bewildered by the Depression. There was no such word as thrift in his vocabulary, costly shows were the only kind he knew how to produce, and he bowed out of the Broadway picture with his 1931 *Follies* and *Hot-Cha,* a heart-broken and sadly perplexed man.

Most of the low-budgeted revues produced during this era of low spirits and empty pockets were shoddy stuff compared with the ostrich-plumed opulence and sable-lined splendor of the Ziegfeld Follies, and served mainly as finishing schools for June Allyson, Henry Fonda, Danny Kaye, Gene Kelly, Carmen Miranda and other newcomers to the Main Street of show business, who capitalized on their Broadway billing in the California gold fields and found a place in Hollywood's star-studded firmament.

Hollywood gave the come-hither eye only to those of marked and proven talent, and the overlooked rank and file also had to work in order to eat. These theatrical orphans of the economic storm found a temporary haven and the price of a meal ticket in a series of unpretentious revues financed by Elsa Maxwell, Heywood Broun and others of an equally sympathetic nature and in three productions sponsored by the Public Works Administration. These WPA shoe-string revues, however, were little more than sounding boards for far-to-the-left propaganda, and one of them, *The Cradle Will Rock,* a violent attack on the capitalistic system, only made the headlines because Washington refused to sanction its presentation and both Actors Equity and the Federation of Musicians barred its members from participation in it. As a result, the show opened with the composer alone on the stage, playing and singing his own songs, and a few insurgents in the cast reciting their lines while seated in the audience.

But eventually, the optimists of Broadway were right. The penny-pinching years didn't last forever. But it took a world war and the inflated pocketbooks the war brought to end them. And as the lights along the Great White Way brightened, Broadway paraphrased one of Al Jolson's gag lines into "You ain't seen nothin' yet!" And future events proved the American theatergoer hadn't.

Harry Akst Score

1934. *CALLING ALL STARS*
Book and lyrics by Lew Brown, and presented by a cast headed by Lew Holtz, Phil Baker, Everett Marshall, Harry McNaughton, Mitzi Mayfair, Gertrude Nie-sen and Martha Raye.
—CALLING ALL STARS
—I'VE NOTHING TO OFFER YOU
—IF IT'S LOVE
—STRAW HAT IN THE RAIN
—I'D LIKE TO DUNK YOU IN MY COFFEE

—I'M STEPPING OUT OF THE PIC-
TURE
—HE JUST BEATS A TOM-TOM
—MY OLD HOSS
—JUST MENTION JOE
—I DON'T WANT TO BE PRESIDENT

Louis Alter Score

1930. *BALLYHOO*
Book and lyrics by Harry Ruskin and
Leighton K. Brill, and starring W. C.
Fields in a cast that included Grace
Hayes.
—I'M ONE OF GOD'S CHILDREN WHO
HASN'T GOT WINGS
Lyrics by Oscar Hammerstein II.
—NO WONDER I'M BLUE
Lyrics by Oscar Hammerstein II.
—THROW IT OUT THE WINDOW
—BLOW HOT, BLOW COLD
—HOW I COULD GO FOR YOU
—THAT TIRED, TIRED FEELING

Harold Arlen Scores

1931. *YOU SAID IT*
Book and lyrics by Sid Silvers and Jack
Yellen, and presented by a cast headed
by Mary Lawlor, Lew Holtz, Lyda Roberti
and George Haggerty.
—SWEET AND HOT
—LEARN TO CROON
—WHAT DID WE COME TO COLLEGE
FOR?
—YOU SAID IT
—WHILE YOU ARE YOUNG
—IT'S DIFFERENT WITH ME
—IF HE REALLY LOVES ME
—WHAT DO WE CARE?
—YOU'LL DO

1934 *LIFE BEGINS AT 8:40*
Book by David Freedman, lyics by Ira
Gershwin and E. Y. Harburg, and pre-
sented by a cast headed by Frances Wil-
liams, Ray Bolger, Brian Donlevy, Luella
Gear, Bert Lahr and Dixie Dunbar.
—SPRING FEVER
—SHOEIN' THE MARE
—THINGS
—YOU'RE A BUILDER-UPPER
—FUN TO BE FOOLED
—WHAT CAN YOU SAY IN A LOVE
SONG?
—LET'S TAKE A WALK AROUND THE
BLOCK
—THE ELKS AND THE MASONS

—IT WAS LONG AGO
—I CAN'T HOLD MY MAN

1937. *HOORAY FOR WHAT?*
Book by Howard Lindsay and Russell
Crouse, lyrics by E. Y. Harburg, and star-
ring Ed Wynn in a cast that included
Paul Haakon, Jack Whiting and June
Clyde.
—HOORAY FOR WHAT?
—I'VE GONE ROMANTIC ON YOU
—VIVE FOR GENEVA
—GOD'S COUNTRY
—MOANIN' IN THE MORNIN'
—LIFE'S A DANCE
—NAPOLEON'S A PASTRY
—DOWN WITH LOVE

Michael Balfe Score

1934. *GYPSY BLONDE*
A modern version of "The Bohemian Girl"
with book by Kenneth Johns, lyrics by
Frank Gabrielson and presented by a cast
headed by Isabel Henderson and George
Trabert.
—IN THE GYPSY'S LIFE
—'TIS SAD TO LEAVE
—THE BROAD HIGHWAY
—COMRADE YOUR HAND
—YOU'LL REMEMBER ME
—OMBO
—IS NO SUCCOR NEAR?
—MALAGUENA
—SILENCE
—DANCE GYPSY
—BLISS FOREVER PAST
—I DREAMT THAT I DWELT IN
MARBLE HALLS
—COME WITH THE GYPSY BRIDE
—THE HEART BOW'D DOWN
—I'M A GYPSY BRIDE

Ralph Benatsky Scores

1936. *WHITE HORSE INN*
A musical comedy with book by David
Freedman, lyrics by Irving Caesar, and
presented by a cast headed by William
Gaxton, Kitty Carlisle, Robert Halliday
and Rags Ragland.
—ARRIVAL OF TOURISTS
—I CANNOT LEAVE WITHOUT YOUR
LOVE
—LEAVE IT TO KATARINA
—BLUE EYES
Music by Robert Stolz.
—ARRIVAL OF STEAMBOAT
—WHITE HORSE INN
—COWSHED RHAPSODY
—MARKET DAY

1930 Follies Show. Of Thee I Sing (1931)

Face the Music (1932)

Oklahoma (1943)

—GOOD-BYE, AU REVOIR, AUF WIEDERSEHN
—HIGH UP IN THE HILLS
—I WOULD LOVE TO HAVE YOU LOVE ME
Music by Gerald Marks.
—ALPINE SYMPHONY
—WELCOME TO THE LANDING STAGE
—SERENADE TO THE EMPEROR
—WE PRIZE MOST THE THINGS WE MISS
—THE WALTZ WE LOVE
1930. *MEET MY SISTER*
A musical comedy with book by Harry Wagstaff Gribble, lyrics by the composer, and presented by a cast headed by Bettina Hall, Walter Slezak, Olive Olsen and Harry Welsh.
—LOVE HAS FADED AWAY
—FIVE THOUSAND FRANCS
—ALWAYS IN MY HEART
—RADZIWILL
—LOOK AND LOVE IS HERE
—THE DEVIL MAY CARE
—I GOTTA HAVE MY MOMENTS
—IT'S MONEY, IT'S FAME, IT'S LOVE
—I LIKE YOU
—FRIENDSHIP
—MY IDEAL
—BIRDS IN THE SPRING

Irving Berlin Scores
1932. *FACE THE MUSIC*
A revue with Mary Boland, J. Harold Murray, Hugh O'Connell and Katherine Carrington.
—LET'S HAVE ANOTHER CUP OF COFFEE
—ON A ROOF IN MANHATTAN
—SOFT LIGHTS AND SWEET MUSIC
—I'LL SAY IT'S SPINACH
—MANHATTAN MADNESS
—LUNCHING AT THE AUTOMAT
—YOU MUST BE BORN WITH IT
—TORCH SONG
—MY BEAUTIFUL RHINESTONE GIRL
—DEAR OLD CRINOLINE DAYS
—I DON'T WANT TO BE MARRIED
1933. *AS THOUSANDS CHEER*
A revue with Marilyn Miller, Helen Broderick, Clifton Webb, Ethel Waters, Hal Forde, J. Harold Murray and Hamtree Harrington.
—HOW'S CHANCES?
—HEAT WAVE
—LONELY HEART
—TO BE OR NOT TO BE

—*EASTER PARADE
The melody for this song was used by Berlin in 1917 for a number that flopped, "Smile and Show Your Dimple."
—WE'LL ALL BE IN HEAVEN WHEN THE DOLLAR GOES TO HELL
—SUPPERTIME
—OUR WEDDING DAY
—THE FUNNIES
—I'VE GOT HARLEM ON MY MIND
—NOT FOR ALL THE RICE IN CHINA

Eubie Blake Scores
1930. *BLACKBIRDS OF 1930*
Book and lyrics by Flourney Miller and Andy Razaf, and presented by a cast headed by Flourney Miller, Broadway Jones, Jazzlips Richardson, Ethel Waters and Buck and Bubbles.
—BABY MINE
—DINAH
—HARLEM
—GREEN PASTURES
—MEMORIES OF YOU
—MY HANDY MAN AIN'T HANDY NO MORE
—ROLL, JORDAN
—THAT LINDY HOP
—YOU'RE LUCKY TO ME
—PAPA DE-DA-DA
By Clarence Todd, Clarence Williams and Spencer Williams.
1938. *SWING IT*
Book and lyrics by Milton Reddie and Cecil Mack, and presented by an all-Negro cast.
—HUGGIN' AND MUGGIN'
—BY THE SWEAT OF YOUR BROW
—GREEN AND BLUE
—AIN'T WE GOT LOVE?

Marc Blitzstein Score
1938. *THE CRADLE WILL ROCK*
A WPA production with book and lyrics by the composer, and with Will Geer playing the heartless capitalist who finally was crushed by organized labor.
—JOE WORKER
—THE CRADLE WILL ROCK
—CROON-SPOON
—GUS AND SADIE'S LOVE SONG
—HONOLULU
—NICKEL UNDER THE FOOT
—THE RICH
—THE FREEDOM OF THE PRESS
—ART FOR ART'S SAKE
—THE DOCTOR AND ELLA

Rube Bloom Score

1936. *BLACKBIRDS OF 1936*
An all-Negro revue with lyrics by Johnny Mercer.
—WHY CAN'T IT BE ME?
—SOUTH WIND
—DIXIE ISN'T DIXIE ANY MORE
—I KNEW
—THE SWING IS THE THING
—JO JO THE CANNIBAL KID
—THE AMERICANA
—KEEP A TWINKLE IN YOUR EYE
—YOUR HEART AND MINE
—AUNT JEMIMA AND YOUR UNCLE CREAM OF WHEAT
—HARLEM TO HOLLYWOOD
—WHERE THE ROAD GOES OVER THE HILL
—YOU'RE MY NECESSARY EVIL
—IF I WAS GOOD ENOUGH FOR UNCLE SAM
—SUNDAY-GO-TO-MEETIN' CLOTHES

Haskell Brown Score

1932. *A LITTLE RACKETEER*
A musical comedy with book by Harry Clarke, lyrics by Edward Eliscu, and presented by a cast headed by Queenie Smith, John Garrick, William Kent, Carl Randall, Grace Hayes and Barbara Newberry.
—BLOW GABRIEL
—MR. MOON
—WHEN THE BAND PLAYS
—THROWING A PARTY
—YOU AND I COULD BE JUST LIKE THAT
—DANGER IS I LOVED YOU
—YOU GOT TO SELL YOURSELF
—SPRING TRA-LA
—WHAT GREAT BIG EYES YOU HAVE
—STARRY SKY
—RIO DE JANEIRO
Music by Dimitri Tiomkin.

Monte Carlo and Alma Sanders Score

1930. *MYSTERY MOON*
A short-lived musical comedy with book by Frederick Herendeen that closed after one performance.
—ONE NIGHT IN THE RAIN
—IT'S ALL OKAY
—MYSTERY MOON

Michael Cleary Scores

1930. *HELLO, PARIS*
With Russell Tarbox. A musical comedy,
based on Homer Croy's novel "They Had To See Paris," with book by Edgar Smith, lyrics by Charles Locke and Ned Washington, and starring Chic Sale in a cast that included Stella Mayhew and Eileen Dougall.
—O-K-L-A-H-O-M-A
—UNACCUSTOMED AS I AM
—DANCE YOUR TROUBLES AWAY
—ROLL ALONG PRAIRIE WAGON
—DEEP PARADISE
—LOVE RACKETEER
—PARIS
—FREE, WHITE AND TWENTY-ONE
—LUCKY LITTLE ME AND YOU
—GOTTA HAVE HIPS
—GIVE IT
—PRAIRIE BLUES
—I KNOW I OUGHT TO SAY NO
—ROSY ROAD
—ME HOT STUFF

1932. *HEY NONNY NONNY*
Book and lyrics by Nat and Max Lief, and presented by a cast that included Frank Morgan, Richie Craig Jr., Ann Seymour and Dorothy McNulty.
—PERSONALLY YOURS
—TELL ME SOMETHING ABOUT YOURSELF
—THIS IS DIFFERENT, DEAR
—MANHATTAN LULLABY
—THREE LITTLE COLUMNISTS
—FOR BETTER OR FOR WORSE
—ON MY NUDE RANCH WITH YOU
—I DIDN'T KNOW THAT IT WAS LOADED
—MINSKY'S METROPOLITAN OPERA
—THE SEASON ENDED
—HEY NONNY NONNY
By Will Irwin and Ogden Nash.
—BE A LITTLE LACKADAISICAL
By Herman Hupfeld.
—LADY IN WAITING
By Mann Holiner and Alberta Nichols.
—I'M REALLY NOT THAT WAY
By Will Irwin and Malcolm McComb.
—WOULDN'T THAT BE WONDERFUL
By Herman Hupfeld.
—IN THOSE GOOD OLD HORSE CAR DAYS
By Will Irwin and Malcolm McComb.
—LET'S GO LOVIN'
By Herman Hupfeld.

Hayden Church Score

1934. *CAVIAR*
Book by Leo Randole, lyrics by Edward Heyman, and presented by a cast headed

by Nanette Guilford and George Houston.
—ONE IN A MILLION
—DREAM KINGDOM
—HERE'S TO YOU
—MY HEART IS AN OPEN BOOK
—SILVER SAILS
—NIGHT WIND
—CARNIVAL
—TARTS AND FLOWERS
—PRINCE CHARMING
—GYPSY
—I FEEL SORTA
—YOUR PRINCE WAS NOT SO CHARMING
—CAVACHAK
—APASSIONETTE
—HAYWIRE
By Edward Heyman.

Noel Coward Scores

1934. *CONVERSATION PIECE*
Book and lyrics by the composer, and presented by a cast headed by Yvonne Printemps.
—I'LL FOLLOW MY SECRET HEART
—NEVERMORE
—REGENCY RAKES
—THERE'S ALWAYS SOMETHING FISHY ABOUT THE FRENCH
1939. *SET TO MUSIC*
Book and lyrics by the composer, and starring Beatrice Lillie.
—I'M SO WEARY OF IT ALL
—STATELY HOMES OF ENGLAND
—MAD ABOUT THE BOY
—NEVER AGAIN
—THREE WHITE FEATHERS
—I WENT TO A MARVELOUS PARTY

Frank d'Armand Score

1934. *SALUTA*
Book and lyrics by Will Morrissey, Eugene Conrad and Maurice Marks, and presented by a cast headed by Milton Berle, Anne Barrie and Charles Chase.
—WE, INCORPORATED
Lyrics by Maurice Sigler and Milton Berle.
—CHILL IN THE AIR
—JUST SAY THE WORD
Lyrics by Milton Berle.
—BLACK HORSE TAVERN
—WALKING THE DECK
—I'LL PRODUCE FOR YOU
—NIGHT
—BALLO MODERNO
—LA VITA
—HELP THE SEAMEN
—MI! MI!

—YOU HAVE MY HEART
—TARANTELLA RHYTHM
—THE GREAT DICTATOR AND ME

Jean Delettre Score

1934. *CONTINENTAL VARIETIES*
With Maurice Aubert. A vaudeville-revue presented by a cast of European stars headed by Lucienne Boyer.
—I NEED NEW WORDS
Lyrics by E. Y. Harburg.
—DANCING WITH MY DARLING
—SPEAK TO ME WITH YOUR EYES
—HANDS ACROSS THE TABLE
Lyrics by Mitchell Parish.
—IS IT THE SINGER OR IS IT THE SONG?
Later, when this production was revived, the following songs were incorporated:
—LET ME DRAW YOU A PICTURE
Lyrics by Irving Taylor.
—IT'S A THRILL ALL OVER AGAIN
Lyrics by Gladys Unger.
—I FOUND A BIT OF PARIS IN THE HEART OF OLD NEW YORK
Lyrics by Gladys Unger.
—THIS IS THE KISS OF ROMANCE
Lyrics by Mitchell Parish.

Gerald Dolin Score

1935. *SMILE AT ME*
Book and lyrics by Eddie Lambert, who with Jack Osterman headed the cast of this production.
—SMILE AT ME
—YOU'RE A MAGICIAN
—I'M DREAMING WHILE I'M DANCING
—DOIN' THE TRUCK
—IS THIS THE END?
—FIESTA IN MADRID
—CALCUTTA
—CARIBBEANA
—TIRED OF THE SOUTH
—GOONA, GOONA

Vernon Duke Scores

1932. *WALK A LITTLE FASTER*
A revue with Beatrice Lillie, Clark and McCullough, Evelyn Hoey, John Hundley and Donald Burr. Lyrics by E. Y. Harburg.
—CAN CAN
—THAT'S THE LIFE
—OFF AGAIN, ON AGAIN
—APRIL IN PARIS
—WHERE HAVE WE MET BEFORE?

—A PENNY FOR YOUR THOUGHTS
—NONCHALANT
—TIME AND TIDE
—END OF A PERFECT DAY
—SPEAKING OF LOVE
—FRISCO FANNY
By Earle Crooker and Henry Sullivan.
—MAYFAIR
By William Waliter and Roland Leigh.

1934. *ZIEGFELD FOLLIES OF 1934*
Presented by Billie Burke (Mrs. Florenz Ziegfeld) with a cast headed by Fanny Brice, Jane Froman, Patricia Bowman, Willie and Eugene Howard, Everett Marshall and Vilma and Buddy Ebsen. Sketches by. H. I. Phillips, Fred Allen and David Freedman. Lyrics by E. Y. Harburg.
—WATER UNDER THE BRIDGE
—I LIKE THE LIKES OF YOU
—SUDDENLY
Lyrics by Billy Rose.
—THIS IS NOT A SONG
—WHAT IS THERE TO SAY?
—THAT'S WHERE WE CAME IN
Music by Samuel Pokrass.
—TO THE BEAT OF MY HEART
Music by Samuel Pokrass.
—THE LAST ROUNDUP
By Billy Hill.
—WAGON WHEELS
By Billy Hill and Peter DeRose.
—SARAH THE SUNSHINE GIRL
By Ballard MacDonald, Billy Rose and Joe Meyer.
—COUNTESS DUBINSKY
By Ballard MacDonald, Billy Rose and Joe Meyer.
—SOUL-SAVING SADIE
By Ballard MacDonald, Billy Rose and Joe Meyer.
—MOON ABOUT TOWN
Music by Dana Suesse.
—TIME IS A GYPSY.
Music by Richard Myers.
—THE FOLLIES ENSEMBLE
Music by Samuel Pokrass.

1936. *ZIEGFELD FOLLIES OF 1936-37*
Sketches by David Freedman, lyrics by Ira Gershwin, and presented by a cast that included Fanny Brice, Bobby Clark, Gypsy Rose Lee, Cass Daley, Jane Pickens and Hugh Cameron.
—TIME MARCHES ON
—HE HASN'T A THING EXCEPT ME
—AN ISLE IN THE WEST INDIES
—THE ECONOMIC SITUATION
—SENTIMENTAL WEATHER
—WORDS WITHOUT MUSIC

—MODERNISTIC MOE
—I CAN'T GET STARTED (WITH YOU)
—MIDNIGHT BLUE
By Edgar Leslie and Joe Burke.
—HARLEM WALTZ
By Richard Jerome and Walter Kent.
—YOU DON'T LOVE RIGHT
By Tot Seymour and Vee Lawnhurst.
—RIDING THE RAILS
By Edward Heyman and Harold Spina.
—ARE YOU HAVIN' ANY FUN?
By Jack Yellen and Sammy Fain.

A. Lehman Engel Score

1938. *A HERO IS BORN*
A WPA production with book by Theresa Helburn and lyrics by Agnes Morgan.
—TRA LA LA
—MATTERS CULINARY
—FIDDLE DEE DEE
—THE ROYAL MARCH
—MUSIC IN THE AIR
—MAGIC GIFTS
—A QUESTION OF GAIT
—WOE IS ME
—FELINE WISDOM
—OFF TO GLUCKSTEIN
—KEEPING PRIGIO COMPANY
—THE SECRET OF SUCCESS
—WE BELIEVE
—A LOVE-LORN MAID
—THEY SAY
—THE BEST DANCE OF ALL
—THE SONG OF PRIGIO
—HURRAH FOR LIFE
—PRIGIO DIDN'T KNOW
—THE LAST WORDS

Gus Edwards Score

1936. *BROADWAY SHOW-WINDOW*
Book and lyrics by Eugene Conrad. A vaudeville revue in which Armida, Thelma Lee and Joe Cook, Jr. were the principal performers. In addition to old numbers from past juvenile revues, these new songs were written for this production:
—POVERTY ROW
—HITCH YOUR WAGON TO A STAR
—SPRING IS IN THE AIR

Sammy Fain Scores

1931. *EVERYBODY'S WELCOME*
A revue with book by Harold Atteridge, lyrics by Irving Kahal, and presented by a cast headed by Frances Williams, Oscar

Shaw, Harriette Lake, Ann Pennington, the Ritz Brothers and Jimmy Dorsey orchestra.
—EVEN AS YOU AND I
—ONE IN A MILLION
—PIE-EYED PIPER
—FEATHER IN A BREEZE
—LEASE IN MY HEART
—DANCE OF THE MIRRORS
—BLUE DANUBE BALLET
—IS RHYTHM NECESSARY?
—NATURE PLAYED A DIRTY TRICK ON ME
By Lippman, Pascal and Sherwin.
—I SHOOT THE WORKS
By Lippman, Pascal and Sherwin.
—ALL WRAPPED UP IN YOU
By Mack Gordon and Harry Revel.
—TA TA, OLD BEAN
By Ed Eliscu and Manning Sherwin.
—AS TIME GOES BY
By Herman Hupfeld.

1938. *RIGHT THIS WAY*
A musical comedy with book by Marianna Brown Waters, lyrics by Irving Kahal, and presented by a cast headed by Tamara, Guy Robertson and Joe E. Lewis.
—I CAN DREAM, CAN'T I?
—I LOVE THE WAY WE FELL IN LOVE
—DOUGHNUTS AND COFFEE
—I'LL BE SEEING YOU
—LOVE DESIGN
Music by Brad Greene.
—LISTEN TO YOUR HEART
Music by Brad Greene.

1939. *BOYS AND GIRLS TOGETHER*
A revue with book by Ed Wynn and Patsy Flick, lyrics by Irving Kahal and Jack Yellen, and starring Ed Wynn in a cast that included Jane Pickens, Dave Apollon, Jerry Cooper and the DeMarcos.
—LIABLE TO CATCH ON
—SUCH STUFF AS DREAMS ARE MADE OF
—THE LATIN IN ME
—TIMES SQUARE DANCE
—CATSUP ON THE MOON
—THE SUN WILL BE UP IN THE MORNING

1939. *GEORGE WHITE'S SCANDALS OF 1939*
A revue with book by Eddie Davis, Matt Brooks and George White, lyrics by Jack Yellen, and presented by a cast that included Willie and Eugene Howard, Ben Blue, Ella Logan and Ann Miller.
—ARE YOU HAVING ANY FUN?
—SMART LITTLE GIRLS

—OUR FIRST KISS
—MEXICONGA
—GOOD NIGHT MY BEAUTIFUL
—SOMETHING I DREAMED LAST NIGHT
—IN WAIKIKI
—THE SONG'S FOR FREE

Fain and Tobias Score

1938. *HELLZ-A-POPPIN*
Music and lyrics by Sammy Fain and Charles Tobias, and starring Olsen and Johnson in a cast that included the Radio Rogues, Ray Kinney and the Hawaiian Maids, the Charioteers, Hal Sherman and Bettymae and Beverly Crane. This revue held the all-time Broadway musical production record of 1,404 performances until "Oklahoma" took over with a 2,246-performance run, and also rang down the final curtain at the historic Auditorium Theater, Chicago, the cradle of grand opera in the Illinois metropolis and scene of Mary Garden's triumphs.
—HELLZ-A-POPPIN
—FUDDLE-DEE-DUDDLE
—THE GAY NINETIES
—ABE LINCOLN
—SHAGANOLA
—IT'S TIME TO SAY "ALOHA"
—WHEN YOU LOOK IN YOUR LOOKING GLASS
By Al Lewis, Stephen Weiss and Paul Mann.

Sylvia Fine Score

1939. *STRAW HAT REVUE*
Book by Max Liebman and Samuel Locke, lyrics by James Shelton, and presented by a cast headed by Imogene Coca, Danny Kaye and Alfred Drake.
—OUR TOWN
—FOUR YOUNG PEOPLE
—CRASHING THROUGH

Rudolf Friml Scores

1930. *LUANA*
An operetta based on the play "The Bird of Paradise," with book and lyrics by J. Keirn Brennan and presented by a cast headed by Ruth Altman, James Macauley, Robert Chisholm and Jans and Whalen.
—HOKU LOA
—LUANA
—ALOHA
—HAWAII'S SHORE
—MY BIRD OF PARADISE

—SHORE LEAVE
—A SON OF THE SUN
—BY WELEWELA
—YANKYULA
—WHERE YOU LEAD
—THE MAGIC SPELL OF LOVE
—DRUMS OF KANE
—IN THE CLOUDS
—WANAPOO BAY

1934. *MUSIC HATH CHARMS*
Book and lyrics by Rowland Leigh, George Rosener and John Shubert and presented by a cast headed by Natalie Hall, Robert Halliday and Harry Mestayer.
—GONDOLIER SONG
—LOVEY DOVEY
—IT'S THREE O'CLOCK
—CAVALIER
—MARIA
—LOVE IS ONLY WHAT YOU MAKE IT
—MY PALACE OF DREAMS
—ROMANCE
—SWEET FOOL
—FRUTTI DI MARE
—LET ME BE FREE
—LADIES, BEWARE
—EXQUISITE MOMENT
—MIDNIGHT FLIRTATION
—IT HAPPENED
—A SMILE, A KISS
—IT'S YOU I WANT TO LOVE TO-NIGHT
—MY HEART IS YOURS

Lewis Gensler Scores

1931. *THE GANG'S ALL HERE*
Book by Russell Crouse, Oscar Hammerstein II and Maurice Ryskind, lyrics by Owen Murphy and Robert A. Simons, and presented by a cast headed by Zelma O'Neill, Tom Howard, Hal LeRoy, Ted Healy, John Gallaudet and Shaw and Lee.
—BY SPECIAL PERMISSION OF THE COPYRIGHT OWNERS (I LOVE YOU)
—ADORABLE JULIE
—IT ALWAYS TAKES TWO
—MORE THAN EVER
—SPEAK EASY
—SPEAKING OF YOU

1932. *BALLYHOO OF 1932*
Book by Norman B. Anthony, lyrics by E. Y. Harburg, and presented by a cast that included Lulu McConnell, Vera Marche, Willie and Eugene Howard, Bob Hope, Donald Stewart, Paul Hartman and Jeanne Aubert.

—THRILL ME
—RIDDLE ME THIS
—FALLING OFF THE WAGON
—OLD FASHIONED WEDDING
—HOW DO YOU DO IT?
—MAN ABOUT YONKERS
—BALLYHUJAH
—NUTS AND NOODLES
—WHAT HAVE YOU GOT TO HAVE?

George Gershwin Scores

1930. *STRIKE UP THE BAND*
Book by Morris Ryskind and George S. Kaufman, lyrics by Ira Gershwin, and presented by a cast that included Clark and McCullough, Blanche Ring and Red Nichols and his band.
—I MEAN TO SAY
—A TYPICAL SELF-MADE AMERICAN
—SOON
—A MAN OF HIGH DEGREE
—THREE CHEERS FOR THE UNION
—THIS COULD GO ON FOR YEARS
—IF I BECOME PRESIDENT
—WHAT'S THE USE OF HANGING AROUND WITH YOU?
—HE KNOWS MILK
—STRIKE UP THE BAND
—IN THE RATTLE OF BATTLE
—MILITARY DANCING GIRL
—MADAMOISELLE IN NEW ROCHELLE
—I'VE GOT A CRUSH ON YOU
—HOW ABOUT A BOY LIKE ME?
—RING A DING A DING-DONG BELL
—THE MAN I LOVE
This song was originally written for "Lady Be Good" and first introduced in that production.
—I WANT TO BE A WAR BRIDE
—YANKEE DOODLE RHYTHM
—SEVENTEEN AND TWENTY-ONE
—NOBODY

1930. *GIRL CRAZY*
Book by Guy Bolton and John McGowan, lyrics by Ira Gershwin, and presented by a cast headed by Allen Kearns, Willie Howard, William Kent and Ethel Merman and Ginger Rogers, both of whom made their Broadway debut in this musical.
—BIDIN' MY TIME
—THE LONESOME COWBOY
—COULD YOU USE ME?
—BRONCHO BUSTERS
—BARBARY COAST
—EMBRACEABLE YOU
—SAM AND DELILAH

—I GOT RHYTHM
—LAND OF THE GAY CABALLERO
—BUT NOT FOR ME
—TREAT ME ROUGH
—BOY, WHAT LOVE HAS DONE TO
   ME
—CACTUS TIME IN ARIZONA
1931. *OF THEE I SING*
   Book by Morris Ryskind and George S.
   Kaufman, lyrics by Ira Gershwin. The first
   musical play to be awarded the Pulitzer
   Prize. With a cast headed by Victor
   Moore, William Gaxton, George Murphy,
   Lois Moran and June O'Dea.
—WINTERGREEN FOR PRESIDENT
—WHO IS THE LUCKY GIRL TO BE?
—THE DIMPLE ON MY KNEE
—BECAUSE, BECAUSE
—NEVER WAS THERE A GIRL SO
   FAIR
—SOME GIRLS CAN BAKE A PIE
—LOVE IS SWEEPING THE COUNTRY
—OF THEE I SING
—HERE'S A KISS FOR CINDERELLA
—I WAS THE MOST BEAUTIFUL
   BLOSSOM
—HELLO, GOOD MORNING
—WHO CARES?
—GARCON, S'IL VOUS PLAIT
—THE ILLEGITIMATE DAUGHTER
—THE ROLL CALL
—JILTED
—WHO COULD ASK FOR ANYTHING
   MORE?
—POSTERITY
—TRUMPETER, BLOW YOUR HORN
1933. *PARDON MY ENGLISH*
   Book by Herbert Fields, lyrics by Ira
   Gershwin, and presented by a cast that
   included Carl Randall, Barbara Newberry,
   Lyda Roberti, Jack Pearl and George
   Givot.
—THREE-QUARTER TIME
—THE LORELEI
—PARDON MY ENGLISH
—DANCING IN THE STREETS
—SO WHAT?
—ISN'T IT A PITY?
—MY COUSIN FROM MILWAUKEE
—HAIL THE HAPPY COUPLE
—THE   DRESDEN   N O R T H W E S T
   MOUNTED
—LUCKIEST MAN IN THE WORLD
—TONIGHT
—WHERE YOU GO I GO
—HE'S NOT HIMSELF
1933. *LET 'EM EAT CAKE*
   Book by Morris Ryskind and George S.
   Kaufman, lyrics by Ira Gershwin, and pre-

sented by a cast that included Lois
Moran, Philip Loeb, Victor Moore and
William Gaxton.
—WINTERGREEN FOR PRESIDENT
—TWEEDLEDEE FOR PRESIDENT
—UNION SQUARE
—DOWN WITH EVERYONE WHO'S UP
—SHIRTS BY MILLIONS
—COMES THE REVOLUTION
—MINE
—CLOISTERED   FROM   THE   NOISY
   CITY
—ON AND ON AND ON
—LET 'EM EAT CAKE
—BLUE, BLUE, BLUE
—WHO'S THE GREATEST?
—NO COMPRENEZ, NO CAPISH
—UP AND AT 'EM
—THAT'S WHAT HE DID
—I KNOW A FOUL BALL
—THROTTLE THROTTLEBOTTOM
—A HELL OF A FIX
—LET 'EM EAT CAVIAR
—HANGING THROTTLEBOTTOM IN
   THE MORNING
1935. *PORGY AND BESS*
   Book by DuBois Heyward, lyrics by Ira
   Gershwin, and with Todd Duncan as
   "Porgy," Anne Wiggins Brown as "Bess'
   and Warren Coleman as "Sporting Life."
—BESS, YOU IS MY WOMAN
—I GOT PLENTY OF NUTTIN'
—IT AIN'T NECESSARILY SO
—SUMMERTIME
—A WOMAN IS A SOMETIME THING
—MY MAN'S GONE NOW
—BUZZARD SONG
—THE REQUIEM
—IT TAKES A LONG PULL TO GET
   THERE
—WHAT DO YOU WANT WID BESS?
—STREET CRIES
—I LOVE YOU, PORGY
—THERE'S A BOAT DAT'S LEAVIN'
   SOON FOR NEW YORK
—WHERE IS MY BESS?

Jay Gorney Scores
1930. *EARL CARROLL'S VANITIES OF
1930*
   With Harold Arlen. Book and lyrics by
   E. Y. Harburg and Ted Koehler, and pre-
   sented by a cast headed by Jimmy Savo,
   Jack Benny, Herb Williams, Patsy Kelly
   and Faith Bacon.
—I CAME TO LIFE
—RING OUT THE NEWS
—KNEE-DEEP IN DAISIES

—ONE LOVE
—THE MARCH OF TIME
—OUT OF A CLEAR BLUE SKY
—GOING UP
—HITTING THE BOTTLE
  Music by Harold Arlen.
—IT'S GREAT TO BE IN LOVE
  By Harold Adamson and Burton Lane.
—TONIGHT OR NEVER
  By Harold Adamson and Burton Lane.
—GOOD NIGHT SWEETHEART
  By James Campbell, Reg Connelly and
  Ray Noble.

Porter Grainger Score

1930. *HOT RHYTHM*
  An all-Negro revue with book by Ballard
  MacDonald, Edward Hurley and Will
  Morrissey, and lyrics by Donald Heywood.
—THE PENALTY OF LOVE
—FOR THE FIRST TIME IN MY LIFE
—I'LL GET EVEN WITH YOU
—WILL YOU BE HATING ME TO-
  MORROW?
—LOVIN' YOU THE WAY I DO
  By Eddie DeLange, Jack Scholl and Eubie
  Blake.

Ray Henderson Scores

1930. *FLYING HIGH*
  Book and lyrics by Jack McGowan, Lew
  Brown and Buddy DeSylva, and present-
  ed by a cast headed by Oscar Shaw, Bert
  Lahr, Grace Brinkley and Kate Smith.
—I'LL KNOW HIM
—WASN'T IT BEAUTIFUL WHILE IT
  LASTED?
—AIR-MINDED
—THE FIRST TIME FOR ME
—FLYING HIGH
—THANK YOUR FATHER
—HAPPY LANDING
—GOOD FOR YOU, BAD FOR ME
—RED HOT CHICAGO
—WITHOUT LOVE
—RUSTY'S UP IN THE AIR
—MR. KRAUSE'S BLUE-EYED BABY
  BOY
—I'LL GET MY MAN
1931. *GEORGE WHITE'S SCANDALS OF
  1931*
  Book by Irving Caesar, Lew Brown and
  George White, lyrics by Lew Brown, and
  starring Ethel Merman in a cast that in-
  cluded Willie and Eugene Howard, Ever-
  ett Marshall, Rudy Vallee and Ray Bol-
  ger.

—LIFE IS JUST A BOWL OF
  CHERRIES
—THIS IS THE MISSUS
—THE THRILL IS GONE
—THAT'S WHY DARKIES WERE
  BORN
—MY SONG
—THE BEGINNING OF LOVE
—LADIES AND GENTLEMEN THAT'S
  LOVE
—SONG OF THE FOREIGN LEGION
—HERE IT IS
—BACK FROM HOLLYWOOD
—GOOD OLD DAYS
1932. *HOT-CHA*
  Book by Lew Brown, H. S. Kraft and
  Mark Hellinger, lyrics by Lew Brown, and
  starring Lupe Velez in a cast that includ-
  ed June Knight, Charles "Buddy" Rogers,
  Bert Lahr and Lynn Overman.
—YOU CAN MAKE MY LIFE A BED OF
  ROSES
—SAY WHAT I WANNA HEAR YOU
  SAY
—SO THIS IS MEXICO
—CONCHITA
—I WANT ANOTHER PORTION OF
  THAT
—JOSE CAN'T YOU SEE?
—FIESTA
—I MAKE UP FOR THAT IN OTHER
  WAYS
—THERE I GO DREAMING AGAIN
—THERE'S NOTHING THE MATTER
  WITH ME
—SONG OF THE MATADORS
1933. *STRIKE ME PINK*
  Book and lyrics by Mack Gordon and
  Lew Brown, and starring Jimmy Durante
  in a cast that included Hal LeRoy, Roy
  Atwell, Eddie Garr, Lupe Velez, Hope
  Williams and George Dewey Washington.
—AN OLD HOLLYWOOD CUSTOM
—IT'S GREAT TO BE ALIVE
—STRIKE ME PINK
—HOME TO HARLEM
—LOVE AND RHYTHM
—LET'S CALL IT A DAY
—RESTLESS
—MEMORIES
—OOH, I'M THINKING
—I HATE TO THINK THAT YOU'LL
  GROW OLD BABY
—HOLLYWOOD, PARK AVENUE AND
  BROADWAY
1934. *SAY WHEN*
  Book by Jack McGowan, lyrics by Ted
  Koehler, and presented by a cast headed
  by Bob Hope, Harry Richman, Betty Dell,

Linda Watkins, Taylor Holmes and Dennis Moore.
—WHEN LOVE COMES SWINGING ALONG
—DECLARATION DAY
—IT MUST HAVE BEEN THE NIGHT
—SAY WHEN
—DON'T TELL ME IT'S BAD
—SUNDAY MORNING
—ISN'T IT JUNE?
—PUT YOUR HEART IN A SONG
—SO LONG FOREVER SO LONG
—TORCH PARADE
—LET'S TAKE ADVANTAGE OF NOW
1935. *GEORGE WHITE'S SCANDALS OF 1935*
Book by George White, William K. Wells and Howard Shiebler, lyrics by Jack Yellen, and presented by a cast that included Rudy Vallee, Bert Lahr, Willie and Eugene Howard, Hal Forde, Cliff Edwards, Gracie Barrie and Peggy Mosley.
—ANYTHING CAN HAPPEN
—CIGARETTE
—I'M THE FELLOW THAT LOVES YOU
—I'VE GOT TO GET HOT
—LIFE BEGINS AT SWEET SIXTEEN
—MAY I HAVE MY GLOVES?
—PIED PIPER OF HARLEM
—TELL THE TRUTH

Ernest Irving Score

1938. *TWO BOUQUETS*
An operetta with book and lyrics by Eleanor and Herbert Farjeon, and presented by a cast headed by Mary Westcott, Patricia Morison, Alfred Drake, Winston O'Keefe and Leslie French.
—TODDY'S THE DRINK FOR ME
—BASHFUL LOVER
—ELEPHANT IN ARCADY
—SWEET BLOSSOMS
Music by M. Pinsuti.
—I SENT A LETTER TO MY LOVE
Music by M. Pinsuti.

Will Irwin Score

1934. *FOOLS RUSH IN*
An intimate revue with lyrics by Norman Zeno, and presented by a cast headed by Imogene Coca.
—TAKE ME
—I'M SO IN LOVE
—RHYTHM IN MY HAIR
—TWO GET TOGETHER
—HARLEM BARCAROLLE
By June Sillman and Bascom Little Jr.

—LET'S HOLD HANDS
By June Sillman and Richard Lewine.
—LOVE CAME
By June Sillman and Richard Lewine.

Donald Heywood Score

1932. *BLACKBERRIES OF 1932*
Book by Lee Posner and Eddie Green, lyrics by Tom Peluse, and presented by an all-Negro cast headed by Eddie Green.
—BLACKBERRIES
—BROWN SUGAR
—FIRST THING IN THE MORNING
—THE ANSWER IS NO
—HARLEM MANIA
—LOVE ME MORE, LOVE ME LESS

Alexander Hill Score

1933. *HUMMING SAM*
A musical comedy of the race tracks with book by Eileen Nutter, and presented by an all-Negro cast headed by Gertrude "Baby" Cox and Madeline Belt.
—DELTA BOUND
—MISTER WILL YOU SERENADE?
With Clarence Williams and Ikey Robinson.
—DIXIE LEE
—MY SWEET HARMONY MAN

Edward A. Horan Score

1934. *ALL THE KING'S HORSES*
Book and lyrics by Frederick Herendeen, and presented by a cast headed by Guy Robertson and Nancy McCord.
—I FOUND A SONG
—CHARMING
—EVENING STAR
—I'VE GONE NUTS OVER YOU
—FAME IS A PHONEY
—TAMBOREE
—THE HAIR OF A HEIR
—YOU'RE ASKING ME
—LANGENSTEIN IN SPRING
—MAMAZELLE PAPAZELLE
—ROMANCE IS CALLING

Jimmy Johnson Scores

1930. *CHANGE YOUR LUCK*
Book by Garland Howard, lyrics by the composer, and presented by an all-Negro cast.
—SWEET BABY OF MINE
—CAN'T BE BOTHERED NOW
—AIN'T PUTTIN' OVER NOTHIN'
—RELIGION IN MY FEET

—YOU SHOULD KNOW
—WAISTIN' AWAY
—WALK TOGETHER, CHILDREN
—HONESTY
—MR. MAMMY MAN
—MY REGULAR MAN
—I'M HONEST
—WE'RE HERE
—LOW DOWN DANCE
—OPEN THAT DOOR
—CHANGE YOUR LUCK
—PERCOLATIN'
—TRAVELLIN'
—ST. LOUIS BLUES
  By William C. Handy.
—WHAT HAVE I DONE?
—RHYTHM FEET

1931. *SUGAR HILL*
  Book by Charles Tazewell, lyrics by Flour-
  ney Miller and Jo Trent, and presented
  by a cast headed by Miller and Lyles.
—APPLE JACK
—SHIVAREE
—KEEP HIM GUESSIN'
—SMILIN' THROUGH MY TEARS
—MY SWEET HUNK O' TRASH
—I DON'T WANT ANY LABOR IN MY
  JOB
—STAY OUT OF THE KITCHEN
—YOU CAN'T LOSE A BROKEN
  HEART
—FAR AWAY LOVE

Joe Jordan Scores

1930. *BROWN BUDDIES*
  An all-Negro revue with book by Carl
  Rickman, and presented by a cast headed
  by Bill Robinson and Adelaide Hall.
—BETTY LOU
—DANCING WAY MY SINS
—DON'T LEAVE YOUR L I T T L E
  BLACKBIRD BLUE
  Lyrics by Porter Grainger.
—HAPPY
—DARKY RHYTHM
  By Peter Tinturin and Victor Young.

Robert Katscher Score

1931. *WONDER BAR*
  Book by Aben Kandel, lyrics by Rowland
  Leigh, and starring Al Jolson in a cast
  that included Trini, Rex O'Malley, Arthur
  Treacher and Patsy Kelly.
—ELIZABETH
—GOOD EVENING FRIENDS
  Lyrics by Irving Caesar.
—OH DONNA CLARA

  By Jimmy Kennedy and J. Peterburski.
—ALONE IN A CROWD
—I'LL BELIEVE IN LOVE
—I'VE GOT A PLAN ABOUT YOU
—TELL ME I'M FORGIVEN
—TURNING NIGHT INTO DAY
—WHO'S TO BLAME?
—WONDER BAR
—DON'T POSE AS A SAINT
—REALLY MINE
—LENOX AVENUE
  By Irving Caesar, Al Jolson and Joseph
  Meyer.
—TRAVELING ALL ALONE
  By Al Jolson.
—SOMETHING SEEMS TO TELL ME
  Lyrics by Irving Caesar.
—MA MERE

Jerome Kern Scores

1931. *THE CAT AND THE FIDDLE*
  Book and lyrics by Otto Harbach, and
  presented by a cast headed by Bettina
  Hall, George Metaxa, George Meador,
  Odette Myrtil, Flora LeBreton and Fred
  Walton.
—SHE DIDN'T SAY YES (SHE DIDN'T
  SAY NO)
—THE NIGHT WAS MADE FOR LOVE
—TRY TO FORGET
—THE BREEZE KISSED YOUR HAIR
—POOR PIERROT
—A NEW LOVE IS OLD
—ONE MOMENT ALONE
—HA! CHA! CHA!
—DON'T ASK ME NOT TO SING
—I WATCH THE LOVE PARADE

1932. *MUSIC IN THE AIR*
  Book and lyrics by Oscar Hammerstein II,
  and presented by a cast headed by Al
  Shean, Reinald Werrenrath, Donald Brian,
  Ann Barry, Gladys Baxter, Walter Slezak,
  Natalie Hall, Tullio Carminati and Kath-
  erine Carrington.
—I'VE TOLD EVERY LITTLE STAR
—AND LOVE WAS BORN
—WE BELONG TOGETHER
—THE SONG IS YOU
—MELODIES IN MAY
—THERE'S A HILL BEYOND A HILL
—I'M COMING HOME
—I'M ALONE
—I AM SO EAGER
—ONE MORE DANCE
—NIGHT FLIES BY
—WHEN SPRING IS IN THE AIR
—IN EGERN ON THE TEGREN SEE

1933. *ROBERTA*
Book and lyrics by Otto Harbach, and
starring Tamara in a cast that included
Lyda Roberti, Fay Templeton, Raymond
Middleton, George Murphy, Bob Hope,
Allan Jones and Fred McMurray.
—LET'S BEGIN
—ALPHA BETA PI
—YOU'RE DEVASTATING
—YESTERDAYS
—SOMETHING'S GOT TO HAPPEN
—THE TOUCH OF YOUR HAND
—HOT SPOT
—SMOKE GETS IN YOUR EYES
While "Roberta" was in rehearsal, the
director insisted on cutting this song from
the score, but Kern was equally adamant
on having it retained. It proved to be
one of the most popular numbers he ever
wrote.
—ASK ME NOT TO SING
—AN ARMFUL OF TROUBLE

1939. *VERY WARM FOR MAY*
Book and lyrics by Oscar Hammerstein
II, and presented by a cast headed by
Grace McDonald, Donald Brian and Jack
Whiting.
—IN OTHER WORDS, SEVENTEEN
—ALL THE THINGS YOU ARE
—MAY TELLS ALL
—HEAVEN IN MY ARMS
—THAT LUCKY FELLOW
—THAT LUCKY LADY
—IN THE HEART OF THE DARK
—ALL IN FUN

Walter Kollo Score

1930. *THREE LITTLE GIRLS*
Book by Marie Hecht and Gertrude Pur-
cell, lyrics by Harry B. Smith, and pre-
sented by a cast headed by Natalie and
Bettina Hall, Charles Hadley and Harry
Puck.
—LOVE'S HAPPY DREAM
—PRINCE CHARMING
—LETTER SONG
—WHISTLE WHILE YOU WORK,
BOYS
—DREAM ON
—ANNETTE
—I'LL TELL YOU
—A LESSON IN LETTER WRITING
—A COTTAGE IN THE COUNTRY
—DOLL SONG
—WALTZ WITH ME
—LOVE COMES ONLY ONCE IN A
LIFETIME
By Stella Unger and Harold Stern.

Franz Lehar Score

1937. *FREDERIKA*
Book and lyrics by Edward Eliscu, and
presented by a cast headed by Helen Glea-
son, Dennis King and Ernest Truex.
—KISS TO REMIND YOU
—ROSE IN THE HEATHER
—ONE
—WHY DID YOU KISS MY HEART
AWAKE?
—RISING STAR
—OH MAIDEN, MY MAIDEN
—WAYSIDE ROSE

Ned Lehac Score

1939. *SING FOR YOUR SUPPER*
With Lee Wainer. A WPA production
with book by Dave Lesan and Turner
Bullock, lyrics by Robert Sour and John
Latouche, and presented by a cast headed
by Paula Laurence.
—AT LONG LAST
—OPENING NIGHT
—BONNIE BANKS
—HOW CAN WE SING IT?
—OH, BOY, CAN WE DEDUCT?
—LEGITIMATE
—YOUNG MAN WITH A HORN
—LUCKY
—IMAGINE MY FINDING YOU HERE
—BALLADE OF UNCLE SAM
By John Latouche and Earl Robinson.

Oscar Levant Score

1930. *RIPPLES*
With Albert Sirmay. Book and lyrics by
Graham John and Irving Caesar, and
starring Mr. and Mrs. Fred Stone in a
cast that included their daughters, Doro-
thy and Paula, Eddie Foy Jr. and Charles
Collins.
—BABYKINS
—I'M AFRAID
—I'M A LITTLE BIT FONDER OF YOU
THAN OF MYSELF
—THERE'S NOTHING WRONG IN A
KISS
—TALK WITH YOUR HEEL AND TOE
—IS IT LOVE?
—YOU NEVER CAN TELL ABOUT
LOVE
By Benny Davis and J. Fred Coots.
—ANYTHING CAN HAPPEN ANY DAY
Music by Jerome Kern.

Richard Lewine Scores

1937. *NAUGHTY NAUGHT*
Good oldtime 10, 20 and 30 cent melo-

drama with music, Manhattans, martinis and vaudeville between the acts, and presented by a cast headed by Alexander Clark, Bartlett Robinson and Eleanor Phelps. Book by John Van Antwerp and lyrics by Ted Fetter.

1938. *THE FIREMAN'S FLAME*
Another Gay Nineties' melodrama with ballads, beer and bourbon served by singing waiters. Book by John Van Antwerp and lyrics by Ted Fetter.

Jerry Livingston Score

1933. *BRIGHT LIGHTS OF 1934*
Book by Charles Sherman and Norman Anthony, lyrics by Mack David, and starring (Joe) Smith and (Charles) Dale in a cast that included James Barton, Frances Williams and Buddy Clark.
—HAVEN'T WE MET BEFORE?
—YOU'D BETTER DANCE
—THOUGHTLESS
—DON'T FORGET THE PUNXSUTAWNEY
—THAT'S BROADWAY
By Gene Herbert and Teddy Hall.
—WE'RE HAVING OUR FLING
—BACK BAY BEAT
—YOUR FACE IS YOUR FORTUNE
—YES, I LOVE YOU HONEY
By James P. Johnson.
—FRANKIE AND JOHNNY
—A LICK, A RIFF AND A SLOW BOUNCE
By Norman Zeno and Al Scofield.

Morgan Lewis Score

1939. *ONE FOR THE MONEY*
An intimate revue with book and lyrics by Nancy Hamilton, and presented by a cast of unknowns that included Gene Kelly.
—ONCE UPON A TIME
—I ONLY KNOW
—TEETER TOTTER TESSIE
—YOO HOO BLUES
—I HATE SPRING
Music by Martha Caples.

Frederick Loewe Score

1938. *GREAT LADY*
Book and lyrics by Lowell Bretano and Earle Crooker, and presented by a cast headed by Norma Terris, Shepperd Strudwick, Irene Bordoni and Tullio Carminati.
—I HAVE ROOM IN MY HEART
—MAY I SUGGEST ROMANCE?

—THERE HAD TO BE THE WALTZ
—WHY CAN'T THIS NIGHT LAST FOREVER?

Jimmy McHugh Scores

1930. *INTERNATIONAL REVUE*
Book by Nat Dorfman and Lew Leslie, lyrics by Dorothy Fields, and presented by a cast that included Florence Moore, Gertrude Lawrence, Harry Richman, Jack Pearl, Moss and Fantana, Jans and Whalen and Argentina.
—MAKE UP YOUR MIND
—THAT'S WHY WE'RE DANCING
—ON THE SUNNY SIDE OF THE STREET
—BIG PAPOOSE IS ON THE LOOSE
—EXACTLY LIKE YOU
—CINDERELLA BROWN
—I'M FEELING BLUE
—GYPSY LOVE
—I'VE GOT A BUG IN MY HEAD
—KEYS TO YOUR HEART
—INTERNATIONAL RHYTHM
—THE MARGINEERS

1930. *VANDERBILT REVUE*
With Jacques Frey and Mario Braggiotti. Lyrics by Dorothy Fields and E. Y. Harburg, and presented by a cast headed by Lulu McConnell, Joe Penner, Teddy Walters and Evelyn Hoey.
—BLUE AGAIN
—BUTTON UP YOUR HEART
—CUT IN
—YOU'RE THE BETTER HALF OF ME

1939. *STREETS OF PARIS*
Lyrics by Al Dubin, and presented by a cast headed by Luella Gear, Carmen Miranda, Yvonne Bouvier, Bobby Clark and Abbott and Costello.
—THE STREETS OF PARIS
—THANKS FOR THE FRANCS
—DANGER IN THE DARK
—THREE LITTLE MAIDS FROM MADRID
—IS IT POSSIBLE?
—RENDEZVOUS TIME IN PAREE
—SOUTH AMERICAN WAY
—IN MY MEMOIRS
—WE HAVEN'T GOT A POT TO COOK IN
—ROBERT THE ROUE (FROM READING, PA.)
—READING, WRITING AND A LITTLE BIT OF RHYTHM
—THREE LITTLE DEBUTANTES
—HISTORY IS MADE AT NIGHT
By Harold Rome.

—THE FRENCH HAVE A WORD FOR
IT
By Harold Rome.

Karl Millocker Score

1932. *THE DU BARRY*
Book and lyrics by Paul Knepler and
Rowland Leigh, and presented by a cast
headed by Grace Moore, Howard Marsh
and Percy Waram.
—I GIVE MY HEART
—IF I'M DREAMING
—GA-GA
—THE DU BARRY
—WITHOUT YOUR LOVE
—TODAY
—ON THE STAGE
—HAPPY LITTLE JEANNE
—GUSTAVE
—PANTALETTES
—DANCE FOR THE GENTLEMEN
—BEAUTY
—THE ROAD TO HAPPINESS
—IN THE BOIS

Jerome Morass Score

1935. *PARADE*
Book by Paul Peters, lyrics by George
Sklar, and presented by a cast headed by
Jimmy Savo, Leon Janney, Evelyn Dall
and Eve Arden.
—ON PARADE
—I'M TELLING YOU, LOUIE
—YOU AIN'T SO HOT
—LIFE COULD BE SO BEAUTIFUL
—BOYS IN BLUE
—MY FEET ARE FIRMLY PLANTED
ON THE GROUND
—MARRY THE FAMILY
—I'M AN INTERNATIONAL ORPHAN
—FEAR IN MY HEART
—JOIN OUR RANKS
—SEND FOR THE MILITIA
Music by Marc Blitzstein.
—SMART SET
Music by Will Irwin.
—I'M ALL WASHED UP WITH LOVE
By Albert Silverman and Kay Swift.

Sam Morrison Score

1936. *SUMMER WIVES*
Book by Mark Linder, lyrics by Dolph
Singer, and presented by a cast headed by
(Joe) Smith and (Charles) Dale.
—LOWEN-GREEN COUNTRY CLUB
—I LOVE YOU
—MY LOVE CARRIES ON

—MICKEY
—THE CHATTERBOX
—PLAY ME AN OLDTIME TWO-STEP
—I WROTE A SONG FOR YOU
—US ON A BUS
By Tot Seymour and Vee Lawnhurst.

Cole Porter Scores

1930. *THE NEW YORKERS*
Book by Peter Arno and E. Ray Goetz,
and presented by a cast headed by Hope
Williams, Ann Pennington, Charles King,
Jimmy Durante, Lew Clayton, Edward
Jackson, Tammany Young, Richard Carle
and Fred Waring's Pennsylvanians.
—GO INTO YOUR DANCE
—SAY IT WITH GIN
—VENICE
—LOVE FOR SALE
—I HAPPEN TO LIKE NEW YORK
—I'M GETTING MYSELF READY FOR
YOU
—THE GREAT INDOORS
—THE SHEIKEN FOOL
—LET'S FLY AWAY
—SING SING FOR SING SING
—TAKE ME BACK TO MANHATTAN
Jimmy Durante also contributed the fol-
lowing songs to this production:
—THE HOT PATATA
—MONEY
—WOOD
—DATA

1932. *THE GAY DIVORCEE*
Book by Dwight Taylor, and presented by
a cast that included Fred Astaire, Grace
Moore, Eric Blore, Luella Gear and Claire
Luce.
—AFTER YOU WHO?
—WHY MARRY THEM?
—SALT AIR
—I STILL LOVE THE RED, WHITE
AND BLUE
—NIGHT AND DAY
—HOW'S YOUR ROMANCE?
—WHAT WILL BECOME OF OUR
ENGLAND?
—I'VE GOT YOU ON MY MIND
—MR. AND MRS. FITCH
—YOU'RE IN LOVE

1934. *ANYTHING GOES*
Book by Guy Bolton, P. G. Wodehouse,
Howard Lindsay and Russell Crouse, and
presented by a cast that included Victor
Moore, William Gaxton, Ethel Merman
and Bettina Hall.
—ALL THOUGH THE NIGHT
—BLOW, GABRIEL, BLOW

—ANYTHING GOES
—I GET A KICK OUT OF YOU
—YOU'RE THE TOP
—BON VOYAGE
—WHERE ARE THE MEN?
—SAILOR'S CHANTEY
—PUBLIC ENEMY NO. 1
—BE LIKE THE BLUEBIRD
—BUDDY, BEWARE
—THE GYPSY IN ME

1935. *JUBILEE*
Book by Moss Hart, and presented by a cast headed by Melville Cooper, Mary Boland, Charles Waters, May Boley, Derck Williams and June Knight.
—OUR CROWN
—WE'RE OFF TO FEATHERMORE
—WHY SHOULDN'T I?
—THE KLING-KLING BIRD IN THE DIVI-DIVI TREE
—WHEN LOVE COMES YOUR WAY
—ME AND MARIE
—JUST ONE OF THOSE THINGS
—A PICTURE OF ME WITHOUT YOU
—WHAT A NICE MUNICIPAL PARK
—WHEN ME, MOWGLI, LOVE
—GATHER YE AUTOGRAPHS
—MY LOULOU
—MY MOST INTIMATE FRIEND
—EV'RYBOD-EE WHO'S ANYBOD-EE
—SWING THAT SWING
—BEGIN THE BEGUINE
—WALTZ DOWN THE AISLE

1936. *RED HOT AND BLUE*
Book by Russell Crouse and Howard Lindsay, and presented by a cast that included Ethel Merman, Jimmy Durante, Bob Hope, Polly Walters and the Hartmans.
—AT YE OLD COFFEE SHOP IN CHEYENNE
—IT'S A GREAT LIFE
—PERENNIAL DEBUTANTES
—OURS
—DEEP IN THE DEPTHS ON THE 90TH FLOOR
—CARRY ON
—YOU'VE GOT SOMETHING
—IT'S DE-LOVELY
—A LITTLE SKIPPER FROM HEAVEN ABOVE
—FIVE HUNDRED MILLION
—RIDIN' HIGH
—WE'RE ABOUT TO START RE-HEARSIN'
—HYMN TO HYMEN
—WHAT A GREAT PAIR WE'LL BE
—THE OZARKS ARE CALLING ME HOME
—RED, HOT AND BLUE

1938. *YOU NEVER KNOW*
Book by Roland Leigh, and presented by a cast headed by Clifton Webb, Rex O'Malley, Lupe Velez and Libby Holman.
—AT LONG LAST LOVE
—I AM GASTON
—AU REVOIR, CHER BARON
—MARIA
—YOU NEVER KNOW
—WHAT IS THAT TUNE?
—FOR NO RHYME OR REASON
—ALPHA TO OMEGA
—DON'T LET IT GET YOU DOWN
—WHAT SHALL I DO?
Lyrics by Roland Leigh.
—LET'S PUT IT TO MUSIC
—YES, YES, YES
—BY CANDLELIGHT
By Robert Katscher.
—GENDARMES
By Robert Katscher.
—NO
By Dana Suesse.
—LADIES' ROOM
By Edwin Gilbert and Alex Fogarty.
—TAKE YOURSELF A TRIP
By Edwin Gilbert and Alex Fogarty.

1938. *LEAVE IT TO ME*
Book by Bella and Samuel Spewack, and presented by a cast headed by William Gaxton, Victor Moore, Mary Martin, Sophie Tucker and Tamara.
—HOW DO YOU SPELL AMBASSA-DOR?
—WE DRINK TO YOU, J. R. BRODY
—VITE, VITE, VITE
—I'M TAKING THE STEPS TO RUSSIA
—GET OUT OF TOWN
—WHEN ALL'S SAID AND DONE
—MOST GENTLEMEN DON'T LIKE LOVE
—COMRADE ALONZO
—FROM NOW ON
—I WANT TO GO HOME
—MY HEART BELONGS TO DADDY
—TOMORROW
—FAR FAR AWAY
—TO THE U.S.A. FROM THE U.S.S.R.

1939. *DU BARRY WAS A LADY*
Book by B. G. DeSylva and Herbert Fields, and starring Ethel Merman and Bert Lahr in a cast that included Betty Grable.
—EVERY DAY A HOLIDAY
—IT AIN'T ETIQUETTE
—WHEN LOVE BECKONS
—DO I LOVE YOU, DO I?
—DU BARRY WAS A LADY

—COME ON IN
—MESDAMES AND MESSIEURS
—BUT IN THE MORNING NO
—GIVE HIM THE OO-LA-LA
—KATIE WENT TO HAITI
—IT WAS WRITTEN IN THE STARS
—FRIENDSHIP
—WELL DID YOU EVAH?
—L'APRES MIDI D'UN BOEF

Harry Revel Scores

1931. *FAST AND FURIOUS*
A revue with an all-Negro cast. Lyrics by
Mack Gordon.
—FAST AND FURIOUS
—WALKING ON AIR
—RUMBATISM
—FROWNS
—DOING THE DUM-BELL
—SHADOWS ON THE WALL
—WHERE'S MY HAPPY ENDING?
—HOT FEET

1931. *ZIEGFELD FOLLIES OF 1931*
This was the last Follies to be produced
by Florenz Ziegfeld. The cast was headed
by Harry Richman, Faith Bacon, Helen
Morgan, Ruth Etting, Jack Pearl, Hal
LeRoy, Mitzi Mayfield, Gladys Glad, Al-
bert Carroll and Buck and Bubbles.
Sketches by Mark Hellinger and lyrics by
Mack Gordon and Gene Buck.
—HELP YOURSELF TO HAPPINESS
—SUNNY SOUTHERN SMILE
—CIGARETTES, CIGARS
—BRING ON THE FOLLIES' GIRL
By Gene Buck and Dave Stamper.
—BROADWAY REVERIE
By Buck and Stamper.
—WAS I?
By Chick Endor and Charles Farrell.
—DOIN' THE NEW YORK
By J. P. Murray, Barry Trivers and Ben
Oakland.
—CHANGING THE GUARD
By Murray, Trivers and Oakland.
—LEGEND OF THE ISLANDS
By Powell and Stevens.
—HALF CASTE WOMAN
By Noel Coward.
—MAILU
By E. Y. Harburg and Jay Gorney.
—I'M WITH YOU
By Walter Donaldson.

1932. *SMILING FACES*
Book by Harry Clarke, lyrics by Mack
Gordon, and starring Fred and Dorothy
Stone in a cast that included Roy Roy-
ston and Charles Collins.

—SPORT IS SPORT
—I'VE FALLEN OUT OF LOVE
—SWEET LITTLE STRANGER
—SHAKIN' THE SHAKESPEARE
—THANK YOU, DON'T MENTION IT
—SMART SET
—POOR LITTLE, SHY LITTLE DE-
  MURE LITTLE ME
—LANDLORD AT MY DOOR
—THERE WILL BE A GIRL
—IN HAVANA
—THINK OF MY REPUTATION
—QUICK HENRY THE FLIT
—CAN'T GET RID OF ME
—LITTLE STUCCO IN THE STICKS
—STUMBLED OVER YOU
—FALLING OUT OF LOVE
—OLD SPANISH CUSTOM

1932. *MARCHING BY*
With Jean Gilbert. Book by Harry B.
Smith and Harry Clarke, lyrics by Mack
Gordon, and starring Desiree Tabor and
Guy Robertson.
—ON THROUGH THE NIGHT
—HERE WE ARE IN LOVE
—MARCHING BY
—IT MIGHT OF BEEN YOU
—WE'RE ON OUR WAY TO HELL
—ALL'S FAIR IN LOVE AND WAR
—LET FATE DECIDE
—I GOTTA KEEP MY EYE ON YOU
—LIGHT UP
—FORWARD MARCH INTO ARMS
—I LOVE YOU

Max Rich Score

1934. *KEEP MOVING*
Book and lyrics by Norman Levy and Jack
Scholl, and presented by a cast headed
by Tom Howard, Billy Taylor, Harriet
Hutchins and the Singer Midgets.
—WAKE UP SLEEPY MOON
—THE PLAY IS THE BUNK
—A PAGE FROM JONATHAN SWIFT
—A BIT OF OPTIMISM
—A LOVELY, LOVELY DAY
—COMMAND TO LOVE
—MOTHER EVE
—MIDTOWN
—HOTCHA CHIQUITA
—SUPERSTITION
—SPRINGTIME AND A LOVE SONG
—COME TO THE AID OF THE PARTY
—KEEP MOVING

Richard Rodgers Scores

1930. *SIMPLE SIMON*
Book by Guy Bolton and Ed Wynn, lyrics

by Lorenz Hart, and starring Ed Wynn in a cast that included Harriet Hoctor, Bobbe Arnst and Will Ahearn.
—CONEY ISLAND
—DON'T TELL YOUR FOLKS
—MAGIC MUSIC
—TEN CENTS A DANCE
—SEND FOR ME
—DULL AND GRAY
—SWEETHEART
—HUNTING THE FOX
—MOCKING BIRD
—FAIRYLAND (I LOVE THE WOODS)
—ON WITH THE DANCE
—LONELY DAYS AND L O N E L Y NIGHTS
—LOVE ME OR LEAVE ME
By Gus Kahn and Walter Donaldson.
—ROPING
—RAGS AND TATTERS
—A COTTAGE IN THE COUNTRY
—MAGIC
—I STILL BELIEVE IN YOU
—I COULD DO WONDERS FOR YOU
—HE WAS TOO GOOD TO ME
—DANCING ON THE CEILING

1930. *AMERICA'S SWEETHEART*
Book by Herbert Fields, lyrics by Lorenz Hart, and co-starring Harriet Lake and Jack Whiting.
—MR. DOLAN IS PASSING THROUGH
—IN CALIFORN-I-A
—MY SWEET
—I'VE GOT FIVE DOLLARS
—SWEET GERALDINE
—THERE'S SO MUCH MORE
—WE'LL BE THE SAME
—HOW ABOUT IT?
—INNOCENT CHORUS GIRLS OF YESTERDAY
—A LADY MUST LIVE
—YOU AIN'T GOT NO SAVOIR FAIRE
—TWO UNFORTUNATE ORPHANS
—I WANT A MAN
—TENNESSEE DAN

1935. *JUMBO*
Billy Rose rings down the final curtain at the New York Hippodrome with a musical spectacle by Ben Hecht and Charles McArthur and lyrics by Lorenz Hart. The cast was headed by Jimmy Durante, Gloria Grafton, Donald Novis, Poodles Hanneford, Bob Lawrence and Paul Whiteman and his band.
—OVER AND OVER AGAIN
—THE CIRCUS IS ON PARADE
—THE MOST BEAUTIFUL GIRL IN THE WORLD

—LAUGH
—MY ROMANCE
—LITTLE GIRL BLUE
—SONG OF THE ROUSTABOUTS
—WOMEN
—DIAVOLO
—THE CIRCUS WEDDING

1936. *ON YOUR TOES*
Book by George Abbott, lyrics by Lorenz Hart, and presented by a cast headed by Luella Gear, Tamara Geva, Ray Bolger, Doris Carson and Monte Wooley, who made his debut as an actor in this production.
—TWO A DAY FOR KEITH
—THE THREE B'S
—IT'S GOT TO BE LOVE
—TOO GOOD FOR THE AVERAGE MAN
—THERE'S A SMALL HOTEL
—THE HEART IS QUICKER THAN THE EYE
—QUIET NIGHT
—GLAD TO BE UNHAPPY
—ON YOUR TOES
—SLAUGHTER ON TENTH AVENUE BALLET

1937. *BABES IN ARMS*
Book by Rodgers and Hart, lyrics by Lorenz Hart, and co-starring Mitzi Green and Ray Heatherton.
—WHERE OR WHEN
—BABES IN ARMS
—I WISH I WERE IN LOVE AGAIN
—ALL DARK PEOPLE
—WAY OUT WEST
—MY FUNNY VALENTINE
—JOHNNY ONE NOTE
—IMAGINE
—ALL AT ONCE
—THE LADY IS A TRAMP
—YOU ARE SO FAIR

1937. *I'D RATHER BE RIGHT*
Book by George Kaufman and Moss Hart, lyrics by Lorenz Hart, and starring George M. Cohan in a cast that included Joy Hodges, Taylor Holmes and Austin Marshall.
—A HOMOGENEOUS CABINET
—HAVE YOU MET MISS JONES?
—TAKE AND TAKE AND TAKE
—SPRING IN VIENNA
—A LITTLE CONSTITUTIONAL FUN
—SWEET SIXTY-FIVE
—WE'RE GOING TO BALANCE THE BUDGET
—WHAT'S IT ALL ABOUT?
—LABOR IS THE THING

—I'D RATHER BE RIGHT
—OFF THE RECORD
—A BABY BOND

1938. *I MARRIED AN ANGEL*
Book by Rodgers and Hart, lyrics by Lorenz Hart, and presented by a cast headed by Vera Zorina, Vivienne Segal, Dennis King and Walter Slezak.
—DID YOU EVER GET STUNG?
—I MARRIED AN ANGEL
—THE MODESTE
—I'LL TELL THE MAN IN THE STREET
—HOW TO WIN FRIENDS AND IN-FLUENCE PEOPLE
—SPRING IS HERE
—ANGELS WITHOUT WINGS
—A TWINKLE IN YOUR EYES
—AT THE ROXY MUSIC HALL

1938. *THE BOYS FROM SYRACUSE*
A musical play based on Shakespeare's "Comedy of Errors" by George Abbott, lyrics by Lorenz Hart, and presented by a cast that included Teddy Hart, Jimmy Savo, Eddie Albert, Wynn Murray, Muriel Angelus, Marcy Westcott and Betty Bruce.
—THIS CAN'T BE LOVE
—FALLING IN LOVE WITH LOVE
—I HAD TWINS
—DEAR OLD SYRACUSE
—WHAT CAN YOU DO WITH A MAN?
—THE SHORTEST DAY IN THE YEAR
—LET ANTIPHOLUS IN
—LADIES OF THE EVENING
—HE AND SHE
—YOU HAVE CAST YOUR SHADOW
—BIG BROTHER
—COME WITH ME
—SING FOR YOUR SUPPER

1939. *TOO MANY GIRLS*
Book by George Marion Jr., lyrics by Lorenz Hart, and presented by a cast that included Marcy Westcott, Hal LeRoy, Eddie Bracken, Mary Jane Walsh, Dick Kollmar, Van Johnson and Desi Arnaz.
—HEROES IN THE FALL
—TEMPT ME NOT
—MY PRINCE
—POTTAWATOMIE
—'CAUSE WE GOT CAKE
—LOVE NEVER WENT TO COLLEGE
—SPICK AND SPANISH
—I LIKE TO RECOGNIZE THE TUNE
—LOOK OUT
—SWEETHEARTS OF THE TEAM
—SHE COULD SHAKE THE MARACAS
—I DIDN'T KNOW WHAT TIME IT WAS

—TOO MANY GIRLS
—GIVE IT BACK TO THE INDIANS

Sigmund Romberg Scores

1930. *NINA ROSA*
Book by Otto Harbach, lyrics by Irving Caesar, and starring Ethelind Terry and Guy Robertson.
—PAY DAY
—PABLO
—NINA ROSA
—WITH THE DAWN
—PAYADOR
—THE SECRET OF LIFE
—YOUR SMILES, YOUR TEARS
—SERENADE OF LIFE
—PIZZARO WAS A VERY NARROW MAN
—A KISS I MUST REFUSE
—LATIGO
—THE ONLY ONE FOR ME
—A GAUCHO'S LOVE SONG
—MY FIRST LOVE, MY LAST LOVE

1931. *EAST WIND*
Book and lyrics by Frank Mandel and Oscar Hammerstein II, and starring Charlotte Lansing and J. Harold Murray.
—IT'S A WONDERFUL WORLD
—EAST WIND
—I SAW YOUR EYES
—THESE TROPICS
—CONGAI
—GOOD NIGHT
—ARE YOU LOVE?
—YOU ARE MY WOMAN
—MINNIE
—TWO SOFT ARMS
—I'D BE A FOOL TO FALL IN LOVE AGAIN
—LOVE WHEN YOUR HEART IS YOUNG

1933. *MELODY*
Book by Edward Childs Carpenter, lyrics by Irving Caesar, and presented by a cast headed by Evelyn Herbert, Everett Marshall, Hal Skelly and Walter Woolf.
—OUR LITTLE LADY UPSTAIRS
—MELODY
—I'D WRITE A SONG
—GOOD FRIENDS SURROUND ME
—ON TO AFRICA
—I AM THE SINGER YOU ARE THE SONG
—NEVER HAD AN EDUCATION
—THE WHOLE WORLD LOVES
—GIVE ME A ROLL ON A DRUM
—TONIGHT MAY NEVER COME AGAIN

1935. *MAY WINE*
Book by Frank Mandel, lyrics by Oscar Hammerstein II, and presented by a cast headed by Nancy McCord, Walter Slezak and Walter Woolf King.
—SOMETHING IN THE AIR IN MAY
—YOU WAIT AND SEE
—I BUILT A DREAM ONE DAY
—DANCE MY DARLINGS
—ALWAYS BE A GENTLEMAN
—SOMEBODY OUGHT TO BE TOLD
—SOMETHING NEW IN MY HEART
—ONCE AROUND THE CLOCK

1936. *FORBIDDEN MELODY*
Book and lyrics by Otto Harbach, and starring Carl Brisson in a cast that included Ruth Weston, June Havoc, Jack Sheehan and Ruby Mercer.
—BUCHAREST
—A LADY IN THE WINDOW
—JUST HELLO
—MOONLIGHT AND VIOLINS
—TWO LADIES AND A MAN
—YOU ARE ALL I'VE WANTED
—HOW COULD A FELLOW WANT MORE
—NO USE PRETENDING
—HEAR THE GYPSIES PLAYING
—SHADOWS
—WHEN A GIRL FORGETS TO SCREAM
—BLAME IT ON THE NIGHT

Harold J. Rome Scores

1937. *PINS AND NEEDLES*
A revue produced by the New York Garment Workers Union with a book by Charles Friedman and lyrics by the composer.
—SUNDAY IN THE PARK
—ONE BIG UNION FOR TWO
—SING ME A SONG OF SOCIAL SIGNIFICANCE
—DOING THE REACTIONARY
—CHAIN STORE DAISY
—WHAT GOOD IS LOVE
—NOBODY MAKES A PASS AT ME
—FOUR LITTLE ANGELS OF PEACE
—PAPA DON'T LOVE MAMA ANY MORE
—I'VE GOT THE NERVE TO BE IN LOVE
—BACK TO WORK
—STAY OUT SAMMY
—IT'S BETTER WITH A UNION MAN
—BERTHA THE SEWING MACHINE GIRL

1938. *SING OUT THE NEWS*
Book by Charles Friedman, lyrics by the composer, and presented by a cast that included Philip Loeb, Joey Faye, Mary Jane Walsh and June Allyson.
—FRANKLIN D. ROOSEVELT JONES
—MY HEART IS UNEMPLOYED
—ORDINARY GUY
—HOW LONG CAN LOVE KEEP LAUGHING
—ONE OF THESE FINE DAYS
—YIP-AHOY
—PLAZA 6-9423

Arthur Schwartz Scores

1930. *PRINCESS CHARMING*
With Albert Sirmay. A musical comedy with book and lyrics by Jack Donahue, and presented by a cast headed by Victor Moore, Evelyn Herbert and Robert Halliday.
—TAKE A LETTER TO THE KING
—PALACE OF DREAMS
—THE PANIC'S ON
—I'LL BE THERE
—TRAILING A SHOOTING STAR
—HERE IS A SWORD
—ONE FOR ALL
—YOU
—I'LL NEVER LEAVE YOU
—WINGS IN THE MORNING
—I LOVE YOU
By Walter O'Keefe and Robert Dolan.

1930. *THREE'S A CROWD*
Book and lyrics by Howard Dietz, and presented by a cast headed by Libby Holman, Tamara Geva, Fred Allen, Clifton Webb, Fred MacMurray and Alan Jones.
—SOMETHING TO REMEMBER YOU BY
—JE T'AIME
—THE MOMENT I SAW YOU
—NIGHT AFTER NIGHT
—THE CALIFORNIA COLLEGIANS
—RIGHT AT THE START OF IT
—FORGET ALL YOUR BOOKS
By Howard Dietz and Burton Lane.
—YALLER
By Henry Myers and Charles Schwab.
—BODY AND SOUL
By Ed Heyman, Robert Sour, Frank Eyton and Johnnie Green.
—PRACTICING UP ON YOU
By Howard Dietz and Phil Charig.
—OUT IN THE OPEN AIR
By Howard Dietz and Burton Lane.
—TALKATIVE TOES
By Howard Dietz and Vernon Duke.

—ALL THE KING'S HORSES
By Howard Dietz, Alex Wilder and Edward Brandt.
1930. *SECOND LITTLE SHOW*
Book and lyrics by Howard Dietz, and presented by a cast headed by Tashamira, Jay C. Flippen, Gloria Grafton and Al Trahan.
—LUCKY SEVEN
—NEW NEW YORK
—SWING YOUR TAILS
—FOOLISH FACE
—YOU'RE THE SUNRISE
—WHAT A CASE I'VE GOT ON YOU
—GOOD CLEAN SPORT
—MY INTUITION
—LONELY HEARTS' BALL
—I STARTED ON A SHOESTRING
—SING SOMETHING SIMPLE
By Herman Hupfeld.
1931. *THE BAND WAGON*
Book by George S. Kaufman, lyrics by Howard Dietz, and starring Fred and Adele Astaire in a cast that included Frank Morgan, Tillie Losch, Philip Loeb and Helen Broderick.
—DANCING IN THE DARK
—NEW SUN IN THE SKY
—I LOVE LOUISA
—HIGH AND LOW DOWN
—HOOPS
—SWEET MUSIC
—WHEN THE RAIN GOES PITTER-PATTER
—THE FLAG
—FOR DEAR OLD NECTAR
—A NICE PLACE TO VISIT
—CONFESSION
—MISERABLE WITH YOU AGAIN
—WHERE CAN HE BE?
—THE BEGGAR WALTZ
—WHITE HEAT
1932. *FLYING COLORS*
Book and lyrics by Howard Dietz, and presented by a cast headed by Clifton Webb, Charles Butterworth, Philip Loeb, Buddy Ebsen, Tamara Geva, Patsy Kelly and Imogene Coca.
—ALONE TOGETHER
—LOUISIANA HAYRIDE
—SHINE ON YOUR SHOES
—TWO-FACED WOMAN
—DAY AFTER DAY
—SMOKIN' REEFERS
—IT WAS NEVER LIKE THIS
—ALL'S WELL
—MOTHER TOLD ME SO
1934. *REVENGE WITH MUSIC*
A musical comedy, based on the Spanish

short-story Classic *Three Cornered Hat*, with book and lyrics by Howard Dietz and presented by a cast headed by Libby Holman, Ilka Chase, George Metaxa and Charles Winninger.
—YOU AND THE NIGHT AND THE MUSIC
—IF THERE IS SOMEONE LOVELIER THAN YOU
—WHEN YOU LOVE ONLY ONE
—NEVER MARRY A DANCER
—IN THE NOONDAY SUN
—THAT FELLOW MANUELO
—THINK IT OVER
—MARIA
—MY FATHER SAID
—ONCE IN A WHILE
—IN THE MIDDLE OF THE NIGHT
—WAND'RING HEART
1935. *AT HOME ABROAD*
Book and lyrics by Howard Dietz, and presented by a cast headed by Beatrice Lillie, Ethel Waters, Eleanor Powell, Paul Haakon, Herb Williams and Eddie Foy, Jr.
—LOVE IS A DANCING THING
—GOT A BRAND NEW SUIT
—GET AWAY FROM IT ALL
—THAT'S NOT CRICKET
—HOTTENTOT POTENTATE
—FAREWELL MY LOVELY
—THE LADY WITH THE TAP
—THIEF IN THE NIGHT
—GET YOURSELF A GEISHA GIRL
During the rendition of this song, Bea Lillie interpolated the show-stopping line: "It's better with your shoes off."
—OH LEO!
—DEATH IN THE AFTERNOON
1937. *VIRGINIA*
An early production at the Radio City Center Theater with a book by Lawrence Stallings and Owen Davis, lyrics by Albert Stillman, and presented by a cast headed by Gene Lockhart, Anne Booth, Nigel Bruce and Ronald Graham.
—GOOD-BYE JONAH
—YOU AND I KNOW HOW SWEET YOU ARE
—AN OLD FLAME NEVER DIES
—VIRGINIA
—WE HAD TO REHEARSE
—SEND ONE ANGEL DOWN
—MY BRIDAL GOWN
—GOOD AND LUCKY
—IT'S OUR DUTY TO THE KING
—IF YOU WERE SOMEONE ELSE
—MY HEART IS DANCING
—MEET ME AT THE FAIR
—FEE-FIE-FO-FUM

—I'LL BE SITTIN' IN DE LAP OF THE
  LORD

1938. *BETWEEN THE DEVIL*
  Book and lyrics by Howard Dietz, and pre-
  sented by a cast headed by Jack Buchan-
  an, Evelyn Laye, Adele Dixon, the Debon-
  aires and the Tune Twisters.
—I SEE YOUR FACE BEFORE ME
—THE NIGHT BEFORE THE MORN-
  ING AFTER
—DON'T GO AWAY MONSIEUR
—EXPERIENCE
—FIVE O'CLOCK
—THE COCKTAIL
—TRIPLETS
—FLY BY NIGHT
—BYE-BYE BUTTERFLY LOVER
—FRONT PAGE NEWS
—WHY DID YOU DO IT?
—CELLINI COULDN'T SAY NO
—BY MYSELF
—I'M AGAINST RHYTHM

1939. *STARS IN YOUR EYES*
  Book by J. P. McAvoy, lyrics by Dorothy
  Fields, and starring Ethel Merman in a
  cast that included Richard Carlson, Jim-
  my Durante, Tamara Toumanova and
  Mildred Natwick.
—PLACES EVERYBODY
—ONE BRIEF MOMENT
—THIS IS IT
—ALL THE TIME
—SELF-MADE MAN
—OKAY FOR SOUND
—A LADY NEEDS A CHANGE
—TERRIBLY ATTRACTIVE
—JUST A LITTLE BIT MORE
—AS OF TODAY
—HE'S GOING HOME
—I'LL PAY THE CHECK
—NEVER A DULL MOMENT
—IT'S ALL YOURS

Sissle and Blake Score

1933. *SHUFFLE ALONG OF 1933*
  A revue with book by Flourney Miller,
  who headed an all-Negro cast.
—LABOR DAY PARADE
—SING AND DANCE YOUR TROUBLES
  AWAY
—CHICKENS COME HOME TO ROOST
—BANDANA WAYS
—BREAKIN' 'EM IN
—IN THE LAND OF SUNNY SUN-
  FLOWERS
—SUGAR BABE
—JOSHUA FIT DE BATTLE
—SORE FOOT BLUES

—GLORY
—SATURDAY AFTERNOON
—HERE 'TIS
—FALLING IN LOVE
—DUSTIN' AROUND
—IF IT'S NEWS TO YOU
—REMINISCING
—HARLEM MOON
—YOU GOTTA HAVE KOO WAH

Sammy Stept Score

1933. *SHADY LADY*
  Book by Estelle Morando, lyrics by Bud
  Green, and presented by a cast headed by
  Helen Kane, Charles Purcell and Lester
  Allen.
—ANY WAY THE WIND BLOWS
—GET HOT FOOT
—SWINGY LITTLE THINGEY
—LIVE, LAUGH AND LOVE
—YOUR TYPE IS COMING BACK
—ONE HEART
—YOU'RE NOT THE ONE
  By Stanley Adams and Jesse Greer.
—I'LL BETCHA THAT I'LL GETCHA
  By Stanley Adams and Jesse Greer.
—ISN'T IT REMARKABLE
  By Stanley Adams and Jesse Greer.
—HIYA SUCKER
  By Stanley Adams and Jesse Greer.
—WHERE, OH WHERE CAN I FIND
  MY LOVE
  By Stanley Adams and Jesse Greer.
—EVERYTHING BUT MY MAN
  By Serge Walter
—ISN'T IT SWELL TO DREAM?
  By Bud Green, Stanley Adams, Sammy
  Stept and Jesse Greer.

Stept and Tobias Score

1939. *YOKEL BOY*
  Book by Lew Brown, music and lyrics by
  Sammy Stept, Charles Tobias and Lew
  Brown, and presented by a cast headed
  by Buddy Ebsen, Judy Canova, Dixie
  Dunbar, Phil Silvers, Jackie Heller and
  Lew Hearn.
—LEM AND SUE
—I KNOW I'M NOBODY
—FOR THE SAKE OF LEXINGTON
—COMES LOVE
—IT'S ME AGAIN
—LET'S MAKE MEMORIES TONIGHT
—JUKIN'
—GRANDPA HAWKINS
—UNCLE SAM'S LULLABY
—HOLLYWOOD AND VINE
—CATHERINE THE GREAT

—THE SHIP HAS SAILED
—I CAN'T AFFORD TO DREAM
—BEER BARREL POLKA
By Lew Brown, Wladimir A. Timm and
Jaromir Vejvoda.

Harold Stern Score

1930. *ARTISTS AND MODELS OF 1930*
With Ernie Golden. A revue presented by a
cast headed by Aileen Stanley, George
Hassell, Harry Welsh, Vera Pearce, Hal-
fred Young and Phil Baker.
—PERFECT MODELS
—UPS AND DOWNS
—BUDAPEST
—MY REAL IDEAL
—NARGILEH
—TWO PERFECT LOVERS
—RO-RO-ROLLIN' ALONG
—JIMMY AND ME
—OLD LADY IN THE SHOE
—THE RUMBA
—IN OLD HAVANA TOWN
—DANCE, DANCE, DANCE
—WITHOUT A SHADOW OF DOUBT
—L-O-V-E
—I WANT YOU TO LOVE ME
—WHERE ARE YOU?
—SEX APPEAL

Johann Strauss Score

1933. *CHAMPAGNE SEC*
An operetta based on "Die Fledermaus"
with book by Lawrence Langner, lyrics
by Robert A. Simon, and presented by a
cast headed by George Meader, Helen
Ford, Peggy Wood and Kitty Carlisle.

J. Strauss Sr. and Jr. Scores

1934. *THE GREAT WALTZ*
Book by Moss Hart, lyrics by Desmond
Carter, and presented by a cast headed
by H. Reeves Smith, Guy Robertson,
Marie Burke and Marion Claire.
—RADETSKY MARCH
—MORNING
—YOU ARE MY SONGS
—LOVE WILL FIND YOU
—ON LOVE ALONE
—LIKE A STAR IN THE SKY
—WITH ALL MY HEART
—NIGHT
—LOVE'S NEVER LOST
—WE LOVE YOU STILL
—WHILE YOU LOVE ME
—LOVE AND WAR
—THE BLUE DANUBE

1937. *THE THREE WALTZES*
Book and lyrics by Claire Kummer and
Roland Leigh. In the score of this oper-
etta, the leading roles of which were
played by Kitty Carlisle and Michael
Bartlett, the waltz melodies of Oscar
Straus were also included.
—I SOMETIMES WONDER
—OUR LAST VALSE
—THE DAYS OF OLD
—TO LOVE IS TO LIVE
—I FOUND MY LOVE
—SPRINGTIME IN THE AIR
—FOREVER
—HOW CAN WORDS CONTENT A
LOVER
—I GAVE MY HEART AWAY

Kay Swift Score

1930. *FINE AND DANDY*
A musical comedy with book by Donald
Ogden Stewart, lyrics by Paul Jones, and
starring Joe Cook in a cast that included
Eleanor Powell.
—STARTING AT THE BOTTOM
—RICH OR POOR
—CAN THIS BE LOVE?
—WHEELS OF STEEL
—FINE AND DANDY
—I'LL HIT A NEW HIGH
—GIDDYUP, BACK
—FORDYCE
—LET'S GO EAT WORMS IN THE
GARDEN
—JIG HOP
—THE THINGS I CAN'T SEEM TO
FORGET
—WEDDING BELLS

Sir Arthur Sullivan Score

1938. *KNIGHTS OF SONG*
A musical biography of Gilbert and Sul-
livan by Glendon Allvine, presented by
a cast headed by Nigel Bruce, Monte
Wooley, John Moore and Natalie Hall,
and reviving songs and scenes from the
following Gilbert-and-Sullivan operettas:
"Pinafore", "The Sorcerer", "Trial By
Jury", "Pirates of Penzance", "Ivanhoe",
"The Mikado", "Yeomen Of The
Guard" and "The Gondoliers".

Joseph Tunbridge Score

1933. *TELL HER THE TRUTH*
With Jack Waller. Book and lyrics by R.
P. Weston and Bert Lee, and presented by
a cast headed by John Sheehan Jr., Lillian Emerson and Andrew Tombes.

—HAPPY THE DAY
—HOCH, CAROLINE!
—SWING, BROTHERS
—WON'T YOU TELL ME WHY?
—THAT'S FINE
—TELL HER THE TRUTH
—HORRORTORIO

Jimmy VanHeusen Score

1939. *SWINGIN' THE DREAM*
A musical version of "Midsummer's Night's Dream" with book by Gilbert Seldes and Eric Charrell, lyrics by Eddie DeLange, and starring Louis Armstrong as "Bottom" in a cast that included Benny Goodman's Sextet and Maxine Sullivan.
—DARN THAT DREAM
—PEACE BROTHER
—THERE'S GOTTA BE A WEDDING
—SWINGIN' A DREAM
—MOONLAND
—LOVE'S A RIDDLE
—DOING THE SABOO
—JUMPIN' AT THE WOODSIDE
—PICK-A-RIB

Harry Warren Scores

1930. *SWEET AND LOW*
Book by David Freedman, lyrics by Billy Rose and Ira Gershwin and presented by a cast headed by James Barton, Fanny Brice, George Jessel and Hannah Williams.
—CHEERFUL LITTLE EARFUL
—WOULD YOU LIKE TO TAKE A WALK?
—OVERNIGHT
Music by Louis Alter.

1931. *THE LAUGH PARADE*
Book by Ed Wynn and Ed Preble, lyrics by Mort Dixon and Joe Young, and starring Ed Wynn in a cast that included Eunice Healy, Bartlett Simmons and Ed Cheney.
—PUNCH AND JUDY MAN
—GOT TO GO TO TOWN
—OOH! THAT KISS
—THE TORCH SONG
—THE LAUGH PARADE
—EXCUSE FOR A SONG AND DANCE
—YOU'RE MY EVERYTHING
—LOVE ME FOREVER

1931. *BILLY ROSE'S CRAZY QUILT*
Book by David Freedman, lyrics by Billy Rose and Mort Dixon, and starring Fanny Brice in a cast that included Phil Baker, Ted Healy, Lew Brice, Ethel Norris and Gomez and Winona.

—SING A LITTLE JINGLE
—I FOUND A MILLION DOLLAR BABY IN A FIVE-AND-TEN CENT STORE
—IN THE MERRY MONTH OF MAYBE
—WOULD YOU LIKE TO TAKE A WALK?
—CRAZY QUILT
Lyrics by Bud Green.
—REST ROOM ROSE
By Lorenz Hart and Richard Rodgers.
—I WANT TO DO A NUMBER WITH THE BOYS
By Ned Wever and Rowland Wilson.
—UNDER THE CLOCK AT THE ASTOR
By Ned Wever and Manning Sherwin.
—PETER PAN
—By Billy Rose, Carroll Gibbons and James Dyrenforth.

Ned Washington and Victor Young Scores

1933. *BLACKBIRDS OF 1933*
Book by Nat Dorfman, Mann Holiner and Lew Leslie, lyrics by Mann Holiner, Joe Young and Alberta Nichols, and presented by an all-Negro cast headed by Bill Robinson.
—GREAT GETTIN' UP MORNIN'
—I'M WALKING THE CHALK LINE
By Mann Holiner and Alberta Nichols.
—I JUST COULDN'T TAKE IT BABY
By Mann Holiner and Alberta Nichols.
—YOUR MOTHER'S SON-IN-LAW
By Mann Holiner and Alberta Nichols.
—TAPPIN' THE BARREL
—VICTIM OF VOODOO DRUMS
—GENTLEMEN OF JAPAN
—A HUNDRED YEARS FROM TODAY
—DOIN' THE SHIM SHAM
—LET ME BE BORN AGAIN
—CONCENTRATE A LITTLE ON LOVE
—WHAT! NO DIXIE

1934. *BLACKBIRDS OF 1934*
This was a revised edition of the "Blackbirds" of the previous season, presented by a cast headed by Edith Wilson, Tim Moore, Valaida, Peg Leg Bates and Bill Robinson. Four songs from the previous edition of this all-Negro revue were retained: "Your Mother's Son-In-Law", "Walking The Chalk Line", "Concentrate A Little On Love" and "Doin' The Shim Sham", and the following new numbers were added:
—ST. JAMES INFIRMARY
By Joe Primrose.
—RHAPSODY IN BLUE
By Ira and George Gershwin.

—PAPA DE DA DA
By Clarence Williams, Clarence Todd and Spencer Williams.
—CHRISTMAS NIGHT IN HARLEM
By Mitchell Parish and Raymond Scott.

Kurt Weill Scores

1938. *JOHNNY JOHNSON*
A protest against war with a book by Paul Green and background music by Kurt Weill, staged by the Group Theater with Russell Collins in the name role and John Garfield and Lee J. Cobb supporting him.

1938. *KNICKERBOCKER HOLIDAY*
Book and lyrics by Maxwell Anderson, and presented by a cast that included Ray Middleton, Walter Huston, Jeanne Madden, Clarence Nordstrom and Richard Kollman.
—CLICKETY-CLACK
—HUSH, HUSH
—THERE'S NOWHERE TO GO BUT UP
—HOW CAN YOU TELL AN AMERICAN?
—ONE TOUCH OF ALCHEMY
—THE ONE INDISPENSABLE MAN
—YOUNG PEOPLE THINK ABOUT LOVE
—SEPTEMBER SONG
—BALLAD OF THE ROBBERS
—WE ARE CUT IN TWAIN
—TO WAR!
—OUR ANCIENT LIBERTIES
—ROMANCE AND MUSKETEERS
—THE SCAR
—DANCE OF THE ABORIGINES
—DIRGE FOR A SOLDIER
—VE VOULDN'T GONTO DO IT

Percy Wenrich Score

1930. *WHO CARES?*
A revue with lyrics by Harry Clark, and presented by a cast headed by Peggy O'Neill, Florenz Ames, William Holbrook and Bobby Edwards.
—NOBODY BUT YOU
—WHO CARES?
—YOUR WAY WILL BE MY WAY
—MAKE MY BED DOWN IN DIXIELAND

Richard Whiting Scores

1931. *FREE FOR ALL*
Book and lyrics by Lawrence Schwab and Oscar Hammerstein II, and presented by a cast headed by Tamara, Dorothy Knapp and Jack Haley.

—I LOVE HIM, THE RAT
—FREE FOR ALL
—THE GIRL NEXT DOOR
—LIVING IN SIN
—JUST EIGHTEEN
—NOT THAT I CARE
—SLUMBER SONG
—WHEN YOUR BOY BECOMES A MAN
—TONIGHT
—NEVADA MOONLIGHT

1932. *TAKE A CHANCE*
With Nacio Herb Brown. Book and lyrics by Lawrence Schwab and B. G. DeSylva, and starring Ethel Merman in a cast that included Jack Whiting, Jack Haley, Sid Silvers (replaced by Olsen and Johnson), June Knight (replaced by Barbara Newberry) and Mitzi Mayfair (replaced by Dorris Groday).
—THE LIFE OF THE PARTY
—SHOULD I BE SWEET?
Music by Vincent Youmans.
—SO DO I
—I GOT RELIGION
—SHE'S NUTS ABOUT ME
—TICKLED PINK
—EADIE WAS A LADY
—TURN OUT THE LIGHTS
—CHARITY
—I LONG TO BELONG TO YOU
—RISE AN' SHINE
Music by Vincent Youmans.
—TONIGHT IS OPENING NIGHT
—YOU'RE AN OLD SMOOTHIE

Al Wilson and Charles Weinberg Score

1932. *YEAH MAN*
With Ken Macomber. An all-Negro revue with sketches by Leigh Whipper and Billy Mills, and lyrics by the composers.
—MISSISSIPPI JOYS
—GOTTA GET DE BOAT LOADED
—DANCIN' FOOL
—AT THE BARBECUE
—I'M ALWAYS HAPPY IN YOUR ARMS
—CRAZY IDEA OF LOVE
—IT'S MODERNISTIC
—COME TO HARLEM
—BABY I COULD DO IT FOR YOU
—SHADY DAN
—SHAKE YOUR BAMBOO
—QUALIFICATINS
By Porter Grainger.
—THAT'S RELIGION
By Porter Grainger.

Vincent Youmans Scores

1930. *SMILES*

Book by William McGuire, lyrics by Clifford Grey, Harold Adamson and Ring Lardner, and presented by a cast headed by Marilyn Miller, Fred and Adele Astaire, Paul Gregory and Tom Howard.

—THE BOWERY
—SAY, YOUNG MAN OF MANHATTAN
—HOTCHA MA CHOTCH
—TIME ON MY HANDS
—BE GOOD TO ME
—THE CHINESE PARTY
—CHINESE JADE
—THE CRYSTAL LADY
—CLEVER THESE CHINESE
—ANYWAY WE HAD FUN
—SOMETHING TO SING ABOUT
—HERE'S A DAY TO BE HAPPY
—IF I WERE YOU LOVE
—I'M GLAD I WAITED
—LA MARSEILLES
—WHY AIN'T I HOME?
—DANCING WEDDING

1932. *THROUGH THE YEARS*

A musical version of "Smiling Through" with book and lyrics by Brian Hooker, and presented by a cast headed by Natalie Hall, Michael Bartlett and Charles Winninger.

—KATHLEEN MINE
—KINDA LIKE YOU
—I'LL COME BACK TO YOU
—HOW HAPPY THE BRIDE
—THROUGH THE YEARS
  This was Vincent Youmans favorite song.
—IT'S EVERY GIRL'S AMBITION
—THE TRUMPETEER AND THE LOVER
—YOU'RE EVERYWHERE
—THE ROAD TO HOME
—DRUMS IN MY HEART

Composite Scores

1930. *GARRICK GAIETIES OF 1930*

An intimate revue with Edith Meiser, Albert Carrol, Imogene Coca, Sterling Holloway, Philip Loeb and Ray Heatherton.

—I'M ONLY HUMAN AFTER ALL
By Ira Gershwin, E. Y. Harburg and Vernon Duke.
—SHAVIAN SHIVERS
By E. Y. Harburg and Vernon Duke.
—ANKLE UP THE ALTAR WITH ME
By E. Y. Harburg and Richard Myers.
—I'VE GOT IT AGAIN
By Allan Boretz and Ned Lehac.
—LAZY LEVEE LOUNGERS
By Willard Robison.
—OUT OF BREATH AND SCARED TO DEATH OF YOU
By Johnny Mercer and Everett Miller.
—PUT IT AWAY TILL SPRING
By Joshua Titzell and Peter Nolan.
—TOO, TOO DIVINE
By E. Y. Harburg and Vernon Duke.
—YOU LOST YOUR OPPORTUNITY
By Henry Myers and Charles M. Schwab.

1930. *NINE-FIFTEEN REVUE*

With Harry McNaughton, Paul Kelly, Fred Keating, Don Voorhees and his orchestra and Ruth Etting.

—ONE WAY STREET TO YOU
By Paul James and Kay Swift.
—UP AMONG THE CHIMNEY POTS
By Paul James and Kay Swift.
—TODDLIN' ALONG
By Ira and George Gershwin.
—TA TA, OL' BEAN
By Edward Eliscu and Manning Sherwin.
—KNOCK ON WOOD
By Edward Eliscu and Richard Myers.
—GET HAPPY
By Edward Eliscu and Harold Arlen.
—WINTER AND SPRING
By Edward Eliscu and Rudolf Friml.
—BOUDOIR DOLLS
By Edward Eliscu and Ned Lehac.
—BREAKFAST DANCE
By Edward Eliscu and Ralph Rainger.
—HOW WOULD A CITY GIRL KNOW
By Paul James and Kay Swift.
—GOTTA FIND A WAY TO DO IT.
By Paul James and Roger Wolf Kahn.
—YOU WILL NEVER KNOW
By Paul James and Vincent Youmans.
—GEE IT'S SO GOOD IT'S TOO BAD
By Ted Koehler and Harold Arlen.

1930. *TATTLE TALES*

An intimate revue with a cast headed by Frank Fay and Barbara Stanwyck.

—I'LL TAKE AN OPTION ON YOU
By Howard Dietz and Ralph Rainger.
—COUNTING THE SHEEP
By Nat Lief and Louis Alter.
—JUST A SENTIMENTAL TUNE
By Nat Lief and Louis Alter.
—ANOTHER CASE OF BLUES
By Johnny Mercer and Richard Myers.
—IN WATERMELON TIME
By Howard Johnson and Archie Gottler.
—ROSE OF THE ROTISSERI
By Joe Goodwin, Jimmy Hussey and James Hanley.

1931. *EARL CARROLL'S VANITIES OF 1931*
Book by Ralph Spence and Eddie Welch, and presented by a cast headed by Will Mahoney, William Demarest, Mitchell and Durante and Lillian Roth.

—HAVE A HEART
By Harold Adamson and Burton Lane.

—GOING TO TOWN WITH ME
By Harold Adamson and Burton Lane.

—LOVE CAME INTO MY HEART
By Harold Adamson and Burton Lane.

—HEIGH HO, THE GANG'S ALL HERE
By Harold Adamson and Burton Lane.

—IT'S GREAT TO BE IN LOVE
By Cliff Friend.

—I'VE GOT ANTS IN MY PANTS
By Cliff Friend.

—PARASOLS ON PARADE
By Clifford Adams and Larry Beeson.

—SANDY MAHATMA GANDY
By Will Mahoney and Bob Geraghty.

—GOOD NIGHT SWEETHEART
By Jimmy Campbell, Reg Connelly and Ray Noble.

—HAVE A HEART
By Ray Klages, Jack Meskill and Vincent Rose.

—TONIGHT OR NEVER
By Ray Klages, Jack Meskill and Vincent Rose.

—I GO HAYWIRE

1931. *SHOOT THE WORKS*
With Heywood Broun, George Murphy, Imogene Coca and Jack Hazzard.

—CHIRP, CHIRP
By Joseph Meyer and Phil Charig.

—MUCHACHA
By E. Y. Harburg, Jay Gorney and Vernon Duke.

—IN THE STARS
By Nat and Max Lief and Michael Cleary.

—TAKEN FOR A RIDE
By Nat and Max Lief and Michael Cleary.

—I WANT TO CHISEL ON YOUR HEART
By Nat and Max Lief and Michael Cleary.

—DOORSTEP BABY
By Nat and Max Lief and Michael Cleary.

—PIE IN THE SKY
By Nat and Max Lief and Michael Cleary.

—THE FIRST LADY OF THE LAND
By Nat and Max Lief and Michael Cleary.

—HOW'S YOUR UNCLE?
By Dorothy Fields and Jimmy McHugh.

—LET'S GO OUT IN THE OPEN AIR
By Ann Ronell.

—DAS LIED IST AUS
By Walter Reisch, A. Robinson and Robert Stolz.

—HOT MOONLIGHT
By E. Y. Harburg and Jay Gorney.

—MY HEART'S A BANJO
By E. Y. Harburg and Jay Gorney.

—DO WHAT YOU LIKE
By Leo Robin and Phil Charig.

—BEGGING FOR LOVE
By Irving Berlin.

1931. *THIRD LITTLE SHOW*
Book and lyrics by Howard Dietz, and presented by a cast headed by Beatrice Lillie, Edward Arnold, Ernest Truex, Carl Randall and Walter O'Keefe.

—WHEN YUBA PLAYED THE TUBA DOWN IN CUBA
By Herman Hupfield.

—YOU FORGOT YOUR GLOVES
By Edward Eliscu and Ned Lehac.

—MAD DOGS AND ENGLISHMEN
By Noel Coward.

—SAY THE WORD
By Harold Adamson and Burton Lane.

—FALLING IN LOVE
By Earle Crooker and Henry Sullivan.

—I'VE LOST MY HEART
By Grace Henry and Morris Hamilton.

—I'LL PUTCHA PITCHA IN THE PAPERS
By Nat and Max Lief and Michael Cleary.

—GOING, GOING, GONE
By Edward Eliscu and Henry Sullivan.

—SEVILLA
By Edward Eliscu and Ned Lehac.

—AFRICA SHRIEKS
By Edward Eliscu and Ned Lehac.

—YOU MIGHT AS WELL PRETEND
By Edward Eliscu, Ted Fetter and William M. Lewis, Jr.

—LITTLE GEEZER
By Nat and Max Lief, Dave Oppenheim and Michael Cleary.

1931. *RHAPSODY IN BLACK*
A vaudeville-revue presented by a cast headed by Ethel Waters and the Cecil Mack Choir.

—I'M FEELIN' BLUE
By Dorothy Fields and Jimmy McHugh.

—WHAT'S KEEPING MY PRINCE CHARMING
By Mann Holiner and Alberta Nichols.

—YOU CAN'T STOP ME FROM LOVIN' YOU
By Mann Holiner and Alberta Nichols.

—TILL THE REAL THING COMES ALONG
By Mann Holiner, Sammy Cahn and Alberta Nichols.

errors in Mr. Burton's original compilation

p. 287—1945 *POLONAISE*—also included *Polonaise* and *Mazurke*.

p. 286—*ZIEGFELD FOLLIES OF 1943*—had Illona Massey in the cast.

p. 285—1941 *CRAZY WITH THE HEAT*—contained *Whos to Blame* by Vernon Duke.

p. 282—1949 *TEXAS LI'L DARLIN'*—contained song *The Yodel Blues*.

p. 280—1949 *MISS LIBERTY*—had *The Honorable Profession of the 4th Estate* cut from the score.

p. 279—1940 *LOUISIANA PURCHASE*—also contained *Wild About You* and *It'll Come to You*.

p. 266—1938 *KNICKERBOCHER HOLIDAY*—also contained *It Never Was You*.

p. 263—1938 *BETWEEN THE DEVIL*—also contained *You Have Everything*.

p. 262—1931 *BAND WAGON*—also contained *It Better Be Good*.

p. 262—1935 *AT HOME ABROAD*—includes the songs: *Paree, Loadin' Time* and *What A Wonderful World*.

p. 158—1934*REVENGE WITH MUSIC*—also contained *I'm A Part of You*.

p. 260—1930 *NINA ROSA*—also contained *Adored One*.

p. 258—*ZIEGFELD FOLLIES OF 1931*—also contained *I'm Good for Nothing But Love*.

p. 255—1939 *STREETS OF PARIS*—included *Doin' the Chamberlain*.

p. 254—1933 *ROBERTA*—includes *I'll Be Hard to Handle, An Armfull of Trouble* which is listed, was cut.

p. 242—1937*HOORAY FOR WHAT*—also contained *In The Shade of the New Apple Tree*.

1932. AMERICANA

A revue by J. P. McAvoy, and presented by a cast that included George Givot, Albert Carroll, Don Barclay, Rex Weber, Georgie Tapps and Peggy Cartwright.

—FIVE MINUTES OF SPRING
By E. Y. Harburg and Jay Gorney.

—BROTHER CAN YOU SPARE A DIME?
By E. Y. Harburg and Jay Gorney.

—LET ME MATCH MY PRIVATE LIFE WITH YOURS
By E. Y. Harburg and Vernon Duke.

—WOULDJA FOR A BIG RED APPLE?
By Johnny Mercer and Henry Souvane.

—WHISTLING FOR A KISS
By Johnny Mercer, E. Y. Harburg and Richard Myers.

—YOU'RE NOT PRETTY BUT YOU'RE MINE
By E. Y. Harburg and Burton Lane.

—GET THAT SUN INTO YOU
By Richard Myers.

p. 228—*ED WYNN'S 1920 CARNIVAL*—also contains *I Love The Land of Old Black Joe*.

p. 229—1923 *WILDFLOWER*—Youmans Harbach - Hammerstein also contains *There's Music In Our Heart*.

p. 213—1926 *DESERT SONG*—also contained *Eastern and Western Love*.

p. 210—1921 *BOMBO*—also contained *Arcady and April Showers*.

p. 308—*Garrick Gaieties for 1926*—also contained *Sleepy Head*.

p. 206—1929 *WAKE UP AND DREAM*—also contains *I Loved Him, Looking at You, and Banjo That Man Joe Plays*.

p. 203—1929 *LAZY FINGERS*—I Love You More Than Yesterday* is by Rodgers and Hart not Joseph Mayer.

p. 199—1927 *SHOW BOAT*—should list *After The Ball* (not by Kern but always included in score).

p. 196—1926*COUNTESS MARITZA*—also contains *Say Yes, Sweetheart Say Yes*.

p. 196—1927 *GOLDEN DAWN*—also contained *It's Always The Way* and *Mulunghu Thabu*.

p. 197—*HITCHY-KOO OF 1920* — also contained *The Old Town*.

p. 189—*GEORGE WHITE'S SCANDALS FOR 1928*—contained *I'm on the Crest of a Wave* and *Blue Grass* and the correct Gershwin title for the 1920 Scandals is *Turn On And Tiss Me* and not *Come On And Kiss Me* as listed on page 179.

p. 304—1950*DANCE ME A SONG*—also contained a song *Lilac Wine* by James Shelton.

p. 337—1948 *INSIDE USA*—also included *Atlanta* and *Protect Me* by Arthur Schwartz and Howard Dietz.

—SATAN'S LITTLE LAMB
By Johnny Mercer, E. Y. Harburg and Harold Arlen.

1932. EARL CARROLL'S VANITIES OF 1932

Book by Jack McGowan, and presented by a cast that included Will Fyffe, Milton Berle, Helen Broderick and Harriet Hoctor.

—ROCKIN' IN RHYTHM
By Ted Koehler and Harold Arlen.

—LOVE YOU ARE MY INSPIRATION
By Ted Koehler and Andre Renaud.

—I'VE GOTTA RIGHT TO SING THE BLUES
By Ted Koehler and Harold Arlen.

—FORSAKEN AGAIN
By Ed Heyman and Richard Myers.

—MY DARLING
By Ed Heyman and Richard Myers.

—TAKE ME AWAY
By Charles Tobias and Peter Tinturin.

—ALONG CAME LOVE
By Charles and Henry Tobias.

1932. *GEORGE WHITE'S MUSIC HALL VARIETIES*
Book by George White and William K. Wells, and presented by a cast that included Bert Lahr, Harry Richman, Eleanor Powell and Lily Damita.
—THERE'LL NEVER BE ANOTHER GIRL LIKE YOU
By Herb Magidson and Cliff Friend.
—SO I MARRIED THE GIRL
By Herbert Magidson and Sammy Stept.
—BIRDS OF A FEATHER
Music by Carmen Lombardo.
—THE WALTZ YOU BROUGHT BACK TO ME
Music by Carmen Lombardo.
—SWEET LIAR
—CABIN IN THE COTTON
Music by Harold Arlen.
—TWO FEET IN TWO-FOUR TIME
Music by Harold Arlen.
—RAH, RAH, RAH
Music by Sammy Stept.
—OH LADY
By Herb Magidson and Sammy Stept.
—HOLD ME CLOSER
By Jack Scholl and Max Rich.
—TURN OUT THE LIGHTS AND GO TO BED
By Herman Hupfeld.

1933. *HOLD YOUR HORSES*
Book by Russell Crouse and Carey Ford, and presented by a cast that included Joe Cook, Harriet Hoctor, Ona Munson and Frances Upton.
—GOOD EVENING, MR. MAN IN THE MOON
—GALLOPING THROUGH THE PARK
—HOLD YOUR HORSES
By Owen Murphy, Robert Simon and Russell Bennett.
—PEANUTS AND KISSES
By Arthur Swanstrom and Louis Alter.
—HAPPY LITTLE WEEK-END
By Arthur Swanstrom and Louis Alter.
—HIGH SHOES
By Owen Murphy, Robert Simon and Russell Bennett.
—SINGING TO YOU
By Robert Simon, Margot Millam and Ben Oakland.
—IF I LOVE AGAIN
By Ben Oakland and J. P. Murray.
—I GUESS I LOVE YOU
By Arthur Swanstrom.
—OLD MAN SUBWAY

1933. *MURDER AT THE VANITIES*
A musical mystery play by Earl Carroll and Rufus King with a cast headed by James Rennie.
—SWEET MADNESS
By Ned Washington and Victor Young.
—SAVAGE SERENADE
By Herman Hupfeld.
—ME FOR YOU FOREVER
By Edward Heyman and Richard Myers.
—YOU LOVE ME
By Herman Hupfeld.
—VIRGINS WRAPPED IN CELLOPHANE
By Paul F. Webster and John J. Loeb.
—WEEP NO MORE MY BABY
By Edward Heyman and Johnny Green.
—DUST IN YOUR EYES
By Irving and Lionel Newman.

1934. *NEW FACES*
An intimate revue with a cast headed by Henry Fonda and Imogene Coca.
—NEW FACES
By Nancy Hamilton and Martha Caples.
—SOMETHING YOU LACK
By Nancy Hamilton, June Sillman and Warburton Guilbert.
—VISITORS ASHORE
By Everett Marcy, Nancy Hamilton and Warburton Guilbert.
—LAMPLIGHT
By James Shelton.
—THE BYRD INFLUENCE
By June Sillman, Nancy Hamilton and Warburton Guilbert.
—THE GANGSTER INFLUENCE
By Viola Shores, June Sillman and Warburton Guilbert.
—MUSIC IN MY HEART
By June Sillman and Warburton Guilbert.
—MY LAST AFFAIR
By Haven Johnson.
—THE VILLAGE GOSSIP
By J. J. Robbins and Sandro Corona.
—EMPEROR JONES
By George Grande, June Sillman and Donald Honrath.
—CAUSE YOU WON'T PLAY HOUSE
By E. Y. Harburg and Morgan Lewis.
—PEOPLE OF TASTE
By Nancy Hamilton and Martha Caples.
—SO LOW
By Nancy Hamilton, June Sillman and Donald Honrath.
—HE LOVES ME
By Nancy Hamilton and Cliff Allen.
—SPRING SONG
By Viola Shores, Nancy Hamilton and Warburton Guilbert.
—ON THE OTHER HAND
By Nancy Hamilton and Martha Caples.

1934. *THUMBS UP*
A revue with sketches by H. I. Phillips and Alan Baxter, lyrics by Ballard Mac-Donald, and presented by a cast headed by Eddie Dowling, Clark and McCullough, J. Harold Murray, Hal LeRoy, Eddie Garr, Ray Dooley, Rose King, Shiela Barrett and the Pickens Sisters.
—CONTINENTAL HONEYMOON
By James Hanley.
—GOTTA SEE A MAN ABOUT HIS DAUGHTER
Lyrics by Jean Herbert and Karl Stark.
—ZING WENT THE STRINGS OF MY HEART   By James Hanley.
—LILY BELLE MAY JUNE
By Earle Crooker and Henry Sullivan.
—EILEEN AVOURNEEN
By J. M. Anderson and H. Sullivan.
—CUTE PEEKIN' KNEES
—AUTUMN IN NEW YORK
By Vernon Duke.
—COTTAGE I CALL JE T'AIME
Music by Arthur Schwartz.
—DO A DUET
Music by Arthur Schwartz.
—I'M A LITTLE MOVIE QUEEN
Music by Arthur Schwartz.

1935. *EARL CARROLL'S SKETCH BOOK OF 1935*
Music and lyrics by Murray Mencher, Charles Tobias and Charles Newman, and presented by a cast that included Ken Murray and Jack Haley.
—THROUGH THESE PORTALS PASS THE MOST BEAUTIFUL GIRLS IN THE WORLD
—LET'S SWING IT
—AT LAST
Music by Henry Tobias and lyrics by Sam Lewis.
—GRINGOLA

—YOUNG IDEAS
—SILHOUETTES UNDER THE STARS
—MOONLIGHT AND VIOLINS
—SUNDAY NIGHT IN NEW YORK
—LET THE MAN WHO MAKES THE GUN
By Ray Egan and Gerald Marks.
—AUNT LOUISE OF LOUISIANA
—THAT RUSTLE OF A BUSTLE
By Will Irwin and Norman Zeno, Jr.

1935. *PROVINCETOWN FOLLIES*
A revue with a cast headed by Beatrice Kay and Billy Green.
—A GAL WITH A PAST
By Frederick Herendeen and Dave Stamper.
—NEW WORDS FOR AN OLD LOVE SONG
By Frede Herendeen & Dave Stamper.
—GOT MYSELF A NEW LOVE
By Frederick Herendeen and Dave Stamper.
—RESTLESS RIVER   By Mary Schaffer.
—POOR PORGY
By Frede Herendeen & Sylvan Green.
—IS IT LOVE OR IS IT APPLE PIE?
—THE NANTUCKET
By Louis Levine and Trevor Jones.
—RAIN OVER MANHATTAN
By Arthur Jones.
—RED SAILS IN THE SUNSET
By Jimmy Kennedy and Hugh Williams.

1936. *NEW FACES OF 1936*
A revue with sketches by Mindret Lord and Everett Marcy, and presented by a cast headed by Imogene Coca and Van Johnson.
—IT'S HIGH TIME I GOT THE LOW DOWN ON YOU
Music by Richard Myers.
—MY LOVE IS YOUNG
By Bix Reichner and Irvin Graham.

The Band Wagon

—YOU BETTER GO NOW
By Bix Reichner and Irvin Graham.
—TONIGHT'S THE NIGHT
By June Sillman and Alexander Fogarty.
—YOUR FACE IS FAMILIAR
By E. Gilbert and Alexander Fogarty.
—LOVE IS A DANCER   By Lew Pollack.
—MY LAST AFFAIR   By Haven Johnson.

1936. *THE SHOW IS ON*
A revue with sketches by David Freed-
man and Moss Hart, and presented by a
cast headed by Bert Lahr, Beatrice Lillie,
Mitzi Mayfair, Gracie Barrie and Paul
Haakon.
—NOW
By Ted Fetter and Vernon Duke.
—WHAT HAS HE GOT?
By Ted Fetter and Vernon Duke.
—CASANOVA
By Ted Fetter and Vernon Duke.
—THE SHOW IS ON
By Hoagy Carmichael.
—RHYTHM
By Larry Hart and Richard Rodgers.
—SONG OF THE WOODMAN
By E. Y. Harburg and Harold Arlen.
—BUY YOURSELF A BALLOON
By Herman Hupfeld
—PARADE NIGHT
By Norman Zeno and Will Irwin.
—BY STRAUSS   By Ira & G. Gershwin.
—WOOF
By Norman Zeno and Will Irwin.
—LITTLE OLD LADY
By Stanley Adams and Hoagy Carmichael.
—JOSEPHINE WATERS
By E. Y. Harburg and Harold Arlen.
—I'VE GOT FIVE DOLLARS
By Larry Hart and Richard Rodgers.

1936. *WHO'S WHO*
A revue produced by Elsa Maxwell with a
cast of Rags Ragland & Imogene Coca.
—THE GIRL WITH THE PAINT ON
HER FACE   By Irvin Graham.
—I DANCE ALONE   By James Shelton.
—I MUST HAVE A DINNER COAT
By James Shelton.
—IF YOU WANT A KISS
By June Sillman and Paul McGrane.
—LET YOUR HAIR DOWN WITH A
BANG
By June Sillman and Baldwin Bergensen.
—ONE SUNDAY IN JUNE
By Neville Fleeson and Paul McGrane.
—RINKA TINKA MAN
By June Sillman and Lew Kesler.
—TRAIN TIME
By June Sillman and Baldwin Bergensen.

—CROUPIER
By June Sillman and Baldwin Bergensen.
—DUSKY DEBUTANTE
By June Sillman and Baldwin Bergensen.

1939. *BLACKBIRDS OF 1939*
Lena Horne made her stage debut in this
all-Negro revue with book by Lew Leslie.
—THURSDAY
By Louis Haber and Dorothy Sachs.
—SHAKE YOUR BLUESIES WITH
DANCING SHOESIES
By Louis Haber and Dorothy Sachs.
—FATHER DIVINE
By Louis Haber and Dorothy Sachs.
—I DID IT FOR THE RED, WHITE
AND BLUE
By Johnny Mercer and Rube Bloom.
—WHEN A BLACKBIRD IS BLUE
By Mitchell Parish and Sammy Fain.
—YOU'RE SO DIFFERENT
By Mitchell Parish and Sammy Fain.
—SWING STRUCK
By Irving Taylor and Vic Mizzy.

Revivals of 1930-1940

1930. *PRINCE OF PILSEN* with Vivian
Hart, Al Shean and Roy Cropper.

1930. *THE CHOCOLATE SOLDIER* with
Vivian Hart and Charles Purcell.

1930. *SARI* with Mitzi and Jack Squires.

1930. *THE SERENADE* with Greek Evans,
C. E. Gallagher, R. Cropper & O. Steck.

1930. *COUNT OF LUXEMBOURG* with
Roy Cropper.

1931. *THE STUDENT PRINCE* with Eliz
Gergely and Edward Nell, Jr.

1931. *THE MERRY WIDOW* with Donald
Brian and Alice McKenzie.

1931. *THE CHOCOLATE SOLDIER* with
Vivienne Segal and Charles Purcell.

1931. *THE GEISHA* with James T. Powers,
Hizi Koyke and Roy Cropper.

1931. *NAUGHTY MARIETTA* with Roy
Cropper and Ilse Marvenga.

1931. *THE FIREFLY* with Ilse Marvenga
and Roy Cropper.

1932. *ROBIN HOOD* with Vivian Hart,
Frank Lalor and Howard Marsh.

1933. *THE CHOCOLATE SOLDIER* with
Bernice Claire and Charles Purcell.

1933. *BITTER SWEET* with Evelyn Herbert and Allan Jones.

1933. *THE ONLY GIRL* with Robert Halliday and Bettina Hall.

PORGY AND BESS. (Score by George Gershwin)
Decca DU-739. Todd Duncan, Anne Brown, the Eva Jessye Choir and Decca Orchestra.
Decca DA-397. The Philharmonic of Los Angeles, Alfred Wallenstein, conductor.
RCA Victor C-25. Lawrence Tibbett and Helen Jepson with chorus and orchestra. (This
is a request album and may be ordered through the dealer.)
Columbia SL-162 (33⅓ rpm). Lawrence Winters, Camilla Williams, Inez Mathews, Avon
Long and Warren Coleman with chorus and orchestra.

RED MILL, THE. (Score by Victor Herbert)
Decca A-411. Wilbur Evans, Eileen Farrell and Felix Knight with chorus and orchestra.
RCA Victor K-1. Martha Briney, Donald Dame, Earl Wrightson, the Mullen Sisters and
the Guild Choristers with Al Goodman's orchestra.

(The albums listed below were available on September 15, 1951, and while numbers refer
to 78 rpm records unless otherwise noted, most are also available in 33⅓ and 45 rpm speeds.)

ANNIE GET YOUR GUN. (Score by Irving Berlin)
RCA Victor DC-38. Audrey Marsh and Maxine Carroll, sopranos; Jimmy Carroll and
Earl Oxford, tenors; Mullen Sisters, Guild Choristers with Al Goodman's orchestra.
Decca A-468. Ethel Merman, Ray Middleton and original cast of "Annie Get Your Gun".

ANYTHING GOES. (Score by Cole Porter)
Columbia MM-967. Mary Martin with chorus and orchestra conducted by Lehman Engel.

BABES IN TOYLAND. (Score by Victor Herbert)
Decca DA-419. Kenny Baker and Karen Kemple with chorus and orchestra.

BANDWAGON, THE. (Score by Arthur Schwartz)
Columbia MM-968. Mary Martin with chorus and orchestra conducted by Lehman Engel.

BLOOMER GIRL. (Score by Harold Arlen)
Decca DL-8015 (33⅓ rpm). Celeste Holm, David Brooks, Joan McCracken, Richard
Huey, Dooley Wilson, Matt Briggs, Toni Hart, Mabel Taliaferro and original cast.

BLOSSOM TIME. (Score by Sigmund Romberg)
RCA Victor K-5. Martha Briney, Blanca Perio, Donald Dame, Earl Wrightson, the Muller Sisters and the Guild Choristers with Al Goodman's orchestra.

BRIGADOON. (Score by Fredrick Loewe)
RCA Victor K-7. Marion Bell, Pamela Britton, Shirley Robbins, Delbert Anderson, David
Brooks, Hayes Gordon and other members of the original Broadway cast.

CALL ME MADAM. (Score by Irving Berlin)
Decca A-813. Dick Haymes and Eileen Wilson with chorus and orchestra.
Decca A-818. Ethel Merman, Dick Haymes and Eileen Wilson with chorus and orchestra.
RCA Victor OC-1. Dinah Shore with Paul Lucas, Galina Talva, Russell Nype, Pat Har-
rison and other members of original cast with chorus and orchestra directed by Jay Blackton.

CALL ME MISTER. (Score by Harold Rome)
Decca DL-7005 (33⅓ rpm). Betty Garrett, Lawrence Winters, Paula Bane, Danny
Scholl, Bill Callahan, Jules Munshin, Harry Clark, Chandler Cowles and original cast.

CARMEN JONES. (Score by Georges Bizet)
Decca DA-366. Muriel Smith, Luther Saxon, C. Franzell, Glenn Bryant, June Hawkins.

CAROUSEL. (Score by Richard Rodgers)
Decca DA-400. John Raitt, Jan Clayton, Jean Darling, Christine Johnson, Eric Matson,
Murvyn Vye, Connie Baxter and other members of the original Broadway cast.

CHOCOLATE SOLDIER, THE. (Score by Oscar Straus)
Columbia MM-482. Risé Stevens and Nelson Eddy with chorus and orchestra.
RCA Victor WK-21 (45 rpm). Ann Ayars, Jimmy Carroll, Charles Fredericks, John
Percival and the Guild Choristers with Al Goodman's Orchestra.

CONNECTICUT YANKEE, A. (Score by Richard Rodgers)
Decca DA-367. Vivienne Segal, Dick Foran, Julie Warren, Robert Chisholm, Chester
Stratton, Vera-Ellen and Crane Calder with chorus and orchestra.

DESERT SONG, THE. (Score by Sigmund Romberg)
Decca DA-370. Kitty Carlisle, Wilbur Evans, Felix Knight, Vicki Vola and chorus.
Columbia MX-260. Dennis Morgan with chorus and orchestra.
RCA Victor K-12. Frances Greer, Jimmy Carroll, Earl Wrightson and the Guild Choristers
with Al Goodman's orchestra.

FINIAN'S RAINBOW. (Score by Burton Lane)
RCA Victor K-3. Audrey Marsh, Jimmy Carroll, Jimmy Blair, the Deep River Boys
and the Guild Choristers with Russell Case orchestra.
Columbia MM-686. Ella Logan, the Lyn Murray Singers, Delores Martin, Donald Richards,
Sonny Terry (harmonica), David Wayne and members of the original Broadway cast.

ROBERTA. (Score by Jerome Kern)
    Decca DL-8007. (33⅓ rpm). Kitty Carlisle, A. Drake, Paula Lawrence and K. Meisle.
    RCA Victor WK-20 (45 rpm). Marion Bell, Eve Young, Jimmy Carroll, Ray Charles
    and the Guild Choristers with Al Goodman's orchestra.
GENTLEMEN PREFER BLONDES. (Score by Jule Styne)
    Columbia MM-895. Carol Channing, Yvonne Adair and members of original cast.
GUYS AND DOLLS. (Score by Frank Loesser)
    Decca DA-825. Vivian Blaine, Robert Alda, Isable Bigley, Sam Levene and other members
    of original cast with chorus and orchestra. Decca A-870. Carmen Cavallaro and his piano.
    RCA Victor K-27. Roy Charles, Audrey Marsh, Donald Richards, Morey Amsterdam and
    the Guild Choristers with Al Goodman's orchestra.
INSIDE U.S.A. (Score by Arthur Schwartz)
    Columbia C-162. Buddy Clark and Pearl Bailey with chorus and orchestra.
KING AND I, THE. (Score by Richard Rodgers)
    RCA Victor K-30. Dinah Shore, Patrice Munsel, Robert Merrill and Tony Martin with
    Al Goodman and Henri Rene orchestras.
    Decca DA-876. Gertrude Lawrence, Yul Brynner and members of the original cast.
    Decca A-881. Carmen Cavallaro and his piano.
KISS ME KATE. (Score by Cole Porter)
    Columbia C-200. Alfred Drake, Patricia Morison, Lisa Kirk, Harold Lang and other
    members of the original Broadway cast with chorus and orchestra.
    Capitol CD-144. Jo Stafford and Gordon MacRae and Paul Weston orchestra.
LUTE SONG (Score by Raymond Scott)
    Decca A-445. Mary Martin with "Lute Song" orchestra under direction of composer.
MAKE A WISH. (Score by Hugh Martin)
    RCA Victor OC-2. Nanette Fabray, Dean Campbell, Stephen Douglass, Helen Gallagher,
    Harold Lang and other members of the original Broadway cast with chorus and orchestra.
MERRY WIDOW, THE. (Score by Franz Lehar)
    Decca DA-364. Kitty Carlisle, Wilbur Evans, Felix Knight and Lisette Verea with chorus.
    Columbia MM-849. Risé Stevens and Dennis Morgan with chorus and orchestra. RCA
    Victor K-28. Donald Richards, Elaine Malbin, Nino Ventura and the Guild Choristers
    with Al Goodman's orchestra.
MEXICAN HAYRIDE. (Score by Cole Porter)
    Decca DL-5232 (33⅓ rpm). June Havoc, Wilbur Evans and Corinna Mura with chorus.
MISS LIBERTY. (Score by Irving Berlin)
    Decca DL-5009 (33⅓ rpm). Fred Waring and his Pennsylvanians.
    Bluebird BN-4. Al Goodman's orchestra.
    Columbia MM-860. Eddie Albert, Allyn McLerie, Mary McCarthy and original cast.
    RCA Victor WK-19 (45 rpm). Sandra Deel, Wynn Murray, Martha Wright, Jimmy
    Carroll, Bob Wright and the Guild Choristers with Al Goodman's orchestra.
NAUGHTY MARIETTA. (Score by Victor Herbert)
    Columbia MM-892. Nelson Eddy and Nadine O'Connor with chorus and orchestra.
    RCA Victor K-22. Elaine Malbin, Jimmy Carroll, Earl Wrightson and Guild Choristers.
NEW MOON, THE. (Score by Sigmund Romberg)
    Decca A-155. Florence George, Paul Gregory and Frank Forest, chorus and orchestra.
    Columbia MM-975. Eleanor Steber and Nelson Eddy with chorus and orchestra.
    RCA Victor K-16. Frances Greer, Donald Dame, Earl Wrightson, Earl Oxford and the
    Guild Choristers with Al Goodman's orchestra.
OKLAHOMA. (Score by Richard Rodgers)
    RCA Victor DM-988. Eleanor Steber, James Melton and John Charles Thomas with
    chorus and orchestra. (This album is a request item to be ordered through dealer.
    Decca DA-359. Alfred Drake, Celeste Holm and other members of the original cast.
    Columbia 7417-M. Andre Kostelanetz and his orchestra.
ON THE TOWN. (Score by Leonard Bernstein)
    Decca DL-8030 (33⅓ rpm). Nancy Walker, Betty Comden and Adolph Green of the
    original Broadway cast and Mary Martin with chorus and orchestra.
OUT OF THIS WORLD. (Score by Cole Porter)
    Columbia MM-980. Charlotte Greenwood, Priscilla Gillette, William Redfield, Barbara
    Ashley, George Jongeyans, David Burns and members of the original Broadway cast.
PAL JOEY. (Score by Richard Rodgers)
    Columbia MM-974. Vivienne Segal, Harold Lang, Barbara Ashley, Beverly Fite, Kenneth
    Remo and Jo Hurt with chorus and orchestra.

The Bonanza Years (1940-1952)

On the night of March 31, 1943, less than sixteen months after the sneak attack on Pearl Harbor, Richard Rodgers and Oscar Hammerstein II dropped a bomb on Broadway that not only rocked the street to its very foundations but pulverized century-old theatrical conventions and traditions.

This atomic blockbuster, which was labeled *Oklahoma,* was pronounced a dud by the prophets of Shubert Alley while it was still in the laboratory stage, and their pessimism was based on seeming logic. Richard Rodgers had tiffed with Larry Hart. His new collaborator, Oscar Hammerstein II, hadn't come up with a real hit for several years. The Theater Guild, which was sponsoring the show, was in dire financial straits. *Green Grow The Lilacs,* the drama on which this musical was based, had finished in the red. And there wasn't a single box office name in the entire cast!

But instead of closing after a two-week run, as these prophets of doom had so freely predicted, *Oklahoma* hung up an all-time endurance record for Broadway musicals of 2248 continuous performances, played to 7,000,000 persons on an 8-year road tour in which 60,000 miles were covered by train, repeated its triumphs in the theaters of three continents—Europe, Africa and Australia, and to date has netted a profit of $4,300,000 on an original investment of $90,000.

The *Oklahoma* success story, however, is far more than a glowing treasurer's report. This phenomenal production set a new pattern for girl-and-music shows in which every line, every song, every dance routine is an indispensible part of a closely knit whole. It was a show that had dramatic substance and never ran off the plot track, and so real, so simple, so engrossing was its story that its narration could be safely entrusted to other than big name stars.

This was a formula that called for meticulous craftsmanship and a passion for perfection with which both Richard Rodgers and Oscar Hammerstein II are uncommonly gifted. Hammerstein especially is a slave to accuracy. He took measurements in the Philadelphia zoo and a field of tasseled maize before writing "The corn grows as high as an elephant's eye", and talked with chowder cooks to make sure there would be no culinary mistakes in the lyrics he wrote for *This Is A Real Nice Clambake.*

And Rodgers and Hammerstein held fast to these high ideals in the later musicals on which they collaborated—*Carousel, Allegro, South Pacific* and *The King And I*—and also in productions they sponsored but did not write, the most notable of which was *Annie Get Your Gun* with songs by Irving Berlin, whose Buick, a piano with a gear-shift lever that transposes keys automatically, carried him to supreme heights during these bonanza years when twenty-five Broadway musicals, paced by *Oklahoma,* hit the 500-or-better continuous performance mark.

Berlin, the most prolific and gifted of the pop song writers, has hung up during the past eleven years a Broadway batting average of .800—four hits out of five times at bat: *Louisiana Purchase, This Is The Army,* the GI revue that netted $10,000,000 for Army War Relief; *Annie Get Your Gun,* which after playing to capacity houses in New York for 1149 performances almost wrecked the English austerity program with a 3-year London run; and *Call My Madam,* which wrings almost as much fun out of lend-lease as the European countries do cash.

Cole Porter, abandoning his Paris town house and Italian villa with the advance of the goose-stepping Nazi armies, found inspiration in his dual apartments in Manhattan's Waldorf-Astoria Towers for three outstanding musicals: *Panama Hattie, Let's Face It* and *Kiss Me Kate,* the staying powers of this latter production being matched by those of a two-year-old filly of the same name who on the afternoon of the night when *Kiss Me Kate* played its 1000th performance, came from out of the ruck to win the third race at Jamaica at odds of 14 to 1.

In this Renaissance of the Broadway musical, sparked by Rodgers and Hammerstein, other Main Stem composers caught fire and came up with music for productions that passed the 500-performance goal, including Kurt Weill's *One Touch Of Venus,* Frederick Loewe's heather-scented *Brigadoon,* Phil Charig's *Follow The Girls,* Robert Wright's *Song of Norway,* Harold Rome's *Call Me Mister,* Burton Lane's *Finian's Rainbow,* Harold Arlen's *Bloomer Girl* and Sigmund Romberg's *Up In Central Park.* Victor Herbert, denied the distinction of a 500-performance run during his lifetime, gained such glory posthumously in the revival of his *Red Mill.* New life was breathed into George Bizet's *Carmen* by the book and lyrics Oscar Hammerstein II wrote for *Carmen Jones.* And musical sprouts from Johann Strauss' *Fledermaus,* which had been transplanted in barren American soil several times in the past, finally took sturdy root and blossomed in *Rosalinda.*

Two songwriters, who left the flesh pots of Hollywood for the bright lights of Broadway, had no reason for regretting the change, Jule Styne taking the Great White Way in stride with *High Button Shoes, Gentlemen Prefer Blondes* and *Two On The Aisle,* while Frank Loesser had unparalleled beginner's luck with *Where's Charley* and *Guys And Dolls.* Even royalty got into the Broadway songwriting act with the King of Siam being credited with several numbers in *Michael Todd's Peep Show*—songs that took harder prat-falls than the burlesque comedians who shared feature billing in this revue with the long-stemmed and scantily clad lovelies.

These bonanza years proved beyond question that Shakespeare was right:

"The play's the thing". Not only are the smash successes of the present era based on pre-tested novels and dramas, but the established stars have faded from the Broadway skies. Both Al Jolson in *Hold On To Your Hats* and Eddie Cantor in *Banjo Eyes* bade Broadway a last farewell in 1940, and of the truly great celebrities of former decades, only Ethel Merman remains to carry on in the grand tradition. Hollywood has the stars or grabs such new-found talent as Celeste Holm and Ezio Pinza, but apparently doesn't know what to do with them. Broadway has musical plays with something to say, and that's what the public not only wants but is willing to pay a top box office price of $6.60 and $7.20 to see.

Gone, too, are the days when a stage success could be built on a shoe-string. The Broadway musical of today represents an outlay of approximately $200,-000 before the opening night, and a hit must run for six months or longer and play to capacity houses before the original investment is recouped.

But in these times when the gambling fever yields a daily pari-mutual take of $2,500,000 at the major race tracks and the ruling passion is to make a fast buck, the Broadway producer doesn't have to pass the hat, as Rodgers and Hammerstein did in seeking financial backing for *Oklahoma,* to interest outside capital. There are more angels on Broadway today than hover around the throne of the Great Jehovah. They are headed by Howard S. Cullman, head of the Port of New York Authority, who has an uncanny gift for putting his money in what prove to be highly profitable hits, and include socialites, celebrated restauranteurs, wardrobe mistresses, press agents, movie tycoons and the heads of radio networks and recording companies. Everybody wants a slice of today's Broadway cake. An up-state New York farmer sold a cow for $1000, invested the money in *Kiss Me Kate,* and skimmed off $2000 in cream. An eye, ear and throat specialist protects his investment in the musical he's helping to finance by going back-stage before each performance to spray the throats of the principals. What a field day Florenz Ziegfeld would have if he were still alive! And George M. Cohan, who produced *Forty-five Minutes From Broadway* for $10,000, would rate as a financial wizard.

But in these years of plenty, the Shubert Alley soothsayers are "viewing with alarm" the astronomical and steadily rising production costs, the scarcity of legitimate playhouses which now have been reduced to thirty, the paucity of stage talent caused by the lure of steady work and fabulous incomes that Hollywood offers, and the great and growing challenge of television, and say the Great White Way may eventually be plunged into darkness. If they haven't misread their crystal ball, the grandfathers of tomorrow may recall Dagmar, the current TV bombshell, with the same nostalgic glow as the grandfathers of yesterday recalled the curvaceous Lillian Russell. But so long as Rodgers and Hammerstein keep healthy, so long as the fear he's about washed-up spurs Irving Berlin to write great songs, so long as Jule Styne and Frank Loesser observe the Stop-and-Go signs, don't sell Broadway and the Broadway musical short.

Harold Arlen Scores

1944. *BLOOMER GIRL*
Book by Sig Herzig and Fred Saidy, lyrics by E. Y. Harburg, and presented by a cast headed by Celeste Holm, David Brooks, Joan McCracken, Mabel Taliaferro and Dooley Wilson.
—WHEN THE BOYS COME HOME
—WELCOME HINGES
—THE EAGLE AND ME
—RIGHT AS RAIN
—PRETTY AS A PICTURE
—SUNDAY IN CICERO FALLS
—SIMON LEGREE
—I NEVER WAS BORN
—EVELINA
—A FARMER'S DAUGHTER
—IT WAS GOOD ENOUGH FOR GRANDMA
—T'MORRA, T'MORRA
—RAKISH YOUNG MAN WITH THE WHISKERS
—I GOT A SONG
—ELIZA CROSSING THE ICE
—MAN FOR SALE
—SATIN GOWN AND SILVER SLIPPERS

1946. *ST. LOUIS WOMAN*
Book by Arna Bontemps and Counter Cullen, lyrics by Johnny Mercer, and presented by a cast that included Ruby Hill, Rex Ingram, Pearl Bailey and Harold and Fayard Nicholas.
—COME RAIN OR COME SHINE
—LI'L AUGIE IS A NATCHAL MAN
—LEGALIZE MY NAME
—ANY PLACE I HANG MY HAT IS HOME
—I FEEL MY LUCK COMIN' DOWN
—TRUE LOVE
—CAKE WALK YOUR LADY
—CHINQUAPIN BUSH
—WE SHALL MEET TO PART, NO NEVER
—LULLABY
—SLEEP PEACEFUL
—LEAVIN' TIME
—A WOMAN'S PREROGATIVE
—RIDIN' ON THE MOON
—LEAST THAT'S MY OPINION
—RACIN' FORM
—COME ON, LI'L AUGIE

Jaques Belasco Score

1945. *THE GIRL FROM NANTUCKET*
Book by Paul Stamford, Harold Sherman and Hi Cooper, lyrics by Kay Twomey, and presented by a cast headed by Adelaide Bishop.
—A HAMMOCK IN THE BLUE
—FROM MORNING TILL NIGHT
—I LIVE ACROSS THE STREET
—SONS OF THE SEA
—TAKE THE STEAMER TO NANTUCKET
—THAT'S HOW I KNOW THAT I'M IN LOVE
—YOUR FATAL FASCINATION

Baldwin Bergensen Scores

1940. *ALL IN FUN*
A revue with sketches by Virginia Faulkner and Everett Marcy, lyrics by S. K. Russell, and presented by a cast headed by Imogene Coca, Bill Robinson, Wynn Murray and Red Marshall.
—IT'S ALL IN FUN
—WHERE CAN I GO FROM YOU?
—LOVE AND I
—APRIL IN HARRISBURG
—THAT MAN AND WOMAN THING
—WHERE'S THE BOY I SAVED FOR A RAINY DAY?
—MY MEMORIES STARTED WITH YOU
—MACUMBA
—HOW DID IT GET SO LATE SO EARLY?
By June Sillman and Will Irwin.
—QUITTIN' TIME
By John Rox.
—IT'S A BIG, WIDE, WONDERFUL WORLD
By John Rox.

1944. *ALLAH BE PRAISED*
Book by George Marion, Jr., lyrics by Don Walker, and presented by a cast headed by Joey Faye, Sid Stone, Jack Albertson, Mary Jane Walsh and Patricia Morison.
—LET'S GO TOO FAR
—SECRET SONG
—ALLAH BE PRAISED
—I'M GETTING ORIENTAL OVER YOU

—KATINKA TO EVA TO FRANCES
—WHAT'S NEW IN NEW YORK?
—THE PERSIAN WAY OF LIFE
—A LEAF IN THE WIND
—SUNRISE ON SUNSET
—I WAS A HAPPIER MAN IN DAN-
NEMORA

1945. *CARIB SONG*
Katherine Dunham, Avon Long and Wil-
liam Franklin head the cast of a musical
play, based on the eternal triangle theme
in the islands of the Caribbean, with book
and lyrics by William Archibald.
—BASKET-MAKIN' BASKET
—GO TO CHURCH ON SUNDAY
—I AM SAD
—INSECT SONG
—LONELY ONE
—WASHERWOMAN SONG
—YOU KNOW, OH LAWD
—WATER MOVIN' SLOW
—SLEEP BABY, DON'T CRY

1948. *SMALL WONDER*
With Albert Selden, and lyrics by Phyllis
McGinley and Billings Brown. A revue
with a cast headed by Tom Elwell, Mary
McCarthy, Alice Pearce, Hayes Gordon
and Marilyn Day.
—FLAMING YOUTH
—SATURDAY'S CHILD
—THINGS
—SOME SWEET DAY
—COMMUTER'S SONG
—WHEN I FALL IN LOVE
—MAN ABOUT TOWN
—BALLAD FOR BILLIONAIRES

Irving Berlin Scores

1940. *LOUISIANA PURCHASE*
A musical comedy with Victor Moore,
William Gaxton, Irene Bordoni, Vera
Zorina and Carol Bruce.
—SEX MARCHES ON
—LOUISIANA PURCHASE
—OUTSIDE OF THAT I LOVE YOU
—IT'S A LOVELY DAY TOMORROW
—YOU'RE LONELY AND I'M LONELY
—TONIGHT AT THE MARDI GRAS
—LATINS KNOW HOW
—WHAT CHANCE HAVE I WITH
LOVE?
—THE LORD DONE FIXED UP MY
SOUL
—FOOLS FALL IN LOVE
—OLD MAN'S DARLING, YOUNG
MAN'S SLAVE
—YOU CAN'T BRUSH ME OFF
—DANCE WITH ME

1942. *THIS IS THE ARMY*
A revue with an all-soldier cast, written
by James McColl and directed by Sgt.
Ezra ("Henry Aldrich") Stone.
—THIS IS THE ARMY, MR. JONES
—I'M GETTING TIRED SO I CAN
SLEEP
—MY SERGEANT AND I
—I LEFT MY HEART AT THE STAGE
DOOR CANTEEN
—THE ARMY'S MADE A MAN OUT OF
ME
—MANDY
—LADIES OF THE CHORUS
—THAT RUSSIAN WINTER
—WHAT THE WELL-DRESSED MAN
IN HARLEM WILL WEAR
—HOW ABOUT A CHEER FOR THE
NAVY?
—AMERICAN EAGLES
—WITH MY HEAD IN THE CLOUDS
—A SOLDIER'S DREAM
—OH HOW I HATE TO GET UP IN
THE MORNING
—THIS TIME (IS THE LAST TIME)

1946. *ANNIE GET YOUR GUN*
A musical comedy by Herbert and Dorothy Fields, starring Ethel Merman as Annie Oakley and with Ray Middleton as
Frank Butler, William O'Neal as Buffalo
Bill and Harry Bellaver as Chief Sitting
Bull. This Richard Rodgers-Oscar Hammerstein production was to have been
composed by Jerome Kern but following
his death, Irving Berlin was commissioned
to write the score. "Annie, Get Your
Gun" ran for 1,147 performances on
Broadway, a record that put it in fourth
place among the longest run musicals.
When it closed on February 12, 1949,
the road company was still on tour in this
country while there were two companies
playing it in England and one in Aus-
tralia with productions scheduled to open
shortly in Sweden, Denmark and South
Africa.
—COLONEL BUFFALO BILL
—I'M A BOLD BAD MAN
—DOIN' WHAT COMES NATUR'LLY
—THE GIRL THAT I MARRY
—YOU CAN'T GET A MAN WITH A
GUN
—THERE'S NO BUSINESS LIKE SHOW
BUSINESS
—MOONSHINE LULLABY
—I'LL SHARE IT ALL WITH YOU
—BALLYHOO
—MY DEFENSES ARE DOWN
—I'M AN INDIAN TOO

—I GOT LOST IN HIS ARMS
—WHO DO YOU LOVE I HOPE
—I GOT THE SUN IN THE MORNIN'
—ANYTHING YOU CAN DO
—THEY SAY IT'S WONDERFUL

1949. *MISS LIBERTY*

Book by Robert Sherwood, and presented by a cast headed by Eddie Albert, Allyn McLerie, Mary McCarthy, Charles Dingle, Philip Bourneuf, Ethel Griffies and Herbert Berghof. This musical comedy marked the debut as a librettist of Robert Sherwood, winner of more Pulitzer prizes than any other writer in the theater and former literary adviser to President Franklin D. Roosevelt.

—EXTRA, EXTRA
—WHAT DO I HAVE TO DO TO GET MY PICTURE TOOK?
—THE MOST EXPENSIVE STATUE IN THE WORLD
—A LITTLE FISH IN A BIG POND
—LET'S TAKE AN OLD FASHIONED WALK
—HOMEWORK
—PARIS WAKES UP AND SMILES
—ONLY FOR AMERICANS
—JUST ONE WAY TO SAY "I LOVE YOU"
—MISS LIBERTY
—THE TRAIN
—YOU CAN HAVE HIM
—THE POLICEMEN'S BALL
—FOLLOW THE LEADER JIG
—ME AND MY BUNDLE
—FALLING OUT OF LOVE CAN BE FUN
—GIVE ME YOUR TIRED, YOUR POOR

The words of this song, written by Emma Lazarus, are inscribed on the base of the Statue of Liberty.

1950. *CALL ME MADAM*

Book by Howard Lindsay and Russell Crouse, and starring Ethel Merman in a cast that included Paul Lukas, Russell Nype and Galina Talva.

—MRS. SALLY ADAMS
—THE HOSTESS WITH THE MOSTES' ON THE BALL
—WASHINGTON SQUARE DANCE
—LICHTENBURG
—CAN YOU USE ANY MONEY TODAY?
—MARRYING FOR MONEY
—THE OCARINA
—IT'S A LOVELY DAY TODAY

—THE BEST THING FOR YOU WOULD BE ME
—SOMETHING TO DANCE ABOUT
—ONCE UPON A TIME TODAY
—THEY LIKE IKE
—YOU'RE JUST IN LOVE

Leonard Bernstein Score

1944. *ON THE TOWN*

Book and lyrics by Betty Comden and Adolph Green, and presented by a cast headed by Betty Comden, Nancy Walker, Adolph Green, Sono Osato, John Battles and Chris Alexander.

—I CAN COOK TOO
—SOME OTHER TIME
—I FEEL LIKE I'M NOT OUT OF BED YET
—COME UP TO MY PLACE
—I GOT CARRIED AWAY
—LONELY TOWN
—PICK-UP SONG
—I'M BLUE
—YOU GOT ME
—I UNDERSTAND
—NEW YORK, NEW YORK

Georges Bizet Score

1943. *CARMEN JONES*

A modernized version of "Carmen" with book and lyrics by Oscar Hammerstein II, played by an all-Negro cast with Muriel Smith and Muriel Rohn alternating in the role of Carmen, Luther Saxon and Napoleon Reed alternating in the role of Joe (Don Jose), and Glenn Bryant playing Husky Miller (Escamillo).

—DAT'S LOVE
—YOU TALK JUS' LIKE MY MAW
—DER'S A CAFE ON THE CORNER
—BEAT OUT DAT RHYTHM ON THE DRUM
—STAN' UP AND FIGHT
—WHIZZIN' AWAY ALONG THE TRACK
—DIS FLOWER
—DE CARDS DON'T LIE MY JOE
—DAT'S OUR MAN

Frank Black Score

1946. *THE DUCHESS MISBEHAVES*

A short-lived musical with book and lyrics by Gladys Shelly and Joe Bigelow in which Joey Faye played the artist Goya and Audrey Christie the Duchess of Alba.

—YOU ARE MY ONLY ROMANCE
—COULDN'T BE MORE IN LOVE

Marc Blitzstein Score

1949. *REGINA*
A musical drama with book and lyrics by the composer, based on Lillian Hellman's "The Little Foxes", wih Jane Pickens in the title role and heading a cast that included Priscilla Gillette, Brenda Lewis, David Thomas, Russell Nype, Donald Clarke, George Lipton and William Wilderman.
—BLUES
—GREEDY GIRL
—SUMMER DAY
—WHAT WILL IT BE?
—CHINKYPIN
—BEST THING OF ALL

Monte Carlo and Alma Sanders Score

1947. *LOUISIANA CARNIVAL*
Book by Isaac Green Jr. and Eugene Berton, and presented by a cast headed by Edith Fellows and Ray Jacquemot.
—I WANT TO LIVE, I WANT TO LOVE
—NO, NO MAM'SELLE
—THE CUCKOO-CHEENA
—GOLD, WOMEN AND LAUGHTER
—THAT'S WHY I WANT TO GO HOME
—MEN ABOUT TOWN
—JUST A LITTLE NAIVE
—THE NIGHT WAS ALL TO BLAME
—BEWARE OF LIPS THAT SAY "CHERIE"
—LOUISIANA'S HOLIDAY
—IT'S MARDI GRAS
—WHEN YOU ARE CLOSE TO ME
—NO ONE CARES FOR DREAMS
—MAMMY'S LITTLE BABY

Hoagy Carmichael Score

1940. *WALK WITH MUSIC*
A musical comedy with a book by Guy Bolton, Parke Levey and Alan Lipscott, lyrics by Johnny Mercer, and presented by a cast headed by Kitty Carlisle, Mitzi Green, Betty Lawford, Art Jarrett, Frances Williams, Marty May and Stepin Fetchit.
—GREETING GATES
—TODAY I AM A GLAMOUR GIRL
—EVEN IF I SAY IT MYSELF
—I WALK WITH MUSIC
—OOH WHAT YOU SAID
—WAIT TILL YOU SEE ME IN THE MORNING
—BREAK IT UP CINDERELLA

—SMILE FOR THE PRESS
—FRIEND OF THE FAMILY
—WAY BACK IN 1939 A. D.
—HOW NICE FOR ME
—WHAT'LL THEY THINK OF NEXT
—THE RHUMBA JUMPS
—EVERYTHING HAPPENS TO ME

Saul Chaplain Score

1948. *BONANZA BOUND*
A musical comedy of the Klondike Gold Rush days with book and lyrics by Betty Comden and Adoph Green, and played by a cast headed by George Coulouris, Carol Raye, Allyn Ann McLerie, and Adolph Green.
—TELL ME WHY
—INSPIRATION
—MISUNDERSTOOD
—UP IN SMOKE
—I KNOW IT'S TRUE
—FILL 'ER UP
—BONANZA

Phil Charig Scores

1943. *ARTISTS AND MODELS OF 1943*
Book by Lou Walters, Don Ross and Frank Luther, lyrics by Dan Shapiro and Milton Pascal, and presented by a cast headed by Jane Froman, Jackie Gleason and the Radio Aces.
—SWING LOW SWEET HARRIET
—YOU ARE ROMANCE
—YOU KNOW THAT IT'S ME
—LET'S KEEP IT THAT WAY
By Milton Berle, Ervine Drake and Abner Silver.
—MY HEART IS ON A BINGE
1944. *FOLLOW THE GIRLS*
Book by Guy Bolton and Eddie Davis, lyrics by Dan Shapiro and Milton Pascal, and presented by a cast headed by Gertrude Niesen, Jackie Gleason, Buster West and Tim Herbert.
—AT THE SPOTLIGHT CANTEEN
—YOU DON'T DANCE
—STRIP FLIPS HIPS
—THANKS FOR A LOUSY EVENING
—YOU'RE PERF
—TWELVE O'CLOCK AND ALL'S WELL
—WHERE YOU ARE
—OUT FOR NO GOOD
—FOLLOW THE GIRLS
—JOHN PAUL JONES
—I WANNA GET MARRIED
—TODAY WILL BE YESTERDAY TO-MORROW

—A TREE THAT GROWS IN BROOK-
LYN

Robert Emmett Dolan Score

1949. *TEXAS, LI'L DARLIN'*
Book by John Whedon and Sam Moore,
lyrics by Johnny Mercer, and presented by
a cast headed by Kenny Delmar and
Mary Hatcher.
—WHOOPIN' AND A-HOLLERIN'
—TEXAS, LI'L DARLIN'
—THEY TALK A DIFFERENT LAN-
GUAGE
—A MONTH OF SUNDAYS
—DOWN IN THE VALLEY
—HOOTIN' OWL TRAIL
—BIG MOVIE SHOW IN THE SKY
—LOVE ME, LOVE MY DOG
—HORSE SHOES ARE LUCKY
—TAKE A CRANK LETTER
—POLITICS
—RIDE 'EM COWBOY
—SQUARE DANCE
—AFFABLE BALDING ME
—WHICHAWAY'D THEY GO?
—IT'S GREAT TO BE ALIVE

Peter DeRose Score

1941. *ICE-CAPADES OF 1941*
An ice skating revue with lyrics by John
LaTouche.
—ORIENTAL MOONRISE
—YIPPI-I-AY
—SWING ME A LULLABY
—SOMEWHERE
—I HEAR AMERICA SINGING
Lyrics by Mitchell Parish.
—THE YANKEE DOODLE POLKA
By Mitchell Parish and Vernon Duke.
FOREVER AND EVER
By Sol Meyer, George Brown and Jule
Styne.

Vernon Duke Scores

1941. *CABIN IN THE SKY*
Book by Lynn Root, lyrics by John La-
Touche, and starring Ethel Waters in a
cast that included Dooley Wilson, Todd
Duncan, Rex Ingram and Katherine Dun-
bar.
—THE GENERAL'S SONG
—PAY HEED
—TAKING A CHANCE ON LOVE
—CABIN IN THE SKY
—DO WHAT YOU WANNA DO
—MY OLD VIRGINIA HOME ON THE
NILE

—IT'S NOT SO GOOD TO BE BAD
—LOVE ME TOMORROW
—LOVE TURNED THE LIGHT OUT
—LAZY STEP
—BOOGY-WOOGY
—HONEY IN THE HONEYCOMB
—SAVANNAH

1941. *BANJO EYES*
A musical version of "Three Men On A
Horse" with book by Joe Quinlan and
Izzy Elinson, lyrics by Harold Adamson
and John LaTouche, and starring Eddie
Cantor in a cast that included June
Clyde, Bill Johnson, Lionel Stander, Ray
Mayer, Audrey Christie and the DeMar-
cos.
—I'LL TAKE THE CITY
—THE TOAST OF THE BOYS AT THE
POST
—I'VE GOT TO HAND IT TO YOU
—WHO STARTED THE RHUMBA?
—IT COULD ONLY HAPPEN IN THE
MOVIES
—BANJO EYES
—MAKE WITH THE FEET
—HAVEN'T A NICKEL TO MY NAME
—NOT A CARE IN THE WORLD
—WE'RE HAVING A BABY (MY BABY
AND ME)
—WE DID IT BEFORE (WE'LL DO IT
AGAIN)
By Charles Tobias and Cliff Friend.

1941. *THE LADY COMES ACROSS*
Book by Fred Thompson and Dawn
Powell, lyrics by John LaTouche, and pre-
sented by a cast headed by Evelyn Wyck-
off, Joe E. Lewis, Ruth Weston and
Mischa Auer.
—YOU TOOK ME BY SURPRISE
—SUMMER IS A-COMIN'
—LADY
—THIS IS WHERE I CAME IN
—I'M FEELING LUCKY TODAY
—MODES MADE IN MANHATTAN
—I'D LIKE TO TALK ABOUT THE
WEATHER

1943. *DANCING IN THE STREET*
Book and lyrics by John Cecil Holm, Matt
Taylor and Howard Dietz, and presented
by a cast headed by Mary Martin, Dud-
ley Digges and Ernest Cossart.
—A FRIENDLY BAR
—BAY OF BOTANY
—INDEFINABLE CHARM
—BOYS, BOYS
—CAN CAN IN THE CANTEEN
—CIVILIAN
—COMFORTS OF HOME

—DANCING IN THE STREETS
—GOT A BRAN' NEW DADDY
—HIP, THE GIRLS ARE MARCHING
—IN MY DREAMS
—IRRESISTIBLE YOU
—KEEP YOUR AMATEUR STANDING
—KISS YOUR BABY GOOD-BYE

1944. *JACK POT*
Book by Guy Bolton, Sydney Shelton and Ben Roberts, lyrics by Howard Dietz, and presented by a cast that included Nanette Fabray, Allen Jones, Jerry Lester, Benny Baker, Betty Garrett and Mary Wickes.
—THE LAST LONG MILE
—BLIND DATE
—I KISSED MY GIRL GOOD-BYE
—A PIECE OF A GIRL
—MY TOP SERGEANT
—SUGAR FOOT
—WHAT HAPPENED?
—GRIST FOR DeMILLE
—HE'S GOOD FOR NOTHING BUT ME
—WHAT'S MINE IS YOURS
—NOBODY EVER PINS ME UP
—IT WAS NICE KNOWING YOU
—ONE TRACK MIND
—THERE ARE YANKS

1944. *SADIE THOMPSON*
A musical version of "Rain" with June Havoc as "Sadie Thompson," Ralph Dumke as "Joe Horn" and Lansing Hatfield as "Rev. Davidson." Book and lyrics by Reuben Mamoulain and Howard Dietz.
—BARREL OF BEADS
—FISHERMAN'S WHARF
—WHEN YOU LIVE ON AN ISLAND
—POOR AS A CHURCH MOUSE
—THE LOVE I LONG FOR
—GARDEN IN THE SKY
—DANCING LESSON
—SIREN OF THE TROPICS
—LIFE'S A FUNNY PRESENT
—BORN ALL OVER AGAIN
—SAILING AT MIDNIGHT
—THE MOUNTAINS OF NEBRASKA

Duke Ellington Score

1946. *BEGGAR'S HOLIDAY*
A modernized version of John Gay's 18th Century "Beggar's Opera" with book and lyrics by John LaTouche, and presented by a cast headed by Alfred Drake, Bernice Parks, Zero Mostel and Avon Long.
—WHEN YOU GO DOWN BY MISS JENNY'S
—I'VE GOT ME
—TNT
—I WANNA BE BAD

—WHEN I WALK WITH YOU
—THE SCRIMMAGE OF LIFE
—WRONG SIDE OF THE RAILROAD TRACKS
—TOOTH AND CLAW
—LULLABY FOR JUNIOR
—MAYBE I SHOULD CHANGE MY WAYS
—TOMORROW MOUNTAIN
—GIRLS WANT A HERO
—QUARREL FOR THREE
—BROWN PENNY
—WOMEN, WOMEN, WOMEN
—THE HUNTED
—TAKE LOVE EASY

Abraham Ellstein Score

1950. *GREAT TO BE ALIVE*
A musical comedy with book by Walter Bullock and Sylvia Regan, lyrics by Walter Bullock, and presented by a cast headed by Valerie Bettis, Vivienne Segal and Stuart Erwin.
—WHEN THE SHEETS COME BACK FROM THE LAUNDRY
—IT'S A LONG TIME TILL TO-MORROW
—HEADIN' FOR A WEDDIN'
—REDECORATE
—WHAT A DAY!
—CALL IT LOVE
—FROM THIS DAY ON
—WHO DONE IT?
—BLUE DAY
—THAT'S A MAN EVERY TIME
—YOU APPEAL TO ME
—THE RIDDLE
—THANK YOU, MRS. BUTTERFIELD

Sammy Fain Scores

1940. *SONS O' FUN*
A revue with book by Olsen and Johnson and Hal Block, lyrics by Jack Yellen and Irving Kahal, and starring Olsen and Johnson in a cast that included Carmen Miranda and Ella Logan.
—HAPPY IN LOVE
—LET'S SAY GOOD NIGHT WITH A DANCE
—IT'S A NEW KIND OF THING
—IT'S A MIGHTY FINE COUNTRY WE HAVE HERE
Music by Will Irwin.
—MANUELO
Music by Will Irwin.
—THE JOKE'S ON US
Music by Will Irwin.

—THANK YOU SOUTH AMERICA
Music by Will Irwin.

1946. *TOPLITSKY OF NOTRE DAME*
Book and lyrics by George Marion, Jr.
and Jack Barnett, and presented by a
cast headed by J. Edward Bromberg, Gus
Van, Betty-Jane Watson, Warde Donovan,
Estelle Sloan, Walter Long, Frank Mar-
lowe and Phyllis Lynne.
—I WANT TO GO TO CITY COLLEGE
—LET US GATHER AT THE GOAL
   LINE
—LOVE IS A RANDOM THING
—YOU ARE MY DOWNFALL
—A SLIGHT CASE OF ECSTASY
—McINERNEY'S FARM
—BABY LET'S FACE IT
—COMMON SENSE
—WOLF TIME
—ALL-AMERICAN MAN

1951. *FLAHOOLEY*
A musical fantasy with book by Fred
Saidy and E. Y. Harburg, lyrics by Har-
burg, and presented by a cast headed by
Ernest Truex, Jerome Courtland, Edith
Atwater, Irwin Corey, Yma Sumac and
Bill Baird's Marionettes.
—HERE'S TO YOUR ILLUSIONS
—FLAHOOLEY
—WHO SAY'S THERE AIN'T NO
   SANTA CLAUS?
—HE'S ONLY WONDERFUL
—THE WORLD IS YOUR BALLOON
—THE SPRINGTIME COMETH
—YOU TOO CAN BE A PUPPET
—B. G. BIGELOW, INC.
—NAJLA'S SONG
—ARABIAN FOR GET HAPPY
—JUMP, LITTLE CHILLUN
—SPIRIT OF CAPSULANTI
—HAPPY HUNTING
—ENCHANTMENT
—SCHEHERAZADE
—COME BACK, LITTLE GENII
—SING THE MERRY

John Fortis Scores

1944. *HATS OFF TO ICE*
An ice skating revue with lyrics by James
Littleford.
—HATS OFF TO ICE
—LOVE WILL ALWAYS BE THE SAME
—YOU'VE GOT WHAT IT TAKES
—ISLE OF THE MIDNIGHT RAINBOW
—HEADIN' WEST
—WITH EVERY STAR
—HERE'S TO LUCK

1946. *ICETIME*
An ice skating revue with lyrics by John
Littleford.
—SONG OF THE SILVER BLADES
—OL' KIND COLE
—MANDY
—CUDDLE UP
—HER DREAM MAN
—MARY, MARY

1947. *ICETIME OF 1948*
This was a revised edition of the 1946
production for which the following open-
ing number was written:
—BREAKIN' THE ICE
By Al Stillman and Paul McGrane.

Charles Gaynor Score

1948. *LEND AN EAR*
An intimate revue with sketches and
lyrics by the composer, first produced on
the straw hat circuit in 1941 and finally
reaching Broadway by way of California
seven years later. The cast included Wil-
liam Eythe, one of the producers, Carol
Channing, Yvonne Adair, Gloria Hamil-
ton and Anne Renee Anderson.
—MOLLIE O'REILLY
—I'M NOT IN LOVE
—WHO HIT ME?
—GIVE YOUR HEART A CHANCE TO
   SING
—WHEN SOMEONE YOU LOVE LOVES
   YOU
—I'M ON THE LOOKOUT
—NEUROTIC YOU AND PSYCHO-
   PATHIC ME
—POWER OF THE PRESS
—FRIDAY DANCING CLASS
—BALLADE
—JOIN US IN A CUP OF TEA
—WHERE IS THE SHE FOR ME?
—I'LL BE TRUE TO YOU
—DOIN' THE OLD YAHOO STEP
—A LITTLE GAME OF TENNIS
—IN OUR TEENY LITTLE WEENY
   NEST
—SANTO DOMINGO
—THREE LITTLE QUEENS OF THE
   SILVER SCREEN
—WORDS WITHOUT SONG

Jay Gorney Scores

1940. *MEET THE PEOPLE*
A topical revue with book and lyrics by
Henry Myers and Edward Eliscu, and
presented in New York with a cast head-
ed by Nanette Fabray, Marion Colby, Jack
Williams, Peggy Ryan and Jack Guilfoil.

This production, which premiered in Hollywood, represented a total outlay of only $3600 on the opening night, December 25, 1939, when the producers vowed they would open on Broadway a year later to the day. After the revue went into three editions and played San Francisco and Chicago, the producers kept their pledge, but they had strenuous competition for their Broadway premiere—*Pal Joey* with music by Rodgers and Hart. Consequently, the major critics didn't catch *Meet The People* until the following week. Then they gave the show their belated OK, and the revue was good for a nine-month run, demonstrating that Hollywood could match New York's vaunted best in the production of stage musicals.
—MEET THE PEOPLE
—IT'S THE SAME OLD SOUTH
—THE BILL OF RIGHTS
—AMERICAN PLAN
—LET'S STEAL A TUNE FROM OFFEN-BACH
—A FELLOW AND A GIRL
—NO LOOKIN' BACK
—IN CHI-CHI CASTENANGO
—THE STARS REMAIN
—UNION LABEL
—SENATE IN SESSION
The following songs were introduced in this revue during its west coast run:
—FOUR FREEDOMS
—THAT MITTEL EUROPA OF MINE
—THE FOUR RIVERS
1948. *HEAVEN ON EARTH*
Book and lyrics by Barry Trivers, and presented by a cast headed by Peter Lind Hayes, David Burns, Dorothy Jarnac and Irwin Corey.
—THE FIRST CUP OF COFFEE IN THE MORNING
—HOME IS WHERE THE HEART IS
—SO NEAR SO FAR
—HEAVEN ON EARTH
—IN THE BACK OF A HACK
—ANYTHING CAN HAPPEN
—DON'T FORGET TO DREAM
—ON A BENCH IN THE PARK
—THE LETTER
—PUSH A BUTTON IN A HUTTON
—APPLE JACK
—WEDDING IN THE PARK
—WHAT'S THE MATTER WITH OUR CITY?
1949. *TOUCH AND GO*
Book and lyrics by Jean and Walter Kerr, and presented by a cast headed by Nancy

Andrews, Kyle MacDonnell, Pearl Lang, Dick Sykes and George Hall.
—AN EVENING FOR EVERYBODY
—THIS HAD BETTER BE LOVE
—FUNNY LITTLE OLD WORLD
—HIGH BROW LOW BROW
—BE A MESS
—BROADWAY LOVE SONG
—IT'LL BE ALL RIGHT IN A HUN-DRED YEARS
—GREAT DANE A-COMIN'
—WISH ME LUCK
—UNDER THE SLEEPING VOLCANO
—MEN OF THE WATERMARK
—MISTER BROWN, MISS DUPREE
—MISS PLATTE SELECTS A MATE

Irvin Graham Score

1941. *CRAZY WITH THE HEAT*
An intimate revue presented by a cast headed by Willie Howard, Carl Randall, Luella Gear, Marie Nash and Tip, Tap and Toe.
—WINE FROM MY SLIPPER
—YOU SHOULD BE SET TO MUSIC
—WITH A TWIST OF THE WRIST
—THE WHISTLING OYSTER
By Walter A. P. Nones.
—THE TIME OF YOUR LIFE
By P. K. Smith and William Provost.
—IT SHOULD HAPPEN TO ME
By Richard Kollmar and Elsie Thompson.
—SOME DAY
Music by Rudi Revil.
—IL PLEURAIT
Music by Rudi Revil.
—CRAZY WITH THE HEAT
Music by Rudi Revil.

Morton Gould Scores

1945. *BILLION DOLLAR BABY*
A musical comedy that looked back upon the Terrific Twenties with their racketeers and gun molls, Charleston dancers and flagpole sitters with book and lyrics by Betty Comden and Adolph Green. The cast included Mitzi Green, Joan Mc-Cracken, William Talbot, Robert Chris-holm, Danny Daniels and Shirley Van.
—MILLION DOLLAR SMILE
—WHO'S GONNA BE THE WINNER?
—DREAMS COME TRUE
—CHARLESTON
—BROADWAY BLOSSOM
—SPEAKING OF PALS
—THERE I'D BE
—BAD TIMING
—ONE TRACK MIND

—A LOVELY GIRL
—HAVIN' A TIME
—THE MARATHON DANCE
—FAITHLESS
—I'M SURE OF YOUR LOVE
—LIFE WITH ROCKY

1950. *ARMS AND THE GIRL*
A musical comedy, based on "The Pursuit of Happiness," by Lawrence Langner and Armina Marshall, with book by Reuben Mamoulian and Dorothy and Herbert Fields, lyrics by Dorothy Fields, and presented by a cast headed by Nanette Fabray, Pearl Bailey and Florenz Ames.
—A GIRL WITH A FLAME
—THAT'S WHAT I TOLD HIM LAST NIGHT
—I LIKE IT HERE
—THAT'S MY FELLA
—A COW AND A PLOW AND A FRAU
—NOTHIN' FOR NOTHIN'
—HE WILL TONIGHT
—PLANTATION IN PHILADELPHIA
—YOU KISSED ME
—I'LL NEVER LEARN
—THERE MUST BE SOMETHING BETTER THAN LOVE
—SHE'S EXCITING
—MISTER WASHINGTON
—UNCLE GEORGE

Johnny Green Score

1942. *BEAT THE BAND*
A revue with book by George Abbott and George Marion Jr., lyrics by George Marion, and presented by a cast headed by Jerry Lester, Jack Whiting, Susan Miller and Eunice Healey.
—LET'S COMB BEACHES
—PROUD OF YOU
—STEAM IS ON THE BEAM
—EVERY OTHER HEARTBEAT
—SONG OF TWO ISLANDS
—DOWN THROUGH THE AGENTS
—FREE, CUTE AND SIZE FOURTEEN
—KEEP IT CASUAL
—BREAK IT UP
—MEN
—AMERICA LOVES A BAND
—I'M PHYSICAL, YOU'RE CULTURED
—THE FOUR FREEDOMS

Maria Grever Score

1941. *VIVA O'BRIEN*
Book by William K. and Eleanor Wells, lyrics by Raymond Levenn, and presented by a cast headed by Marie Nash.

Ray Henderson Score

1943. *ZIEGFELD FOLLIES OF 1943*
Lyrics by Jack Yellen, and presented by a cast headed by Milton Berle, Eric Blore and Sue Ryan.
—THIRTY-FIVE SUMMERS AGO
—THIS IS IT
—LOVE SONGS ARE MADE IN THE NIGHT
—COME UP AND HAVE A CUP OF COFFEE
—SWING YOUR LADY MISTER HEMINGWAY
—BACK TO THE FARM
—HINDOO SERENADE
—HOLD THAT SMILE
—THE MICROMANIAC
By Harold J. Rome.

Victor Herbert Score

1946. *GYPSY LADY*
An operetta with book and lyrics by Henry Myers, based on melodies from five Victor Herbert scores: "The Fortune Teller," "The Serenade," "The Idol's Eye," "The Singing Girl" and "The Ameer," and presented by a cast headed by Helena Bliss and Melville Cooper.

Gordon Jenkins Score

1949. *ALONG FIFTH AVENUE*
A revue with sketches by Charles Sherman and Nat Hiken, lyrics by Tom Adair, and presented by a cast headed by Jackie Gleason, Nancy Walker, Hank Ladd, Carol Bruce, Donald Richards and Johnny Coy.
—FIFTH AVENUE
—THE BEST TIME OF DAY
—IF THIS IS GLAMOUR
—SKYSCRAPER BLUES
—I LOVE LOVE IN NEW YORK
—A FUGITIVE FROM FIFTH AVENUE
—SANTO DINERO
—IN THE LOBBY
—WEEP NO MORE
—CHANT d'AMOUR
—VACATION IN THE STORE
—CALL IT APPLE FRITTERS
—A TRIP DOESN'T MIND AT ALL
—MAYBE IT'S BECAUSE
By Harry Ruby and Johnny Scott.

Emmerich Kalman Score

1945. *MARINKA*
Karl Farkas and George Marion Jr., who wrote the book and lyrics, found their

inspiration for this operetta in the Mayerling tragedy in which Harry Stockwell played Crown Prince Rudolph of Austria and Joan Roberts his mistress, Maria Vetsera.

—CAB SONG
—ONE LAST LOVE SONG
—ONE TOUCH OF VIENNA
—SIGH BY NIGHT
—TREAT A WOMAN LIKE A DRUM
—TURN ON THE CHARM
—MY PRINCE CAME RIDING
—IF I NEVER WALTZ AGAIN
—OLD MAN DANUBE

Bronislaw Kaper Score

1945. *POLONAISE*
A musical romance with book by Gottfried Reinhardt and Anthony Veiller, lyrics by John LaTouche, and based on Frederick Chopin's music in which Jan Kiepura and Marta Eggerth were co-starred in the roles of General Kosciusko and the dancing girl with whom the Polish patriot fell in love.

—NEXT TIME I CARE I'LL BE CAREFUL
—WAIT FOR TOMORROW
—STRANGER
—NOW I KNOW YOUR FACE BY HEART
—AU REVOIR SOLDIER
—JUST FOR TONIGHT
—I WONDER AS I WANDER
—OH HEART OF MY COUNTRY!

Walter Kent Score

1951. *SEVENTEEN*
A musical comedy, based on Booth Tarkington's novel and play of the same title, with book by Sallie Benson, lyrics by Kim Gannon, and presented by a cast headed by Ann Crowley, Harrison Muller, Kenneth Nelson, Doris Dalton and Frank Albertson.

—WEATHERBEE'S DRUG STORE
—THIS WAS JUST ANOTHER DAY
—THINGS ARE GONNA HUM THIS SUMMER
—HOW DO YOU DO, MISS PRATT?
—SUMMERTIME IS SUMMERTIME
—RECIPROCITY
—ODE TO LOLA
—HEADACHE AND HEARTACHE
—OO-OOO-OOO, WHAT YOU DO TO ME
—THE HOOSIER WAY

—I COULD GET MARRIED TODAY
—IF WE COULD ONLY STOP THE OLD TOWN CLOCK
—AFTER ALL, IT'S SPRING

E. Wolfgang Korngold Score

1944. *HELEN GOES TO TROY*
An operetta based on Jacques Offenbach's "Le Bella Helene" with Jarmila Novotna as Helen, William Horne as Paris and Ernest Truex as Menelaus. Lyrics by Herbert Baker.

—LOVE AT LAST
—JUDGMENT OF PARIS
—WHAT WILL THE FUTURE SAY?
—IF HELEN ONLY KNEW!

Fritz Kreisler Score

1944. *RHAPSODY*
An operetta with book by Leonard L. Levinson and Arnold Sundgard, lyrics by John LaTouche, Russell Bennett and Blevins Davis, and presented by a cast headed by Annamary Dickey, George Dickey and Eddie Mayehoff.

—THEY'RE ALL THE SAME
—MY RHAPSODY
—SCHERZO
—HEAVEN BLESS OUR HOME
—THE WORLD IS YOUNG AGAIN
—TO HORSE!
—SONG OF DEFIANCE
—BECAUSE YOU'RE MINE
—WHEN MEN ARE FREE
—HAPPY ENDING
—CAPRICE VIENNOIS

Burton Lane Scores

1940. *HOLD ON TO YOUR HATS*
Book by Guy Bolton, Matt Brooks and Eddie Davis, lyrics by E. Y. Harburg, and starring Al Jolson in a cast that included Martha Raye, Eunice Healey, Jinx Falkenburg, Bert Gordon and Jack Whiting.

—WAY OUT WEST WHERE THE EAST BEGINS
—HOLD ON TO YOUR HATS
—WALKIN' ALONG MINDIN' MY BUS'NESS
—THE WORLD IS IN MY ARMS
—WOULD YOU BE SO KINDLY
—LIFE WAS PIE FOR THE PIONEER
—DON'T LET IT GET YOU DOWN
—THERE'S A GREAT DAY COMING MANANA
—THEN YOU WERE NEVER IN LOVE
—DOWN ON THE DUDE RANCH

—OLD TIMER
—SHE CAME, SHE SAW, SHE CAN-
CANNED

1944. *LAFFING ROOM ONLY*
Book by Olsen and Johnson and Eugene
Conrad, lyrics by Burton Lane, and star-
ring Olsen and Johnson in a cast that
included Betty Garrett, Frank Libuse,
Mata and Hari, Jean Moorehead and the
Fred Waring Glee Club.
—HOORAY FOR ANYWHERE
—GO DOWN TO BOSTON HARBOR
—STOP THAT DANCING
—THIS IS AS FAR AS I GO
—GOTTA GET JOY
—GOT THAT GOOD TIME FEELING
—SUNNY CALIFORNIA
—THE STEPS OF THE CAPITOL
—FEUDIN' AND FIGHTIN'
Lyrics by Al Dubin. This song was never
put on the air until 1947, the Shuberts,
who produced the show, being at odds
with the American Society of Composers,
Authors and Publishers and refusing to
release the broadcasting rights. In 1947,
however, Lane, who had been "feudin'
and fightin'" with the Shuberts over the
number, gave Dorothy Shay permission
to sing it on the Bing Crosby program.
It soon became among the top ten sheet
music and coin-machine sellers.

1947. *FINIAN'S RAINBOW*
A musical comedy with book and lyrics
by Fred Saidy and E. Y. Harburg, and
presented by a cast headed by Albert
Sharpe, David Wayne, Ella Logan, Don-
ald Richards, Robert Pitkin and Anita
Alvarez.
—HOW ARE THINGS IN GLOCCA
MORRA?
—LOOK TO THE RAINBOW
—WHEN THE IDLE POOR BECOME
THE IDLE RICH
—SOMETHING SORT OF GRANDISH
—WHEN I'M NOT NEAR THE GIRL I
LOVE
—THE BEGAT
—OLD DEVIL MOON
—IF THIS ISN'T LOVE
—THAT GREAT COME-AND-GET-IT
DAY
—NECESSITY
—THIS TIME OF THE YEAR

Lester Lee Score
1949. *ALL FOR LOVE*
A revue with sketches by Ted Luce, the
Hartmans, Max Shulman, Jane Bishir and

Billy Wells, lyrics by Allan Roberts, and
starring Bert Wheeler, who replaced the
ailing Willie Howard during rehearsals,
in a cast that included Grace and Paul
Hartman, Patricia Wymore, Bert Wheeler,
Milada Mladova, Dick Smart and Leni
Lynn. Anthony M. Farrell, one of the pro-
ducers and heir to an Albany fortune,
spent $2,150,000 on the show before the
rise of the opening night curtain: $1,500,-
000 for the old Warner Theater he re-
named the Mark Hellinger; $250,000 for
renovations; $200,000 on "Hold It," a
flop that goaded him into buying the
theater; and $200,000 to produce "All
For Love."
—ALL FOR LOVE
—MY BABY'S BORED
—THE BIG FOUR
—WHY CAN'T IT HAPPEN AGAIN?
—MY HEART'S IN THE MIDDLE OF
JULY
—IT'S A LIVING
—BENJAMIN B. O'DELL
—PRODIGAL DAUGHTER
—RUN TO ME MY LOVE
—NO TIME FOR LOVE
—A DREAMER WITH A PENNY
—THE FARRELL GIRL
—OH HOW FORTUNATE YOU MOR-
TALS BE

Richard Lewine Score
1948. *MAKE MINE MANHATTAN*
A review with book and lyrics by Arnold
B. Horwitt, and presented by a cast head-
ed by David Burns, Sid Caesar, Joshua
Shelley, Jack Kilty, Kyle MacDonald,
Danny Daniels and Shiela Bond.
—I DON'T KNOW HIS NAME
—THE GOOD OLD DAYS
—I FELL IN LOVE WITH YOU
—SATURDAY NIGHT IN CENTRAL
PARK
—TAKE IT BACK, WE'RE THROUGH
—GENTLEMAN FRIEND
—PHIL THE FIDDLER
—MOVIE HOUSE IN MANHATTAN
—TRAFTZ
—RINGALEVIO
—NOISES IN THE STREET
—SUBWAY SONG
—A NIGHT OUT

Franz Lehar Score
1946. *YOURS IS MY HEART*
An operetta with book and lyrics by Harry
Graham, Ira Cobb and Karl Farkas, and

presented by a cast headed by Richard
Tauber. Alexander D'Arcy, Sammy White,
Stella Andreva and Fred Keating.
—MUSIC BOX WALTZ
—GOODBYE, PAREE
—FREE AS THE AIR
—CHINESE MELODY
—PATIENTLY SMILING
—YOURS IS MY HEART ALONE
—A CUP OF CHINA TEA
—UPON A MOONLIGHT NIGHT IN
  MAY
—LOVE, WHAT HAS GIVEN YOU
  THIS MAGIC POWER?
—MEN OF CHINA
—CHINGO-PINGO
—WEDDING CEREMONY
—PARIS SINGS AGAIN
Music by Alfred Gruenwald.

George Lesser Score

1948. *SLEEPY HOLLOW*
A musical comedy based on Washington
Irving's "Legend of Sleepy Hollow" with
book and lyrics by Russell Maloney and
William Battista, and presented by a cast
headed by Gil Lamb, Betty Jane Watson,
Hayes Gordon, Mary McCarthy, Ward
Garner, Ruth McDevitt, Ellen Repp and
James Starbuck.
—MY LUCKY LOVER
—HERE AND NOW
—ALONE
—THE THINGS THAT LOVERS SAY
—TIME STANDS STILL
—YOU'VE GOT THAT KIND OF A
  FACE
—IN THE HAY
—THERE'S HISTORY TO BE MADE
—POOR MAN
—GOOD-NIGHT

Morgan Lewis Scores

1941. *TWO FOR THE SHOW*
Book and lyrics by Nancy Hamilton, and
presented by a cast headed by Betty Hut-
ton, Richard Haydn, Keenan Wynn and
Brenda Forbes.
—HOW HIGH THE MOON
—HOUSE WITH A LITTLE RED BARN
—AT LAST IT'S LOVE
—CALYPSO JOE
—FOOL FOR LOVE
1946. *THREE TO MAKE READY*
Book and lyrics by Nancy Hamilton, and
starring Ray Bolger in a cast that includ-
ed Brenda Forbes, Gordon MacRae and
Arthur Godfrey.

—IT'S A NICE NIGHT FOR IT
—TELL ME THE STORY
—THE OLD SOFT SHOE
—BARNABY BEACH
—IF IT'S LOVE
—A LOVELY LAZY KIND OF DAY
—AND WHY NOT I

Sidney Lippman Score

1947. *BAREFOOT BOY WITH CHEEK*
A musical comedy of the college campus
where Communism raises its ugly head
with book by Max Shulman, lyrics by
Sylvia Dee, and presented by a cast that
included Nancy Walker, Billy Redfield,
Red Buttons, Ellen Hanley and Tommy
Farwell.
—I KNEW I'D KNOW
—I'LL TURN A LITTLE COG
—STORY OF CARROT
—STAR OF THE NORTH STAR STATE
—WHEN YOU ARE EIGHTEEN
—YETTA'S GONNA GET A MAN
—LOTS OF THINGS YOU CAN DO
  WITH TWO
—ALICE IN BOOGYLAND
—AFTER GRADUATION DAY
—TOO NICE A DAY TO GO TO
  SCHOOL
—EVERYTHING LEADS RIGHT BACK
  TO LOVE
—WHO DO YOU THINK YOU ARE?

Frank Loesser Scores

1948. *WHERE'S CHARLIE?*
A musical comedy, based on Brandon
Thomas' successful farce of 1893, "Char-
ley's Aunt," by George Abbott, starring
Ray Bolger in a cast that included Byron
Palmer, Allyn Ann McLerie, Doretta Mor-
row and Jane Lawrence.
—THE YEARS BEFORE US
—BETTER GET OUT OF HERE
—THE NEW ASHMOLEAN MARCHING
  SOCIETY AND STUDENTS' CON-
  SERVATORY BAND
—SERENADE WITH ASIDES
—WHERE'S CHARLEY?
—THE GOSSIPS
—THE WOMAN IN HIS ROOM
—PERNAMBUCO
—AT THE RED ROSE COTILLON
—MY DARLING, MY DARLING
—LOVELIER THAN EVER
—MAKE A MIRACLE
—ONCE IN LOVE WITH AMY
1950. *GUYS AND DOLLS*
A musical comedy, based on Damon Run-

yon characters, with book by Jo Swerling and Abe Burrows, and presented by a cast headed by Robert Alda, Vivian Blaine, Sam Levene, Isabel Bigley and Pat Rooney Sr.
—FUGUE FOR TINHORNS
—FOLLOW THE FOLD
—THE OLD ESTABLISHED
—I'LL KNOW
—A BUSHEL AND A PECK
—ADELAIDE'S LAMENT
—GUYS AND DOLLS
—HAVANA
—IF I WERE A BELL
—MY TIME OF DAY
—I'VE NEVER BEEN IN LOVE BEFORE
—TAKE BACK YOUR MINK
—MORE I CANNOT WISH YOU
—LUCK BE A LADY
—SUE ME
—SIT DOWN YOU'RE ROCKIN' THE BOAT
—MARRY THE MAN TODAY

Frederick Loewe Scores

1943. *WHAT'S UP?*
A revue with sketches and lyrics by Alan Jay Lerner and Arthur Pierson, and presented by a cast headed by Jimmy Savo and Gloria Warren.
—FROM THE CHIMNEY TO THE CELLAR
—HOW TIME FLIES
—A GIRL IS LIKE A BOOK
—MISS LANGLEY'S SCHOOL FOR GIRLS
—ILL-TEMPERED CLAVICHORD
—YOU WASH AND I'LL DRY
—JOSHUA
—MY LAST LOVE
—YOU'VE GOT A HOLD ON ME
—THREE GIRLS IN A BOAT

1945. *THE DAY BEFORE SPRING*
Book and lyrics by Alan Jay Lerner, and presented by a cast headed by Irene Manning, Bill Johnson, John Archer and Patricia Marshall.
—THE DAY BEFORE SPRING
—GOD'S GREEN WORLD
—YOU HAVEN'T CHANGED AT ALL
—MY LOVE IS A MARRIED MAN
—FRIENDS TO THE END
—A JUG OF WINE
—I LOVE YOU THIS MORNING
—WHERE'S MY WIFE?
—THIS IS MY HOLIDAY

1947. *BRIGADOON*
A whimsical musical fantasy with book

and lyrics by Alan Jay Lerner that was laid in the land of the bluebell and heather and had Broadway theater-goers tossing their tam-o-shanters in the air. The cast included Marion Bell, David Brooks, George Keane, Pamela Britton, Lee Sullivan, William Hansen and James Mitchell.
—THE HEATHER ON THE HILL
—COME TO ME, BEND TO ME
—THERE BUT FOR YOU GO I
—DOWN ON MacCONNECHY SQUARE
—FROM THIS DAY ON
—ALMOST LIKE BEING IN LOVE
—WAITIN' FOR MY DEARIE
—BRIGADOON
—I'LL GO HOME WITH BONNIE JEAN
—THE LOVE OF MY LIFE

Paul McGrane and Paul VanLoane Score

1942. *STARS ON ICE*
An ice skating revue with lyrics by Albert Stillmann.
—BROAD SMILE
—GIN RUMMY (I LOVE YOU)
—JUKE BOX SATURDAY NIGHT
—LIKE A LEAF FALLING IN THE BREEZE
—LITTLE JACK FROST
—THE WORLD WALTZES
Music by Irving Graham.

Jimmy McHugh Scores

1940. *KEEP OFF THE GRASS*
Book and lyrics by Howard Dietz and Al Dubin, and starring Jimmy Durante in a cast that included Ray Bolger, Larry Adler, Jane Froman and Ilka Chase.
—THE CABBY'S SERENADE
—THIS IS SPRING
—CRAZY AS A LOON
—A FUGITIVE FROM ESQUIRE
—I'LL APPLAUD WITH MY FEET
—TWO IN A TAXI
—THE OLD PARK BENCH
—RHETT, SCARLET AND ASHLEY
—LOOK OUT FOR MY HEART
—OLD JITTERBUG
—I'M IN THE MOOD
—THIS IS WINTER
—CLEAR OUT OF THIS WORLD
Lyrics by Harold Adamson.

1948. *AS THE GIRLS GO*
A musical comedy in which Bobby Clark played the harrassed huband of the first woman president of the United States, a

role in which Irene Rich made her stage debut. The cast also included Betty Lou Barto, Bill Callahan and Kathryn Lee. Book by William Roos and lyrics by Harold Adamson.

—I GOT LUCKY IN THE RAIN
—NOBODY'S HEART BUT MINE
—AS THE GIRLS GO
—IT TAKES A WOMAN TO MAKE A MAN
—FATHER'S DAY
—AMERICAN CANNES
—YOU SAY THE NICEST THINGS BABY
—THERE'S NO GETTING AWAY FROM YOU
—ROCK, ROCK, ROCK
—IT'S MORE FUN THAN A PICNIC
—BRIGHTEN UP AND BE A LITTLE SUNBEAM

Gerald Marks Score

1948. *HOLD IT!*
A musical comedy with book by Matt Brooks and Art Arthur, lyrics by Sam Lerner, and presented by a cast headed by Johnny Downs, Red Buttons, Jet McDonald and Patricia Wymore.

—ALWAYS YOU
—FRIENDLY ENEMY
—IT WAS SO NICE HAVING YOU
—ABOUT FACE
—YOU TOOK POSSESSION OF ME
—FUNDAMENTAL CHARACTER
—DOWN THE WELL
—NEVERMORE
—BUCK IN THE BANK
—HOLD IT!
—HEAVEN SENT
—ROLL 'EM

Hugh Martin Scores

1941. *BEST FOOT FORWARD*
A musical comedy with book by John Cecil Holm and lyrics by Ralph Blane in which June Allyson made her Broadway stage debut in a cast that included Gil Stratton Jr., Rosemary Lane, Jack Jordan Jr., Maureen Cannon, Nancy Walker and Marty May.

—DON'T SELL THE NIGHT SHORT
—THAT'S HOW I LOVE THE BLUES
—EVERYTIME
—THE GUY WHO BROUGHT ME
—I KNOW YOU BY HEART
—SHADY LADY BIRD
—BUCKLE DOWN WINSOCKI

—MY FIRST PROMISE
—WHO DO YOU THINK I AM?
—JUST A LITTLE JOINT WITH A JUKE BOX
—WHERE DO YOU TRAVEL?
—I'D GLADLY TRADE

1948. *LOOK, MA, I'M DANCIN'*
A musical comedy with book by Jerome Lawrence and Robert E. Lee, lyrics by the composer, and starring Nancy Walker in a cast that included Harold Lang, Loren Welch, Virginia Gerski, Don Liberto, Robert Harris and Alice Pearce.

—I'M THE FIRST GIRL
—JAZZ
—GOTTA DANCE
—LITTLE BOY BLUES
—I'M TIRED OF TEXAS
—SHAUNY O'SHAY
—I'M NOT SO BRIGHT
—TINY ROOM
—THE NEW LOOK
—IF YOU'LL BE MINE
—THE TWO OF US

1951. *MAKE A WISH*
A musical comedy, based on Molnar's "The Good Fairy," with book by Preston Sturges, lyrics by the composer, and presented by a cast headed by Nanette Fabray, Harold Lang, Helen Gallagher, Melville Cooper and Stephen Douglass.

—THE TOUR MUST GO ON
—I WANNA BE GOOD'N BAD
—THE TIME STEP
—WHAT WAS I WARNED ABOUT?
—WHO GIVES A SOU?
—FOLIES LEBICHE OVERTURE
—TONIGHT YOU ARE IN PAREE
—WHEN DOES THE FEELING GO AWAY?
—SUITS ME FINE
—PARIS, FRANCE
—THAT FACE!
—MAKE A WISH
—I'LL NEVER MAKE A FRENCHMAN OUT OF YOU
—OVER AND OVER
—TAKE ME BACK TO TEXAS WITH YOU

Alan Moran Scores

1948. *HOWDY MR. ICE*
An ice skating revue with lyrics by Albert Stillman.

—IN THE PINK
—PLENTY MORE FISH IN THE SEA
—THE FORTY-EIGHT STATES
—ROCKED IN THE CRADLE OF JAZZ

—IF I ONLY KNEW
—WORLD'S GREATEST SHOW
1950. *HOWDY MR. ICE OF 1950*
    A revised edition of the 1948 ice skating
    revue, "Howdy Mr. Ice," with lyrics by
    Albert Stillman.
—WE'RE THE DOORMEN OF NEW
    YORK
—YOU WAS

Al Moritz Score

1945. *BLUE HOLIDAY*
    Ethel Waters, Mary Lou Williams, Josh
    White, the Chocolateers and the Kathe-
    rine Durham Dancers headline the cast
    of a Negro revue.
—BLUE HOLIDAY
—THAT'S WHERE MY HEART WILL
    BE
—SLEEP TIME LULLABY
—FREE AND EQUAL BLUES
    By E. Y. Harburg and Earl Robinson.

Larry Morey Scores

1949. *ICE FOLLIES OF 1949*
    An ice skating revue with lyrics by the
    composer.
—ME AND MY HEART WENT A GAD-
    DING
—SONG BIRD SINGING IN A BAMBOO
    TREE
—SMOOTH SAILIN'
—WHEN YOU'RE YOUNG AND IT'S
    SPRING
—LOLLIPOP POLKA
—CANDY CHOO-CHOO
—UPSIDE DOWN SONG
—WITH A ROSE IN YOUR HAIR
—CHICKADY CHAY
—I'M GONNA FIND A GAL IN CALI-
    FORNY
—SWING WALTZ
—ICICLE SONG
—CANDY SOLDIERS ON PARADE
1950. *ICE FOLLIES OF 1950*
    An ice skating revue with lyrics by the
    composer.
—IT'S A GOOD, GOOD MORNING
—WALKING WITH MARIAH
—COME TO THE BOWERY TONIGHT
—THE BUILDIN' BEE
—SHAKE 'EM OFF
—CIRCUS DAY
—MILK BOTTLE PARADE

John Mundy Score

1950. *THE LIAR*
    A musical comedy with book by Edward
    Eager and Alfred Drake, lyrics by Ed-
    ward Eager, and presented by a cast head-
    ed by William Eythe, Paula Lawrence and
    Melville Cooper.
—MARCH OF THE GUARDS
—THE LADIES' OPINION
—YOU HAVE STOLEN MY HEART
—THE LIAR'S SONG
—SUPPER TRIO
—TRUTH
—LACKADAY
—STOP HOLDING ME BACK
—WHAT'S IN A NAME?
—WOMEN'S WORK
—SPRING
—STOMACHS AND STOMACHS
—A JEWEL OF A DUEL
—OUT OF SIGHT, OUT OF MIND
—A PLOT TO CATCH A MAN IN
—FUNERAL MARCH
—'TWILL NEVER BE THE SAME

Harold Orlob Score

1943. *HAIRPIN HARMONY*
    Book by Don Witty, lyrics by the com-
    poser, and presented by a cast headed by
    Lennie Kent, Carlyle Blackwell and Mau-
    reen Cannon.
—HAIRPIN HARMONY
—WHAT-A-YA-SAY?
—YOU'RE THE REASON
—I'M TICKLED PINK
—I'M A BUTTER HOARDER
—WITHOUT A SPONSOR
—I CAN BE LIKE GRANDPA
—THAT'S MY APPROACH TO LOVE
—WHAT DO THE NEIGHBORS SAY?
—PICKANINNY PIE

Cole Porter Scores

1940. *PANAMA HATTIE*
    Book by Herbert Fields and B. G. De-
    Sylva, and starring Ethel Merman in a
    cast that included James Dunn, Pat Har-
    rington, Frank Hyers, Rags Ragland, Vir-
    ginia Field, Betty Hutton, Joan Carroll
    and Arthur Treacher.
—JOIN IT RIGHT AWAY
—VISIT PANAMA
—MY MOTHER WOULD LOVE YOU
—I'VE STILL GOT MY HEALTH
—FRESH AS A DAISY
—LET'S BE BUDDIES

—WHO WOULD HAVE DREAMED?
—MAKE IT ANOTHER OLD FASHIONED, PLEASE
—ALL I'VE GOT TO GET NOW IS MY MAN
—GOD BLESS THE WOMEN

1941. *LET'S FACE IT*
Book by Herbert and Dorothy Fields. A musical version of "The Cradle Snatchers" with Eve Arden, Vivian Vance, Ethel Meiser, Danny Kaye, Benny Baker, Jack Williams and Mary Jane Walsh.
—MILK, MILK, MILK
—A LADY NEEDS A REST
—JERRY, MY SOLDIER BOY
—LET'S FACE IT
—BABY GAMES
—FAIRY TALE
—RUB YOUR LAMP
—CUTTIN' A PERSIAN RUG
—I'VE GOT SOME UNFINISHED BUSINESS WITH YOU
—MELODY IN FOUR F
—FARMING
—EVERYTHING I LOVE
—ACE IN THE HOLE
—YOU IRRITATE ME SO
—A LITTLE RUMBA NUMBA
—I HATE YOU, DARLING
—LET'S NOT TALK ABOUT LOVE

1943. *SOMETHING FOR THE BOYS*
Book by Herbert and Dorothy Fields, and starring Ethel Merman in a cast that included Paula Laurence, Betty Bruce, Betty Garrett and Allen Jenkins.
—COULD IT BE YOU?
—HE'S A RIGHT GUY
—HEY, GOOD LOOKIN'
—SOMETHING FOR THE BOYS
—BY THE MISSISSINIWAH
—SEE THAT YOU'RE BORN IN TEXAS
—WHEN MY BABY GOES TO TOWN
—WHEN WE'RE HOME ON THE RANGE
—THE LEADER OF THE BIG TIME BAND
—I'M IN LOVE WITH A SOLDIER BOY
—THERE'S A HAPPY LAND IN THE SKY

1944. *MEXICAN HAYRIDE*
Book by Herbert and Dorothy Fields, and presented by a cast headed by Bobby Clark, George Givot, Paul Haakon, June Havoc and Ethel Meiser.
—SING TO ME, GUITAR
—THE GOOD WILL MOVEMENT
—I LOVE YOU

—THERE MUST BE SOMEONE FOR ME
—WHAT A CRAZY WAY TO SPEND SUNDAY
—ABRACADABRA
—COUNT YOUR BLESSINGS
—CARLOTTA
—GIRLS

1944. *SEVEN LIVELY ARTS*
Billy Rose reopens the Ziegfeld Theater as a legitimate playhouse with magnums of champagne and a musical review in with Beatrice Lillie, Bert Lahr, Doc Rockwell, Albert Carroll and Benny Goodman were starred or featured. Sketches by Moss Hart and Ben Hecht.
—FRAHNGEE-PAHNEE
—BIG TOWN
—EV'RY TIME WE SAY GOODBYE
—IS IT THE GIRL OR IS IT THE GOWN?
—ONLY ANOTHER BOY AND GIRL
—WOW-OOH-WOLF
—DRINK
—WHEN I WAS A LITTLE CUCKOO
—DANCIN' TO A JUNGLE DRUM
—HENCE IT DON'T MAKE SENSE
—THE BAND STARTED SWINGING A SONG

1946. *AROUND THE WORLD IN EIGHTY DAYS*
A musical play, based on Jules Verne's book of the same name by Orson Welles, who starred in a cast that included Arthur Margetson, Mary Healy, Julie Warren, Larry Laurence and Victoria Cordova.
—LOOK WHAT I FOUND
—THERE HE GOES, PHILEAS FOGG
—MEERAHLAH
—SEA CHANTEY
—SHOULD I TELL YOU I LOVE YOU?
—PIPE DREAMING
—IF YOU SMILE AT ME
—WHEREVER THEY FLY THE FLAG OF OLD ENGLAND
—THE MARINES HYMN

1948. *KISS ME, KATE*
Musical comedy by Bella and Samuel Spewack, vaguely based on Shakespeare's "The Taming of the Shrew" and starring Alfred Drake and Patricia Morison in a cast in which Harold Lang and Lisa Kirk were featured.
—ANOTHER OP'NIN', ANOTHER SHOW
—WHY CAN'T YOU BEHAVE?
—WUNDERBAR

—SO IN LOVE AM I
—WE OPEN IN VENICE
—TOM, DICK OR HARRY
—I'VE COME TO WIVE IT WEALTH-
  ILY IN PADUA
—I HATE MEN
—WERE THINE THAT SPECIAL FACE
—I SING OF LOVE
—KISS ME, KATE
—TOO DARN HOT
—WHERE IS THE LIFE THAT LATE I
  LED?
—ALWAYS TRUE TO YOU (IN MY
  FASHION)
—BIANCA
—BRUSH UP ON YOUR SHAKE-
  SPEARE
—I AM ASHAMED THAT WOMEN
  ARE SO SIMPLE

1950. *OUT OF THIS WORLD*
A musical comedy with book by Dwight
Taylor and Reginald Lawrence, and pre-
sented by a cast headed by Charlotte
Greenwood, William Redfield, Priscilla
Gillette and David Burns.
—I JUPITER, REX
—USE YOUR IMAGINATION
—HAIL, HAIL, HAIL
—I GOT BEAUTY
—MAIDEN FAIR
—WHERE, OH, WHERE
—I AM LOVED
—THEY COULDN'T COMPARE TO
  YOU
—WHAT DO YOU THINK ABOUT
  MEN?
—I SLEEP EASIER NOW
—CLIMB UP THE MOUNTAIN
—NO LOVER FOR ME
—CHERRY PIE OUGHT TO BE YOU
—HARK, THE SONG OF THE NIGHT
—NOBODY'S CHASING ME

M. and L. Portnoff Score

1950. *HAPPY AS LARRY*
A musical fantasy by Donagh McDonagh,
starring Burgess Meredith in a cast that
included Marguerite Piazza, Irwin Corey
and Gene Barry.
—NOW AND THEN
—I REMEMBER HER
—OCTOBER
—WITHOUT A STITCH
—MRS. LARRY, TELL ME THIS
—A CUP OF TEA
—HE'S WITH MY JOHNNY
—AND SO HE DIED
—THREE OLD LADIES FROM HADES

—IT'S PLEASANT AND DELIGHTFUL
—THE DIRTY DOG
—THE FLATULENT BALLAD
—THE LOYALIST WIFE
—OH, MRS. LARRY
—HE'S A BOLD ROGUE
—THE TOBACCO BLUES

David Raskin Score

1946. *IF THE SHOE FITS*
A musical comedy with book and lyrics
by John Duke and June Carroll, and pre-
sented by a cast headed by Florence Des-
mond, Leila Ernst, Erward Dew, Joe Bes-
ser, Jack Williams and Barbara Perry.
—THIS IS THE END OF THE STORY
—BUT I TOOK ANOTHER LOOK
—I'M NOT MYSELF TONIGHT
—MY BUSINESS MAN
—I WISH
—IN THE MORNING

Harry Revel Score

1945. *ARE YOU WITH IT?*
A musical comedy, based on George Mal-
colm Smith's novel "Slightly Perfect,"
with a book by Sam Perrin and George
Balzar, lyrics by Arnold B. Horwitt, and
presented by a cast that included Joan
Roberts, Johnny Downs, Lew Parker,
Dolores Lee, Jane Dulo and June Rich-
mond.
—FIVE MORE MINUTES IN BED
—NUTMEG INSURANCE
—SLIGHTLY PERFECT
—WHEN A GOOD MAN TAKES TO
  DRINK
—POOR LITTLE ME
—ARE YOU WITH IT?
—THIS IS MY BELOVED
—SLIGHTLY SLIGHTLY
—SEND US BACK TO THE KITCHEN
—HERE I GO AGAIN
—YOU GOTTA KEEP SAYING NO
—JUST BEYOND THE RAINBOW
—IN OUR COZY LITTLE COTTAGE
  OF TOMORROW

Richard Rodgers Scores

1940. *HIGHER AND HIGHER*
Book by Gladys Hurlbut and Joshua Lo-
gan, lyrics by Lorenz Hart, and presented
by a cast that included Jack Haley, Hilda
Spong, Shirley Ross, Lee Dixon and Marta
Eggert, who was replaced by Marie Nash
during the run of this production.
—A BARKING DOG NEVER BITES

—FROM ANOTHER WORLD
—MORNINGS AT SEVEN
—NOTHING BUT YOU
—DISGUSTINGLY RICH
—BLUE MONDAY
—EV'RY SUNDAY AFTERNOON
—A LOVELY DAY FOR MURDER
—HOW'S YOUR HEALTH?
—IT NEVER ENTERED MY MIND
—I'M AFRAID

1940. *PAL JOEY*
Book by John O'Hara, lyrics by Lorenz Hart, and presented by a cast that included Vivienne Segal, June Havoc, Leila Ernst, Gene Kelly, Jack Durant and Van Johnson.
—YOU MUSTN'T KICK IT AROUND
—I COULD WRITE A BOOK
—CHICAGO
—THAT TERRIFIC RAINBOW
—LOVE IS MY FRIEND
—HAPPY HUNTING GROUND
—BEWITCHED, BOTHERED AND BEWILDERED
—THE FLOWER GARDEN IN MY HEART
—ZIP
—PLANT YOU NOW, DIG YOU LATER
—IN OUR LITTLE DEN
—DO IT THE HARD WAY
—TAKE HIM

1942. *BY JUPITER*
Book by Rodgers and Hart, based on Julian F. Thompson's "The Warrior's Husband," with lyrics by Lorenz Hart. Presented by a cast that included Constance Moore, Benay Venita, Bertha Delmore, Ray Bolger and Ronald Graham.
—JUPITER FORBID
—LIFE WITH FATHER
—NOBODY'S HEART BELONGS TO ME
—HERE'S A HAND
—NO, MOTHER, NO
—THE BOY I LEFT BEHIND
—EV'RYTHING I'VE GOT
—BOTTOMS UP
—CARELESS RHAPSODY
—WAIT TILL YOU SEE HER
—NOW THAT I'VE GOT MY STRENGTH

1943. *OKLAHOMA*
Book and lyrics by Oscar Hammerstein II, and presented by a cast that included Betty Garde, Alfred Drake, Joseph Buloff, Joan Roberts, Lee Dixon, Howard De Silva, Celeste Holm, Ralph Riggs, Marc Platt, Katherine Sergava and Vladimir Kostenko.

—OH, WHAT A BEAUTIFUL MORNING
—THE SURREY WITH THE FRINGE ON TOP
—KANSAS CITY
—I CAN'T SAY NO
—MANY A NEW DAY
—IT'S A SCANDAL IT'S AN OUTRAGE
—PEOPLE WILL SAY WE'RE IN LOVE
—PORE JUD
—LONELY ROOM
—OUT OF MY DREAMS
—THE FARMER AND THE COWMAN
—ALL OR NOTHIN'
—OKLAHOMA

1945. *CAROUSEL*
A musical play based on Ferenc Molnar's "Liliom" with book and lyrics by Oscar Hammerstein II. The cast was headed by Jan Clayton as "Julie" and John Raitt as "Billy Bigelow," the carnival barker.
—YOU'RE A QUEER ONE, JULIE JORDAN
—WHEN I MARRY MR. SNOW
—IF I LOVED YOU
—JUNE IS BUSTIN' OUT ALL OVER
—WHEN THE CHILDREN ARE ASLEEP
—BLOW HIGH, BLOW LOW
—THIS IS A REAL NICE CLAMBAKE
—SOLILOQUE
—GERANIUMS IN THE WINDER
—THERE'S NOTHIN' SO BAD FOR A WOMAN
—WHAT'S THE USE OF WONDERIN'
—YOU'LL NEVER WALK ALONE
—THE HIGHEST JUDGE OF ALL

1947. *ALLEGRO*
A musical play with book and lyrics by Oscar Hammerstein II, and presented by a cast that included Annamary Dickey, William Ching, John Battles, Roberta Jonay, Muriel O'Malley, Gloria Wills, John Conte and Lisa Kirk.
—JOSEPH TAYLOR JR.
—I KNOW IT CAN HAPPEN AGAIN
—ONE FOOT OTHER FOOT
—A FELLOW NEEDS A GIRL
—A DARN NICE CAMPUS
—THE PURPLE AND BROWN
—SO FAR
—YOU ARE NEVER AWAY
—WHAT A LOVELY DAY FOR A WEDDING
—IT MAY BE A GOOD IDEA FOR JOE
—TO HAVE AND TO HOLD
—WISH THEM WELL
—MONEY ISN'T EVERYTHING
—YATATA YATATA YATATA
—THE GENTLEMAN IS A DOPE

—ALLEGRO
—COME HOME
1949. *SOUTH PACIFIC*
A musical play based on James A. Michener's Pulitzer prize book "Tales of the South Pacific" with libretto by Oscar Hammerstein II and Joshua Logan and lyrics by Hammerstein. Ezio Pinza of the New York Metropolitan Opera Co. and Mary Martin were co-starred in a cast that included Myron McCormick, Bill Tabbert, Martin Wolfson, Harvey Stephens, Juanita Hall, Betta Striegler, Henry Slate and Archie Savage.
—DITES-MOI POURQUOI
—A COCKEYED OPTIMIST
—SOME ENCHANTED EVENING
—BLOODY MARY IS THE GIRL I LOVE
—THERE IS NOTHING LIKE A DAME
—BALI HA'I
—I'M GONNA WASH THAT MAN RIGHT OUT OF MY HAIR
—I'M IN LOVE WITH A WONDERFUL GUY
—YOUNGER THAN SPRINGTIME
—HAPPY TALK
—HONEY BUN
—YOU'VE GOT TO BE TAUGHT
—THIS NEARLY WAS MINE
1951. *THE KING AND I*
A musical based on Margaret Landon's novel, "Anna And The King Of Siam," with book and lyrics by Oscar Hammerstein II, and presented by a cast headed by Gertrude Lawrence, Yul Brynner, Doretta Morrow, Dorothy Sarnoff and Larry Douglas.
—I WHISTLE A HAPPY TUNE
—MY LORD AND MASTER
—HELLO, YOUNG LOVERS
—THE ROYAL SIAMESE CHILDREN
—THE ROYAL BANKOK ACADEMY
—A PUZZLEMENT
—SHALL I TELL YOU WHAT I THINK OF YOU?
—GETTING TO KNOW YOU
—SOMETHING WONDERFUL
—WESTERN PEOPLE FUNNY
—I HAVE DREAMED
—WE KISS IN A SHADOW
—THE SMALL HOUSE OF UNCLE THOMAS
—SHALL WE DANCE?

Sigmund Romberg Scores

1942. *SUNNY RIVER*
Book and lyrics by Oscar Hammerstein

II, and presented by a cast that included Muriel Angelus, Helen Claire, Ethel Levey and Bob Lawrence.
—MY GIRL AND I
—CALL IT A DREAM
—IT CAN HAPPEN TO ANYONE
—THE BUTTERFLIES AND BEES
—ALONG THE WEDDING ROAD
—BUNDLING
—CAN YOU SING?
—MAKING CONVERSATION
—LET ME LIVE TODAY
—BOW-LEGGED SAL
—SUNNY RIVER
—SHE GOT HIM
—TIME IS STANDING STILL
1945. *UP IN CENTRAL PARK*
Book and lyrics by Herbert and Dorothy Fields, and presented by a cast headed by Betty Bruce, Maureen Cannon, Charles Irwin, Wilbur Evans and Noah Beery Sr.
—UP FROM THE GUTTER
—CAROUSEL IN THE PARK
—IT DOESN'T COST ANYTHING TO DREAM
—BOSS TWEED
—WHEN SHE WALKS IN THE ROOM
—CURRIER AND IVES
—CLOSE AS PAGES IN A BOOK
—RIP VAN WRINKLE
—THE FIREMAN'S BRIDE
—WHEN THE PARTY GIVES A PARTY
—THE BIG BACK YARD
—APRIL SNOW
—THE BIRDS AND THE BEES
1948. *MY ROMANCE*
A musical play with book and lyrics by Rowland Leigh, based on Edward Sheldon's "Romance," with a cast headed by Anne Jeffreys in the role of the diva created by Doris Keane in 1913, Luella Gear, Lawrence Brooks and Hazel Dawn Jr.
—SOUVENIR
—1898
—DEBUTANTE
—WRITTEN IN YOUR HAND
—LOVE AND LAUGHTER
—FROM NOW ONWARD
—LITTLE EMMALINE
—DESIRE
—IF ONLY
—BELLA DONNA
—PARADISE STOLEN
—IN LOVE WITH ROMANCE

Harold Rome Scores

1942. *LET FREEDOM RING*
A production of the Youth Theater in

which Mitzi Green was starred.
—RING UP THE CURTAIN
—IT'S FUN TO BE FREE
—THE LADY IS A WAC
—I DID IT FOR DEFENSE
—BE CALM
—HISTORY EIGHT TO THE BAR
—LITTLE MISS VICTORY JONES
—GIVE A VIVA
—JOHNNY IS A HOARDER
—OF THE PEOPLE STOMP
—FRAUGHT
  By Marc Blitzstein.
—MITTEL EUROPA
  By Henry Myers, Edward Eliscu and
  Jay Gorney.
—GRANDPA GUERRILA
  By Hy Zaret and Walter Kent.
—WE HAVE A DATE
  By Roslyn Harvey and Lou Cooper.
—THE LITTLE THINGS WE LIKE
  By Roslyn Harvey and Lou Cooper.
—FLOWERS IN BLOOM
  By David Gregory and Jack Gerald.
—THE HOUSE I LIVE IN
—By Lewis Allan and Earl Robinson.
1946. *CALL ME MISTER*
  A revue that made light of the GI's post-
  war problems with book by Arnold Auer-
  bach, lyrics by the composer, and pre-
  sented by a cast headed by Betty Garrett,
  Jules Munshin and Bill Callahan.
—THE JODY CHANT
—GOIN' HOME TRAIN
—ALONG WITH ME
—SURPLUS BLUES
—THE DRUG STORE SONG
—THE RED BALL EXPRESS
—MILITARY LIFE
—CALL ME MISTER
—YULETIDE PARK AVENUE
—WHEN WE MEET AGAIN
—THE FACE ON THE DIME
—HIS OLD MAN
—SOUTH AMERICA, TAKE IT AWAY
—THE SENATORS' SONG
1950. *BLESS YOU ALL*
  A revue with sketches by Arnold Auer-
  bach, lyrics by the composer, and pre-
  sented by a cast headed by Jules Munshin,
  Mary McCarthy, Pearl Bailey, Valerie
  Bettis, Jane Harvey, Byron Palmer and
  Robert Chisholm.
—BLESS YOU ALL
—DO YOU KNOW A BETTER WAY TO
  MAKE A LIVING?
—DON'T WANNA WRITE ABOUT THE
  SOUTH
—I CAN HEAR IT NOW

—WHEN
—LITTLE THINGS MEANT SO MUCH
  TO ME
—LOVE LETTER TO MANHATTAN
—A ROSE IS A ROSE
—LOVE THAT MAN
—JUST A LITTLE WHITE HOUSE
—VOTING BLUES
—SUMMER DRESSES
—TAKE OFF THE COAT
—THE NOBBIEST HOBBY
—YOU'LL NEVER KNOW WHAT HIT
  YOU
—THE ROARING TWENTIES STRIKE
  BACK

Ann Ronell Score
1943. *COUNT ME IN*
  Book by Walter Kerr, Leo Grady and
  Nancy Hamilton, lyrics by Will Irwin, and
  presented by a cast headed by Charles
  Butterworth, Hal LeRoy, Luella Gear,
  June Preisser, Mary Healy and Jean
  Arthur.
—TICKETYBOO
—YOU'VE GOT IT ALL
—THE WOMAN OF THE YEAR
—SOMEONE IN THE KNOW
—ON LEAVE FOR LOVE

David Rose Score
1943. *WINGED VICTORY*
  A U. S. Army Air Force show presented
  by an all-soldier cast, and produced to
  raise money for the U. S. O.
—WINGED VICTORY
—MY DREAM BOAT OF MEMORIES
—YOU'RE SO SWEET TO REMEMBER
  Lyrics by Leo Robin.
—ARMY AIR CORPS SONG
  By Robert Crawford.

Harry Ruby Score
1941. *THE HIGH KICKERS*
  Book and lyrics by George Jessel and Bert
  Kalmar, and starring Sophie Tucker in a
  cast that included George Jessel, Betty
  Bruce, Chic York and Rose King.
—MY SWEETHEART MAMIE
—DON'T TELL YOUR MOTHER
  NOTHIN'
—YOU'RE ON MY MIND
—A PANIC IN PANAMA
—THE GIRLS
—TIME TO SING
—I GOT SOMETHING
—CIGARETTES
—WALTZING IN THE MOONLIGHT

Arthur Schwartz Scores

1940. *AMERICAN JUBILEE*
A New York World's Fair production with book and lyrics by Oscar Hammerstein II, and presented by a cast headed by Lucy Monroe, Ray Middleton, Paul Haakon, Joe Jackson, Wynn Murray and Harry Meehan.
—HOW CAN I EVER BE ALONE?
—WE LIKE IT HERE
—TENNESSEE FISH FRY
—JENNY LIND
—MY BICYCLE GIRL
—BY THE PEOPLE
—ONE IN A MILLION
—THE FIREMAN'S SERENADE

1946. *PARK AVENUE*
A satire with music on short-lived marriages and multiple divorces with a book by George S. Kaufman and Nunnally Johnson, lyrics by Ira Gershwin, and presented by a cast headed by Leonora Corbett, Arthur Margetson, Mary Wilkes, Raymond Walburn, Ray McDonald and Martha Stewart.
—DON'T BE A WOMAN IF YOU CAN
—TOMORROW IS THE TIME
—LAND OF OPPORTUNITEE
—SWEET NEVADA
—THERE'S NO HOLDING ME
—FOR THE LIFE OF ME
—THE DEW WAS ON THE ROSE
—THERE'S NOTHING LIKE MARRIAGE FOR PEOPLE
—HOPE FOR THE BEST
—MY SON-IN-LAW
—GOOD-BYE TO ALL THAT

1948. *INSIDE U.S.A.*
A revue with sketches by Arnold Auerbach, Moss Hart and Arnold Horwitt, lyrics by Howard Dietz, and starring Beatrice Lillie and Jack Haley in a cast that included Valerie Bettis and John Tyers.
—INSIDE THE U.S.A.
—LEAVE MY PULSE ALONE
—COME OH COME
—BLUE GRASS
—RHODE ISLAND IS FAMOUS FOR YOU
—HAUNTED HEART
—MASSACHUSETTS MERMAID
—FIRST PRIZE AT THE FAIR
—THE MARDI GRAS
—MY GAL IS MINE ONCE MORE
—WE WON'T TAKE IT BACK

1951. *A TREE GROWS IN BROOKLYN*
A musical drama, based on Betty Smith's novel of the same name, with book by Betty Smith and George Abbott, lyrics by Dorothy Fields, and presented by a cast headed by Marcia van Dyke, Johnny Johnston, Shirley Booth and Nomi Mitty.
—PAYDAY
—MINE 'TIL MONDAY
—MAKE THE MAN LOVE ME
—I'M LIKE A NEW BROOM
—LOOK WHO'S DANCING
—LOVE IS THE REASON
—IF YOU HAVEN'T GOT A SWEETHEART
—I'LL BUY YOU A STAR
—THAT'S HOW IT GOES
—HE HAD REFINEMENT
—GROWING PAINS
—IS THAT MY PRINCE?
—HALLOWEEN
—DON'T BE AFRAID

Raymond Scott Score

1946. *LUTE SONG*
A modern version of the old Chinese fantasy "Pi-Pa-Ki," with book by Sidney Howard and Will Irwin, lyrics by Bernard Hanighen, and starring Mary Martin in a cast that included McKay Morris and Rex O'Malley.
—MOUNTAIN HIGH, MOUNTAIN LOW
—MONKEY SEE, MONKEY DO
—WHERE YOU ARE
—BUTTERFLY AND THE BIRDIE
—DIRGE SONG
—IMPERIAL MARCH
—LION DANCE
—LUTE SONG
—BITTER HARVEST
—VISION SONG
—WILLOW TREE

Carl Sigman Score

1947. *ANGEL IN THE WINGS*
A revue starring the Hartmans and Hank Ladd with lyrics by Bob Hilliard.
—BIG BRASS BAND FROM BRAZIL
—CIVILIZATION (BONGA, BONGA, BONGA)
—THOUSAND ISLAND SONG (OH, FLORENCE)
—BREEZY
—ONCE AROUND THE MOON
—IF IT WERE EASY TO DO
—LONG GREEN BLUES
—HOLLER BLUE MURDER
—TAMBOURINE

Manning Sherwin Score

1947. *UNDER THE COUNTER*
Book by Arthur MacRae, lyrics by Harold
Purcell and starring Cicely Courtneidge.
—EVERYWHERE
—NO ONE TO KISS ME
—THE MOMENT I SAW YOU
—LET'S GET BACK TO GLAMOUR
—AI YI YI

Fred Spielman Score

1945. *A LADY SAYS YES*
Book by Clayton Ashley and Stanley
Adams, lyrics by Arthur Gershwin, and
presented by a cast headed by Carole
Landis and Arthur Maxwell.
—I WONDER WHY YOU WANDER
—TAKE MY HEART WITH YOU
—WITHOUT A CARESS
—YOU'RE MORE THAN A NAME AND
   ADDRESS

Johann Strauss Score

1942. *ROSALINDA*
An operetta with book by John Meehan
Jr., lyrics by Paul Kerby, and presented
by a cast headed by Dorothy Sarnoff and
Everett West.
—ROSALINDA, LOVE OF MINE
—OH JIMINY!
—DRINKING SONG
—WINE AND SONG, SONG AND
   DANCE
—ORLOFSKY'S SONG
—LAUGHING SONG
—CSARDAS
—WATCH DUET
—IN A LEAGUE OF FRIENDS
—ADELE'S AUDITION

Robert Stolz Scores

1941. *NIGHT OF LOVE*
An operetta with book and lyrics by
Roland Leigh, and presented by a cast
headed by Martha Errolle, Helen Gleason,
Robert Chisholm, John Lodge and Mar-
guerite Namara.
—MY LOVED ONE
—CHIQUITA TRIO
—I'M THINKING OF LOVE
—THE ONE MAN I NEED
—TONIGHT OR NEVER
—SERENADE FOR YOU
—WITHOUT YOU
—LOOSEN UP
—STREAMLINED POMPADOUR

1945. *MR. STRAUSS GOES TO BOSTON*
George Rigaud, the French tenor, makes
his American debut as Johann Strauss in
a musical comedy with book by Leonard
L. Levison and lyrics by Robert Sour, in-
spired by the visit of the Waltz King to
America in 1872 to serve as the guest
conductor of the World Peace Jubilee, a
musical festival in which a 1000-piece or-
chestra, forty brass bands and 20,000
vocalists participated.
—CAN ANYONE SEE?
—RADETSKY MARCH-FANTASIE
—FOR THE SAKE OF ART
—LAUGHING WALTZ
—MR. STRAUSS GOES TO BOSTON
—DOWN WITH SIN
—WHO KNOWS?
—MIDNIGHT WALTZ
—INTO THE NIGHT
—COLORATURA WALTZ
—THE GOSSIP POLKA
—GOING BACK HOME
—YOU NEVER KNOW WHAT COMES
   NEXT
—WHAT'S A GIRL SUPPOSED TO DO?
—THE GRAND AND GLORIOUS
   FOURTH
—WALTZ FINALE

Sir Arthur Sullivan Score

1945. *HOLLYWOOD PINAFORE* or
   THE LAD WHO LOVED A SALARY
A modernized version of "H. M. S. Pina-
fore" with book and lyrics by George S.
Kaufman, and presented by a cast that
included Victor Moore, William Gaxton,
Annamary Dickey and Shirley Booth.

Jule Styne Scores

1947. *HIGH BUTTON SHOES*
Book by Stephen Longstreet, lyrics by
Sammy Cahn, and presented by a cast
headed by Phil Silvers, Joey Faye, Na-
nette Fabray, Mark Dawson, Jack Mc-
Cauley and Lois Lee.
—HE TRIED TO MAKE A DOLLAR
—CAN'T YOU SEE YOURSELF IN
   LOVE WITH ME?
—A SUMMER INCIDENT
—NEXT TO TEXAS I LOVE YOU
—THERE'S NOTHING LIKE A MODEL
   T
—I STILL GET JEALOUS
—BIRD WATCHERS' SONG
—YOU'RE MY BOY
—POPPA WON'T YOU DANCE WITH
   ME?

—GET AWAY FOR A DAY IN THE COUNTRY
—SECURITY
—ON A SUNDAY BY THE SEA
—YOU'RE MY GIRL
—NOBODY EVER DIED FOR DEAR OLD RUTGERS
—CASTLE WALK

1949. *GENTLEMEN PREFER BLONDES*
A musical version of the comedy hit of the 1920s of the same title with a book by Anita Loos and Joseph Fields, lyrics by Leo Robin, and presented by a cast that included Carol Channing, Yvonne Adair, Eric Brotherson, Jerry Cooper and Alice Pearce.
—IT'S HIGH TIME
—BYE, BYE BABY
—A LITTLE GIRL FROM LITTLE ROCK
—I LOVE WHAT I'M DOING
—JUST A KISS APART
—IT'S DELIGHTFUL DOWN IN CHILE
—SUNSHINE
—IN THE CHAMPS DE MARS
—I'M A-TINGLE I'M A-GLOW
—THE HOUSE ON RITTENHOUSE SQUARE
—YOU SAY YOU CARE
—MAMIE IS MIMI
—DIAMONDS ARE A GIRL'S BEST FRIEND
—COQUETTE
—GENTLEMEN PREFER BLONDES
—KEEPING COOL WITH COOLIDGE
—BUTTON UP WITH ESMOND

1951. *TWO ON THE AISLE*
A revue with book and lyrics by Betty Comden and Adolph Green, and starring Bert Lahr and Dolores Gray in a cast theat included Collette Marchand and Elliott Reid.
—SHOW TRAIN
—HOLD ME TIGHT
—EAST RIVER HOE-DOWN
—THERE NEVER WAS A BABY LIKE MY BABY
—IF YOU HAD'NT BUT YOU DID
—CATCH OUR ACT AT THE MET
—EVER-LASTING
—GIVE A LITTLE, GET A LITTLE LOVE
—HOW WILL HE KNOW?

Peter Tschaikowsky Score

1947. *MUSIC IN MY HEART*
An operetta with book by Patsy Ruth Miller, lyrics by Forman Brown, and pre-sented by a cast headed by Martha Wright, Vivienne Segal and Robert Carroll.
—SONG OF THE TROIKA
—WHERE THERE'S A SONG TO SING
—BALALAIKA SERENADE
—STOLEN KISSES
—ONCE UPON A TIME
—UNREQUITED LOVE
—FLOWER WALTZ
—LOVE IS A GAME FOR SOLDIERS
—NO, NO, NO
—TREPAK
—AM I ENCHANTED?
—GOSSIP
—THREE'S A CROWD
—THE BALLERINA'S SONG
—SONG OF THE CLAQUE
—BEAUTY AND THE BEAST
—LOVE IS THE SOVEREIGN OF MY HEART

Jimmy VanHeusen Scores

1940. *BILLY ROSE'S AQUACADE*
The New York World's Fair water carnival, starring Eleanor Holm and Johnny Weismuller with Vincent Lopez and his orchestra and the Fred Waring Glee Club. Lyrics by Joseph McCarthy.
—YOU THINK OF EVERYTHING
—THERE'S A NEW GANG ON THE WAY
—ELEANOR I ADORE YOU
—WHEN THE SPIRIT MOVES ME
—YOURS FOR A SONG
By Ted Fetter, Billy Rose and Dana Suesse.
—YOU'RE TOO GOOD TO BE TRUE
By Billy Rose and Dana Suesse.

1946. *NELLIE BLY*
A musical comedy inspired by the round-the-world trip of Nellie Bly, the girl reporter on the *New York World,* who beat the 80-day record of the hero of the Jules Verne novel. Book by Joseph Quinlan, lyrics by Johnny Burke, and starring William Gaxton and Victor Moore in a cast that included Joy Hodges and Benay Venuta.
—JUST MY LUCK
—YOU MAY NOT LOVE ME
—THERE'S NOTHING LIKE TRAVEL
—ALL AROUND THE WORLD
—FOGARTY THE GREAT
—THAT'S CLASS
—NELLIE BLY
—MAY THE BEST MAN WIN
—HOW ABOUT A DATE?
—YOU NEVER SAW THAT BEFORE

—L'EXPOSITION UNIVERSALLE
—SKY HIGH
—NO NEWS TODAY
—CHORAL RUSSE
—ALADDIN'S DAUGHTER
—START DANCING
—HARMONY

Victor Young Score

1950. *PARDON OUR FRENCH*
A revue with lyrics by Edward Heyman, and starring Olsen and Johnson in a cast that included Denise Darcel.
—I'M GONNA MAKE A FOOL OUT OF APRIL
—A FACE IN THE CROWD
—THERE'S NO MAN LIKE A SNOW-MAN
—I OUGHTA KNOW MORE ABOUT YOU

Villa-Lobos Score

1948. *MAGDALENA*
A musical romance of the Magdalena jungle with book by Frederick Hazlitt Brennan and Homer Curran, lyrics by Robert Wright and George Forrest, and presented by a cast headed by Irra Petina, John Raitt, Dorothy Sarnoff and Hugo Haas.
—WOMEN WEAVING
—PETECAL
—THE SEED OF GOD
—THE OMEN BIRD
—MY BUS AND I
—THE EMERALD
—FOOD FOR THOUGHT
—COME TO COLUMBIA
—PLAN IT BY THE PLANETS
—BON SOIR, PARIS
—TRAVEL, TRAVEL, TRAVEL
—MAGDALENA
—THE BROKEN PIONOLITA
—GREETING
—RIVER SONG
—CHIVOR DANCE
—THE FORBIDDEN ORCHID
—LOST
—THE SINGING TREE
—FREEDOM
—VALS de ESPANA
—PIECE de RESISTANCE
—THE BROKEN BUS

Don Walker Score

1951. *COURTIN' TIME*
A musical comedy, based on Eden

Phillpots' "The Farmer's Wife", with book by William Roos, lyrics by Jack Lawrence, and starring Joe E. Brown in a cast that included Billy Worth and Carmen Mathews.
—TODAY AT YOUR HOUSE, TO-MORROW AT MINE
—FIXIN' FOR A LONG, COLD WINTER
—ARAMINTA TO HERSELF
—AN OLD-FASHIONED GLIMMER IN YOUR EYE
—GOODBYE, DEAR FRIEND, GOOD-BYE
—THE WISHBONE SONG
—SMILE AWHILE
—TOO MUCH TROUBLE
—CHOOSE YOUR PARTNER
—I DO, HE DOSN'T
—JOHNNY RIDE THE SKY
—GOLDEN MOMENT
—THE SENSIBLE THING TO DO
—MASCULINITY
—MAINE WILL REMEMBER THE MAINE
—HEART IN HAND

"Fats" Waller Score

1943. *EARLY TO BED*
A musical comedy with book and lyrics by George Marion, Jr., and presented by a cast headed by Mary Small, Muriel Angelus, Richard Kollmar and George Zivich.
—A GIRL WHO DOESN'T RIPPLE WHEN SHE BENDS
—THERE'S A MAN IN MY LIFE
—MY OLD WORLD CHARM
—SUPPLE COUPLE
—SLIGHTLY LESS THAN WONDER-FUL
—THIS IS SO NICE
—HI-DE-HO-HIGH
—THE LADIES WHO SING WITH THE BAND
—THERE'S "YES" IN THE AIR
—GET AWAY YOUNG MAN
—LONG TIME NO SONG
—EARLY TO BED
—WHEN THE NYLONS BLOOM AGAIN

Clay Warwick Scores

1944. *DREAM WITH MUSIC*
A musical fantasy with book by Sidney Shelton, Ben Roberts and Dorothy Kilgallen, lyrics by Edward Edgar, and presented by a cast headed by Vera Zorina and Jay Hodges.
—BABY DON'T COUNT ON ME

—I'M AFRAID I'M IN LOVE
—LOVE AT SECOND SIGHT
—BE GLAD YOU'RE ALIVE
—COME WITH ME

1945. *MEMPHIS BOUND*
Bill Robinson is starred in a jive version of "Pinafore" with book by Albert Barker and Sally Benton and lyrics by Don Walker.
—GROWIN' PAINS
—THE NIGHTINGALE, THE MOON AND I
—OLD LOVE
—FAREWELL MY LOVE

Kurt Weill Scores

1940. *RAILROADS ON PARADE*
A New York World's Fair production in which historical locomotives and trains were displayed with a musical setting. Lyrics by C. Alan and Buddy Bernier.
—MILE AFTER MILE

1941. *LADY IN THE DARK*
Book by Moss Hart, lyrics by Ira Gershwin, and starring Gertrude Lawrence in a cast that included Danny Kaye, Victor Mature and Bert Lytell.
—OH FABULOUS ONE IN YOUR IVORY TOWER
—THE WORLD'S INAMORATA
—ONE LIFE TO LIVE
—GIRL OF THE MOMENT
—IT LOOKS LIKE LIZA
—MAPLETON HIGH CHORAL
—THIS IS NEW
—THE PRINCESS OF PURE DELIGHT
—MY SHIP
—SAGA OF JENNY
—THIS WOMAN AT THE ALTAR
—THE GREATEST SHOW ON EARTH
—THE BEST YEARS OF HIS LIFE
—TSCHAIKOWSKY

1944. *ONE TOUCH OF VENUS*
Book by A. J. Perelman and Ogden Nash, lyrics by Ogden Nash, and presented by a cast headed by Mary Martin, John Boles, Kenny Baker, Teddy Hart and Paula Laurence.
—NEW ART IS TRUE ART
—ONE TOUCH OF VENUS
—HOW MUCH I LOVE YOU
—I'M A STRANGER HERE MYSELF
—FORTY MINUTES FOR LUNCH
—SPEAK LOW
—WEST WIND
—WAY OUT WEST IN JERSEY
—FOOLISH HEART
—THE TROUBLE WITH WOMEN

—DOCTOR CRIPPEN
—VERY, VERY, VERY
—CATCH HATCH
—THAT'S HIM
—WOODEN WEDDING
—VENUS IN OZONE HEIGHTS

1945. *FIREBRAND OF FLORENCE*
A musical version of "The Firebrand" with book and lyrics by Edwin Justin Mayer and Ira Gershwin, and presented by a cast that included Earl Wrightson as Cellini, Melville Cooper as The Duke and Beverly Tyler as Angela.
—SONG OF THE HANGMAN
—COME TO FLORENCE
—MY LORDS AND LADIES
—THERE WAS LIFE, THERE WAS LOVE, THERE WAS LAUGHTER
—YOU'RE FAR TOO NEAR ME
—ALESSANDRO THE WISE
—I AM HAPPY HERE
—SING ME NOT A BALLAD
—WHEN THE DUCHESS IS AWAY
—THERE'LL BE LIFE, LOVE AND LAUGHTER
—I KNOW WHERE THERE'S A COZY NOOK
—THE NIGHTIME IS NO TIME FOR THINKING
—DIZZILY BUSILY
—THE LITTLE NAKED BOY
—MY DEAR BENVENUTO
—JUST IN CASE
—A RHYME FOR ANGELA
—THE WORLD IS FULL OF VILLIANS
—YOU HAVE TO DO WHAT YOU DO DO
—LOVE IS MY ENEMY
—COME TO PARIS

1947. *STREET SCENE*
A folk opera of the sidewalks of New York, based on the Pulitzer prize-winning drama of the same name, with book by Elmer Rice, lyrics by Langston Hughes, and presented by a cast headed by Norman Cordon, Anne Jeffreys, Hope Emerson, Polyna Stoska and Brian Sullivan.
—REMEMBER THAT I CARE
—THE WOMAN WHO LIVED UP THERE
—WOULDN'T YOU LIKE TO BE ON BROADWAY?
—GET A LOAD OF THAT
—SOMEHOW I NEVER COULD BELIEVE
—WHAT GOOD WOULD THE MOON BE?
—I GOT A MARBLE AND A STAR

—CATCH ME IF YOU CAN
—ICE CREAM
—THERE'LL BE TROUBLE
—MOON-FACED AND STARRY-EYED
—AIN'T IT AWFUL—THE HEAT?
—WRAPPED IN A RIBBON AND TIED
    IN A BOW
—LONELY HOUSE
—A BOY LIKE YOU
—WHEN A WOMAN HAS A BABY
—LET THINGS BE LIKE THEY
    ALWAYS WAS
—WE'LL GO AWAY TOGETHER
—LULLABY
—I LOVED HER TOO
—DON'T FORGET THE LILAC BUSH

1948. *LOVE LIFE*
    Book and lyrics by Alan Jay Lerner, and
    starring Nanette Fabray and Ray Middle-
    ton.
—WHO IS SAMUEL COOPER
—MY NAME IS SAMUEL COOPER
—HERE I'LL STAY
—PROGRESS
—I REMEMBER IT WELL
—GREEN UP TIME
—ECONOMICS
—MOTHER'S GETTING NERVOUS
—MY KIND OF NIGHT
—WOMAN'S CLUB BLUES
—LOVE SONG
—I'M YOUR MAN
—HO, BILLY, O
—IS IT HIM OR IS IT ME?
—THIS IS THE LIFE
—MINSTREL PARADE
—MADAME ZUZU
—TAKING NO CHANCE
—MR. RIGHT

1949. *LOST IN THE STARS*
    A musical tragedy by Maxwell Anderson
    based on Alan Paton's novel, "Cry The
    Beloved Country," and presented by a cast
    headed by Todd Duncan, Leslie Banks,
    Warren Coleman, Herbert Coleman, Wil-
    liam Greaves, Inez Matthews, Frank
    Roane, Julian Mayfield and Shelia Guyse.
—THE HILLS OF IXOPO
—THOUSANDS OF MILES
—TRAIN TO JOHANNESBURG
—THE SEARCH
—THE LITTLE GREY HOUSE
—WHO'LL BUY?
—TROUBLE MAN
—MURDER IN PARKWOLD
—FEAR
—LOST IN THE STARS
—THE WILD JUSTICE

—OH, TIXO, TIXO, HELP ME
—STAY WELL
—CRY, THE BELOVED COUNTRY
—BIG MOLE
—A BIRD OF PARADISE

Jacques Wolfe Score

1944. *JOHN HENRY*
    A Negro folk musical by Roark Bradford,
    co-starring Paul Robeson and Ruby Elzy.
—CARELESS LOVE
—GOT A HEAD LIKE A ROCK
—I'VE TROMPLED ALL OVER
—SUNDOWN IN MY SOUL

Robert Wright Score

1944. *SONG OF NORWAY*
    An operetta, based on the life and melo-
    dies of Edvard Grieg, with book by Mil-
    ton Lazarus, lyrics by George Forrest, and
    presented by a cast headed by Irra Patina,
    Lawrence Brooks, Robert Shafer, Helena
    Bliss and the Ballet Russe de Monte
    Carlo.
—THE LEGEND
—HILL OF DREAMS
—FREDDY AND HIS FIDDLE
—NOW
—STRANGE MUSIC
—MIDSUMMER'S EVE
—MARCH OF THE TROLLGERS
—HYMN OF BETROTHAL
—BON VIVANT
—THREE LOVES
—DOWN YOUR TEA
—NORDRAAK'S FAREWELL
—CHOCOLATE PAS DES TROIS
—WALTZ ETERNAL
—PEER GYNT
—I LOVE YOU
—AT CHRISTMASTIME
—SONG OF NORWAY

Composite Scores

1940. *IT HAPPENS ON ICE*
    A skating revue, produced by Sonja
    Henie and Arthur Wirtz, with Joan Ed-
    wards and Joe Cook heading a cast of
    skaters. Lyrics by Al Stillman.
—SO WHAT GOES?
    Music by Fred Ahlert.
—BETWEEN YOU AND ME AND THE
    LAMPPOST
    Music by Fred Ahlert.
—WHAT'S ON THE PENNY?
    Music by Fred Ahlert.

—DOUBLE OR NOTHING
Music by Vernon Duke.
—LONG AGO
Music by Vernon Duke.
—ADAGIO DAN
Music by Vernon Duke.
—DON'T BLOW THAT HORN, GABRIEL
Music by Will Hudson and Vernon Duke.
—THE MOON FELL IN THE RIVER
By Mitchell Parish and Peter DeRose.
1940. *EARL CARROLL'S VANITIES*
A revue with sketches by Earl Carroll, and presented by a cast of Hollywood starlettes.
—I WANT MY MAMA
By Albert Stillman and Jararaca and Vincente Paiva.
—STARLIT HOUR
By Mitchell Parish and Peter DeRose.
—ANGEL
By Mitchell Parish and Peter De Rose.
1942. *STAR AND GARTER*
A burlesque-revue starring Gypsy Rose Lee in a cast that included Marjorie Knapp, Bobby Clark, Pat Harrington and Prof. Lamberti.
—I DON'T GET IT.
By Sis Willner and Doris Tauber.
—THE BUMP IN THE BALLET
By Irving Gordon, Allan Roberts and Jerome Brainin.
—DON'T TAKE ON MORE THAN YOU CAN DO
By Irving Gordon, Allan Roberts and Jerome Brainin.
—ON A SATURDAY NIGHT
By Jerry Seelan and Lester Lee.
—STAR AND GARTER
—By Jerry Seelan and Lester Lee.
—BUNNY, BUNNY, BUNNY
By Harold J. Rome.
—IT WAS MARVELOUS
By Allan Roberts and Doris Fisher.
1942. *OF V WE SING*
An American Youth production in which Betty Garrett appeared in one of the principal roles.
—YOU CAN'T FOOL THE PEOPLE
By Alfred Hayes and George Kleinsinger.
—SISTERS UNDER THE SKIN
By Sylvia Marks and Beau Bergensen.
—DON'T SING SOLO
By Roslyn Harvey and George Kleinsinger.
—RED, WHITE AND BLUES
By Lewis Allan.
—BROOKLYN CANTATA
By Mike Stratton and George Kleinsinger.
—PRIORITIES

—By Roslyn Harvey and Lou Cooper.
—QUEEN ESTHER
By Beatrice Goldsmith and George Kleinsinger.
—GERTIE, THE STOOL PIGEON'S DAUGHTER
By Joe Darian and Ned Lehac.
—YOU'VE GOT TO APPEASE WITH A STRIP TEASE
By Lewis Allan and Toby Sacher.
—WE HAVE A DATE
By Roslyn Harvey and Lou Cooper.
—JUKE BOX
By Alfred Hayes and Alex North.
—OF V WE SING
By Arthur Zipser and Lou Cooper.
1944. *SING OUT SWEET LAND*
A musical history of America, based on a story by Walter Kerr, with Alfred Drake playing the role of an immortal minstrel and Burl Ives reviving old American folk songs. The cast also included Bibi Osterwald, Philip Coolidge and Alma Kaye.
1950. *DANCE ME A SONG*
A revue with songs by James Shelton, Herman Hupfeld, Albert Hague, Maurice Valency and Bud Gregg, and presented by a cast headed by Joan McCracken, Marion Lorne, Lee Goodman, Jimmy Kirkwood, Eric Rhodes, Ann Thomas, Cynthia Rogers and Wally Cox.
—AVERAGE FAMILY
—SHE'S NO LADY
—GLEE CLUB
—STRANGE NEW LOOK
—I'M THE GIRL
—THE LUNTS ARE THE LUNTS ARE THE LUNTS
—DOCUMENTARY
—ONE IS A LONELY NUMBER
—TEXAS
—THE FOLKS AT HOME
—HELLO FROM HOLLYWOOD
—IT'S HIS MONEY
1950. *ALIVE AND KICKING*
A revue with songs by Hal Borne and Irma Jurist, Sammy Fain, Harold Rome, and Ray Golden and Sonny Burke, and presented by a cast that included David Burns, Lenore Lonergan, Jack Gifford and Carl Reiner.
—A WORLD OF STRANGERS
—I'M ALL YOURS
—ONE WORD LED TO ANOTHER
—CRY BABY CRY
—FRENCH WITHOUT TEARS
—ALIVE AND KICKING
—PALS OF THE PENTAGON
—I DON'T WANT HIM

—CALYPSO CELEBRATION
—ONCE UPON A TIME
—COAL SCUTTLE BLUES
—PROPINQUITY
—ONE, TWO, THREE

1950. *MICHAEL TODD'S PEEP SHOW*
A revue in which the King of Siam made
his Broadway debut as a popular songwriter under the pseudonym of Bhumibol,
and presented by a cast of former burlesque stars that included Lilly Christine,
June Allen, "Red" Marshall, "Hi Wilber-
force" Conley, "Bozo" Snyder and "Peanuts" Mann.

—YOU'VE NEVER BEEN LOVED
By Sammy Stept.
—WE'VE GOT WHAT IT TAKES
By Sammy Stept.
—A BRAND NEW RAINBOW IN THE
SKY

Revivals of 1940-1951

1942. *PORGY AND BESS* with Todd Duncan and Anne Brown.
1942. *THE CHOCOLATE SOLDIER* with
Helen Gleason and Allan Jones.
1942. *THE MERRY WIDOW* with Helen
Gleason, Wilbur Evans and Eddie Garr.
1942. *THE NEW MOON* with Ruby Mason
and Wilbur Evans.
1942. *THE TIME, THE PLACE AND
THE GIRL* with Vickie Cummings, Clarence Nordstrom and Red Marshall.
1943. *THE STUDENT PRINCE* with
Frank Hornaday, Barbara Scully, Everett
Marshall and Ann Pennington.
1943. *THE VAGABOND KING* with John
Brownlee.
1943. *THE MERRY WIDOW* with Melville Cooper, Marta Eggerth and Jan
Kiepura.
1943. *BLOSSOM TIME* with Alexander
Gray.
1943. *PORGY AND BESS* with Avon Long,
Etta Moten and Todd Duncan.
1943. *CONNECTICUT YANKEE* with
Dick Foran and Vivienne Segal.
1944. *THE NEW MOON* with Earl Wrightson and Dorothy Kirsten.
1945. *THE RED MILL* with Michael
O'Shea, Eddie Foy, Jr. and Dorothy Stone.
1946. *THE DESERT SONG* with Walter
Cassel and Dorothy Sandlin.
1946. *SHOW BOAT* with Ralph Dumke,
Carol Bruce and Jan Clayton.
1947. *SWEETHEARTS* with Bobby Clark.
1947. *THE CHOCOLATE SOLDIER* with
Keith Andes and Frances McCann.
1947. *THE CRADLE WILL ROCK*

—FRANCIE
By Bob Hilliard and Jule Styne.
—VIOLINS FROM NOWHERE
By Herb Magidson and Sammy Fain.
—FALLING RAIN —DREAM OF YOU
By Chakraband, Tongyai & Bhumibol.
—LOVE AT SUNDOWN
By Chakraband, Tongyai & Bhumibol.
—BLUE NIGHT
By Chakraband, Tongyai & Bhumibol.
—SONG WITHOUT WORDS
By Chakraband, Tongyai & Bhumibol.
—THE MODEL HASN'T CHANGED
By Harold Rome.
—GIMME THE SHIMMY
By Harold Rome.
—POCKETFUL OF DREAMS
By Harold Rome.
—I HATE A PARADE

1942. *PRIORITIES OF 1942*
With Lew Holtz, Willie Howard, Phil
Baker, Jean Merrill, Hazel Scott and the
Helen Raymond Skaters. Later, during the
353-run, Gloria Swanson was headlined.

1942. *NEW PRIORITIES OF 1943*
With Harry Richman, Bert Wheeler,
Johnny Burke, Hank Ladd, Carole Bruce,
Imogene Carpenter, the Radio Aces and
The Bricklayers.

1943. *LAUGH TIME*
With Ethel Waters, Bert Wheeler, Frank
Fay, Buck & Bubbles & The Bricklayers.

1944. *TAKE A BOW*
With Jay C. Flippen, Chico Marx, Pat
Rooney and Think-a-drink Hoffman.

1945. *KEEP 'EM LAUGHING*
With Hildegarde, Zero Mostel, the Hartmans, The Bricklayers and William Gaxton and Victor Moore, who were replaced
in run by Gracie Fields and Argentina.

1945. *CONCERT VARIETIES*
Produced by Billy Rose, and with the
Katherine Durham Dancers, Imogene
Coca, Deems Taylor, Eddie Mayehoff and
Zero Mostel headlining the bill.

1948. *HILARITIES*
With Morey Amsterdam, Sid Stone, Gali
Gali, Betty Jane Watson and Al Kelly.

1949. *KEN MURRAY'S BLACKOUTS
OF 1949*
A vaudeville-revue that ran for more than
seven years in Hollywood, and presented
in New York by a cast that included
Owen McGivney in his protean perform-
ance of characters in "Oliver Twist,"
Nick Lucas, Peg Leg Bates and Shelton
Brooks. Songs by Ray Foster and Charles
Henderson.

INDEX OF MUSICALS through 1950 (With number of continuous Broadway performances in parentheses.)

* Performances through November 3, 1951.

New Broadway Shows 1951-1969

Irving Berlin Scores (1889-   )

1962. *MR. PRESIDENT*
A musical based on the book by Crouse and Lindsay with music and lyrics by Berlin. Mr. Berlin is now 80 years of age and this will probably be his last new musical; he started in 1915 and produced 20 other Broadway shows.
—LET'S GO BACK TO THE WALTZ, IN OUR HIDE-A-WAY, THE FIRST LADY, MEAT AND POTATOES, I'VE GOT TO BE AROUND, THE HEART SERVICE, HE'S THE ONLY MAN IN THE WORLD, THEY LOVE ME, PIGTAILS AND FRECKLES, DON'T BE AFRAID OF ROMANCE, EMPTY POCKETS, GLAD TO BE HOME, THE WASHINGTON TWIST, THE ONLY DANCE I KNOW, I'M GONNA GET HIM, THIS IS A GREAT COUNTRY, LAUGH AT US, IT GETS LONELY IN THE WHITE HOUSE

Leonard Bernstein Scores (1918-   )

1953. *WONDERFUL TOWN*
A musical with music by Bernstein and lyrics by Betty Comden and Adolph Green.
—CHRISTOPHER STREET, OHIO, CONQUERING NEW YORK, ONE HUNDRED EASY WAYS, WHAT A WASTE, NEVER FELT THIS WAY BEFORE, PASS THE FOOTBALL, A QUIET GIRL, CONGA, MY DARLIN' EILEEN, SWING, IT'S LOVE, WRONG NOTE RAG
1956. *CANDIDE*
A musical with music by Bernstein and lyrics by Richard Wilbur, John Latouche and Dorothy Parker.
—THE BEST OF ALL POSSIBLE WORLDS, O HAPPY ME, IT MUST BE SO, IT MUST BE ME, GLITTER AND BE GAY, YOU WERE DEAD YOU KNOW, MY LOVE, I AM EASILY ASSIMILATED, QUIET, ELDORADO, BON VOYAGE, WHAT'S THE USE?, MAKE OUR GARDEN GROW
1957. *WESTSIDE STORY*
A musical with music by Bernstein and lyrics by Sondheim
—MARIA, I FEEL PRETTY, A LITTLE BIT OF LOVE, AMERICA, LOVELY TOWN, YOU GOT ME, COOL, SOMEWHERE SOMETHING'S COMING

Jerry Bock Scores (1930-   )

1956. *MR. WONDERFUL*
A musical comedy with lyrics by Larry Holofcener & George Weiss.
—1617 BROADWAY
—WITHOUT YOU, I'M NOTHING
—JACQUES D'IRAQ
—ETHEL BABY
—MR. WONDERFUL
—CHARLIE WELCH
—TALK TO HIM
—TOO CLOSE FOR COMFORT
—THERE
—MIAMI
—I'VE BEEN TOO BUSY
1957. *BODY BEAUTIFUL*
A Broadway show with a Bock Score.
—HIDDEN IN MY HEART
THE HONEYMOON IS OVER
—JUST MY LUCK
—LEAVE WELL ENOUGH ALONE
—OOH MERCI BEAUCOUP
—SUMMER IS
—UH-HUH, OH YEAH
1959. *FIORILLO*
A musical comedy from a book by J. Weidman & G. Abbott. Lyrics by S. Harrick.
—BUSINESS FUNDAMENTALLY SOUND
—I LOVE A COP
—THE BUM WON
—IMPATIENT
—LITTLE TIN BOX (overture)
—MARIE'S LAW
—POLITICS AND POKER
—ON THE SIDE OF ANGELS
—GENTLEMEN JIMMY
—TILL TOMORROW
—TILL THE BOOTLEGGER COMES
—TIRESTI
—UNFAIR
—I'LL MARRY
—WHEN DID I FALL IN LOVE
—WHERE DO I GO FROM HERE
—HORA, HORA
—NAME'S LAGUARDIA
—THE VERY NEXT MAN
—HOME AGAIN
1960. *TENDERLOIN*
A musical with book by Abbott & Weidman (from novel by S. H. Adams). Lyrics by S. Harrick.
—BLESS THE LAND
—ARTIFICIAL FLOWER
—ARMY OF THE JUST
—FINALLY
—FIRST THINGS FIRST
—I WONDER WHAT ITS LIKE
—LITTLE OLD NEW YORK

—LORD OF ALL CREATION
—THE MONEY CHANGES HANDS
—GOOD CLEAN FUN
—NOBODY CARES (overture)
—PICTURE OF TENDERNESS
—REFORM
—SEA SHELL
—TOMMY, TOMMY
—THE TRIAL
—WHAT'S IN IT FOR ME
—DR. BROCK
—THE TENDERLOIN CELEBRATION

1963. *SHE LOVES ME*
A musical based on a Parfumerie play, with lyrics by S. Harrick.
—I DON'T KNOW HER NAME
—THE TOUCH OF MAGIC
—I RESOLVE
—THREE LETTERS
—VANILLA ICE CREAM
—MERRY CHRISTMAS BELLS
—I LONG FOR LETTERS
—MR. NOWACH
—IF YOU PLEASE
—MUSIC BOX MELODY
—CHRISTMAS EVE
—DAYS GONE BY
—DEAR FRIEND
—GOOD MORNING (reprise)
—GOODBYE GEORGE
—GRAND KNOWING YOU
—HEADS I WIN
—MY DRUG STORE
—NO MORE CANDY
—POPSICLES IN PARIS
—PERSPECTIVE
—A ROMAN ATMOSPHERE
—TRY ME
—SEASONAL PLEASURES
—SOUNDS WHILE SELLING
—THANK YOU MADAM
—WILL HE LIKE ME
—TANGO TRAGIQUE
—TRIP TO THE LIBRARY
—12 DAYS TO CHRISTMAS
—TONIGHT AT EIGHT
—ATMOSPHERE
—WHERE'S MY SHOE
—SHE LOVES ME

1964. *FIDDLER ON THE ROOF*
A musical (book by J. Stein) with lyrics by S. Harrick.
—IF I WERE A RICH MAN
—IF I WERE A WOMAN
—MATCHMAKER
—MIRACLE OF MIRACLES
—NOW I HAVE EVERYTHING
—THE RUMOR
—SABBATH PRAYER
—SUNRISE—SUNSET
—THE DREAM
—TO LIFE
—TRADITION
—WHEN MESIAH COMES
—ANALIOKA

—AS MUCH AS THAT
—GOSSIP
—DEAR SWEET SEWING MACHINE
—DO YOU LOVE ME
—FAR FROM THE HOME I LOVE
—FIDDLER ON THE ROOF
—GET THEE OUT

Jerry Herman Scores (1931-   )

1959. *PARADE*
A musical with words and music by Herman.
—THE NEXT TIME I LOVE, YOU HAD ONE, THE ANTIQUE MAN

1961. *MILK AND HONEY*
A musical based on Appell's book with music and lyrics by Herman.
—SHEPARD'S SONG, SHALON, MILK & HONEY, THERE'S NO REASON IN THE WORLD, LETS NOT WASTE A MOMENT, THAT WAS YESTERDAY, CHIN UP LADIES, THE WEDDING, LIKE A YOUNG MAN, I WILL FOLLOW YOU, HYMN TO HYMIE, AS SIMPLE AS THAT

1964. *HELLO DOLLY*
A musical based on M. Stewart's book with music and lyrics by Herman.
—PUT MY HAND IN, IT TAKES A WOMAN, PUT ON YOUR SUNDAY CLOTHES, RIBBONS DOWN MY BACK, MOTHERHOODS, DANCING, BEFORE THE PARADE PASSES BY, ELEGANCE, THE WAITERS GALLOP, HELLO DOLLY, COME AND BE MY BUTTERFLY, IT ONLY TAKES A MOMENT, SO LONG DEARIE

1966. *MAME*
The musical version of the Pat Dennis novel with music and lyrics by Herman.
—ITS TODAY, OPEN A NEW WINDOW, MAME, MY BEST GIRL, BOSOM BUDDIES, THE MAN IN THE MOON

Frank Loesser Scores (1910-   )

1956. *THE MOST HAPPY FELLA*
A musical based on Sidney Howard's "They Knew What They Wanted" with music and lyrics by Loesser.
—I LOVE HIM, THE MOST HAPPY FELLA

1959. *GREENWILLOW*
A musical based on book, music and lyrics by Loesser.
—THE MUSIC OF HOME, WHAT A BLESSING, GIDEON BRIGGS I LOVE YOU

1961. *HOW TO SUCCEED IN BUSI-
NESS WITHOUT REALLY TRYING*
A musical based on Mead's novel with
music and lyrics by Loesser.
—HOW TO, HAPPY TO KEEP YOUR
DINNER WARM, COFFEE BREAK,
THE COMPANY WAY, A SECRETARY
IS NOT A TOY, BEEN A LONG DAY,
GRAND OLD IVY, ROSEMARY,
FINALETTO, CINDERELLA - DAR-
LING, LOVE FROM A HEART OF
GOLD, I BELIEVE IN YOU, THE YO
HO HO, BROTHERHOOD OF MAN

Frederick Loewe Scores (1904-   )

1951. *PAINT YOUR WAGON*
A musical with music by Frederick Loewe
and lyrics by Alan Jay Lerner.
—I'M ON MY WAY, I TALK TO THE
TREES, THEY CALL THE WIND
MARIA, I STILL SEE ELSA, HOW
CAN I WAIT, WHOOP-TI-AY, CAR-
INO MIO, THERE'S A COACH
COMIN' IN, HAND ME DOWN THAT
CAN O' BEANS, ANOTHER AUTUMN,
MOVIN', ALL FOR HIM, WAND'RIN
STAR
1956. *MY FAIR LADY*
A musical with music by Loewe and
lyrics by Alan Jay Lerner.
—WHY CAN'T THE ENGLISH,
WOULDN'T IT BE LOVERLY, WITH
A LITTLE BIT OF LUCK, I'M AN
ORDINARY MAN, JUST YOU WAIT,
THE RAIN IN SPAIN, I COULD
HAVE DANCED ALL NIGHT, ASCOT
GAVOTTE, ON THE STREET WHERE
YOU LIVE, THE EMBASSY WALTZ,
YOU DID IT, SHOW ME, GET ME
TO THE CHURCH ON TIME, A
HYMN TO HIM, WITHOUT YOU,
I'VE GROWN ACCUSTOMED TO
HER FACE
1960. *CAMELOT*
A musical based on book and lyrics by
Lerner and music by Loewe.
—WONDER WHAT THE KING IS DO-
ING TONIGHT, SIMPLE JOYS OF
MAIDENHOOD, FOLLOW ME, THE
LUSTY MONTH OF MAY, TAKE ME
TO THE FAIR, HOW TO HANDLE A
WOMAN, THE JOISTS, BEFORE I
GAZE ON YOU AGAIN, IF EVER I
WOULD LEAVE YOU, GUENEVERE,
THE PERSUASION, FIE ON GOOD-
NESS, I LOVED YOU ONCE IN SI-
LENCE, WHAT DO SIMPLE FOLK
DO

Robert Merrill Scores (1920-   )

1957. *NEW GIRL IN TOWN*
A musical with both words and music by
Merrill.
—ROLL YOUR SOCKS UP, ANNA
LILLA, SUNSHINE GIRL, ON THE
FARM, FLINGS, ITS GOOD TO BE
ALIVE, LOOK AT 'ER, YER MY
FRIEND AINTCHA?, DID YOU
CLOSE YOUR EYES, AT THE CHECK
APRON BALL, THERE AIN'T NO
FLIES ON ME, VEN I VALSE, IF
THAT WAS LOVE, CHESS AND
CHECKERS
1959. *TAKE ME ALONG*
A musical comedy based on "Ah Wilder-
ness" with Merrill doing both music and
lyrics.
—PARADE, I GET EMBARRASSED,
PROMISE ME A ROSE, TAKE ME
ALONG
1961. *CARNIVAL*
A musical based on M. Stewart's book
with songs and words by Merrill.
—DIRECT FROM VIENNA, A VERY
NICE MAN, FAIRYLAND, I'VE GOT
TO FIND A REASON, EVERYBODY
LIKES YOU, MIRA, HUMMING, YES
MY HEART, MAGIC MAGIC, TANZ,
MIT MIR, THEME FROM CARNI-
VAL, BEAUTIFUL CANDY, HER
FACE, I HATE HIM, GRAND IM-
PERIAL CERQUADE PARIS, AL-
WAYS ALWAYS YOU, SHE'S MY
LOVE

Cole Porter Scores (1893-1964)

1953. *CAN-CAN*
A musical with music and lyrics by
Porter.
—MAIDENS TYPICAL OF FRANCE,
NEVER GIVE ANYTHING AWAY,
C'EST MAGNIFIQUE, COME ALONG
WITH ME, LIVE AND LET LIVE, I
AM IN LOVE, IF YOU LOVED ME
TRULY, MONTMART, ALLEZ-VOUS
EN, NEVER NEVER BE AN ARTIST,
ITS ALL RIGHT WITH ME, EVERY
MAN IS A STUPID MAN, I LOVE
PARIS, CAN-CAN
1955. *SILK STOCKINGS*
A musical with music and lyrics by
Porter.
—TOO BAD, PARIS LOVES LOVERS,
STEREAPHONIC SOUND, IT'S A
CHEMICAL REACTION THAT'S ALL,
ALL OF YOU, SATIN AND SILK,

WITHOUT LOVE, HAIL BIBINSKI, AS ON THROUGH THE SEASONS WE SAIL, JOSEPHINE, SIBERIA, SILK STOCKINGS, THE RED BLUES

Richard Rodgers Scores (1902-   )

1953. *ME AND JULIET*
A musical show with music by Rodgers and lyrics by Oscar Hammerstein II.
—A VERY SPECIAL DAY, THAT'S THE WAY IT HAPPENS, MARRIAGE TYPE LOVE, KEEP IT GAY, THE BIG BLACK GIANT, NO OTHER LOVE, IT'S ME, IT FEELS GOOD, INTERMISSION TALK, THE BABY YOU LOVE, WE DESERVE EACH OTHER, I'M YOUR GIRL

1955. *PIPE DREAM*
A musical with music by Rodgers and lyrics by O. Hammerstein II.
—ALL KINDS OF PEOPLE, THE TIDE POOL, EVERYBODY'S GOT A HOME BUT ME, A LOPSIDED BUS, BUM'S OPERA, THE MAN I USED TO BE, SWEET THURSDAY, SUZY IS A GOOD THING, ALL AT ONCE YOU LOVE HER, THE HAPPIEST HOUSE ON THE BLOCK, THAT PARTY WE'RE GONNA HAVE TOMORROW, MASQUERADE BRAWL AT THE FLOPHOUSE, HOW LONG?, THINKIN', THE NEXT TIME IT HAPPENS

1959. *THE SOUND OF MUSIC*
A musical based on a book by Lindsay and Crouse with music by Rodgers and lyrics by O. Hammerstein II.
—PRELUDIUM, THE SOUND OF MUSIC, MARIA, DO RE MI, SO LONG FAREWELL, CLIMB EVERY MOUNTAIN, EDELWEISS, HOW CAN LOVE SURVIVE, PROCESSIONAL, YOU ARE SIXTEEN

1962. *NO STRINGS*
A musical based on the book of S. Taylor with music and lyrics by R. Rodgers.
—THE SWEETEST SOUNDS, HOW SAD, LOADS OF LOVE, THE MAN WHO HAS EVERYTHING, BE MY HOST, LA LA LA, YOU DON'T TELL ME, LOVE MAKES THE WORLD GO ROUND, NOBODY TOLD ME, LOOK NO FURTHER, MAINE, ANOTHER FOOL, EAGER BEAVER, NO STRINGS

1965. *ON A CLEAR DAY*
A musical comedy with music by Rodgers and Burton Lane and lyrics by A. J. Lerner.
—ON A CLEAR DAY, WHAT DID I HAVE THAT I DON'T HAVE NOW, COME BACK TO ME, WHEN I'M BEING BORN AGAIN

Harold Rome Scores (1908-   )

1952. *WISH YOU WERE HERE*
Musical with music & lyrics by Rome.
—CAMP KAREFREE, GOODBYE LOVE, SOCIAL DIRECTOR, SHOPPING AROUND, BRIGHT COLLEGE DAYS, MIX AND MINGLE, COULD BE, TRIPPING THE LIGHT FANTASTIC, WHERE DID THE NIGHT GO, CERTAIN INDIVIDUALS, THEY WON'T KNOW ME, SUMMER AFTERNOON, DON JOSE, EVERYBODY FOR EVERYBODY, WISH YOU WERE HERE, RELAX, FLATTERY, FINALE, GLIMPSE OF LOVE

1954. *FANNY*
A musical with music & lyrics by Rome.
—NEVER TOO LATE FOR LOVE, COLD CREAM JAR SONG, OCTOPUS SONG, RESTLESS HEART, WHY BE AFRAID TO DANCE, SHIKA SHIKA, WELCOME HOME, I LIKE YOU, I HAVE TO TELL YOU, FANNY, THE LOVERS, THE SAILING, TO MY WIFE, LOVE IS A VERY LIGHT THING, OYSTERS COCKLES AND MUSSELS, PANISSE AND SON, BIRTHDAY SONG, THE THOUGHT OF YOU, OTHER HANDS OTHER HEARTS, BE KIND TO YOUR PARENTS, WELCOME HOME

1959. *DESTRY RIDES AGAIN*
A musical with music & lyrics by Rome.
—ANYONE COULD LOVE YOU, ARE YOU READY, BALLAD OF A GUN, GYP WATSON, BOTTLENECK, FAIR WARNING, EVERY ONCE IN A WHILE, A GOOD GOOD THING, A HANDY THING, HOOP DE DINGLE, I HATE HIM, I SAY HELLO, LET'S TALK ABOUT A WOMAN, NOT GUILTY, ONCE KNEW A FELLA, ONLY TIME WILL TELL, RING ON THE FINGER, ROSE LOVEJOY OF PARADISE VALLEY, THE SUNSHINE SONG, SWAP HER FOR A MULE, TOMORROW MORNING, WE'RE LADIES, THE SOCIAL, RESPECTABILITY

1962. *I CAN GET IT FOR YOU WHOLESALE*
A musical based on J. Weidman's novel with music & lyrics by Rome.
—BALLAD OF THE GARMENT TRADE, EAT A LITTLE SOMETHING, THE FAMILY WAY, A FUNNY THING HAPPENED, A GIFT TODAY, GRAB THEM WHILE YOU CAN, I'M NOT A WELL MAN, MISS MARMELSTEIN, MOMMA MOMMA, SOMEBODY ELSE, THE SOUND OF MONEY,

TOO SOON, WHO KNOWS, WHEN
GENINI MEETS , CAPRICORN
WHAT'S IN IT FOR ME, WHAT ARE
THEY DOING TO US, NOW, THE
WAY THINGS ARE, DANCE

Jule Styne Scores
(1905-   )

1953. *HAZEL FLAGG*
A musical satire with music by Styne and
lyrics by Bob Hilliard.
—A LITTLE MORE HEART, THE
WORLD IS BEAUTIFUL TODAY, I'M
GLAD I'M LEAVING, THE RUTLAND
BOUNCE, HELLO HAZEL, PARIS
GOWN, EVERY STREET'S A BOULE-
VARD IN OLD NEW YORK, HOW DO
YOU SPEAK TO AN ANGEL?, AUTO-
GRAPH CHANT, I FEEL LIKE I'M
GONNA LIVE FOREVER, YOU'RE
GONNA DANCE WITH ME WILLIE,
WHO IS THE BRAVEST, SALOME,
EVERYBODY LOVES TO TAKE A
BOW, LAURA DE MAUPASSANT
1956. *BELLS ARE RINGING*
A musical with music by Styne and
lyrics by Betty Comden and Adolph
Green.
—IT'S A PERFECT RELATIONSHIP,
ON MY OWN, YOU'VE GOT TO DO
IT, IT'S A SIMPLE LITTLE SYSTEM,
IS IT A CRIME, HELLO HELLO
THERE, I MET A GIRL, LONG BE-
FORE I KNEW YOU, MU-CHA-CHA,
JUST IN TIME, DROP THAT NAME,
THE PARTY'S OVER, SALZBURG,
THE MIDAS TOUCH, I'M GOIN'
BACK
1960. *DO RE MI*
A musical based on a book by Kaner with
music by Styne and lyrics by B. Comden
and A. Green.
—WAITING, ALL YOU NEED IS A
QUARTER, TAKE A JOB, THE
JUKE BOX HOP, ITS LEGITIMATE,
I KNOW ABOUT LOVE, THE AUDI-
TION, CRY LIKE THE WIND, AM-
BITION, SUCCESS, FIREWORKS,
WHAT'S NEW AT THE ZOO, ASK-
ING FOR YOU, THE LATE LATE
SHOW, ADVENTURE, MAKE SOME-
ONE HAPPY, DO RE MI, DON'T BE
ASHAMED OF A TEARDROP, V.I.P.,
ALL OF MY LIFE
1961. *SUBWAYS ARE FOR SLEEPING*
A musical based on book and lyrics by
Comden and A. Green with music by
Styne.
—SUBWAYS ARE FOR SLEEPING,
GIRLS LIKE ME, STATION RUSH,
I'M JUST TAKIN' MY TIME, I WAS
A SHOO-IN, SUBWAY DIRECTIONS,
RIDE THRU THE NIGHT, WHO

KNOWS WHAT MIGHT HAVE BEEN,
SWING YOUR PROJECTS, SUBWAY
INCIDENT, I JUST CAN'T WAIT,
COMES ONCE IN A LIFETIME,
WHAT IS THIS FEELING IN THE
AIR
1964. *FUNNY GIRL*
A musical based on the original story by
J. Lenmart with music by Styne and
lyrics by Bob Merrill.
—IF A GIRL ISN'T PRETTY, I'M THE
GREATEST STAR, CORNET MAN,
WHO TAUGHT HER EVERYTHING,
HIS LOVE MAKES ME BEAUTIFUL,
I WANT TO BE SEEN WITH YOU
TONIGHT, HENRY STREET, PEO-
PLE, YOU'RE A WOMAN, DON'T
RAIN ON MY PARADE, SAIDE-
SAIDE, RAT-A TAT—TUT, THE
MUSIC THAT MAKES ME DANCE,
WHO ARE YOU, FIND YOURSELF
A MAN
1964. *FADE OUT-FADE IN*
A musical based on book and lyrics of
B. Comden and A. Green and music by
Styne.
—THE 30'S, ITS GOOD TO BE BACK
HOME, FEAR-FEAR, CALL ME SAV-
AGE, THE USHER FROM THE MEZ-
ZANINE, I'M WITH YOU, MY FOR-
TUNE IS MY FACE, GO HOME
TRAIN, CLOSE HARMONY, YOU
MUSN'T BE DISCOURAGED, FADE
OUT-FADE IN, IN QUEST OF HIS
YOUTH, THE FIDDLER AND THE
FIGHTER, THE DANGEROUS AGE

Meridith Willson Scores
(1902-   )

1957. *THE MUSIC MAN*
A musical with music and lyrics by Will-
son. This Broadway show 'made' Mr.
Willson.
—TROMBONES-TONIGHT, ITS YOU,
LEDA RIS, TILL THERE WAS YOU,
ROCK ISLAND ROCK, THE SADDER
BUT WISER GIRL FOR ME, YA GOT
TROUBLE, MARIAN — LIBRARIAN,
GOOD NIGHT LADS, PICK A LIT-
TLE-TELL A LITTLE, THE WELLS
FARGO WAY, WILL I TELL YOU,
IOWA STUBBORN, MY WHITE
KNIGHT, IF YOU DON'T MIND MY
SAYING SO, WALK HER THERE,
THE PIANO OVERTURE, FINALE
1960. *UNSINKABLE MOLLY BROWN*
A musical based on the book by R. Morris
with music and lyrics by Willson.
—AIN'T DOWN YET, BELLY UP TO
THE BAR BOYS, I'VE ALREADY
STARTED IN, I'LL NEVER SAY NO,
MY OWN BRASS BED, BEAUTIFUL
PEOPLE OF DENVER, ARE YOU

SURE, BON JOUR, IF I KNEW,
KEEP-A-HOPPIN', UP WHERE THE
PEOPLE ARE, DOLCE FAR NIENTI,
COLORADO, MY HOME
1963. *HERE'S LOVE*
A musical with music and lyrics by Will-
son.
—EXPECT THINGS TO HAPPEN, LOVE
COME TAKE ME AGAIN, HERE'S
LOVE, MY WISH, PINE CONES AND
HOLLY BERRIES, THE MAN OVER
THERE, THE BIG CLOWN'S BAL-
LOON, SHE HAD TO GO BACK,
DEAR MR. SANTA CLAUS, YOU
DON'T HAVE TO PROVE IT, LOOK
LITTLE GIRL

Miscellaneous Scores

1951. *SEVENTEEN*
A musical comedy with music by Walter
Kent & lyrics by Kim Gannon.
—WEATHERBEE'S DRUG STORE, THIS
WAS JUST ANOTHER DAY, THINGS
ARE GONNA HUM THIS SUMMER,
HOW DO YOU DO MISS PRATT?,
SUMMERTIME IS SUMMERTIME,
RECIPROCITY, ODE TO LOLA,
HEADACHE AND HEARTACHE, OO-
OOO-OOO WHAT YOU DO TO ME,
THE HOOSIER WAY, I COULD GET
MARRIED TODAY, AFTER ALL IT'S
SPRING, IF WE COULD STOP THE
OLD TOWN CLOCK
1951. *TOP BANANA*
A musical with lyrics and music by
Johnny Mercer.
—THE MAN OF THE YEAR THIS
WEEK, YOU'RE SO BEAUTIFUL
THAT, TOP BANANA, ELEVATOR
SONG, HAIL TO MAC CRACKEN'S,
ONLY IF YOU'RE IN LOVE, MY
HOME IS IN MY SHOES, I FOUGHT
EVERY STEP OF THE WAY, O K.
FOR T.V., SLOGAN SONG, SANS
SOUCI, A DOG IS A MAN'S BEST
FRIEND, THATS FOR SURE, A
WORD A DAY
1951. *COURTIN' TIME*
A musical with lyrics by Jack Lawrence
and music by Don Walker.
—TODAY AT YOUR HOUSE TOMOR-
ROW AT MINE, FIXIN' FOR A LONG
COLD WINTER, ARAMINTA TO
HERSELF, AN OLD-FASHIONED
GLIMMER IN YOUR EYE, GOODBYE
DEAR FRIEND GOODBYE, THE
WISHBONE SONG, SMILE AWHILE,
TOO MUCH TROUBLE, CHOOSE
YOUR PARTNER, I DO HE DOESN'T,
GOLDEN MOMENT, JOHNNY RIDE
THE SKY, THE SENSIBLE THING TO
DO, MASCULINITY, MAINE WILL
REMEMBER THE MAINE, HEART IN
HAND

1952. *THREE WISHES FOR JAMIE*
A musical with lyrics and music by Ralph
Blane.
—THE WAKE, THE GIRL THAT I
COURT IN MY MIND, MY HOME'S
A HIGHWAY, WE'RE FOR LOVE, MY
HEART'S DARLIN', GOIN' ON A
HAYRIDE, LOVE HAS NOTHING TO
DO WITH LOOKS, I'LL SING YOU
A SONG, IT MUST BE SPRING, THE
ARMY MULE SONG, WHAT DO I
KNOW, ITS A WISHING WORLD,
TROTTIN' TO THE FAIR, APRIL
FARE
1953. *MAGGIE*
A musical comedy with music and lyrics
by William Ray.
—I NEVER LAUGHED IN MY LIFE,
LONG AND WEARY WAIT, THIM-
BLEFUL, HE'S THE MAIN, WHAT
EVERY WOMAN KNOWS, ANY AF-
TERNOON ABOUT FIVE, SMILE FOR
ME, YOU BECOME ME, ITS ONLY
THIRTY YEARS, THE NEW ME, THE
TRAIN WITH THE CUSHIONED
SEATS, PEOPLE IN LOVE, PRACTI-
CAL, CHARM, FUN IN THE COUN-
TRY
1953. *KISMET*
A musical show with lyrics and musical
adaptation by Robert Wright and George
Forrest. Music by Aleksandr Borodin.
—SANDS OF TIME, RHYMES HAVE I,
FATE, BAZAAR OF THE CARAVANS,
NOT SINCE NINEVEH, BAUBLES,
BANGLES AND BEADS, STRANGER
IN PARADISE, HE'S IN LOVE, GES-
TICULATE, NIGHT OF MY NIGHTS,
WAS I WAZIR, RAHADLAKUM, AND
THIS IS MY BELOVED, THE OLIVE
TREE, CEREMONIAL OF THE
CALIPH'S DIWAN, PRESENTATION
OF PRINCESSE'S
1953. *CARNIVAL IN FLANDERS*
A musical with lyrics by Johnny Burke,
music by James VanHeusen.
—RING THE BELL, THE VERY NECES-
SARY YOU, IT'S A FINE OLD IN-
STITUTION, I'M ONE OF YOUR
ADMIRERS, THE PLUNDERING OF
THE TOWN, THE STRANGER SEX,
THE SUDDEN THRILL, IT'S AN OLD
SPANISH CUSTOM, A SEVENTEEN
GUN SALUTE, YOU'RE DEAD,
RAINY DAY, TAKE THE WORD OF
A GENTLEMAN
1954. *THE GIRL IN PINK TIGHTS*
A musical show with music by Sigmund
Romberg and lyrics by Leo Robin.
—THAT NAUGHTY SHOW FROM GAY
PAREE, LOST IN LOVELINESS, I
PROMISED THEIR MOTHERS, UP
IN THE ELEVATED RAILWAY, IN
PARIS AND IN LOVE, YOU'VE GOT
TO BE A LITTLE CRAZY, WHEN I

AM FREE TO LOVE, OUT OF THE WAY, ROLL OUT THE HOSE BOYS, MY HEART WON'T SAY GOODBYE, WE'RE ALL IN THE SAME BOAT, LOVE IS THE FUNNIEST THING, THE CARDINAL'S GUARD ARE WE

1954. *THE PAJAMA GAME*
A musical comedy with lyrics and music by Richard Adler & Jerry Ross.
—THE PAJAMA GAME, RACING WITH THE CLOCK, A NEW TOWN IS A BLUE TOWN, I'M NOT AT ALL IN LOVE, I'LL NEVER BE A JEALOUS AGAIN, HEY THERE, HER IS, SLEEP —TITE, ONCE A YEAR DAY, SMALL TALK, THERE ONCE WAS A MAN, STEAM HEAT, THE WORLD AROUND US, THINK OF THE TIME I SAVE, HERMANDO'S HIDEAWAY, JEALOUSY BALLET, 7 1/2 CENTS

1954. *THE GOLDEN APPLE*
A musical show with music by Jerome Moross and lyrics by John Latouche.
—NOTHING EVER HAPPENS IN ANGEL'S ROOST, MY LOVE IS ON THE WAY, IT WAS A GLAD ADVENTURE, COME ALONG BOYS, IT'S THE GOING HOME TOGETHER, HELEN IS ALWAYS WILLING, INTRODUCIN' MR. PARIS, LAZY AFTERNOON, MY PICTURE IN THE PAPERS, WHEN WE WERE YOUNG, STOREBOUGHT SUIT, BY GOONA-GOONA LAGOON, DOOMED DOOMED DOOMED, CIRCE-CIRCE, WE'VE JUST BEGUN

1954. *THE BOY FRIEND*
A musical show with music and lyrics by Sandy Wilson.
—PERFECT YOUNG LADIES, THE BOY FRIEND, WON'T YOU CHARLESTON ME?, FANCY FORGETTING, I COULD BE HAPPY WITH YOU, SUR LA PLAGE, A ROOM IN BLOOMSBURG, YOU DON'T WANT TO PLAY WITH ME BLUES, SAFETY IN NUMBERS, RIVIERA, IT'S NEVER TOO LATE TO FALL IN LOVE, CARNIVAL TANGO, POOR LITTLE PIERRETTE

1954. *HIT THE TRAIL*
A musical with lyrics by Elizabeth Miele and music by Frederica Valerio.
—ON WITH THE SHOW, MR. RIGHT, DYNAMIC, BLUE SIERRAS, NO! NO! NO!, THE WIDE OPEN SPACES, GOLD CANNOT BUY, REMEMBER THE NIGHT, TELL ME HOW, IT WAS DESTINY, JUST A WONDERFUL TIME, NEVADA HOE DOWN, NEW LOOK FEELING, SET ME FREE, SOMEHOW I'VE ALWAYS KNOWN, MY FATAL CHARM, MEN ARE A PAIN IN THE NECK, WHEREVER I MAY GO, TAKE YOUR TIME, HAPPY BIRTHDAY

1954. *HOUSE OF FLOWERS*
A musical with lyrics by Messrs. Capote and Arlen, music by Harold Arlen.
—WAITIN', ONE MAN AIN'T QUITE ENOUGH, MADAME TANGO'S TANGO, A SLEEPIN' BEE, BAMBOO CAGE, HOUSE OF FLOWERS, TWO LADIES IN DE SHADE OF DE BANANA TREE, WHAT IS A FRIEND FOR? MARDI GRAS, I NEVER HAD SEEN SNOW, HUSBAND CAGE, HAS I LET YOU DOWN, VANDOU, SLIDE BOY SLIDE, DON'T LIKE GOODBYES, TURTLE SONG

1954. *BY THE BEAUTIFUL SEA*
A musical with lyrics by Dorothy Fields. Music by Arthur Schwartz.
—MONA FROM ARIZONA, THE SEA SONG, OLD ENOUGH TO LOVE, CONEY ISLAND BOAT, ALONE TOO LONG, HAPPY HABIT, GOOD TIME CHARLIE, I'D RATHER WAKE UP BY MYSELF, HOORAY FOR GEORGE THE THIRD, HANG UP, MORE LOVE THAN YOUR LOVE, LOTTIE GIBSON SPECIALTY, THROW THE ANCHOR AWAY

1955. *THE VAMP*
A musical with lyrics by John Latouche. Music by James Mundy
—THE SPIEL, THE FLICKERS, KEEP YOUR NOSE TO THE GRINDSTONE, THATS WHERE A MAN FITS IN, I'VE ALWAYS LOVED YOU, YOU'RE COLOSSAL, FAN CLUB CHANT, HAVE YOU MET DELILAH?, YEEMY YEEMY, THE VAMPS, DELILAH'S DILEMMA, FOUR LITTLE MISFITS, SAMPSON AND DELILAH, WHY DOES IT HAVE TO BE YOU, RAGTIME ROMEO, I'M EVERYBODY'S BABY, THE IMPOSSIBLE SHE

1955. *SEVENTH HEAVEN*
A musical with lyrics by Stella Unger and music by Victor Young
—C'EST LA VIE, WHERE IS THAT SOMEONE FOR ME?, CAMELLE, CALLETTE, FIFI, MAN WITH A DREAM, REMARKABLE FELLOW, IF IT'S A DREAM, HAPPY LITTLE CROOK, SUN AT MY WINDOW LOVE AT MY DOOR, GLOVE DANCE, A MISS YOU KISS, LOVE SNEAKS UP ON YOU

1955. *DAMN YANKEES*
A musical with lyrics and music by Richard Adler.
—SIX MONTHS OUT OF EVERY YEAR, GOODBYE OLD GIRL, HEART, SHOELESS JOE FROM HANNIBAL MO., A MAN DOESN'T KNOW, A LITTLE BRAINS—A LITTLE TALENT, WHATEVER LOLA WANTS, NOT MEG, WHO'S GOT THE PAIN, THE AMERICAN LEAGUE, THE

GAME, NEAR TO YOU, THOSE
WERE THE GOOD OLD DAYS, TWO
LOST SOULS

1955. *ANKLES AWEIGH*

A musical show with lyrics by Dan Shapiro and music by Sammy Fain.

—ITALY, OLD-FASHIONED MOTHERS,
SKIP THE BUILD-UP, NOTHING AT
ALL, WALK LIKE A SAILOR, HE
ADIN' FOR THE BOTTOM, NOTH-
ING CAN REPLACE A MAN, HERE'S
TO DEAR OLD US, HIS AND HERS,
LA FESTA, READY CASH, KISS ME
AND KILL ME WITH LOVE, HONEY-
MOON, THE VILLAIN ALWAYS
GETS IT, THE CODE, ELEVEN
O'CLOCK SONG

1955. *PLAIN AND FANCY*

A musical with lyrics by Arnold B. Horwitt & music by Albert Hague.

—YOU CAN'T MISS IT, IT WONDERS
ME, PLENTY OF PENNSYLVANIA,
YOUNG AND FOOLISH, WHY NOT
KATIE?, BY LANTERN LIGHT, ITS
A HELLUVA WAY TO RUN A LOVE
AFFAIR, THIS IS ALL VERY NEW
TO ME, PLAIN WE LIVE, THE
SHUNNING, HOW DO YOU RAISE A
BARN, FOLLOW YOUR HEART,
CITY MOUSE COUNTRY MOUSE,
I'LL SHOW HIM, CARNIVAL BAL-
LET, ON THE MIDWAY, TAKE
YOUR TIME AND TAKE YOUR PICK

1956. *SHANGRI-LA*

A musical with lyrics by Mr. Hilton,
Jerome Lawrence, Robert E. Lee and
music by Harry Warren.

—OM MANI PADME HUM, LOST
HORIZON, THE MAN I NEVER MET,
EVERY TIME YOU DANCED WITH
ME, THE WORLD OUTSIDE, I'M
JUST A LITTLE BIT CONFUSED,
THE BEETLE RACE, SOMEWHERE,
WHAT EVERY OLD GIRL SHOULD
KNOW, SECOND TIME IN LOVE,
TALKIN WITH YOUR FEET, WALK
SWEET, LOVE IS WHAT I NEVER
KNEW, WE'VE DECIDED TO STAY,
SHANGRI-LA

1956. *LI'L ABNER*

A musical comedy with lyrics by Johnny
Mercer, music by Gene de Paul.

—A TYPICAL DAY, IF I HAD MY
DRUTHERS, JUBILATION T. CORN-
PONE, RAG OFFEN THE BUSH,
NAMELY YOU, UNNECESSARY
TOWN, WHAT'S GOOD FOR GEN-
ERAL BULLMOOSE, THE COUN-
TRY'S IN THE VERY BEST OF
HANDS, SADIE HAWKINS DAY, OH
HAPPY DAY, I'M PAST MY PRIME,
LOVE IN A HOME, PROGRESS IS
THE ROOT OF ALL EVIL, PUT 'EM
BACK, THE MATRIMONIAL STOMP

1956. *HAPPY HUNTING*

A musical with lyrics by Matt Dubey and
music by Harold Karr.

—POSTAGE STAMP—PRINCIPALITY,
DON'T TELL ME, ITS GOOD TO BE
HERE, MUTUAL ADMIRATION SO-
CIETY, FOR LOVE OR MONEY, BI-
KINI DANCE, IT'S LIKE A BEAUTI-
FUL WOMAN, WEDDING-OF-THE-
YEAR-BLUES, MR. LIVINGSTONE,
IF'N, THIS IS WHAT I CALL LOVE,
A NEW-FANGLED TANGO, SHE'S
JUST ANOTHER GIRL, THE GAME
OF LOVE, HAPPY HUNTING, I'M A
FUNNY DAME, JUST ANOTHER
GUY, EVERYONE WHO'S "WHO'S
WHO"

1957. *COPPER AND BRASS*

A musical with lyrics by David Craig and
music by David Baker.

—CAREER GUIDANCE, WEARING OF
THE BLUE, I NEED ALL THE HELP
I CAN GET, COOL COMBO MAMBO,
YOU WALKED OUT, COOL CREDO,
BRINGING UP DAUGHTER, DON'T
LOOK NOW, BABY'S BABY, CALL
THE POLICE, UNMISTAKABLE SIGN,
WHY HER?, ME AND LOVE, RE-
MEMBER THE DANCING, HONG
KONG, ARGENTINE TANGO, SWEET
WILLIAM, LITTLE WOMAN

1957. *LIVIN' THE LIFE*

A musical with lyrics by Mr. Geller and
music by Jack Urbont

—SOMEONE, WHISKEY BUG, LIVIN'
THE LIFE, STEAMBOAT, TAKE
KIDS, PROBABLY IN LOVE, DON'T
TELL ME, ALL OF 'EM SAY, LATE
LOVE, AIN'T IT A SHAME, SUPER-
SATIONAL DAY, MAC DOUGAL'S
CAVE

1957. *SHINBONE ALLEY*

A musical with lyrics by Mr. Darion
music by George Kleinsinger.

—WHAT DO WE CARE, TANJOURS
GAI, QUEER LITTLE INSECT, BIG
BILL, TRUE ROMANCE, THE LIGHT-
NING BUG SONG, I GOTTA BE,
FLOTSAM AND JETSAM, COME TO
MEE-OW, SUICIDE SONG, SHINE-
BONE ALLEY, THE MOTH SONG, A
WOMAN WOULDN'T BE A WOMAN;
THE LULLABY, WHAT THE HELL,
PRETTY KITTY, WAY DOWN BLUES,
THE LADY BUG SONG, VACANT
LOT BALLET, QUIET STREET, BE A
PUSSYCAT

1957. *SIMPLY HEAVENLY*

A musical with lyrics by Langston Hughes
and music by David Martin.

—LOVE IS SIMPLY HEAVENLY, LET
ME TAKE YOU FOR A RIDE, BROK-
EN STRING BLUES, DID YOU EVER
HEAR THE BLUES, I'M GONNA BE
JOHN HENRY, WHEN I'M IN A
QUIET MOOD, LOOK FOR THE

MORNING STAR, LETS BALL AWHILE, THE MEN IN MY LIFE, I'M A GOOD OLD GIRL

1957. *RUMPLE*
A musical with lyrics by Frank Reardon, music by Ernest G. Schweikert.
—IT'S YOU FOR ME, IN TIMES LIKE THESE, RED LETTER DAY, THE FIRST TIME I SPOKE OF YOU, OBLIVIA, PECULIAR STATE OF AFFAIRS, HOW DO YOU SAY GOODBYE, GENTLEMEN OF THE PRESS, TO ADJUST IS A MUST, COAX ME, WISH, ALL DRESSED UP

1957. *JAMAICA*
A musical with lyrics by E. Y. Harburg, music by Harold Arlen.
—SAVANNAH, SAVANNAH'S WEDDING DAY, PRETTY TO WALK WITH, PUSH THE BUTTON, INCOMPATIBILITY, LITTLE BISCUIT, COCOANUT SWEET, PITY THE SUNSET, YANKEE DOLLAR, WHAT GOOD DOES IT DO, MONKEY IN THE MANGO TREE, TAKE IT SLOW JOE, AIN'T IT THE TRUTH, LEAVE THE ATOM ALONE, FOR EVERY FISH, I DON'T THINK I'LL END IT ALL TODAY, NAPOLEON

1958. *OH CAPTAIN*
A musical with lyrics and music by Jay Livingston and Ray Evans.
—A VERY PROPER TOWN, LIFE DOES A MAN A FAVOR, A VERY PROPER WEEK, CAPTAIN HENRY ST. JAMES, THE DARK DANCE, THREE PARADISES, SURPRISE, HEY MADAME, FEMININITY, IT'S NEVER QUITE THE SAME, WE'RE NOT CHILDREN, GIVE IT ALL YOU GOT, LOVE IS HELL, KEEP IT SIMPLE, THE MORNING MUSIC OF MONTMARTRE, YOU DON'T KNOW HIM, I'VE BEEN THERE AND I'M BACK, DOUBLE STANDARD, ALL THE TIME, YOU'RE SO RIGHT FOR ME

1959. *LITTLE MARY SUNSHINE*
A musical comedy based on book with music, lyrics by Rick Resoyan.
—COLORED LOVE CALL, LOOK FOR A SKY OF BLUE, HOW DO YOU DO, TELL A HANDSOME STRANGER, EVERY LITTLE NOTHING, ONCE IN A BLUE MOON, THE FOREST RANGER, NAUGHTY NAUGHTY NANCY

1959. *NAUGHTY 42ND STREET*
A musical with lyrics by Bud Freeman, music by L.Probes.
BEG BORROW OR STEAL, NAUGHTY 42ND STREET, 5 PROOF

1959. *HAPPY TOWN*
A musical with music by G. Duffy and lyrics by H. M. Haldane.
—IT ISN'T EASY, SOMETHING SPECIAL, CAN'T WIN, OPPORTUNITY,

THE BEAT OF THE HEART, I'M STUCK WITH LOVE

1959. *SARATOGA*
A musical based on the Ferber book with music by H. Arlen, lyrics by J. Mercer.
—PETTICOAT HIGH, GAME OF POKER, LOVE HELD LIGHTLY, THE MAN IN MY LIFE, COUNTIN' OUR CHICKENS

1960. *VALMOUTH*
A musical with lyrics by H. Grove, lyrics by S. Wilson.
—SOB, LOVE, VALMOUTH

1960. *CHRISTINE*
A musical—lyrics by P. F. Webster and music by Sammy Fain.
—UNICEF SONG, I NEVER MEANT TO FALL IN LOVE

1960. *EARNEST IN LOVE*
Based on Oscar Wilde's "The Importance of Being Earnest" with music and lyrics by L. Pockriss.
—EARNEST LOVE, MY ETERNAL DEVOTION

1960. *BYE BYE BIRDIE*
A musical comedy with music by C. Strouse, lyrics by Lee Adams.
—AN ENGLISH TEACHER, ONE BOY, HONESTLY SINCERELY, ONE LAST KISS, KIDS, WHAT DID I EVER SEE IN HIM

1960. *OH KAY*
A musical comedy based on Wodehouse's book with music by the Gershwins used in a new setting.
—OH KAY ** YOU'RE OK, THE 20'S ARE HERE TO STAY, MAYBE

1960. *WILDCAT*
A musical with music by C. Colman, lyrics by C. Leigh.
—YOU'VE COME HOME, TIPPY TIPPY TOES, HEY LOOK ME OVER, WILDCAT, WHAT I WANT FOR JANIE

1961. *SING MUSIC*
A musical based on the book and lyrics of E. Segal and music by J. Reposo.
—YOUR NAME MAYBE PARIS, TOO BAD, THE WRATH OF ACHILLES

1961. *LET IT RIDE*
A musical based on Abbott's book "Three Men on a Horse". Music and lyrics by Jay Livingston.
—RUN RUN RUN, HE NEEDS YOU, IF FLATTERY WINS, THERE'S SOMETHING ABOUT A HORSE, JUST AN HONEST MISTAKE, I'LL LEARN YA, LOVE LET ME KNOW

1961. *SAIL AWAY*
A musical based on Noel Coward's book, music and lyrics also by him.
—WHEN YOU WANT ME, WHY DO THE WRONG PEOPLE TRAVEL, LATER THAN SPRING, DON'T TURN AWAY FROM LOVE, COME TO ME, SAIL AWAY, BEATNIK LOVE AF-

FAIRS, WHEN SHALL I FIND HIM, THE CUSTOMER'S ALWAYS RIGHT

1961. *THE CONQUERING HERO*
A musical with music by M. Charlaf and lyrics by N. Gimbel.
—ONLY RAINBOWS, THE CONQUERING HERO

1961. *13 DAUGHTERS*
Musical with music and lyrics by E. Magoon, Jr.
—MY HAWAII, 13 DAUGHTERS

1961. *DONNYBROOK*
A musical with music and lyrics by Johnny Burke.
—THE DAY THE SNOW IS MELTIN', HE MAKES ME FEEL I'M LOVELY, DEE-LIGHTFUL IS THE WORD, FOR MY OWN, I QUIT LIFE, WISHA-WURRA

1961. *KWAMINA*
A musical based on R. A. Auther's book with music & lyrics by R. Adler.
—NOTHING NOW TO LOOK FORWARD TO, WHAT HAPPENED TO ME TONIGHT

1961. *OH MARRY ME*
A musical with music by P. Kessler and lyrics by Pergamet.
—OH MARRY ME, A CHILD'S WORST FRIEND IS HIS MOTHER

1961. *KEAN*
A musical based on Dumas Play with music & lyrics by P. Wright and G. Foreil.
—PENNY PLAIN TWO PENCE COLORED, SWEPT AWAY, THE FOG IN THE GROG

1961. *ALL IN LOVE*
A musical based on the book, "The Rivals" with music and lyrics by I. Urbont.
—ALL IN LOVE, I LOVE A FOOL, WHY WIVES

1961. *THE GAY LIFE*
A musical with music and lyrics by A. Schwartz and H. Sietz.
—I'M READY FOR A FRAU, WHO CAN YOU CAN, MAGIC MOMENTS, I COULDN'T MARRY YOU

1962. *THE BANKER'S DAUGHTER*
A musical with music by Sol Kaplar and lyrics by E. Elisar.
—SAY NO MORE, FATHER'S DAUGHTER, SUCH A BEAUTIFUL WORLD, SLEEP OH SLEEP, ITS SO HEART WARMING

1962. *A FAMILY AFFAIR*
A musical with music and lyrics by J. Goldman.
—HARMONY, EVERY GIRL WANTS TO GET MARRIED, WHAT I SAY GOES

1962. *RIVERWIND*
A musical based on the book, music & lyrics of John Jennings.

—I CANNOT TELL HER SO, I WANT A SURPRISE, RIVERWIND, AMERICAN FAMILY PLAN, WISHING SONG, ALMOST BUT NOT QUITE, A WOMAN MUST THINK OF THESE THINGS, A WOMAN NEED NEVER GROW OLD, I'D FORGOTTEN HOW BEAUTIFUL SHE COULD BE, LAUGHING FACE, PARDON WHILE WE DANCE

1962. *LITTLE ME*
A musical based on N. Simon's book with music by C. Coleman and lyrics by C. Leigh.
—THE TRUTH, THE OTHER SIDE OF THE TRACK, BOOM, BOOM, POOR LITTLE HOLLYWOOD STAR, HERES TO US

1962. *NOWHERE TO GO BUT UP*
A musical with music by S. Berkowitz, lyrics by J. Lipton.
NOWHERE TO GO BUT UP, WE'RE MAKING CASH WITH SOUR MASH

1963. *FLY BLACKBIRD*
A musical based on the book, music & lyrics by C. Jackson & J. Hatch.
—LOUISIANA, WHOSE THE FOOL?, WAKE UP, NATCILLOCHES

1963. *OLIVER*
Based on the Dickens novel with book, music, lyrics by Lionel Bart.
—FOOD GLORIOUS FOOD, OLIVER, I SHALL SCREAM, BOYS FOR SALE, THAT'S YOUR FUNERAL, WHERE'S LOVE, CONSIDER YOURSELF, YOU'VE GOT TO PICK A POCKET OR TWO, IT'S A FINE LIFE, I'LL DO ANYTHING, AS LONG AS HE NEEDS ME, REVIEWING THE SITUATION

1963. *STREETS OF NEW YORK*
A musical with music by R. B. Chodesh, lyrics by B. A. Grabel.
LOVE WINS AGAIN, IF I MAY, CHRISTMAS CAROL

1963. *IN THE SHADE*
A musical based on "The Rainmaker" with music by H. Schmidt.
—FINALE, THE RAIN SONG, SIMPLE LITTLE SONG

1963. *JENNIE*
A musical with music and lyrics by H. Dietz and A. Schultz.
—JENNIE, BEFORE I KISS THE WORLD GOODBYE

1963. *HOT SPOT*
A musical with music by Mary Rodgers & J. M. Charnin and lyrics by J. Wensell.

1963. *SOPHIE*
A musical based on the life of Sophie Tucker with music and lyrics by Steve Allen.

1964. *ANYONE CAN WHISTLE*
A musical based on A. Laurent's book with music & lyrics by S. Sandheim.

—COME PLAY WITH ME, MAIN STREET, EVERYBODY SAYS DON'T, THE COOKIE CHAIRS

1964. *FLAHOOLEY* (with lyrics & music by Sammy Fain)

1964. *JO* (Based on LITTLE WOMEN with lyrics & music by W. Dyer).

1964. *CAPE CROWN* (Music by A. Hage).

1964. *HIGH SPIRITS* (Based on "Blythe Spirit" by N. Coward).

1964. *CINDY* (Music & lyrics by J. Brandon).

1964. *WHAT MAKES SAMMY RUN* (Music by E. Drake).

1964. *FOXY* (Music & lyrics by R. Dolan and J. Mercer).

1965. *THE YEARLING*
A musical comedy based on M. Rawling's novel, with songs and lyrics by Martin & Leonard.

—SOME DAY I'M GOING TO FLY

1965. *MAN OF LA MANCHA*
A musical comedy based on Don Quixote story with music by M. Leigh and lyrics by J. Darwin.

—TO DREAM THE IMPOSSIBLE DREAM

1966. *TOVARICH*
A musical based on the Sherwood play with music by L. Pockriss and lyrics by A. Crosswell.

—NITCHEVO, I GO TO BED, TOVARICH, THAT FACE, I KNOW THE FEELING, STUCK WITH EACH OTHER, THE ONLY ONE, ALL FOR YOU

1966. *THE EDUCATION OF HYMAN KAPLAN*
A musical with music & lyrics by P. Nassai & Oscar Biard.

—I NEVER FELT BETTER IN MY LIFE, OLD-FASHIONED HUSBAND

1967. *YOU'RE A GOOD MAN, CHARLIE BROWN*
A musical based on book by Persson and Whitelaw (based on *PEANUTS* comic strip by Schultz) with words and music by Clark Gesner.

—YOU'RE A GOOD MAN CHARLIE BROWN, HAPPINESS, PEANUTS

1968. *GOLDEN RAINBOW*
A musical based on E. Kinoy's book with music and lyrics by Walter Marks.

—24 HOURS A DAY, WE GOT US, HE NEEDS ME NOW, I'VE GOTTA BE ME, HOW COULD I BE SO WRONG, KID, TAKING CARE OF YOU, ALL IN FUN, DESERT MOON

1968. *CURLEY MC DIMPLE*
A musical comedy spoof on Shirley Temple, with music and lyrics by Robert and Dale Boylan.

—LOVE IS THE LOVELIEST LOVE SONG, THE MEANEST MAN IN TOWN, THERE ARE NO MORE ROSIE O'GRADY'S

1968. *HOW NOW DOW JONES*
A musical comedy based on book by Max Shulman. Lyrics and music by C. Leigh and Elmer Bernstein.

—ABC, LIVE A LITTLE, THE PLEASURE'S ABOUT TO BE MINE, A LITTLE INVESTIGATION, WALK AWAY, GOODBYE FAILURE GOODBYE, SHAKESPEARE LIED, STEP TO THE REAR, BIG TROUBLE, CREDO ONE OF THOSE MOMENTS, HE'S HERE, PANIC, THAT'S GOOD ENOUGH FOR ME

Other Broadway musicals in production for 1968-69 include HER FIRST ROMAN (based on show of Anthony & Cleopatra) and GOOD WORLD. One might further consult "Critics Theatre Reviews" in the Theatre Division of the New York Public Library for later extensions of this list of shows, many of which survive only a few days after opening on Broadway.

(The albums listed below were available on September 15, 1951, and while numbers refer to 78 rpm records unless otherwise noted, most are also available at other speeds. Recordings of later shows are given in the discography section (starting on page 991) of Heineman's Encyclopedia (mentioned in the Foreword). It lists all platters made by original casts of all Broadway and off-Broadway Musical Shows beginning with Decca's Oklahoma album in 1943 through 1964.)

TREE GROWS IN BROOKLYN, A. (Score by Arthur Schwartz)
Columbia MM-1000. Shirley Booth, Johnny Johnston, Marcia Van Dyke and chorus.

TWO ON THE AISLE. (Score by Jule Styne)
Decca DA-886. Bert Lahr, Dolores Gray, Elliott Reid, Colette Marchand and chorus.

UP IN CENTRAL PARK. (Score by Sigmund Romberg)
Decca DL-8016 (33⅓ rpm.) Wilbur Evans and Betty Bruce, Eileen Farrell and Celeste Holm.
RCA Victor M-991. Jeanette MacDonald and Robert Merrill with chorus and orchestra.

VAGABOND KING, THE. (Score by Rudolf Friml)
RCA Victor K-17. Earl Wrightson, Frances Greer, Guild Choristers and Al Goodman.
Decca DA-855. Mimi Benzell and Frances Bible with Jay Blackton orchestra.

INDEX OF SHOWS 1951-69

Errata:

p. 247—*ZIEGFELD FOLLIES OF 1936*— also contained *That Moment of Moments* with Josephine Baker, Bob Hope and Gertrude Niesen in the cast and *ZIEGFELD FOLLIES OF 1934* also contained *The House Is Haunted*.

p. 164—*ZIEGFELD FOLLIES of 1927*— contained *It Ali Belongs to Me*.

p. 157—1950*OUT OF THIS WORLD*— contained *You Don't Remind Me* which was cut.

p. 293—1948 *KISS ME KATE*—had *From This Moment On* cut from it.

p. 290—1940 *KEEP OFF THE GRASS*— contained *A Latin Tune and Moon And You* by Jimmy McHugh and Al Dubin.